MODERN FINANCIAL MARKETS
Prices, Yields, and Risk Analysis

THE WILEY BICENTENNIAL—KNOWLEDGE FOR GENERATIONS

Each generation has its unique needs and aspirations. When Charles Wiley first opened his small printing shop in lower Manhattan in 1807, it was a generation of boundless potential searching for an identity. And we were there, helping to define a new American literary tradition. Over half a century later, in the midst of the Second Industrial Revolution, it was a generation focused on building the future. Once again, we were there, supplying the critical scientific, technical, and engineering knowledge that helped frame the world. Throughout the 20th Century, and into the new millennium, nations began to reach out beyond their own borders and a new international community was born. Wiley was there, expanding its operations around the world to enable a global exchange of ideas, opinions, and know-how.

For 200 years, Wiley has been an integral part of each generation's journey, enabling the flow of information and understanding necessary to meet their needs and fulfill their aspirations. Today, bold new technologies are changing the way we live and learn. Wiley will be there, providing you the must-have knowledge you need to imagine new worlds, new possibilities, and new opportunities.

Generations come and go, but you can always count on Wiley to provide you the knowledge you need, when and where you need it!

WILLIAM J. PESCE
PRESIDENT AND CHIEF EXECUTIVE OFFICER

PETER BOOTH WILEY
CHAIRMAN OF THE BOARD

MODERN FINANCIAL MARKETS

Prices, Yields, and Risk Analysis

DAVID W. BLACKWELL

Texas A&M University

MARK D. GRIFFITHS

Miami University

DREW B. WINTERS

Texas Tech University

JOHN WILEY & SONS, INC.

Associate Publisher	*Judith R. Joseph*
Associate Editor	*Brian Kamins*
Senior Production Editor	*Patricia McFadden*
Executive Marketing Manager	*Christopher Ruel*
Creative Director	*Harry Nolan*
Senior Designer	*Kevin Murphy*
Editorial Assistant	*Emily Horowitz*
Senior Media Editor	*Allison Morris*
Production Management Services	*Suzanne Ingrao*
Cover Design	*David Levy*
Cover Photo	*Roy Ooms/Masterfile*

This book was set in *10/12 New Times Roman* by *Techbooks* and printed and bound by *Malloy Lithographing*. The cover was printed by *Phoenix Color*.

The book is printed on acid free paper. ∞

To order books or for customer service please, call 1-800-CALL WILEY (225-5945)

ISBN-13   978-0-470-00010-6
ISBN-10   0-470-00010-4

Printed in the United States of America

10 9 8 7 6 5 4 3 2 1

PREFACE

MOTIVATION AND VISION

The title tells it all. The purpose of this book is to explain to students, many of whom will have literal or virtual careers on Wall Street, how to

- Calculate the prices of financial assets;
- Calculate the yields of those assets;
- Measure the risk associated with owning the assets; and
- Manage those risks.

The term "modern" in the title is intended to imply that this book takes a new approach to the topics that have typically been covered in a variety of university courses with titles such as "Money and Capital Markets," "Financial Markets," or "Financial Markets and Institutions." Unlike the more traditional approach, which focuses on how specific financial institutions measure and manage risk, this book takes the common-sense approach that knowledge of prices, yields, and risk in the various financial markets can be applied at a wide variety of institutions, including commercial banks, investment banks, investment funds, insurance companies, etc. Thus, the book is organized around the major financial markets. The first half of the book focuses on understanding how to calculate prices and yields in the financial markets, with just enough institutional detail to facilitate understanding the calculations. The last half of the book focuses on understanding the risks involved in these same financial markets and provides some introduction to techniques for managing those risks. This book does not attempt to teach a student how to be a CFO of a major financial institution. Rather, it is more focused on the types of issues that an analyst or associate at a major financial firm might be asked to analyze by the CFO, chief risk officer, or portfolio manager.

Like most textbooks, this one has its origins from the frustrations of the authors who could never find exactly the right book to match the way they wanted to teach a course in financial markets. Currently and historically, books for financial markets or capital markets courses have been wide-reaching survey-style books with a lot of emphasis on institutional detail. This style of book fits the traditional teaching of this type of course, which typically focuses on institutional details about the various institutional players and how they interact. This more traditional approach means that there is usually a limited discussion on valuing the assets and that any discussion of risk management focuses on a particular financial institution. In addition, most finance courses are designed so that the valuation of different financial assets is covered in separate courses, such as "Fixed Income," "Investments," "Real Estate Finance," and "Derivative Securities." By treating valuation and risk management issues "under one roof," so to speak, the professor is better able to reinforce the key valuation, risk measurement, and risk management concepts. It also allows for easier comparisons across financial markets, further reinforcing the key concepts of valuation and risk management.

ORGANIZATION

The first three chapters provide some background. The book's first chapter explains the purpose of the book to the student and reviews some useful concepts from earlier finance courses, including risk, return, and market efficiency. Chapter 2 then describes the basic structure and risks faced by the major types of financial firms. Having some basic institutional knowledge allows the student to put concepts and examples presented later in the book into an institutional context. Because many of the securities addressed in the book are fixed-income securities, chapter 3 describes the major influences on the level and structure of interest rates.

The next five chapters (4–8) introduce the major financial markets and address prices and yields in those markets: money markets, bond markets, mortgage markets, equity markets, and foreign exchange markets. The emphasis in these chapters is not on institutional detail, but rather on understanding the basics of valuation in those markets. Where appropriate in these chapters, students are also exposed to the major risks faced by institutions owning securities from those markets. The chapters have sufficient institutional detail to allow the reader to understand the terminology used in each market and how the most important market mechanisms function.

Chapters 9–11 introduce the tools of risk management in financial markets and provide an overview of the importance of risk management to financial institutions. Chapter 9 introduces forward and futures contracts and provides a number of examples of how these instruments are used by financial institutions. Chapter 10 does the same for options. In Chapter 11, a general concept of risk is defined and describes the risk management function for financial institutions. Equipped with the tools and concepts developed in Chapters 1–11, the student is prepared to move into the last half of the book, which addresses how risks are measured and managed in the various financial markets.

Chapters 12–16 focus on measuring and managing risks in each of the major financial markets: money markets, bond markets, mortgage markets, equity markets, and foreign exchange markets. These chapters apply the concepts developed in the first half of the book, including how to use futures, forwards, and swaps to manage risks in the various markets. The concept of value-at-risk is also developed and applied in the context of equity markets.

The book ends with three chapters (17–19) on some advanced applications of derivative securities to risk management. Chapter 17 addresses some of the practical problems associated with hedging using options. Chapter 18 goes into greater detail in the valuation and use of interest rate derivatives such as caps and floors. The book concludes with an introduction to credit derivatives in Chapter 19.

TARGETED STUDENTS

The book is aimed at undergraduate students with at least an introductory course in finance under their belts, along with the usual prerequisites in accounting, economics, and statistics typical in most business school curriculums. The book is also appropriate for use at the master's level, including MBA or MS Finance programs. While the entire book is intended to be accessible to undergraduates, there is some material that is more advanced and may not be appropriate for undergraduates in all programs. Certainly Chapters 1–16 should be appropriate for undergraduates at most institutions, while Chapters 17–19 may be best suited for MBAs or MS students at most institutions or for an advanced course in risk management.

PEDAGOGICAL FEATURES

To motivate student interest, help students to understand the material, and to build appreciation for how the concepts can be applied in the "real world," the book provides a number features:

- The chapter introductions provide guideposts throughout the book by showing how the chapter relates to earlier or later chapters or by providing a motivating example from industry. Each chapter introduction ends with a list of the valuation and risk management skills that are developed. These skills are highlighted with the heading "Developing Valuation and Risk Management Skills."

- There are featured examples as appropriate to each chapter to take students step-by-step through complex calculations and applications.

- Where appropriate, there are "Industry Application" boxed items that illustrate how chapter concepts are used in practice or that highlight implications of those concepts for financial firms.

- "In the News" boxed items appear in appropriate places throughout the book to show students the contemporary relevance of the concepts they are studying.

- Each chapter ends with a "Summary of Valuation and Risk Management Skills," which provides an overview of the key takeaways from the chapter. These summaries directly tie to the "Developing Valuation and Risk Management Skills" section found in the introduction to each chapter.

- There are questions and problems at the end of each chapter. The solutions are available in the instructor's manual.

- A list of annotated references appears at the end of each chapter.

- Each chapter concludes with a list of key terms used in the chapter. The first time a key term is used, it is indicated in boldface.

ANCILLARY PACKAGE

There is a package of ancillary materials that will assist students and instructors who use this book:

- The Instructor's Manual with Test Bank contains a number of teaching aids, including a chapter overview and some advice on how to best use each chapter, a summary of the valuation and risk management skills, and solutions to end-of-chapter questions and problems. The test bank includes at least one thousand true-false, multiple-choice, or short-answer examination questions involving definitions of key terms, understanding of key concepts, applications of the concepts, and calculations. A computerized version of the test bank is available to instructors on the companion web site.

- PowerPoint® presentations are available for each chapter on the companion web site. The presentations provide lecture notes and selected figures, tables, and graphs from the text, ready for classroom presentation.

- A companion web site accompanies this book. It is located at www.wiley.com/college/blackwell and provides instructors adopting the book access to an electronic version of the instructor's manual and test bank, the computerized test bank, and each chapter's PowerPoint® presentation. Students will also be able access the PowerPoint® presentations on the website.

ACKNOWLEDGMENTS

We are grateful to the many people who have assisted us with bringing this book to fruition. First, we thank the reviewers whose many useful comments have substantially improved the book as it evolved from the proposal to the published version:

Armand Picou	University of Central Arkansas
Francis Laatsch	Bowling Green State University
James McNulty	Florida Atlantic University
K. Thomas Liaw	St. John's University
John Halstead	Southern Connecticut State University
Murat Aydogdu	Bryant University
Matej Blasko	Oakland University
Deanne Butchey	Florida International University
Vijaya Subrahmanyam	Mercer University

At John Wiley & Sons, we are grateful to Judith R. Joseph, Associate Publisher, and Brian Kamins, Associate Editor who superbly guided us to completing this book. We also greatly appreciate the efforts of Patricia McFadden, our production editor at Wiley and Suzanne Ingrao of Ingrao Associates, both, who guided the manuscript through the production process.

We gratefully acknowledge the contributions of Professor James H. Gilkeson of the University Central Florida. Professor Gilkeson, an expert in real estate finance, prepared the initial drafts of chapter 6 (Mortgage Valuation) and chapter 14 (Mortgage Risk Management). We sincerely appreciate his outstanding work on these chapters.

We also appreciate the tremendous assistance of Patrick Cary. While working as Blackwell's graduate assistant at Texas A&M University, Patrick meticulously read the entire manuscript, error checking and copy editing. His work resulted in substantial improvements. In addition, we appreciate the diligent research assistance of Kerrine Schroeder Herber. The very first draft of the book was carefully read and edited by Barbara Winters.

She helped us get the book on the right track in terms of readability and we sincerely appreciate her help.

We thank our current and previous colleagues, mentors and students who, like us, were constantly trying to figure out the best ways to teach and learn the subject of this book. Certainly some of their ideas and techniques have influenced our work and are reflected in the book. We appreciate them taking the time over the years to share techniques, approaches, questions, answers and methods. This book could not have been written without what we learned from them.

Last, but not least, we gratefully acknowledge the support, encouragement, and mentoring of our families, friends, colleagues, and former professors as we labored on this project.

David W. Blackwell
College Station, Texas
dblackwell@mays.tamu.deu

Mark D. Griffiths
Oxford, Ohio
griffim2@muohio.edu

Drew B. Winters
Lubbock, Texas
Drew.Winters@TTU.edu

ABOUT THE AUTHORS

DAVID W. BLACKWELL

Dave Blackwell is the James W. Aston/RepublicBank Professor of Finance and Head of the Department of Finance at Texas A&M University's Mays Business School. Prior to joining Texas A&M, Dr. Blackwell worked for several years as a consultant with Pricewaterhouse-Coopers LLP and KPMG LLP. Before his stint in the Big 4, he served on the faculties of the University of Georgia, the University of Houston, and Emory University. He was also a visiting professor at the University of Rochester. His publications have appeared in the leading scholarly journals of finance and accounting such as *Journal of Finance, Journal of Financial Economics, Journal of Financial and Quantitative Analysis, Financial Management, Journal of Financial Research, Journal of Accounting Research,* and *Journal of Accounting and Economics.* While in the Big 4, Dr. Blackwell consulted on a broad range of issues including intellectual property valuation, securities and business valuation, corporate governance, and executive compensation. Dr. Blackwell received a Ph.D. in Finance and a B.S. in Economics from the University of Tennessee, Knoxville. He is a past president of the Southern Finance Association and a former Associate Editor of the *Journal of Financial Research.*

MARK D. GRIFFITHS

Mark Griffiths is the Jack Anderson Professor of Finance at Miami University's Richard T. Farmer School of Business. His research focuses primarily on issues in market microstructure, money markets and short-term interest rates. Dr Griffiths' publications appear in leading academic journals including *Journal of Business, Journal of Finance, Journal of Financial Economics, Journal of Banking and Finance,* and *Journal of Financial Intermediation.* He received undergraduate degrees in French and administrative studies from the University of Western Ontario and from York University, Canada, respectively. He completed an MBA in finance at York University before earning a master's degree in economics at the University of Waterloo and a Ph.D. in finance from the University of Western Ontario.

DREW B. WINTERS

Drew Winters is the Jerry S. Rawls Professor of Finance and Area Coordinator of Finance at Texas Tech University's Rawls College of Business. His research focuses on the behavior of short-term interest rates and the determinants of interest rates on bank lines of credit. His publications appear in leading journals such as *Journal of Business, Journal of Accounting Research, Journal of Banking and Finance, Journal of Financial Research,* and the *Economic Review of the Federal Reserve Bank of St. Louis.* Before joining Texas Tech, Dr. Winters served at the University of Central Florida, University of Southern Mississippi,

University of Wisconsin-Milwaukee, and Western Illinois University. He has also served as a Visiting Research Economist at the Federal Reserve Bank of St. Louis. Before he entered academic life, Dr. Winters was a loan officer at First Union National Bank and a staff accountant for a public accounting firm. Dr. Winters received a Ph.D. in finance and the MBA from the University of Georgia, and a B.S. in computer science and accounting from Duke University.

BRIEF CONTENTS

CONTENTS

CHAPTER 1

OVERVIEW OF RISK, RETURN, AND EFFICIENCY IN FINANCIAL MARKETS

1.1 INTRODUCTION

The purpose of this book is to give you some initial preparation for a career in the financial services industry by introducing you to the myriad financial markets in which financial institutions operate. To do this, we will teach you how to determine the price or market value of the securities that are traded in those markets, guide you through the calculation of rates of return or yields for the securities, and then introduce you to a set of tools used by financial institutions to manage the risks of operating in the financial markets. The book is not designed to train you to be the CEO or CFO of a commercial bank or investment company after graduation. It is intended to guide someone with an introductory understanding of finance and provide them with the necessary theoretical foundation and practical skills for functioning as a financial analyst in a financial institution such as Goldman Sachs or Wells Fargo. If you successfully plow through this book, you will be farther down the "learning curve" in your first Wall Street job and you will be much more valuable to the organization that hires you.

We emphasize the themes of valuation and risk management in this book. Valuation means determining what a financial asset or security is worth. Virtually all participants in any type of market hope to buy a good (a product or a security) for less than it is worth and either sell it for more than it is worth or, more generally, derive a benefit from owning the good that is worth more than its cost. In the financial markets, the valuation process involves identifying all relevant cash flows from owning a security and determining what someone should be willing to pay for the right to receive those cash flows after adjusting for the risk of the security, which determines the appropriate required rate of return. Remember, the greater the risk, the higher the required rate of return. Let's turn to the second major theme, risk management. Although it is nice to expect a particular set of cash flows from owning a security, what market participants expect (or hope) to happen, can vary from what actually happens. The news can be good or bad. Sometimes prices go up or down more than expected, borrowers unexpectedly fail to make payments to lenders, or interest rates or foreign currency exchange rates change more than anticipated.

This book takes you beyond the introductory finance course and gives you a tool kit for survival in the financial markets. There are three basic elements of your tool kit. First you need to know how to calculate the prices or values of various financial instruments such as stocks, bonds, and options. This skill will allow you to determine whether these securities are fairly priced in the market. Second, you need to be aware of the risk from owning the securities and be able to calculate and quantify the amount of risk. Finally, once the risk is identified and measured, you must be able to manage that risk, keeping the value of your position in the security within some desirable limits.

The structure of this book is simple. In the first half of the book (Chapters 1–10) we provide a review of some fundamentals required to understand financial institutions, the functioning of the various financial markets, and show you how to determine the prices or yields of various securities, including bonds, stocks, money market instruments, and mortgages. In the first half of the book, we also introduce the financial instruments that institutions use to manage their risks: forward contracts, futures contracts, and options. By the time you finish reading the first half of the book, you will be well along the way toward being conversant in the language of Wall Street and understand the basics of the various financial markets. The second half of the book (Chapters 11–19) is focused on measuring and managing the risks that financial institutions face in the financial markets. After providing a general framework for risk management, the second half of the book shows how instruments such as futures, forwards, options, and swaps and how tools such as value-at-risk are used by institutions to manage risks in the debt, equity, currency, and mortgage markets. The book ends by introducing what are called credit derivatives, which are financial instruments that institutions use to manage the risk that transaction counter parties are unable to make promised payments. The second half is very applied—demonstrating how real-world institutions manage the risks they face.

Before you are ready to tackle how to value various financial instruments, we need to briefly review some concepts that you have probably seen in earlier finance courses. This review, which covers the remainder of this chapter and Chapter 2, will set up the landscape on which the tools developed later in the book are used. In Chapter 1, we define some measures of risk and return for different classes of securities and provide some historical perspective on the relationship between risk and return. We also discuss the importance of risk management, providing a concrete example, and we review the concept of market efficiency—how do prices in financial markets react to new information? The chapter ends with a detailed efficient markets example. Chapter 2 then describes the key characteristics of the financial institutions that use the concepts described in this book and provides an overview of the major risks those institutions face. Note that we will begin each chapter with a box, like the one appearing below, that highlights some of the chapter's most important concepts.

DEVELOPING VALUATION AND RISK MANAGEMENT SKILLS

1. What classes of securities historically have the highest risk premiums and why?
2. What is the basic approach to valuing a security?
3. Define the three aspects of market efficiency and explain their importance.

1.2   SOME LESSONS FOR A HISTORY OF RETURNS AND RISK

When investors place their money in financial assets they are "renting" out their money and require the user pay an appropriate amount of "rent". The question is "How much rent should I require for the use of my money?" Figure 1-1 provides historical data on different classes of financial securities. The figure provides a historical perspective of how much rent (**return**) investors require for the use of their money and the relationship between returns and risk.

Figure 1-1 provides the *average return, risk premium*, and *standard deviation* for five classes of financial assets. Panel A covers the period from 1926 to 1997, while Panel B extends the sample to cover from 1926 to 2002.

Several important observations can be made from this data. First, U.S. Treasury bills are considered the least risky financial assets and, accordingly, Treasury bills have the lowest historical average return. Why is this? The United States has a large and relatively stable economy and has a long history of paying its debts. Where does the money to pay the debt come from? The source is the tax revenue collected by the U.S. government. So, if the U.S. government has difficulty paying back the money it owes,[1] it can always raise taxes and enforce payment. This taxing ability is not without consequences, however, as many lesser-developed countries have discovered. Raising taxes and enforcing payment can cause inflation and higher interest rates in an economy and unrest in a population.

Second, as we move down Figure 1-1, the average return increases. Since we are moving to classes of securities that are more risky than Treasury bills, the assumption can be made that the return increases are for additional levels of **risk**. Accordingly, column 3 (Panel A) is labeled as the **risk premium**; it measures the difference in average return for each class of securities from the Treasury bill average return. For example, the risk premium on large-company stocks is $8.9\% = 12.7\% - 3.8\%$.

Third, the **standard deviation** of the returns is a proxy for the risk of an individual security and we can see that, in general, a higher risk premium is associated with a higher standard deviation.[2] That is, we see a positive **correlation** between risk and return. At this point the introduction of the concept of **risk aversion** is important. What is the meaning of being risk averse? In finance, the usual assumption is that people fall into one of three categories. The three categories are risk taking, risk neutral, and risk averse. Risk takers are easy to understand; they will choose whichever alternative provides the greatest amount of

---

[1] At the end of the 1990s, the U.S. economy was performing very well. In fact, the government found itself with annual budget surpluses and chose to use part of the surplus to buy back the public debt in advance of the debts' maturity dates. The plan from the Treasury Department was to reduce the amount of the public debt by $216 billion during the fiscal year 2000. If achieved, public debt would have been reduced by $355 billion over the three-year period ending with fiscal year 2000. However, we note that even with the debt reduction the public debt still is enormous. In fact, on 5/30/2000 the public debt was $5.66 trillion. With recent increases in government spending the public debt stands at $7.14 trillion on 4/26/04. For more information on the public debt visit www.publicdebt.treas.gov. For more information on the debt reduction plan visit www.ustreas.gov.

[2] Recall from your statistics class that 68.4% of the observations in a normally distributed population are within one standard deviation of the average (mean), 95% are within two standard deviations, and 99% are within three standard deviations.

(Panel A) 1926–1997

Asset class	Average return (%)	Risk premium (%)	Standard deviation (%)
U.S. Treasury bills	3.8	na	3.3
Long-term government bonds	5.4	1.6	9.2
Long-term corporate bonds	6.0	2.2	8.7
Large-company stocks	12.7	8.9	20.3
Small-company stocks	17.7	13.9	34.1

Source: *Stocks, Bonds, Bills, and Inflation 1997 Yearbook,* Ibbotson Associates, Inc, Chicago, Ibbotson department at 800 758 3557, or send an email to source@ibbotson.com to ask for a Data Request Application.

(Panel B) 1926–2002

Asset class	Average return (%)	Risk premium (%)	Standard deviation (%)
U.S. Treasury bills	3.8	na	3.2
Long-term government bonds	5.8	2.0	9.4
Long-term corporate bonds	6.2	2.4	8.7
Large-company stocks	12.2	8.4	20.5
Small-company stocks	16.9	13.1	33.1

Source: *Stocks, Bonds, Bills, and Inflation 2003 Yearbook,* Ibbotson Associates, Inc.

FIGURE 1-1 Risk and return for selected classes of financial assets.

risk. Risk-neutral people are also easy to understand; they will always choose the alternative that has the highest return. But risk-averse people are really interesting. These people make a trade-off between risk and return, and the really interesting thing is that people with varying degrees of risk aversion will demand different levels of return for taking on the same amount of risk. The average of these demands determines what the average return should be. Because of the positive correlation between risk and return, it is standard practice in finance to assume that the average investor is risk averse.

Fourth, Treasury bills are often assumed to be risk free. However, the return of a risk-free security is constant through time, which results in a standard deviation of zero. Treasury bill yields, and therefore returns, change daily so Treasury bills are not a risk-free asset, which can be seen from the Treasury bill standard deviation of 3.3%. Remember that Treasury bills are free of default risk but are exposed to interest rate and inflation risk. Therefore, Treasury bills should properly be referred to as our *least* risky asset.

Fifth, long-term corporate bonds have a smaller standard deviation than long-term government bonds but have a larger risk premium. The reason for the larger risk premium on corporate bonds is default risk. But what about their lower standard deviation? Many government bonds have maturities of more than 20 years, yet long maturity corporate bonds rarely have maturities more than 20 years. So, government bonds are subject to more interest rate risk than are corporate bonds; therefore, their prices change more and they have a larger standard deviation.

Finally, note the slight difference between the data in Panel A and the data in Panel B even though the additional five years covered in Panel B saw major changes (both positive

INDUSTRY APPLICATION

THE IMPORTANCE OF TRANSACTIONS COSTS

In most textbooks, including this one, the authors tend to overlook transactions costs because they are "just cost of doing business" or because they might cloud the "essence of the problem." In their book, *Equity Markets in Action*,[3] Professors Robert Schwartz and Reto Francioni refer to a report by The Plexus Group, which is a wholly owned subsidiary of JP Morgan Chase & Co. This company analyzed the trading decisions and trading costs for a large group of institutional investors that accounted for approximately 25% of worldwide exchange volume.

They found that for a $30 stock transaction, costs averaged 1.57% — roughly 47 cents per share — on each of the buy and sell sides of the trade. Therefore, total round-trip costs would be 3.14% or 94 cents per trade. This information would be important to anyone attempting to estimate the expected return on a portfolio — this is a task usually assigned to junior associates. Here is how the costs break down for a purchase of a $30 share.

Transaction cost	Cost in basis points	Cost in cents
Commissions	17	5
Market impact	34	10
Delay	77	23
Missed trades	29	9
Total	**157**	**47**

Wayne Wagner, chairman of The Plexus Group, in testimony before the House Committee on Financial Services stated, "... total transaction cost is the largest cost borne by investors over time, in most cases being a larger drag on performance than management and administrative fees. Yet these figures are never disclosed, and often are dismissed by the manager as merely 'part of the process.'"[4]

Commissions are funds paid to brokers for facilitating a trade on an exchange. These funds go to paying for the operation of a cash and securities account for the investor and to cover the cost of any research or advice (if any) provided. Market impact refers to the additional cost over and above the bid-ask spread that an investor may incur to have a large order executed quickly. That is, a higher price may have to be paid for a purchase or a lower price accepted for a sale than currently exists in the market. This premium is often viewed as the cost of having the market absorb the unusually large order. The cost of delay is an opportunity cost incurred if the execution of an order is delayed. This usually happens when an attempt is made to get execution at a better price than currently exists in the market. The buyer incurs an opportunity cost if the stock price rises during the delay while a seller incurs the cost if the stock price falls. The final cost of a missed trade is not relevant when a trade does occur and perhaps could be eliminated from the cost calculation. However, the cost is relevant at the end of the holding period when the portfolio attempts to unwind the position but is unable to do so. The Plexus Group includes the cost as presented.

and negative) in the financial markets. This suggests that the relationships documented in Figure 1-1 are relatively stable across time.

So, what has been learned by looking at a 75-year history of returns and standard deviations? First, different classes of securities provide different average returns. Second, higher average returns are associated with higher levels of risk. Third, the average

[3] Schwartz, R. A., and R. Francioni, 2004, *Equity Markets in Action: The Fundamentals of Liquidity, Market Structure & Trading*, pp. 66–67. John Wiley & Sons, Hoboken, NJ.

[4] Testimony of Wayne H. Wagner, House Committee on Financial Services, March 12, 2003 as reported in Schwartz and Francioni (2004).

relationship between classes of securities is relatively stable. Now, the next logical question is, "What does this have to do with the pricing of financial assets?" This question will be answered in the next section.

1.3 RISK, RETURN, AND THE PRICING OF FINANCIAL ASSETS

The value (or price) of any asset is the present value of all of its future cash flows. To calculate the present value of the future cash flows, three features of the future cash flows must be identified: (1) the amount of each of the future cash flows, (2) the timing of the future cash flows, and (3) the risk of the future cash flows. The amount and timing of the future cash flows result in a timeline of cash flows, but what should be done with the risk of the cash flows? Two choices exist; however, the standard procedure is to use the risk of the future cash flows to determine the appropriate discount rate for calculating the present value of those cash flows.

So, why did we start with a history lesson on the link between returns and risk? First, different classes of securities earn different average returns. Second, the average returns increase with increases in risk. These discoveries suggest that investors demand compensation for bearing risk. In other words, an investor's required rate of return for investing in a security is based on that security's risk. Since investors expect to earn their required rate of return, their risk-based required rate of return is the appropriate discount rate for calculating the present value of the future cash flows of a financial asset. The present value of the future cash flows is our estimate of the security's price. Paying the correct price for an asset is a very important first step toward earning the expected rate of return on the security.

The first half of the book concentrates on learning to identify the expected future cash flows and the appropriate risk-adjusted discount rates for the different classes of financial assets. Along with this discussion, institutional details about each market will be provided.

1.4 MANAGING THE RISK OF OWNING A FINANCIAL ASSET

Once an investor has purchased an asset, that investor has put their financial resources at risk. The second half of the book discusses how the investor can determine the amount of the investment that is at risk and techniques that an investor can use to manage or, in some situations, eliminate the risk. That is, the second half of the book focuses on value-at-risk and techniques in managing the risk of a financial investment.

As seen in Figure 1-1, different classes of securities historically have different levels of risk. This suggests that different classes of securities face different amounts of risk and different types of risk. For this reason, the chapters in the second half of the book are divided along market lines.

One of the main points of this book is to learn how to manage potential losses when investing in financial assets. This point is often lost on investors that came to the financial markets during the 1990s because across the decade, the financial markets experienced the largest and longest period of growth in the history of the financial markets. However, the dramatic decline in value across most financial markets during 2000 and 2001 emphasized the point that losses are possible and that the size of losses is potentially large. Accordingly, many of the **In the News** items throughout the book come from 2000 and 2001 because these are the most recent and dramatic examples of the risk potential in financial markets.

The April 9, 2001, edition of *Business Week* contains an article titled "There's Hardly Anywhere to Hide." The article states that when the stock market turns down, as it did in the first quarter of 2001, almost all stocks go down and there is almost no safe place for investing. However, there are a few positives in this market and the size of the loss depends on the amount of risk taken. For example, we provide the following partial lists from the article:

Funds	Return
Big Funds	
Fidelity Magellan	−10.85%
Vanguard 500	−10.24%
Janus	−13.83%

Funds	Return
Worst Performers	
Berkshire Technology	−53.91%
Profunds Ultra OTC	−52.54%
Van Wagner Technology	−51.92%
Best Performers	
Potomac Internet Short	30.15%
Profunds Ultrashort OTC	27.89%
Profunds Ultrabear	22.79%

The list shows us that the big funds, which are considered broad-based market funds, had negative returns, but not nearly as negative as the worst performers. The worst performers are the technology funds and the small stock funds. These funds are considered the most risky, which means in *good times* they tend to do quite well, but in *bad times* they tend to perform quite poorly. This vacillation is the nature of risk and the reason we are going to show you how to manage risk in this book. The best performers are short or bearish funds. These funds "bet" the market is going to decline, and if it does (which it did in the first quarter of 2001), they gain from their position. Later in the book, you will learn how taking short positions can be used as a technique to manage your risks.

1.5 PRICES, RISK, AND EFFICIENT MARKETS

The focus of this book is on the techniques for valuing financial assets and managing the risk inherent in investments in financial assets. A key element of the process that we generally will not discuss is market efficiency because we generally assume that markets are reasonably efficient and well functioning. In this section, market efficiency will be briefly discussed so the reader will have an understanding of why market efficiency is an important part of the process. Three aspects of market efficiency are discussed next: (1) **allocational efficiency**, (2) **informational efficiency**, and (3) **operational efficiency**.

1.5.1 Allocational Efficiency

Allocational efficiency exists when society cannot be made better off by a different allocation of the investable funds. In other words, funds flow to their highest valued use. In financial terms we say that funds are flowing to the highest net present value (NPV) projects on a risk-adjusted basis. In general, this means that businesses are investing in their highest NPV projects and individuals are investing in financial assets that provide the highest return for a given level of risk. For allocational efficiency to occur, informational efficiency and operational efficiency must exist.

1.5.2 Informational Efficiency

Informational efficiency exists when the investor (individual or business) has sufficient, timely, and accurate information about the project or financial assets being considered to value the project or financial asset correctly. That is, the investor has the proper information to determine the amount, timing, and riskiness of the future cash flows of the project or financial assets. Notice that this does not mean that the investor can predict the future accurately and consistently—even fortune tellers cannot do this.[5] This means only that the investor is basing financial decisions on the best information currently available.

Three levels of informational efficiency are generally discussed in finance: (1) strong-form efficiency, (2) semistrong-form efficiency, and (3) weak-form efficiency. The concept of market efficiency can be summed up by saying, "*An investor cannot make abnormal profits (outperform the market return on a risk-adjusted basis) in the stock market on a consistent basis.*" Fama (1970) defines the different levels of informational efficiency in financial markets.[6] His definitions describe the amount of information inherent in a security price. The levels of informational efficiency are defined as:

Strong-form efficiency implies that all information (public and private) of every kind is embedded in the security price.

Semistrong-form efficiency implies that all publicly available information is in the security price.

Weak-form efficiency implies that all information about past prices is in the security price.

Strong-form efficiency is the most extreme form of informational efficiency and, as Fama (1970, p. 410) points out, is quickly rejected by evidence from various sources, indicating that insiders do profit from monopolistic access to inside information. Then, Fama suggests that the important question is how far away from strong-form efficiency do we have to move before reaching actual financial market conditions.

Weak-form efficiency suggests that an investor cannot profit solely by tracking past prices. Academics have historically assumed that financial markets are at least weak-form efficient. The logic behind this assumption is based on the ease of creating profitable trading strategies based on trends in prices. That is, investors could easily form strategies of

---

[5] One of our colleagues points out that the *Psychic Friends Network*—a group of phone-in fortune tellers who advertised extensively on the television in the late 1990s could not predict the bankruptcy of their own company—since if they could they would never have gone into business in the first place.

[6] Fama notes that Roberts (1959) first suggested the distinction between strong- and weak-form efficiency.

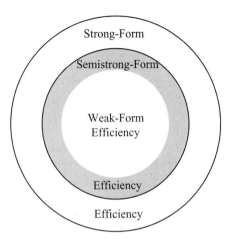

FIGURE 1-2 The relation between forms of informational efficiency.

selling overvalued assets and buying undervalued assets in sufficient volume to change the existing levels of supply and demand, thereby eliminating any mispricing (inefficiencies). Eliminating profits from simple strategies based on price trends leaves us with financial markets that are semistrong-form efficient to some degree.

A semistrong-form efficient market implies that finding incorrectly priced securities is difficult, but that profits exist for the investor who first uncovers valuable new information. What this suggests is that, on average, beating the market is very difficult, but in the situations where someone uncovers new information, substantial profits can be made.

In Figure 1-2, the relationship among the various forms of informational efficiency is shown. You should not think of the weak-, semistrong- and strong-form efficiency arguments as separate theories. Rather, semistrong-form efficiency reflects all of the historical price data that is reflected in weak-form efficiency, plus all of the other publicly available information that is reflected in the semistrong-form. Strong-form reflects all information that is reflected in semistrong-form, plus all of the other publicly-available information.

At this point, two academic papers will be briefly discussed to present what we think are the important issues in a semistrong-form efficient market. First, Jensen (1969) examines the performance of a group of mutual funds. The idea is that mutual fund managers actively search for new information about securities and then trade on the information in an attempt to enhance their fund's performance. Professor Jensen started with 115 mutual funds and identified the group that beat the market the first year. Reasoning that he may have identified the better fund managers, he examined their performances for the following year. After measuring the funds' performances, he again kept the group that beat the market and looked at their performances for the third year. He repeated this process until he had very few survivors. From this process, Professor Jensen finds that, on average, about 50 percent of the mutual funds beat the market each year, a conclusion that would be expected in a semistrong-form efficient market. In a semistrong-form efficient market we expect that investors cannot consistently beat the market because of the difficulty in finding valuable new information. However, few funds could consistently equal the return of their competitors ("beat the market").

Second, Ritter (1996) discusses an apparently profitable trading strategy that later turned unprofitable. Professor Ritter had developed a stock index futures trading strategy that had been profitable for a few years in the mid-1980s. In 1986, Professor Ritter again entered into his trading strategy. Unexpectedly, he incurred large losses. When Professor Ritter investigated, he found that one of the stock indexes in his strategy had been incorrectly priced and his large losses occurred because another investor, Fischer Black, identified the pricing error and was trading against Ritter based on this new information. What this tells us is that pricing errors are possible and that substantial profits are available to investors that discover them. This finding supports the notion of a semistrong-form efficient market.

Before moving on to operational efficiency, we should mention some recent findings on some profitable (i.e., market-beating) trading strategies. These strategies are based, in large part, on stock price trends. While this is an active area of research that is still open for debate, the evidence on these trading strategies suggests that stock markets may not be as informationally efficient as was previously thought.[7]

1.5.3　Operational Efficiency

Operational efficiency relates to the **transaction costs** required to trade. An operationally efficient market has the lowest possible cost because the lower the transaction cost, the more freely investable funds will flow to their most productive use. However, when lowest possible transaction costs are discussed, we must remember that dealers and brokers are a necessary part of trading, so transaction costs must be large enough to provide the dealers and brokers a fair profit.

In our current financial markets some trades can be conducted for an $8 online trading fee. However, remember that the trading fee is only one component of transaction costs. Transaction costs also include **search costs, information costs**, and **opportunity costs**.

EXAMPLE　*Efficient Markets*

As an example of how investors react to new information, let's look at Yahoo!, Inc. Yahoo! is known as one of the best and most popular Internet search engines. The company is a publicly traded corporation whose stock is listed on NASDAQ. As with all publicly traded companies, the press maintains a continual flow of news about and announcements from Yahoo!; but we want to focus on two major announcements at the end of 2000 and the beginning of 2001 to emphasize the role and importance of new information in changing security prices.

Announcement 1: On October 11, 2000, four stock analysts that actively follow Yahoo! downgraded their recommendation for Yahoo!.
Announcement 2: In the evening (after the close of trading) of January 10, 2001 in a conference call with Wall Street, Yahoo! informed the market that estimates for its financial performance for 2001 needed to be adjusted down by a substantial amount.

Figure 1-3 provides Yahoo! stock prices from the week of each announcement. Take a look at the prices for Yahoo! around the two announcement dates to see how the market reacted to these two "bad news" events for Yahoo!. The stock price data in Figure 1-3 suggest that the market reacts quickly to new information. In these two cases the new information is bad news, so the price of Yahoo! declined quickly, which suggests that the stock market is reasonably efficient.

---

[7] For some of the recent work on momentum and contrarian trading strategies see De Bondt and Thaler (1985), Grinblatt, Titman, and Wermers (1995), Chan, Jeegadeesh, and Lakonishok (1996), and La Porta Lakonishok, Shleifer, and Vishny (1997).

(Announcement 1)   **Analysts Downgrade**

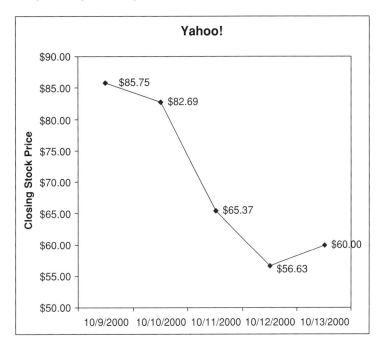

(Announcement 2)   **Earnings Downgrade**

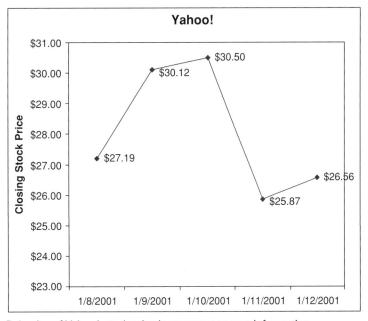

FIGURE 1-3 Behavior of Yahoo! stock price in response to new information.

SUMMARY OF VALUATION AND RISK MANAGEMENT SKILLS

1. What classes of securities historically have the highest risk premiums and why?

Investors require higher returns for securities with greater risks. Generally, investors associate higher risk with higher return volatility, which can be measured with the standard deviation of returns. With risk-averse investors, classes of securities with greater risk must offer greater compensation in the form of return in excess of the risk-free rate. This "extra" return above the risk-free rate is the risk premium. U.S. Treasury bills are the lowest-risk security and generally considered risk free and have the lowest standard deviation historically. Corporate securities are considered more risky and have higher risk premiums.

2. What is the basic approach to valuing a security?

The value (or price) of any asset is the present value of all future expected cash flows from that asset. The value of an asset depends on the amount of cash flow, the timing of the cash flows, and the risk associated with those cash flows. In general, larger cash flows are worth more; cash flows received sooner are worth more than those received later; and riskier cash flows are worth less than those with less risk. To adjust cash flows for risk, the typical approach is to discount the cash flows with the interest rate that reflects the amount of risk.

3. Define the three aspects of market efficiency and explain their importance.

There are three important aspects of market efficiency. Allocational efficiency means that funds invested in the financial markets tend to flow to their highest valued use, thereby maximizing the economic impact of the investments. Informational efficiency means that asset prices quickly reflect all information relevant to the value of the asset. This means that prices are a good indicator of value, which provides investors with the accurate information for making smart investment decisions. Operational efficiency means that the costs of conducting financial transactions are as low as possible, thereby making it easier for funds to flow to the highest valued use.

QUESTIONS

1. What is the standard deviation of the returns of a truly risk-free security? Explain why Treasury bills are not risk free but instead the least risky security.

2. Define risk and explain why standard deviation is a good measure for the risk of a security.

3. Define the term risk-averse investor. Use the information in Figure 1-1 to explain why a risk-averse investor would expect a higher return on small-company stocks than on large-company stocks.

4. Define allocational efficiency. Explain why informational efficiency and operational efficiency are necessary for the allocational efficiency.

5. If you had a trading strategy that beat the market every year, would you tell anyone? Would you write a book about your strategy? Given your answer, explain why Jensen examined the performance of mutual funds managers when he wanted to test for informational efficiency.

6. Peter Lynch is considered an outstanding investor because his mutual fund beat the market 11 out of 19 years. Your job is to see if you can achieve this level of success. Using the random number generator in a spreadsheet, create 19 columns of 50 random numbers and then calculate the average for each column. What is the expected average for a column of random numbers? Now look at the rows. How many rows beat the column averages more often than 50% of the time? How many rows underperformed the column averages more than 50% of the time? How would you define a great stock picker?

7. In a recent insider trading scandal, insiders made substantial profits trading on information not available to diligent, informed, outside investors. Does this situation reflect a violation of one of the forms of informational market efficiency? If so, which one? If not, why not?

REFERENCES

CHAN, L. K. C., N. JEEGADEESH, and J. LAKONISHOK, 1996, Momentum strategies, *Journal of Finance*, *51*, 1681–1713.
They find a large positive drift in future returns and conclude that the market responds gradually to new information.

DE BONDT, W., and R. THALER, 1985, Does the stock market overreact?, *Journal of Finance*, *40*, 793–805.
De Bondt, and Thaler examine the hypothesis that people overreact to unexpected and dramatic news events. They find evidence consistent with the overreact hypothesis, which supports contrarian investing.

FAMA, E., 1970, Efficient capital markets: A review of theory and empirical work, *Journal of Finance*, *25*, 383–417.
This is the classic article in which Fama identifies and defines the forms of market efficiency that dominate finance texts today.

GRINBLATT, M., S. TITMAN, and R. WERMERS, 1995, Momentum investment strategies, portfolio performance and herding, *American Economic Review*, *85*, 1088–1105.
They find that mutual funds tend to be momentum buyers but not momentum sellers of stocks. They find weak evidence of herding by mutual funds (funds buying and selling the same stocks at the same time).

JENSEN, M., 1969, Risk, the pricing of capital assets, and the evaluation of investment portfolios, *Journal of Business*, *42*, 167–247.
Jensen analyzes mutual fund performance across time relative to appropriate benchmarks to determine if informed investors (mutual fund managers) can consistently beat the market. He finds that mutual fund managers cannot consistently beat the market.

LA PORTA, R., J. LAKONISHOK, A. SHLEIFER, and R. VISHNY, 1997, Good news for value stocks: Further evidence on market efficiency, *Journal of Finance*, *52*, 859–874.
They examine price reactions to earnings announcements for value and glamour stocks and find that earnings surprises are systematically more positive for value stocks. The authors conclude that the differences between value and glamour stocks result from expectational errors by investors from extending trends too far.

RITTER, J., 1996, How I helped make Fischer Black wealthier, *Financial Management*, *25*, 104–107.
Ritter explains how he tried to profit from his knowledge of the turn-of-the-year anomaly in small stocks, but that in the end he provided profits for the truly informed investor (who he later found out was Fisher Black).

KEY TERMS

Allocational Efficiency Allocation efficiency means investment flows to the projects with the highest NPVs.

Correlation Correlation measures the relationship between items. If the items' returns move in the same direction, then the two items are positively correlated; and if the items move in opposite directions, then the two items are negatively correlated.

Information Costs Information costs are the costs associated with acquiring and processing the information needed to value a security.

Informational Efficiency Information efficiency means that investors have timely, accurate, and sufficient information to determine the value of a project.

Informational efficiency is broken down into three forms: (1) strong form, (2) semistrong form, and (3) weak form.

Operational Efficiency Operational efficiency is minimizing transaction costs with the constraint that brokers and dealers must be able to earn a fair profit.

Opportunity Costs Opportunity costs are the implied cost of bypassing another investment. Remembering the opportunity costs ensures that investors analyze various opportunities to pick the best opportunity.

Return A return is the total gain or loss to an investor from a security across a period of time. A return includes the change in price of the security plus any additional cash flows received by the investor during a time period. The total change is compared to the price at the beginning of the time period. For example, the return on a stock is often calculated as:

$$r = \frac{(P_1 - P_0 + \text{dividend})}{P_0}.$$

Risk Risk is the chance that an investor will earn something other than that which was expected. However, risk is often referred to as a double-edge sword because the chance for decline in value (risk) is accompanied by the opportunity for an increase in value (reward).

Risk Aversion Risk aversion means that the investor considers the trade-off between risk and return. A risk-averse investor will demand a higher expected return when taking on higher risk.

Risk Premium A risk premium is the return on a security after subtracting the risk-free rate of return.

Search Costs Search costs are the cost of finding someone to trade with at an acceptable price.

Semistrong-Form Efficiency Semistrong-form efficiency implies that all publicly available information is included in the security price.

Standard Deviation Standard deviation measures the dispersion of values relative to the average (mean). It is used as a measure of risk because it provides information about how likely a single return is to be near the average return for the security.

Strong-Form Efficiency Strong-form efficiency implies that all information of every kind is included in the security price.

Transaction Costs Transaction costs are the total cost of trading a security. Transaction costs include the cost of the trade, search costs, information costs, and opportunity costs.

Weak-Form Efficiency Weak-form efficiency implies that all information about past prices is reflected in the security price.

CHAPTER 2

OVERVIEW OF FINANCIAL INSTITUTIONS

2.1 INTRODUCTION

This chapter describes the major types of financial institutions with a focus on the assets they own, the financial obligations they create, and the risks that they must manage. Our discussion provides a context for the valuation and risk management techniques that follow in this book's remaining chapters. Since many of you reading this book will eventually start your careers at a financial institution, it is important that you understand how financial institutions make money and the risks that they take. As a financial analyst, you will be asked to value securities and manage the risks of these institutions, so read this chapter carefully and refer back to it as needed when you encounter applications of the valuation and risk management techniques in future chapters.

At their essence, financial institutions transfer funds from those that have excess funds to those that need funds. The process of transferring these excess funds is vitally important to the well-being of the economy, ensuring that the funds are invested in the most valuable projects. Financial institutions make up a significant portion of the largest corporations in the United States and around the world. At the beginning of 2005 there were 13 financial institutions among the S&P 100 firms, 82 financial institutions among the S&P 500, and 228 financial institutions among the S&P Global 1200.

The chapter proceeds in the next section by discussing the process of financial intermediation, which transfers funds from those with excess funds to those needing funds. In the remaining sections, we describe the balance sheets and the risks faced by depository institutions (e.g., commercial banks), insurance companies and pension funds, finance companies, securities firms, and mutual funds.

DEVELOPING VALUATION AND RISK MANAGEMENT SKILLS

1. Understand the financial intermediation process.
2. Understand the risks faced by the five major types of financial institutions.

2.2 FINANCIAL INTERMEDIATION AND ITS ASSOCIATED RISKS

So that you get an idea of the types of organizations that engage in the process of transferring funds, turn to Figure 2-1, which lists the 13 financial institutions among the S&P 100 and classifies them according to type. The list gives you examples of the types of financial

Allstate Corporation	Insurance
American Express	Finance
American International Group (AIG)	Insurance
Bank of America	Depository
Citigroup	Depository
Goldman Sachs	Securities
Hartford Financial Services Group	Insurance
JP Morgan Chase & Company	Depository
Lehman Brothers	Securities
Merrill Lynch	Securities
Morgan Stanley	Securities
US Bancorp	Depository
Wells Fargo	Depository

FIGURE 2-1 Financial institutions in the S&P 100.
Source: www.S&P.com.

institutions that use the valuation and risk management tools developed later in this book: depository institutions, insurance companies, finance companies, and securities firms. The remainder of this chapter discusses these four types of financial institutions and mutual funds. Before we begin discussing specific financial institutions, we introduce the process of financial intermediation, which is the formal term for the funds transfer process.

One major function of the financial markets is to handle timing problems. Those that have extra money (surplus-spending units or SSUs) at the current time are looking for ways to lend or invest their excess funds. Those that need money (deficit-spending units or DSUs) at the current time are looking for ways to borrow or raise capital. When SSUs and DSUs find each other in the financial markets and agree on the terms of a financial transaction, the timing problem is solved.

SSUs and DSUs can be brought together directly or indirectly. In a direct process SSUs and DSUs search independently for a transaction partner. When they find a partner they conduct the transaction with the partner. It is easy to see that the direct process can be time consuming and costly, which is why an indirect process exists. In the indirect process a middleman (intermediary) channels the funds from SSUs to DSUs without the need for the two to meet. This process is referred to as **financial intermediation**, the topic of this section.

Figure 2-2 provides a simple diagram of financial intermediation. One key feature of financial intermediation is that a financial institution stands between the SSUs and DSUs as a central location for financial transactions. This dramatically reduces the search costs of a financial transaction. A second key feature is that both the SSU and DSU transact with financial institutions, which dramatically alters the risks of the financial transactions.

FIGURE 2-2 Financial intermediation.

```
Credit Risk
Interest-Rate Risk
Market Risk
Liquidity Risk
Exchange-Rate Risk
Operational Risk
```

FIGURE 2-3 Risk faced by financial institutions.

Transacting indirectly through a financial institution instead of directly between a SSU and DSU provides three additional benefits: (1) denomination intermediation, (2) risk intermediation, and (3) maturity intermediation. Denomination intermediation refers to the fact that working through a financial institution allows both the SSU and DSU to get the size of financial transaction they need. For example, a SSU can put $100 in a savings account at a bank. That $100 is unlikely to meet the needs of a business DSU. However, the bank can put one thousand $100 deposits together and lend the business $100,000. Risk intermediation exists because the SSU has a claim on the financial institution instead of a claim on the DSU, which dramatically alters the risk of the SSU's claim. The primary feature for altering risk is the portfolio diversification available to the financial institution. Maturity intermediation means that the claims of the SSUs can have different maturities than the obligations of the DSUs. Referring back to the preceding savings account example, the depositor may want to access their money in the next month, while the business is unlikely to want to repay the loan within one month. Working through a financial institution allows both to have their maturity preferences.

Providing financial intermediation exposes financial institutions to a wide variety of risk. Figure 2-3 lists the risk that financial institutions are exposed to. The remainder of this chapter discusses the major financial institutions—examining their balance sheets and analyzing the specific risks that the institutions are exposed to. Then the remainder of this book discusses how to value those assets and how to manage the associated risks.

2.3 DEPOSITORY INSTITUTIONS

Depository institutions take in deposits and make loans. The depository institutions listed in Figure 2-1 are all banks. However, banks are not the only form of depository institution. Other common forms of depository institutions are savings banks, thrifts, and credit unions. The various types of depository institutions differ based on the rules under which they operate. For example, to have a deposit account with a credit union you must be a member of the group served by the credit union, while having a deposit account at a bank is not restricted to a particular group. However, once you have a deposit account with a credit union, the deposit account functions in a similar manner to a deposit account in any other type of depository institution. The point is that differences exist between the types of depository institutions, but all depository institutions take in deposits and make loans.

Since all depository institutions conduct the same basic operations, we can discuss the assets owned (loans and securities), financial obligations created (deposits), and risks to manage for one type of depository institution, and this discussion will generalize to

	All %	Large domestic (%)	Small domestic (%)
Assets			
Cash	4.07	3.48	3.91
Securities	23.95	22.77	23.14
Loans	59.61	57.69	64.77
Interbank loans	4.46	6.05	2.39
Other	7.90	10.01	5.79
Liabilities			
Transaction deposits	8.42	7.64	11.24
Nontransaction deposits	56.24	49.16	63.51
Borrowings from banks	5.72	5.24	6.19
Borrowings from others	14.46	13.88	9.79
Net due to foreign offices	0.56	4.69	0.35
Other	6.12	7.80	2.55
Equity	8.48	11.60	6.37

FIGURE 2-4   Banking industry assets and liabilities (as a percentage of total assets).
Source: Federal Reserve Board of Governors H8 report.

all depository institutions. The discussion that follows focuses on banks, which typify depository institutions.

Banks take in deposits and make loans. Traditionally, bank profits came from the spread between the rate charged on loans and the rate paid on deposits. However, in recent years, nonbank competition for loans and deposits have reduced the spread banks can charge, so banks now need to generate profits from other activities. Thus, banks now charge fees for services such as check processing, automatic teller machines, and lockboxes.

Figure 2-4 provides aggregate balance sheet percentages for: all banks operating in the United States, large domestic U.S. banks, and small domestic U.S. banks. The balance sheets show three primary risks faced by banks: (1) credit risk, (2) interest-rate risk, and (3) liquidity risk. These risks are easily understood through an analysis of the balance sheet.

2.3.1 Loans and Credit Risk

Figure 2-4 shows that banks hold about 60% of their assets in loans, by far the largest asset category. There are many different types of loans in this asset category including consumer loans (car, boat, education, etc.), commercial loans (lines of credit, revolvers, term, etc.), and mortgages (single-family, multiunit, commercial, etc.). However, even though a bank makes many types of loans, for our purposes loans can be viewed as one asset category because all loans have the same basic risk: credit risk (default risk).

Credit risk is important to banks for two reasons. First, credit risk is the primary risk in the largest asset category. Second, making loans is the primary business of a bank, so credit risk is a bank's primary **business risk**. We discuss a variety of techniques for managing credit risk throughout the remainder of the book.

Since making loans is the primary business of a bank, it is important to the bank to properly price its product. The typical bank loan is made in the amount requested by the borrower, and the pricing of a bank loan is based on the interest rate charged on the loan.

Chapter 3 discusses how to properly determine an interest rate, and how to determine the proper rate of return on a financial asset is discussed throughout the remainder of this book.

2.3.2 Interest-Bearing Assets and Liabilities and Interest-Rate Risk

The interest earned on loans is the primary revenue source for a bank. Nontransaction deposits are the primary liability category for a bank, and the interest paid on these deposits is their primary expense. The potential for changes in the difference between interest earned and interest paid creates **interest-rate risk** for banks.

Market interest rates change regularly, which changes the interest earned and the interest paid by a bank. However, the interest earned by the bank and the interest paid by the bank may not change by the same amount when market interest rates change. For example, a popular type of mortgage loan is a 30-year fixed-rate mortgage, which means the interest rate from the mortgage is set at the beginning of the loan and does not change over its 30-year life. A common deposit is a savings account. A savings account earns interest based on current market rates, which means when market interest rates change the interest expense on the savings account changes. Now, if market interest rates increase, a bank will not earn more on the fixed-rate mortgage but it will pay more on the savings account, reducing its net interest income. This illustrates interest-rate risk.

A typical bank is exposed to interest-rate risk because the rates on their loans change less frequently than the rates on their deposits. The timing of the rate changes on loans and deposits means that banks are less profitable when interest rates increase and more profitable when interest rates decline. There are a number of techniques available to banks to reduce the exposure of the bank's profits to changes in interest rates, and these techniques are discussed in various places throughout the remainder of this book.

2.3.3 Deposits, Securities, and Liquidity Risk

The primary liability of a typical bank is deposits. Figure 2-4 shows two types of deposits: (1) transaction (demand) deposits and (2) nontransaction (time) deposits. These deposits are used to fund the bank's loans, which creates a problem that is referred to as **liquidity risk.**

Liquidity risk is a problem for banks because the time to maturity of the deposits is substantially less than the time to maturity of the loans. For example, transaction deposits are often referred to as demand deposits because depositors can take their money out of the bank any time they want (on demand). Nontransaction deposits are typically time deposits, which means the deposits must stay in the bank for a specified time period.[1] However, the time period is relatively short and seldom exceeds five years. Conversely, the time to maturity of many loans exceeds five years. This means the deposits used to fund the loans can leave the bank before the bank receives the principal back on the loans. This problem is called liquidity risk because the deposits become cash before the loans become cash.

---

[1] Depositors can withdraw their money before the specified date, but the early withdrawal must be accompanied by penalty paid to the bank.

Liquidity risk is a critical risk for banks because they are required to meet the withdrawal demands of their deposits and they must do this every business day. If a bank does not have the cash to meet its daily withdrawals it risks going out of business because of a lack of confidence in the bank created when a bank runs out of cash. To manage liquidity risk, banks hold some cash, but cash is an idle (nonearning) asset so banks store cash in earning assets that earn lower interest and can quickly convert to cash. These highly liquid low-interest earning assets are called money market securities and they make up the majority of the assets in a bank's security portfolio. Figure 2-4 shows that these securities make up about 20 percent of the total assets of a bank, which indicates how important managing liquidity risk is to banks. Chapters 4 and 12 discuss money market securities.

2.4 INSURANCE AND PENSION FUNDS

Three of the financial institutions listed in Figure 2-1 are insurance companies. An **insurance company** can handle all types of insurance, but companies often specialize in one type of insurance, such as life, property/casualty, or health. Insurance companies sell policies to their customers and these policies become the primary liability of the company. The premiums paid for the insurance policies are invested in financial assets that generate income and store value to cover future claims on the policies sold and the operating expenses of the insurance company.

Pension funds work in a similar manner. Customers put money in the pension fund and the pension fund agrees to make future payments to its customers when they retire. Pension fund payments come in one of two basic forms: (1) defined benefit and (2) defined contribution. In a defined benefit pension the customers receive a contract defining the payments they will receive when they retire. In a defined contribution plan the customers' retirement payments depend on the value of the investment portfolio that the pension fund holds for them. The payments to the pension fund are invested in financial assets that generate income and store value to cover future retirement payments of the fund and the operating expenses of the pension fund.

As with the depository institutions, there are a variety of different types of insurance companies and pension funds. However, they all function in basically the same manner. Accordingly, the discussion can focus on one type of insurance company or pension fund. This section will discuss the assets, liabilities, and risk of life insurance companies. Figure 2-5 provides the life insurance industry's aggregate balance sheet.

2.4.1 Liabilities of Life Insurance Companies

Figure 2-5 shows that the primary liability of life insurance companies is the obligations under the insurance policies. Specifically, that means the death benefits of the company's policyholders.

The death benefit under a life insurance policy is a defined amount payable at an unknown future date (the date of death), which would appear to make predicting future payments (cash outflows) difficult. However, actuarial methods applied to a large portfolio of life insurance policies allows life insurance companies to predict their annual death benefit payments reasonably well. That is, life insurance companies have specific obligations under

Assets	%	%
Investments		75.91
Real estate	4.68	
Stocks	7.32	
Bonds	35.72	
Mortgage loans	16.03	
Other loans	4.18	
Deposits with financial institutions	7.98	
Current assets		23.17
Liabilities		71.59
Provisions for life insurance		1.45
Other provisions		14.37
Current liabilities		
Equity		9.65

FIGURE 2-5   Life insurance industry assets and liabilities (as a percentage of total assets).

each policy that, when combined in a large portfolio of obligations, creates predictable cash flows for the company. This means that life insurance companies must invest the policy premiums (payments to the company) so that the company can cover the predicted death benefits, have sufficient liquidity for unexpectely large death benefits, and provide a reasonable return to the owners of the insurance company.

2.4.2 Investments, Credit Risk, and Liquidity Risk

Figure 2-5 shows about 23% of the assets of a typical life insurance company in current assets with the remainder of the assets in investments. This section discusses this asset mix.

The current assets of a life insurance company are cash and near-cash securities (money market securities). As was discussed about banks, money market securities are assets that can be converted to cash quickly to cover liquidity needs. In the case of life insurance companies, the liquidity needs result from an unusually high death rate among policyholders.

The investment portfolio of a life insurance company is for covering the predictable policy payments and to generate the income needed to cover expenses and provide a return to the owners. Because the obligations of a life insurance company are defined in each policy and the payment patterns are reasonably predictable, life insurance companies invest in financial assets with reasonably predictable returns. Figure 2-5 shows that about 76% of the assets of a life insurance company are in the company's investment portfolio. The figure also shows that the vast majority of the investments are in fixed-income (debt) securities. The reason for investing in fixed-income securities is that these securities make regular interest payments over the life of the security and make a repayment the face value (loan principal) of the security at the end of the life of the security. This pattern of payments provides predictable payments and a predictable rate of return on investments for the life insurance company which matches well with their predictable death payment obligations. How to invest to meet defined obligations is discussed in various places throughout the remainder of this book.

Notice that the only investment category in Figure 2-5 that is not a fixed-income category is stock, which makes up only about 7 percent of total assets. The popular financial news frequently tells us about spectacular gains in the stock market. However, these spectacular gains are unpredictable and are also accompanied by the potential for spectacular losses. The unpredictable nature of stocks does not fit well with the defined obligations of a life insurance company, so stocks are only a small part of a life insurance company's investment portfolio.

2.5   FINANCE COMPANIES

Finance companies are the third type of financial institution covered in this chapter. Figure 2-1 listed only one finance company (American Express) among the S&P 100. However, that does not mean the finance companies are not an important form of financial institution or that finance companies are all small in size. Instead, it is the corporate form of finance companies that keeps them out of the S&P 100—large finance companies are almost always subsidiaries of other large corporations. For example, GMAC, Ford Credit, and GE Credit are huge finance companies that would be among the largest companies in the United States if they were independent companies. However, each of these finance companies is a subsidiary of a major corporation.

Finance companies make loans for a living so, like a bank, credit risk is the primary business risk of finance companies. However, instead of funding their loans with deposits, finance companies raise funds in the financial markets. This means finance companies do not face the liquidity risk that banks face and instead are exposed to credit risk on the funding (liability) side of the balance sheet. Because finance companies earn and pay interest, they are exposed to interest-rate risk. Also, because finance companies earn and pay interest in their primary business activity, their profit comes from the spread between the loan interest rate and the funding interest rate.

2.5.1   Loans and Credit Risk

Figure 2-6 provides the industry averages of assets and liabilities for finance companies. The figure shows four primary asset categories: three loan categories and other assets. These categories suggest that loans are the primary assets of finance companies. Figure 2-6 shows that about 24% of finance company assets are in consumer loans. The majority of these loans are car loans. The second loan category for finance companies is business loans, which make up about 26% of total assets. The majority of the business loans are for equipment, but this category also includes motor vehicle loans to businesses. The third loan category for finance companies is real estate loans, the vast majority of which are home loans (this type of loan is discussed in detail in Chapter 6 on mortgage loans). Real estate loans make up about 13% of finance company assets.

The primary assets of finance companies are loans. Therefore, the primary business risk of finance companies is credit risk. Interestingly, the primary loan categories for finance companies are similar to those for banks. Accordingly, finance companies face the same concerns about credit risk that banks face. However, some finance companies specialize in

Assets	%
Consumer loans	23.60
Business loans	25.86
Real estate loans	12.72
Other	41.84
Liabilities	
Bank loans	3.63
Commercial paper	8.55
Debt to parent	6.37
Other	67.68
Equity	13.77

FIGURE 2-6 Finance company industry assets and liabilities (as a percentage of total assets).

Source: Federal Reserve Board of Governors G20 report.

lending to higher risk customers (some times referred to as subprime lending), and therefore face higher levels of credit risk.

2.5.2 Liabilities, Credit Risk, and Interest-Rate Risk

Figure 2-6 shows four liability categories for finance companies. These categories are bank loans (3.63% of total assets), commercial paper (8.55%), debt to parent (6.37%), and other (67.68%). The majority of the other category is long-term debt. Accordingly, almost all of a finance company's liabilities carry an explicit interest-rate charge. Since a finance company's primary asset category is its loan portfolio, finance companies are exposed to interest-rate risk in the same way as banks.

Finance companies are also exposed to credit risk on their liabilities. However, the credit risk here is their own credit risk. The bank loans and commercial paper on the finance companies' balance sheet will have a time to maturity of less than one year, which means these liabilities will need to be repaid quickly. However, the loans (assets) funded by these liabilities likely will not be repaid within one year. This means the finance companies will need to rollover (refinance) these liabilities when they come due, which exposes the finance companies to credit risk because they will only be able to rollover their liabilities if their credit quality remains acceptable. Acceptable credit quality (default risk) is discussed in a number of places throughout the remainder of this book.

2.6 SECURITIES FIRMS

Securities firms are firms that are in the business of trading financial assets. This is different from owning financial assets. For example, life insurance companies own fixed-income securities for the purpose of generating returns and covering obligations. Securities firms own fixed-income securities so that they are ready to trade these securities with customers. Thus, securities firms own securities so that the securities can be traded and the trading process generates the profits for the business.

Figure 2-1 lists four securities firms among the S&P 100. These firms are Goldman Sachs, Lehman Brothers, Merrill Lynch, and Morgan Stanley. All of these firms are in the business of making trades on financial assets. Figure 2-7 provides the aggregate balance

Assets	%
Cash	1.04
Receivables—dealers, brokers, etc.	38.59
Receivables—customers	4.88
Receivables—noncustomers	0.47
Reverse repurchase agreements	24.73
Securities owned	26.20
Other	4.09
Liabilities	
Bank loans	1.61
Repurchase agreements	41.29
Payables—dealers, brokers, etc.	19.38
Payables—customers	11.87
Payables—noncustomers	1.94
Securities sold short	11.21
Accounts payable and accruals	6.29
Notes and mortgage	1.48
Other	2.10
Equity	2.83

FIGURE 2-7 Securities company industry assets and liabilities (as a percentage of total assets).

sheet for the securities firms and shows that the assets of securities firms are related to trading securities and the liabilities are related to financing the trading process.

2.6.1 Assets for the Business of Trading Securities and Inventory Risk

The largest single asset category (38.59% of total assets) for securities firms is receivables from dealers, brokers, etc. This asset category is for security trades that are in process, but for which the firm has not yet been paid. This occurs because the trading of financial assets typically takes a couple of days to settle (complete).

The next large asset category for securities firms is reverse repurchase agreements (reverse repos), which make up about 25% of total assets. A reverse repo occurs when a securities firm borrows securities and is typically associated with a short sale. A **short sale** is selling a security that you do not own (its "borrowed") and is done when the price of the security is expected to fall. The idea behind a short sale is that the security is sold at today's price and repurchased later after the price has declined, thus creating a profit.[2] When a short sale occurs the seller is selling a security that they do not own. However, the buyer of the security expects to receive the security sold, which means the short seller must borrow the security. Thus, the creation of a reverse repurchase agreement occurs. Discussions of short selling occur in various places throughout this book.

The final major asset category for securities firms is the portfolio of securities owned, which are about 26% of total assets. However, these firms do not own a securities portfolio for long-term investment. Instead, this portfolio is inventory that the firm uses to trade. When a securities portfolio is held for investment, the typical investor is accepting risk for the opportunity to earn long-term gains. However, the portfolio of a securities firm is held

---

[2] An old adage in finance is buy low, sell high. However, the transactions do not have to be in the order of a buy followed by a sale. A short sale is an attempt to sell high, buy low.

to accommodate trading instead of long-term gains. Accordingly, securities firms want to protect their portfolios against short-term losses, and there are a variety of techniques to do this which are discussed later in this book.

2.6.2 Liabilities and Changes in Interest Rates

The primary liability category of a securities firm is repurchase agreements (repos), which are about 41% of total assets. A repo occurs when the owner of a security lends the security and receives (borrows) cash.[3] When the loan is due the cash is repaid plus interest and the security is returned. A repo is a method for an investor to use a security that the investor owns to borrow funds. Accordingly, a repo is an easy way to borrow funds because the securities firm has an inventory of securities that can be used to structure a repo. Because a repo requires the payment of interest at the end of the loan, the extensive use of repos exposes securities firms to changes in interest rates. Techniques for managing changes in interest rates are discussed throughout the book, and repurchase agreements are discussed in detail in Chapter 4.

Payables make up the other major liability category of securities firms. Figure 2-7 shows three payables categories that make up about 33% of total liabilities. These categories are the securities transactions that a firm has started, but has not paid for. These accounts occur because of the time it takes to settle a securities transaction.

2.7 MUTUAL FUNDS

The mutual fund industry is the final type of financial institution to be discussed in this chapter. Figure 2-1 lists the 13 financial institutions in the S&P 100, which does not contain a single mutual fund (or family of funds).[4] This is not to suggest that mutual funds are not an important type of financial institution, but instead, this reflects the nature of the mutual fund business.

A **mutual fund** is a portfolio of securities owned by the fund's investors. A mutual fund competes for investors (and their money) against other similar funds. The competition for investors is based on the return a fund generates for its investors, and history suggests that the funds with the highest returns (within a category of funds) attract the most investors. Large funds have more difficulty than small funds in generating high returns because of the limited number of investment opportunities that are large enough to significantly alter the return for a large fund. Accordingly, the mutual fund industry is made up of many small funds instead of a few large funds.

Figures 2-8 and 2-9 provide an overview of the mutual fund industry. Figure 2-8 shows the four basic asset categories of mutual funds: equity, hybrid, bond, and money market; it also shows that the industry has about $7,414 billion ($7.4 trillion) in securities under management. Figure 2-9 provides a further breakdown of the fund categories and provides the number of funds in each category. The list of the number of funds in each category suggests that in 2003 there were over 8,000 mutual funds in existence.

[3] Note, a repurchase agreement works in the opposite direction of a reverse repurchase agreement.
[4] The Janus Capital Group is a mutual fund family that is listed in the S&P 500.

Equity funds	$3,684.80
Hybrid funds	$436.68
Bond funds	$1,240.92
Money market funds	$2,051.68

FIGURE 2-8   Mutual fund industry assets (2003) ($ billion).

Source: Investment Company Institute, *Mutual Fund Fact Book* (2004).

The assets of a mutual fund are a portfolio of securities held for investment. The liabilities of a mutual fund are the claims that investors have against the fund's portfolio of securities. A mutual fund attracts investors by generating returns and makes a profit by charging fees for its services that exceed the costs of operating the fund.

2.7.1   Securities Held for Investment and Portfolio Risk

The primary asset of a mutual fund is its securities portfolio. As shown in Figure 2-9, a mutual fund specializes in a category of securities. Within each category the fund selects the securities that it believes will best achieve its stated objective. For example, a capital appreciation fund will select stocks that it believes will dramatically increase in price. Investors interested in this objective will consider the fund for investment, and potential investors typically look at past fund performance as well as the securities in the current portfolio.

The major risk to a mutual fund is an extraordinary event that dramatically decreases the value of its portfolio. Of course, exposure to extraordinary events is what provides the opportunity for huge increases in portfolio value. Later in this book, methods to reduce the long-term exposure to significant events are discussed along with some short-term hedges that eliminate decreases in value.

Equity funds	
Capital appreciation	2,933
World	863
Total return	805
Hybrid funds	509
Bond funds	
Corporate	290
High yield	198
World	106
Government	316
Strategic income	355
State municipal	527
National municipal	251
Money market funds	
Taxable	661
Tax-exempt	312

FIGURE 2-9   Number of mutual funds by investment classification (2003).

Source: Investment Company Institute, *Mutual Fund Fact Book* (2004).

	Net investment $ Billion	Redemptions $ Billion	%	Liquidity ratio (%)
Equity funds				
Capital appreciation	1,858.84	362.05	20	4.1
World	517.70	179.61	35	5.7
Total return	1,308.26	168.98	13	3.9
Hybrid funds	436.68	65.33	15	6.7
Bond funds				
Corporate	200.06	71.71	36	6.3
High yield	153.70	43.67	29	5.3
World	27.56	10.78	39	3.7
Government	224.71	87.67	39	1.1
Strategic income	300.79	94.10	31	12.7
State municipal	150.94	26.86	18	2.2
National municipal	183.16	37.163	20	3.7

FIGURE 2-10 Redemptions and liquidity ratios of mutual funds by investment classification (2003).

Source: Investment Company Institute, *Mutual Fund Fact Book* (2004).

Note: Liquidity ratio is the ratio of liquid assets divided by total net assets.

2.7.2 Claims against the Portfolio and Liquidity Risk

The primary liability of a mutual fund is its investors' claims against the investment portfolio, referred to as shares of the mutual fund. Mutual fund investment increments can be of any dollar size, but a common size is $100. The small dollar size of a mutual fund investment increment provides small investors the ability to diversify at low cost. These benefits are discussed in detail later in this book.

Investors purchase claims against (shares of) a mutual fund investment portfolio. Investors can also redeem their claims, requesting that the mutual fund pay them the value of their claim in cash. The ability to redeem their claim is available to investors at any time (similar to bank demand deposits) and therefore creates liquidity risk for mutual funds.

Figure 2-10 provides the net investment by mutual fund category for 2003 and the dollar value of redemptions for 2003. The figure shows that the redemption rates for equity funds in 2003 is between 13 and 35%, whereas the redemption rate for bond funds is between 18 and 39%. These redemption rates represent the percentage of the mutual fund investment portfolio that must be converted to cash and paid to investors during the year. This conversion to cash can create timing problems for the fund managers, so the funds hold some portion of their portfolio in liquid assets to handle redemptions. Figure 2-10 shows that the funds hold between 1.1 and 12.7% (average of about 5%) of their assets in liquid assets.

Retirement plan	48%
Sales force/advice	37%
Direct	10%
Discount broker	5%

FIGURE 2-11 Primary mutual fund purchase channel.

Source: Investment Company Institute, *Mutual Fund Fact Book* (2004).

One mitigating factor that helps mutual funds manage their liquidity risk is the form of ownership of mutual funds. Figure 2-11 shows that 48% of the mutual fund purchases in 2003 were through retirement plans. Retirement plans have restrictions on how and when money in the plans can be withdrawn. The limitations on retirement plan withdrawal reduce the redemption problem for mutual funds.

SUMMARY OF VALUATION AND RISK MANAGEMENT SKILLS

1. Understand the financial intermediation process.

Financial intermediation is an indirect process of SSUs and DSUs coming together for a financial transaction. Financial intermediaries exist because they are often more efficient than a direct search. There are three types of financial intermediation: (1) denomination intermediation, (2) risk intermediation, and (3) maturity intermediation.

2. Understand the risks faced by the five major types of financial institutions.

There are five major types of financial institutions that provide intermediary services: depository institutions, insurance companies, finance companies, securities firms, and mutual funds. Financial institutions face a variety of risks: credit risk, interest-rate risk, market risk, liquidity risk, exchange-rate risk, and operational risk. A financial institution's assets and liabilities determine the specific risks it faces.

QUESTIONS

1. What is the primary function of a financial intermediary?

2. A financial intermediary reduces the cost of a financial transaction. What other benefits are available for a financial transaction done through a financial intermediary?

3. What does a bank do for a living and what risks are a bank exposed to?

4. How do banks make a profit and how has this changed through time?

5. The primary liability of a life insurance company is the death benefits of its policyholders. Explain how the characteristics of death benefits determine the type of assets life insurance companies invest in.

6. What is the difference between a defined benefit pension plan and a defined contribution pension plan?

7. Banks and finance companies often make similar types of loans. However, they fund their loans differently. What is the primary funding source of each and what are the different risks that occur because of the different funding sources?

8. Most financial institutions own financial assets for investment purposes. Why do securities firms hold financial assets and how does this alter their risk concerns?

9. What is a mutual fund and what are a mutual fund's primary benefits for investors?

10. Bank depositors and mutual fund investors can withdraw their funds when desired. How do banks and mutual funds handle this problem?

REFERENCES

ALLEN, F., and A. SANTOMERO, 1997, The theory of financial intermediation, *Journal of Banking and Finance*, *21*, 1461–1485.

HANNAN, T., and G. HANWECK, 1988, Bank insolvency risk and the market for large certificates of deposit, *Journal of Money, Credit, and Banking*, 20, 203–212.

SAUNDERS, A., and M. CORNETT, 2003, *Financial Institutions Management*, 4th Ed. McGraw-Hill Irwin, New York.
A good textbook on the management of financial institutions that focuses on the risks faced by financial institutions.

KEY TERMS

Business Risk The risk faced by a business from their primary business activity.

Credit Risk The risk of default on a loan contract.

Depository Institution The type of financial institution that takes in deposits and makes loans.

Finance Companies Finance companies are in the business of making loans. However, unlike banks, finance companies must borrow their funds from the market.

Financial Intermediation The process of bringing those that have excess funds together with those that need funds working through a financial institution.

Insurance Company Insurance companies sell protection to policyholders against major financial obligations.

Interest-Rate Risk The risk associated with changes in market rates of interest.

Liquidity Risk The risk that an asset cannot be converted to cash quickly enough to pay a financial obligation.

Mutual Fund A mutual fund is a portfolio of securities and is created so investors can buy into the fund.

Pension Funds Pension funds receive payments that are invested to provide retirement cash flows for fund participants.

Securities Firms A securities firm is a financial institution that is in the business of trading financial assets.

Short Sell A short sell of a security is selling a security that the seller does not own. Instead, the seller borrowers the security for the sale and later repurchases the security so it can be returned to the original lender of the security.

THE LEVEL AND STRUCTURE OF INTEREST RATES

3.1 INTRODUCTION

This chapter examines the factors that determine the level of interest rates and explains the characteristics that cause interest rates to vary widely across different types of securities, which defines what analysts call the structure of interest rates. Understanding interest rates is essential for valuing financial assets in general, and interest-bearing financial assets in particular. In later chapters you will apply your understanding of the level and structure of interest rates to measuring and managing the risk of holding or issuing securities.

An example of a situation you might have faced as a young analyst in the mid-1990s is explaining to a portfolio manager why you believe interest rates on U.S. Treasury bonds are declining. Consider the second term of the Clinton administration, during which the U.S. federal government achieved budget surpluses for the first time in decades. The Clinton administration decided to use a portion of the surplus to retire part of the federal government debt, focusing its efforts on retiring long-term Treasury bonds. The resulting increased demand for these bonds increased bond prices and decreased yields. In fact, the yield on the long-term bonds decreased below shorter-term bonds, a relatively unusual occurrence in the bond markets. When you finish reading this chapter, you will have the tools you need to give your boss a coherent explanation of this phenomenon, among many others that you may face.

To begin the discussion of interest rates, the next section uses a simple supply–demand framework called the loanable funds theory to explain the market forces that determine the level of interest rates. We also explain the relationship between interest rates and expected average price levels in the economy. Next you will read about factors that cause interest rates to vary across different securities: time (or term) to maturity, default (or credit) risk, taxes, marketability, and embedded options.

DEVELOPING VALUATION AND RISK MANAGEMENT SKILLS

1. Explain the major factors that determine the level of interest rates in the economy.
2. Understand the relationship between the time to maturity of a security and its interest rate.
3. Understand how default risk (or credit risk) of a security issuer (or borrower) is measured and how it affects the interest rate.

4. Describe how differential tax treatment of interest income causes interest rates to vary across securities.

5. Describe what is meant by marketability and understand the relationship between marketability and interest rates on securities.

6. Explain how various imbedded options cause interest rates to vary across securities.

3.2 LOANABLE FUNDS THEORY OF INTEREST RATES

What is an **interest rate**? Interest rate has a variety of useful definitions, including: the time value of consumption, an opportunity cost, and the rental price of money. We believe the most insightful description is as the rental price for money. In a debt instrument, the borrower is using a lender's money during a period of time specified in the loan contract and returns their money at the end of the contract. This process is similar to renting an apartment. During the time the borrower has the use of the lender's money, the borrower makes periodic interest payments, similar to monthly rent payments on an apartment.[1] Just as some renters are more likely to pay the rent, so, too, are some borrowers more likely to pay their obligations. Hence, there should be no surprise that different borrowers pay different rental rates for the same amount of money (principal).

The **loanable funds theory** of interest rates states that, in the short-run, interest rates are determined by the supply and demand of loanable funds. When all the factors that determine the supply and demand of loanable funds at a given point in time are considered, the theory suggests that the equilibrium interest rate is a combination of (1) a long-run base interest rate, (2) various short-term factors of supply and demand, and (3) current financial market risks. This approach to building interest rates has led to wide use of the loanable funds theory by market analysts and interest rate forecasters.

In loanable funds theory, the economy is divided into three sectors: (1) households, (2) businesses, and (3) government. Households, as a group, are generally net suppliers of funds and are referred to as SSUs (surplus-spending units). Businesses and the government are typically net demanders of funds and are referred to as DSUs (deficit-spending units). Figure 3-1 provides a more complete list of sources of and demanders for loanable funds.

SSUs have surplus funds (income exceeds expenses) in the current period and are looking to earn a return on their surplus funds. SSUs purchase financial assets to earn interest on their surplus funds. Since a portion of the SSU's investments are discretionary, the supply of funds made available by them increases with increasing interest rates. On the other hand, DSUs have a shortage (expenses exceed income) of funds and are looking for sources of funds to finance their shortages. As with the SSUs, a portion of the DSUs expenditures are discretionary, so the demand for loanable funds will increase with decreasing interest rates. The result is an equilibrium level of loanable funds (Q^*) and an equilibrium interest rate (r^*) determined by the supply and demand of loanable funds. This is shown in Figure 3-2.

---

[1] When the borrower is done using the lender's money, the money is returned to the lender, which is similar to moving out of the apartment.

Supply of Loanable Funds
    Consumer savings
    Business savings
    State and local government surpluses
    Federal government surpluses
    Federal Reserve increases in the money supply
Demand for Loanable Funds
    Consumer credit
    Business investment
    State and local government budget deficits
    Federal government budget deficits

FIGURE 3-1 Loanable funds theory. Sources of supply of and demand for loanable funds.

Note: Each of the three sectors of the economy appear as both suppliers and demanders of loanable funds. However, as mentioned previously, households are typically net suppliers of funds and businesses and governments are net demanders of funds.

From the standard supply and demand graph depicted in Figure 3-2, the effect of a change in either the supply or demand of loanable funds on the equilibrium interest rate can easily be seen. For example, if the Federal Reserve decides to increase the money supply, what will happen to interest rates in the short run? The answer, depicted in Figure 3-3, shows that the increase in the money supply will shift the curve for the supply of loanable funds to the right (from supply$_0$ to supply$_1$), which will result in a lower interest rate (r_1).

The loanable funds theory describes the process for determining the equilibrium interest rate at a given point of time as the rate that equates the supply and demand for loanable funds. The remainder of this chapter will consider the various components that determine the level of rates and the structure of rates.

3.3 THE LEVEL OF INTEREST RATES

The level of interest rates is determined by a number of economic factors. The loanable funds theory of interest rates states that an interest rate is a combination of (1) a long-run base rate, (2) various factors including inflation that affect short-run supply and demand,

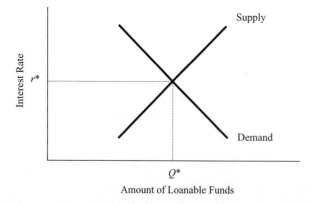

FIGURE 3-2 Loanable funds theory. Equilibrium interest rate.

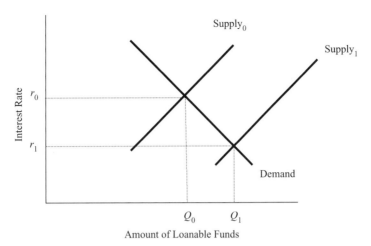

FIGURE 3-3 Loanable funds theory. The effect of an increase in the supply of loanable funds.

and (3) various financial market risks. From this list, there are two factors that affect the level of interest rates: (1) the long-run base rate, and (2) inflation.

3.3.1 The Long-Run Base Rate

The long-run base rate from loanable funds theory is referred to as the **real rate of interest.** The real rate of interest is the equilibrium rate that equates the desire of individuals to save with the desire of businesses to invest. Figure 3-4 depicts the real rate of interest.

From a business viewpoint, Figure 3-4 shows that their desire to invest increases with lower interest rates. Businesses invest in projects that they believe will generate real output in the future. Real output includes the return on investment which, in turn, increases as interest rates decrease.

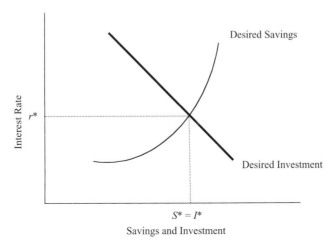

FIGURE 3-4 Determinants of the real rate of interest.

From the viewpoint of individuals, who have the choice to either consume or save, Figure 3-4 shows that their desire to save increases with increases in interest rates. The upward sloping savings curve results from the assumption that individuals, all else equal, would prefer to consume today rather than delay their consumption (this is referred to as a positive time preference). Therefore, individuals must be compensated for delaying their consumption. The higher the compensation, the more individuals are willing to delay their consumption. Thus, an upward-sloping desire to save curve. The real rate of interest is labeled as $r*$ in Figure 3-4 and is the equilibrium interest rate that equates the desire to save with the desire to invest.

3.3.2 Inflation and the Fisher Equation

The real rate of interest compensates the investor for the time preference of consumption. However, in addition to receiving rent on the invested money, the investor wants to be able to purchase the same goods in the future as can be purchased today. This is not a problem if the prices for goods are constant; however, if prices increase then the investor must adjust the contract (rental) rate to ensure that the investor's buying power keeps up with the price increases. The contract rate on a loan is an example of a nominal interest rate. **Nominal interest rates** (or contract interest rates) are the rates that lenders (investors) receive and borrowers pay in the market. The specific adjustment to the nominal (contract) rate that is necessary to keep up with inflation is described as the **Fisher Effect**

The Fisher equation for the contract rate is as follows:

$$(1 + r) = (1 + R)(1 + E(i)) \tag{3-1}$$

where

$$r = \text{the nominal interest rate (contract rate)},$$
$$R = \text{the real interest rate},$$
$$E(i) = \text{the expected annual rate of inflation}.$$

Solving the Fisher equation for the nominal rate (r), we obtain the following equation:

$$r = R + E(i) + (R \times E(i)) \tag{3-2}$$

Equation (3-2) provides the method for calculating the annual contract rate on a loan when inflation exists. The following example calculates the contract rate on a loan and calculates the related cash flows for a one-year $1,000 loan.

EXAMPLE *Fisher Equation Calculation and Loan Cash Flows*

Assume that the real interest rate is 6% and the inflation rate is 7%, then the contract rate should be $r = 0.06 + 0.07 + (0.06 \times 0.07) = 0.1342$, or 13.42%.

Now, assume that a lender wants to make a one-year loan for $1,000. The interest is paid at the end of the year; the real interest rate is 6%; the inflation rate at 7%. What are the cash flows on this loan and what do they compensate for? The answers are in the following table.

Cash flows at the end of the year	Calculation	Amount
Principal		$1,000.00
Compensation for delaying consumption	$1,000 × 6%	$60.00
Compensation for the loss of purchasing power on principal	$1,000 × 7%	$70.00
Compensation for the loss of purchasing power on interest	$1,000 × (6% × 7%)	$4.20
Total compensation	$1,000 × 13.42%	$1,134.20

The preceding loan example shows that the annual compensation on a loan with inflation includes three components: (1) compensation for delaying consumption, (2) loss of the purchasing power on the loan amount, and (3) loss of the purchasing power on interest when the interest payment is made at the end of the year. Note that the contract rate from the Fisher equation does not include an adjustment for risk, so the Fisher equation provides the contract rate for a loan with no risk of default. In other words, it provides the calculation of what is commonly referred to as the *risk-free interest rate*.

3.3.3 Details about Uses of the Fisher Equation

3.3.3.1 The Approximate Fisher Equation
The Fisher equation provides the appropriate contract rate for a default-free loan in an environment that includes inflation. However, many situations arise in finance where the precision of the Fisher equation is not necessary, so people use an approximate Fisher equation as a "rule of thumb." The approximate Fisher equation is as follows:

$$r = R + E(i). \qquad (3\text{-}3)$$

In the approximate Fisher equation, the third term of the Fisher equation is dropped because the value of the third term, especially during periods of low inflation, is approximately zero.

In the Western world, most people are not accustomed to high rates of inflation. Many still regard the mid-1970s as an unusual period of high inflation when rates were in the 10 to 15% range. Other parts of the world would not consider these inflation rates to be high. In 1993, Yugoslavian inflation was exceeding 313 million percent per month at its peak. On December 23, 1993, the Yugoslavian central bank issued a 500 billion dinar note, marking a milestone in their economic chaos. At the time of issue, this note was worth about $6 U.S. It would buy 10 loaves of bread, or less than 4 ounces of poor quality pork, or a gallon of milk, or two dozen eggs. In 1992, before this economic chaos in Yugoslavia, one U.S. dollar was equivalent to 1,000 dinar. By the end of 1993, 180 trillion of the same 1,000 dinar notes—factoring in the missing zeroes—would be needed to equal one U.S. dollar.

3.3.3.2 Estimating the Real Rate of Interest
The interest payments, received or paid, are based on nominal interest rates which, by definition, include an adjustment for inflation. So, to determine the actual (or realized) real rate of interest in any nominal risk-free rate, the adjustment for inflation must be removed. This adjustment

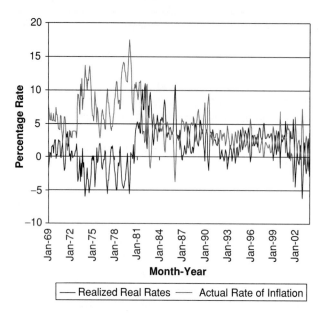

FIGURE 3-5 The relationship between inflation and realized real interest rates.

is generally done using the approximate Fisher equation with the actual nominal rate and the actual inflation rate as follows:

$$R_a = r_a - i_a. \tag{3-4}$$

Using Equation (3-4), Figure 3-5 plots the realized real rate of interest on three-month Treasury bills from January 1969 through December 2003. Figure 3-5 also includes the rate of inflation, which is estimated from the Consumer Price Index (CPI).

Figure 3-5 provides two useful insights. First, the average real rate appears to be about 2%. However, the figure shows that the actual real rate is seldom precisely 2%, which suggests that forecasting the actual rate of inflation is difficult. Second, during the 1970s and early 1980s, the real rate was frequently negative. During these times, investors dramatically underestimated the actual rate of inflation; therefore, they actually paid for delaying consumption rather than being compensated for delaying consumption.

3.3.3.3 *Price Declines or Deflation*

In developing the Fisher equation, the impact of inflation (or rising prices) on nominal interest rates was discussed. However, from Figure 3-5, we see some points in time where inflation is negative. The following example details how to handle negative inflation (deflation) in the Fisher equation.

EXAMPLE *Deflation and Interest Rates*

The CPI decreased for four months from January 1986 through April 1986. This negative inflation means that prices were declining and is referred to as deflation. The Fisher equation handles deflation by attaching a negative sign to the expected rate of inflation ($E(i)$). For example, if the real rate is 3% and the expected deflation is 1%, then the Fisher equation suggests the following nominal rate:

$$r = 0.03 + (-0.01) + (0.03 \times (-0.01)) = 0.0197 \text{ or } 1.97\%.$$

3.3.3.4 *Multiperiod Contract Rates*   The example in Section 3.2 uses the Fisher equation to calculate a nominal rate for a one-year loan. However, many loans cover several years with a fixed contract rate set at the beginning of the loan. So, what is done if there is a multiyear fixed-rate loan?

The answer depends on the expectation for inflation over the life of the loan. If a constant rate of inflation is expected, then the lender would need to receive the same rate in each year to cover inflation, so the earlier example for a one-year loan would be followed. However, a problem arises when the lender expects the annual inflation rates to change over the life of the loan. To be properly compensated for the different inflation rates, a different contract rate for each year is needed. However, in this example, a fixed-rate loan is being made, so different rates are not possible. So, what needs to be done to compensate the lender for the potentially different rates of inflation?

Remember, the objective when adjusting for inflation is to maintain the purchasing power of money so that when the lender gets their principal back they can purchase the same goods as when they loaned it. This means that we do not have to keep up our purchasing power every year. Instead, it means that purchasing power must be maintained on average over the life of the loan. Consequently the annual expected rates of inflation should be averaged over the life of the loan and that average used for the expected rate of inflation in the Fisher equation.

Understanding that multiyear loan rates include the average of the expected annual inflation rates over the life of the loan provides a powerful insight into the relation between inflation rates and interest rates on securities with different terms to maturity. Figure 3-6 graphs inflation rates with three-month Treasury bill and 10-year Treasury note yields. In the figure, a positive relationship is seen between changes in inflation and changes in interest rates. In addition, short-term rates are seen to have a larger response to changes in inflation than do long-term rates. This result occurs because the current rate of inflation is a much smaller portion of the inflation premium in the long-term rates than in short-term rates.

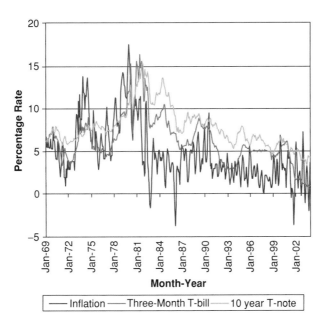

FIGURE 3-6 The sensitivity of long- and short-term interest rates to inflation.

INDUSTRY APPLICATION

NEGATIVE INTEREST RATES[2]

Working in the capital markets is very different from studying in the classroom. One of the major skills a junior associate on a fixed income desk must master is an in-depth understanding of the different forces at work in the market.

In 2003, short-term interest rates hit the lowest level in 45 years. This fact combined with a marked increase in intermediate-term yields resulted in significant settlement problems in repurchase agreements involving the $3\frac{5}{8}\%$ 10-year Treasury note issued in May 2003. Specifically, from early August through mid-November 2003, repurchase agreements for this specific note were sometimes arranged at *negative* interest rates.

There are basically two types of repurchase agreements; general collateral repos and special collateral repos. General acceptable collateral repos commonly include all Treasury securities although there could be limitations such as Treasuries maturing in less than 10 years or it might include agency issues as well. These types of repos are attractive to lenders concerned with earning interest on money and having assets that can be sold quickly in the event of a default by the borrower. The interest rates on these agreements are usually quite close to overnight loan rates in the federal funds market.

In the case of a special collateral repo, the lender designates a specific security as the *only* acceptable collateral. Here, the lender is interested in borrowing a specific security for delivery against a short sale. As a result, the owner of the security may not have any interest at all in borrowing money but is convinced to lend the security because the interest rate is even less than that on general collateral repos. For example, if the special repo rate is 3% and the general repo rate is 4%, an investor can earn a 100 basis points spread by borrowing money on the special collateral repo and lending it on a general collateral repo.

Generally, special collateral repo rates are nearly always greater than zero because, instead of lending money at a negative interest rate to borrow a particularly scarce issue, a short seller can choose to fail on its delivery obligation. In a *fail* a seller does not deliver the promised securities as required and consequently does not receive payment for the securities. The convention in the market is to reschedule delivery for the next day at an *unchanged* price. Thus, the cost of failing is about the same as the cost of borrowing a security on a special collateral repo at a zero interest rate. As a consequence, broker/dealers found failing is usually preferable to borrowing a security at a negative special collateral interest rate.

Unfortunately, the situation is not quite so simple because opportunity costs should also be considered. The Securities and Exchange Commission sets out capital requirement rules that state that a dealer must maintain additional capital for fails to deliver that are more than five business days old and for fails to receive that are more than 30 business days old. In addition, because fails on the $3\frac{5}{8}\%$ 10-year note were becoming so prevalent by August 2003, dealers were experiencing increased labor costs (because more attention had to be paid to unsettled trades) and perhaps just as important, customer relations were beginning to deteriorate because customers were not receiving the securities that they had purchased even after long delays.

To resolve this situation, some dealers decided that they would *pay* interest on money *lent* to *borrow* the 10-year note. The reasoning was that it would be less expensive to pay interest to borrow the notes needed to settle than it was to continue to incur capital charges, labor costs, and continued customer dissatisfaction.

At noon each business day, the Federal Reserve offers by auction to lend for one day up to 65% of the amount of each Treasury that it has in its account and is not out on loan. Dealers who borrow from the Federal Reserve pay an annualized fee that is equivalent to the difference between the rate paid for borrowing money in the general collateral market and the rate earned by ending in the special collateral market. The loan fee that dealers pay the Federal Reserve normally does not rise above the general collateral rate because the special collateral rate for the security will not go below zero. On August 5, 2003, the auction loan fee was 1.25%. The general collateral rate was 0.95% that day, so the implied special collateral rate for the note was -30 basis points. Nor was this a one-day phenomenon; on August 11 through August 13 inclusive the implied special collateral rate was less than -20 basis points. On August 15, 2003 a new $4\frac{1}{4}\%$ 10-year note was issued that eased the stress temporarily—average auction loan fees for the $3\frac{5}{8}\%$ note fell to approximately 1%, which suggests an implied special collateral rate of roughly 0%.

(continued)

NEGATIVE INTEREST RATES[2]

However, on September 11 the Treasury department re-opened the 4¼% 10-year note but not the earlier note, hence there was no chance that fails would cease occurring in the 3⅝% note. That same day the loan fee for this note moved back above the general collateral repo rate and the implied special collateral repo rate fell to −11 basis points. The implied special collateral repo rate remained below zero through the beginning of October and reached a low of −146 basis points on September 26, 2003. Why did this occur? Dealers were willing to pay a premium to borrow from the Federal Reserve because it *never fails to deliver securities.*

In mid-September 2003, some dealers were willing to enter into *"guaranteed delivery"* repos for the 3⅝% note at interest rates as low as −3%. Several other aspects of the usual repo contract were also changed should the collateral lender fail to deliver the notes as scheduled. The use of negative interest rates also likely created an incentive for holders of the note to lend their securities, and further reduce the lack of availability of this note.

This unique scenario should serve to remind people that negative interest rates can occur under reasonable and possible economic conditions. It also shows how the market will react to such conditions by changing pricing and the nature of business contracts.

3.4   THE STRUCTURE OF INTEREST RATES

The structure of interest rates refers to factors that cause interest rates to vary across different securities. Five factors are generally discussed as factors that affect the structure of interest rates. These five factors are (1) time to maturity, (2) default risk, (3) taxes, (4) marketability, and (5) embedded options. Each factor will be independently discussed in the remainder of this chapter.

Before discussing the specifics of each factor, let's look at some interest rates on different classes of debt securities (Figure 3-7) to see what, if any, differences are initially apparent in the rates. Figure 3-7 provides rates from different classes of debt securities for May 2000 and April 2004. Marketability or embedded options cannot be discussed using data on classes of securities because both are security specific. However, time, default risk, and taxes can be discussed using rates from different classes of securities.

Starting at the top of Figure 3-7 with Treasury securities of different maturities, notice that the rates tend to increase with the length of time to maturity. This relationship between rates and time to maturity suggests a time or term premium in interest rates; however, the May 2000 rates show that the interest rate on Treasury securities does not always increase with an increase in the time to maturity. This is an example of rates that result in a twist in the yield curve like the twist mentioned in the first paragraph of this chapter. A closer look

---

[2]This Industry Application is a synopsis of Fleming, M.J., and K.D. Garbade 2004, *Repurchase agreements with negative interest rates, Current Issues in Economics and Finance, 10(5), April, 1–7* (published by the Federal Reserve Bank of New York, New York).

Debt security yield (interest rates)	May 2000 (%)	April 2004 (%)
Three-month Treasury bill	5.99	0.91
Six-month Treasury bill	6.39	1.17
One-year Treasury bill	6.33	1.53
Two-year Treasury note	6.81	2.21
Three-year Treasury note	6.77	2.74
Five-year Treasury note	6.69	3.52
Seven-year Treasury note	6.69	4.01
Ten-year Treasury note	6.44	4.43
Aaa Municipal bonds (20 years)	4.89	4.46
Aaa Corporate bonds (20 years and above)	7.64	5.80
Aa Corporate bonds	7.82	6.04
A Corporate bonds	8.07	6.13
Baa Corporate bonds	8.40	6.51

FIGURE 3-7 Yields on various securities.

will be taken at twists in the yield curve later when the theories that attempt to explain the term premium are discussed.[3]

Next, look at the corporate bond rates. These bond classes have similar maturities, but different bond ratings. The bond ratings measure default risk. As bond ratings change from Aaa to Baa, interest rates tend to increase, suggesting that investors are compensated for default-risk with a default-risk premium.

Finally, notice that municipal bonds, which do have default risk, carry interest rates that are significantly less than similarly rated corporate bonds. Municipal bond interest payments are exempt from federal tax, whereas corporate bond interest payments are taxed as income by the federal government. Thus, municipal bonds can pay lower rates and still compete with corporate bonds.

3.4.1 Time to Maturity

Figure 3-7 shows that a time premium exists in interest rates. The relation between the rates on securities with different times to maturity is referred to as the **term structure** of interest rates. Three main theories have developed to explain the term structure of interest rates. These theories, which will be discussed in the remainder of this section, are referred to as: (1) expectations theory, (2) liquidity preference theory, and (3) preferred habitat theory.

Before moving on to term structure theory, the difference between the term structure of interest rates and the **yield curve** needs to be discussed. The term structure refers to the relationship between rates on debt securities that are identical in all characteristics except the time to maturity. The yield curve is the plot of yields for securities of varying maturities.

3.4.1.1 Expectations Theory
The **expectations theory** was the first theory developed to explain the term structure of interest rates.[4] The expectations theory assumes

---

[3] Figure 3-7 provides interest rates (yields) on Treasury securities with different times to maturity. The yield curve is a plot of these rates.

[4] Expectations theory was first proposed by Irving Fisher in 1930.

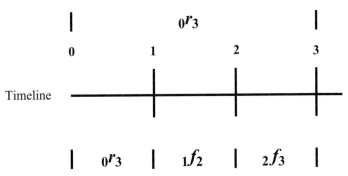

FIGURE 3-8 Timeline for a three-year interest rate.

that investors are indifferent to risk and in efficient markets they will buy and sell debt securities of different maturities until the expected return on all assets is equal across all time periods. Therefore, current long-term rates are based on current and expected future short-term rates. This means that the structure of interest rates at any point in time is based on the market's expectation of future interest rates. The expectations theory is the principal theory underlying the calculation of future and forward rates (see Chapter 9).

The expectations theory can explain three different shapes for the yield curve. When investors expect rates to increase in the future, the yield curve will be upward sloping. When investors expect rates to remain constant, the yield curve will be flat. Finally, when investors expect rates to fall, the yield curve will be downward sloping.

One of the important implications of expectations theory is that current long-term rates are a combination of current and expected future short-term rates. Before moving on, some time must be spent on this point. Specifically, long-term rates are the geometric average of the current and future short-term rates.[5] Thus, the formula for a long-term interest rate under expectations theory is as follows:

$$(1 + {_0}r_t)^t = (1 + {_0}r_1)(1 + {_1}f_2)(1 + {_1}f_3)\ldots(1 + {_{(t-1)}}f_t) \tag{3-5}$$

where

> r = a **spot rate**,
>
> f = an expected one-period future short-term rate,
>
> t = number of time periods in the long-term rate.

In this notation, the prescript to the rate is the beginning of the time period that the rate covers and the postscript is the ending of the time period that the rate covers on a timeline. For example, a three-year rate would be $(1+{_0}r_3)^3 = (1+{_0}r_1)(1+{_1}f_2)(1+{_2}f_3)$ and would appear on a timeline as shown in Figure 3-8.

The expectations theory defines the long-term rate as the geometric average of current and expected future short-term rates. This feature can be used to calculate an unbiased estimate of future short-term interest rates. Specifically, the last expected future short-term

---

[5] As a point of information, the general formula is provided for the arithmetic and geometric averages typically used in finance for average rates of return. The arithmetic average is $\bar{r} = \left(\frac{1}{n}\right)\sum_{t=1}^{n} r_t$ and the geometric average is $\bar{r} = \left[\sqrt[n]{\prod_{t=1}^{n}(1 + r_t)}\right] - 1$.

rate embedded in the long-term rate can be found, which is done by solving Equation (3-5) for the last short-term rate on the right-hand side of the equation. The result is

$$(1 + {}_{t-1}f_t) = \frac{(1 + {}_0r_t)^t}{(1 + {}_0r_1)(1 + {}_1f_2)\cdots(1 + {}_{t-2}f_{t-1})} = \frac{(1 + {}_0r_t)^t}{(1 + {}_0r_{t-1})^{t-1}}. \tag{3-6}$$

Thus, Equation (3-6) can be used to calculate expected future interest rates as in the following example.

EXAMPLE *Expected Future Interest Rates*

Calculate the expected one-year rate for next year using the Treasury yields from Figure 3-9. In May, 2000, the two-year Treasury note has a yield of 6.81% and the one-year Treasury bill has a yield of 6.33%. Therefore, the one-year rate for next year is

$$(1 + {}_1f_2) = \frac{(1 + {}_0r_2)^2}{(1 + {}_0r_1)^1} = \frac{(1 + 0.0681)^2}{1 + 0.0633} = 1.0729 \text{ so } {}_1f_2 \text{ is } 7.29\%.$$

Before moving on, a point about the long-term rate needs to be clarified. All interest rates are presented as annualized interest rates, so a long-term rate is expressed as the annualized interest rate on a long-term security. For the preceding example, the two-year rate is the annualized rate on a Treasury security with two years to maturity.

3.4.1.2 *Liquidity Preference*
The expectations theory assumes that investors are indifferent to risk, which is usually referred to as being risk neutral. However, as seen in Figure 3-9, investors demand additional returns for taking on higher levels of risk. This insight suggests that the average investor is risk averse instead of risk neutral. **Liquidity preference theory** extends expectations theory by assuming that investors are risk averse. In other words, they prefer liquidity.

The essence of liquidity preference theory is that a risk-averse investor will never extend the maturity of a debt investment beyond the desired holding period of the investment unless the investor can expect to receive a risk premium. The reason for the risk premium is that if the maturity extends beyond the desired holding period, the investor is exposed to

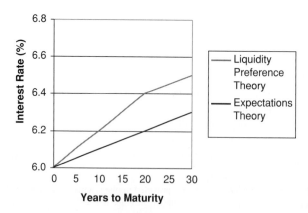

FIGURE 3-9 The effect of liquidity preference in the term structure.

price risk because the investor must sell the investment at the end of the holding at the then prevailing market price. The need for a risk premium implies that the future short-term rates embedded in a long-term rate are upward-biased predictors of the expected future short-term rate because the embedded short-term rates must include the expected risk premium.

Another important assumption underlying the liquidity preference theory is that the demand for long-term debt exceeds the supply (lenders prefer shorter maturities than borrowers), and that the supply and demand differential increases as the time to maturity increases. This suggests that the risk premium from liquidity preference increases with time to maturity. Defining lp as the risk premium expected for increasing the time to maturity of a debt instrument by one period, the relationship for liquidity preference risk premiums (using the same pre- and postscript notation developed above) is $0 \leq {}_1lp_2 \leq {}_2lp_3 \leq {}_3lp_4 \leq$ .... Thus, for liquidity preference theory the Equation (3-5) from expectations theory can be modified to include the liquidity risk premiums as follows:

$$(1 + {}_0r_t)^t = (1 + {}_0r_1)(1 + {}_1f_2 + {}_1lp_2)(1 + {}_2f_3 + {}_2lp_3)\cdots(1 + {}_{t-1}r_t + {}_{t-1}lp_t). \quad (3\text{-}7)$$

The implication of Equation (3-7) is that the yield curve assuming risk aversion will always be above the yield curve assuming risk neutrality and the spread between the curves either increases or remains constant with increasing time to maturity. Figure 3-9 plots two yield curves: one for expectations theory and one for liquidity preference theory.

3.4.1.3 *Preferred Habitat Theory*   The liquidity premiums for risk aversion might seem to fully correct for the deficiencies of the pure expectations theory. However, empirical evidence shows that the liquidity premiums frequently do not increase monotonically with increasing time to maturity. In addition, as seen in the May 2000 Treasury rates in Figure 3-7, rates may increase initially with increasing time to maturity and then begin to decrease with increasing maturity. A hump or twist in the term structure is only possible if risk-averse investors have maturity preferences based on their desired holding periods.[6]

Traditionally, a discussion of maturity preferences begins with **market segmentation theory.** Market segmentation theory assumes that investors are completely risk averse. This means that investors will *never* mismatch the maturity of their investments relative to their desired holding period. The problem with market segmentation is that complete risk aversion is an overly restrictive assumption that does not fit well with the interest rate data or with the realities of the real world. The **preferred habitat theory** was developed to overcome the problems with the market segmentation theory.[7]

The preferred habitat theory assumes that investors are risk averse and that investors have maturity preferences equal to the desired holding period of the investment. This means the investor will prefer a debt investment that matches the desired holding period, but will purchase securities of different maturities if adequately compensated for the additional risk. This differs from the liquidity preference theory because the investor may choose an investment with a maturity either shorter or longer than the desired holding period. In either

---

[6] SmartMoney.com has a feature called the Living Yield Curve that shows the yield curve change through time at http://www.smartmoney.com/onebond/index.cfm?story=yieldcurve.

[7] A preferred habitat was first suggested by Modigliani and Sutch (1966). Recently, Ogden (1987) and Griffiths and Winters (1997) have suggested that a preferred habitat can explain time-based anomalies in short-term interest rates.

case, the investor takes on additional risk with an investment that does not match the desired holding period. If the maturity of the security is less than the desired holding period, the investor faces reinvestment rate risk because when the security matures before the end of the desired holding period, the investor will have to reinvest for the remainder of the holding period. Note that the investor will reenter the market at the prevailing current interest rate with an investment that reaches the desired initial maturity. If the actual maturity is longer than the desired holding period, the investor faces price risk because the investor must sell the investment at the market price at the end of the desire holding period.

The bottom line with preferred habitat theory is that investors prefer debt securities which have maturities that match the investors's desired holding period. However, investors will consider reasonable substitutes if adequately compensated for the additional risk caused when the security's maturity does not match the investor's holding period. Investors' preferences for specific maturities create the twists in the yield curve. However, investors' willingness to move into other maturities for additional compensation prevents dramatic differences in adjacent interest rates across the yield curve.

3.4.1.4 Which Theory Is Correct?

Figure 3-10 provides the yield curve from the Treasury security term structure in Figure 3-7. The May 2000 yield curve includes a hump or twist. The only theory available that could explain this term structure is the preferred habitat theory. Does this mean that preferred habitat theory is the only theory consistent with actual term structure data? The answer is no. In Figure 3-10, the April 2004 yield curve clearly shows a curve that either the expectations theory or the liquidity preference theory can explain.

Recall that the preferred habitat theory was developed from extensions of expectations theory and liquidity preference theory; therefore, a term structure consistent with a preferred habitat should contain elements of both the expectations and the liquidity preference theories. Historical interest rate data suggest that this is, in fact, true. The data suggest that day-to-day changes in the term structure contain patterns that are most consistent with

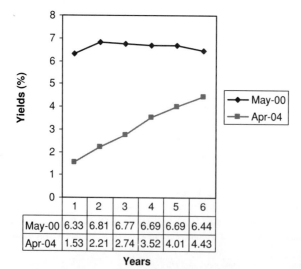

	1	2	3	4	5	6
May-00	6.33	6.81	6.77	6.69	6.69	6.44
Apr-04	1.53	2.21	2.74	3.52	4.01	4.43

Years

FIGURE 3-10 Various shapes of yield curves.

a preferred habitat. Over the long run, however, evidence exists that supports a role for expectations and liquidity preferences in interest rates.

3.4.2 Default Risk

At the beginning of the discussion of the structure of interest rates, Figure 3-7 showed that interest rates increased with a change in corporate bond ratings. The increase was described as a default-risk premium. Since the link between risk and expected returns is already understood, this section will discuss the meaning of **default risk** and its link to **bond ratings.**

A default on a debt contract occurs when the borrower violates any of the conditions contained in the loan contract. The concern for investors (lenders) in a debt contract is how much the default impairs the expected cash flows from the contract. A wide range of possible effects may occur on cash flows from a default. At one end of the range is a one-day late payment. This is a default. However, this type of default is unlikely to impair future cash flows. At the other end of the range is bankruptcy. Here the investors are unlikely to receive the expected future interest payments and may lose part or all of the principal originally loaned.

When the risk of default exists, investors will demand compensation for the potential impairment of their expected future cash flows. However, with the wide range of possible impacts on cash flows from default, the risk premium that investors will demand varies substantially with the expected impact of default on their cash flows. Thus, a way is needed to measure the default risk of a borrower. Bond ratings are used as our proxy for a borrower's risk of default on a debt contract.

3.4.2.1 Bond Ratings
Bond ratings are determined by rating agencies. Several agencies exist, but two agencies are the most well-known because they dominate the market for bond ratings: Moody's Investor Services and Standard and Poor's.[8] In this section, we focus on the ratings by Moody's and Standard and Poor's (S&P).

S&P defines a bond rating as a current opinion of the borrower's overall financial ability to pay its obligations. Moody's states that a rating measures the total expected credit loss over the life of the debt security. Moody's method includes both the likelihood of default and the expected loss from default. Both agencies do a thorough financial analysis of the borrower to determine the default risk of the borrower; and then, based on this determination, the agency assigns a bond rating to the borrower.

Figure 3-11 provides the bond ratings used by Moody's and S&P and includes a brief description of the credit quality associated with each rating. In Figure 3-11, the lowest default risk rating is listed at the top, and the highest default risk is at the bottom. Also, note that the figure has subheadings that divide that rating into two grades: investment grade and speculative grade. Investment grade ratings suggest a low risk of default and associated losses, and speculative grade ratings suggest that a reasonable chance of default exists.

---

[8] We note that both agencies also provide ratings for short-term debt and other useful information about credit quality. We focus on bond ratings because these ratings focus on the long-term financial strength of the borrower. If you want more of the information available from these rating agencies, you can visit their websites: www.standardandpoors.com and www.moodys.com.

Moody's rating	S&P rating	Explanation
		Investment grades
Aaa	AAA	Extremely strong, best quality
Aa	AA	Very strong, high quality
A	A	Strong, upper-medium grade
Baa	BBB	Adequate, medium-grade
		Speculative grades
Ba	BB	Judged to have speculative elements
B	B	Lack the characteristics of a desirable investment
Caa	CCC	Currently vulnerable, of poor standing
Ca	CC	Currently highly vulnerable, marked shortcomings
C	C	Extremely poor prospects

FIGURE 3-11   Description of major bond rating categories.

The rating agencies assign bond ratings based on their opinions of the default risk of the borrowers. However, for there to be a link between bond ratings and risk premiums, the lower quality ratings must be associated with higher levels of actual defaults. Moody's reports various default statistics for its bond ratings and Figure 3-12 provides a small portion of that information. From Moody's statistics, a clear link can be seen between the bond ratings and default rates, with the lower quality ratings associated with higher rates of default.[9]

Bond and credit ratings have many practical applications that will be discussed throughout the remainder of this book. These ratings are particularly important in bond pricing, money market risk management, and the evolving market for credit derivatives.

3.4.3 Taxes

The third factor in the structure of interest rate is taxes. Figure 3-7 showed **municipal bonds** to have a significantly lower interest rate than corporate bonds with similar time to maturity and the same bond rating. The primary difference between municipal bonds and corporate bonds is the federal tax treatment of interest payments. Investors pay federal tax on interest received from corporate bonds, but interest received from municipal bonds is exempt from federal tax.

In a world with taxes, investors care about their after-tax rate of return because the after-tax return is the portion of the total return on their investments they get to keep. The formula for after-tax returns is as follows:

$$r_{at} = r_{bt}(1 - t) \tag{3-8}$$

where

r_{at} = after-tax return,
r_{bt} = before-tax return, and
t = the investor's marginal tax rate.

---

[9] We recognize that the data in Figure 3-12 include the Great Depression, which is a time period with a high level of defaults; therefore, we examined data from different time periods. The numbers change across different time periods (although the numbers are surprisingly similar), but the link between the bond ratings and levels of default remains across all of the time periods.

Years	1	5	10	15	20
Aaa	0.00	0.20	1.09	1.89	2.38
Aa	0.08	0.97	3.10	5.61	6.75
A	0.08	1.37	3.61	6.13	7.47
Baa	0.30	3.51	7.92	11.46	13.95
Ba	1.43	10.04	19.05	25.95	30.82
B	4.48	20.89	31.90	39.17	43.70

FIGURE 3-12 Cumulative default rates percentages by rating for the years after the rating (1920–1999).

Restating Equation (3-8), the relationship between municipal bond rates of return and corporate bond rates of return when an investor would be indifferent between the two investments is as follows:

$$r_{\text{municipal}} = r_{\text{corporate}} \times (1 - \text{investor's marginal federal tax rate}) \qquad (3\text{-}9)$$

Equation (3-9) shows that municipal bonds can pay lower coupon interest rates and still be competitive with similar corporate bonds because of their favorable federal tax treatment.

The tax effect shown in Figure 3-7 shows the average reduction in coupon interest that municipal bonds pay at the time the data were collected. This is an average effect. It does not provide the specific reduction an individual investor is willing to accept because that choice is based on the individual investor's marginal federal tax rate. The following example provides the calculation an individual investor would make to determine whether a tax-exempt bond or a taxable bond is a better investment.

EXAMPLE   *Taxable vs. Tax-Exempt Returns*

Assume AAA corporate bonds pay 7.50% interest and an investor's marginal federal tax rate is 30%. Then the indifference rate for AAA municipal bonds would be 5.25% [5.25% = 7.50% (1−30%)].

This means this investor, with a 30% marginal tax rate, would prefer AAA municipal bonds if their coupon rate is above 5.25% and would prefer corporate bonds if the AAA municipal coupon rate is below 5.25%. Of course, the decision point (the municipal bond rate) would be different for individuals with different marginal tax rates.

3.4.4 Marketability

Marketability is the fourth factor that affects the structure of interest rates. Less marketable securities are more difficult to sell at market prices and, therefore, must pay higher interest rates to compensate the investor for the additional risk. Often, long-term debt securities are assumed to be less marketable than short-term debt securities and thus would be part of the discussion of the general structure of rates associated with the interest rates in Figure 3-7. However, marketability is based on the ability to trade and the assumption should not be made that all short-term debt securities are easier to trade than all long-term debt securities. Accordingly, marketability is not discussed as a factor in the general structure of interest rates, and instead marketability for each debt security should be examined individually.

Marketability refers to the cost and speed with which an investor can sell the security without a significant loss of value. Highly marketable securities have a low cost and high speed of trading. As the trading cost increases and/or the speed declines, securities are less marketable. To make certain the entire cost of trading is considered, the following set of costs must be examined:

- price concessions necessary for the sale,

- the cost of the executing the trade,
- search costs, and
- information costs.

After considering all the marketability factors, investors (lenders) demand higher interest rates on less marketable securities. In other words, lenders include a marketability premium in interest rates with the marketability premium increasing as the marketability of the security declines.

3.4.5 Embedded Options

The fifth and final factor in the structure of interest rates is the effect of embedded options in the debt contract on interest rates. An embedded option in a debt contract provides one party in the debt contract with the right to modify their position. Because different types of options are available, each type of option is examined individually instead of discussing them in general. The three types of embedded options we discuss are (1) an embedded call option (a **callable bond**), (2) an embedded put option (a **putable bond**), and (3) an embedded conversion option (a **convertible bond**).

The embedded call option in a callable bond provides the issuer of the bond the right to retire (or call) the bond at a predetermined price before its maturity date. This is a valuable right for the borrower that creates additional risk for the lender (the investor) relative to a noncallable bond. This additional risk is that the investor may not receive all the cash flows originally expected from the debt contract. In addition, borrowers tend to call bonds when interest rates are decreasing so that they can replace the bond with a bond paying a lower interest rate. This means the investor would also have to reinvest at a lower rate. Because of this additional risk, the investor will demand a higher interest rate on a callable bond relative to a similar noncallable bond. The increase in the interest rate is referred to as the *call interest premium.*

The embedded put option in a putable bond provides the investor (buyer of the bond) the right to sell (or put), at a predetermined price, the bond back to the issuer before its maturity date. This embedded option provides the investor with a valuable right and creates additional risk for the borrower. The investor would put the bond when interest rates have increased, which would cause the borrower to refinance the bond at a higher interest rate. Because of the additional risk to the borrower, the borrower will pay a lower interest rate than on similar nonputable debt. The interest rate reduction is referred to as the *put interest discount.* Usually only companies with good credit ratings issue putable bonds.

The embedded conversion option in a convertible bond provides the investor the right to convert the bond, at a predetermined conversion rate, into another type of security before the bond's maturity date. The most common conversion is a conversion to common stock. The conversion option is a valuable right for the investor; therefore, the investor will pay a higher price for a convertible bond relative to a similar nonconvertible bond. The higher price means a lower rate of return (yield) on the convertible bond, and the decrease in the yield is referred to as the *conversion yield discount.* The convertible bond also provides value to the issuer as it allows the company to raise more funds (than a nonconvertible bond of similar risk) when issued and pay lower amounts of interest during the life of the bond. Companies issue convertible bonds when they are trying to fund positive NPV projects that require major capital outflows over several years.

IN THE NEWS

Following is a classic example of how the Federal Reserve manages interests rates and the importance of interest rates to the financial markets as a whole. The example illustrates why the financial news media closely follows the interest rate management activities of the Federal Reserve.

Between 10:00 A.M. and 11:00 A.M. on Wednesday, April 18, 2001, the Federal Reserve made a surprise announcement during their morning conference call that they had agreed to reduce their policy target fed funds rate by 50 basis points from 5.00 to 4.50%. The Fed said that the reduction was made because of concerns that lackluster corporate investment could make the economy "unacceptably weak." The stock markets responded with an immediate across-the-board upturn. Immediately following the announcement, the S&P 500 increased in value by about 2%. A chart of the S&P 500 index for April 17, 18, and 19, 2001, is provided as a representative example of the stock market response.

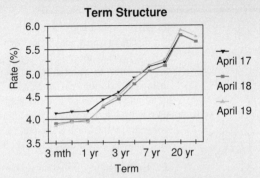

Term Structure

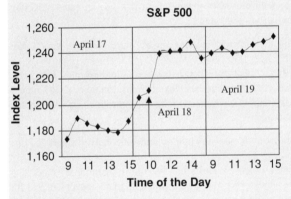

S&P 500

One interesting question following the Fed's announcement and the stock market's reaction is whether the target rate change caused a change in the market's forecast of future cash flows or a change in the market's forecast of future interest rates? From the expectations theory of the term structure, an expected change in future interest rates would appear as a change in the position or shape of the term structure of interest rates.

From the chart of the term structure of interest rates for April 17, 18, and 19, the expectations of future interest rates for the next two years appeared to have changed following the Fed's announcement. Terms of two years or less had lower rates after the Fed target rate decrease. For terms of more than two years, very little difference can be seen between, before, or after the target rate change. The term structure picture combined with a relatively stable S&P 500 level from 11 A.M. on the 18th through the end of the day of the 19th suggests that the stock market responded to lower interest rates.

Before leaving this brief news item, one more point needs to be made. The Federal Reserve did not change the position of the term structure through trading. Instead, the Fed changed the position of the term structure through changing market expectations of future interest rates through a change in the policy target interest rate.

The Federal Reserve continued to lower the target rate through 2001, reaching a target rate of 1.75% on December 11, 2001. The next target rate change was a decrease to 1.25% on November 6, 2002, which was followed by one final decrease to 1.00% on June 25, 2003. On March 24, 2004 the president of the Federal Reserve Bank of Atlanta commented that he believes that it is time to begin raising the target rate again to accompany the recovery of the economy. His concern is that as businesses plan and expand with the recovery of the economy they will use reasonable expectations for future interest rates instead of the historical lows seen over the last year or two. He believes that increases in the target rate will serve as a useful reminder to businesses about realistic future interest rates.

SUMMARY OF VALUATION AND RISK MANAGEMENT SKILLS

1. Explain the major factors that determine the level of interest rates in the economy.

   The two principal factors that determine the level of interest rates are the real rate and inflation. The real rate is the rate demanded for delaying consumption and is the base rate for all nominal interest rates. In general, increases (decreases) in the demand for (supply of) loanable funds result in increases in the real interest rate. Inflation, the expected change in prices of goods, is included in all interest rates so that the lender's purchasing power is protected over the life of the loan (the time period during which consumption is delayed). The Fisher equation shows that the risk-free (or nominal) interest rate is the real rate plus the expected rate of inflation. Generally, nominal interest rates increase when the expected rate of inflation increases.

2. Understand the relationship between the time to maturity of a security and its interest rate.

   There are three major theories to explain the term (time) structure of interest rates: expectations theory, liquidity preference theory, and preferred habitat theory. The historical data on interest rates provide some support for each theory. Investor expectations about future interest rate movements tend to be associated with the shape of the yield curve. When interest rates are expected to increase, long-term rates tend to be higher than short-term and the yield curve slopes upward. The opposite tends to occur when interest rates are expected to decline. Liquidity preference and preferred habitats may cause deviations from this simple explanation.

3. Understand how default risk (or credit risk) of a security issuer (or borrower) is measured and how it affects the interest rate.

   Bond ratings tend to be lower for securities with more default risk. Lower rated securities exhibit more defaults and tend to have higher interest rates.

4. Describe how differential tax treatment of interest income causes interest rates to vary across securities.

   Differential tax treatment of interest payments affects the structure of interest rates. Generally, securities with favorable tax treatment on interest payments have lower yields. Municipal bond interest is exempt from federal income tax, so they tend to have lower yields than corporate (taxable) bonds with similar terms to maturity and bond ratings.

5. Describe what is meant by marketability and understand the relationship between marketability and interest rates on securities.

   Marketability refers to the ease with which a security can be sold in a secondary market. A security that is highly marketable is easy for an investor to sell. Since this is a convenience to the investor, highly marketable securities tend to have lower yields than less marketable securities.

6. Explain how various options embedded cause interest rates to vary across securities.

   A security can contain embedded options that affect the interest rate. Three types of embedded options are discussed in the chapter: a call option, a put option, and a conversion option. Securities with call (put) options tend to have higher (lower) yields than otherwise similar securities without these options. A conversion option is a benefit to the investor, so they generally require lower yields on convertible securities compared to otherwise similar non-convertible securities.

QUESTIONS

1. What is an interest rate?

2. What is the real rate of interest and how is it used to build a nominal interest rate?

3. The Fisher Effect states that the risk-free nominal rate of interest has three components. Define each component in terms of the compensation it provides the lender (investor).

4. You have agreed to make a one-year loan with principal and interest due at the end of the year. You and the borrower agree that the real interest rate is 3.5% and expected inflation is 1.7%. In addition, you believe that the probability of default on the loan is zero. What is the contract rate you will request on the loan? What would be your contract rate if the borrower has a Baa bond rating and the Baa default premium over a risk-free loan rate is 1.9%?

5. Using a spreadsheet, prepare a chart of real interest rates and rates of inflation to demonstrate the levels of inflation necessary for the third term in the Fisher equation to exceed 1%.

6. What is the appropriate annual risk-free rate on a three-year default-free loan under the following conditions? Real interest rate = 3%, first year expected inflation is 1.7%, second year expected inflation is 2.2%, third year expected inflation is 1.9%.

7. Using Equation 3-6 and the data in Figure 3-7 for May 2000, calculate the one-year interest rate expected for year three.

8. Using Equation 3-6 and the data in Figure 3-7 for April 2004, calculate the one-year interest rate expected for year two.

9. In this chapter, we discussed using expectations theory to find expected future interest rates, but we only discussed estimating expected rates covering a one-year period. However, the process can be generalized to estimate future interest rates over multi-year periods. Use the data in Figure 3-7 for April 2004 to estimate the expected annualized interest for a two-year security that starts three years in the future. (Hint: this security spans years four and five and the figure contains current rates for three- and five-year securities.)

10. Explain why the preferred habitat theory is a necessary extension to the expectations theory and the liquidity preference theory for explaining a twisted term structure. See the term structure for May 2000 in Figure 3-10 as an example.

11. Define default and explain why default-risk premiums vary across different borrowers.

12. The current marginal tax rates for individuals in the United States are 10, 15, 25, 28, 33, and 35%. Figure 3-7 reports an Aa corporate bond return of 7.82% in May 2000. Calculate the municipal bond yield yields at which a taxpayer in each marginal tax rate would be indifferent between the 7.82% corporate bond yield and a municipal Aa bond.

13. A city government with an Aa bond rating is considering a bond issue to build two new schools. The city knows that the interest payments on its bonds are exempt from federal income tax and thus its bonds are an attractive investment to high income investors wishing to shelter income from federal income tax. The city determines that investors in the marginal tax brackets of 33 and 35% are the most likely investors for the city's bonds. Using the April 2004 data from Figure 3-7, determine the lowest interest rate the city can pay on its bonds and still be an attractive investment to investors in the 33 and 35% tax brackets.

14. Explain why an investor would demand a higher coupon rate on a bond that the investor anticipates would be difficult to sell, if the need to sell occurred.

15. Explain who has the valuable right in a putable bond and why this right leads to a lower coupon rate on a putable bond than on a comparable nonputable bond.

16. Explain who has the valuable right in a callable bond and why that right leads to a higher coupon rate on a callable bond than for a comparable noncallable bond.

REFERENCES

Asquith, P., D. Mullins, Jr., and E. Wolff, 1989, Original issue high yield bonds: Aging analyses of defaults, exchanges, and calls, *Journal of Finance, 44*, 923–952.

The authors examine the argument that high yield bonds default at a much lower rate than suggested by their coupon rate. The authors are able to reject the notion of low default rates on high yield bonds. They find that 34% of the high yield bonds issued in 1977 and 1978 had defaulted by the end of 1988.

Fleming, M., and K. Garbade, 2004, Repurchase agreements with negative interest rates, *Federal Reserve Bank of New York Current Issues in Economics and Finance, 10*, 1–7.

The authors discuss the market conditions that lead to negative interest rates on repurchase agreements on the 10-year Treasury note issued in May of 2003. The repurchase agreements on this 10-year T-note became what is known as a "special collateral" repurchase agreement.

Griffiths, M., and D. Winters, 1997, On a preferred habitat for liquidity at the turn-of-the-year: Evidence from the term-repo market, *Journal of Financial Services Research, 12*, 21–38.

The authors examine the market for term repos at the turn-of-the-year and find that repos that mature after the turn-of-the-year carry a substantial interest rate premium relative to repos of the same term that mature before the year-end. The authors conclude that their results derive from a general year-end desire for liquidity.

Kane, E., and B. Malkiel, 1967, The term structure of interest rates: An analysis of a survey of interest-rate expectations, *Review of Economics and Statistics, 49*, 343–355.

The authors' survey informed investors about interest rate expectations. They find that investors form interest rate expectations and these expectations influence maturity choices for investment. They also find a term premium that increases with time to maturity.

MacDonald, R., and P. Macmillan, 1994, On the expectations view of the term structure, term premia, and survey-based expectations, *The Economic Journal, 104*, 1070–1086.

The authors use U.K. interest rate survey data to examine the short end of the term structure. They find that 30% of the movement in the forward premium is explained by time-varying term premium and 70% is explained by expected changes in interest rates.

Modigliani, F., and R. Sutch, 1966, Innovations in interest rate policy, *American Economic Review, 56*, 178–197.

This is the paper where the preferred habitat theory was proposed. The authors suggest that maturity matters to investors and not all investors focus on the short term. They propose this hypothesis in the framework of the Kennedy Administration's policy known as *Operation Twist,* which was an attempt to twist the yield curve.

Nelson, C., and W. Schwert, 1977, Short-term interest rates as predictors of inflation: On testing the hypothesis that the real rate of interest is constant, *American Economic Review, 67*, 478–486.

The authors revisit Fama's (*American Economic Review, 1975*) finding that the real rate of interest is constant, using more powerful tests, and conclude that the real rate of interest is not constant. A nonconstant real rate is consistent with the view that the real rate varies over time and can be related to economic variables such as real output and monetary policy.

Ogden J., 1987, The end of the month as a preferred habitat: A test of operational efficiency in the money market, *Journal of Financial and Quantitative Analysis, 22*, 329–344.

Ogden relates the observed turn-of-the-month effect in T-bills to regular corporate cash flow cycles that concentrate payments at the turn-of-the-month and concludes that the cash flow cycle creates a preferred habitat for the last T-bill that matures each month.

Rose, A. 1988, Is the real interest rate stable? *Journal of Finance, 43*, 1095–1112.

The author concludes that the real rate of interest has a unit root and therefore cannot be constant.

Russell, S., 1992, Understanding the term structure of interest rates: The expectations theory, *Federal Reserve Bank of St. Louis-Review, July/August*, 36–50.

The author provides an excellent practical explanation of expectations theory and finds evidence that expectations influence the term structure and that uncertainty about expectations leads risk-averse investors to demand risk premiums.

Santoni, G., and C. Stone, 1982, The fed and the real rate of interest, *Federal Reserve Bank of St. Louis-Review, December*, 8–18.

The authors provide a good discussion of (1) what the real rate is, (2) why it is important, and (3) what influence the Fed can have on it.

KEY TERMS

Bond Ratings Bond ratings provide a relative measure of default risk. The ratings are provided by a rating agency after a thorough financial analysis of the borrower.

Callable Bond A callable bond is a bond where the issuer has the right the retire (call) the bond before maturity at a predetermined price.

Convertible Bond   A convertible bond is a bond where the owner has the right to convert the bond into another security before maturity at a predetermined conversion rate. Typically, the bond is convertible to common stock.

Default Risk   Default risk is the risk that the borrower will not meet the obligations of the debt contract. The severity of default ranges from a payment being late to bankruptcy.

Expectations Theory   The expecations theory is the theory for the term structure that states that long-term rates are based on investors' expectations of future interest rates.

Fisher Effect   The Fisher Effect describes the relationship between nominal rates and inflation rates using the real rate of interest as the base rate.

Interest Rate   An interest rate is the rental price of money. It is the rent a borrower pays during the time period the borrower is using the lender's money.

Liquidity Preference Theory   The liquidity preference theory is a theory for the term structure that assumes that investors are risk averse and, therefore, demand higher rates on riskier securities. Long-term debt is riskier than short-term debt, so liquidity preference suggests a risk premium on long-term debt.

Loanable Funds Theory   The loanable funds theory is the theory that interest rates are set by the supply and demand for theory loanable funds.

Marketability   Marketability is the relative ease or difficulty in trading a security. Marketability relates to the cost and speed with which an investor can sell the security.

Market Segmentation Theory   The market segmentation theory is a theory for the term structure that suggests that investors have maturity preferences and the preferences dominate the investment decision.

Municipal Bond   A municipal bond is a bond issued by a state or local government. These bonds have a tax advantage because their interest payments are exempt from federal income tax.

Nominal Interest Rate   A nominal interest rate is a market interest rate that includes an adjustment rate for inflation.

Preferred Habitat Theory   The preferred habitat theory is a theory for the term structure that suggests that investors have maturity preferences, but that investors will leave their preferred maturity if adequately compensated for the additional risk.

Putable Bond   A putable bond is a bond where the owner of the bond has the right to sell (put) the bond back to the issuer before maturity at a predetermined price.

Real Rate of Interest   The real rate of interest is the rate paid for delaying consumption. It is used as the long-run base rate for building nominal interest rates.

Spot Rate   A spot rate is an interest rate that is available today.

Term Structure   The term structure describes the time premia in nominal interest rates.

Yield Curve   A yield curve is a plot at a point in time of nominal interest rates relative to different times to maturity holding all other factors constant. In other words, a yield curve is a plot of the term structure.

CHAPTER 4

MONEY MARKETS

4.1 INTRODUCTION

In times of turmoil, some money will exit the stock market. During the agitated stock market of 2001, a headline in *BusinessWeek Online* described the stock market exit as "money on the sidelines." But where are the sidelines? Or, put another way, where would investors park their cash while waiting to reenter the stock market? One common answer to this question is the **money markets**. This chapter explains why the money markets are a preferred place to invest temporary and otherwise idle cash. By reading on, you will gain an understanding of the characteristics of money market securities that follow from their economic function. In addition, you will learn how to calculate the prices and yields of money market securities. These skills are important at most financial institutions, but are particularly important in the balancing of liquidity and credit risk on the balance sheet of a typical commercial bank, where money market securities typically make up 20% of assets and 40% of liabilities.

By convention, the money markets are defined as the markets for short-term debt, which are debt instruments with an initial maturity of one year or less. Because the securities are debt instruments, lenders (investors) charge borrowers (issuers) interest. Any instrument with an initial maturity of more than one year (long-term debt, equity, and mortgages) is referred to as a **capital market** instrument. Capital markets are covered in the following three chapters.

This chapter begins with a discussion of the economic role of the money markets and the key features of money market securities. Next, we show you how to determine the price and yield of a money market security given market conventions. Finally, the chapter explains seven types of money market securities with a focus on the relative default risk and marketability of each class.

DEVELOPING VALUATION AND RISK MANAGEMENT SKILLS

1. Understand the economic role of the money markets and the characteristics of money market securities stemming from that economic role.
2. Calculate the prices and yields of money market securities using the bank discount method.
3. Know the main institutional features of the different types of money market securities and explain the relative default risk and marketability of each type.

4.2 ECONOMIC ROLE OF THE MONEY MARKETS

The economic role of the money markets is to facilitate the trading of **liquidity**. As discussed under the loanable funds theory in Chapter 3, SSUs have excess funds that they are looking to lend (invest) and DSUs have shortages they are looking to cover by borrowing (or raising) capital. Typically, when speaking about lending or investing, the discussion concerns the placing of funds for an extended period of time in a risky investment for the purpose of earning a return on the investment. However, in the money markets, issues are a little different. In the money markets, SSUs lend temporary excesses and DSUs borrow to cover temporary shortages. SSUs are lending excess funds to prevent the funds from being idle assets; however, the SSUs' primary concern is the ability to retrieve all of their cash when they need it. The ability to turn a financial asset into cash quickly without a price concession is referred to as liquidity. Therefore, the money markets are described as the markets for trading liquidity, SSUs are described as lenders (storers) of liquidity, and DSUs are described as borrowers of liquidity.

4.2.1 Primary Features of a Market for Liquidity

The money markets are markets for liquidity. These are markets for liquidity because liquidity is what the investors demand when they make their funds available in the money markets. To ensure the liquidity of these investments, money markets have been developed around three primary features: (1) **short-term debt** instruments, (2) low **default risk**, and (3) high **marketability**.

First, money market investors only make short-term loans. Using only short-term loans ensures that their cash is scheduled to return in a short amount of time (by definition, one year or less). Typically, money market investors pick securities with an initial maturity that matches the period of time that they expect to have excess funds.

Second, money market investors have a temporary excess. This means that money market investors expect to need their current excess within the next year. Because they expect to need their current excess to meet their own future cash flows obligations, they will only invest these temporary excesses in securities with very low default risk. In other words, since the investors expect to have to use their current excess funds in the near future, they are unwilling to place these funds at risk.

Third, while money market investors pick initial maturities that match the time they expect to need their cash, they require the ability to sell the securities before maturity without price concession just in case they need their cash sooner than originally planned. That is, money market investors require that their securities are marketable.

4.2.2 Supporting Features

To ensure that investors in the money markets receive the liquidity they demand, the money markets have several other common features that support liquidity. First, within each of the seven money markets, the debt contracts are standardized. Standardized contracts mean that all the contracts have the same basic features. This standardization allows traders to understand and value each individual contract quickly, which allows for fast trading of securities. Second, trades are done in immediately available funds. To allow trading in immediately available funds, physical possession of money market securities seldom occurs. Instead, the securities are warehoused in a central location and ownership is recorded electronically, which allows ownership to change hands as rapidly as the funds. Finally, many **brokers** and **dealers** trade money market securities. Since numerous outlets exist for trading money market securities, the competition between the brokers and dealers minimizes the transaction costs of a trade.[1]

4.2.3 Major Players in the Money Markets

Almost all lenders and borrowers use the money markets at some point in time to store or borrow liquidity. However, four major "players" actively participate in the money markets to manage their cash flows. The four players are (1) commercial banks, (2) the Federal Reserve, (3) securities dealers, and (4) corporations. In this section, each of the four major players who actively participate in the money markets will be discussed.

Commercial banks have the need to both store and borrow liquidity in the money markets. First, banks store liquidity to ensure that they can meet any withdrawal needs. Its primary earning assets are loans, which are illiquid. One of its primary funding sources for its loans are deposits, which are highly liquid. Therefore, since deposits can be withdrawn with little notice, banks must store some liquidity to meet potential withdrawal demands. Holding cash would ensure that the bank could meet withdrawal demands, but cash is a nonearning asset. Therefore, instead of holding cash, banks purchase money market securities which earn a modest return and can quickly be converted to cash. Second, banks borrow liquidity in the money markets to fund peaks in loan demand. Bank loan demand is often seasonal, and although deposits also vary, the changes in deposits seldom match the changes in loan demand. This difference in timing between loan demand and deposits leaves the bank with attractive loan requests that sometimes cannot be funded from deposits. Rather than let the loans go unfunded, banks borrow from the money markets to fund the loans. That is, the banks borrow liquidity to meet their seasonal loan demand peaks. An important related issue to banks borrowing in the money markets is Regulation D (Reg D, 12 CFR 204).[2]

Reg D defines the reserve requirements for banks as defined by the Board of Governors of the Federal Reserve System. The reserve requirements are the percentage of bank deposits and reservable liabilities that banks must hold in reserve on a daily basis either as deposits at a Federal Reserve Bank or as vault cash.[3] Bank borrowings in the money market are subject to Reg D. However, the different money securities, which are discussed in detail below, are subject to different reserve requirements; therefore, Reg D influences a bank's choice of instrument when borrowing in the money markets.

The second major player in the money markets is the Federal Reserve (Fed). One of the primary roles of the Federal Reserve is monetary policy, and one of the tools the Fed uses for this is open market operations. Open market operations (described as either permanent

---

[1] Minimizing transaction costs in markets with dealers and brokers does not mean zero transaction costs. In these markets, the dealers and brokers provide valuable services that allow the markets to function efficiently. Investors must pay the dealers and brokers for their services or the dealers and brokers will leave the market. Accordingly, the level of transaction costs in a competitive dealer or broker market is the minimum transaction cost that provides a reasonable profit to the dealers and brokers for their services.

[2] 12 CFR 204 means that Regulation D is available in the Code of Federal Regulations (CFR) Chapter 12, Section 204.

[3] Interestingly, cash in automatic teller machines (ATMs) counts as vault cash.

or temporary) involve the buying or selling of U.S. Treasury securities and federal agency securities. A permanent open market operation is the outright purchase or sale of securities and may be done with money market securities. A temporary purchase is conducted with repurchase agreements (repos) on Treasury or agency securities while a temporary sale is conducted with matched sale–purchase agreements on Treasury and agency securities. A matched sale–purchase agreement is a form of a repurchase agreement and is classified as money market securities. The discussion of the details of repurchase agreements will occur later in this chapter.

Securities dealers are the third major player in the money markets. Securities dealers are referred to as "market makers" because they stand ready to trade (or make a market) in the securities they trade. Money market dealers are security dealers who stand ready to trade (buy or sell) money market securities. Securities dealers generally have substantial inventories of securities ready for sale to accommodate the buying demands of investors. For money market dealers their inventories would be money market securities. Securities dealers who also stand ready to buy the securities in which they make a market often fund the securities that they purchase by borrowing liquidity in the money markets, usually through repurchase agreements.

Corporations are the final major player in the money markets. Corporations use the money markets to manage their operating (day-to-day) cash flows. They will place their temporary cash excesses in the money markets to eliminate idle cash on hand. Corporations also borrow operating cash flows from the money markets to cover temporary cash flow shortages. Corporate borrowing in the money markets is usually limited to businesses with high credit ratings because of the demand by money market investors for low default risk.

4.3 PRICING MONEY MARKET SECURITIES

The price of a money market instrument has two components: (1) the **face value** (loan principal) and (2) one interest payment. With a face value and one interest payment, two possible cash flow combinations are possible. One combination forms an instrument known as a **discount instrument**. The cash flow combination for a discount instrument sets the price at the face value minus the interest payment and repays the face value. The second cash flow combination forms an add-on instrument. The cash flow combination for an add-on instrument sets the price at the face value and repays the face value plus the interest payment. Each will be discussed separately in this section.

All debt securities, including money market securities, have a stated amount that the borrower agrees to pay at the maturity of the security. That amount is referred to as face value. Debt securities that trade at prices above the face value are described as trading at a premium, and debt securities that trade at prices below the face value are described as trading at a discount (premiums and discounts will be discussed in detail in Chapter 5 on bond pricing). Therefore, by definition, a debt security that is described as a discount instrument is one that always trades at a price that is less than face value. A debt security that repays the face value at maturity but has no interest payments (no contractual payments between purchase and maturity) will always trade at a discount. Thus, in the money market, a discount instrument is one where the investor (lender) pays less than face value for the right to receive the face value when the security matures at some point that is less than or equal to one year in the future. Now, how is the price of a money market discount security determined?

The price of a financial asset is the present value of the future cash flows and a discount security is a financial asset; therefore, the price of a money market discount security is determined by finding the present value of the future cash flows. Since the investor in a discount security is purchasing the right to receive the face value at maturity without an intervening interest payment, one might expect to find the price using the formula for the present value of a single future cash flow which is

$$PV = \frac{FV_t}{(1+r)^t} \tag{4-1}$$

where

t = time when the investor expects to receive the future cash flow, and

r = the discount rate.

However, as logical a choice as the formula seems to be, it is not the market convention for money market instruments. Instead, the market convention is to price money market instruments on a **bank discount** basis. The convention stems from the Treasury's choice to price Treasury bills on a bank discount basis. The Treasury began auctioning Treasury bills in 1929 and, at that time, the bank discount method was common practice. The bank discount method uses simple interest and a 360-day year which simplified calculations in a time that predated modern computers and financial calculators. Obviously, the simplification is not necessary today, but for consistency the Treasury continues the convention on its bills. Since the Treasury continues the convention, the other money market instruments are also priced on a bank discount basis for comparability with Treasury bills. The formula for pricing a money market discount instrument on a bank discount basis is

$$\text{Price} = \text{FaceValue} - \text{Discount} = \text{FaceValue} - \left(\text{FaceValue} \times r \times \left(\frac{t}{360} \right) \right) \tag{4-2}$$

where

t = the number of days to maturity, and

r = the current annualized market rate.

EXAMPLE *Pricing a Money Market Discount Instrument*

The following example demonstrates the pricing of a six-month money market discount instrument with a face value of $1,000 when the annualized market rate is 3.87%. A typical six-month instrument has 182 days to maturity. However, because of holidays and weekends, six-month securities may have slightly more or less than 182 days to maturity. The exact number of days to maturity will be specified in the contract. For this example, 182 days to maturity will be used. The price of this security is

$$\text{Price} = \$1,000 - \text{Discount} = \$1,000 - \left(\$1,000 \times 0.0387 \times \left(\frac{182}{360} \right) \right)$$

$$= \$1,000 - \$19.57 = \$980.43.$$

The discount is the amount of simple interest on the face value over the life of the security based on a 360-day year. Obviously, 360 days does not make a year, but remember that a 360-day year is part of the bank discount basis.

Now that the price of a money market discount instrument can be determined, the next question is what is the rate of return on a money market discount instrument? The first inclination of most readers is to answer r, which is the market rate of interest. This is incorrect. Returns are calculated based on the price paid an investment, whereas r calculates the discount based on what the investor will receive from the investment. The standard formula for a security's return is

$$\text{return} = \frac{(\text{Price}_{t+1} - \text{Price}_t)}{\text{Price}_t}. \tag{4-3}$$

EXAMPLE *continued* **Return on a Money Market Discount Instrument**

In the previous example, a 182-day money market discount instrument with a face value of $1,000 with the annualized market rate 3.87%, has a price of $980.43. Using Equation (4-3) the annualized return for the instrument in the example is

$$\text{return} = \frac{(\$1,000 - \$980.43)}{\$980.43} \times \left(\frac{360}{182}\right) = 0.0395 \text{ or } 3.95\%.$$

Since investors generally use annualized returns to compare investments, a formula has been developed to translate the annualized market interest rate on a money market discount instrument into an annualized rate of return. The annualized rate of return here is referred to as the **money market yield** and is calculated as follows:

$$\text{Money market yield} = \frac{360 \times r}{360 - (r \times t)}. \tag{4-4}$$

In the money market yield formula r must be entered in decimal form.

EXAMPLE *continued* **Money Market Yield Calculation**

Continuing the example for the discount instrument, the money market yield on the instrument is

$$\text{Money market yield} = \frac{(360 \times 0.0387)}{360 - (0.0387 \times 182)} = 0.0395 \text{ or } 3.95\%,$$

which agrees with our return calculation using the instrument's cash flows.[4]

Four of the seven types of money market securities are priced as discount instruments, namely: (1) Treasury bills, (2) short-term federal agency debt, (3) commercial paper, and (4) banker's acceptances (BAs). The remaining three types, negotiable certificates of deposits (CDs), repurchase agreements (repos), and fed funds, are sold at face value as add-on instruments. The price and yield (return of a debt security) of money market add-on instruments will be discussed now.

---

[4]The money market yield is calculated based on a 360-day year. The 360-day year continues to be used because a 360-day year is the market convention even though a calendar year has more than 360 days. The formula that calculates the return of money market instruments on a 365-day year is called the bond equivalent yield. The bond equivalent yield calculation that substitutes for Equation (4-4) is Bond equivalent yield = $\frac{(365 \times r)}{360 - (r \times t)}$. This equation is important because the *Wall Street Journal* reports money market yields based on the bond equivalent yield *instead* of the market convention of the money market yield.

The initial price of an add-on instrument is the face value. When an add-on instrument is bought, the investor buys the right to receive at maturity the face value plus the interest payment. The interest payment is a simple interest calculation as follows:

$$\text{Interest} = \text{FaceValue} \times r \times \left(\frac{t}{360}\right) \tag{4-5}$$

where r and t are defined as before. Note that the interest payment calculation is identical to the calculation of the discount in Equation (4-2).

EXAMPLE *Interest Amount and Return for an Add-on Money Market Instrument*

Assume a three-month add-on instrument with $1,000 face value and 4.65% interest is to be purchased. A typical three-month instrument covers 91 days, so 91 days will be used to calculate the interest payment on this instrument. The interest calculation for this example is

$$\text{Interest} = \$1,000 \times 0.0465 \times \left(\frac{91}{360}\right) = \$11.75.$$

Therefore, $1,000 is paid at the time of purchase for the right to receive $1,011.75 in 91 days. The rate of return on this investment will be

$$\text{return} = \frac{(\$1,011.75 - \$1,000)}{\$1,000} \times \left(\frac{360}{91}\right) = 0.0465 \text{ or } 4.65\%.$$

Notice, with add-on instruments, the interest rate and the return on the investment are the same.

4.4 THE CLASSES OF MONEY MARKET SECURITIES

In this section, the institutional details for each of the seven basic classes of money market securities will be discussed. The seven classes of securities are (1) Treasury bills, (2) short-term federal agency debt, (3) commercial paper, (4) banker's acceptances (BAs), (5) negotiable certificates of deposit (CDs), (6) federal (fed) funds, and (7) repurchase agreements (repos). Money market investors demand that money market securities are short-term debt with low default risk and high marketability. Since, by definition these securities are short-term debt, the discussion of the seven different classes of money market securities will focus on the default risk and marketability of each class of money market securities.

4.4.1 Treasury Bills: The Ideal Money Market Security

The three primary features required by investors of all money market securities are (1) short-term debt, (2) low default risk, and (3) high marketability. **Treasury bills** (T-bills) are often described as the ideal money market instrument because T-bills have the lowest default risk and highest marketability of any money market instrument. In this section, the specific features that make T-bills the ideal money market instrument are discussed.

4.4.1.1 The Initial Maturity of T-bills

The Treasury Department issues debt securities for the U.S. government with initial maturities ranging from one month to 30 years. These securities are named based on their initial maturity. Instruments with initial maturities of one year or less are called *bills*. Instruments with initial maturities of more than one year but less than or equal to 10 years are called *notes*, and instruments with initial maturities of more than 10 years are called *bonds*. Only bills will be discussed here since this discussion concerned short-term debt. Since Treasury bills (T-bills) have initial maturities of one year or less, these instruments are by definition money market securities. T-bills are issued in a minimum denomination of $1,000 and increase in increments of $1,000. The interdealer market is a wholesale market where T-bills trade in a round lot of $5 million.

Originally, T-bills were available in three initial maturities: (1) 13-week bills, (2) 26-week bills, and (3) 52-week bills. However, in 2001 the Treasury discontinued issuing 52-week bills and began issuing 4-week bills. A 13-week bill is often described as a three-month bill or a 91-day bill. Nevertheless, the Treasury describes the bills based on weeks because this is the most accurate description of the initial maturity of a T-bill. Remember, from an earlier example, that the exact number of days to maturity in money market instruments varies due to holidays and weekends.

The Treasury Department sells new T-bills through auctions. The 13- and 26-week bills are auctioned weekly. The weekly auction process works as follows (see Figure 4-1 for a timeline of the weekly auction process): Each Thursday, the Treasury announces the amount (in dollars) of 13- and 26-week bills that are available for that auction. Noncompetitive bidders have until noon on Monday (New York time) and competitive bidders have until 1:00 P.M. on Monday (New York time) to place orders at a Federal Reserve Bank. The auction results are typically announced by 1:30 P.M. on Monday. These new bills are issued on Thursday (three days after results are announced). Historically, 52-week bills were auctioned every four weeks, with the new bills issued on the third Thursday of the month. However, on February 29, 2000, the Treasury changed the auction schedule for 52-week bills to a quarterly scheduling; then January 31, 2001, the Treasury announced the elimination of the 52-week bill, with the last 52-week bill auction occurring on February 27, 2001. After the elimination of the 52-week bill the Treasury introduced a 4-week bill. The first 4-week bill was auctioned on July 31, 2001. Since its introduction, the new 4-week bill has been auctioned weekly on the same cycle as the 13-week and 26-week bills.

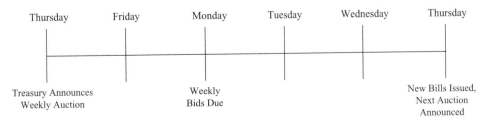

FIGURE 4-1 Timing of weekly treasury bill auctions.

As mentioned before, the Treasury accepts two types of bids: (1) competitive and (2) noncompetitive. A **competitive bid** specifies the quantity of bills sought and the discount rate the bidder is willing to accept. A competitive bid is limited to 35% of the dollar value of the auction and is usually submitted by a primary dealer. Security dealers are designated as a primary dealer if they do the following: (1) make a reasonably good market with the Federal Reserves Open Market Desk, (2) participate meaningfully in Treasury auctions, and (3) provide the Open Market Desk with information that is useful in the formulation and implementation of monetary policy. A current list of the primary dealers is provided in Figure 4-2. A **noncompetitive bid** specifies only the quantity of bills sought. The purpose of a noncompetitive bid is to allow small investors who are not familiar with the current money market rates to purchase Treasury bills without substantial risk of (1) paying too much or (2) bidding too low and not receiving any bills in the auction. Historically, a noncompetitive bidder agreed to accept the average discount rate (which equates to the average price) in the auction from the accepted competitive bids in return for a guarantee of receiving the quantity of bills desired. However, the process for determining the auction price has changed. Figure 4-3 shows the results of a Treasury security auction, as reported on the website of the U.S. Treasury Department.

ABN AMRO Inc.
Aubrey G. Lanston & Co., Inc.
Bear, Stearns & Co., Inc.
BT Alex. Brown Inc.
Barclays Capital Inc.
Chase Securities Inc.
CIBC Oppenheimer Corp.
Credit Suisse First Boston Corp.
Daiwa Securities America Inc.
Deutsche Bank Securities Inc.
Donaldson, Lufkin & Jenrette Securities
Dresdner Kleinwort Benson North America LLC.
First Chicago Capital Markets Inc.
Fuji Securities Inc.
Goldman, Sachs & Co.
Greenwich Capital Markets Inc.
HSBC Securities Inc.
JP Morgan Securities Inc.
Lehman Brothers Inc.
Merrill Lynch Government Securities Inc.
Morgan Stanley & Co. Incorporated
NationsBanc Montgomery Securities LLC.
Nesbitt Burns Securities Inc.
The Nikko Securities Co. International Inc.
Nomura Securities International Inc.
Paine Webber Inc.
Paribas Corp.
Prudential Securities Inc.
Salomon Smith Barney Inc.
Warburg Dillon Read LLC.
Zions First National Bank

FIGURE 4-2 List of the primary government securities dealers.

PUBLIC DEBT NEWS

Department of the Treasury • Bureau of the Public Debt • Washington, DC 20239

```
                    TREASURY SECURITY AUCTION RESULTS
                 BUREAU OF THE PUBLIC DEBT - WASHINGTON DC

FOR IMMEDIATE RELEASE                    CONTACT:     Office of Financing
September 05, 2000                                    202-691-3550

              RESULTS OF TREASURY'S AUCTION OF 13-WEEK BILLS

      Term:                      91-Day Bill
      Issue Date:                September 07, 2000
      Maturity Date:             December 07, 2000
      CUSIP Number:              912795EJ6

      High Rate:   6.065%   Investment Rate 1/:   6.245%   Price:  98.467

    All noncompetitive and successful competitive bidders were awarded
securities at the high rate.  Tenders at the high discount rate were
allotted  43%.  All tenders at lower rates were accepted in full.

               AMOUNTS TENDERED AND ACCEPTED (in thousands)
```

Tender Type	Tendered	Accepted
Competitive	$ 26,296,999	$ 6,891,409
Noncompetitive	1,229,265	1,229,265
PUBLIC SUBTOTAL	27,526,264	8,120,674 2/
Foreign Official Refunded	1,400,000	1,400,000
SUBTOTAL	28,926,264	9,520,674
Federal Reserve	4,453,744	4,453,744
Foreign Official Add-On	0	0
TOTAL	$ 33,380,008	$ 13,974,418

```
    Median rate   6.060%: 50% of the amount of accepted competitive tenders
was tendered at or below that rate.  Low rate   6.030%:   5% of the amount
of accepted competitive tenders was tendered at or below that rate.

Bid-to-Cover Ratio = 27,526,264 / 8,120,674 = 3.39

1/ Equivalent coupon-issue yield.
2/ Awards to TREASURY DIRECT = $984,335,000
```

FIGURE 4-3 Results of a treasury security auction.

The process for accepting bids is as follows: First, all noncompetitive bids are accepted (up to $1 million) and the amount of these bids is subtracted from the amount of bills available in the auction. Then, competitive bids are sorted from highest to lowest price and are accepted starting with the highest price bid (lowest discount rate) and continuing down in price until all the bills in the auction are sold. Historically, this meant the bidders paid different prices for the same bills. Beginning in November 1998, the Treasury switched all auctions to uniform-price auctions where all bidders pay the same price. Under the uniform-price auctions, noncompetitive and competitive bids are made and accepted, as in the past; but once the bids are accepted, all bidders pay the same price. The common price is based on the stop-out discount rate (lowest price accepted) for the auction. The switch was made to uniform-price auctions to eliminate the so-called **winner's curse** in the multiple price auction process. The winner's curse is that the winner of the auction paid more for the asset than anyone else was willing to pay, creating concern that the winner ends up paying more than the asset is worth.

4.4.1.2 No Default Risk for T-bills

The second primary feature of a money market instrument is low default risk. T-bills are backed by the full faith and credit of the U.S. government. The U.S. government has never failed to pay its debts. Since, in the over 200-year existence of the United States, the federal government has always paid its debts, the debt of the U.S. government is considered default free.[5] This makes T-bills the ideal money market instrument from the standpoint of default risk.

Often, T-bills are referred to as a risk-free security. T-bills are not risk free; they are default free. However, T-bills, like all debt securities, are exposed to interest-rate risk. The discussion of interest-rate risk will be delayed until the next chapter and will then be discussed in detail as part of the discussion of bonds.

4.4.1.3 High Marketability of T-bills

The third primary feature of money market instruments is high marketability. High marketability means that an investor can sell the security quickly without a major price concession. T-bills are considered the most marketable money market security because of their large and active secondary market.

While money market investors typically purchase securities with initial maturities that match their investment horizon, money market investors demand marketability in money market instruments if the need to sell arises. A large and active secondary market ensures high marketability, and T-bills have the largest and most active secondary market of all money market securities.

There are approximately 2,000 securities brokers and dealers that are registered to trade government securities. Many of the dealers *make markets* in T-bills. This means they stand ready to trade at their quoted bid and ask prices. The large number of dealers in this market creates competition in prices, which ensures that T-bill investors can sell their bills quickly without a major price concession relative to the current market conditions. Data on T-bill activity by dealers show an active market with the average daily volume in T-bills traded among primary dealers at $29.5 billion in the second quarter of 1999.[6,7] The daily volume in T-bills continues to grow with the Federal Reserve Bank of New York reporting that the average daily volume among primary dealers was $44.5 billion in 2003.

4.4.2 Federal Agency Obligations

Leaving the discussion of T-bills and progressing to the other money market instruments, the progression is from the ideal money market characteristics of T-bills to instruments

---

[5] There is a fine point about U.S. government defaults that needs to be made. The debt is considered default free because no loss of principal (face value) has ever occurred on U.S. government debt. However, from time to time, technical defaults have occurred. A technical default occurs when the government is late with a payment. Late payments on bills usually occur when Congress is slow in raising the debt ceiling, which prevents the rolling over of the bill in times of rising national debt. With each technical default, the government has paid the full amount of the obligation a few days after maturity.

[6] Primary dealers are registered government securities dealers that are selected by the Federal Reserve Bank of New York to serve as counterparties in the open market operations conducted by the Federal Reserve.

[7] See, Dupont, D., and B. Sack, 1999, The Treasury securities market: Overview and recent developments, *Federal Reserve Bulletin, December*, 785–806.

that have more default risk, less marketability, or both. The first of the other money market instruments to be discussed is federal agency obligations.

Federal agencies are credit granting intermediaries established by Congress to supply funds to specific classes of borrowers that Congress deems to be disadvantaged. When Congress deems a specific class of borrowers is disadvantaged, they believe the supply of credit available to that group is (1) too limited, (2) too variable, or (3) too expensive. The federal agencies' job is to provide a dependable supply of credit to their specific disadvantaged groups at the lowest possible cost. The two areas that have received the most focus for agency credit are housing and farming.

4.4.2.1 *Default Risk of Federal Agency Debt*
Federal agencies are credit agencies established by Congress to supply credit to the disadvantaged groups. This description implies that the agencies are part of the federal government and are therefore backed by the full faith and credit of the U.S. government. This is not always the case. Some agencies are owned and directed by the federal government and their debt is indeed backed by the full faith and credit of the U.S. government. Other agencies are federally sponsored but privately owned. The debt of these agencies is not guaranteed by the federal government. However, it is unlikely the federal government would allow a sponsored agency to default on its debt, so these agencies have a de facto government guarantee.

A good example of the difference between a federal agency and a federally sponsored agency is the comparison between the Government National Mortgage Association and the Federal National Mortgage Association. The Government National Mortgage Association (GNMA or Ginnie Mae) is a wholly government-owned corporation within the Department of Housing and Urban Development. Its debt is guaranteed by the federal government. The Federal National Mortgage Association (FNMA or Fannie Mae) started as a wholly government-owned entity in 1938 but evolved through the years and in 1968 became privately owned. Accordingly, its debt is no longer guaranteed by the federal government. Fannie Mae continues to have government supervision and has a role as a government policy tool, so Fannie Mae has the de facto government guarantee of its debt.

4.4.2.2 *Marketability of Federal Agency Debt*
The marketability of federal agency debt varies from one agency's securities to another's securities. Some agencies have well-established and active secondary markets; however, none of the agencies' securities have the marketability of T-bills.[8] Agency securities trade at a positive spread above the same maturity T-bill. The spread in recent years has been between 3 and 20 **basis points**. Although agency securities are not obligations of the federal government and, therefore, have more default risk than T-bills, the size of the spread is generally considered to result from the existence of less marketability for agency securities.

4.4.2.3 *Some Prominent Agencies and What They Do*
As mentioned earlier, Congress has focused its efforts for agency debt in the areas of housing and farming. In this section, the discussion centers on the primary agencies in these areas and their roles

---

[8] The agencies with the most active secondary markets are the Federal Land Bank, the Federal Intermediate Credit Banks, Banks for Cooperatives, the Federal Home Loan Banks, and the Federal National Mortgage Association. The most active agencies issue short-term debt offer securities daily with initial maturities typically between three and six months and in minimum denominations between $5,000 and $100,000.

in providing credit for housing or farming. This section ends with a brief mention of some prominent agencies outside of housing and farming.

The oldest farm credit agency is the Federal Land Bank, which was created by the Federal Farm Loan Act of 1916. Today, 12 Federal Land Banks are in existence and make credit available for land, equipment, and livestock. Federal Intermediate Credit Banks and the Bank for Cooperatives are other agencies that extend credit to farmers.

Originally, all of the capital for the farm banks was provided by the federal government. However, the capital is now provided by its member farmers who are required to purchase capital when obtaining a loan. These agencies are federally sponsored but their debt is not guaranteed by the federal government. The farming crisis of the early 1980s raised concerns about the default risk of credit issued by these agencies, and to alleviate this concern Congress passed the 1985 Farm Bill which provides a line of credit with the Department of the Treasury. This bill also provides for direct borrowing for these agencies from the Farm Credit Bank. These provisions created an implicit guarantee for the debt of these agencies.

The Federal National Mortgage Association (Fannie Mae) was started in 1938 to create a secondary market for FHA mortgages (mortgages insured by the Federal Housing Administration). In 1954, Fannie Mae was divided into three divisions: secondary market operations, special assistance functions, and management and liquidation functions. In 1968, the Government National Mortgage Association (Ginnie Mae) was created and was assigned the special assistance functions and the management and liquidation functions from Fannie Mae. In addition to these functions, Ginnie Mae was asked to make real estate investment more attractive to institutional investors which, in turn, led to the development of mortgage-backed securities. With the establishment of Ginnie Mae, the primary function of Fannie Mae was to provide liquidity for government-insured mortgages (secondary market operations). To carry out this function, Fannie Mae bought and sold mortgages insured or guaranteed by the Federal Housing Administration, the Veterans Administration, and the Farm Home Administration. In 1970, Freddie Mac (Federal Home Loan Mortgage Corporation, or FHLMC) was established. The primary function of Freddie Mac is to promote a nationwide secondary market in conventional mortgages.

Some other prominent federal agencies are the Community Development Corporation (CDC), the Export-Import Bank (Eximbank), the Small Business Administration (SBA), the Tennessee Valley Authority (TVA), and the Student Loan Marketing Association (Sallie Mae). Each of these agencies was established to provide funds to a specific sector of the economy to enhance the development of that sector.

4.4.3 Commercial Paper (CP)

Commercial paper (CP) is unsecured corporate debt which is typically issued to finance short-term working capital. Commercial paper is issued as an alternative to short-term bank credit and is often used because the firms that have access to this market can issue commercial paper at a lower rate than they can borrow from a bank. Commercial paper is cheaper than bank debt because it avoids the middleman (the bank) and thus, the middleman's markup. However, because commercial paper is unsecured debt and money market investors demand low default risk, the commercial paper market is not available to most firms because their default risk is too high. From 1998 through 2003 the average number of companies with outstanding commercial paper was 575.

Rating	Description
	Moody's
Prime-1	Superior ability to repay senior short-term debt
Prime-2	Strong ability to repay senior short-term debt
Prime-3	Acceptable ability to repay senior short-term debt
Not prime	Issuer not in prime rating categories
	Standard and Poor's
A-1	Strong capacity to meet financial commitments
A-2	Satisfactory capacity to meet financial commitments
A-3	Adequate capacity to meet financial commitments
B	Vulnerable and has significant speculative characteristics
C	Currently vulnerable to nonpayment

FIGURE 4-4 Commercial paper credit ratings.

The commercial paper market is a wholesale market with common denominations of $100,000, $250,000, $500,000, and $1 million and with initial maturities ranging from 1 to 270 days.[9] Some readers may think these characteristics, along with the small number of issuers, are restrictive enough to create a relatively small market. However, this is not the case. From 1998 through 2003 the average dollar amount of commercial paper outstanding was $1,346 billion.

4.4.3.1 Commercial Paper Default Risk

Commercial paper is unsecured corporate debt. This means that the only backing it has is the creditworthiness of the issuing firm. Since money market investors demand low default risk, commercial paper ratings have been developed to provide investors information about the issuing firm's creditworthiness for commercial paper. As with bond ratings, Moody's and Standard and Poor's are the primary providers of commercial paper ratings. Figure 4-4 provides the Moody's and Standard and Poor's commercial paper rating scales. Recent evidence suggests these ratings are important to money market investors with their demand for low default risk because 97% of the commercial paper issued was rated in the top two rating categories.

Almost all commercial paper is issued with a backup line of credit from a bank because investors demand it. Having a backup line of credit would seem to protect investors from default risk and thus make commercial paper secured. However, this is not the case. The backup line of credit exists to handle timing problems because most commercial paper is rolled over. What this means is that when commercial paper comes due, the paper that is due is paid off by issuing new commercial paper. If new paper cannot be issued in time to pay off the paper that has come due, the firm borrows from its backup line of credit and pays off the commercial paper that has come due. Then, when the new commercial paper is issued, the proceeds from the issue pay off the backup line of credit.

If the issuing firm has an adverse change in its financial condition to the point where it cannot service its debt obligations, the bank that issued the backup line of credit does not have to loan the firm money under the backup line of credit. This is common practice in lending

---

[9] Commercial paper with initial maturity of 270 days or less is referred to as 3(a)(3) paper because it is exempt from SEC registration under Section 3(a)(3) of the Securities Act of 1933, which exempts commercial paper used to finance current transactions.

because all loan agreements for lines of credit allow the bank to deny requests under the line of credit if the borrowing firm has experienced an adverse change in its financial condition.

4.4.3.2 *Commercial Paper Marketability*

Marketability is the ability to sell an asset quickly without a major price concession. To assess the marketability of a financial asset, the daily trading volume of the asset in the secondary market is generally examined. However, actual trading volume may not always measure the marketability of a financial asset.

Hahn (1993) reports that the secondary market in commercial paper is small. He notes that investors know how long they want to invest cash and, barring some unforeseen cash need, hold commercial paper to maturity. First Chicago Capital Markets, Inc. (1994) agrees that commercial paper is usually purchased with the intent of holding it to maturity. However, they contend there is a highly liquid secondary market for dealer-placed commercial paper because dealers for commercial paper are expected to stand ready to trade (make a secondary market in) their clients' notes.[10]

Stigum (1990) notes that in recent years dealers have worked to promote the liquidity of the commercial paper secondary market. One change designed to improve liquidity was the decrease in the bid-ask spread from 12.5 basis points to 5 basis points. With the activities of the dealers, the commercial paper market has evolved from a buy-and-hold-to-maturity market to a market where some buyers will take longer-term commercial paper with the intent to trade for a profit. This technique argues in favor of the commercial paper market having sufficient marketability for an investor to sell their commercial paper quickly and without a price concession.

4.4.3.3 *Commercial Paper Spreads*

Previously, a T-bill was described as the ideal money market instrument because it has no default risk and has high marketability. In the previous section, the idea was discussed that agency debt traded at a positive spread (between 3 and 20 basis points) over T-bill yields because the agency debt has less marketability. Now, the point has been made that commercial paper is unsecured corporate debt and therefore has default risk. It also has lower secondary market volume, suggesting that it may be less marketable than both T-bills and agency debt. Hence, from a money market investor's point of view, commercial paper is a less desirable money market instrument than T-bills or agency debt.

Because commercial paper is less desirable from the point of view of the money market investor, it would be expected to trade at a larger positive spread relative to T-bills than agency debt. Figure 4-5 provides a graph of the weekly spread between 13-week commercial paper and 13-week T-bills from January 1997 through March 2004. Figure 4-5 shows that from January 1997 through June 2001 the spread was always greater than 20 basis points (0.2%), with a maximum at 125 basis points. The average spread over that time period was 49 basis points. As expected, the spread on commercial papers during that time period was substantially higher than the spread on agency debt. Then, in June of 2001 the spread went below 20 basis points with the exception of the two weeks following September 11, 2001, and the average spread from June 2001 through March 2004 was 10 basis points.

---

[10] At June 2000, dealer-placed commercial paper accounted for over 80% of the commercial paper outstanding.

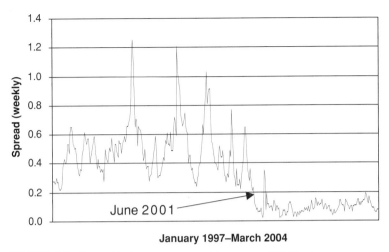

FIGURE 4-5   Spread between commercial paper and T-bill rates.

The drop below 20 basis points aligns with a decline in the number of issuers of commercial paper, which suggests that money market investors (lenders) increased their standards for the necessary credit quality for borrowing in the commercial paper market at that time as the economy continued to decline.

4.4.4 Bankers' Acceptances

A **bankers' acceptance** begins with an actual business transaction where the seller has difficulty determining the creditworthiness of the buyer and therefore requests special assurances with receiving payments. The special assurance of a bankers' acceptance is that the bank accepts the responsibility to make the payment for the business transaction. That is, when the bank accepts the transaction, payment for the transaction becomes a direct obligation of the bank. Thus, the bank's creditworthiness replaces the creditworthiness of the buyer. The need for a bankers' acceptance almost always arises in foreign trade; however, Federal Reserve regulations also allow their use in domestic trade.

4.4.4.1 The Process for and the Benefits of a Bankers' Acceptance
The process for creating a bankers' acceptance is quite involved and requires a substantial amount of specialized knowledge. So, if there is to be a transaction that requires a bankers' acceptance, this transaction should be made through a knowledgeable bank. Less than 200 banks worldwide have staffs that specialize in bankers' acceptances, and most of the U.S. bankers' acceptances originate in New York, Chicago, and San Francisco.

To provide some insight into the involved process for creating a bankers' acceptance and the reason these transaction should involve a knowledgeable bank, the primary steps in a bankers' acceptance are described. The steps for a bankers' acceptance for international trade are

1. The importer (buyer) requests that its bank send an irrevocable letter of credit to the exporter (seller) to cover the cost of the goods to be purchased,

2. The exporter, on receipt of the letter of credit, ships the goods and is paid by its own bank when it presents the letter of credit along with proof the goods were shipped,

3. The exporter's bank creates a time draft based on the letter of credit and sends it with proof of shipment to the importer's bank,

4. The importer's bank stamps the time draft ACCEPTED. This makes the time draft an obligation of the importer's bank. The importer's bank then either returns the accepted time draft to the exporter's bank (which it can then sell) or pays the exporter's bank the discounted amount of the face value of the time draft, and

5. The importer's bank collects funds from the importer to cover the bankers' acceptance when the time draft matures.

There are three primary benefits in foreign trade for going through this involved process. The benefits are

1. The exporter does not have to determine the creditworthiness of the importer. Instead, the importer's bank guarantees payment,

2. The exporter gets paid immediately, and

3. The exporter is not exposed to foreign exchange risk because it receives payment from its bank in its local currency.

4.4.4.2 *Default Risk of Bankers' Acceptances*

Because a bankers' acceptance is a direct obligation of the accepting bank, the default risk of a bankers' acceptance is based on the creditworthiness of the accepting bank. Because bankers' acceptances are almost always done between large banks, which seldom default on their obligations, bankers' acceptances have very low default risk. In fact, in the over 60 years that bankers' acceptances have traded in the United States, no investor has ever suffered a loss of principal.

One additional caveat for the default risk of a bankers' acceptance needs to be noted. The caveat occurs when the accepting bank is outside the United States and in a country with a national banking system, for example, Canada. When a Canadian bank accepts the time draft and creates the bankers' acceptance, payment of the acceptance is indirectly guaranteed by the Canadian government because all banks in Canada are part of a national banking system.

4.4.4.3 *The Marketability of Bankers' Acceptances*

The initial maturity of a bankers' acceptance can be whatever time-span best fits the transaction. Historically, almost all bankers' acceptances came with initial maturities of six months or less. The reason for the six-month or less initial maturities is a restriction on bankers' acceptances in **Regulation D** of the Federal Reserve Act. Under Regulation D, a bankers' acceptance is defined as a nonpersonal time deposit and, historically, nonpersonal time deposits carried a 3% reserve requirement, which means that a bank must keep 3% of the total amount of its nonpersonal time deposits on reserve at the Federal Reserve. Regulation D exempts bankers' acceptances with initial maturities of six months or less from a bank's **reserve requirements** when they are traded. Therefore, banks create bankers' acceptances with

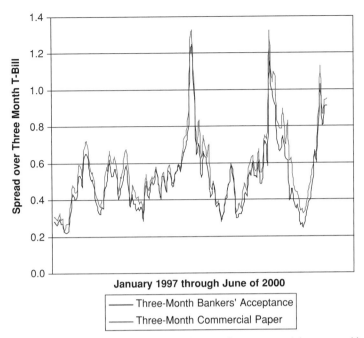

FIGURE 4-6 Yield spreads over T-bill rates for commercial paper and bankers acceptances.

Note: Figure 4-6 ends with June of 2000 because at that time the Federal Reserve stopped collecting rate information on bankers' acceptances. This was because the market had dramatically declined in size and had reached a point where the Fed no longer considered the bankers' acceptance a major financial market.

initial maturities of six months or less for the ability to trade bankers' acceptances without a reserve requirement.[11]

The secondary market for bankers' acceptances is a dealer market. Currently, about a dozen primary dealers in bankers' acceptances make the ongoing market. However, other dealers and banks are active in the bankers' acceptance market. This market is generally considered to have a similar marketability as commercial paper. Stigum (1990) notes that bankers' acceptance volume declined through the last half of the 1980s as the commercial paper market gained in importance. Figure 4-6 plots the spreads on three-month bankers' acceptances and three-month commercial paper relative to three-month T-bills. It shows that the commercial paper spread is usually below the bankers' acceptance spread. This suggests that bankers' acceptances are less marketable than commercial paper, given that bankers' acceptances are not more risky.[12]

[11] In December 1990, the Federal Reserve reduced the reserve requirement on nonpersonal time deposits from 3 to 0%. This currently removes the need to limit bankers' acceptances to initial maturities of six months or less. However, the Federal Reserve can reinstate a positive reserve requirement on nonpersonal time deposits at any time, which creates a practical reason for retaining the limit on initial maturities.

[12] Commercial paper is unsecured corporate debt of high quality borrowers. Bankers' acceptances are unsecured corporate debt of major banks. These banks are generally considered high quality borrowers because major banks seldom default on their obligations. Therefore, it is unlikely that the banks obligated to make payments on bankers' acceptance are more risky than the businesses obligated to make payments on commercial paper.

4.4.5 Negotiable Certificates of Deposit

Certificates of deposits (CDs) are time deposits at a bank. **Negotiable CDs** are time deposits at a bank that are negotiable and, therefore, can trade in the secondary market. Negotiable CDs come in denominations between $100,000 and $10 million. However, negotiable CDs seldom trade in denominations of less than $1 million because $1 million is deemed to be a round lot for trading in this market.

The negotiable CD was started by Citibank in 1961. The purpose was to counter the long-term trend at large banks of declining demand deposits. This trend is important and troublesome because demand deposits are a primary funding source for a bank's lending activities. Citibank established the market by getting securities dealers to agree to make a market in negotiable CDs.

4.4.5.1 *The Default Risk of Negotiable Certificates of Deposit*   Deposits at banks are FDIC (Federal Deposit Insurance Corporation) insured up to $100,000 per depositor. This fact is important because deposits covered by FDIC insurance are default free. However, negotiable certificates of deposit do not receive FDIC coverage because their minimum denomination exceeds the deposit limit for insurance. Negotiable certificates of deposit are unsecured bank debt backed only by the creditworthiness of the bank.

The creditworthiness of the bank is an important issue as money market investors seek to limit default risk exposure in their money market investments. Research on negotiable CD rates has found tiers of rates: money center banks pay the lowest rates, regional banks pay higher rates, and small banks pay the highest rates. In the banking industry, bank size is viewed as a good proxy for credit risk. The tiering of rates represents investors demanding higher rates from riskier banks.

4.4.5.2 *The Marketability of Negotiable Certificates of Deposit*
During the 1970s, negotiable CDs were a major source of funds for banks, which meant an active secondary market was available for negotiable CDs. However, in the early 1980s, several things occurred that dramatically reduced the market for negotiable CDs. First, the Mexican debt crisis created questions about the credit quality of major U.S. banks. Second, the Monetary Control Act of 1980 allowed banks to pay interest on restricted-use demand deposits, which allowed banks to recapture deposits that were lost to money market mutual funds (more on these funds later in this chapter). Finally, the Federal Reserve increased reserve requirements on bank time deposits to 3%, which created a regulatory tax on time deposits. These events combined to dramatically reduce the volume of negotiable CDs to a point where Stigum (1990) describes the market as very illiquid.

To provide some insight about the cost of not being liquid in this market, the spread of three-month negotiable CDs of large banks over three-month T-bills is compared to the spread of three-month bankers' acceptances over three-month T-bills. Because negotiable CDs and bankers' acceptances are unsecured obligations of banks, any difference in spread must be the cost of a difference in marketability. Using weekly data from January 1997 through June of 2000, the data showed that the average spread on bankers' acceptances was 57 basis points (bps) with a minimum spread of 23 bps and maximum spread of 133 bps. Over the same time period, the average spread on negotiable certificates of deposits was 65 bps with a minimum spread of 32 bps and a maximum spread of 142 bps. Therefore, negotiable CDs must be less marketable than bankers' acceptances. Over the same time period, the spreads on commercial paper averaged 52 bps with a minimum at 22 basis points and a maximum at 125 basis points. Thus, negotiable CDs are the least marketable of the money market instruments that have been discussed so far.

4.4.6 Federal Funds

The Monetary Control Act of 1980 requires that all depository institutions place reserves on deposit at the Federal Reserve following the reserve requirements specified in Regulation D. The **federal (fed) funds** market is a market for trading these reserve deposits. Thus, the only participants in the fed funds market are depository institutions.

Regulation D specifies that depository institutions must place a percentage of their deposits on reserve at the Federal Reserve. The deposits that Reg D states banks must place at the Federal Reserve are referred to as required reserves. Required reserves are calculated daily, at the close of business, by the Federal Reserve, and the daily required reserves are summed (accumulated) over a two-week period. The Federal Reserve also tracks the depository institution's actual reserve deposits on a daily basis and the actual reserves are also accumulated over a corresponding two-week period. The two-week period for actual reserves tracking begins on Thursday and ends two weeks later on Wednesday and is called the reserve maintenance period. The Federal Reserve compares the accumulated actual and required reserves at the close of business on the second Wednesday (referred to as settlement Wednesday) of the reserve maintenance period to determine if the institution has meet its legal reserve requirement. Successfully meeting one's reserve requirement is known as settling with the Fed.

A depository institution has successfully settled with the Federal Reserve when it has met two requirements. First, the institution's accumulated actual reserves over the reserve maintenance period must be within +/−4% of accumulated required reserves. Second, the institution must oscillate between settling with excess accumulated actual reserves and accumulated actual reserves less than accumulated required reserves. Griffiths and Winters (1995) recognize that excess reserves are lost investment opportunities, while shortages of reserves are investments using an interest-free loan from the Federal Reserve. They note the clear strategic difference between excess reserves and shortages, which creates a daily pattern in the market clearing rate for fed funds.

A market clearing rate is by definition the rate that the marginal borrower would pay on fed funds. However, this is not the fed funds rate that is reported daily in the news. Instead, the Federal Reserve calculates a transaction-weighted daily average rate called the effective fed funds rate, and reports this rate daily to the news media.

4.4.6.1 Default Risk in Federal Funds   The typical transaction in the fed funds market is an overnight (one-day) trade on reserve deposits. These trades are done so that depository institutions can manage their reserve positions to meet their settlement requirements. Because the primary objective for trading fed funds is successful settlement of reserve requirements with the Federal Reserve, low default risk is very important in this market. Depository institutions are unwilling to take on default risk in this market. So, how do they limit default risk?

The fed funds market is a market where institutions with excess reserves lend these reserves to institutions that need reserves. The loans are accommodated through open lines of credit. Requiring that the loans operate under an existing line of credit is the technique the institutions use to limit default risk. Having a line of credit means that the lender has done a credit analysis on the borrower and determined that the borrower is creditworthy. In addition, once the lender has determined that the borrower is creditworthy, the lender sets a limit on the amount that the lender is willing to lend under the line of credit. This means that lenders in the fed funds market only trade with borrowers that they have determined to be creditworthy.

4.4.6.2 *Marketability of Fed Funds*   A secondary market in fed funds does *not* exist. Instead, market liquidity is directly related to the maturity of the loan. Accordingly, most fed funds transactions are for one day, which is described as overnight. Historically, fed funds borrowed for one day would be returned at the open of business the next day, so the transaction was referred to as an overnight loan. However, in 1994, the Federal Reserve began charging fees to banks for daylight overdrafts in their reserve accounts and the overnight market for fed funds began shifting toward a 24-hour market for fed funds. A process was begun where one-day funds that were borrowed at 2 P.M. would be returned the next day at 2 P.M., so that the borrower would have had the funds for 24 hours. This 24-hour market helps banks reduce their daylight overdrafts and thus reduce their overdraft fees. Longer-term fed funds transactions are available, but the term of these transactions (loans) seldom exceeds one week.

4.4.7 Repurchase Agreements (Repos)

A **repurchase agreement (repo)** is the sale of securities with the simultaneous agreement to repurchase the securities at an agreed on price at an agreed on future date. The typical securities for a repo are government and agency securities. The reason government and agency securities are typically used is that repos using government and agency securities are exempted from reserve requirements under Regulation D. Repos using other securities are treated like deposits for depository institutions under Regulation D and, therefore, are subject to the same reserve requirements as deposits.[13] The repurchase price is the initial sale price plus an interest payment. Thus, repos are add-on interest instruments and are quoted in terms of the interest used to calculate the interest payment. The length of the repo is negotiated between the buyer and seller at the time of the initial sale. Approximately 80% of all repos are overnight (one-day) repos. Any repo agreement longer than overnight is called a term repo. Term repos usually extend for less than 30 days.

In a repo, cash and securities trade at the initial sale, with the securities and the initial cash amount plus interest returned on the specified future date. This process is the same as a collateralized loan, with the securities as collateral. Repos are most easily understood when they are thought of as a short-term loan backed by collateral.

---

[13] See Griffiths and Winters (1997) for a discussion of the role of government and agency repos in the settlement process.

INDUSTRY APPLICATION

FINANCING TREASURY POSITIONS: USING REPURCHASE
AGREEMENTS[14]

Perhaps one of the most difficult things to learn when just starting out in the world of finance is how all the different products fit together. Peter Barker of the Chicago Mercantile Exchange provides the following example of how a repurchase agreement can be used to finance Treasury positions (investments). It is important to remember that a repurchase agreement comprises the selling of securities to one party who simultaneously agrees to buy them back at a particular date in the future. The seller is actually borrowing money for the term of the agreement. The interest paid by the borrower is the difference between the selling price and the higher repurchase price.

Buy a Treasury Note and Finance the Position for One Day

Instrument:	five-year T-note $6\frac{5}{8}$ of 3/31/02,
Trade date:	April 2, 1997
Settlement date:	April 3, 1997
Note price:	99-19+
Accrued interest (three days):	$543.03 (3/183 × 0.033125 × $1,000,000)
Full price:	$996,636.78

What has just happened? The trader has bought a five-year T-note on April 2 for $99 and 19.5/32nds plus accrued interest that has to be paid on the next business day and agreed to pay $996,636.78. However, let's assume that the trader does not have the $996,636.78 in the business account to pay for the note. The solution is to finance the position by using the T-note that was just purchased as collateral in a loan. Here's how it works.

The trader enters into an overnight repurchase (repo) agreement where the agreement is made to sell the T-note and receive cash on April 3, and buy the T-note back on April 4. Note that the original sale of the T-note

is the same as borrowing money, whereas buying it back is the same as repaying the loan. The difference between the selling price and the buying price is the overnight rate of interest. Using an overnight rate of 5.5%, we can calculate the values of the different legs of the transaction.

Sell price:	$996,636.78 (receive cash on 4/3)
Buy price:	$996,789.04 (to be paid on 4/4)
Difference:	−$ 152.26 (overnight interest)

April 3 (Thursday)

On April 3, the $1 million (face value) of the five-year T-note is delivered to the trader's clearing firm account. The T-note is then transferred (this is called being *repo'd out*) to the repo counterparty in exchange for cash. The trader's clearing firm wires the $996,636.78 from the repo counterparty to the original T-note seller's bank account. Thus, the original seller has now been paid. However, the T-note buyer is obligated to pay back the $996,636.78 plus overnight interest of $152.26 to the repo counterparty on April 4.

Now assume that the trader sells the T-note on April 4 and that the Note price has not changed, but the full price has changed because of additional accrued interest.

Trade date:	April 3, 1997
Settlement date:	April 4, 1997
Note price:	99-19+
Accrued interest (three days):	$724.04 (4/183 × 0.033125 × $1,000,000)
Full price:	$996,817.79

What happens on April 4?

(continued)

INDUSTRY APPLICATION (*continued*)

FINANCING TREASURY POSITIONS: USING REPURCHASE AGREEMENTS[14]

April 4 (Friday) Settlement Day

On settlement day, the trader receives $996,817.79 from the previous day's sale of the five-year T-note. The trader then repays the $996,789.04 to the overnight repo loan, and receives back the T-note. The Treasury note is then sent out to the new buyer, so there is no outstanding Treasury position. Because the note price of the T-note did not change from April 2 to April 3 in this exam-

ple, the profit to the trade is equal to the difference between the accrued coupon interest received for one day and the overnight repo interest paid out on the loan. Hence:

One day's accrued interest:	$181.01
One day's repo interest:	$152.26
Profit:	$ 28.75

4.4.7.1 Default Risk in Repos The money lender in a repo is subject to the default risk of the borrower. The securities in the repo act as collateral that reduces default risk. The lender does not own the securities but instead has the securities as collateral. During the time covered (the tenor) by the repo, the securities are held for safe keeping by a third party custodian. Therefore, in the case of default by the borrower, the lender must precede with legal procedures to take ownership of the securities. Having a custodian hold the securities provides protection for the lender because the borrower is prevented from pledging the securities as collateral for more than one repo contract. As further protection for the lender, the value of the securities provided as collateral exceeds the dollar value of the loan. This excess value protects the lender against adverse market movements in interest rates which reduce the value of the collateral. With all of this protection, Stigum (1989) notes that repo traders still advise that repos should only be conducted with parties who are known to be creditworthy.

4.4.7.2 Marketability of Repos Repos do *not* have a formal secondary market.[15] A repo is a secured loan with specific collateral pledged which prevents a secondary market. However, since the future repurchase date is negotiated at the beginning of a repo, the length of a repo is set to fit the lender's needs. In addition, should the lender need their money back before the end of a term repo, the borrower usually will accommodate the lender by repaying the loan early.

4.4.7.3 Players in the Repo Market Four major players are in the repo market. These players are the Federal Reserve, depository institutions, security dealers, and corporations.

---

[14]This example is adapted from Peter Barker's *Financing Treasury Positions: Using Repurchase and Reverse Repurchase Agreements,* which appears in *CME Interest Rate Products Advanced Topics* available at www.cme.com.

[15] Fleming and Garbade (2003) discuss a recent innovation in repos (GCF repo) which they conclude enhances the liquidity of the repo market.

The Federal Reserve conducts monetary policy through trading by the Federal Open Market Trading Desk to create permanent and temporary changes in the money supply. Permanent changes are done through buying and selling securities while temporary changes are done through repos.

Depository institutions must settle with the Federal Reserve every two weeks. Regulation D sets the rules for reserve requirements for depository institutions and the requirements for successful settlement with the Federal Reserve. Regulation D allows government- and agency-backed repos as a substitute for the fed funds market. These allowances permit depository institutions a secured substitute for unsecured fed funds transactions.

Securities dealers use the repo market as a source of short-term borrowing to finance their inventories, which allows them to more readily *make a market*. Finally, corporations often use repos as part of their regular banking activities. Because banks are prohibited by law from paying interest on corporate checking accounts, cash in a corporate checking account is a nonearning (idle) asset. Therefore, to avoid idle cash, corporations use sweep accounts as a part of their regular banking activities. Sweep accounts remove (sweep) all excess cash from corporate checking accounts overnight and invest the cash. The overnight instrument typically used for investing the excess cash in sweep accounts is an overnight repo.

IN THE NEWS

Federal Reserve interest rate change announcements are always big news items for the financial press. In 2001, the economy slowed and these announcements weighed even more heavily on the markets. These announcements need to be understood clearly. The May 15, 2001 rate reduction where the Federal Reserve reduced its target fed funds rate from 4.5 to 4.0% is used to examine what the Federal Reserve does with a target interest rate change announcement. This announcement, as with *all* target rate change announcements, was a change in the Federal Reserve's policy target rate. It was not a change in a market rate.

To attempt to change a market rate, the Federal Reserve must use one of its monetary policy tools. The three monetary policy tools available to the Federal Reserve are (1) a change in reserve requirements, (2) open market operations, and (3) a change in the discount rate. A change in the reserve requirements changes the amount of a bank's deposits that the bank must keep on reserve at the Federal Reserve. The Federal Reserve seldom uses this tool because it has such a big effect on the amount of money in circulation that it shocks the system. The second tool, open market operations, is the buying and selling of securities to change the money sup-

ply. Temporary changes in the money supply are done with repos or matched sale repurchases, and permanent changes are generally done with Treasury and agency securities. Temporary changes, done through repos or matched sale repurchases, automatically reverse themselves; therefore, they are temporary by definition. The discount rate is the rate that banks pay for borrowing from the Federal Reserve. Changing the discount rate should change a bank's desire to borrow from the Federal Reserve and thus change the amount of money in circulation. *A target rate change is not one of the Federal Reserve's monetary policy tools, so a target rate change will not directly cause a change in the fed funds rate.*

Now, looking at market rate responses to Federal Reserve actions, on May 15, 2001, the Federal Reserve reduced their fed funds target rate from 4.5 to 4.0%. The fed funds market rate opened on May 15 at 4.25% and closed at 4.25% and the daily low rate was 4.1875%. Therefore, there was little, if any, reaction in the fed funds market to the Federal Reserve policy change. Interesting to note is that the open on May 15 was 3/16 of a percent (0.1875%) lower than the previous day's close, suggesting that the market either anticipated the policy change or was already moving down on its own.

(continued)

On May 16, the Federal Reserve conducted an open market operation to increase the available money supply and thus reduce interest rates toward the new policy target. At 10:17 A.M., the Federal Reserve did an eight-day system term repo and at 10:18 A.M. they did an overnight system repo. The fed funds market rate at 10:00 A.M. was 4.25%. At 11:00 A.M. was it 4.25% suggesting no immediate effect from the open market operations. Rates did fall in the afternoon on May 16 and closed at 4.0%. On the following day the market rate rose to 4.0625% by 9 A.M. and closed at that same rate.

The point is that the Federal Reserve does not change the fed funds market rate when it makes an announcement of a target rate change. Instead, to change the fed funds rate, the Federal Reserve must use one of its monetary policy tools to change the money supply, which in turn may alter rates in the overnight markets. In other words, this is an indirect process where the Federal Reserve attempts to suggest (target rate change) and nudge (open market operations) the overnight fed funds rates to the level desired by the Federal Reserve.

4.4.8 Money Market Mutual Funds

The money markets are primarily wholesale markets because the instruments are typically written in large denominations. The large denominations of money market securities make the money markets a corporate or institutional market. However, individual investors also have interest in investing in money market instruments. This investing is accomplished through **money market mutual funds**. Individual investors make investments in a money market mutual fund. The fund accumulates the individual investments and invests in money market securities.

Money market mutual funds are a substitute for bank deposits for individual investors. However, bank deposits are insured and money market mutual funds are not; so, money market mutual funds are riskier than bank deposits. The money market mutual fund industry began in the early 1970s when interest rates were fairly low. The beginning of the industry was slow because depositors were unwilling to give up the deposit insurance and convenience offered by bank deposits for an investment that offered a low interest rate. Then, in the mid to late 1970s, market interest rates skyrocketed and banks were prohibited from matching the market rates because of the interest rate ceiling in Regulation Q (e.g., in March of 1980 the effective overnight fed funds rate was 17.29%, while Reg Q limited banks to 5.25% on deposits). Since money market instruments were not prohibited from paying the market rates, individual investors switched from insured bank deposits to money market mutual funds and earned the substantially higher market rate of interest. Once individual investors switched to using money market mutual funds for investing their excess cash and became comfortable with them, they have continued to use them. By the end of 2001, more than $2.2 trillion was invested in money market mutual funds.

SUMMARY OF VALUATION AND RISK MANAGEMENT SKILLS

1. Understand the economic role of the money markets and the characteristics of money market securities stemming from that economic role.

The economic role of the money market is the trading of liquidity. Three dominant characteristics in money market securities meet the demands of investors storing liquidity. These three characteristics are (1) short maturity, (2) high marketability, and (3) low default risk.

2. Calculate the prices and yields of money market securities using the bank discount method.

You should now be an expert on calculating prices and yields of money market securities. Money market securities provide investors a single cash flow at maturity. For discount securities, investors pay less than face value (by the amount of the interest payment) and then receive face value at maturity. For add-on securities, investors pay face value for the security and receive face value plus an interest payment at maturity. The interest payments are calculated using the simple interest convention.

3. Know the main institutional features of the different types of money market securities and explain the relative default risk and marketability of each type.

Treasury bills are the ideal money market security because they have no default risk and high marketability. Six other types of money market securities are available and, relative to Treasury bills, each either has more default risk, less marketability, or both. The six classes of securities are (1) federal agency debt, (2) commercial paper, (3) bankers' acceptances, (4) negotiable CDs, (5) repos, and (6) fed funds.

QUESTIONS

1. Explain the primary difference between money markets and capital markets.

2. What is the economic role of the money markets?

3. Since money market investors are providing their temporary cash surpluses to the money markets, what characteristics will investors demand in money market securities?

4. Describe the two methods for pricing money market securities.

5. What is the price of a $1,000 T-bill with 91 days to maturity when the annualized market rate is 3.65%?

6. A negotiable CD is an add-on interest instrument with the price equal to the face value. Calculate what you would receive at maturity if you purchase a $1,000 negotiable CD with 91 days to maturity at a rate of 3.65%.

7. Calculate the price of a $1,000 T-bill with 182 days to maturity when the annualized market rate is 4.25%. What is the annualized rate of return on this investment?

8. If six-month (182 day) T-bills have an annualized market rate of 4.25%, what is the money market yield on this T-bill? Compare your answer to your answer for Question 7.

9. Discuss why T-bills are considered the ideal money market instrument.

10. What is the default risk of federal agency debt in the money market?

11. Whose creditworthiness backs commercial paper and how would you determine their creditworthiness? Commercial paper is accompanied by a bank line of credit. How does this effect the default risk of commercial paper?

12. Is commercial paper highly marketable? Discuss.

13. When would you use a bankers' acceptance and what is its purpose?

14. Do negotiable CDs have default risk and if so, whose default risk are investors concerned with?

15. What are fed funds and who are the participants in the fed funds market?

16. How is default risk controlled in the fed funds market?

17. A repo can be thought of as a secured loan. Describe why.

18. What role do money market mutual funds serve for individual investors?

REFERENCES

BRYAN, W., and T. GALLAGHER, 1978, The role of the federal funds market: Note, *Journal of Money, Credit and Banking, 10*, 102–104.
The authors discuss three possible functions for the Fed funds market. They find that the market functions to distribute reserves across the system as needed. That is, the market is a mechanism for financial intermediation.

CARGILL, T., 1989, CAMEL ratings and the CD market, *Journal of Financial Services Research, 3*, 347–358.
Cargill shows that CD rates reflect the riskiness of the issuing bank and the risk reflected in the CD rates is consistent with the regulators' confidential CAMEL rating for the riskiness of the bank.

CRABBE, L., and M. POST, 1994, The effect of a rating downgrade on outstanding commercial paper, *Journal of Finance, 49*, 39–56.
The authors show that after banks experience a commercial paper downgrade they issue less commercial paper in subsequent months. The finding suggests that quality/reputation is an important factor in the commercial paper market.

DUFFIE, D., 1996, Special repo rates, *Journal of Finance, 51*, 493–526.
Duffie defines what is meant by a *special* repo. The article discusses that collateral shortages cause the specials.

DUPONT, D., and B. SACK, 1999, The treasury securities market: Overview and recent developments, *Federal Reserve Bulletin, December* 785–806.
This article provides a nice overview of the current conditions and processes in the Treasury securities markets.

First Chicago Capital Markets, Inc., 1994, *U.S. Commercial Paper: An Overview*, First Chicago Capital Markets Inc., Chicago IL.
This article provides an overview of the commercial paper market.

FLEMING, M., and K. GARBADE, 2003, The repurchase agreement refined: GCF repos, *Federal Reserve Bank of New York Current Issues in Economics and Finance, 9*, 1–7.
The authors discuss a recent innovation in the repo market (GCF repos) designed to enhance liquidity in the repo market.

The authors began by describing the typical process for repos and then describe the process for GCF repos. They conclude that GCF repos reduce transaction costs and enhance liquidity.

GARBADE, K., and J. HUNT, 1978, Risk premiums on federal agency debt, *Journal of Finance, 33*, 105–116.
The authors examine the spread between short-term agency debt and Treasury bills and conclude that the spread is driven by the illiquidity of the agency debt and not by credit risk.

GOULD, L., 1969, Banks and the commercial paper market, *Financial Analysts Journal, 25*, 25–28.
Gould discusses the various roles of banks in commercial paper.

GRIFFITHS, M., and D. WINTERS, 1995, Day-of-the-week effects in federal funds rates: further empirical findings, *Journal of Banking and Finance 19*, 1265–1284.
The authors show that excess reserves and reserve shortages are not equivalent and use the difference to model the trading behavior of banks. They show that an optimizing bank will run reserve deficits across a reserve maintenance period and then borrow to settle, which results in rates falling on Fridays and the Tuesday before settlement and then rising on settlement Wednesday.

GRIFFITHS, M., and D. WINTERS, 1997, The effects of Federal Reserve accounting rules on the equilibrium level of overnight repo rates, *Journal of Business Finance and Accounting, 24(6)*, 813–830.
The authors find Federal Reserve settlement effects in overnight government repos rates, which shows that Federal Reserve rules reach into the money markets other than Fed funds.

HAHN, T., 1993, Commercial paper, *Federal Reserve Bank of Richmond Economic Quarterly, 79*, 45–67.
This article is a nice overview of the commercial paper market that includes a discussion of the characteristics of commercial paper, the market participants, the role of dealers, and the risks. The paper concludes with recent innovations such as asset-backed commercial paper, swaps, and foreign commercial paper.

LAW, W., and C. CRUM, 1963, New trend in finance: The negotiable CD, *Harvard Business Review, 41*, 115–126.

This article provides a nice history lesson on the origins of the negotiable CD market.

LONGSTAFF, F., 1995, How much can marketability affect security values? *Journal of Finance, 50(5)*, 1767–1774.

Longstaff shows that price discounts for lack of marketability can be large even when the illiquidity period is very short.

SIMON, D., 1991, Segmentation in the treasury bill market: Evidence from cash management bills, *Journal of Financial and Quantitative Analysis, 26(1)*, 97–108.

Simon finds that investors do not trade in cash management bills to pick up the additional yield on these bills. His conclusion is that segmentation is widespread in the Treasury bill market.

SHEN, P., and R. STARR, 1998, Liquidity of the treasury bill market and the term structure of interest rates, *Journal of Economics and Business, 50*, 401–417.

The authors use the bid-ask spread as a measure of liquidity and find a liquidity premium that is distinct and separate from the term premium in the Treasury bill market.

SPINDT, P., and R. HOFFMEISTER, 1988, The micromechanics of the Federal funds market: Implications for day-of-the-week effects in funds rate variability, *Journal of Financial and Quantitative Analysis, 23*, 401–416.

The authors show that the rules for periodically counting reserves create heteroscedastic daily and intraday variances.

They predict that daily variance will increase as settlement approaches with settlement Wednesday having the largest daily variance and that afternoon variances are larger than morning variances.

STIGUM, M., 1989, *The Repo and Reverse Market*, Dow Jones/Irwin, New York.

In this book, Stigum tells you everything you need to know about the operations of the repo market.

STIGUM, M., 1990, *The Money Market*, 3rd Ed., Dow Jones/Irwin, New York.

This book is *the* reference text for the money markets. It provides an extraordinary amount of institutional detail about each of the money markets.

SUMMERS, B., 1980, Negotiable certificates of deposit, *Federal Reserve Bank of Richmond Economic Review, 66*, 8–19.

This article provides a nice overview of the negotiable CD market. It describes the different types of CDs, the different issuers, and the risks.

WHYTE, A., 1998, The impact of dealer failures on primary dealers and on the market for repurchase agreements, *Review of Financial Economics, 7*, 35–53.

The author finds increased repo spreads around dealer failures, which is consistent with the concern that dealer failures could disrupt the operations of the repo market.

KEY TERMS

Bank Discount The bank discount method calculates simple interest and uses only a 360-day year.

Bankers' Acceptance A bankers' acceptance is a direct obligation of the accepting bank that arises from an international trade by one of the accepting bank's customers.

Basis Point A basis point is an interest rate increment, and 100 basis points equals 1%.

Brokers A broker is someone that brings traders together so they can trade. Brokers helps facilitate a trade but are not part of the trade.

Capital Market Capital markets are markets for long-term securities (long-term debt, equity, and mortgages). These are securities with initial maturity of more than one year.

Commercial Paper Commercial paper is unsecured short-term corporate debt.

Competitive Bid A competitive bid in a treasury auction is a bid that specifies both the discount rate and the quantity desired of the auctioned security.

Dealers Dealers are often referred to as *market makers* because they stand ready to trade securities. In other words, they stand ready to buy or sell a security; therefore, a dealer is on one side of a trade.

Default Risk Default risk is the risk that a borrower will not honor all the terms of a debt contract. The lender is concerned about the probability that a borrower will default and the expected loss from that default.

Discount Instrument A discount instrument is one that always sells for less than the face value.

Face Value The face value of a debt security is the equivalent to the principal amount of a loan.

Federal Agencies Federal agencies are agencies established by Congress to assist in providing funds to specific sectors of the economy.

Federal (fed) Funds The fed funds market is a market where depository institutions trade reserve account deposits.

Liquidity Liquidity is the ability to convert an asset to cash quickly without a price concession from current price.

Marketability Marketability is the ability to sell quickly to recover investor's funds.

Money Market Mutual Funds A money market mutual fund is a mutual fund that only contains (owns) money market securities.

Money Markets Money markets are the markets for short-term debt. Short-term debt has initial maturity of one year or less.

Money Market Yield Money market yield is the annualized rate of return on a money market discount instrument.

Negotiable CD A negotiable certificate of deposit (CD) is a time draft from a bank that is created for secondary market trading. Negotiable CD are not covered by FDIC deposit insurance because the minimum CD size exceeds the insurance limit.

Noncompetitive Bid A noncompetitive bid in a treasury auction specifies only the quantity desired of the auctioned security.

Regulation D Regulation D is the federal regulation that defines the reserve process for all institutions taking domestic deposits.

Repurchase Agreement (repo) A repo is the sale of a security with a simultaneous agreement to later repurchase the security. The repurchase price is the original sales price plus interest, so repos function like a secured loan.

Reserve Requirements Reserve requirements are the minimum percentage of a bank's deposits that the bank must keep on deposit at the Federal Reserve.

Short-Term Debt Short-term debt is a debt contract with initial maturity of one year or less.

Treasury Bill A Treasury bill (T-bill) is a short-term debt obligation of the U.S. government.

Winner's Curse The winner's curse in an auction refers to the fact that the winner paid more than anyone else was willing to pay. Thinking about this in capital budgeting terms suggests that the winner paid a price that made the investment a negative NPV project for all the other bidders, which is why they stopped bidding. The possibility exists that the winner paid too much for the asset.

CHAPTER 5

BOND VALUATION

5.1 INTRODUCTION

The purpose of this chapter is to teach you how to determine the value of a bond, calculate bond yields, and analyze bond risk. These skills are essential for bond portfolio managers at mutual funds, such as the Fidelity Investment Grade Bond Fund or at life insurance companies, such as MetLife. As you saw in Chapter 2, over a third of life insurance industry assets are invested in bonds, so you can bet that life insurance companies are in tune with the concepts we develop in this chapter. To manage a bond portfolio, these firms use analysts to calculate and analyze bond values, yields, and various measures of risk. As a fixed-income security analyst at a pension fund or life insurance company, for example, you might be called on to analyze the profitability of a bond trading strategy, such as the "barbell" strategy, which we will discuss in the Industry Application box later in this chapter. You will be able to apply the valuation and risk analysis skills developed in this chapter and in Chapter 13, where you will read about specific techniques used by bond portfolio managers to increase returns and minimize risk.

This chapter begins by defining the terms of a bond contract and explaining some institutional features of the bond market. We then show you how to use the basis bond valuation formula and then use that formula to calculate various bond yield measures, which are useful in understanding the risk and return from bond investments. Next we explain the interest-rate risk associated with bond investing and show you how to calculate duration and convexity, which measure the amount and nature of the sensitivity of a bond's value to changes in market interest rates. Finally, we show you how to value a bond using what is called the theoretical spot rate curve, which allows for a more sophisticated analysis of the yields and risks of a bond. Pricing a bond with theoretical spot rates is an application of the term structure of interest rates, which you read about in Chapter 3.

DEVELOPING VALUATION AND RISK MANAGEMENT SKILLS

1. Calculate the value of a bond and the different yield measures important for analyzing a bond's investment performance.
2. Understand how interest rate changes affect a bond's value and calculate and interpret the measures of bond interest-rate risk: duration and convexity.
3. Apply term structure theory to the valuation of a bond using theoretical spot rates.

5.2 BOND TERMINOLOGY AND INSTITUTIONAL FEATURES OF THE BOND MARKETS

This chapter moves from the money markets to the bond market. This is a move from the short-term debt markets into the first capital market to be discussed. Capital markets are the markets for securities with initial maturities of more than one year. Therefore, the capital markets are the markets for long-term debt and equity. Bond valuation and bond ownership risk will be discussed in this chapter.

This section continues with a discussion of the various terms associated with bonds. These terms allow an investor to understand thoroughly the bond contract that they are considering as an investment. This section will conclude with a discussion of some institutional features of bond markets.[1]

5.2.1 A Bond Is a Loan

A **bond** is a loan contract between the issuer (borrower) of the bond and the investor (lender). A loan that makes periodic interest payments is referred to as an **interest-only loan**. The term interest-only refers to the periodic payments made during the loan. These periodic payments are only for the interest due on the loan. No principal reduction occurs during the life of the loan. Instead, the entire amount of principal is due at the end of the loan (maturity).

The most common bond is a loan contract that calls for periodic interest payments over the life of the loan, with the entire amount of principal due at maturity. This type of loan contract is referred to as an interest-only loan. Even though interest-only describes the basic cash flow pattern of the loan, it does not fully describe the contract between the borrower and the lender. The discussion of the terms associated with bonds in the remainder of this section will provide for the complete description of a bond contract.

5.2.1.1 Bond Coupons

Historically, bond contracts contained a fixed interest rate for interest payments with a regular schedule (usually semiannually) of payments. A fixed interest rate with regular payments on an interest-only loan means that the interest payment is the same for every payment. Having a fixed interest rate allows the amount of the interest payment to be specified in the contract. This prespecification is important because of the method of payment that was used for bonds in the past. The method of payment was coupon redemption. The payment amount was prespecified and **coupons** for each interest payment for the bond were attached around the outside border of the bond. When a payment was due, the owner of the bond would detach the coupon for the payment and take the coupon to a bank. The bank would then pay the bond owner the amount of the coupon and subsequently recover the payment from the bond issuer. This method of payment is the historical source of the term clipping coupons and is the reason bond interest payments are known as coupon payments and the bond interest rate is called the **coupon rate** (see Figure 5-1).

Presently, two other forms of coupon arrangements exist for bonds although fixed rate coupons is still the dominant form. One form contains no coupon at all. A bond without a coupon is called a **zero-coupon bond**. An investor purchases a zero-coupon bond for an amount that is less than the stated principal amount of the bond. At maturity, the investor

---

[1] The Bond Market Association provides a substantial amount of institutional detail about the various bond markets. The association also maintains a site related specifically to the process of investing in bonds (http://www.investinginbonds.com/).

FIGURE 5-1 Example of a coupon bond.

receives the principal amount of the loan, the only payment the investor receives over the life of the bond. The difference between the purchase price and the principal amount of the bond is the interest earned on the bond.[2] Zero-coupon bonds are also called discount bonds since they always sell for a price that is less than the principal amount due at maturity.

The other form of bonds that exists is the variable rate coupon bonds. These bonds do not have predetermined coupon amounts. The amount of the coupon payment varies based on an interest rate index. Basing the coupon payment on an index allows the payment to change as market interest rates change. Allowing coupons to change with market rate changes reduces the risk to a bond owner that is associated with market rate increases. This method of determining coupon payments also reduces the risk to the bond issuer if market interest rates decline.

One important issue for the investor in a variable rate bond is the choice of the index for determining the coupon payment. A good index meets two criteria. First, the index must be easy to verify and second, it must be market determined. Accordingly, a popular choice for the index of a variable coupon rate bond is the London Interbank Offer Rate (LIBOR). LIBOR is the rate banks offer each other for deposits in the London market. LIBOR will be discussed in more detail in Appendix 5-A at the end of this chapter.

---

[2] Investors in zero-coupon bonds must be careful about the income tax consequences of owning zero-coupon bonds. For income tax purpose, the interest earned on a zero-coupon bond is assumed to accrue evenly over the life of the bond and the annual amount of accrued interest is considered taxable income even though the owner does not receive an interest payment. For this reason, zero-coupon bonds are typically held in tax-deferred accounts.

5.2.1.2   *Bond Principal Amount (Face Value)*   The **principal** amount of the
loan in the bond contract is referred to as the **face value**. In a typical bond issue, all the
bonds in the issue mature on the same date, with the entire face value of the issue due at
maturity. These bonds are known as **term bonds**. Having the entire face value of a bond
issue due at one time creates an enormous cash outflow for the issuer of the bond. Two
alternatives exist that address the problem of this large cash outflow that occurs at the end
of a term bond issue.

One alternative is to issue a **serial bond**. Serial bonds are popular with state and local
governments. These bond issues contain a variety of maturity dates. In a serial bond issue,
the issue is divided into several groups (series) of bonds with each series having a different
maturity date. The staggered maturity dates force the issuer to repay a portion of the face
value periodically over the life of the issue as each series matures, thereby reducing the
cash flow burden at the end of the life of the issue.

The second alternative for addressing the large cash outflow at the end of a term bond
issue is to use a **sinking fund** for a term bond issue. A sinking fund requires that the bond
issuer periodically retires a portion of the face value. The issuer generally has two options:
(1) make a cash payment to the bond trustee for the face value of the bonds to be retired and
the trustee will call the bonds using a lottery, or (2) purchase the bonds on the open market
and deliver the repurchased bonds to the trustee.

5.2.1.3   *Source of Bond Payments*   To cover bond payments, the issuer of a
bond must generate cash flows. For corporate bonds, the source of the cash flows is expected
to be the project that the bonds funded. However, for government bonds, many of the projects
funded by bonds do not generate specific cash flows, for example, when the government
builds a dam. Therefore, with government bonds, the source of the cash flows for repayment
has to be identified. The three classes of cash flow sources for government bonds are (1)
general obligation bonds, (2) *revenue bonds*, and (3) *industrial revenue bonds*.

General obligation bonds are repaid from the general tax revenue of the issuing
government. Therefore, the quality of the cash flows for repayment comes from the taxing
authority of the issuer. However, since the ability to impose taxes does not guarantee repayment, state and local government bonds have bond ratings. **Revenue bonds** are repaid
from the cash flows generated by the specific government project funded by the issued
bond. A well-known example of a revenue bond is a bond for a toll road. A government
issues a bond to build the road and then makes the bond payments from the tolls collected.
Industrial revenue bonds are bonds issued by a government that are used to fund private
projects such as a nursing home or an assisted-living center for senior citizens. The cash
flows from the private project repay the bond. These industrial revenue bonds are often used
by a government to attract new businesses because of the lower interest rates available on
them. These rates are lower because interest payments made by the issuing state or local
government are exempt from federal income tax.

5.2.1.4   *Bond Collateral and the Order of Priority*   Bonds, like all loans,
can be either secured or unsecured and this is stated in the title of the bond issue. Unsecured
bonds are described in the bond issue title as **debentures**. Secured bonds have specific
collateral pledged to support the bond. Mortgage bonds are secured by real estate; equipment
trust bonds are secured by equipment (e.g., aircraft); collateral trust bonds are secured by
stocks or bonds.

Having collateral attached to a bond gives the bond owners first claim to the specific collateral in the event of a default by the issuer. However, since not all bonds are collateralized, a procedure exists that determines the order of claims of the unsecured bond owners against the unpledged assets of the bond issuer. The procedure is known as the order of priority. The order of priority identifies the order of the claims of the unsecured bondholders and is determined by the bond issue date. The bond issue date is used because all loan contracts contain a *me first* clause, which specifies that all future loans made by the borrower come after the current loan when claims are made against the borrower's unpledged assets.[3]

The order of priority among a borrower's debentures is described by the terms **senior** and **subordinated**. The senior debenture stands first in the order of priority of the unsecured claims. The claims of subordinated debentures come after the claims of the senior debenture. The order of the subordinated debentures is based on the issue date of the bonds.

5.2.1.5 *Options Embedded in Bonds*

A typical bond is an interest-only loan with the face value of the bond due at maturity. However, not all bonds require their face value to be repaid at maturity. Instead, some bonds have **embedded options** that allow for retiring the bond before maturity or for converting the bond to another type of security. In this section, the three major types of options that can be embedded in a bond are discussed. The three types of options are (1) a call option, (2) a put option, and (3) a conversion option.

When a call option is embedded in a bond, the bond is described as a callable bond. The call option of a callable bond gives the issuer of the bond the right to retire (call) the bond before it matures at a predetermined price specified in the bond contract. In exchange for the opportunity to retire the debt earlier than expected, the issuer generally pays a higher coupon rate than a similar bond without the call option. The difference between the rates on callable bonds and similar noncallable bonds is referred to as the *call interest premium*. This call option creates two additional risks for the investor over a similar noncallable bond. The two risks are (1) reinvestment risk and (2) price compression. These risks occur for the investor when market interest rates are falling.

In a market with falling interest rates, the issuer can call the bond and replace it with a new bond that has a lower coupon rate. This is an advantage to the issuer. However, investor's funds must now be reinvested in a market that is paying lower interest rates. This is a disadvantage to the investor. This risk to the investor is known as reinvestment risk. In addition, when interest rates fall, asset values rise. However, as interest rates fall, the price of a callable bond increases at a decreasing rate because the bond is more likely to be called; and, when called, the investor gets the prespecified call price. That is, the price of the bond does not increase as much as it should based on the decline in market interest rates. This risk to the investor is known as price compression.

A put option on a bond creates the same risks and advantages as a call option except the advantages go to the investor and the risks to the issuer. A putable bond allows the investor to sell (put) the bond back to the issuer before maturity at a predetermined price specified in the bond contract. Investors are likely to sell (put) the bond back to issuer when interest rates are rising so they can get their money back and reinvest at the now higher

---

[3] Secured bond owners have a claim against a specific set of pledged assets. If the proceeds from the sale of the pledged assets do not pay the full amount of the obligation to the secured bond owner, the unpaid amount of the obligation becomes an unsecured claim against the borrower's assets and is paid based on its order of priority using the bond issue date.

market rates. This means the issuer will need to borrow new funds at the now higher market rates. Because the investor is reducing their risk with the embedded put option, the issuer will provide a lower coupon (the *put interest discount*) on putable bonds than on comparable nonputable bonds.

A conversion option is the third type of option that can be embedded in a bond. A conversion option gives the investor the right to convert the bond into another type of security before the bond matures. Typically, convertible bonds convert to common stock, which allows the investor the protection of the bond contract if the issuer is performing poorly but with an opportunity to capture the stock price gain if the issuer performs well. Since this is clearly an advantage for the investor, convertible bonds carry lower coupons than comparable nonconvertible bonds. The difference between the coupons is referred to as the *conversion yield discount*.

All convertible bonds have an embedded call option. Otherwise the issuer would not be able to force the investors to convert their bonds into shares. Although the usual statement is that the investor has the option to convert, convertible bonds are issued to be converted. The purpose of issuing a convertible bond is to sell shares at a higher price than the shares are currently selling in the market. When the company decides the time has come to have the shares converted, it calls the bond. In essence, the company says to the investor, "Which do you prefer, $1,050 in cash or shares that you can sell right away for $1,200?" The rational investor will always choose the stock. The investor is offered $1,050 instead of the face value of $1,000 because most issuers usually offer a call premium to compensate the investor for the reinvestment risk. It is a safe assumption that if exercising the call option is good for the issuer, it will be less than optimal for the investor.

In this chapter and throughout this book the focus is on the pricing of bonds without embedded options. For the reader interested in pricing bonds with embedded options, a book that focuses specifically on bonds, such as Fabozzi (1996), is recommended but only after mastering the topics in this chapter.

5.2.1.6 Bond Ownership

The record of ownership is the final piece of terminology for the bond contract to be discussed. The record of bond ownership comes in two forms: (1) registered and (2) bearer. A **registered bond** has a written record of ownership of the bond, and when the bond trades, the register is updated to reflect the new owner. A **bearer bond** has no written record of ownership. The owner of a bearer bond is the person who has physical possession of the bond. In the past, bearer bonds were the more popular form of ownership. However, in recent years the bond market has moved to registered ownership.[4]

5.2.2 Bond Markets

A bond is a loan contract between the issuer of the bond and the investor. However, for a contract to exist, the issuer and the investor must be able to find each other. Financial markets provide this meeting place. In this section, the different parts of the market for

---

[4] Advances in technology have aided in the move to registered ownership, but a primary force is the need of law enforcement to be able to track ownership of financial assets. Bearer bonds are an ideal way to launder illegal profits because no record of ownership exists.

bonds are discussed. Specifically discussed are primary vs. secondary bond markets and exchange-based vs. the over-the-counter bond markets.

5.2.2.1 *The Primary Market for Bonds*   The **primary market** for bonds is the market for the initial sale of the bond from the issuer to the investor. This sale from the issuer to the investor occurs either through a private placement or a public offer.

The **private placement** of a bond issue is the direct sale of the entire issue to one investor or a small group (usually less than 35) of investors. One significant advantage to a private placement is that they are not required to be registered with the Securities and Exchange Commission (SEC). Not having to register with the SEC substantially reduces the cost of the bond issue. However, one potentially large drawback to private placements exists. Without SEC registration, private placements have limits on their resale. Prior to 1990, private placements could not be resold. However, in 1990 the SEC adopted rule 144A which allows for the trading of private placements between qualified institutional buyers. Rule 144A creates liquidity in the private placements market, which has undoubtedly enhanced the recent trend toward more bond private placements.

If a bond is not issued through a private placement, it is issued through a **public sale**. The term public sale means that the bond issue is offered to the public and is available for resale, which requires SEC registration. However, when an issuer does not have the people and processes in place to offer the bond issue to the public, public sales go through an investment banker. Most offers done through investment bankers are described as **underwritten offers**. When an investment banker underwrites a public offer, the investment banker first buys the entire bond offer from the issuer and then sells it to investors. The price that the investment banker pays the issuer is determined in one of two ways. The first way is by having different investment bankers bid to acquire the bond issue and the issuer choosing the most attractive bid. The price from this bidding process is called a *competitive price*. The second way to set the price is for the issuer to select an investment banker and then negotiate a sales price with that banker. The price from this process is known as a *negotiated price*.

5.2.2.2 *Secondary Markets for Bonds*   The **secondary markets** are resale markets. The secondary market for bonds has two forms: (1) exchanges and (2) over-the-counter.

Because financial news focuses on stock **exchanges**, the assumption often made is that all trades of financial assets occur on exchanges. This assumption is not true for bonds. While some corporate bonds are listed on exchanges, the majority of secondary market bond trading occurs **over-the-counter**. Over-the-counter means that the bond market operates through dealer and broker networks whose roles are to facilitate the trading of bonds.

5.3 THE BASICS OF BOND PRICING

Now that the various components of a bond contract and the various bond markets have been described, how to value a bond needs to be discussed. Because of the many different components of the bond contract, a few assumptions must be made to clearly define the task. The assumptions to start the process are as follows:

1. all rates are stated as annual interest rates,
2. coupon rates are fixed,
3. the first coupon is one coupon period from today, and
4. the bond does not have embedded options.

With these assumptions we are ready to price a bond.

5.3.1 Valuing a Fixed Coupon Bond with Annual Coupons

The discussion of bond valuation begins by valuing a fixed coupon bond that has annual coupon payments. Remembering that the value of an asset is the present value of its future cash flows, the task is to determine (1) the amount of the future cash flows, (2) the timing of the future cash flows, and (3) the riskiness of the future cash flows. The process begins by valuing the cash flows assuming that the appropriate discount rate is available. The riskiness of the cash flows enters the pricing process through the discount rate. The discussion of how to select the appropriate *risk-adjusted discount* rate is delayed until later in this section.

As previously discussed, the cash flows of bonds come in two forms: (1) coupons and (2) face value. To determine the value of a bond, the amount and timing of payment of the coupons and the face value must be determined. For a fixed coupon bond with annual coupon payments starting one year from today, the bond pays the same coupon at the end of each year through the maturity date. At maturity the bond repays the face value of the bond. Therefore, the formula for valuing a fixed coupon bond with annual coupons is

$$B_0 = \frac{C}{(1+r)} + \frac{C}{(1+r)^2} + \frac{C}{(1+r)^3} + \cdots + \frac{C}{(1+r)^n} + \frac{F}{(1+r)^n}, \qquad (5\text{-}1)$$

where

B_0 = price of the bond at $t = 0$,

C = annual fixed-rate coupon payment (coupon rate $\times$ face value),

F = face value of bond,

r = risk-adjusted discount rate, and

n = the number of years until maturity.

However, this formula can be shortened. Notice that the series of coupon payments is a fixed cash flow occurring at a regular interval for a fixed number of periods. This type of payment stream is known as an annuity. Therefore, the formula for the present value of an annuity shortens the formula for the price of a fixed coupon bond to

$$B_0 = C \left[\frac{1 - \left(\frac{1}{(1+r)^n} \right)}{r} \right] + \frac{F}{(1+r)^n}. \qquad (5\text{-}2)$$

EXAMPLE *Pricing a Fixed-Rate Annual Coupon Bond*

Assume a bond has: (1) 5.25% fixed coupon rate with annual coupons, (2) $1,000 face value, (3) 20 years until maturity, and (4) a risk-adjusted discount rate of 6%. The price of this bond is

$$B_0 = 52.50 \left[\frac{1 - \left(\frac{1}{(1 + 0.06)^{20}} \right)}{0.06} \right] + \frac{1,000}{(1 + 0.06)^{20}} = 602.17 + 311.80 = \$913.97.$$

The price of the bond in this example is $913.97, which is less than the face value of the bond. A bond that sells for less than its face value is said to sell at a *discount*. A fixed coupon bond will sell at a discount whenever its coupon rate is less than the discount rate. A coupon rate may also equal the discount rate or exceed the discount rate. When the coupon rate equals the discount rate, the bond price equals the face value and the bond is said to sell at *par*. When the coupon rate is greater than the discount rate, the bond price is greater than the face value and the bond is said to sell at a *premium*.[5]

5.3.2 Valuing a Fixed Coupon Bond with Semiannual Coupons

Section 5.3.1 discussed the basics of valuing a fixed coupon bond. This section will discuss how to modify the formula to fit coupon timings other than annual and provide an example with semiannual coupons. Semiannual coupons are the most common coupon timing for bonds.

Three changes to Equation (5-2) are necessary to adjust from annual coupons to other timings for coupons. The three adjustments are made to (1) the coupon payments, (2) the discount rate, and (3) the number of periods until maturity. The adjustment to the coupon payment is to take the annual coupon and divide it by the number of coupon payments per year. To match the discount rate to the timing of the coupon payments, divide the annual discount rate by the number of coupons per year. The last adjustment is to adjust the number of periods to maturity to fit the timing of coupons. This adjustment is made by multiplying

---

[5] For our example, when the discount rate is 5.25% the price of the bond is

$$B_0 = 52.50 \left[\frac{1 - \left(\frac{1}{(1 + 0.0525)^{20}} \right)}{0.0525} \right] + \frac{1,000}{(1 + 0.0525)^{20}} = 640.62 + 359.38 = \$1,000,$$

and if the discount rate is 4.75% then the price of the bond is

$$B_0 = 52.50 \left[\frac{1 - \left(\frac{1}{(1 + 0.0475)^{20}} \right)}{0.0475} \right] + \frac{1,000}{(1 + 0.0475)^{20}} = 668.36 + 395.29 = \$1,063.65.$$

the number of years to maturity by the number of coupons per year. The adjusted formula is

$$B_0 = \left(\frac{C}{m}\right)\left[\frac{1 - \left(\dfrac{1}{\left(1 + \left[\frac{r}{m}\right]\right)^{(n \times m)}}\right)}{\left(\dfrac{r}{m}\right)}\right] + \frac{F}{\left(1 + \left[\frac{r}{m}\right]\right)^{(n \times m)}}, \qquad (5\text{-}3)$$

where

B_0 = price of the bond,

C = annual coupon payment,

r = annual discount rate,

n = number of years to maturity, and

m = number of coupons per year.

EXAMPLE   *Pricing a Fixed-Rate Semiannual Coupon Bond*

Use Equation (5-3) to value a fixed coupon bond with semiannual coupon payments. Assume a semiannual bond with an annual coupon rate of 5.8%, a face value of $1,000, 17 years to maturity, and an annual discount rate of 6.15%. From this information, the price of the bond is

$$B_0 = \left(\frac{58}{2}\right)\left[\frac{1 - \left(\dfrac{1}{\left(1 + \left[\frac{0.0615}{2}\right]\right)^{(17 \times 2)}}\right)}{\left(\dfrac{0.0615}{2}\right)}\right] + \frac{1,000}{\left(1 + \left[\frac{0.0615}{2}\right]\right)^{(17 \times 2)}}$$

$$= 606.31 + 357.10 = \$963.41.$$

5.3.3 Valuing a Bond When the Next Coupon Is Not a Full Coupon Period Away

In Section 5.3.1, the assumption was made that the first coupon was one coupon period away from today. Another way to state this assumption is that today is a coupon payment day. This assumption is often made to simplify the pricing of a bond; however, this assumption is not realistic since there are many days on which an investor might wish to purchase a bond that are not coupon payment days. This section will discuss how to price a bond between coupon payment days.

Being between coupon payment days, the number of days to the first coupon is less than the number of days in a coupon payment period. In other words, the number of days until the next coupon payment is less than the number of days between all subsequent coupon payments. The coupon stream is no longer an annuity because an annuity requires the same length of time from today to the first cash flow as the length of time between all remaining cash flows. Since the coupon stream is not an annuity, Equation (5-3) can no longer be used to price the bond. Instead, Equation (5-1) must be used and its time increments must be modified. The modified formula is

$$B_0 = \frac{(c/m) \times (a/b)}{(1 + [r/m])^{(a/b)}} + \frac{(c/m)}{(1 + [r/m])^{(1+a/b)}} + \frac{(c/m)}{(1 + [r/m])^{(2+a/b)}} + \frac{(c/m)}{(1 + [r/m])^{(3+a/b)}}$$

$$+ \cdots + \frac{(c/m)}{(1 + [r/m])^{(n-1+a/b)}} + \frac{F}{(1 + [r/m])^{(n-1+a/b)}} \qquad (5\text{-}4)$$

where

B_0 = price of the bond,

C = annual coupon,

m = number of coupons per year,

n = number of coupons remaining on the bond,

a = number of days from today until the first coupon, and

b = number of days between coupons.

EXAMPLE *Pricing a Semiannual Coupon Bond When the First Payment Is Not a Full Period Away*

Use Equation (5-4) to price a semiannual coupon bond between coupon payments. The bond is a 9% coupon, two-year corporate $1,000 bond with a discount rate of 10%. There are 145 days until the first coupon payment. Furthermore, the example will assume a 182-day coupon payment period for semiannual coupon bonds. Accordingly, for this bond our pricing inputs are[6]

$$C = \$90,$$
$$m = 2,$$
$$n = 4,$$
$$a = 145,$$
$$b = 182, \text{ and}$$
$$F = \$1,000,$$

and the price of the bond is

$$B_0 = \frac{(90/2) \times (145/182)}{(1 + [0.1/2])^{(145/182)}} + \frac{(90/2)}{(1 + [0.1/2])^{(1 + 145/182)}} + \frac{(90/2)}{(1 + [0.1/2])^{(2 + 145/182)}}$$

$$+ \frac{(90/2)}{(1 + [0.1/2])^{(3 + 145/182)}} + \frac{1,000}{(1 + [0.1/2])^{(3 + 145/182)}}$$

$$= \$34.48 + \$41.22 + \$39.26 + \$37.39 + \$830.90 = \$983.25.$$

---

[6] Because this is just a simple example, assume a 365-day year. Later the assumption will be relaxed to allow for the pricing of corporate bonds. Suffice it to say here that part of the problem with pricing a bond is that different conventions are used for calculating the number of days in the year.

$983.25 is the price of the bond based on the present value of the remaining cash flows. However, $983.25 is not the price an investor would pay for the bond. An adjustment must be made for accrued interest. The investor that purchases this bond today will receive a $45 coupon in 145 days and the $45 coupon represents 182 days of interest on the bond, of which 37 (182–145) days of interest were earned while the seller still owned the bond. Thus, the sale price of the bond must be adjusted to pay the seller the interest due for the portion of the next coupon payment that accrued before the sale. For the bond in the example, the accrued interest is $9.15 [$45 × (37/182)], so the adjusted sales price is $992.40 ($983.25 + $9.15).

Several interesting points from the above example should be noted here. First, the first coupon is adjusted downward for the amount of the accrued interest belonging to the seller—the first term is multiplied by 145/182. This price ($983.25) is known as the *flat* or *clean* price. This is also the bond price quotation that appears in the newspaper. Second, the amount of accrued interest ($9.15) payable to the seller is added directly to the clean price to get the *full* or *dirty* price ($992.40). This is the amount immediately payable on purchase by the buyer to the seller. Market convention handles the transaction in this way. Also, the seller does *not* earn compound interest on the accrual—another market convention. Finally, notice that if the general rule that the value of a financial asset is equal to the present value of *all* future funds flows was blindly applied, a price of $992.05 would have been calculated which is equal to neither the clean price nor the dirty price.[7]

5.3.4 Yield to Maturity

Now that pricing a fixed coupon bond is understood, another important question for the investor that can be addressed is the expected rate of return on the bond. The expected rate of return is the rate of return the investor expects to earn if purchasing the bond at today's price and holding it until the bond's maturity. In bond market terminology, the **yield to maturity** (YTM) is the expected rate of return on a bond. In this section, the yield to maturity of a fixed coupon bond will be discussed.

The yield to maturity is the discount rate that equates today's price for the bond to the present value of the future cash flows on the bond. In other words, the yield to maturity of a bond is equivalent to the internal rate of return (IRR) for a capital budgeting project. To find the yield to maturity, Equation (5-3) is modified by replacing the discount rate with the term YTM as follows:

$$B_0 = \left(\frac{C}{m}\right)\left[\frac{1 - \left(\frac{1}{(1 + YTM)^{n \times m}}\right)}{YTM}\right] + \frac{F}{(1 + YTM)^{n \times m}}. \tag{5-5}$$

To find the yield to maturity, Equation (5-5) is solved for YTM. However, YTM cannot be found using a simple algebraic solution. Either a financial calculator or trial and error must be used. The use of a financial calculator is preferential.

---

[7] The value of $992.05 is determined by finding the present value of all future cash flows without the adjustment to the first payment.

EXAMPLE   *Yield to Maturity Calculation*

The following is an example of yield to maturity of a semiannual fixed coupon bond. The bond has a coupon rate of 7.15%, a face value of $1,000, 12 years to maturity, and a current price of $1,060.44. Substituting this information into Equation (5-5) results in the following equation

$$1,060.44 = \left(\frac{71.50}{2}\right)\left[\frac{1 - \left(\frac{1}{(1 + YTM)^{12 \times 2}}\right)}{YTM}\right] + \frac{1,000}{(1 + YTM)^{12 \times 2}} \quad \text{then} \quad YTM = 3.21\%.$$

Solving for YTM in the preceding example provides a yield to maturity for this bond of 3.21% on a semiannual basis. This rate is a semiannual rate because all of the cash flows and the time periods are semiannual. However, annual rates of return are normally used for comparisons among different securities; therefore, the YTM must be adjusted to an annual figure. The bond market convention is to take the yield to maturity of the bond and multiply it by the number of coupon periods per year. For this example, the yield to maturity is multiplied by 2 (3.21% × 2). The annualized rate is 6.42%. This resulting annualized rate is referred to as the **bond equivalent yield**. Even though the bond equivalent yield is a simple interest calculation that understates the actual annual yield on the bond because it ignores the effect of compounding, it is the market convention.[8]

The calculation of the yield to maturity of a bond is a very specific rate of return calculation. The calculated rate is the rate of return the investor expects to earn if the investor purchases the bond today at its current price, holds the bond to maturity, and reinvests all the coupons at the yield to maturity. The good news is that this calculation summarizes all the investor's sources of returns from the bond in one number. The bad news is that if the investor sells before the bond matures or if the investor cannot reinvest the coupons at the yield to maturity, the investor's return will differ from the yield to maturity. A calculation referred to as the **realized compound yield** has been developed to address the problems faced by each individual investor with yield to maturity.

The realized compound yield is a five-step process for estimating an investor's expected rate of return on a bond. The steps are as follows:

Step 1.   Calculate the future value of the coupon payments received from the bond during the investor's expected holding period (investment horizon) using the interest rate the investor will receive from reinvesting the coupons.

Step 2.   Calculate the sales price of the bond at the end of the investment horizon,

Step 3.   Add the answers from Steps 1 and 2.

Step 4.   Find the discount rate that equates the purchase price of the bond with the sum of the future sales price and the future value of the coupon payments. This is an application of the formula of the present value of a single cash flow. The formula

---

[8] The annual rate of return with compounding is referred to as the effective annual rate (EAR) and is calculated as follows:

$$EAR = (1 + YTM)^m = (1 + 0.0321)^2 = 1.0652 \text{ or } 6.52\%.$$

for this application is

$$\text{purchase price} = \frac{(\text{future value of coupons} + \text{sales price})}{(1+r)^n},$$

where n = number of coupons received during the investment horizon. This is the realized compound yield.

Step 5. If the bond is not an annual coupon bond, the realized compound yield must be converted to an annual rate by multiplying the realized compound yield from Step 4 by the number of coupons per year.

EXAMPLE *Realized Compound Yield Calculation*

For this example, a semiannual fixed coupon bond with 6.5% coupon rate, $1,000 face value, 20 years to maturity, and a current price of $950 will be used. The investor expects to hold the bond for five years, reinvest the coupons at 4.5%, and sell the bond for $975. What is the investor's anticipated realized compound yield?

Step 1. Determine the future value of the semiannual coupons reinvested at 4.5% over a five-year period. The coupon payment stream is an annuity, so the future value is calculated using the formula for the future value of an annuity. The future value of the coupon stream is

$$FVA = 32.5 \left[\frac{((1+0.0225)^{10} - 1)}{0.0225} \right] = \$359.96.$$

Step 2. The sales price is estimated to be $975; therefore,

Step 3. Add Steps 1 and 2. The result is ($975.00 + $359.96) = $1,334.96, which is the value of the investment at the end of the investment horizon.

Step 4. Find the realized compound yield by solving for r in the following formula:

$$\$950.00 = \frac{(359.96 + 975.00)}{(1+r)^{10}}$$

$r = 3.46\%$.

Step 5. Since the bond has semiannual coupons, the realized compound yield is converted to an annualized return by multiplying by 2 (3.46% × 2). The annualized rate of return is 6.92%.

5.3.5 Risk-Adjusted Discount Rate

The discussion of the appropriate risk-adjusted discount rate for pricing a bond was delayed until now because we use yield to maturity to determine the appropriate discount rate. Specifically, the appropriate risk-adjusted discount is the yield to maturity of a similar bond.

Chapter 3 discussed the five factors that determine the structure of interest rates. These factors were (1) time to maturity, (2) default risk, (3) tax treatment of interest payments, (4) marketability, and (5) embedded options. These factors must be used to determine what bonds are equivalent (similar). Once a similar bond is found, the yield to maturity of that similar bond is used as the risk-adjusted discount rate. The logic behind this process is that the market has determined the appropriate return on the similar bond based on these five factors; therefore, the market will demand the same return on the bond that is being priced.

Issuer	Coupon (%)	Maturity	Price	YTM (%)/C	Duration
ITT Corp.	6.500	5/1/2011	94.811	7.24 C	0.39
Georgia Pacific	7.700	6/15/2015	92.884	8.58 M	11.60
Nabisco	7.550	6/15/2015	101.388	7.39 M	10.56
Ralston Purina	7.875	6/15/2025	109.946	7.01 M	13.54
Burlington Northern	7.290	6/1/2036	109.981	6.98 P	14.45

FIGURE 5-2 Baa rated corporate bonds.

5.3.6 Bond Quotes

Before moving on, some bond quotes are provided to relate the textbook details to the real-world bond market. Figure 5-2 provides market quotes for some well-known companies. The last column of the figure lists each bond's duration. Duration will be discussed in detail in Section 5.4.1 of this chapter.

Several items from Figure 5-2 need to be discussed briefly. First, the companies that issued the bonds listed in this figure are well-known companies that are generally thought of as being financially strong, yet their bonds are rated Baa. This point is made to provide a feel for the financial quality needed to have investment grade bonds because these bonds are in the lowest investment grade rating class. Second, the price quote is a percentage of the face value. Third, the yield to maturity (YTM) is accompanied by the letters M (maturity), C (call), and P (put). This tells the investor if the bond has an embedded option and thus how the yield is calculated. M means the yield is a standard yield-to-maturity calculation and the C and P provide yields calculated to the option date with the assumption that the embedded option will be exercised. The embedded option also affects the duration calculation because duration is also calculated assuming that the option is exercised.

5.4 THE RELATIONSHIP BETWEEN MARKET INTEREST RATES AND BOND PRICES

Once an investor has determined the appropriate price for a bond given its risks, and acquired the bond, the issues for the investor to consider change. The new considerations are (1) how different risk factors affect the value of the bond and (2) how the investor can manage those risks. In this section, the risk factors that affect bond value are identified and measures of the impact of the risks on price are discussed. Chapter 13 will discuss how to manage the risks inherent in bond ownership.

The risks that affect bond value can be identified by taking another look at Equation (5-2). Equation (5-2) is the price of a fixed coupon bond without embedded options and is written as:

$$B_0 = C \left[\frac{1 - \left(\frac{1}{(1 + r)^n} \right)}{r} \right] + \frac{F}{(1 + r)^n}.$$

In the press release following the August 12, 2003, FOMC meeting the Fed stated that it could continue its current policy of maintaining low interest rates for "a considerable period." The reason for the considerable period statement is that the Fed was concerned that the bond market was not correctly interpreting its signals as the yield on the 10-year Treasury note increased 150 basis points from its low yield in June of 2003. Even though the considerable period statement made the point the Fed wanted to make, many people at the Fed did not like the statement because they did not like the inference that the Fed is committed to a specific policy for a given period of time. On January 28, 2004, the Fed changed its language from "a considerable period" to "it can be patient in removing its policy accommodation." This new statement suggests that the Fed is in no hurry to raise interest rates as the economy continues to recover.

Nevertheless, the market responded to the Fed's new statement by increasing the yield on the 10-year Treasury note by 11 basis points, which Merrill Lynch economist David Rosenberg notes rivals the 14 basis point jump on February 4, 1994, when the Fed raised the target rate (by 25 basis points) to begin a period of target rate increases. The 11 basis point increase is a huge market increase compared to the average 3 basis point increase during the first day of the last three times when the Fed increased the target rate. This large increase suggests that the market viewed the change in the Fed wording as a signal of the Fed moving toward increasing interest rates.

The point of this *In the News* item is that the bond market is very sensitive to any change in market interest rates. One important point that should be taken from this chapter is that interest rates affect the price of a bond and therefore bondholders are concerned about changes in interest rates.

Therefore, the price of a fixed coupon bond is determined by the contractual cash flows from the bond, the timing of the contractual cash flows, and the discount rate. The cash flows from the bond (the coupon payments and the face value) are fixed in the bond contract and change only if the bond issuer defaults. The impact of a default on a bond's cash flows, and therefore its price, is situation specific and cannot be addressed in a general manner. The method for addressing default risk when owning a bond is to hold the bond in a well-diversified portfolio that includes assets other than bonds. On the other hand, discount rates change with changes in market interest rates without altering bond cash flows and therefore can be addressed in a general manner. The remainder of this section will address the relationship between changes in interest rates and changes in bond prices.

5.4.1 Duration

As the discount rate increases, the present value of a series of cash flows declines. Because the price of a bond is the present value of a series of cash flows, then as market rates increase, the price of the bond declines. However, the relationship is not linear. Instead, it is curved, with the price declining at a decreasing rate as market rates increase. This means the bond price curve will be convex, but the exact shape is bond specific. Figure 5-3 provides a representative curve for a fixed coupon bond without embedded options. Figure 5-3 is for a 9% fixed-rate annual coupon bond that has a face value of $1,000 and 25 years to maturity.

---

[9]This *In the News* item is from Rosenberg, D. (Chief North American Economist), 2004, *Merrill Lynch Fixed Income Weekly*, January 30, 10.

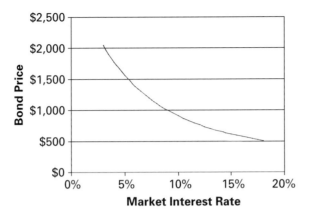

FIGURE 5-3 The relationship between bond price and the market interest rate.

Figure 5-3 provides a clear picture of the relationship between bond prices and market rates. However, an investor usually wants to know the change in value of the bond when the market rate changes. While the change in value can be estimated from the information in the curve, the exact answer is not immediately obvious from observing Figure 5-3. However, if a bond price/market rate pair on the curve is chosen and a tangent line to the curve is drawn at that point, the slope of the tangent line provides an approximation for the change in price that coincides with a change in the market rate. In Figure 5-4, a tangent line is added to the curve from Figure 5-3 at the price/rate pair of $1,000/9%.

Adding the tangent line to the bond price curve provides a general idea of the bond price change from a change in market rates. However, a specific estimate of the price change is needed, which means the slope of the tangent line must be calculated. The first derivative

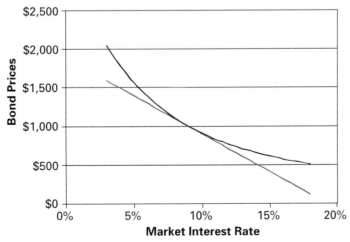

FIGURE 5-4 Linear approximation of the change in the bond price for a given change in market interest rates.

of the pricing equation that creates the bond price curve provides the formula for the slope of the tangent line. The simplest place to start to find the first derivative of the bond price formula is with Equation (5-1). Equation (5-1) is

$$B_0 = \frac{C}{(1+r)} + \frac{C}{(1+r)^2} + \frac{C}{(1+r)^3} + \cdots + \frac{C}{(1+r)^n} + \frac{F}{(1+r)^n}.$$

Then the first derivative of this equation is

$$\frac{dB}{dr} = -\frac{1}{(1+r)}\left[\frac{1C}{(1+r)} + \frac{2C}{(1+r)^2} + \frac{3C}{(1+r)^3} + \cdots + \frac{nC}{(1+r)^n} + \frac{nF}{(1+r)^n}\right]. \quad (5\text{-}6)$$

Equation (5-6) provides the change in the bond price for a change in the market interest rate. However, changes in bond prices are often analyzed on a percentage basis. To get the percentage change in the value of a bond, Equation (5-6) needs to be modified. It is modified by dividing both sides of the equation by the price of the bond and then multiplying both sides by the change in the market rate. Then, after some strategic grouping of terms, the resulting equation for the percentage change in the price of a bond is[10]

$$\frac{\Delta B}{B} \approx -\left[\frac{\frac{1C}{(1+r)} + \frac{2C}{(1+r)^2} + \frac{3C}{(1+r)^3} + \cdots + \frac{nC}{(1+r)^n} + \frac{nF}{(1+r)^n}}{B}\right]\left[\frac{\Delta r}{(1+r)}\right]. \quad (5\text{-}7)$$

The first term on the right-hand side of Equation (5-7) is often referred to as *Macaulay's duration* (*D*). The Macaulay's duration of a bond is often calculated separately from Equation (5-7) because **duration** provides an indication of the bond's price sensitivity to changes in interest rates with larger duration bonds being more sensitive to a given change in interest rates. The formula for Macaulay's duration is

$$D = \left[\frac{\frac{1C}{(1+r)} + \frac{2C}{(1+r)^2} + \frac{3C}{(1+r)^3} + \cdots + \frac{nC}{(1+r)^n} + \frac{nF}{(1+r)^n}}{B}\right] \quad (5\text{-}8)$$

or more generally Macaulay's duration is

$$D = \left[\frac{\left(\sum_{t=1}^{n}\frac{t \times C}{(1+r)^t}\right) + \frac{n \times F}{(1+r)^n}}{B}\right]. \quad (5\text{-}9)$$

Substituting *D* into Equation (5-7) provides the traditional form of that equation and shows that the percent change in the price of a bond from a change in interest rate is a function of

[10] Note that in moving from Equation (5-6) to (5-7) the equals sign changes to an approximation sign. The reason is that the equals sign is true for only very small changes in interest rates (*dr*). However, the Δr in Equation (5-7) is not restricted to be a very small change, so the equation becomes an approximation.

the bond's duration. The rewritten Equation (5-7) using D is

$$\frac{\Delta B}{B} \approx -D\left[\frac{\Delta r}{(1+r)}\right]. \qquad (5\text{-}10)$$

EXAMPLE *Using Duration to Estimate the Percent Change in the Value of a Bond*

As an example, apply Equation (5-10) to the bond pictured in Figures 5-3 and 5-4. The duration of the bond in Figures 5-3 and 5-4 is 10.71 for the price/rate pair of $1,000/9%. So, how will this bond respond to an increase in the market rate of 25 basis points (0.25%)? The answer from Equation (5-10) is

$$\frac{\Delta B}{B} \approx -10.71\left[\frac{0.0025}{(1+0.09)}\right] = -0.0246 \quad \text{or} \quad -2.46\%.$$

The preceding example estimated a change in value of -2.46%. However, by calculating the new price and comparing it to the old price we find that the correct answer is -2.41%. What is the problem? The problem is that the first derivative provides the slope of the tangent line only at the tangent point. Moving away from the tangent point, the slope of the curve changes as the curve moves away from the tangent line and thus the slope of the tangent line is only an approximation for the slope of the curve.

Figure 5-4 shows the farther the tangent line extends away from the tangent point the larger the gap becomes between the curve and the tangent line. This widening gap depicts how well (or how poorly) Equation (5-10) approximates the percent change in the price of the bond. For small changes in market rates, the curve and the tangent line are close together and Equation (5-10) provides a good approximation for the percent change in the price of the bond. However, for large changes in market rates a large gap exists between the curve and the tangent line, which means Equation (5-10) will not provide a good approximation for the percent change in the price of the bond. To provide a reasonable estimate of the effect of larger changes in market rates, something is needed to fill the gap between the curve and the tangent line. In other words, an error correction factor needs to be added to Equation (5-10). The error correction factor is referred to as convexity. However, before discussing convexity, a list of facts about duration needs to be presented.

The following is a brief list of some important facts known about duration.

1. Duration is the weighted time to maturity for a bond. It can also be thought of as the effective length of the payment stream. However, for examining bond interest-rate risk duration should be considered an elasticity measure.

2. The duration of a zero-coupon bond is its time to maturity. For coupon bonds, duration is less than the bond's time to maturity.

3. Duration increases with maturity but at a decreasing rate.

4. A bond has a shorter duration when
   a. the coupon rate is higher,
   b. the coupons occur more frequently, or
   c. the yield to maturity is higher.

5. For very long maturities, a low-coupon bond begins to resemble a perpetual annuity.

6. The duration of a bond portfolio is the weighted average of the individual bond durations with each weight equal to the percent of portfolio value invested in each bond.

7. As time elapses, duration will initially decline slowly and then will decline more rapidly as the bond approaches maturity.

8. Macaulay duration measures the absolute dollar volatility of a bond. However, the investor is more often interested in the percentage price volatility which leads to another duration calculation. The alternative duration calculation is referred to as the modified duration. The modified duration is calculated as: modified duration $= \frac{\text{Macaulay duration}}{1+r}$. The modified duration provides the percent change in the price of a bond for a given change in the yield.[11]

5.4.2 Convexity

As stated before, **convexity** is used to fill the gap between the tangent line and the bond price curve. However, before the convexity formula is presented and the associated error correction factor is added to Equation (5-10), some background on the source of the convexity formula and the error correction factor is presented.

The problem at this point is trying to determine the effect of moving along the bond price curve using a straight line at the tangent point. This does not work well; therefore, the process for estimating the percent change in the price of a bond needs to be adjusted. Fortunately, calculus offers a solution to our problem. The solution is called a Taylor's series expansion and it provides the mathematical solution for moving along a curve. A Taylor's series is a series of the derivatives of the formula that creates the curve that is being estimated. For estimating the percent change in the price of a bond, only the first and second derivatives of the bond price formula are used in a Taylor's series. The first derivative leads to the duration formula and the second derivative is the convexity formula.

The formula for convexity (the second derivative of the bond price formula) is

$$\text{Convexity} = \left[\frac{\left(\sum_{t=1}^{n} \frac{t \times (t+1) \times C}{(1+r)^{(t+2)}} \right) + \frac{n \times (n+1) \times F}{(1+r)^{(n+2)}}}{B} \right]. \tag{5-11}$$

---

[11] Modified duration provides a percentage volatility measure by substituting the modified duration into Equation (5-10). Equation (5-10) becomes

$$\frac{\Delta B}{B} = -(\text{modified duration}) \times \Delta r$$

then by dividing the equation through by Δr we get

$$\left(\frac{\Delta B}{B} \right) \left(\frac{1}{\Delta r} \right) = -(\text{modified duration}).$$

The result is that the modified duration equals the percent change in the price of the bond for a given change in the yield.

The adjustment to Equation (5-10) for the second term of a Taylor's series using convexity results in the following formula:

$$\frac{\Delta B}{B} \approx -D\left[\frac{\Delta r}{(1+r)}\right] + \frac{1}{2}(\text{convexity})(\Delta r)^2. \qquad (5\text{-}12)$$

The second term on the right side of Equation (5-12) is the error correction factor to fill the gap between the curve and the tangent line in Figure 5-4.

EXAMPLE *continued* Using Duration and Convexity to Estimate the Percent Change in the Value of a Bond

Continuing the example of the bond with 9% annual coupons, $1,000 face value, 25 years to maturity, and duration equal to 10.71, use Equation (5-12) to find the percent change in the price of the bond for a 25 basis point change in the market rate of interest. The convexity of the bond is 159.17. Equation (5-12) suggests the percent change in the price of the bond is

$$\frac{\Delta B}{B} \approx -10.71\left[\frac{0.0025}{(1+0.09)}\right] + \frac{1}{2}(159.17)(0.0025)^2 = -0.0245 + 0.0005 = -0.0240 \text{ or } -2.40\%.$$

As previously mentioned, the correct change in value for the bond in the preceding example is −2.41%; therefore, the correction factor worked reasonably well.[12] But, the example considered was a small change in the market rates where the curve and the tangent line are close together. The question that remains is, "how well does Equation (5-12) works for large changes in interest rates?"

EXAMPLE *continued* Percent Change from a Large Change in Interest Rates

To address the preceding question Equation (5-12) needs to be estimated for the percent change in the price of the bond for a 150 basis point (1.5%) increase in the market rate. The estimate from Equation (5-12) is

$$\frac{\Delta B}{B} \approx -10.71\left[\frac{0.015}{(1+0.09)}\right] + \frac{1}{2}(159.17)(0.015)^2 = -0.1474 + 0.0179 = -0.1295 \text{ or } -12.95\%.$$

The actual percent change in the price of the bond from a 150 basis point increase in the market rate is a decrease of 13.11%. Therefore, Equation (5-12) only estimates the percent change. This is a good estimate but only an estimate.

If Equation (5-12) only estimates the percent change in the price of a bond, then why is Equation (5-12) important? Equation (5-12) is important because it also works for a portfolio of bonds. That is, once the duration and convexity of a bond portfolio is known, Equation (5-12) is used to estimate the percent change in the value of the portfolio for a

---

[12] The reason that the error correction formula only works reasonably well is because of the very nature of convexity. Reexamine Figure 5-4. Notice that as interest rates decline from the point of intersection, duration projects the bond's price to rise (per the tangent line) but the actual increase in price (per the curved line) is greater than duration projects. Alternately, if rates rise, the duration line projects that the bond price will fall, but the actual decline in price is less than duration projects. This characteristic, a larger increase in price than a decrease in price for the same change in rates, is known as positive convexity and is common to all bonds without embedded options. The amount of convexity is, of course, a function of the maturity of the bond.

change in the market rate of interest. This very useful tool for bond portfolio managers enables them to estimate the impact of a change in interest rates in their portfolio value with one calculation. Without Equation (5-12) they would have to calculate the impact of an interest rate change on the value of each individual bond in their portfolio.

One final point about Equation (5-12) needs to be made. The rates, and therefore, the rate changes in Equation (5-12) are in terms of annual rates. Because the rates and rate

INDUSTRY APPLICATION

BOND ARBITRAGE—BARBELL

One of the tasks of a junior associate on a fixed income desk is to explain to clients how bond prices are determined. Unlike equities, bonds have a defined maturity date and hence the arbitrage opportunities in the fixed income market are also a function of time. For example, in an equity-based arbitrage, an investor would set up a risk-free arbitrage by selling over-valued stocks and buying under-valued stocks of similar risk.

In the case of bonds, interest rate risk is also a factor since the effect on bond prices of a change in interest rates is also a function of the maturity of the bond. As we know, short-term interest rates are more volatile than long-term interest rates but long-term bond prices are more volatile than short-term bond prices.

Suppose that today a 1-year zero-coupon bond costs $96.15 and a 3-year zero costs $88.92. Your computer says a 2-year zero should cost $91.85, but it is trading in the market at $92.47. Suppose further that in 1 year rates could go to 5% at which the 1-, 2- & 3-year bonds would be worth $100, $95.24 and $90.70, respectively. Alternately, rates could fall to 3% and the bonds would be worth $100, $97.09, and $94.26.

Your task would be to design an illustrative example to show how an investor could set up a risk-free arbitrage in such a situation. Since the 2-year bond is over-valued, you would want to sell this instrument. The trick is to buy enough of the 1-year and 3-year instruments so that when you unwind the position in 1-year's time, the cash flow from the sale of the longer and shorter maturity instruments will be enough to cover the cost of covering the short position on the 2-year instrument, *regardless of which interest rate regime is in existence in 1-year's time.*

So, what you want to do is set up a system of equations and solve for x [the amount of 1-year zero coupon bonds you want to buy] and y [the number of 3-year zero coupon bonds you want to buy] that will insure that re-

gardless of which interest rate regime occurs, you will be able to cover the short position you created by selling the 2-year bonds short. This is why we set the equations equal to zero. Note that we use the value of zero-coupon bonds that will exist in 1 year's time when we unwind the arbitrage position because that is when you will buy back the 2-year bond.

Sell the 2-year note and buy the 1-year and the 3-year notes

$$-95.24 + 100x + 90.70y = 0$$
$$-97.09 + 100x + 94.26y = 0$$
$$y = 0.5197$$
$$x = 0.4811$$

The position earns $92.47 − $91.85 = $0.62 per bond risk-free.

What is it that you have done? At the present time, you believe that the 2-year bond trading at $92.47 is over-valued, so you sell it because you believe it is currently worth $91.85. However, what happens in 1 year's time? You will have to buy the bond back at either $95.24 [if rates are at 5%] or at $97.09 [if rates fall to 3%]. At the time you set up the arbitrage, you buy roughly $x = 0.48$ of the 1-year zero [for every 2-year bond you sell short] because you know that this instrument will guarantee a payoff of $100 when it matures. Similarly, you buy $y = 0.52$ of a 3-year bond [for every 2-year bond you sell short] because in 1 year's time you will be able to sell it for $90.70 [if rates are at 5%] or $94.26 [if rates fall to 3%]. Notice that the differential amount that you earn by buying the 3-year zero and then selling it in 1-year's time helps to offset the differential amount you have to spend on buying back the 2-year bond that you sold short. Check to see that when you use the correct values of x and y, that each equation equals zero.

changes in Equation (5-12) are in terms of annual rates, duration and convexity must also be in annual terms. For convenience, the previous examples used annual coupon bonds so the duration and convexity would already be annualized. However, most bonds pay semiannual coupons; therefore, how to handle semiannual coupons needs to be discussed. The process takes two steps. The first step is to calculate duration and convexity using semiannual coupons, semiannual discount rates, and semiannual time periods in Equations (5-9) and (5-11). The adjustment to the duration and the convexity formulas are the same as the adjustments needed to change from the pricing formula from annual coupons to semiannual coupons. The second step is to annualize the duration and convexity. To annualize the semiannual duration the semiannual duration is divided by 2. To annualize the semiannual convexity, the semiannual convexity is divided by 4.[13]

5.5 ADVANCED BOND PRICING: PRICING FROM THE THEORETICAL SPOT RATE CURVE

Earlier, to price a bond, the cash flows were discounted at a constant rate r. This was done so focus would be on the process of bond pricing with a minimum of complications. However, using one rate to discount the bond's cash flows is equivalent to assuming that the yield curve is flat, which seldom occurs. Therefore, a change to Equation (5-1) is needed to modify our pricing method to allow for a term structure of interest rates that is not constant (i.e., a yield curve that is not flat).

Equation (5-1) is

$$B_0 = \frac{C}{(1+r)} + \frac{C}{(1+r)^2} + \frac{C}{(1+r)^3} + \cdots + \frac{C}{(1+r)^n} + \frac{F}{(1+r)^n}.$$

The change needed to Equation (5-1) to allow for different discount rates is as follows:

$$B_0 = \frac{C}{(1+r_1)} + \frac{C}{(1+r_2)^2} + \frac{C}{(1+r_3)^3} + \cdots + \frac{C}{(1+r_n)^n} + \frac{F}{(1+r_n)^n}. \tag{5-13}$$

Equation (5-13) shows that the price of a bond is still the present value of its coupons and its face value. However, now the discount rate is allowed to change. Specifically, the discount rates change to align with the term structure of interest rates. So, the question now is how to find the various discounts rates.

The answer is a two-stage process. First, the **theoretical spot rate curve** for Treasury securities is constructed from the term structure. This provides the default-free rate for each time period that is needed to discount a cash flow. Second, a premium for the risks and other features of the bond are added to the default-free discount rate for each time period. The remainder of this section details this two-stage process.

---

[13] Duration and convexity can be calculated for any frequency of coupon payment by matching the timeframe of the discount rate and the number of periods to the frequency of the coupon payment and then calculating Equations (5-9) and (5-11). Then the duration and convexity are annualized as follows:

$$\text{Annualized duration} = \frac{\text{calculated duration}}{\text{number of coupons per year}}$$

and

$$\text{Annualized convexity} = \frac{\text{calculated convexity}}{(\text{number of coupons per year})^2}.$$

5.5.1 Constructing the Theoretical Spot Rate Curve

In this section, the theoretical spot rate curve (which is often referred to as constructing the zero curve) is constructed. However, before the mechanics of the process is begun, the logic behind the process needs to be discussed.

The logic is that in an efficient market, two investments of the same risk with the same cash flows must have the same price. For the theoretical spot rate curve, the first investment is a coupon paying Treasury security. The second investment is a series of *zero-coupon* Treasury securities with cash flows that duplicate the cash flows of the coupon security. In an efficient market, these two investments must have the same price. With this logic in mind, the theoretical spot rate curve can be constructed.

First, the yield to maturity of the Treasury securities (the term structure) that matches the timing of the cash flows of our bond must be determined. This means two facts about the bond to be valued must be known. These two facts are (1) timing of coupons and (2) the time to maturity. Therefore, to construct a theoretical spot rate curve assume that a 7.5% semiannual coupon Treasury bond with five years to maturity will be priced. This means the yield to maturity of Treasury securities in six-month increments starting at six months to maturity and increasing through five years to maturity will be used to calculate the theoretical spot rate curve. Figure 5-5 lists a series of (artificial) rates that will be used as the example to construct the theoretical spot rate curve. These artificial rates will be used to demonstrate the specific points for calculation, but it should be noted that a real yield curve would not normally have this much change in yields over so short a period of time—this point will be discussed later. Assume also that from period three onward, par value coupon bonds will be examined and that the first two bonds are discount-value Treasury bills. Using these rates, a theoretical spot rate curve will be constructed.

The process for finding the theoretical spot rate curve divides into a logical process for defining the spot rates and a mechanical process for calculating the spot rates. The logic behind the theoretical spot rate curve is

1. Assume a Treasury coupon paying security and a series of zero-coupon Treasury securities with the same cash flows must sell for the same price.

2. Solve for the discount rate that equates the prices of each term. The discount rates found in the process are the theoretical spot rates.

Period	Time to maturity	Yield to maturity (%)
1	6 months	8.00
2	1 year	7.50
3	1 1/2 years	7.00
4	2 years	6.50
5	2 1/2 years	6.00
6	3 years	5.50
7	3 1/2 years	5.00
8	4 years	4.50
9	4 1/2 years	4.00
10	5 years	3.50

FIGURE 5-5 Hypothetical yield curve.

Then the mechanical process for calculating (constructing) the theoretical spot rate curve is a multistep process. The steps for the process are as follows:

Step 1. Start with first coupon period and move through each coupon period to the time to maturity of the bond to be priced.

Step 2. Treasury securities with initial maturities of one year or less are T-bills. T-bills are zero-coupon securities, so T-bill yields can be used without any additional calculations. Therefore, when pricing a semiannual coupon bond (as in this example), the six-month T-bill yield is the first discount rate and the one-year T-bill yield is the second discount rate.

Step 3. The first discount rate (theoretical spot rate) that must be calculated is the $1\frac{1}{2}$ year rate.

Step 4. To calculate a theoretical spot rate assume a face value of $1,000 and assume the bond is selling at par. This means that the price of the bond is $1,000 and that the coupon rate equals the yield to maturity of the bond. Accordingly, the coupon equals (face value × coupon rate)/number of coupons per year.

Step 5. Use the known theoretical spot rates as discount rates and solve for the discount rate associated with the last bond cash flow. That discount rate is the next theoretical spot rate.

Step 6. Extend the bond one coupon period and repeat Steps 4 through 6 until the end of the term of the bond to be priced is reached.

This process is difficult at first, but with a little work can be mastered.

Applying the process for the theoretical spot rate curve to the example of a 7.5% semiannual coupon Treasury bond with five years to maturity and the term structure of interest rates in Figure 5-5, the theoretical spot rates are calculated next and listed in Figure 5-6. Pricing a semiannual bond requires a theoretical spot rate every six months. Since T-bill yields can be used directly, $r_1 = 8\%$ and $r_2 = 7.5\%$ (see Step 2). Accordingly, the first theoretical spot rate that must be calculated is the $1\frac{1}{2}$ year rate (r_3) (see Step 3). Following

Period	Time to maturity	Bond equivalent yield theoretical spot rate (%)
1	6 months	8.00
2	1 year	7.50
3	1 $\frac{1}{2}$ years	6.98
4	2 years	6.46
5	2 $\frac{1}{2}$ years	5.94
6	3 years	5.42
7	3 $\frac{1}{2}$ years	4.90
8	4 years	4.38
9	4 $\frac{1}{2}$ years	3.87
10	5 years	3.36

FIGURE 5-6 Theoretical spot rates implied by the yield curve in Figure 5-5.

Steps 4 and 5 the formula for calculating r_3 is[14]

$$B = \frac{[C/2]}{(1 + [r_1/2])} + \frac{[C/2]}{(1 + [r_2/2])^2} + \frac{([C/2] + F)}{(1 + [r_3/2])^3} \quad \text{and with the cash flows is}$$

$$\$1,000 = \frac{35}{(1 + [0.08/2])} + \frac{35}{(1 + [0.075/2])^2} + \frac{1,035}{(1 + [r^3/2])^3}.$$

Now, we solve for r_3. The solution is

$$\$1,000 = \$33.6538 + \$32.5156 + \frac{\$1,035}{(1 + [r_3/2])^3}$$

$$933.8306 = \frac{\$1,035}{(1 + [r_3/2])^3}$$

$$(1 + [r_3/2])^3 = 1.108338 \quad \text{then}$$

$$r_3 = 0.069757 \quad \text{or} \quad 6.98\%.$$

Step 6 says that after finding a theoretical spot rate, extend the analysis one time period and repeat Steps 4 through 6 until the term to maturity of the bond is reached. Accordingly, the two-year theoretical spot rate must be calculated next. The calculation of the two-year rate is presented below. Note that the coupon changes to match the two-year yield from the term structure and that r_1, r_2, and r_3 are the identified theoretical spot rates.

$$\$1,000 = \frac{32.50}{(1 + [0.08/2])} + \frac{32.50}{(1 + [0.075/2])^2} + \frac{32.50}{(1 + [0.0698/2])^3} + \frac{1,032.50}{(1 + [r_4/2])^4}$$

$$\$1,000 = \$31.25 + \$30.1931 + \$29.3216 + \frac{\$1,032.50}{(1 + [r_4/2])^4}$$

$$909.2353 = \frac{\$1,032.50}{(1 + [r_4/2])^4}$$

$$(1 + [r_4/2])^4 = 1.13557 \quad \text{then}$$

$$r_4 = 0.064588 \quad \text{or} \quad 6.46\%.$$

The theoretical two-year spot rate is 6.46%. The process is continued through the time of maturity for the bond. The resulting theoretical spot rates for a five-year semiannual coupon Treasury security are shown in Figure 5-6.

This example uses a downward-sloping yield curve. With a downward-sloping yield curve, the theoretical spot rate curve lies below the yield curve like an open pair of scissors pointing down. When the yield curve is upward sloping, the theoretical spot rate curve lies above the existing yield curve like an open pair of scissors pointing upwards. When the yield curve is flat, the spot curve matches exactly with (plots right on top of) the yield curve.

With the theoretical spot rates calculated (see Figure 5-6), the appropriate discount rates to price a five-year semiannual coupon Treasury note have been determined. The next step is to price the bond in the example. Recall that the bond in the example is a 7.5%

---

[14] Remember, the convention in the bond market is to divide annual rates by 2 to find semiannual rates. We continue with that convention here.

semiannual coupon Treasury note with five years to maturity. The price of this bond using the theoretical spot rates is

$$
\begin{aligned}
B = {} & \frac{37.50}{(1 + [0.08/2])} + \frac{37.50}{(1 + [0.075/2])^2} + \frac{37.50}{(1 + [0.0698/2])^3} + \frac{37.50}{(1 + [0.0646/2])^4} \\
& + \frac{37.50}{(1 + [0.0594/2])^5} + \frac{37.50}{(1 + [0.0542/2])^6} + \frac{37.50}{(1 + [0.049/2])^7} + \frac{37.50}{(1 + [0.0438/2])^8} \\
& + \frac{37.50}{(1 + [0.0387/2])^9} + \frac{1{,}037.50}{(1 + [0.0336/2])^{10}} = \$1{,}175.11.
\end{aligned}
$$

The process for calculating the theoretical spot rates used a five-year semiannual coupon Treasury note. However, the process will work for any frequency of coupon payments and any time to maturity with proper modification of the coupon payment, the discount rates, and the time periods.

As a final comment, notice that the 10th period theoretical spot rate of the 3.36% is 14 basis points different from the 10th period rate YTM of 3.5% in Figure 5-5. Earlier, it was stated that the yield curve rates used in the example were not very realistic (have extreme changes) but were used to make a point. The point is that the theoretical spot rates differ from the YTMs in the yield curve. In reality, YTMs in the yield curve seldom differ as much as the example. Instead, the actual yield curve for six-month through five-year Treasuries from November 2000 contained the rates of 6.34%, 6.07%, 6.00%, 5.87%, 5.83%, 5.83%, 5.79%, 5.76%, 5.72%, and 5.65%. If the theoretical spot rate curve is calculated using these rates the 10th period theoretical spot rate was 5.63%, which is only a difference of 2 basis points for the yield curve rate. Does a 2 basis point difference matter? Why does this occur? Yes, the difference matters because bonds are usually traded in millions of dollars; therefore, small differences in the discount rate can make a big difference to the price. Second, the difference occurs because of the relative sizes of the coupons and the principal repayment.

The authors have a colleague who refers to why this 2 basis point difference matters as the horse and rabbit stew problem. The rabbits represent the coupon payments and the horse represents the principal repayment. Begin with one horse (face value) and one rabbit (one coupon payment) in the cooking pot. This stew tastes a lot like horse. Even when the cooking/maturity time is extended and more rabbits are put into the stew, a very long time elapses before enough rabbits are in the pot to offset the taste of that really big horse.

5.5.2 Pricing a Bond with Default Risk Using the Theoretical Spot Rate Curve

In Section 5.5.1, the process to price Treasury securities using the theoretical spot rate curve was presented. However, many bonds that are not Treasury securities are available and need to be priced. To price these other bonds, the theoretical spot rate curve must be adjusted to reflect the specific risks and other features of these bonds. This section covers the process of adjusting the theoretical spot rate curve to price bonds that are not Treasury securities.

The process follows from the one discussed in Section 5.3.5 of this chapter for determining risk-adjusted discount rates. Recall, five factors determine the structure of interest rates. These factors are (1) time to maturity, (2) default risk, (3) tax treatment of interest payments, (4) marketability, and (5) attached options. These factors are used to determine *what is a similar bond*. Once a similar bond is found, the yield difference (spread) between that bond and a Treasury security of the same maturity is calculated. This spread will contain the premium on the similar bond for default risk, tax differences, marketability, and attached options. The spread is then added to each rate in the theoretical spot rate curve to arrive at the risk-adjusted discount rates.[15]

EXAMPLE *Pricing a Risky Bond Using the Theoretical Spot Rate Curve*

Assume that an AAA rated five-year $1,000 corporate bond with semiannual coupons at 7% and no embedded options needs to be priced. At the time the theoretical spot rates were calculated, the spread on five-year AAA corporate bonds was 1.05%. Therefore, to price this bond the AAA spread is added to the theoretical spot rate curve to find the risk-adjusted discount rates. Using the theoretical spot rate curve construct from the November 2000 term structure (mentioned earlier), the following risk-adjusted discount rates were determined.

Period	Years to maturity	Theoretical spot rate November 2000 (%)	Risk-adjusted discount rate (%)
1	6 months	6.34	7.39
2	1 year	6.07	7.12
3	1½ years	6.00	7.05
4	2 years	5.86	6.91
5	2½ years	5.82	6.87
6	3 years	5.82	6.87
7	3½ years	5.78	6.83
8	4 years	5.75	6.80
9	4½ years	5.70	6.75
10	5 years	5.63	6.68

Then using these discount rates, the price of the AAA corporate bond is

$$B = \frac{35.00}{(1 + [0.0739/2])} + \frac{35.00}{(1 + [0.0712/2])^2} + \frac{35.00}{(1 + [0.0705/2])^3} + \frac{35.00}{(1 + [0.0691/2])^4}$$

$$+ \frac{35.00}{(1 + [0.0687/2])^5} + \frac{35.00}{(1 + [0.0687/2])^6} + \frac{35.00}{(1 + [0.0683/2])^7} + \frac{35.00}{(1 + [0.0680/2])^8}$$

$$+ \frac{35.00}{(1 + [0.0675/2])^9} + \frac{1,035.00}{(1 + [0.0668/2])^{10}} = \$1,012.21.$$

[15] It is very important to make sure we find the spread on a bond with the same time to maturity. We know from previous discussions that this is important due to the term structure of interest rates. However, there is an additional time factor that is often ignored, and that is the term structure of the credit spread. Long-term bonds of similar initial default risk have a higher probability of default than short-term bonds because there is more time for bad things to happen to the bond issuer, so the credit spread increases with time to maturity. However, when we find the total spread using a bond of the same maturity, this spread will include the appropriate credit spread for compensating the investor, on average, over the life of the bond.

SUMMARY OF VALUATION AND RISK MANAGEMENT SKILLS

1. Calculate the value of a bond and the different yield measures important for analyzing a bond's investment performance.

You should now have a thorough understanding of the bond valuation formula and how to use it to calculate the value of a bond. The value of a bond is just the present value of its future cash flows. For a bond, the future cash flows are periodic interest payments (coupons) and a principal payment at maturity (face value). In addition, you should have mastered calculation of the yield to maturity, one of the key measures of return used by bond investors. Yield maturity is the annual rate of return on a bond assuming that the bond is purchased today at the current market price, held to maturity, and all coupon payments are reinvested at the yield to maturity. Yield to maturity is equivalent to internal rate of return (IRR).

2. Understand how interest rate changes affect a bond's value and calculate and interpret the measures of bond interest-rate risk: duration and convexity.

Bond investors are exposed to interest rate risk—when interest rates increase, the value of the bond decreases and vice versa. Analysts predict the effect of a change in interest rates on bond value using duration and convexity calculations. These measures help portfolio managers understand how the maturity and coupon rate of the bond affect how sensitive bond prices are to interest rates. The evolution of interest rates over the life of a bond determine the realized yield of the investment. You should now be able to calculate duration and convexity and interpret what they mean for a bond's risk.

3. Apply term structure theory to the valuation of a bond using theoretical spot rates.

The basic bond pricing formula assumes a flat term structure of interest rates. However, the term structure is seldom flat. The theoretical spot rate curve is used to price a bond with any term structure. You should be able to derive the theoretical spot rates from bond market data and use them in the valuation of a coupon bond, recognizing that a coupon bearing bond is similar to a portfolio of zero-coupon bonds.

QUESTIONS

1. A bond is an interest-only loan. Define in loan terms a bond coupon and face value.

2. A corporate bond is repaid from the cash flows of the project it funds. Government bonds descriptions are based on the source of the cash flows used to repay a specific government bond. List the three types of government bonds that were discussed and describe the source of their cash flows for repayment. Which source of cash flows is the least risky?

3. Describe a subordinated debenture. Which of the firm's assets do debenture investors have a claim to in bankruptcy?

4. List the three types of embedded options in bonds that were discussed. Describe for each what the valuable option is, who has the option, and what effect the option has on the coupon rate of the bond.

5. What is a primary market and what are the two main methods used in a primary market to sell the bonds to investors?

6. What is a secondary market and what are the two forms of secondary markets in the bond market?

7. What is the major benefit of a private placement? What is the major limitation of a private placement?

8. List the three pieces of information that an investor needs to determine the price of a bond. Also, list the assumptions that need to be made to simplify the pricing of bonds as discussed in this chapter.

9. Find the price of the following bond:

coupon rate of 7.75%,
pays annual coupons,
face value of $1,000,
risk-adjusted discount rate of 8.25%, and
14 years to maturity.

Before you begin pricing the bond, determine if the bond will sell at a discount, a premium, or at par. You should always do this as a reality check for the bond price you calculate.

10. Find the price of the following bond:

coupon rate of 8.75%,
pays semiannual coupons,
face value of $1,000,
risk-adjusted discount rate of 8.0%, and
10 years to maturity.

Before you begin pricing the bond, determine if the bond will sell at a discount, a premium, or at par. You should always do this as a reality check for the bond price you calculate.

11. Find the yield to maturity (YTM) of the following bond:

coupon rate of 6.25%,
pays semiannual coupons,
face value of $1,000,
seven years to maturity, and
a price of $1,125.

Before beginning to find the yield to maturity, determine if the YTM is less than the coupon rate, greater than the coupon rate, or equal to the coupon rate.

12. You are considering the purchase of a bond with 10 years to maturity. The bond's YTM is 7%. However, your investment horizon is four years, your reinvestment rate for the bond coupons is 5%, and the yield curve is upward sloping. In this situation is the yield to maturity of the bond a good estimate of the yield you would expect to earn on the bond? Explain.

13. Calculate the realized compound yield for the following investment:

Investment horizon	$3\frac{1}{2}$ years,
Bond purchased	6.5% coupon rate paying semiannual coupons,
	face value of $1,000,
	10 years to maturity,
	7.5% yield to maturity,
	current price of $930.52.
Coupon reinvestment rate	3.75%,
Bond YTM at sale	8.25%.

14. You need to determine the price of a bond. You know the bond rating of the issuing firm but the firm does not have any existing publicly traded debt. Explain how you would determine the appropriate risk-adjusted discount rate for the bond.

15. For the following bond, calculate the bond's duration and convexity:

    8% coupon rate
    pays annual coupons,
    $1,000 face value,
    9% yield to maturity,
    seven years to maturity.

16. For the following bond, calculate the bond's duration and convexity:

    7.50% coupon rate,
    pays semiannual coupons,
    $1,000 face value,
    9% yield to maturity,
    three years to maturity.

Your answer is based on semiannual coupons, so both calculations are semiannual. What are the annualized duration and convexity of the bond?

17. You own a bond with duration of 10.7 years and convexity of 159.17. The duration and convexity were calculated at a YTM of 9%. Estimate the percent change in value of your bond for a 50 basis point increase in the market yield. Next, calculate the percent change in value for a 50 basis point decrease in the market yield. You will not get the same percent change, why?

18. What assumption is made about the term structure when a bond is priced using Equation (5-2)? What is the problem with this assumption?

19. Using the following term structure of interest rates, construct the theoretical spot rate curve for each of the six periods.

Period	Time to Maturity	Yield to Maturity (%)
1	6 months	3.97
2	1 year	3.94
3	1½ years	4.10
4	2 years	4.30
5	2½ years	4.43
6	3 years	4.55

Note: one method for calculating the theoretical spot rates from the YTMs in the term structure is to use the SOLVER tool in an Excel spreadsheet.

20. Use the theoretical spot rates from Figure 5-6 to price the following bond:

    10-year U.S. Treasury Note with four years remaining until maturity,
    8% coupon rate,
    pays semiannual coupons,
    $1,000 face value.

21. Use the theoretical spot rates in Figure 5-6 to price the following corporate bond:

20-year BBB rated corporate bond with three years remaining until maturity,
10% coupon rate,
pays semiannual coupons,
$1,000 face value,
1.89% spread for three-year BBB corporate bonds.

REFERENCES

BOARDMAN, C., and R. McENALLY, 1981, Factors affecting seasoned corporate bond prices, *Journal of Financial and Quantitative Analysis, 16*, 207–226.
The authors find that default risk is included in the price of bonds. Specifically, they find that cash flows are considered uncertain and the degree of uncertainty increases until the cash flow occurs. Also, they find that the cash flows of lower rated bonds are considered more uncertain.

CARAYANNOPOULOS, P., 1996, A seasoning process in the US Treasury bond market: The curious case of newly issued ten-year notes, *Financial Analysts Journal, January/February,* 48–55.
The author finds that *on-the-run* notes and bonds trade at higher prices than equivalent seasoned notes and bonds. Over time, as the on-the-run security trades, the on-the-run price moves to the seasoned price. The price adjustment process generally takes about the length of time a security is on-the-run.

EDERINGTON, L., J. YAWITZ, and B. ROBERTS, 1987, The informational content of bond ratings, *Journal of Financial Research, Fall*, 211–226.
The authors find that bond ratings contain useful information for investors but that investors do not rely totally on bond ratings. Investors also use other available sources of financial information about the bond issuer.

FABOZZI, F., 1996, *Bond Markets, Analysis and Strategies*, 3rd Ed., Prentice-Hall, Englewood Cliffs. NJ.
This book provides a thorough discussion of all the important issues in the bond market.

FULLER, R., and J. SETTLE, 1984, Determinants of duration and bond volatility, *Journal of Portfolio Management, Summer,* 66–72.
They authors state that duration is a direct measure of bond volatility and show that duration is a function of the coupon rate, the term to maturity, and the yield to maturity.

HITE, G., and A. WARGA, 1997, The effect of bond-rating changes on bond price performance, *Financial Analysts Journal, May/June*, 35–51.
The authors find that bond prices begin declining six months prior to a rating downgrade, yet there is still a significant price reaction to the downgrade announcement.

LITTERMAN, R. and T. IBEN, 1991, Corporate bond valuation and the term structure of credit spreads, *Journal of Portfolio Management, Spring*, 52–64.
The authors show that the credit spread for risky bonds is not constant. Instead it increases as time to maturity increases. This article shows a term structure of credit spreads.

MOSER, J., and J. LINDLEY, 1989, A simple formula for duration: An extension, *Financial Review, 24(4)*, 611–615.
The authors provide a shortcut calculation of Macaulay's duration that allows for coupons periods of less than a year.

RICH, S., and J. ROSE, 1991, A note on finance principles, bond valuation, and the appropriate discount rate, *Financial Practice and Education, Fall/Winter*, 99–101.
The authors discuss the standard practice in finance texts of pricing semiannual coupons using the annual discount rate divided by two. The point made is that this process ignores compounding and thus incorrectly values the bond.

STANHOUSE, B., and D. STOCK, 1999, How changes in bond call features affect coupon rates, *Journal of Applied Corporate Finance, Spring*, 92–99.
The authors discuss that the coupon rate on callable bonds is higher than the coupon rate on noncallable bonds. Also discussed is that the size of the premium is a function of length of the protection period and the first call price.

WHITE, M., and J. TODD, 1995, Bond pricing between coupon payment dates using a "no-frills" financial calculator, *Financial Practice and Education, Spring/Summer*, 148–152.
The authors provide the steps on a financial calculator for calculating the price of a bond when the arrival of the first coupon is not a full coupon period away.

KEY TERMS

Bearer Bond   A bearer bond is a bond without a record of ownership. The owner of a bearer bond is the person in physical possession of the bond.

Bond   A bond is a loan. The details of the loan are specified in the bond contract. A bond is an interest-only loan. This means periodic payments of interest will be made with the full amount of the principal due at the maturity date of the loan.

Bond Equivalent Yield The bond equivalent yield is an annualized return on a bond based on simple (instead of compound) interest.

Convexity Convexity is the second derivative of the bond price formula. It is used with duration to estimate the change in value of a bond or bond portfolio from a change in interest rates.

Coupon Rate The coupon rate is the specific rate of interest for the interest payments on a fixed rate bond.

Coupons Coupons are the periodic interest payments on bonds.

Debentures A debenture is an unsecured bond. Debentures are described as either senior or subordinated, which designates the order of priority of claims against the borrower's assets.

Duration Duration is the weighted time to maturity for a bond. It can also be thought of as the effective length of the payment stream. However, to examine bond interest-rate risk, think of duration as an elasticity measure.

Embedded Options Embedded options are rights attached to a bond that give the holder of the bond the right or opportunity to change the contract. The common embedded options in a bond are a call option, a put option, or a conversion option.

Exchange An exchange is a physical location for trading securities.

Face Value The face value of a bond is the principal amount of the loan and is the amount repaid to the lender at maturity.

General Obligation Bond A municipal bond backed by the taxing authority of the issuer.

Industrial Revenue Bond A bond issued by a municipal government for a private project and the bond is repaid from the cash flows of the private project.

Interest-Only Loan An interest-only loan is a loan with periodic payments of only interest and with the entire amount of principal repayment at the maturity of the loan.

Over-the-Counter A network of dealers and brokers for trading securities.

Primary Market A primary market is the market for the original sale of the security.

Principal Principal is the agreed-on amount of the loan. In a bond, the principal amount is called the face value of the bond.

Private Placement A private placement of a bond issue is the direct sale of the entire issue to one investor or to a small group (less than 35) of investors.

Public Sale A public sale means that the bond issue is offered to the public.

Realized Compound Yield A rate of return on a bond that corrects for the shortcomings of yield to maturity. Specifically, it allows for the sale of the bond before maturity and for the coupons to be reinvested at a rate different from the yield to maturity.

Registered Bond A registered bond is a bond that maintains a record of ownership.

Revenue Bond A municipal bond repaid by the cash flows of the specific project that the bond funds.

Secondary Market A secondary market is a market for the resale of a security.

Senior Senior refers to a debenture that is first in the order of priority.

Serial Bond A serial bond is a bond issue that has different maturity dates. A serial bond is issued in different series with each series having a different maturity date.

Sinking Fund A sinking fund is a method that provides for the periodic retirement of a portion of the bond principal.

Subordinated Subordinated refers to debentures that are not first in the order of priority. For a subordinated debenture to exist, there must first be a senior debenture.

Term Bond A term bond is a bond with the entire amount of principal due at maturity. Most bonds are term bonds.

Theoretical Spot Rate Curve The set of interest rates derived from the term structure for pricing a bond.

Underwritten Offer An underwritten offer is a public offer that is sold through an investment banker. Underwriting means that the investment banker buys the entire security offering and then sells it to the public.

Yield to Maturity The rate of return on a bond purchased today and held through maturity.

Zero-coupon Bond A bond that does not pay periodic interest is called a zero-coupon bond. A zero-coupon bond always sells at a discount.

FLOATING RATE DEBT

Floating-rate notes (FRN) are securities with a coupon or interest rate that is adjusted periodically due to changes in a base or benchmark. In general, there are two categories of *variable-rate* debt issues.

1. Floating-rate notes with coupons based on a short-term index. These coupons may be at a spread over the base or index rate or at a discount to the base or index rate. These coupon rates are reset more than once per year.

2. *Adjustable-rate notes or variable-rate notes* with coupons based on a longer-term index. These coupon rates are usually not reset more than once a year. They are not reset for a much longer period of time than one year.

   Several different types of indices are used with FRNs but the most popular are

- Prime rate,
- LIBOR (one, three, and six month),
- LIBID[16] (one, three, and six month),
- LIMEAN (average of LIBID and LIBOR),
- Federal funds,
- Commercial paper,
- Certificates of deposit,
- 11th district cost of funds (used to calculate mortgage rates),
- 91-day Treasury bills.

The most common of all these indices for debt issues is LIBOR. LIBOR (London Interbank Offer Rate) is the rate that the primary London banks offer to other banks on deposits in the Eurocurrency market. That is, the average interest rate on nondomestic deposits. For example, dollars deposit outside of the United States in, say, London or Panama would be considered Eurodollar deposits.[17]

The LIBOR rate quoted in the *Wall Street Journal* is an average of rate quotes from five major banks: Bank of America, Barclays, Bank of Tokyo, Deutsche Bank, and Swiss Bank. Because LIBOR is an average, it is really a form of an index and is quoted for one-month, three-months, six-months, as well as one-year periods.

---

[16] The London Interbank Bid Rate.

[17] Hence, the Euro prefix should not be considered as referring to the geographic location of the funds.

TABLE 5A-1

Date	LIBOR rate (%)	Floating cash flow (%)
March 1, 2003	4.5	
September 1, 2003	4.75	4.5
March 1, 2004	4.4	4.75
September 1, 2004	4.5	4.4

One common assumption is that LIBOR and Eurodollar rates are the same thing. This assumption is *not* true. LIBOR is for interbank loans in London and can occur in a variety of currencies. Eurodollar rates are rates on dollar-based time deposits outside the United States, and Eurodollar rates are available in all the major financial markets around the world. The Eurodollar market has been in existence for over 40 years and is a major component of the international financial market.

For investors, the most attractive feature of the FRN is the fact that the FRN normally reprices to par every time the coupon is reset. Hence, there is reasonable certainty of the recapture of principal.

Let's consider a four-period bond with floating coupons f_1, f_2, f_3, and f_4, and a notional face value of P. The amount of floating interest paid in any period will be $f_k = P \times r_k$ (the then prevailing one-period interest rate). At maturity, the bondholder receives $P + f_4 = P(1 + r_4)$. One period earlier, the investor would have received $PV\{P(1 + r_4)\} = P$. In general notation then, if f_{n-1} is paid one period prior to maturity, then two periods prior to maturity this bond is again worth $P = PV\{P(1 + r_{n-1})\}$. And so on.

Let's assume we are dealing with LIBOR on Eurodollar deposits. Obviously, this rate can and will change on a daily basis. However, this does not mean that we cannot value a variable-rate bond whose interest rate coupon is tied to the LIBOR index. For example, consider Table 5A-1.

Table 5A-1 shows that although we may only have expected values for the floating rates in the future, we always know what the interest payment will be on the next reset date. On March 1, 2003, the six-month LIBOR rate is 4.5%. Thus, on September 1, 2003, the issuer will pay $(4.5\% \times 1/2) = 2.25\%$ times the principal amount of the debt outstanding. At that same time, the issuer and the investor will both know that the current value of the FRN is par and that the annualized coupon payment to be paid on March 1, 2004, is 4.75%, and so on until the instrument matures. The only problem that arises is when the FRN has to be valued between the coupon/reset dates.

Suppose that the rates in Table 5A-1 are the LIBOR rates on Eurodollar deposits and there are 91 days until the coupon payment date on September 1, 2003. What would be the clean price of the FRN, if the current LIBOR rate is 4.6%?

$$B_0 = \frac{(\$45/2) \times (91/182)}{(1 + [0.046/2])^{(91/182)}} + \frac{\$1{,}000}{(1 + [0.046/2])^{(91/182)}}$$

$$= \$11.12 + \$988.69 = \$999.81.$$

As can be ascertained, the fact that the FRN resets to par at the next coupon date makes the FRN both very attractive and easy to value for an investor.

CHAPTER 6

MORTGAGE VALUATION

6.1 INTRODUCTION

The purpose of this chapter is to explain how to value and evaluate the risk of one of the most prevalent securities traded in U.S. financial markets, the mortgage. In simple terms, a mortgage is a loan that is secured by real property. When a borrower pledges property as collateral for a loan and does not repay the loan as promised, the collateral can be seized by the lender and sold to cover the outstanding debt. At the end of 2003 there were $9.4 trillion of mortgages outstanding, about 42% of the U.S. fixed income market. This means that the mortgage market was bigger than the combined markets for U.S. Treasury, municipal, and corporate bonds.

Many financial institutions hold mortgages, but they are owned primarily by commercial banks and government-sponsored enterprise mortgage pools (e.g., Federal National Mortgage Association or Fannie Mae and Federal Home Loan Mortgage Corporation or Freddie Mac). While mortgages are conceptually simple, you will find out from this chapter that valuing and measuring the risk of mortgages is more complicated than for bonds; although in analyzing mortgages, we use the same basic framework for valuation and risk measurement that we developed for bonds in Chapter 5. This chapter covers concepts that are vital for a financial analyst at any institution that originates mortgages or invests in them.

Effectively managing the risk of a portfolio of mortgages requires understanding how to identify and predict the cash flows from mortgages and how to quantify the various risks from owning them. This chapter begins with a description of the mortgage markets and the characteristics of mortgages that define the cash flows followed by an explication of the predominant types of residential mortgages. We then turn to showing you the basics of mortgage valuation and conclude this chapter by explaining the factors that cause mortgage cash flows and values to change, which is essential to quantifying their risks. We also provide a detailed example of how to value a portfolio of mortgages and how to measure and interpret the duration and convexity of a mortgage portfolio. The duration and convexity discussion follows from similar discussions in Chapter 5.

DEVELOPING VALUATION AND RISK MANAGEMENT SKILLS

1. Understand the primary features of a mortgage loan and how each feature affects mortgage cash flows.
2. Understand the different types of residential mortgages.
3. Calculate the value and duration of a mortgage portfolio and understand the risk implications of the duration measure.

4. Understand the convexity of a mortgage portfolio and its valuation and risk implications.

6.2 MORTGAGE TERMINOLOGY AND INSTITUTIONAL FEATURES OF MORTGAGE MARKETS

Going from Chapter 4 to Chapter 5 moved the discussion from money markets to bond markets, adding a layer of complexity. This chapter moves on to the mortgage market, which adds more layers of complexity.

The security commonly called a **mortgage loan** contains two parts, a loan agreement and the collateral assignment or mortgage. Through the loan agreement, the borrower, or mortgagee, agrees to receive a fixed amount of money at origination and repay it through a series of payments to the lender, or mortgagor, over a fixed period of time. Through the **mortgage**, the mortgagee pledges a piece of real property as collateral for the loan. The mortgage places a **lien** on the property. With a lien in place, the borrower cannot sell the property or transfer it to another person or corporation until the loan is repaid. In addition, if the borrower fails to make the promised payments, the lender can seize the collateral, sell it, and use the proceeds of the sale to repay the loan. Mortgage loans and other loans for which the borrower posts collateral are types of **secured lending**.

6.2.1 Types of Mortgages

The four main types of mortgage loans are residential, multifamily, commercial, and farm. Farm mortgages are not a significant part of the sector, so farm mortgage will be essentially ignored in the remainder of the discussion of mortgages.

Commercial mortgages and multifamily mortgages are similar to other bank loans in that the structure can vary widely from one loan to the next. The maturity of the loan, how frequently payments are made, whether any principal is repaid before the loan matures, and other features will depend on the needs of the borrower and the requirements of the lender. The only feature in common is that each mortgage is secured by a piece of real estate. Essentially, **commercial** and **multifamily mortgages** are secured commercial and industrial (C&I) loans that have real estate collateral.

In contrast, the residential mortgage market has become quite standardized. In most cases, borrowers choose from a limited number of options. For example, almost all **residential mortgages** are issued with an initial maturity of either 30 years or 15 years, with 30 years being the most common. As another example, almost all residential mortgages require monthly payments.[1] Because of this standardization and because residential mortgages comprise more than three-quarters of the total mortgage market, the rest of the discussion will consider only residential mortgages.

---

[1] It would be nice to say "all residential mortgages...," but in a $7.3 trillion market, there are always exceptions. Some mortgages are issued with 10-, 20-, or 25-year maturities and a few are issued that require quarterly payments, rather than monthly payments.

Rather than continuing to use phrases such as "most mortgages" or "almost all mortgages," the discussion will simply describe what is most common and talk about exceptions only when they occur with a reasonably high frequency. Also, the discussion is about U.S. residential mortgage practices and markets and may not be accurate for foreign mortgage markets. Indeed, many of the features that are common for U.S. mortgages, such as the embedded prepayment option that will be discussed in great detail in this chapter and in Chapter 14, do not exist in many European mortgages.

6.2.2 Scheduled Principal and Interest Payment

The most common type of residential mortgage requires the borrower to give the lender level or fixed monthly payments of principal and interest based on the initial size or principal balance of the mortgage, its initial term to maturity, and its fixed coupon interest rate. This is known as a **fixed-rate mortgage** and the scheduled monthly payment is called the **P&I payment**. For a fixed-rate mortgage, a portion of each P&I payment is used to pay the interest that has accrued and the remainder goes toward repaying the principal balance of the loan. Over time, as the principal balance is repaid, the amount of interest that accrues each month gets smaller and a larger part of the P&I payment goes toward principal repayment.

The scheduled P&I payment amount (which is the cash flow received by the lender) can be determined at any time during the life of the mortgage using the formula for calculating an annuity payment or

$$PICF_{t+1} = F_t \left/ \left[\frac{1 - \left(\frac{1}{(1+r)^{T-t}} \right)}{r} \right], \right. \tag{6-1}$$

where F_t is the principal balance remaining at the end of the previous month, r is the monthly coupon rate, T is the initial term to maturity of the mortgage measured in months, and $PICF_{t+1}$ is the next principal and interest or P&I payment.[2]

EXAMPLE   *Calculating the P&I Payment on a Fixed-Rate Mortgage*

Using Equation (6-1), what is the P&I payment for a new 30-year fixed-rate mortgage with an initial principal balance of $150,000 and a simple annual coupon rate of 6.0%? We are at the beginning of the life of the mortgage, or $t = 0$, and want to calculate the first payment. The initial principal balance is $F_0 = 150,000$, the term to maturity is $T = 360$ (= 30 years × 12 months per year), and the monthly coupon rate is $r = 0.005$ (= 6.0%/12 = 0.06/12). Putting all of this together in Equation (6-1), this

---

[2] Any financial calculator will also calculate the P&I payment for a mortgage using its annuity functions. However, each calculator uses different sets of keys for these calculations, so instructions for using a financial calculator are not included in this textbook. In general, using your calculator's built-in functions is preferable, because it helps you to avoid rounding error in your calculations.

mortgage's scheduled monthly P&I payment is calculated to be

$$PICF_1 = 150,000 \left/ \left[\frac{1 - \left(\frac{1}{(1.005)^{360}} \right)}{0.005} \right] \right. = \$899.3258$$

or \$899.33 rounded to the nearest penny.

EXAMPLE *Calculating the P&I Payment on a Fixed-Rate Mortgage during the Life of the Mortgage*

Calculate the monthly P&I payment for a 15-year fixed-rate mortgage that is four years old, has a remaining principal balance of \$141,163, and a coupon rate of 5.40%. In this case, $t = 48$ ($= 4$ years $\times$ 12 months per year have passed), $F_{48} = 141,163$, $T = 180$ ($= 15$ years $\times$ 12 months per year), and $r = 0.0045$ ($= 5.4\%/12 = 0.054/12$). Putting all of this into Equation (6-1), this mortgage's next monthly P&I payment (the 49th payment) is calculated to be

$$PICF_{49} = 141,163 \left/ \left[\frac{1 - \left(\frac{1}{(1.0045)^{180 - 48}} \right)}{0.0045} \right] \right. = \$1,420.6292$$

or \$1,420.63 rounded to the nearest penny.

6.2.3 Secured Lending and Default

As stated earlier, residential mortgages are loans secured by real estate. When purchasing a residence or 1–4 family investment property, it is rare for an individual or family to have enough savings to pay the full purchase price. In most cases, the purchaser pays a portion of the purchase price from savings and borrows the rest through a residential mortgage loan. The purchaser also pays closing costs for the real estate transaction and the creation of the mortgage, including local (city/county) taxes related to the deed transfer and mortgage lien registration, any fees charged by the lender, and any costs associated with securing the loan (such as for required inspections or lender's title insurance). The portion of the purchase price paid by the borrower is known as the **down payment**. The amount borrowed divided by the purchase price of the property is known as the **loan-to-value ratio** or LTV ratio. Because mortgages have LTV ratios that are less than 100% (less than 1.00), they are said to be **overcollateralized**. That is, the collateral is worth more than the loan balance.

Residential mortgages are quite safe loans. People are very protective of their homes and will generally make sure that the mortgage is paid even if the car payment or credit card bill isn't. In addition, although the borrower's down payment may only represent 10 or 20% of the value of the home (or even less) it is often one of the biggest investments the borrower has ever made. Borrowers do not want to lose this investment. In fact, the borrower can always sell the property, use part of the proceeds of the sale to repay the loan, and keep the rest rather than defaulting on the mortgage.

Further, as shown earlier, mortgages require monthly payments of principal and interest, which means that the amount owed by the borrower is decreasing every month. On top of that, real estate prices have generally risen over time, often by much more than the rate of inflation. While an increase in prices is not guaranteed, widespread declines in real estate prices are exceedingly rare. What a safe loan! The amount owed decreases each month and the value of the collateral can reasonably be expected to rise over time.

Despite the safety provided by real estate collateral, residential mortgage lenders have occasionally lost money when a borrower stops making required payments. Although the lender has a first lien on the property, that lien does not take priority over the government's claim if the borrower fails to pay required property taxes or assessments. Further, a property might lose significant value because of a fire or natural disaster. For these reasons, lenders typically require that borrowers have insurance on the property and that they make a monthly escrow payment toward the insurance premium and property taxes. These escrow payments are accumulated by the lender or its agent and used to pay the tax or insurance bill when it is due. Lenders also require the borrower to purchase and maintain flood insurance if the property is found to be in a flood-prone location.

Despite taking these precautions, borrowers do, on occasion, stop making the P&I payments that are due to the lender. In this case, the borrower is said to be in default on the loan. When a borrower defaults, the lender will ask the appropriate court to foreclose on the property that has served as collateral. In **foreclosure** proceedings, the property title is transferred to the lender, which typically sells it and uses the proceeds to repay all or part of the unpaid principal balance. Despite overcollateralization, scheduled repayment of principal over time, increases in property values, and tax and insurance escrow payments, lenders can still lose money when a borrower defaults.

Typically, a mortgage default will occur when the borrower has lost employment. In such cases, it is not uncommon for the borrower to have neglected property maintenance or even to have caused physical damage in frustration as foreclosure proceedings began. This is known as the **distressed collateral** problem. In addition, as mentioned earlier, regional declines in property values are not common but do occasionally occur. Such losses in value are typically associated with severe local economic problems and high local unemployment rates. Finally, default losses are positively related to the mortgage's initial loan-to-value ratio. Loans with higher LTV ratios, representing lower down payments, are more likely to suffer losses than similar loans with lower LTV ratios.

As a final layer of protection, lenders may require that a borrower purchase **private mortgage insurance,** or PMI, if the borrower makes a down payment of less than 20% (initial LTV ratio greater than 80%). The borrower pays for PMI each month in addition to the scheduled P&I payment and escrow payments for taxes and insurance. The lender can legally require that PMI be maintained by the borrower until the principal balance falls below 80% of the collateral's value.

6.2.4 Prepayment Option

In Chapter 5, embedded options in bonds were discussed. One embedded option that was discussed is a call option that allows a bond's issuer to retire the bond before maturity. Most residential mortgages contain an embedded option that is similar to the one in a callable corporate bond.

Residential mortgages contain a **prepayment option** that allows the borrower to pay off the mortgage at any time and without penalty. This means that the borrower can retire the mortgage by repaying the remaining principal balance plus any interest that has accrued

Coupon rate (%)	P&I payment ($)
5.0	536.82
6.0	599.55
7.0	*665.30*
8.0	733.76
9.0	804.62

FIGURE 6-1 P&I payment (30-year, fixed-rate, $100,000 mortgage).

since the last payment was made. The prepayment option is a call option because it allows the borrower to buy back (call) the mortgage. As with a callable bond, the advantage lies with the issuer of the security (the borrower). The advantage gained by the borrower through the prepayment option is balanced by a disadvantage for the lender or investor.

A borrower may prepay a mortgage for liquidity reasons or for financial reasons. Liquidity-motivated **prepayments** occur when the borrower sells the collateral property. There are many reasons why a borrower might sell the property. Individuals and families may move to a new house because of new job opportunities, growth in the family, shrinkage in the family as children grow up and leave home, retirement, improved economic circumstance leading to a more expensive lifestyle, poor economic circumstances because of loss of employment, and so on. The motivating factor for such prepayments is the desire to sell the property being used as collateral for the mortgage. Even if the sale of the property is motivated by a desire to realize a financial gain from increasing real estate prices, the prepayment of the mortgage is liquidity motivated. Mortgages have a *due-on-sale clause* to ensure that the lender is repaid if the property is sold.

Alternatively, a borrower may prepay a mortgage because the coupon rate on new mortgages has fallen significantly below the rate on the borrower's existing mortgage. Such a financially motivated prepayment occurs because the borrower wants to take out a new mortgage at the current, lower interest rate and use the proceeds of that mortgage to prepay the existing, high cost mortgage. To see why a borrower would have a financial motivation to prepay an existing mortgage, consider a 30-year, fixed-rate mortgage with a $100,000 principal balance and a coupon rate of 7.0%. As Figure 6-1 shows, the scheduled monthly P&I payment on this mortgage is $665.30.

The table also shows what the P&I payment would be on a new 30-year mortgage with higher and lower coupon rates. For example, if the coupon rate on a new 30-year fixed-rate mortgage fell to 6.0%, the borrower could reduce his or her monthly P&I payment to $599.55 by **refinancing** the mortgage, a savings of $65.75 or almost 10%. Obviously, if mortgage interest rates were to increase, the borrower would not want to refinance, because the monthly payment would increase. Because prepayment is an option that benefits the borrower, the borrower will only refinance when it is to his or her financial advantage.

Residential mortgage contracts typically require no explicit penalty for prepayment,[3] but the lack of an explicit prepayment penalty does not mean that refinancing is costless

---

[3] In recent years, a few mortgage lenders (including Countrywide) have experimented with offering mortgages that charge prepayment penalties during the first three to five years of the mortgage's life. The borrower is rewarded for accepting this penalty by a small reduction in the mortgage coupon rate, usually about 0.125%. These mortgages have not gained widespread appeal.

for borrowers. The borrower will have expenses totaling one or more thousands of dollars associated with the creation of the new mortgage, including fees for the mortgage application, property inspection and/or appraisal, credit check, loan underwriting and processing, lender's title insurance, taxes for filing the new mortgage lien, and so on. Some of these fees are required, but others (such as loan processing, loan underwriting, courier fees, etc.) are simply ways that the lender tries to disguise the profit being made from the transaction.

When considering whether to refinance, the borrower must weigh the total costs of obtaining the new mortgage against the monthly savings coming from a lower scheduled P&I payment. Because mortgage interest is deductible from taxable income for federal and most state income taxes, the after-tax cost savings from refinancing will usually be lower than before tax. The borrower must decide whether he or she is likely to keep the new mortgage long enough for the accumulated monthly savings to exceed the cost of refinancing.

Borrowers may also be motivated to refinance a mortgage loan to extract equity from their home or real estate investment. If the collateral's value has increased since the original mortgage was created, a way to turn this increased value into cash without selling the property is to take out a new mortgage for an amount higher than the remaining principal balance on the existing mortgage. This sort of refinancing is both liquidity-motivated and financially motivated. Alternatively, a borrower could take out a **home equity loan**, also known as a **second mortgage**.

A borrower may choose to make an extra payment in addition to the scheduled P&I payment. Such an extra payment is used to pay down the principal balance and is called a **curtailment**. The motivation for making curtailments varies from borrower to borrower but may include the desire to pay off the loan more quickly than scheduled or the desire to reduce mortgage debt using savings that are generating lower returns than the mortgage's coupon rate. Some borrowers make curtailment payments every month as a regular savings/investment vehicle, while others do so only once or on rare occasions: using an inheritance, for example, or an income tax refund.

6.2.5 Mortgage Origination and Investment

Traditionally, an individual or family who wanted a mortgage loan for the purchase of a home would apply to a local commercial bank or savings and loan. This financial institution borrowed money from local individuals and businesses in the form of savings and checking deposits and used that money to make various kinds of loans to other individuals and businesses, including mortgage loans. The local institution handled all three major aspects of mortgage lending, including

- **Origination**. Making the decision to accept or reject a loan application on the basis of underwriting standards set by the institution.
- **Servicing**. Accepting payments over the life of a mortgage, pursuing late payments, and handling foreclosure if the borrower defaulted on the loan.
- **Investment**. Making sure that the net return generated (after any defaults) by the mortgage loan and other loans in the institution's portfolio was sufficient to pay the

interest due to depositors, the overhead costs of running the institution (buildings, salaries, etc.), and the return required by the institution's shareholders.

In the traditional market, each financial institution was a **financial intermediary**. Financial intermediaries stand between savers and borrowers, writing contracts with each side that are very different from one another. A checking account allows a saver to deposit or withdraw money at will, so the account may have a lot of money in it one day and very little money the next. On the other hand, a mortgage loan provides money to the borrower for many, many years. A checking account and a mortgage do not look at all alike. Yet a bank, savings and loan, or other financial intermediary creates mortgages (and car loans, business loans, etc.) out of checking accounts (and savings accounts, CDs, etc.).

This was not a particularly efficient way of handling mortgage lending because each intermediary was forced to handle every part of the mortgage business, whether it was good at it or not. Further, supply and demand imbalances were common. One local market might contain a lot of younger people with little savings and high demand for mortgage loans (and automobile loans and so on). Interest rates on deposits and loans would be high in such a market, yet many deserving borrowers would still be unable to obtain loans because of the lack of available funds. Another local market might contain a high proportion of retired people with high levels of savings and little demand for mortgages, car loans, and such. Interest rates on deposits and loans would be low in such a market, hurting the retirees who depend on earnings from their savings.

Fortunately, over the last 20 years, the market for mortgage loans has undergone a process of **disintermediation**. Disintermediation means that a business can choose to specialize in only one or two of the three major aspects of mortgage lending. Disintermediation has been made possible by the tremendous growth in mortgage securitizations, a process that we will discuss in detail in Chapter 14. Securitization allows funds to flow efficiently from investors to borrowers and has resulted in lower mortgage rates that more closely track other market interest rates. Securitization has also facilitated disintermediation in financial markets.

Figure 6-2 provides the strong evidence of the extent of disintermediation in the **home mortgage** market. It shows the total value of existing U.S. residential mortgages for 1988 through 2003. It also shows what sort of institution held those mortgages. In 1988, depository intermediaries (commercial banks, savings and loans, and credit unions) held more than 45% of all residential mortgages, but by 2003 that share had dropped to about 30%. In contrast, the share of home mortgages held by government and private agencies

	2003	1998	1993	1988
Total home mortgages	7,282.6	4,362.9	3,119.3	2,157.7
Depository intermediaries	2,231.4	1,427.4	1,058.2	1,002.7
(percentage of total)	30.6%	32.7%	33.9%	46.5%
Government agency or ABS	4,578.5	2,889.3	1,714.7	863.2
(percentage of total)	62.9%	66.2%	55.0%	40.0%

FIGURE 6-2 Holdings of home mortgages (in $billions).

Source: Federal Reserve System, Z-1 Releases, L.218.

that securitize mortgages grew from 40% to more than 60% during the same time period. Banks and savings and loans still hold a lot of home mortgages, but the trend is clearly away from such intermediaries.

Many different financial service providers compete to offer mortgage origination services, including private mortgage brokers, insurance agents, online services, as well as banks, savings and loans, and credit unions. These mortgage originators work with a borrower to complete his or her application, process the application according to fixed (often nationally applied) standards, and make sure that money gets to the closing for the property purchase or refinancing. Originators work on a fee basis, typically earning a few hundred dollars for each mortgage they help to create.

Mortgage servicers handle the mundane processing of monthly payments, separating each check into its principal, interest, and escrow components. Servicers keep track of escrow accounts and make sure that taxes and insurance premiums get paid on time. They are the contact point for borrowers who have questions about any aspect of their loans. They also contact borrowers if payments are late and pursue foreclosure if a borrower goes into default. Servicers earn a small fee each month that is based on the remaining principal balance of the loan. They also earn any late payment fees that are collected or fees for other services such as providing a payoff statement for a prepayment. Servicing is a business driven by economies of scale. Servicers typically invest a lot of money in sophisticated computer and telecommunications systems in an attempt to reduce the marginal cost of handling each additional account.

The primary investors in mortgages are depository intermediaries, federal agencies such as the Government National Mortgage Association (GNMA or Ginnie Mae), federally sponsored enterprises like the Federal National Mortgage Association (FNMA or Fannie Mae) and the Federal Home Loan Mortgage Corporate (FHLMC or Freddie Mac), and pools that are used to create mortgage-backed securities (MBS). Other institutional investors, such as pension funds and insurance companies, invest in mortgages by purchasing MBS. The investment mortgages and mortgage-backed securities will be discussed in detail in Chapter 14.

It is rare for an individual investor to own mortgages. An individual investor might own a mortgage if he or she has sold a piece of real estate and provided some of the financing to the buyer. In 1988, this kind of financing was significant, representing about $108 billion, or 5.0% of the residential mortgage market. In 2003, however, the volume of home mortgages held by the household sector declined to about $81 billion, or 1.1% of the total market. Individuals also rarely purchase MBS because the minimum required investment is large and the characteristics of mortgages make them more difficult to manage than other fixed-income securities like Treasury bonds and corporate bonds.

One reason why individual investors do not hold mortgages is the lack of a secondary market for them. Once a mortgage is originated, there are only a very few institutions that will buy them—GNMA, FNMA, FHLMC, and a few private MBS issuers. These issuers do not buy single mortgages and prefer to work only with originators who can provide either a large portfolio of mortgages at one time or a steady stream of new mortgages over time. Even commercial banks and savings and loans are extremely reluctant to purchase mortgages, and the few finance companies that will purchase them do so at a steep discount to the face value. Essentially, single residential mortgages are very illiquid: it would take a long time to find a buyer for one and the selling price would be well below the true value.

INDUSTRY APPLICATION

FANNIE MAE (THE FEDERAL NATIONAL MORTGAGE ASSOCIATION)

As you have learned, Fannie Mae does not lend money directly to home buyers. This agency makes mortgage funds available and affordable by buying mortgages from a variety of institutions that do lend money directly to home buyers. How Fannie Mae does this is often a question that newly hired interns and associates in the real estate finance field are expected to know.

Primary market lenders include mortgage companies, savings and loans, commercial banks, credit unions, and state and local housing finance agencies. After making the mortgage loan to the home buyer, these lenders sell mortgages into the secondary market—the market where mortgages are bought and sold by various investors. The secondary market participants include not only Fannie Mae but also various pension plans, insurance companies, securities dealers, and other financial institutions. When the lenders sell their mortgages, they no longer have their funds tied up in their loan portfolios but once again have cash to make additional loans. Hence, these lenders are making a return on the origination of the mortgage and not necessarily off of the repayment of the loan.

Fannie Mae buys mortgages made to low-, moderate-, and middle-income people. For example, their loan limits[4] for 2005 (effective January 1, 2005) are

First Mortgages

- One-family loans: $359,650
- Two-family loans: $460,400
- Three-family loans: $556,500
- Four-family loans: $691,600

Second Mortgages

- $179,825
- In Alaska, Hawaii, Guam, and the U.S. Virgin Islands: $269,725

Fannie Mae pays cash for the mortgages it buys and holds them in their portfolio. Fannie Mae and other secondary market securitization firms have very large and sophisticated fixed income departments. Fannie Mae then issues mortgage-backed securities (MBS) in exchange for pools of mortgages from lenders. These MBS provide the lenders with a more liquid asset to hold or sell. To fund the original purchase of the mortgages, Fannie Mae also issues debt securities to the investing public. Much of Fannnie Mae's earnings are derived from the difference between the yield on the mortgages it buys and the yield on the bonds issued to buy them. When the MBS is issued, Fannie Mae guarantees that investors will receive principal and interest payments on a timely basis regardless of what happens to the underlying mortgages—for this, Fannie Mae earns a fee which is another source of income.

How Do the MBS Work?

Recall that Fannie Mae buys pools of loans that conform to its guidelines and converts them into single-class mortgage-backed securities with a guarantee on timely payment. Essentially, the security passes through to the investors at a specific coupon rate, scheduled principal and interest that the mortgagors pay each month on their outstanding balance (plus any unscheduled prepayments). So, an investor in a Fannie Mae MBS owns an undivided interest in a pool of mortgages that serve as the underlying asset for the security and receives a pro-rata share of the cash flows from those mortgages.

Each pool of fixed-rate, single-family mortgages has a passthrough rate which is lower than the interest rate on the underlying pool of mortgages. The interest differential covers the guarantee fee paid to Fannie Mae, and the fee paid to the servicing institution (often the originating bank) for collecting payments from home owners and performing other servicing functions. The following simple schematic indicates how one particular pool of mortgages might be securitized by Fannie Mae.

(continued)

---

[4] These data were taken from www.fanniemae.com. Note that one- to four-family mortgages in Alaska, Hawaii, Guam, and the U.S. Virgin Islands are 50% higher than the limits for the rest of the country.

INDUSTRY APPLICATION (*continued*)

FANNIE MAE (THE FEDERAL NATIONAL MORTGAGE ASSOCIATION)

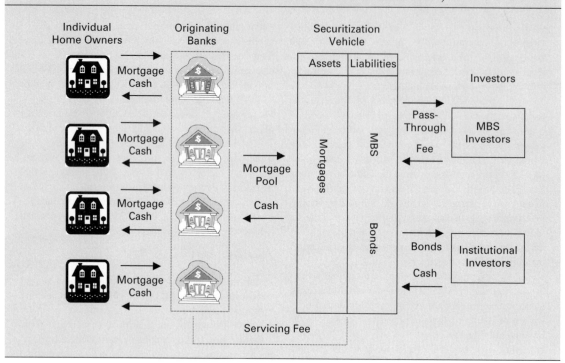

6.3 TYPES OF RESIDENTIAL MORTGAGES

It was stated in Section 6.2.1 of this chapter that the most common type of residential mortgage is the fixed-rate mortgage. Other reasonably common types of mortgages include the **adjustable-rate mortgage,** or ARM, and the **balloon mortgage**. Recently, another type of mortgage has grown in popularity, the **interest-only mortgage**. Each of these types of mortgages will be discussed in turn.

6.3.1 Fixed-Rate Mortgages

There are three critical pieces of information needed to evaluate a fixed-rate mortgage: its remaining principal balance, coupon rate, and remaining term to maturity (or the original maturity and the number of months that have passed since origination). These three items will seem familiar because they are the same information needed to calculate a fixed-rate mortgage's scheduled P&I payment using Equation (6-1). In addition, because the P&I payment for a fixed-rate mortgage will never change, the original principal balance of the mortgage, its coupon rate, and its original term to maturity can always be used to calculate the scheduled P&I payment for every month.

However, as discussed in Section 6.2.4 of this chapter, a mortgage borrower has a right or option to prepay the remaining balance of the mortgage at any time and without penalty. What is not immediately apparent is how much will be owed at any given point in time. Luckily, the remaining principal balance on the loan can be calculated using the scheduled P&I payment, the coupon rate, and the remaining maturity (or the original maturity and the number of months that have elapsed since the mortgage was originated). Assuming that all monthly P&I payments have been made on schedule and no curtailments (additional payments of principal) have been made, the remaining principal balance after t payments have been made is

$$F_t = PICF \times \left[\frac{1 - \left(\frac{1}{(1+r)^{T-t}} \right)}{r} \right], \tag{6-2}$$

where F_t is the principal balance remaining at the end of month t, r is the monthly coupon rate, T is the initial term to maturity of the mortgage measured in months, and $PICF$ is the fixed P&I payment.

EXAMPLE   *Calculating the Remaining Principal Balance*

Recall the first example in Section 6.2.2, which used a 30-year, fixed-rate mortgage with an initial $150,000 principal balance and a 6.0% coupon rate to calculate that the scheduled monthly P&I payment for this mortgage is $899.33, rounded to the nearest penny. What will be the remaining principal balance on this loan after one year has passed? The answer to this question is found using Equation (6-2). The inputs to Equation (6-2) in this example are $PICF = 899.33$, $T = 360$, $t = 12$ (one year is 12 months), and $r = 0.005$. Putting all of this into Equation (6-2), the remaining principal balance on the mortgage after one year has passed (and 12 monthly payments have been made) is calculated to be

$$F_{12} = 899.33 \times \left[\frac{1 - \left(\frac{1}{(1.005)^{360-12}} \right)}{0.005} \right] = \$148,158.68,$$

rounded to the nearest penny.

EXAMPLE   *Calculating the Amount of Principal Repaid*

Another question that can be asked about this mortgage is "how much principal will be paid back after five years?" Again, Equation (6-2) is used, but this time with $t = 60$, because there are 60 months in five years. The principal balance after 60 months is

$$F_{60} = 899.33 \times \left[\frac{1 - \left(\frac{1}{(1.005)^{360-60}} \right)}{0.005} \right] = \$139,582.19,$$

rounded to the nearest penny. But this doesn't precisely answer the question about how much principal has been repaid. The original principal balance was $150,000.00 and $139,582.19 remains after five years, so $10,417.81 ($= 150,000.00 - 139,582.19$) will have been repaid.

There are two aspects of calculating Equation (6-2) that must be well-understood. First, it assumes that each monthly P&I payment has been made exactly on the first of the month. If payments are made even a few days earlier or later than scheduled, there will be a change in accrued interest. Over time, this will cause the remaining principal balance to deviate from what has been calculated. Second, the monthly P&I payment in the calculations is a rounded amount. Rounding will create an error in the calculation compared to the more precise answer that would be found using a financial calculator or spreadsheet program. The actual remaining principal balance after five years, calculated without rounding error, is $139,581.54, meaning that $10,418.46 in principal is scheduled to be repaid. The difference between these two answers is only $0.65, but it is important to recognize that the answers calculated using Equations (6-1) and (6-2) are subject to some error.

6.3.2 Adjustable-Rate Mortgages

The second most popular type of residential mortgage is the adjustable-rate mortgage, more commonly known as an ARM. As the name suggests, the coupon rate on an ARM is not fixed over its life; instead, the coupon rate rises or falls periodically to reflect changes in market interest rates. This means that an ARM's scheduled P&I payment may rise or fall over time, depending on how market interest rates change during the life of the ARM.

For a fixed-rate mortgage, the coupon rate was a fixed percentage. For an ARM, the coupon rate is equal to a specified market index rate plus a fixed spread. The ARM contract must specify both the index and the spread. For example, a common index is the London Interbank Offer Rate, known as LIBOR. An ARM contract might specify its index as the 12-month LIBOR plus a spread of 2.50%. Actually, spreads are more typically quoted in **basis points** or bps, where 1% equals 100 basis points (100 bps). So the ARM would have 12-month LIBOR as its index and 250 bps as its spread.

The next question that must be answered in the ARM contract is how often the payment will be recalculated using the current market value of the index. Logistically, it would be difficult to recalculate the payment each month, because the borrower needs to be notified about the payment amount in advance. An ARM contract will specify a **repricing frequency** (also known as an adjustment interval) which states how often the payment will be recalculated. The most common repricing frequency is 12 months (annually), but ARMs that reprice twice a year or once every two years are not uncommon. The ARM contract will also specify the exact dates on which the coupon rate will change and a new payment will be calculated. This typically occurs at least one month before the new payment is due, so that there is time to notify the borrower. The maturity of the index and repricing frequency will usually match, so that a one-year ARM (one that reprices every 12 months) will use a 12-month index like the 12-month LIBOR or the one-year constant maturity Treasury (CMT) yield, and a six-month ARM will use the six-month LIBOR or the six-month CMT yield.

Each time an ARM reprices, the new P&I payment is calculated by assuming that the ARM's coupon rate will stay at the new level for the rest of the ARM's life. When the value of the index rises, the ARM's P&I payment will rise to reflect the higher interest cost. When the index falls, the P&I payment will fall. Understanding how the P&I payment is recalculated is probably easiest through an example.

EXAMPLE *Calculating P&I Payments on an ARM*

The example will look at a one-year ARM with an original maturity of 15 years, an original principal balance of $120,000, an index equal to 12-month LIBOR, and a spread of 300 bps. On the day that the ARM's first payment is determined, the 12-month LIBOR rate is 2.10%, so the initial coupon rate is the index plus the spread, or 5.10% (= 2.10% + 3.00%).

Equation (6-1) is used to calculate the monthly payment that will be required for the first 12 months (until the first repricing occurs). The calculation assumes that 5.10% will be the coupon rate for the entire life of the ARM, so $F_0 = 120,000$, $r = 0.00425$ (= 0.0510/12), and $T = 180$ (15 × 12). Putting all of this together, the initial P&I payment is calculated to be

$$PICF_{(1-12)} = 120,000 \Bigg/ \left[\frac{1 - \left(\frac{1}{(1.00425)^{180}}\right)}{0.00425}\right] = \$955.22.$$

The borrower will make this scheduled P&I payment for the first 12 months.

If the borrower makes this P&I payment as scheduled for the first year, a part of the principal balance will be repaid. The remaining principal balance after 12 monthly P&I payments of $955.22 can be calculated using Equation (6-2) to be

$$F_{12} = 955.22 \times \left[\frac{1 - \left(\frac{1}{(1.00425)^{180-12}}\right)}{0.00425}\right] = \$114,531.33.$$

Now suppose that on the next repricing date, 12 months after the date on which the initial value of the index was determined, 12-month LIBOR has risen to 2.70%. This means that the new coupon rate will be 5.70% (= 2.70% + 3.00%) or $r = 0.00475$. This new coupon rate will be used to calculate the P&I payment for the next 12 months. Remember that one year has passed on the mortgage, so only 14 years will remain of the ARM's original 15-year maturity or $T - t = 168$.

Because the assumption for calculating ARM payments is that the new coupon rate will remain fixed for the remainder of the life of the mortgage, Equation (6-1) is again used with the new inputs to calculate the monthly P&I payment for the second year of the ARM's life. The new payment amount is

$$PICF_{(13-24)} = 114,531.33 \Bigg/ \left[\frac{1 - \left(\frac{1}{(1.00475)^{168}}\right)}{0.00475}\right] = \$991.08.$$

The payment has increased by $35.86. This is as expected, because the index rate rose from the first year to the second.

Many of the ARMs now being originated are actually **fixed/adjustable hybrids**. This type of mortgage acts like a fixed-rate mortgage for a period of time and then acts like an adjustable-rate mortgage for the remainder of its life. That is, the coupon rate on the mortgage is initially fixed for three, five, seven, or even ten years, and then adjusts periodically to a specified market index plus a fixed spread. An ARM of this type will be named to indicate the period of time during which its coupon rate will be fixed and its repricing frequency once the coupon begins to adjust. For example, a 5/1 ARM will have a fixed coupon rate for five years and then reprice annually for the remainder of the ARM's life. Similarly, a 7/2 ARM will have a fixed coupon rate for seven years and then reprice every two years thereafter.

One concern that a borrower might have about entering into an adjustable-rate mortgage agreement is that the coupon rate on the mortgage could (in theory) increase without limit. Similarly, the lender might be concerned that the coupon rate could drop to a very small amount. To address these concerns, most ARM contracts contain a pair of **rate caps** and a pair of **rate floors**. An ARM will have a periodic rate cap that limits the amount by which the ARM's coupon rate can increase from one repricing date to the next. It will also have a lifetime rate cap that limits the amount by which the coupon rate can increase from its initial level. In addition, the ARM will have a periodic rate floor that limits the amount by which the coupon rate can decrease from one repricing date to the next and a lifetime rate floor that limits the amount by which the coupon rate can decrease over the life of the mortgage.

For example, consider an ARM with 5/2 lifetime/periodic caps and floors and an initial coupon rate of 6.50%. The rate caps mean that the coupon rate cannot rise to more than 8.50% at the next repricing (the initial coupon rate of 6.50% plus the 2.00% periodic cap) and can never rise above 11.50% (the initial coupon rate plus the 5.00% lifetime cap). The rate floors mean that the coupon rate cannot fall below 4.50% at the next repricing and can never fall below 1.50%.

It is also not uncommon for an ARM to offer an artificially low initial coupon rate that is much less than the current index rate plus the spread. This is called a **teaser rate** and means that the initial P&I payment will be artificially low.[5] In addition, because the lifetime rate cap is based on the initial coupon rate, a teaser rate limits the maximum coupon rate the borrower can ever be charged. The downside of a teaser rate is that the artificially low P&I payment may encourage a borrower to borrow too much. When an ARM has a teaser rate, the coupon rate (and therefore the P&I payment) is almost certain to go up by a lot at the first repricing date, often by as much as the periodic rate cap will allow. A borrower who barely qualified for a loan based on the low "teaser" payment may not be able to afford the new, higher payment.

6.3.3 Other Types of Mortgages

In addition to traditional fixed-rate mortgages and ARMs, two other types have gained a level of popularity in recent years—the balloon mortgage and the interest-only mortgage. A balloon mortgage is one that has a fixed-rate and scheduled P&I payments calculated for a 30-year mortgage, but requires repayment of the remaining principal balance in full after a certain amount of time. For example, a 7-year balloon mortgage would have the same P&I payments as a 30-year mortgage for the first seven years, but would then have to be paid off

---

[5] A teaser rate is a rate that is artificially low and therefore is expected to rise in the future. Not all ARMs start with teaser rates. However, all ARMs start at rates that are lower than similar term fixed rate loans. Under a fixed rate mortgage the lender takes on all the interest rate risk of the mortgage while under an ARM some of the interest rate risk is transferred to the borrower. The lower starting rate on an ARM is compensation to the borrower for taking on some interest rate risk. When the starting rate on an ARM is not a teaser rate, the rate on the ARM will not automatically be expected to increase in the future.

in full. As the name suggests, an interest-only mortgage requires no repayment of principal until the maturity date. The upside of such a mortgage is that the payment amount is small, allowing the borrower to qualify for a larger loan. The downside is that the borrower builds no savings or equity in the property beyond the initial down payment, unless the property value increases.

It would be virtually impossible to describe every other type of residential mortgage that is available in the current market. There are ARMs that adjust only once during the life of the mortgage and ARMs that can be converted to fixed-rate mortgages. There are graduated payment mortgages in which the scheduled P&I payment increases over time and reverse-amortization mortgages in which the principal balance grows over time because the scheduled P&I payment is too low to cover accrued interest.

One advantage for borrowers of strong competition in the mortgage marketplace is that various participants continually create new products that they hope will suit the needs of various types of borrowers. This can be a bit of a problem for a borrower; however, because it can be difficult to sort through all of the available options and decide which product offers the features the borrower most needs or desires (lowest payment vs. quickest repayment vs. greatest flexibility, etc.). If you struggle to understand some of the material in this chapter, imagine what it can be like for an average mortgage borrower who has never had a finance class.

6.4 BASICS OF MORTGAGE VALUATION

The discussion of mortgage valuation will focus on fixed-rate mortgages. In Chapter 5, Equation (5-3) was used to value a fixed coupon bond with semiannual coupon payments. That equation valued a bond by using an appropriate risk-adjusted discount rate to discount back to the present all of the contractually promised coupon payments and the repayment of face value at maturity. The appropriate risk-adjusted discount rate for a bond is the average yield to maturity (YTM) of recently traded bonds with the same maturity and credit rating. The discount rate will be higher for bonds with more risk of default, reflecting the lower expected cash flows of such bonds. It will also typically be higher for bonds with longer maturities, because the yield curve is typically upward sloping.

Both coupon bond and fixed-rate mortgage contracts contain an agreement by the borrower to make a series of scheduled payments to the lender over the life of the contract. In addition, both are subject to default risk. Mortgages, however, are more complicated than coupon bonds because of the embedded prepayment option, discussed in Section 6.2.4 of this chapter, which allows the borrower to buy back the mortgage from the lender at any time by repaying the remaining principal balance. Most mortgages are prepaid; in fact, well over 90% of mortgages are repaid before their scheduled maturity date.

In order to properly value a single fixed-rate mortgage using an approach that is similar to Equation (5-3), the credit quality of the individual borrower must be known so that the proper default-risk premium can be estimated. In addition, the timing of anticipated prepayments must be determined, assuming there is no default. Some prepayments are financially motivated, so a way to predict changes in mortgage rates is needed, indicating whether the borrower will have an incentive to refinance.

Although prepayment is sometimes financially motivated, at other times it is motivated by liquidity needs (the need to sell the house). To obtain a good estimate of the expected liquidity-motivated prepayment date (if any), a lot about the borrower's personal circumstances would need to be known. Does the borrower have children who will leave for college? Does the borrower plan to have more children? Is the borrower getting ready to retire? Is the borrower getting ready to change jobs? And so on. These extremely detailed questions are essential for the proper estimation of a borrower's likely prepayment. And all of the answers are subject to change because they describe the borrower's behavior, not hard financial data.

This is a lot of detailed information that would be time-consuming and expensive to collect. It would also be a terribly intrusive process. Can you imagine calling a borrower up and saying, "Hi, it's your mortgage company. Would you please tell me if and when you plan to have children?"

When detailed information is collected to evaluate a coupon bond issuer's credit quality, the reward is that the same information can be used to value all of the bonds of that issuer. This means that the cost of the evaluation is spread over tens (or hundreds) of millions of dollars of bonds. When similar information is collected to evaluate a mortgage borrower, it can be used only to value a single mortgage. Clearly, it is not only difficult to obtain good estimates of the prepayment behavior of a single borrower, the cost of doing so is prohibitive.

6.4.1 Valuing a Mortgage Portfolio

Because valuing a single mortgage is difficult, costly, and subject to large errors, analysts focus on determining the value of a portfolio of similar mortgages. The approach used is to group together mortgages that have similar characteristics and then estimate the average or aggregate behavior of the group of borrowers, rather than trying to determine what any individual borrower will do in the future. As the insurance industry learned a long time ago, it is much easier to predict the average behavior of a group than the specific behavior of an individual.

Generally speaking, each type of mortgage will be valued separately. Fixed-rate mortgages will not be mixed with ARMs. Nor will 30-year mortgages be mixed with 15-year mortgages. An example of an appropriate grouping would be every fixed-rate mortgage held by a particular financial institution that had an original maturity of 30 years and was originated within the last three years. It's true that there will be considerable variation in the coupon rate, remaining maturity, LTV ratio, remaining principal balance, and other characteristics of mortgages in this portfolio, but this set of mortgages is similar enough to be grouped together.

The portfolio valuation approach that will be discussed is called the **adjusted cash flow (ACF) approach**. This approach starts by estimating the **expected cash flow** of the mortgage portfolio for each month of its life. The expected cash flow will reflect the likelihood of prepayments and defaults, based on the characteristics of the portfolio and on the state of the mortgage market and the rest of the economy. The expected cash flows are discounted back to the present using an appropriate risk-adjusted discount rate to determine the value of the portfolio.

6.4.2 Scheduled Portfolio P&I Payment

The first step in determining the expected cash flow of a portfolio of fixed-rate mortgages is to determine the next scheduled P&I payment for the portfolio. As previously mentioned, each mortgage in the portfolio may have a different remaining maturity, coupon rate, and remaining principal balance; and therefore, a different P&I payment. To avoid having to calculate the P&I payment for every mortgage in the portfolio, the portfolio valuation process uses the P&I payment of the portfolio.

The next scheduled P&I payment for the portfolio is calculated using the aggregate remaining principal balance, the **weighted-average coupon rate (WAC)**, and the **weighted-average maturity (WAM)** of the portfolio. The aggregate remaining principal balance is simply the total of the remaining principal balances of the individual mortgages. The weights used to calculate the portfolio's WAC and WAM are each mortgage's remaining principal balance divided by the aggregate remaining principal balance of the portfolio. To calculate the WAC of the portfolio, multiply each mortgage's coupon rate by its weight and then add up these weighted coupon rates. To calculate the WAM of the portfolio, multiply each mortgage's remaining maturity by its weight and then add up these weighted maturities.

EXAMPLE *Calculating Portfolio P&I Payments*

Figure 6-3 provides an example of these three calculations for a portfolio containing three fixed-rate mortgages. Mortgage A has a remaining principal balance of $75,000 out of the $400,000 total for the portfolio, so its weight is 0.1875 (= 75,000/400,000). Multiplying its weight by its 7.5% coupon rate gives a weighted coupon rate of 0.0141 (rounded off). Multiplying its weight by its 348-month remaining maturity gives a weighted remaining maturity of 65.25. Adding up all of the weighted coupon rates and weighted remaining maturities gives a WAC (weighted-average coupon) of 6.94% for the portfolio and a WAM of 341 months. Please note that the WAM of a portfolio must be rounded to the closest whole number.

Once the aggregate remaining principal balance, WAC, and WAM of the portfolio are calculated, Equation (6-1) can be used to calculate the next scheduled P&I payment. The remaining principal balance will be F_0, the WAC will be r (after adjusting it to a monthly rate), and the WAM will be T. For the example in Figure 6-3, $F_0 = 400,000$, $r = 0.005783$ (= 0.0694/12, rounded off), and $T = 341$. Using Equation (6-1), the next schedule P&I payment is calculated to be

$$PICF_1 = 400,000 \left/ \left[\frac{1 - \left(\frac{1}{(1.005783)^{341}} \right)}{0.005783} \right] \right. = \$2,689.68.$$

Mortgage	Remaining principal balance ($)	Weight	Coupon rate (%)	Weighted coupon rate	Remaining maturity (months)	Weighted remaining maturity
A	75,000	0.1875	7.50	0.0141	348	65.25
B	125,000	0.3125	6.50	0.0203	354	110.63
C	200,000	0.5000	7.00	0.0350	330	165.00
Total	400,000			6.94% WAC		341 WAM

FIGURE 6-3 Portfolio WAC and WAM calculations (portfolio with three fixed-rate mortgages).

6.4.3 Expected Prepayment

The next step in calculating the expected cash flow for a fixed-rate mortgage portfolio is to estimate the volume of prepayments. For a large portfolio of mortgages, it is relatively easy (for an expert) to estimate the proportion of borrowers who will choose to prepay for liquidity-motivated reasons each year.

The proportion of borrowers in the portfolio who will choose to prepay for financially motivated reasons each year will depend on the level of rates available on new mortgages relative to the WAC of the portfolio. If current market rates are higher than the WAC of the portfolio, none of the borrowers will have a reason to refinance and, indeed, these borrowers may rethink plans to buy a bigger house or take a job in a new location. If current market rates are lower than the WAC of the portfolio, then the borrowers in the portfolio will have a financial incentive to refinance, as long as they plan to stay in the house long enough to justify the time and cost required to refinance. The lower market interest rates fall, the higher the incentive for borrowers to refinance and the higher the proportion of borrowers who are expected to prepay their mortgages each year.

The reader should not take the above discussion on financially motivated prepayments to mean that it is easy to estimate expected prepayments for a portfolio of mortgages. It is not. Indeed, very smart people are paid a lot of money to develop such estimates. But the basic rule of thumb is that the level of prepayments will rise if market interest rates fall and vice versa. Also, the reader needs to understand that prepayment expectations are not intended to be an exact prediction of the future. The future actions of a group of borrowers are not perfectly predictable. Instead, when analyzing a mortgage portfolio, prepayment estimates are intended to be the best guess of what will happen in the future. The actual future will usually be different from the expectations, but the hope is that, on average, the expectations of the future will be reasonably accurate.

The expected prepayment activity for a portfolio of mortgages is typically quoted as an annual **cumulative prepayment rate (CPR)**. This includes both prepayments of the entire balance of a mortgage and curtailments. Prepayments are assumed to occur each month immediately following the scheduled P&I payment. Also, it is assumed that these monthly prepayments occur at a rate that, over the course of 12 months, would equal the estimated annual *CPR*. This monthly prepayment rate is known as a **single monthly mortality (SMM)** and is equal to

$$SMM = 1 - (1 - CPR)^{1/12}. \tag{6-3}$$

For example, if prepayments for a mortgage portfolio are estimated at a *CPR* of 20%, the *SMM* is calculated using Equation (6-3) to be

$$SMM = 1 - (1 - 0.20)^{1/12} = 0.018423 = 1.8423\%.$$

Remember that the monthly prepayment rate (*SMM*) is *not* equal to the annual prepayment rate (*CPR*) divided by 12. Using *CPR*/12, rather than the actual *SMM* that is calculated using Equation (6-3) will drastically underestimate prepayments.

Once the *SMM* is calculated, the expected prepayment cash flow for the portfolio for the current month can be calculated. Remember the assumption is that prepayments occur after the scheduled P&I payment is made. This means that the remaining principal balance needs to be adjusted to reflect the principal part of the P&I payment. The interest part of the P&I payment is equal to the coupon rate multiplied by the remaining principal balance at the beginning of the month, or $r \times F_0$. So the principal portion of the P&I payment is the total cash flow less the interest portion or $PICF_1 - (r \times F_0)$. Putting all of this together, the prepayment cash flow (PCF) to be received by the portfolio during the next month is expected to be

$$PCF_t = SMM \times [F_{t-1} - (PICF_t - (r \times F_{t-1}))].$$ (6-4)

EXAMPLE *continued* *Calculating Prepayment Cash Flow*

Continue the previous example of a fixed-rate mortgage portfolio that contains three mortgages with a remaining principal balance of $F_0 = 400,000$. The next scheduled P&I payment of this portfolio was calculated to be $PICF_1 = 2,689.68$ using Equation (6-1). Also, the CPR is estimated to be 20%, which means $SMM = 0.018423$. Given these inputs, the expected prepayment cash flow using Equation (6-4) is calculated to be

$$PCF_1 = 0.018423 \times [400,000 - (2,689.68 - (0.005783 \times 400,000))] = \$7,362.26.$$

Notice in this example that the expected prepayment cash flow is significantly larger than the scheduled P&I payment. This is not unusual, especially during the first five or even ten years of a mortgage portfolio's life. As mentioned earlier, most borrowers prepay their mortgage rather than making all of the scheduled P&I payments.

IN THE NEWS

EFFECT OF THE REFI BOOM

What kept the U.S. economy going in the early 2000s, despite little job growth and an anemic stock market? In such a complex economy, it was surely more than one thing, but record low residential interest rates that allowed consumers to refinance home mortgages and reduce monthly debt payments certainly helped. In 2002, U.S. borrowers refinanced more than $1 trillion in mortgages. In 2003, they refinanced another $1 trillion.

Moreover, during the late 1990s and early 2000s, a lot of home owners refinanced more than once, reducing their monthly mortgage payment each time. And many borrowers withdraw some or all of the equity they have in their home (from rising home prices, for the most part) when they refinance. In many cases, neither the monthly savings nor the extracted equity value was used to reduce credit card or other debts. Instead, it was spent like an end-of-year bonus. Just as the rising stock market in the 1990s fueled consumer spending, ongoing, high levels of mortgage refinancing in 2000–2003 bolstered consumer confidence and put money in consumer wallets.

The "refi boom" has gone on for so long that it's sometimes hard to imagine the economy (or consumer spending) without it. But it may be coming to a close. Mortgage rates flattened out during 2002–2003 and began to rise in 2004. As expected, mortgage prepayment rates have fallen (see, e.g., Coy and Palmeri, 2003). If long-term rates continue to rise, as economists expect they will, the boom will be over, housing prices will stabilize, and consumers (and the U.S. economy) will learn to live without a magic piggy bank that refills every couple of years.

6.4.4 Default and Recovery

The final piece of the expected cash flow puzzle is default. Each month, it is possible that one or more borrowers will have reached a point at which the investor believes that foreclosure is inevitable and that no further cash flow will be received from that borrower until the collateral is seized and sold. The frequency of default will depend on many things: the state of the economy, housing prices, unemployment rates, the loan-to-value ratios of mortgages in the portfolio, and so on. As has already been mentioned, mortgage default is relatively rare, because borrowers can usually sell the property for more than the remaining principal balance of the loan.

The default rate is usually quoted in a manner similar to the prepayment rate: a cumulative, annual percentage of the outstanding balance. This means that it must be converted to a monthly rate using an equation similar to Equation (6-3). If AD is the annual cumulative default rate, than the monthly default rate is equal to

$$MD = 1 - (1 - AD)^{1/12}. \tag{6-5}$$

The expected default amount (DA) in a mortgage portfolio is this percentage of the remaining principal balance of the portfolio, after accounting for the amount of principal repaid as part of the scheduled P&I payment, or

$$DA_t = MD \times [F_{t-1} - (PICF_t - (r \times F_{t-1}))]. \tag{6-6}$$

But investors do not lose everything when a mortgage borrower defaults. As discussed earlier, when a borrower defaults, the investor will foreclose on the collateral and sell it. The proceeds from this sale will be used to pay the costs of foreclosure and to repay as much of the remaining principal balance of the loan as possible. The amount repaid represents a cash flow to the investor and must be included in the expected monthly cash flow of the mortgage portfolio. A fixed percentage of the amount defaulted is assumed to be recovered by the investor.

The **recovery rate** (rr) reflects any expected decline in property values, the typically distressed nature of property that is foreclosed on (i.e., the house is usually in poor condition), and the delay between the date that the mortgage is considered to be in default and the date that the money from the sale of the collateral is received by the investor. The amount of time it takes to go through a foreclosure proceeding varies from state to state. The longer the expected delay, the lower will be the recovery rate because of time value of money effects. The expected recovery cash flow is the expected default amount multiplied by the recovery rate or

$$RCF_t = rr \times DA_t. \tag{6-7}$$

EXAMPLE *continued*   *Calculating Recovery Cash Flows*

Again, continue the three-mortgage portfolio example with the additional assumptions that the expected annual default rate is 2.0% and the recovery rate is 70% or $rr = 0.70$. Using Equation (6-5), the monthly default rate is calculated to be

$$MD = 1 - (1 - 0.02)^{1/12} = 0.001682.$$

Using Equation (6-6), the expected default amount is calculated to be

$$DA_1 = 0.001682 \times [400,000 - (2,689.68 - (0.005783 \times 400,000))] = \$672.17.$$

Finally, using Equation (6-7), the expected recovery cash flow is calculated to be

$$RCF_1 = 0.70 \times 672.17 = \$470.52.$$

6.4.5 Total Expected Cash Flow

At this point all of the calculations needed to determine the first expected cash flow for a portfolio of mortgages have been discussed. The first expected cash flow for a portfolio of mortgages is the sum of three components: the scheduled P&I payment calculated using Equation (6-1), the expected prepayment cash flow calculated using Equation (6-4), and the expected recovery cash flow calculated using Equations (6-6) and (6-7), or

$$E[CF_t] = PICF_t + PCF_t + RCF_t. \tag{6-8}$$

EXAMPLE *continued* **Calculating Expected Cash Flows on a Mortgage Portfolio**

Continuing the three-mortgage portfolio example, the first expected cash flow is

$$E[CF_1] = \$2,689.68 + \$7,362.26 + \$470.52 = \$10,522.46.$$

6.4.6 Calculating the Rest of the Expected Cash Flows

Having learned how to calculate the first expected cash flow for a portfolio of mortgages, the process moves on to how to calculate the second expected cash flow, the third expected cash flow, and so on. There are three components of each expected cash flow, the scheduled P&I payment, the expected prepayment cash flow, and the expected recovery cash flow.

In calculating the scheduled P&I payment for the second expected cash flow, it is important to recognize two changes to the inputs for the calculations. First, the weighted-average maturity or WAM of the portfolio gets smaller over time, so as each month passes, the WAM used in the calculations must decrease by one. In the example, the WAM of the portfolio is 341 months. This is the maturity (T) in the calculation of the first scheduled P&I payment. When the second scheduled P&I payment is calculated, however, this must be decreased by one, to 340 months. For the third payment, it will be decreased to 339 months, and so on.

The second issue to be addressed is the remaining principal balance. It is tempting to use Equation (6-2) to calculate the principal balance remaining after the first month, but this is not proper. Equation (6-2) is based on the assumption that no prepayments or defaults occur and the calculation of the first expected cash flow includes an expected amount of prepayment and an expected amount of default. In order to calculate the expected remaining principal balance after the first cash flow occurs, the principal portion of the first scheduled P&I payment, the expected prepayment, and the expected default must be subtracted from the principal balance, or

$$F_{t+1} = F_t - [PICF_t - (r \times F_t)] - PCF_t - DA_t. \tag{6-9}$$

Notice that the full expected default amount is subtracted, which is larger than the recovery cash flow. The default amount represents the principal balance that will no longer be contributing to scheduled P&I payments, so it must all be deducted from the remaining principal balance.

EXAMPLE *continued* **Calculating the Second Expected Cash Flow of a Mortgage Portfolio**

Continuing with the example, the expected remaining principal balance of the three-mortgage portfolio after the first cash flow is

$$F_1 = 400{,}000 - [2{,}689.68 - (0.005783 \times 400{,}000)] - 7{,}362.26 - 672.17 = \$391{,}589.09.$$

Using this expected principal balance, the second expected cash flow can now be calculated. Using Equation (6-1), the second expected P&I payment is calculated as

$$PICF_2 = 391{,}589.09 \left/ \left[\frac{1 - \left(\frac{1}{(1.005783)^{340}} \right)}{0.005783} \right] = \$2{,}635.60. \right.$$

Next, using Equation (6-4), the second expected prepayment cash flow is calculated as

$$PCF_2 = 0.018423 \times [391{,}589.09 - (2{,}635.60 - (0.005783 \times 391{,}589.09))] = \$7{,}207.41.$$

Next, using Equation (6-6), the second expected default amount is calculated as

$$DA_2 = 0.001682 \times [391{,}589.09 - (2{,}635.60 - (0.005783 \times 391{,}589.09))] = \$658.03.$$

Finally, using Equation (6-7), the second expected recovery cash flow is calculated as

$$RCF_2 = 0.70 \times 658.03 = \$460.62.$$

Putting these items together, using Equation (6-8), the second expected cash flow of the mortgage portfolio is calculated to be

$$E[CF_2] = \$2{,}635.60 + \$7{,}207.41 + \$460.62 = \$10{,}303.63.$$

Next, the process continues to the third expected cash flow using the steps just presented. Calculating the expected cash flows for the portfolio by this method is an iterative process. That is, the step-by-step process for the first iteration (the first cash flow) must be completed before the second iteration (the second cash flow) can be started. One cannot jump ahead in the process and calculate the 50th cash flow, because the expected principal balance will not be known without first calculating the 1st through 49th expected cash flows.

The mortgage portfolio used in the example has a WAM of 341 months. This means that 341 expected cash flows need to be calculated. This is not a task to be done by hand. The table in Appendix 6-A of this chapter lists the expected cash flows (and individual components of expected cash flow) for this portfolio for the first 24 months. This table was created using an Excel spreadsheet. Spreadsheet software is designed precisely for this sort of iterative (repetitive) process. Once the proper formulas are written to calculate the first expected cash flow, they can be copied down the spreadsheet rows and the spreadsheet will automatically calculate the 2nd through 341st cash flows. Anytime you are faced with a problem that requires repeating the same calculations over and over again, you would be smart to create a spreadsheet to do the work for you!

6.4.7 Present Value of Expected Cash Flows

Once all of the expected cash flows of the mortgage portfolio have been calculated, they must be discounted back to the present using an appropriate risk-adjusted discount rate. As was discussed in Chapter 5, selecting the appropriate discount rate or discount rates is an important part of the valuation process. The discount rate should represent the market return that, investor would earn on an alternative investment that has similar characteristics, in terms of maturity and risk, to the security being valued.

The adjusted cash flow method for valuing a mortgage portfolio requires that expected cash flows be calculated rather than using contractually promised cash flows. The expected cash flows take into account all expected prepayments and defaults. This means that the expected cash flows are theoretically stripped of prepayment risk and default risk. Therefore, the appropriate discount rate should be for a security that has no prepayment risk or default risk.

U.S. Treasury securities have no prepayment risk or default risk. For that reason, it is natural to think of using a Treasury yield to discount the expected cash flows of the mortgage portfolio. One option is to calculate the theoretical spot rate curve, as described in Section 5.5.1 of Chapter 5 and then discount each expected cash flow for the mortgage portfolio using the appropriate spot yield. This process is described for U.S. Treasury securities in Section 5.5.2 of Chapter 5. For the mortgage portfolio example in this chapter, this would require the calculation of 341 spot yields, one for each expected cash flow.

An alternative is to use a single U.S. Treasury yield to maturity to discount all the mortgage portfolio expected cash flows back to the present. But which maturity Treasury yield should be used? Treasury bonds are coupon paying bonds which repay principal only at maturity, whereas mortgages have annuity-like payments that include principal and interest each month. This means we should not discount the cash flows of a portfolio of 30-year mortgages with a 30-year Treasury bond yield or the cash flows of a portfolio of 15-year mortgages with the 15-year Treasury bond yield. Further, prepayment risk complicates matters significantly. When interest rates fall, prepayments rise and the expected maturity of a mortgage portfolio gets shorter. When interest rates rise, prepayments fall and the expected maturity of a mortgage portfolio gets longer.

Most analysts recommend using the Treasury yield that is best tracked by the mortgage rate as the discount rate. Often, the 10-year Treasury yield is used because, historically, it and the 30-year fixed-rate mortgage rate have moved together closely. Figure 6-4 graphs the three-month Treasury bill yield and the 10-year Treasury bond yield against the 30-year fixed-rate mortgage rate for the 22 years from 1982 through 2003. Clearly, the 30-year fixed-rate mortgage rate tracks the 10-year Treasury yield closely, but hardly tracks the three-month Treasury yield at all.

Figure 6-5 shows the difference between the 30-year fixed-rate mortgage rate and the 10-year Treasury bond yield over the same period of time. During the early period (1982–1987 or so), before disintermediation caused a single, national mortgage market to develop, the difference between the 10-year Treasury yield and the 30-year fixed-rate mortgage rate changed dramatically from month to month. Since that time, the spread between the two has been fairly stable at between 1.2 and 2.2%. This suggests that the 10-year Treasury bond yield is a reasonable discount rate for the expected cash flows of a fixed-rate mortgage portfolio.

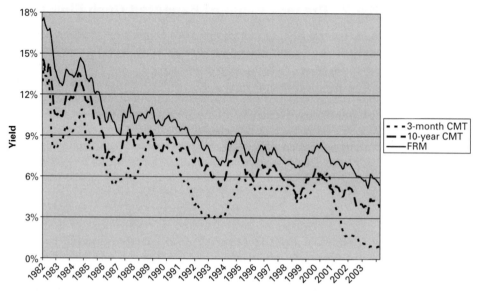

FIGURE 6-4 Fixed-rate mortgage yield vs. three-month and 10-year constant maturity treasury yields.

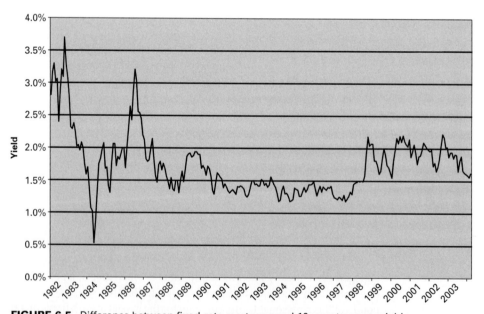

FIGURE 6-5 Difference between fixed-rate mortgage and 10-year treasury yields.

6.4.8 Closed-Form Solution

The valuation process described in this chapter is reliable for valuing a fixed-rate mortgage portfolio. The basic steps can also be modified to calculate the expected cash flows and value of a portfolio of ARMs, balloon mortgages, or other types of mortgages. It is fair to say, however, that the process is fairly complicated, very repetitive, and is best accomplished using spreadsheet software. Because of this, it would be useful to have a single equation to use.

It turns out that a closed-form solution exists for valuing a portfolio of fixed-rate mortgages, but only for a portfolio that is never expected to experience any loss when a borrower defaults. That is, the recovery rate must be 100%, so that a default acts just like a prepayment. A closed-form solution is another way of saying that a single equation can be used to calculate the desired answer. Instead of calculating each expected cash flow using the iterative process described earlier, the present value of the portfolio can be calculated as

$$PV_0 = CF_1 \times \left[\begin{array}{l} \left(\left(1 + \dfrac{SMM}{r} \right) \times \left(\dfrac{1 - \left[\dfrac{1 - SMM}{1 + i} \right]^T}{i + SMM} \right) \right) \\[2em] - \left(\left(SMM + \dfrac{SMM}{r} \right) \times \dfrac{1}{(1+r)^T} \right. \\[2em] \left. \times \left(\dfrac{1 - \left[\dfrac{1 + r - SMM - (SMM \times r)}{1 + i} \right]}{i - r + SMM + (SMM \times r)} \right) \right) \end{array} \right], \qquad (6\text{-}10)$$

where i is the monthly discount rate, CF_1 is the first P&I cash flow calculated using Equation (6-1), and the rest of the inputs are defined as they were before. Equation (6-10) is very complex, but when remembering that it's replacing a spreadsheet with hundreds of rows of equations, it doesn't seem that bad.

Because it cannot be used to value a portfolio of mortgages that can suffer losses when a default occurs, this equation is of limited practical value. It is tempting to use Equation (6-10) for portfolios that are insured against default losses. However, such portfolios typically pay a premium to the insurer each month and this equation cannot be modified or adapted to allow for such a fee.

6.4.9 Importance of Assumptions

In Chapter 5, a valuation process for U.S. Treasury bonds and corporate bonds was discussed that was fairly straightforward. If a group of analysts was each asked to value a particular bond using this process, it is reasonable to assume that each would calculate much the same value as the others. This is not necessarily the case with the process described for valuing mortgage portfolios.

As discussed, calculating the value of a mortgage portfolio is complicated and depends on assumptions made at each step. When using the valuation process described in this chapter, assumptions were made about the annual prepayment rate, the annual default rate, the recovery rate, and the appropriate discount rate. None of these are driven by a market price or yield in the way that the discount rate for a corporate bond is set by observing the yields to maturity on bonds with similar maturities and credit ratings.

Further, the assumptions made when valuing a mortgage portfolio will change from portfolio to portfolio, depending on the characteristics of the mortgages in the portfolio. For example, mortgages with higher LTV ratios (i.e., lower initial down payments) are more likely to default and will have lower recovery rates than those with lower LTV ratios. As another example, mortgages with higher coupon rates are more likely to prepay than those with lower coupon rates.

These assumptions will also change over time, as economic conditions change. When market interest rates fall, the prepayment rate assumed will increase for all mortgage portfolios, as will the discount rate applied to the expected cash flows. When economic conditions deteriorate (e.g., falling GDP growth or rising unemployment), the assumed default rate will increase for all portfolios and the assumed recovery rate will decrease.

This means that mortgage pricing is much less efficient than is pricing of Treasury bonds and corporate bonds. Opinions of value will differ widely across analysts. On the one hand, this can seem like a good thing if an investor can buy a portfolio at a price significantly below the value the investor has estimated. On the other hand, this can be problematic if an investor has to sell a portfolio and no one will pay what the investor thinks the portfolio is worth.

It is very important to remember that mortgage valuation is not an exact science. The answer calculated will always have as much to do with the assumptions being made by the analyst as with economic facts.

6.5 MORTGAGE PRICE CHARACTERISTICS

In Chapter 5 we discussed three measures that are commonly used to evaluate fixed-income securities: yield to maturity (YTM), duration, and convexity. Unfortunately, because of the embedded prepayment option, none of these measures can be used in the same way to describe mortgage portfolios.

6.5.1 Yield to Maturity

In Chapter 5 we discussed that a common measure of the return that will be earned on a fixed-income security is its yield to maturity (YTM). The YTM is the discount rate that equates the security's market price to its promised cash flows. It can also be thought of as the internal rate of return on the security, assuming that the investor receives all of the promised payments on schedule.

Unfortunately, YTM is not a useful measure of the return that will be earned on a mortgage portfolio. This is because no one believes that the mortgage borrowers (who are the issuers of the securities in the portfolio) will make all of the promised payments. Almost all, if not all, of the mortgages in the portfolio are expected to prepay before their scheduled maturity date. But how many will be prepaid and when they will be prepaid is a matter of opinion, not fact. It is possible to calculate a mortgage return measure that is similar to a YTM using a spreadsheet like the one that was used to create the table in Appendix 6-A.

In order to do so, the spreadsheet would have to contain a column for calculating the discounted present value of each expected cash flow using a fixed monthly discount rate. The spreadsheet would also have to contain the market price of the mortgage portfolio, which is difficult to determine. The SOLVER function in Excel (or a similar function in other spreadsheet software) would then be used to find the discount rate that equates the expected cash flows to the market price.

This solution is not a yield to maturity, because it is based on expected cash flows, not promised cash flows. Further, as already discussed, different analysts will determine different expected cash flows for the same portfolio, because their prepayment rate assumptions and default and recovery assumptions will differ. Finally, there is no established marketplace for mortgage portfolios. A YTM is a discount rate that equates cash flows to a market price. Without a market price for the mortgage portfolio, the process cannot work.

6.5.2 Duration

All fixed income securities are sensitive to changes in discount rates because higher discount rates imply lower present values and vice versa. Mortgages are doubly sensitive to interest rates because the prepayment rate is tied to the level of interest rates. In fact, because borrowers use their prepayment option to their best advantage when interest rates rise or fall, mortgage investors are always hurt more by interest rate increases and helped less by interest rate decreases than are bond investors.

If interest rates decline, bond investors are happy. They will continue to receive the old, high coupon rate for the life of the bond. The present value of these coupon payments is higher because the discount rate has gone down. In contrast, when interest rates decline, mortgage borrowers have a greater incentive to prepay their mortgages and refinance. Just when mortgage investors thought they would get to receive high coupon payments for the life of the mortgage, increased prepayment activity returns principal to them today. That returned principal must be reinvested at new, lower rates.

If interest rates rise, bond investors are unhappy, because they must continue to receive lower coupon payments until the bond matures. The present value of the coupon payments is lower because the discount rate has gone up. Mortgage investors, however, are more unhappy. Higher interest rates mean that mortgage borrowers are less likely to prepay than before. Families will delay moving to a new house if interest rates are high and borrowers may turn down new jobs if the cost of moving and buying a new house is prohibitive. This means that mortgage investors will continue to receive low coupon payments for even longer than they had originally anticipated. And these extended payments will be worth less because the discount rate has risen.

For most fixed-income securities, Equation (5-9) from Chapter 5 is used to calculate duration. Equation (5-9) will not work for mortgage portfolios because one of the major assumptions behind Equation (5-9) is that the cash flows of the security do not change when interest rates change. Clearly, this assumption will be violated, and in a significant way, for a mortgage portfolio.

Duration, however, is too important a measure to do without. Fixed-income managers and managers of financial institutions rely on duration to give them a snapshot of their interest rate sensitivity. Further, it is possible to calculate the combined duration of a group of dissimilar portfolios—for example, a portfolio of Treasury bonds, a portfolio of corporate bonds, a portfolio of fixed-rate mortgages, and a portfolio of ARMs—so that an investor with a lot of different fixed income investments can see a single measure of interest rate sensitivity for the entire set of investments. It is also possible to find the net duration or interest rate sensitivity of an entire financial institution, like a commercial bank or savings and loan. But to do this, an estimate of the duration of a mortgage portfolio is required.

The only way to estimate the duration of a mortgage portfolio in a somewhat reliable way is to calculate the portfolio's **effective duration**. Recall from Chapter 5 that the relationship between a change in interest rates and the resulting change in the present value of a security is described in Equation (5-10). A slightly changed version of this equation, modified for this chapter, is

$$\frac{\Delta PV}{PV} \cong -D \times \frac{\Delta i}{(1+i)}, \qquad (6\text{-}11)$$

where PV is the present value of the portfolio at this time, D is the Macaulay duration of the portfolio, i is the annual discount rate used to calculate the present value of the portfolio, and the relationship is approximate because it is exactly true only for very small changes in interest rates.[6]

In order to calculate the effective duration of a portfolio of mortgages, three valuations of the mortgage portfolio are required. The three values are the present value of the portfolio at today's interest rates, the value assuming a hypothetical increase in interest rates, and the value assuming a hypothetical decrease in interest rates of the same size as the increase. Remember that when rates rise, the mortgage portfolio valuation process requires a lower prepayment rate assumption. When rates fall, a higher rate of prepayment is assumed.

EXAMPLE   *Calculating the Effective Duration of a Portfolio of Mortgages*

Figure 6-6 continues the earlier example of the three-mortgage portfolio with the assumption of prepayments at a CPR of 20%. The value of this portfolio has been calculated, assuming an annual discount rate of 7.0%, to be $391,815. Figure 6-6 also includes the recalculated value of this portfolio for two interest rate changes, an increase of 0.5% and a decrease of 0.5%. When interest rates increase by 0.5%, the discount rate rises to 7.5% and the assumed prepayment rate declines by half to a CPR of 10%. The value of the portfolio is calculated to fall to $378,604 in this scenario, a decline of $13,211. When interest rates decrease by 0.5%, the discount rate falls to 6.5% and the assumed prepayment rate increases by half to a CPR of 30%. In this circumstance, the value of the portfolio is calculated to rise to $398,512, an increase of $6,697.

---

[6] Note that in Chapter 5, Equation (5-10) is $\dfrac{\Delta B}{B} \approx -D\left[\dfrac{\Delta r}{(1+r)}\right]$ where r is referred to as the market rate. In Chapter 5, r is also the discount rate for pricing the bond. Throughout Chapter 6, r is the coupon rate for a mortgage so i is used as the discount rate in the closed-form solution [Equation (6-10)] for valuing a fixed-rate mortgage and the use of i as the discount rate is continued through the duration of Equation (6-11) for continuity.

Discount rate (%)	Change in discount rate (%)	Assumed CPR (%)	Discounted present value (%)	Change in DPV (%)
6.50	−0.50	30.0	398,512	6,697
7.00		*20.0*	*391,815*	
7.50	0.50	10.0	378,604	−13,211

FIGURE 6-6   Portfolio value as interest rates change (portfolio with three fixed-rate mortgages).

These estimated portfolio values are used to calculate the effective duration of the portfolio. Equation (6-11) can be rearranged to reveal the duration of the portfolio or

$$D \cong -\left[\frac{\Delta PV}{PV} \Big/ \frac{\Delta i}{(1+i)}\right]. \tag{6-12}$$

Equation (6-12) can be used to calculate the duration of a portfolio using estimates from a hypothetical increase in interest rates and then used again to calculate the duration using estimates from a hypothetical decrease in interest rates. The average of these two answers provides the effective duration of the portfolio. In essence, we use the valuation model to tell us how sensitive the portfolio is to changes in interest rates.

Using the values provided in Figure 6-6 for the 0.5% increase in interest rates, the duration is calculated using Equation (6-12) to be

$$D \cong -\left[\frac{-13,211}{391,815} \Big/ \frac{0.005}{1.07}\right] = 7.22.$$

Using the values for the decrease in interest rates, the duration is calculated to be

$$D \cong -\left[\frac{6,697}{391,815} \Big/ \frac{-0.005}{1.07}\right] = 3.66.$$

The average of these is 5.44 (= (7.22 + 3.66)/2), so the effective duration of this mortgage portfolio is 5.44 years.

Oddly, although it is difficult to estimate the effective duration of a portfolio of fixed-rate mortgages, it is trivially easy to measure the approximate duration of a portfolio of ARMs. The duration of an ARM portfolio is approximately one-half of the average repricing frequency of the ARMs in the portfolio. In other words, a portfolio that contains only one-year ARMs has a duration of approximately 0.5 years and a portfolio that contains half six-month ARMs and half one-year ARMs (average repricing frequency of nine months) has a duration of approximately 0.375 years.

6.5.3   Convexity

As discussed in Chapter 5 and again in the previous section of this chapter, duration is a measure of the sensitivity of a portfolio's value to a change in interest rates. The relationship

Discount rate (%)	Assumed CPR (%)	Present value (%)	PV (%) for CPR = 20%
5.00	30.0	104.8	108.8
6.00	20.0	103.4	104.2
7.00	15.0	100.0	100.0
8.00	10.0	95.1	96.1
9.00	7.0	89.0	92.5

FIGURE 6-7 Prepayments and negative convexity. ($1 million portfolio, 7.0% WAC, 350-month WAM, no default).

between a change in interest rates, duration, and the resulting change in present value was shown in Equation (5-10). This is, however, only an approximate relationship, because the duration of a portfolio changes as market interest rates change. In Chapter 5, convexity was introduced to improve the duration model.

Unfortunately, it is no more possible to calculate the convexity of a mortgage portfolio than it is to calculate its duration. Equation (5-11) in Chapter 5 assumes that the cash flows of the portfolio do not change as interest rates change. However, the cash flows of a mortgage portfolio will change significantly if interest rates change, because of the effect that changes in interest rates have on borrower prepayments.

As previously discussed, mortgage investors are always hurt by prepayments. Borrowers pay investors back more quickly when interest rates fall and more slowly when interest rates rise. This is the opposite of what investors want. This is why the duration of a mortgage portfolio changes so quickly when interest rates change. In the last example, the mortgage portfolio acted like it had a duration of 3.66 years when interest rates fell, but acted like it had a duration of 7.22 years when interest rates rose.

To see the asymmetric impact of prepayments on the interest rate sensitivity of mortgages more clearly, a new example of a $1 million portfolio of fixed-rate mortgages with a WAC of 7.00%, and a WAM of 350 months is provided. In order to focus only on the effect of prepayments, assume that there will be no defaults in this portfolio.

Figure 6-7 shows the present value of this portfolio for various changes in the discount rate under two alternative assumptions. If the assumption that the prepayment rate will increase when the discount rate falls and decrease when the discount rate rises is correct, the values in the third column of the table are generated. If the assumption is not correct and the prepayment rate stays the same, regardless of whether the discount rate rises or falls, the values in the fourth column of the table are generated.

Clearly, investors would rather live in the world in which the prepayment rate does not change. In this fixed-prepayment world, the value of the portfolio is always higher than in the floating-prepayment world. Figure 6-8 compares these values graphically. The solid line shows the real world, in which prepayments rise when interest rates fall and vice versa. The dashed line represents the fantasy world in which the prepayment rate never changes.

In the fantasy world, mortgage portfolios have fixed cash flows, just like Treasury bonds and non-callable corporate bonds. In the fantasy world, the duration and convexity of the mortgage portfolio can be calculated and can be used to estimate the effect of a change in market interest rates on the value of the portfolio.

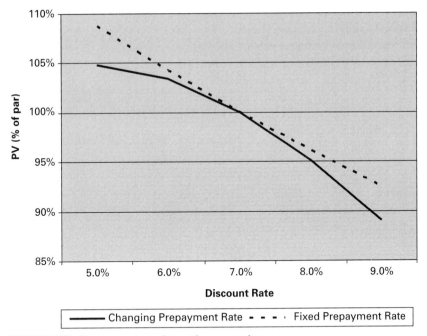

FIGURE 6-8 Prepayments and negative convexity.

In the real world, prepayment rates change as interest rates change, which means that expected cash flows change as interest rates change. In the real world, the duration or convexity of a mortgage portfolio cannot be calculated. In the real world, the prepayment decisions of mortgage borrowers are always the opposite of what mortgage investors would want.

Figure 6-8 also provides insights about the convexity of mortgage portfolios. In Chapter 5, the convexity of a Treasury bond or noncallable corporate bond portfolio was shown to be positive. That means that when interest rates change, the actual present value of a Treasury bond or noncallable corporate bond is always higher than is predicted by the duration model.

Figure 6-8 clearly shows that the present value of a real mortgage portfolio is concave; that is, it looks like an upside-down bowl. In the language of fixed-income investors, mortgages are said to have **negative convexity**. That is, if the convexity of a mortgage portfolio could be calculated, it would be a negative number. Negative convexity means that the actual present value of a mortgage portfolio is always lower than is predicted by the duration model.

Another way to think about duration and convexity is that duration is a pessimistic measure for bonds and an optimistic measure for mortgages. That is, duration overstates the damage that an increase in interest rates will have on bond investors and understates the damage on mortgage investors. Similarly, duration understates the benefits of a decrease in interest rates for bond investors and overstates the benefits for mortgage investors. It is generally not a good idea to use an optimistic risk measure.

SUMMARY OF VALUATION AND RISK MANAGEMENT SKILLS

1. Understand the primary features of a mortgage loan and how each feature affects mortgage cash flows.

Residential mortgages are complex fixed-income securities that are secured by real estate. Mortgage borrowers promise investors monthly, annuity-like payments of principal and interest. Residential mortgages contain an embedded option that allows the borrower to prepay the mortgage at any time and without penalty. This embedded prepayment option is similar to the embedded call option in callable bonds.

2. Understand the different types of residential mortgages.

The primary type of residential mortgage is a fixed-rate mortgage, which means that the interest on the mortgage is fixed for the life of the loan. The other common type of residential mortgage is an adjustable rate mortgage (ARM). In an ARM the interest rate on the mortgage changes periodically to reflect current market interest rates. The interest rate in an ARM has annual and lifetime caps and floors which limit the adjustments in the interest rates.

3. Calculate the value and duration of a mortgage portfolio.

The value of a mortgage portfolio is the present value of the expected future cash flows of the portfolio. Prepayments and defaults can have a significant effect on the expected cash flows of the portfolio. Mortgage portfolios can be valued using the adjusted cash flow approach. This method follows an iterative process to calculate expected cash flows based on the assumption of a constant level of prepayment and default and a fixed recovery rate on defaulted mortgages. Expected cash flows are discounted back to the present using the appropriate prepayment-risk free and default-risk free yield, usually the yield on a U.S. Treasury security. The duration of a mortgage portfolio cannot be calculated directly. Instead, an effective duration of the portfolio is estimated.

4. Understand the convexity of a mortgage portfolio.

Fixed-rate mortgage portfolios have negative convexity, whereas bond portfolios have positive convexity. The negative convexity of mortgage portfolios occurs because the mortgage prepayment decisions are always the opposite of what mortgage investors would want.

QUESTIONS

1. What are the first, second, and third largest sectors of the U.S. fixed income market and what proportion of the market does each make up?

2. What are the first, second, and third largest subsectors of the U.S. mortgage market? What is the size of each?

3. What are the common features of a residential mortgage?

4. How do residential, commercial, and multifamily mortgages differ from one another?

5. What three characteristics of a fixed-income mortgage determine its scheduled P&I payment?

6. What characteristics make residential mortgage loans safe investments?

7. Define the two general reasons why mortgage borrowers prepay a mortgage.

8. Describe the three components of the mortgage business.

9. How is the U.S. mortgage market an example of disintermediation?

10. Why are individual mortgage loans illiquid?

11. Describe the main differences between a fixed-rate mortgage and an adjustable-rate mortgage.

12. Describe the main differences between a fixed-rate mortgage and a balloon mortgage.

13. Describe the three components of expected cash flow for a portfolio of residential mortgages.

14. Discuss the different ways that the expected default amount and the expected recovery cash flow affect the value of a mortgage portfolio.

15. Why is mortgage pricing less efficient than bond pricing?

16. Why is it difficult to calculate the yield to maturity (YTM) of a mortgage portfolio?

17. Why do we calculate the effective duration of a mortgage portfolio rather than its actual duration (as described in Chapter 5)?

18. What is negative convexity? Why do mortgage portfolios have negative convexity?

19. What is the scheduled P&I payment of a residential mortgage with an initial principal balance of $200,000, a coupon rate of 7.20%, and a maturity of 15 years? What will be the remaining principal balance after two years?

20. What is the scheduled P&I payment of a residential mortgage with a remaining principal balance of $140,000, a coupon rate of 6.60%, and a remaining maturity of $26\frac{1}{2}$ years? How much of this principal balance will be paid off in three more years?

21. What is the scheduled P&I payment for the first year of a one-year ARM with an initial principal balance of $175,000, an initial maturity of 30 years, the one-year LIBOR rate as its index (currently 2.90%), and a fixed spread of 250 bps? If, one year from now, the one-year LIBOR rate has fallen to 2.30%, what will be the scheduled P&I payment for the second year?

22. What is the scheduled P&I payment for the next two years of a two-year ARM with a remaining principal balance of $220,000, a remaining maturity of 13 years, the two-year Constant Maturity Treasury yield as its index (currently 2.40%), and a fixed spread of 300 bps? If, two years from now, the two-year CMT yield has risen to 3.00%, what will be the scheduled P&I payment for the following two years?

23. What is the WAC and WAM of a portfolio containing the four mortgages described in the following table?

Mortgage	Remaining principal balance ($)	Coupon rate (%)	Remaining maturity (months)
A	110,000	8.00	340
B	80,000	6.10	355
C	150,000	7.50	325
D	160,000	6.80	330

24. A portfolio of residential mortgages has a total remaining principal balance of $1,200,000, a WAC of 5.70%, and a WAM of 172 months. What is the next scheduled P&I payment of the mortgage?

25. If the mortgage portfolio described in Question 24 has an expected CPR of 23%, what is its expected SMM? What is the portfolio's next expected prepayment cash flow?

26. If the mortgage portfolio described in Question 24 has an expected annual default rate of 2.5% and an expected recovery rate of 92%, what is the portfolio's next expected recovery cash flow.

27. Using the information in Questions 24–26, what is this portfolio's next expected cash flow and what is the expected total remaining principal balance of the portfolio at the end of the month?

28. Using all of the information in Questions 24–27, calculate this portfolio's second expected cash flow.

29. A portfolio of residential mortgages has the following characteristics: total remaining principal balance = $2,500,000; WAC = 6.60%; WAM = 350 months; expected CPR = 18%; expected default rate = 3.0%; and expected recovery rate = 85%. What is the next expected cash flow for this portfolio? (Hint: for more practice, calculate the second expected cash flow as well.)

30. Using a sophisticated valuation model, we have determined that the current value of a portfolio of residential mortgages is $2,100,000. The current mortgage rate is 7.30%. Using the same valuation model, we determine that the value of the portfolio would rise to $2,300,000 if the mortgage rate fell 1% to 6.30% and would fall to $1,975,000 if the mortgage rate rose 1% to 8.30%. Using these valuations, what is the effective duration of this portfolio?

REFERENCES

Coy, P., and C. Palmeri, 2003, Say goodbye to refi madness. *Business Week, November*, 42.
    This article discusses the relationship between refinancing and mortgage rates.
DeRosa, P., L. Goodman, and M. Zazzarino, 1993, Duration estimates on mortgage-backed securities, *Journal of Portfolio Management 19(2)*, 32–38.
    This was the first paper to closely examine MBS durations in the presence of changing prepayment rates.
Gilkeson, J. H., P. Jacob, and S. D. Smith, 1994, Buy, sell, or hold? Valuing cash flows from mortgage lending, Federal Reserve Bank of Atlanta *Economic Review 79(6)*, 1–16.
    This paper discusses the impact of securitization on the traditional, intermediated model of mortgage lending.
Newell, J. E., 1991, *Encyclopedia of Mortgage & Real Estate Finance*, Probus Publishing, Chicago.

This book serves as a comprehensive resource for mortgage banking and related real estate issues.
O'Brian, T. J., 1992, Elementary growth model valuation expressions for fixed-rate mortgage pools and derivatives, *Journal of Fixed Income 2(June)*, 68–79.
    This paper provides closed-form solutions for common MBS structures, including passthroughs and IO and PO strips. Very useful in modeling.
Richard, S. F., and R. Roll, 1989, Prepayments on fixed-rate mortgage-backed securities, *Journal of Portfolio Management 15(3)*, 73–82.
    This is the classic paper that showed that more than 90% of the variation in prepayment rates could be explained by two things: (1) the difference between the mortgage coupon rate and the current market rate and (2) the remaining maturity of the mortgage.

KEY TERMS

Adjustable-Rate Mortgage (ARM) A residential mortgage with a coupon rate (and, therefore, a P&I payment) that changes periodically to reflect a specified market rate of interest.

Adjusted Cash Flow (ACF) Approach A valuation process in which the expected cash flows of a portfolio of similar securities is discounted back at the yield of an optionless, riskless security of the same maturity.

Balloon Mortgage A residential mortgage that requires the same P&I payments as a fixed-rate mortgage but also requires repayment of the remaining principal balance after a predetermined period of time.

Basis Point One hundredth of 1%—1% equals 100 basis points or bps.

Commercial Mortgages Mortgage loans secured by commercial property such as factories, shopping malls, or office buildings.

Cumulative Prepayment Rate (*CPR*) The proportion of a portfolio of mortgages that is expected to prepay in one year.

Curtailment Prepayment of a part of a mortgage's principal balance.

Disintermediation Market trends that lead to direct agreements between savers and borrowers (as when investors buy bonds issued by a corporation) as opposed to more traditional markets in which savers lend money to a financial intermediary such as a bank which then lends the money to a borrower.

Distressed Collateral Collateral for a loan that is in poor condition relative to similar assets in the market. In residential mortgage lending, a house that has significant structural problems and needs major repairs would be called distressed.

Down Payment The portion of the real estate purchase price that the buyer pays for out of savings. This represents the borrower's initial equity position in the property.

Effective Duration The duration implied by price changes observed in the market place or estimated by a valuation model.

Expected Cash Flow The probability weighted-average of all possible cash flow outcomes.

Financial Intermediary A financial institution that borrows from savers and then lends the money to borrowers, maintaining an ongoing contractual relationship with both sides.

Fixed/Adjustable Hybrid A residential mortgage that acts like a fixed-rate mortgage for the first years of its life and an ARM for the remainder of its life.

Fixed-Rate Mortgage A residential mortgage with a coupon rate (and, therefore, a P&I payment) that does not change during its life.

Foreclosure The process by which ownership of a mortgage's real estate collateral is transferred from a borrower who is in default to the lender.

Home Equity Loan A loan that is typically secured by a second lien on real estate collateral.

Home Mortgage See residential mortgage.

Interest-Only Mortgage A residential mortgage that requires the borrower to pay the accrued interest each month, but not any part of the principal balance.

Lien The interest in an asset held by the lender in a secured loan transaction.

Loan-to-Value (LTV) Ratio The ratio of the principal balance of a mortgage to the market value of the real estate that secures the mortgage.

Mortgage The agreement that assigns a particular piece of real estate as collateral for a loan.

Mortgage Loan A paired loan agreement and mortgage.

Multifamily Mortgage A mortgage secured by an apartment building or apartment complex with more than four residential units.

Negative Convexity Used to describe a portfolio whose duration decreases as interest rates decrease, such as a portfolio of mortgages that contain a prepayment option.

Origination The process whereby a new loan is created.

Overcollateralized A secured loan for which the value of the collateral is higher than the loan balance.

Prepayment Repayment of a loan before its stated maturity.

Prepayment Option The right commonly granted to residential mortgage borrowers to prepay their loan balance at will and without penalty.

Principal and Interest (P&I) Payment The payment owed on a self-amortizing residential mortgage. The payment is applied first to accrued interest and then to the remaining principal balance of the loan.

Private Mortgage Insurance (PMI) Default insurance paid for by the mortgage borrower that is required by most lenders if the borrower's initial down payment is less than 20% of the value of the property used as collateral.

Rate Cap A limit on the amount that the coupon rate on an ARM can increase at each repricing (i.e., periodic cap) or over the life of the mortgage (i.e., lifetime cap).

Rate Floor A limit on the amount that the coupon rate on an ARM can decrease at each repricing (i.e., periodic floor) or over the life of the mortgage (i.e., lifetime floor).

Recovery Rate The portion of the remaining principal balance of the loan that the lender expects to receive when the collateral is foreclosed on and sold, after all fees are paid and after discounting is considered.

Refinance   The process in which a home owner takes out a new mortgage and uses a part or all of the proceeds to prepay the existing mortgage.

Repricing Frequency   How frequently an ARM's P&I payment is recalculated.

Residential Mortgages   A loan that requires monthly, self-amortizing payments of principal and interest and which is secured by real property containing one to four separate residences.

Second Mortgage   A loan secured by real estate that serves as collateral for an earlier loan. The first lender has a priority claim on the property (called a first lien) should the borrower default.

Secured Lending   Loans backed by a specific asset rather than a general, subordinated claim on the borrower's assets.

Servicing   The process whereby loan payments are collected from borrowers and disbursed to investors.

Loan servicers also answer questions for borrowers, pursue late payments, and proceed to foreclosure on behalf of the investor, should the borrower default.

Single Monthly Mortality (*SMM*)   The proportion of a portfolio of mortgages that is expected to prepay each month.

Teaser Rate   An initial coupon rate on an ARM that is less than the value of the ARM's index plus its fixed spread.

Weighted-Average Coupon Rate (WAC)   The sum of the coupon rates of the mortgages in a portfolio, each weighted by the remaining principal balance of the individual mortgage divided by the total remaining principal balance of the portfolio.

Weighted-Average Maturity (WAM)   The sum of the remaining maturities of the mortgages in a portfolio, each weighted by the remaining principal balance of the individual mortgage divided by the total remaining principal balance of the portfolio.

The amounts for the first and second expected cash flows are slightly different from those calculated in Section 4 of this chapter. The spreadsheet calculations that appear in Table 6A-1 are free from rounding error, while those presented in Section 4 contain small rounding errors.

TABLE 6A-1 Expected Cash Flows of Mortgage Portfolio[a]

t	Expected P & I cash flow	Interest part	Principal part	Expected prepayment cash flow	Expected default amount	Expected recovery cash flow	Expected cash flow	Remaining principal balance
0								400,000.00
1	2,689.12	2,312.50	376.62	7,362.45	672.22	470.56	10,522.13	391,588.71
2	2,635.05	2,263.87	371.18	7,207.58	658.08	460.66	10,303.30	383,351.86
3	2,582.08	2,216.25	365.82	7,055.93	644.24	450.97	10,088.97	375,285.86
4	2,530.16	2,169.62	360.54	6,907.43	630.68	441.47	9,879.06	367,387.22
5	2,479.29	2,123.96	355.33	6,762.00	617.40	432.18	9,673.47	359,652.49
6	2,429.44	2,079.24	350.20	6,619.59	604.40	423.08	9,472.12	352,078.29
7	2,380.60	2,035.45	345.15	6,480.15	591.67	414.17	9,274.91	344,661.34
8	2,332.73	1,992.57	340.16	6,343.59	579.20	405.44	9,081.76	337,398.39
9	2,285.83	1,950.58	335.25	6,209.87	566.99	396.89	8,892.60	330,286.28
10	2,239.88	1,909.47	330.41	6,078.93	555.03	388.52	8,707.33	323,321.90
11	2,194.84	1,869.20	325.64	5,950.71	543.33	380.33	8,525.88	316,502.23
12	2,150.71	1,829.78	320.93	5,825.16	531.86	372.30	8,348.17	309,824.28
13	2,107.47	1,791.17	316.30	5,702.21	520.64	364.45	8,174.13	303,285.13
14	2,065.10	1,753.37	311.73	5,581.82	509.64	356.75	8,003.67	296,881.93
15	2,023.58	1,716.35	307.23	5,463.94	498.88	349.22	7,836.73	290,611.89
16	1,982.89	1,680.10	302.79	5,348.50	488.34	341.84	7,673.23	284,472.25
17	1,943.03	1,644.61	298.42	5,235.47	478.02	334.61	7,513.11	278,460.34
18	1,903.96	1,609.85	294.11	5,124.79	467.92	327.54	7,356.29	272,573.53
19	1,865.68	1,575.82	289.86	5,016.41	458.02	320.61	7,202.70	266,809.23
20	1,828.17	1,542.49	285.68	4,910.29	448.33	313.83	7,052.29	261,164.93
21	1,791.41	1,509.86	281.55	4,806.38	438.84	307.19	6,904.98	255,638.16
22	1,755.40	1,477.91	277.49	4,704.63	429.55	300.69	6,760.71	250,226.49
23	1,720.10	1,446.62	273.48	4,605.00	420.46	294.32	6,619.42	244,927.55
24	1,685.52	1,415.99	269.53	4,507.45	411.55	288.08	6,481.05	239,739.02

[a](F, 400,000; WAC, 6.94%, WAM, 341 months; CPR, 20%; Default, 2%; Recovery, 70%).

CHAPTER 7

EQUITY VALUATION

7.1 INTRODUCTION

This chapter explains the basic structure of the stock market and shows you how to price a stock using some standard valuation models that are employed by industry professionals in financial institutions such as investment banks, pension funds, or mutual funds. During the 1990s the stock market exploded. The S&P 500 Index earned an annual return of 18.84%, the S&P MidCap 400 earned an annual return of 19.11%, and the S&P SmallCap 600 earned an annual return of 14.16%. In addition, the news media reported that technology stocks had performed extremely well during that period, and while some might have expected them to dominate any list of annual top 10 stock price increases, a quick check shows that nontech stocks, such as Gap Inc., Navistar, Bally Entertainment, Chrysler, Home Depot, and Goodyear Tire & Rubber, were among the annual leaders.

Who made all the money in this broad-based market surge? While it is well known that people like Bill Gates and Warren Buffett made a lot of money, the majority of the benefits went to the average worker and investor. The Federal Reserve generates a report called the *Flow of Funds Account of the United States* that provides the market value of stocks held by different classes of investors. A small portion of this information is provided in Figure 7-1. This figure shows the different investor groups that have benefited from the dramatic rise in the stock market during the 1990s. Figure 7-1 shows that households held $1,760 billion of stock in 1990 and the amount held by households had increased to $9,052 billion by 1999. Over the same period life insurance company holdings of stock increased from $98 billion to $904 billion, and private pension fund holdings increased from $593 billion to $2,269 billion. These numbers clearly indicate that the average worker and average investor benefited substantially from the rise in the stock market across the 1990s. However, by 2003 the average worker and average investor experienced a reversal. The holdings of households decreased to $5,709 billion and the holdings of private pension funds decreased to $1,872 billion, in part, because of the major downturn in the market in 2001.

Given the importance of the stock market, two important questions arise. First, how can stocks be valued so that a decision can be made concerning which to buy, sell, or keep? Second, as a stock owner, what do you have at risk and how do you manage that risk? Stock valuation is the topic of this chapter and continues the valuation process developed in the preceding three chapters on valuation in the money market, bond market, and mortgage market. As with all the valuation chapters in this book, this chapter begins with explaining "how the markets operate." This institutional detail is followed by the methods for valuing stocks and the process for finding the risk-adjusted discount rate needed to value a stock. The chapter ends with a detailed stock pricing example for two stocks. Later, in Chapter 15, we will discuss techniques for measuring and managing the risks of a stock portfolio.

Stock holdings at market value ($billion)	1990	1994	1999	2003
Households	$1,760	$3,168	$9,052	$5,709
Life insurance companies	$98	$274	$904	$956
Private pension funds	$593	$921	$2,269	$1,872

FIGURE 7-1 Stock holdings of households and major financial institutions.

DEVELOPING VALUATION AND RISK MANAGEMENT SKILLS

1. Understand the institutional features of stock markets.
2. Know the various methods available for valuing stock and be able to use each method to determine the value of a stock.
3. Understand the CAPM (capital asset pricing model) and be able to use it to calculate the appropriate risk-adjusted discount rate for a stock.

7.2 INSTITUTIONAL DETAILS

Every financial market has unique features and terms that must be understood before an investor can become an informed investor in a specific market. In this section some of the important institutional features of the equity markets will be discussed.

7.2.1 Primary vs. Secondary Markets

The **primary market** for equity is the market for the original issue of a security. In this market, the company sells new issues of its stock and receives the proceeds from the sale. The primary market is commonly thought of as the market for **initial public offers** (IPOs); however, other offers, referred to as **seasoned offers**, can also occur in the primary market. The difference between an IPO and a seasoned offer is the number of times the company has issued stock to the public. An IPO is the first offer of stock to the public by the company and the seasoned offers are all subsequent offers of stock to the public by the company.

The primary market is also used for **secondary offerings**. In many countries, governments are the original shareholders of a company. When these firms privatize—issue shares to the general public for the first time—the funds raised through this secondary offering is used to "buy out" the government's position.

Almost all stock offers in the primary market go through an investment banker because the investment banker has the distribution system in place to distribute the shares to the public. The investment banker has one of two roles in a primary market transaction: (1) **marketer** or (2) **underwriter**. As a marketer of the issue, the investment banker makes a "best effort" to sell the issue to the public. When acting as an underwriter, the investment banker buys the entire offer from the firm and then resells the offer to the public. A main difference between marketing and underwriting is "who bears the risk of selling the new shares of stock." When the investment banker acts as a marketer, the issuing company bears the risk. When the investment banker is an underwriter, the investment banker bears the risk. When underwriting the new issue, the investment banker and the issuing company must

Issue date	Company	Ticker	Offer price($)	Price one day after offer ($)	Price one year after offer ($)
		1999			
1/15/99	MarketWatch.com	MKTW	17.00	97.50	40.13
2/1/99	Perot Systems	PER	16.00	43.50	21.44
2/4/99	Del Monte Foods	DLM	15.00	15.63	10.25
2/4/99	Delphi Automotive	DPH	17.00	18.63	17.50
2/10/99	Prodigy Comm.	PRGY	15.00	28.13	25.56
2/19/99	Pinnacle Holdings	BIGT	14.00	14.06	51.50
3/11/99	Infosys Tech.	INFY	34.00	46.63	660.00
3/24/99	Ducati Motor	DMH	31.67	31.06	28.50
3/29/99	Priceline.com	PCLN	16.00	69.00	81.81
5/3/99	Goldman Sachs	GS	53.00	70.38	91.13
5/10/99	TheStreet.com	TSCM	19.00	60.00	6.75
5/19/99	eToys	ETYS	20.00	76.56	6.25
5/25/99	barnesandnoble.com	BNBN	18.00	25.63	9.81
5/26/99	Edgar Online	EDGR	9.50	9.31	5.81
		2003			
1/8/03	Bridge Street Fin	OCNB	10.00	10.18	14.50
2/11/03	Bancshares Florida	BOFL	10.00	10.19	13.99
2/12/03	Infinity P & C	IPCC	16.00	15.90	30.54
2/14/03	Accredited Home Lenders	LEND	8.00	7.25	27.64
2/28/03	Endurance Specialty	ENH	23.00	23.00	33.79
3/4/03	Telkom SA	TKG	13.98	13.90	45.75

FIGURE 7-2 IPO prices in 1999 and 2003.

reach an acceptable price for the offer. To determine the price, the issuing company will either negotiate the price with an investment banker, or the issuing company entertains bid prices from several investment bankers and accepts the best bid which then sets the price.

In Figure 7-2, a partial list of the IPO deals that took place in 1999 and 2003 are provided. First consider the IPOs in 1999. In many cases in 1999 the price at which the investment banker and the company agree to issue the shares in the primary market was very different from the price at which the shares closed on the first day the stocks were traded in the secondary market (the market where investors trade with each other). Also, the initial offer price was very different from the price at which the stock closed one year later. In most cases, the shares closed at a substantially higher price after one day in the secondary market than the issue price. The difference in these amounts does not go to the company; rather, it goes to the investor who initially purchased the stock. There are two ways to interpret this difference. First, the company has to issue the shares at a discount in order to ensure that all the shares will be purchased and, hence, the amount of money needed to be raised will be raised. This is usually the situation when the firm has a very specific investment plan. Second, at the time of these issues there was, as Federal Reserve Chairman Alan Greenspan stated, considerable "irrational exuberance in the market."[1] That is, investors in the secondary market were not using the same rational valuation techniques as the company and its investment advisors were using.

[1] Alan Greenspan's remarks on irrational exuberance appear in a speech at the Annual Dinner and Francis Boyer Lecture of The American Enterprise Institute for Public Policy Research, Washington, D.C., December 5, 1996.

Now look at the IPOs in 2003. The first day prices from the IPOs in 2003 are quite similar to their offer prices, which supports Greenspan's concern about irrational exuberance in the 1990s. That is, when all the stock markets were rising rapidly, investors believed (irrationally) that all stocks would go up substantially in the future. Then there was the huge stock market downturn in 2001. Investors are now much more cautious about the future prospects of IPOs even thought this set of firms in Figure 7-2 with 2003 IPOs have done well since their IPO.

The **secondary market** is a resale market. A colleague refers to this as the *used securities* market. All trades after the initial sale of the stock occur in a secondary market. The markets that the news media generally focus on, such as the NYSE and NASDAQ, are secondary markets. Despite the fact that companies do not gain any additional funds from stock transactions in the secondary market, the firms' stock performance in this market is of crucial importance. As secondary market prices increase, a firm's leverage decreases; therefore, a firm gains access to more debt. Conversely, if a firm's share price declines in the secondary market, the firm's leverage increases and limits the firm's access to new debt. The NYSE and NASDAQ are two of our main stock markets, but these two markets differ in several significant ways. Section 2.2 and Figures 7-3 and 7-4 will cover some important differences.

INDUSTRY APPLICATION

OPENING A MARKET[2]

In a call auction, orders are batched for a simultaneous execution. This is a common method of trading on many European exchanges such as the Deutsche Börse and the Paris, Amsterdam, Brussels, and Lisbon exchanges. It is also the means by which the NYSE is opened every morning. It is the task of specialists and their staffs on the floor of the NYSE to determine where a stock should open.

The most common criterion for setting the opening price is that of *maximizing the order turnover*. Consider the following preopening snapshot of an order book.

Buy orders, # of shares				Sell orders, # of shares		
Individual orders	Total size at price	Cumulative orders from highest price	Price (limit)	Cumulative orders from lowest price	Total size at price	Individual orders
200 + 150	350	350	Market			
			>47.45			
100	100	450	47.45			
150	150	600	47.40			
200	200	800	47.35	2,100	250	100 + 150
100 + 150	250	1,050	47.30	1,850	350	350
400 + 50	450	1,500	47.25	1,500	250	250
500	500	2,000	47.20	1,250	150	50 + 100
350 + 100	450	2,450	47.15	1,100	150	150
			47.10	850	150	50 + 100
			47.00	800	50	100
			<47.00			
			Market	750	750	350 + 400

(continued)

INDUSTURY APPLICATION (*continued*)

OPENING A MARKET[2]

Consider the buy side, where there are orders from investors to buy 350 shares at the market's opening price, and then various limit orders at different prices. Because these are buy orders, an investor who is willing to buy the stock at say $47.45 would also be willing to buy the stock at $47.40. Hence, the buy orders are aggregated in the third column in descending price order. Now consider the sell side. There are orders from investors to sell 750 shares at the opening market price, and then various limit orders at different prices. Because these are sell orders, an investor who is willing to sell at $47.00 would also be willing to sell at say, $47.15. Hence, the sell

orders are aggregated in the fifth column in ascending price order.

Now take a look at the cumulative number of buy and sell orders at $47.25. If the market were to open at this price, 1,500 shares would be bought and sold. This would result in an opening bid-ask spread of $47.20 − $47.30.

Unfortunately, it is sometimes the case that two or more prices could satisfy the maximization of turnover criterion. In such cases, a second criterion is used, the *minimization of the order surplus*. Consider the following revised table.

Buy orders, # of shares			Price	Sell orders, # of shares		
Individual orders	Total size at price	Cumulative orders from highest price	(limit)	Cumulative orders from lowest price	Total size at price	Individual orders
200 + 150	350	350	Market			
			>47.45			
100	100	450	47.45			
150	150	600	47.40			
200	200	800	47.35	2,350	250	100 + 150
100 + 150	250	1,050	47.30	2,100	350	350
400 + 50	450	1,500	47.25	1,750	250	250
500	500	2,000	47.20	1,500	400	50 + 350
350 + 100	450	2,450	47.15	1,100	150	150
			47.10	850	150	50 + 100
			47.00	800	50	100
			<47.00			
			Market	750	750	350 + 400

In this case, opening at either of $47.25 and $47.20 would result in a trading volume of 1,500 shares. But, if the opening price is set at $47.25 there would be a surplus of only 250 shares on the sell side (the bid-ask spread would be $47.20 − $47.25). However, if the opening price is set at $47.20 there would be a surplus of 500 shares on the buy side. Clearly, more investors' orders are satisfied at the higher price.

Sometimes it is possible for even these two criteria to provide two different potential opening prices. A third criterion, of *market pressure* can then be used. If two prices both provide the same trading volume and

the same minimum surplus, then if the surplus is on the buy side the higher of the two prices is used and if the surplus is on the sell side then the lower of the two prices is used. In the unlikely event that these three criteria fail to identify a satisfactory opening price, then either the price closest to the most recent traded price is used or the exchange uses additional specialized rules.

This process is important to understand because the NYSE now makes this order information available through their OpenBook service. Thus, brokerage firms can now determine the opening price of a security and provide this information to their customers.

[2] This example is derived from one in Schwartz, R. A., and R. Francioni, 2004, *Equity Markets in Action: The Fundamentals of Liquidity, Market Structure & Trading,* pp. 172–173. John Wiley & Sons, Hoboken, NJ.

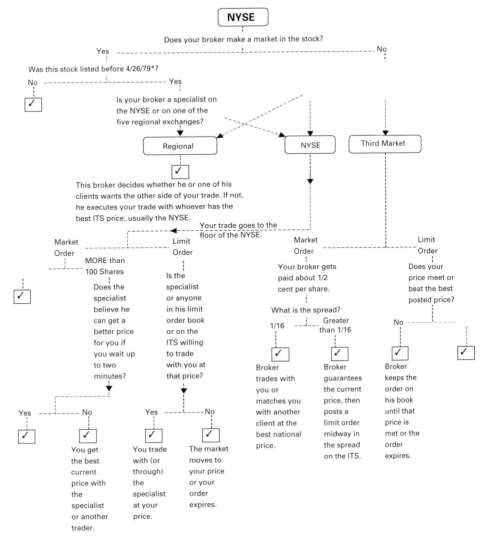

FIGURE 7-3 Order execution on the NYSE.

Source: *Fortune,* April 2000.

7.2.2 Dealer Markets vs. Exchanges

The primary difference between the NYSE (New York Stock Exchange) and the NASDAQ (National Association of Securities Dealers Automated Quotation system) is reflected in their names. The NYSE is an **exchange** while NASDAQ is a **dealer network**.

Most exchanges, including the NYSE, are auctions. Generally, they have a physical location that brings all traders to one location, offers stock for sale, and then sells the offered stock to the highest bidder. Auctions provide the best price to the seller on a given day. Since an auction provides the best price, an assumption could be that all stock would trade at an exchange. However, maintaining the physical location of an exchange is costly and the

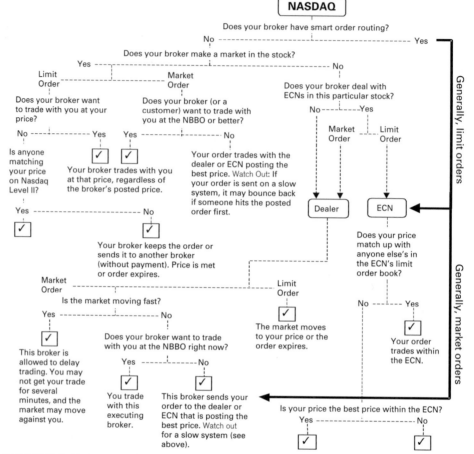

FIGURE 7-4 Order execution on the NASDAQ.

Source: *Fortune,* April 2000.

cost is paid through transaction fees; therefore, only high volume stocks can trade on an exchange and maintain competitive trading fees.[3]

The alternative to an exchange is a dealer or a dealers' network. NASDAQ is a prominent dealer network. At a dealer network, many different dealers submit their quotes that include both the prices and the quantities of shares they are willing to buy or sell. The quotes with the best prices form the best bid-ask spread. That is, these quotes represent the lowest price at which an investor can buy a share and the highest price at which the stock can be sold. The same dealer does not have to offer the best bid and ask prices.

Price differences are not the only difference that exists between exchanges and dealer networks. To demonstrate another difference, Figures 7-3 and 7-4 show the path a buy or a sell order takes on the NYSE and NASDAQ markets.

---

[3] The two major exceptions to this are the Toronto Stock Exchange and the Paris Bourse, both of which are exchanges but do not have a physical trading floor. All transactions for these two exceptions are routed through a network of computer systems.

INDUSTRY APPLICATION

ORDER-DRIVEN MARKETS

An order-driven market (such as the NASDAQ) is one where everyone is an investor attempting to buy or sell shares for their own account. Although everyone wants to either buy or sell shares, they can do so in two different ways. First, they can place either a limit buy or sell order, or, second, they can place a market buy or sell order. The investors who place the limit orders define the maximum price at which a share can be purchased (the bid price) and the minimum price at which the share can be sold (the ask price). Examine the following table which represents a limit order book. A limit order book simply shows all of the prices and quantities at which limit order investors are willing to trade. The desires of market order investors are not shown since they execute immediately against the limit orders. We will give an example of this next.

Notice that there are three occurrences where no orders are placed. At $30.45 there are no ask orders and at $30 there are no bid orders. Limit orders simply were not placed at these prices—this occurs purely by chance. However, there are also no orders at $30.20 and $30.25; this is not by chance. These orders are within the bid-ask spread.

Suppose that an investor who is eager to sell places a limit order for 500 shares at $30.25. The bid-ask spread would then narrow to $30.15–$30.25. A market order is an unpriced order. Let's say that a market order to buy 1,700 shares arrives. This order would

Bid orders (hundreds)	Price	Ask orders (hundreds)
	30.50	105
	30.45	No orders
	30.40	76
	30.35	47
	30.30	12
Bid-ask spread	30.25	
(30.15–30.30)	30.20	
41	30.15	
82	30.10	
23	30.05	
No orders	30.00	
77	29.95	
53	29.90	
66	29.85	

execute immediately against the recently placed limit order of 500 shares at $30.25 and against the order(s) at $30.30. The bid-ask spread would then become $30.15–$30.35. The bid-ask spread would widen.

Investors seeing this and anticipating increased demand and therefore rising prices, might then place a limit buy order for, say, 2,000 shares at $30.20. The bid-ask spread would then become $30.20–$30.35, reverting to the earlier 15 cent spread but at a higher level.

Another venue for trading securities is the **over-the-counter** (OTC) market or third market. In this market all trades are made with a specific dealer. However, unlike an auction or a dealer network, an individual dealer may not provide the best prices. Dealers in an OTC stock will quote different prices based on their current need to buy or sell a given stock. Accordingly, the investor must search for the dealer with the best price. Even though the time spent searching increases the search costs to the investor, the OTC market provides a market for lower-volume stocks.

7.3 VALUING STOCKS

In this section, the process for valuing stocks will be discussed. In the previous chapters covering money market instruments, bonds, and mortgages, the discussion taught that the value of a financial asset is the present value of its future cash flows. The same is true for stock. Therefore, the cash flows a stock owner can expect to receive must be identified and we must determine the appropriate risk-adjusted discount rate for discounting the expected cash flows. In this section, the expected future cash flows and the formulas for finding the present value of those cash flows will be identified. The discussion that follows will be divided into two segments: (1) stocks that pay dividends and (2) stocks that do *not* pay a dividend. The discussion of the appropriate risk-adjusted discount rate will be delayed until Section 7.4 of this chapter.

7.3.1 Pricing Dividend-Paying Stocks

An investor in a **dividend** paying stock expects to receive two sets of future cash flows: (1) a stream of future dividends and (2) a sales price when the stock is sold. To find the present value of these cash flows, the expected amount of the dividends and the timing of the dividend payments must be identified. These determinations are quite difficult because of the uncertainty of both the amount and the timing of the expected cash flows. In addition, the further into the future the estimates are to be made, the more likely the estimations will be inaccurate.

Stock owners have the right to sell their stock at any time at the then prevailing market price. This sale will be the last cash flow to the current owner of the stock, and this sale price must be considered when determining the current price of this stock. However, no reliable method is available for determining the optimal timing of a stock sale or its sales price. That is the bad news for an investor attempting to determine the current price of a stock. However, the good news for the investor is that the future sale price of the stock does not have to be known to determine the current purchase price, and the following explains why. Each owner of a dividend-paying stock buys the stock expecting to receive a stream of dividends and a future sale price. The sale price will be based on the dividends and the sale price the purchaser expects to receive. Importantly, this pattern will repeat itself for every subsequent sale of the stock. Thus, since a stock has an infinite life, a dividend-paying stock can be valued on the basis of an infinite stream of expected future dividends.

Reducing the problem of the timing and the amount of the expected future cash flows to an infinite stream of future dividends better defines the situation, but the timing and amount of the expected future dividends still must be determined. Luckily, most dividend-paying stocks pay dividends at regular intervals; therefore, the assumption will be made that dividends are paid at regular intervals. Then, one of three assumptions about dividend growth will be used to value a dividend paying stock: (1) no growth in dividends, (2) constant growth in dividends, or (3) nonconstant growth in dividends.

7.3.1.1 *No Growth in Dividends*   The first assumption, the **no growth in dividends assumption**, assumes that the amount of the future dividend will be constant. Given the assumption of a regular dividend forever, the assumption of constant dividends (no growth) means that the expected dividend stream is a perpetuity.

The present value of a perpetuity is

$$PV = \frac{CF}{r}.$$
(7-1)

To convert the formula to standard stock price notation, the following formula is used

$$P_0 = \frac{D}{r},$$ (7-2)

where

P_0 = stock price at time 0 (today),

D = dividend,

r = risk-adjusted discount rate.

The assumption of no growth in dividends may seem unrealistic, and for most common stock it is unrealistic. However, the assumption of constant dividends fits perfectly with the characteristics of **preferred stock**.

Preferred stock carries a stated dividend of a fixed amount and all preferred stock dividends must be fully paid before any dividend on **common stock** can be paid. Often, preferred stock dividends are cumulative, which means if any arrears exist, they must be paid before a common stock dividend can be paid.[4] Nevertheless, the cumulative nature of preferred stock dividends is seldom an issue because the vast majority of firms with preferred stock dividends also pay regular common stock dividends and thus remain current with the preferred stock dividend.

EXAMPLE *Calculating the Price of Preferred Stock*

Assume a company pays a quarterly preferred dividend of $0.25 and further assume that the company's risk-adjusted discount rate is 8%. Then the price of the company's preferred stock should be

$$P_0 = \$0.250/0.02 = \$12.50.$$

7.3.1.2 *Constant Growth in Dividends* The second common assumption possible for expected future dividends is the assumption that dividends increase at a **constant rate**. Historical evidence suggests that this is a reasonable assumption for the large, stable, dividend-paying companies. These companies are often referred to as "blue chip" firms.

Assuming that dividends grow at a constant rate (g), then dividends at any point in the future can be calculated as

$$D_t = D_0(1 + g)^t,$$ (7-3)

where

D_t = dividend at time t,

g = expected growth rate in dividends.

Since the price of the stock is the present value of expected future dividends, then under the assumption of constant growth in dividends, the price of the stock is

$$P_0 \frac{D_0(1 + g)}{(1 + r)} + \frac{D_0(1 + g)^2}{(1 + r)^2} + \frac{D_0(1 + g)^3}{(1 + r)^3} + \frac{D_0(1 + g)^4}{(1 + r)^4} + \cdots$$ (7-4)

---

[4] Although preferred stock is technically equity, it is not unusual for bankers to consider preferred shares as a form of subordinated debt when computing debt/equity and times interest earned ratios.

In Equation (7-4), the price of the stock is the sum of the present value sum of an infinite series of dividends which cannot immediately be solved for a numerical answer. However, if $[r > g]$ then the sum of the infinite series converges and the following formula can be used for pricing a stock with a constant growth rate in expected future dividends:

$$P_0 = \frac{D_1}{(r - g)},$$ (7-5)

where[5]

$$D_1 = D_0(1 + g).$$

If $(g > r)$ then the series will not converge and the third common assumption about future dividends, which will be discussed in Subsection 7.3.1.3, must be used.

EXAMPLE *Calculating the Price of a Stock with a Constant Growth Rate in Dividends*

Assume the current quarterly dividend on the common shares of your company is $0.50, the risk-adjusted discount rate is 10%, and a new and untapped market for your company has been discovered. The management of the firm believes that the new market will allow it to increase the dividend by 0.25% per quarter. Also, the company has decided to leave the next quarterly dividend at $0.50. What is the current share price of this company? The answer is

$$P_0 = \frac{\$0.50}{(0.025 - 0.0025)} = \$22.22.$$

7.3.1.3 *Nonconstant Growth Dividends*   Now the assumption of $(g > r)$ will be discussed. When $(g > r)$, dividends are said to grow at a **nonconstant rate**. This assumption is used because when $(g > r)$, dividends are growing at a high rate that cannot be sustained over the long run. Thus, the rate of growth must decline at some point in the not too distant future. This unsustainable growth results in a nonconstant growth rate for dividends. In a nonconstant growth rate situation, the growth rate in dividends is generally assumed to decline to a rate of growth that is sustainable over the long run. A further assumption is that the long-term growth rate is a constant rate g where $(g < r)$. Under these assumptions, the price of the stock is calculated as follows:

$$P_0 = \sum_{t=1}^{n} \frac{D_t}{(1 + r)^t} + \left[\frac{(D_{n+1}/(r - g))}{(1 + r)^n} \right],$$ (7-6)

where

$$g = \text{growth rate in dividends in the later period where } (g < r),$$
$$D_{n+1} = D_n(1 + g),$$
$$n = \text{number of periods of high } (g > r) \text{ growth.}$$

---

[5] We note that the constant growth formula can be rearranged to solve for r and the result is

$$r = \frac{D_1}{P_0} + g.$$

This formula provides the implied discount rate. However, we do not recommend its use because risk is not explicitly considered. An approach for calculating a risk-adjusted discount rate that explicitly considers risk is discussed in Section 7.4 of this chapter.

EXAMPLE *Calculating the Price of a Stock with Nonconstant Dividends*

Now consider an example where the management reviews their financial projections and realizes that the firm can pay quarterly dividends starting in the next quarter at $0.50 and then increasing 2.5% every quarter for the next three quarters before the earnings and dividends stabilize. When earnings stabilize, management believes that dividends will grow at a rate of 1% per quarter into the foreseeable future.[6] Using the assumption as stated, what should the current price of this stock be? The answer is

$$
\begin{aligned}
P_0 &= \$0.50/(1.025) + (\$0.50 \times 1.025)/(1.025)^2 + (\$0.50 \times 1.025)^2/(1.025)^3 \\
&\quad + (\$0.50 \times 1.025)^3/(1.025)^4 + [(\$0.50 \times 1.025)^3 \times (1.01)/(0.025 - 0.01)] \times [1/(1.025)^4] \\
&= \$0.4878 + \$0.4878 + \$0.4878 + \$0.4878 + \$32.84 \\
&= \$34.79.
\end{aligned}
$$

7.3.1.4 *Three-Stage Nonconstant Growth in Dividends* The noncon-stant growth formula in the previous section contains two stages of dividend growth: (1) high growth and (2) mature (low) growth. An assumption underlying dividend growth is that dividend growth is directly linked to earnings growth. Therefore, a high dividend growth firm is a high earnings growth firm and a mature dividend growth firm is a mature earnings growth firm. Considering earnings, a reasonable assumption can be made that an intermediate stage of earnings growth exists between high and mature. If an intermediate stage of earnings growth exists, then an intermediate stage of dividend growth should also exist. Several choices are available for including the decline in the growth rate phase (the intermediate phase) in the pricing model, but the simplest approach is to include the intermediate phase with the high growth dividends in the first n dividends in Equation (7-6).

EXAMPLE *Alternative Approach to Pricing a Stock with Nonconstant Dividends*

For example, assume a firm's current dividend is $1.00 and the dividend is expected to grow at 6% per quarter for the next four quarters. Then the dividend growth rate is expected to decline 1% per quarter for the following four quarters. After the four quarters of growth rate decline, the growth rate is expected to settle at 2% where it will remain. If the risk-adjusted discount rate for this firm is 12%, then what is its current stock price? Using the assumptions as stated, the current stock price is

$$
\begin{aligned}
P_0 &= \frac{\$1.00(1.06)}{(1.03)} + \frac{\$1.00(1.06)^2}{(1.03)^2} + \frac{\$1.00(1.06)^3}{(1.03)^3} + \frac{\$1.00(1.06)^4}{(1.03)^4} + \frac{\$1.00(1.06)^4(1.05)}{(1.03)^5} \\
&\quad + \frac{\$1.00(1.06)^4(1.05)(1.04)}{(1.03)^6} + \frac{\$1.00(1.06)^4(1.05)(1.04)(1.03)}{(1.03)^7} \\
&\quad + \frac{\$1.00(1.06)^4(1.05)(1.04)(1.03)(1.02)}{(1.03)^8} \\
&\quad + \left[\frac{\$1.00(1.06)^4(1.05)(1.04)(1.03)(1.02)(1.02)}{0.03 - 0.02} \times \frac{1}{(1.03)^8} \right] \\
&= 1.0291 + 1.0591 + 1.0899 + 1.1217 + 1.1435 + 1.1546 + 1.1546 + 1.1434 + 116.6234 \\
&= \$125.52.
\end{aligned}
$$

---

[6] Technically speaking, it is not correct to assume that the risk-adjusted discount rate will remain constant throughout both the high growth and the sustainable growth periods. However, we set this technicality aside at this point.

7.3.2 Pricing Stocks That Do Not Pay Dividends

Historically, most publicly traded stocks paid a dividend. However, in today's high growth, high-tech world, many publicly traded stocks do not pay any form of a dividend. In the previous subsection, discussion concerned how to value a stock when the investor expects to receive dividends. In this subsection, discussion will center on how to value a stock that does not pay dividends.

Some companies do not pay dividends, retaining the cash flow to invest in company expansion. Basically a company has one of two reasons for deciding *not* to pay a dividend. First, the company is very new and does not have an adequate credit rating; therefore, borrowing from banks would be very expensive. Second, the company is growing very quickly and their rate of return is greater than other companies of similar risk. Therefore, the company retains their earnings for reinvestment in the company instead of paying dividends because the shareholders would otherwise have to invest in the lower-return alternatives. A different approach must be used to value non-dividend-paying company's stock.

From dividend-paying stocks, stockholders receive cash flows in the form of dividends and a sales price at the end of their holding period. When a company does not pay a dividend, the only cash flow stockholders receive is the sale price. With no dividends, an investor buys a stock based on expected capital gains, and each subsequent investor will buy the stock based on expected capital gains. Therefore, the value of the stock of a non-dividend-paying company will be based on an infinite stream of expected capital gains.

Consider these facts. Net income is the portion of annual earnings that remains after all of the current year's obligations are paid. Earnings per share (**EPS**) is net income divided by the number of common shares outstanding. EPS belongs to the owners of the common stock because the owners, as residual claimants, get the portion of annual earnings remaining after all other current year obligations are paid. Because EPS belongs to the stockholder, EPS is used to proxy for the annual capital gains that an owner can expect. Therefore, the calculation of the stock price of a non-dividend-paying stock is based on the stream of EPS.

A standard conceptual method for valuing non-dividend-paying stock is

$$P_0 = \text{PV(cash flows from assets in place)} + \text{PV(cash flows from growth opportunites)}. \tag{7-7}$$

Using EPS, the present value of the cash flows from the assets in place is EPS_0/r. The calculation for the present value of the growth opportunities depends on the rate of growth. If the rate of growth is less than the discount rate, then a modification of the dividend constant growth formula is used and, if the growth rate is greater than the discount rate, then a modification of the dividend nonconstant growth formula is used. The formula is either

$$\text{if } (r > g) \text{ then } \quad P_0 = \frac{EPS_0}{r} + \frac{(EPS_1) - EPS_0}{(r - g)}$$

or

if $(g > r)$ for n periods followed by $(r > g)$ for all periods thereafter then

$$P_0 \frac{EPS_0}{r} + \sum_{t=1}^{n} \frac{(EPS_t - EPS_0)}{(1 + r)^t} + \frac{((EPS_{n+1} - EPS_0)/(r - g))}{(1 + r)^n}. \tag{7-8}$$

where g is the annual rate of growth in earnings-per-share.

Now methods for valuing dividend paying stocks and nondividend stocks have been discussed. However, before moving on to the determination of the appropriate risk-adjusted discount rate (which is done in Section 7.4 below), a few comments need to be made about the current levels of dividends available in the market.

Historically, the firms in the Dow Jones Industrial Average (DJIA) and the firms in the S&P 500 paid a dividend that was a significant portion of their investors' annual returns. However, times have changed. During the late 1990s, the dividend yield on the S&P 500 was less than 2% while the total yield was above 20%. [7] The average dividend yield for the firms in the DJIA for 1999 was 1.78%. This suggests that as the market has evolved, dividends have become a very small portion of the investors' total return. This further suggests that even when a firm pays dividends, and if the dividend is a small portion of the investor's expected annual return, the dividend stream may not adequately describe the cash flows to the investors. Therefore, investors should consider the valuation method presented in Equation (7-7) when a firm pays a dividend that is a very small portion of the total expected return.

IN THE NEWS

The *BusinessWeek* cover story for May 14, 2001 is titled "The Numbers Game." The subtitle continues by stating "Companies use every trick to pump earnings and fool investors. The latest abuse: 'Pro forma' reporting." Providing misleading earnings is a particularly important topic in today's stock market because, as we have seen in this chapter, dividends are a very small portion of an investor's return. Stock values are driven by earnings and, in particular, by expecting future earnings.

What is pro forma reporting? Well, one accounting text defines pro forma statements as hypothetical statements. These are financial statements as they would appear if some event occurred, such as a merger or increased production and sales. In finance texts, forecasted financial statements are referred to as pro forma statements. However, pro forma literally means "as a matter of form" and these discrepancies in the definition appear to be the root of the problem. Companies are creating information that looks like financial statements, but that doesn't accurately reflect the entire financial picture of the company.

Accounting courses teach that financial statements are prepared according to GAAP (Generally Accepted Accounting Principles). This statement is true for accounting statements required by the SEC (Securities

and Exchange Commission). However, pro forma statements are not for the SEC and, therefore, are not required to conform to GAAP. Instead, companies seem to be adjusting their GAAP numbers to provide a more favorable view of their company's earnings and are providing these numbers to investors and Wall Street in the form of pro forma statements. To make this point, the article provides the following table of pro forma earnings in comparison to GAAP earnings.

Company	Pro forma EPS ($)	GAAP EPS ($)
JDS Uniphase	0.14	−1.13
Checkfree	−0.04	−1.17
Terayon	−0.43	−1.01
Amazon.com	−0.22	0.66
PMC-Sierra	0.02	−0.38
Corning	0.29	0.14
Qualcomm	0.29	0.18
Cisco Systems	0.18	0.12
eBay	0.11	0.08
Yahoo!	0.01	−0.02

(*continued*)

[7] Dividend yield equals the firm's annual dividend divided by the current price of the firm's stock.

IN THE NEWS (*continued*)

Now, a few cents of difference between pro forma EPS and GAAP EPS does not on the surface appear to be important. However, Yahoo! has 566.9 million shares outstanding; therefore, the three cent difference represents a difference in net income of about $17 million. Amazon.com has 359.2 million shares outstanding, so an 88 cent difference in EPS is about a $316 million difference in net income. These differences in net income are substantial and raise two questions. First, what creates the differences? Second, why are the differences important?

To answer the first question we use a statement in the article by SEC Chief Accountant Lynn Turner who describes the pro forma EPS as EBS earnings— "Everything but Bad Stuff." What this means is that companies are creating their pro forma statements to emphasize positive aspects of company performance while ignoring negative aspects of company performance. The companies justify this process by also including in the news releases of their GAAP numbers. One company spokesman attempted to explain the use of pro forma financial statements with the comment that "The pro forma numbers are how we think about our business." Turner also answers the second question with the opinion that pro forma statements appear to be used to distract investors from the actual firm performance. This point is important because the use of misleading financial statements affects the integrity of the stock markets, and integrity is a necessity for the markets' continued successful operation.

7.4 RISK-ADJUSTED DISCOUNT RATES

Investors demand compensation for the risk they bear from owning a stock. In this section, discussion concerns the risk a stock owner is compensated for bearing and how that risk translates into a risk-adjusted discount rate.

The primary risk to a stock owner is that the stock price will fall. However, stock prices can also rise. Price changes are measured as returns and the average return (mean) across several periods is often the measure used as the normal or expected return on the stock. Next, the standard deviation of returns is calculated as a measure of the dispersion of returns. This standard deviation is used as a proxy for risk.[8]

Under the assumption that returns are normally distributed (a common and fairly reasonable assumption about stock returns), the mean and the standard deviation of returns fully describe the return behavior of the stock. That is, the mean and standard deviation provide the expected return (the mean) and the probabilities of the possible returns relative to the mean (from the normal distribution and the standard deviation). Under a normal distribution, 68% of returns are within one standard deviation of the mean and 95% of the

[8] The standard calculation for the average return is

$$\bar{r} = \frac{1}{n}\left[\sum_{t=1}^{n} r_t\right],$$

and the standard calculation for standard deviation is

$$\sigma = \sqrt{\frac{\sum_{t=1}^{n}(r_t - \bar{r})^2}{(n-1)}},$$

where n equals the number of returns periods used.

returns are within two standard deviations of the mean. These facts allow the probable range of returns to be calculated. For example, if a stock has an expected return of 14% with a standard deviation of 2%, 68% of the possible returns are between 12 and 16% and 95% of the possible returns are between 10 and 18%. This information provides the investor the expected return and total risk of the stock. However, even though the standard deviation provides a measure of **total risk**, standard deviation is not the appropriate measure of risk for determining risk-adjusted discount rates.

7.4.1 Diversification

The standard deviation of a stock's returns is a measure of the total risk of the individual stock. However, investors seldom, if ever, hold just one asset. Instead, investors own portfolios of assets. Therefore, the changes to the standard deviation as a portfolio expands from a single stock to many stocks must be understood.

Figure 7-5 presents the change in a portfolio's standard deviation as stocks are added to the portfolio and provides a description of the decomposition of risk. As stocks are added to the portfolio, the standard deviation of the portfolio's return declines. However, the decline is not linear. Instead, portfolio standard deviation declines at a decreasing rate as stocks are added to the portfolio until a point is reached where adding more stocks to the portfolio no longer significantly reduces the portfolio's standard deviation. The process of adding stocks that reduce a portfolio's standard deviation is called **diversification**. The maximum amount of diversification occurs when 25–30 randomly chosen securities are placed in a portfolio.

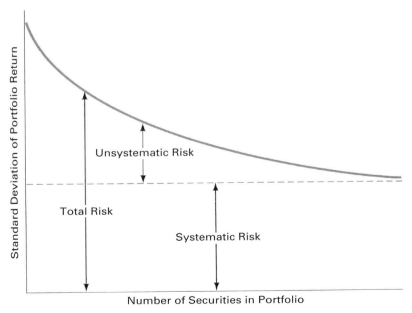

FIGURE 7-5 Components of portfolio risk.

Diversification reduces, but does not eliminate, the risk of the portfolio. This fact suggests that through diversification some risks can be elimited while other risks cannot be eliminted. The risk that cannot be eliminated through diversification is referred to as **systematic**, nondiversifible, or market **risk**. The risk that can be eliminated is referred to as **unsystematic**, diversifible, or company-specific **risk**.

The risk reduction from diversification operates through the **correlation** of the assets in the portfolio. Correlation measures how the returns of two stocks move relative to each other and is a standardized measure that ranges from -1 (perfect negative correlation) to $+1$ (perfect positive correlation).[9] Perfect positive correlation means the returns of two stocks follow identical patterns in the percent change in their returns, and perfect negative correlation means identical return patterns in the percent change in their returns but with the opposite sign.

If a portfolio is formed of two stocks with exactly the same pattern of returns (this is one example of perfect positive correlation), the portfolio return pattern is the same as either stock and no risk reduction occurs (see Figure 7-6).[10] On the other hand, if a portfolio of two stocks is formed with the exact same pattern but with changes in the opposite direction (this is one example of perfect negative correlation), the return pattern of the portfolio is a straight line and risk has been eliminated (see, Figure 7-7). In reality, the correlation between most pairs of stock returns varies between 0.2 and 0.8; therefore, risk can be reduced, but not eliminated, through diversification.

Diversification occurs when portfolios are formed from stocks that are not highly positively correlated. A portfolio is said to be well-diversified when it eliminates company-specific risk and, in today's financial market with the vast array of available stock mutual funds, holding a well-diversified portfolio is both cheap and easy. In a market where it is cheap and easy to be well-diversified, will investors be compensated for the total risk of a stock? Will they be compensated only for the market risk of the stock? The answer is that the investor is compensated only for the market risk of the stock, because the assumption is

---

[9] The correlation of two stock is usually denoted as $\rho\{r_a, r_b\}$ and is calculated as follows:

$$\rho\{r_a, r_b\} = \frac{Cov(r_a, r_b)}{\sigma_a \sigma_b},$$

where σ_a and σ_b are the standard deviation of the returns of stocks a and b and

$$Cov(r_a, r_b) = \frac{\sum_{t=1}^{n}(r_{a,t} - \overline{r_a})(r_{b,t} - \overline{r_b})}{(n-2)}.$$

[10] Perfect positive correlation occurs when the percent change in the returns of two stocks are identical. This statement is different from saying the two stocks have an identical pattern of returns, as in Figure 7-6. With identical patterns, no risk reduction is possible from forming a portfolio. However, when two stocks have perfect positive correlation but not identical return patterns, risk reduction is possible by forming a portfolio of the two stocks. The problem with forming a portfolio of two perfectly positively correlated stocks is that by adding the lower risk stock to the portfolio to reduce risk, a linear reduction in portfolio returns occurs. However, when a portfolio of two stocks that are not perfectly positively correlated is formed, as the lower risk stock is added to the portfolio to reduce risk, reduction in portfolio return is not linear. In fact, as positive correlation declines, portfolio returns decline at a slower rate as the lower risk stock is added to the portfolio. Correlation and portfolio risk is revisited in more detail in Chapter 15.

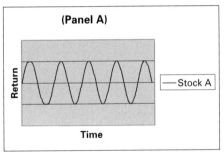

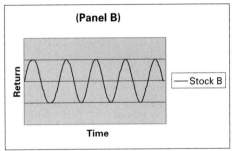

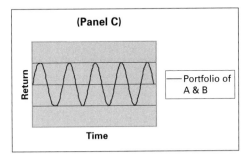

FIGURE 7-6 Effect on return of combining two perfectly positively correlated stocks in a portfolio.

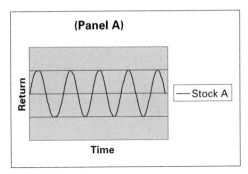

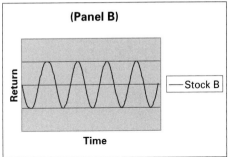

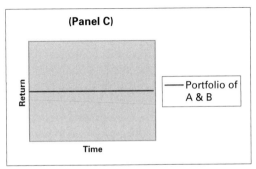

FIGURE 7-7 Effects on return of combining two perfectly negatively correlated stocks in a portfolio.

that the investor is rational and thus will eliminate company-specific risk since that risk can be eliminated at almost no cost to the investor. Remember, there are no "free lunches" in the stock market. The market will not compensate investors for risk that can be eliminated at almost no cost.

7.4.2 Diversification with Mutual Funds

Mutual funds provide a cheap and easy method for investors to diversify. Currently, there are more than 6,200 different mutual funds, which is more than the number of stocks listed on the New York Stock Exchange. Given the popularity of mutual funds and their benefits toward diversification, investors must understand the basics of mutual funds. This subsection diverts from the development of the appropriate risk-adjusted discount for valuing stock to discuss the basics of mutual funds because mutual funds provide a simple method for diversification. After this subsection on mutual funds the discussion returns to the development of the risk-adjusted discount in the next section with a discussion of beta.

A mutual fund is an investment company that uses the funds contributed by hundreds, if not thousands of small investors and invests that money in a diversified portfolio of assets. In general, there are three main types of mutual funds: stock or equity; bond or income; and money market. Stock mutual funds are the most popular.

An investor in a mutual fund buys shares of the fund where each share represents a proportional ownership in the underlying securities in the fund. As a result, the investor assumes the investment risk, including the possible loss of principal. Unlike bank deposits, mutual funds are *not* guaranteed by the Federal Deposit Insurance Corporation or any other government agency. Neither are they guaranteed by the bank or any financial institution regardless of how or where they are sold. Just like a straightforward investment in shares, the greater the investment risk, the greater the potential returns. However, all U.S. mutual funds are subject to strict regulation and oversight by the Securities and Exchange Commission. As part of this regulation, all mutual funds are required to provide investors with full and complete disclosure about the fund in a written prospectus. This document describes the funds investment objective, its investment methods, information about how to purchase and redeem shares, information about the investment advisors, and the level of risk the fund is willing to take on, among other things. The SEC also requires that the all fees and expenses are clearly outlined in the prospectus.

One primary advantage to investing in mutual funds comes from the professional management team that decides the investment strategy on behalf of the shareholders. The investment strategy is described in the prospectus for each fund. Types of mutual funds based on investment strategy include: tax-exempt funds; U.S. Treasury funds; small-capitalization funds; growth funds; value funds; equity income funds; and science and technology funds. The managers of the funds are usually professionals with years of investing experience. They engage in extensive market research and financial analysis of the performance of individual firms. As a result, it is not unusual to see that the funds can and will adjust their mix of investments to become more aggressive or more defensive as economic conditions change.

A second main advantage for a small investor to investing in mutual funds comes from the ability to benefit from the advantages of a diversified portfolio. Mutual funds are an economical way for average investors to attain the same kind of professional money management and diversification that is available to large institutions and wealthy investors.

Mutual funds calculate the price of their shares as of the end of every business day. Investors can then sell some or all of their shares and receive this current share price, which may be more or less than the price they originally paid for the shares. The share price of a mutual fund is called the *net asset value* (NAV) and is the market value of all the fund's securities minus expenses divided by the total number of shares outstanding. The NAV is published in major newspapers on a daily basis.

When a fund earns a return on its portfolio, it distributes these earnings to the shareholders as dividends or, if the investments have been sold at a profit, the earnings are distributed as capital gains. The distributions to the shareholders are treated in the same fashion as dividends or capital gains from any other investments for tax purposes. If the overall value of the mutual fund increases, then the individual mutual fund share values increase and thus, an investor with a $1,000 investment earns the same rate of return as an investor with a $10,000 investment.

All fees and expenses are charged directly against a mutual fund's earnings before distribution to the investor, which reduces the investor's return. The most common types of expenses (although not all funds charge all of the these fees) include: *a front-end sales charge or "load"* which can be attached to the investor's initial purchase of the fund's shares and is designed to compensate the financial professional for services rendered; *a contingent deferred sales charge* which is levied at the time of redemption and is an alternate way to reimburse the financial professional for the services rendered; *a redemption fee* which is another type of back end fee; and an *exchange fee* which is levied when the investor wishes to transfer funds from one type of mutual fund to another within the same mutual fund family. In addition, there are also *annual operating expenses* which are ongoing fees charged by the fund's investment advisor for managing the fund and selecting the portfolio of securities. Finally, there may be *12b-1 fees* that are charged by some funds to cover marketing and advertising expenses, which often include compensation to sales agents.

This brief detour into mutual funds was to provide the reader a basic understanding of features of this very popular investment tool. Now, the discussion returns to the development of the risk-adjusted discount rate for valuing stock with a discussion of beta.

7.4.3 Beta

Investors are assumed to be well-diversified and therefore are only compensated for bearing market risk. Bearing market risk is the only relevant risk for well-diversified investors. But a measure is still needed to quantify the exposure to market risk of a well-diversified investor and a method is needed to turn that measure into a risk-adjusted discount rate. This measure is known as **beta** (β) and the method for converting β into a risk-adjusted discount rate is the CAPM. This subsection will develop β and the next subsection will develop the CAPM.

Remembering that risk in stocks is relative price movement, then the risk in the market is relative changes in the value of the market. Since the compensation on an individual stock is based only on market risk, the relevant risk on an individual stock is its price movement relative to changes in the general market value. In other words, a measure similar to the correlation for a stock's movements relative to market movements is needed. Our measure

Company	Beta (from 5/04)
Best Buy	2.338
Microsoft	1.620
Citigroup	1.387
Ford	1.293
Neiman Marcus	1.263
Kohl's	1.088
Wal-Mart	0.811
Sears	0.561
Campbell Soup	0.441
Eli Lilly	0.391

FIGURE 7-8 Betas of selected stocks.

of a stock's price changes relative to changes in market value, beta (β), is calculated as follows:

$$\beta_j = \frac{Cov(r_j, r_m)}{\sigma_m^2}, \tag{7-9}$$

where j represents an individual stock and m represents the market.

The market β equals 1. Why? Because the covariance of the market with itself is its variance! Then when a stock β equals 1, the stock has the same risk as the general market. In other words, the stock returns mirror the general market's change in value. A stock β greater than 1 means that the stock's price changes in the same direction as the change in market value and the stock return is larger than the market return. That is, the stock is more risky than the market. A stock β less than 1 means the stock's price changes less than the market and thus is less risky than the market.[11] Figure 7-8 provides stock βs for some well-known firms.

7.4.4 CAPM

In this section, our measure of the relevant risk (β) is used to develop a method for determining a risk-adjusted discount rate for valuing stock. The method that will be developd is referred to as the capital asset pricing model (**CAPM**).

The development of the CAPM begins with a discussion of the reward/risk ratio for a stock. The reward/risk ratio is defined as

$$\text{reward/risk ratio for stock } j = \frac{E(r_j) - r_f}{\beta_j}, \tag{7-10}$$

where

$E(r_j) =$ the expected return of stock j,

$r_f =$ the risk-free rate.

---

[11] Recall, that most stocks have correlation coefficients between 0.2 and 0.8, which means that the price changes are in the same direction. A positive correlation requires a positive covariance (*Cov*). Thus, while it is mathematically possible to have a negative β, this fact is almost never observed in practice. Accordingly, a common and reasonable assumption is that β is positive ($\beta > 0$).

In an efficient market, the reward/risk ratio for each stock must be the same. That is, with the common measure of the relevant risk (β), the reward for each unit of risk must be the same for each and every stock. This statement is a very important point. It does not state that all stocks have the same risk nor does it state that all stocks provide that same reward. Both of these statements are clearly not true. It says that the reward $[E(r_j) - r_f]$ expected from each stock per unit of risk is the same. Two facts have to be noted here. First, the only concern that is important is the amount of risk the security contributes to the investor's portfolio. There is no concern about whether the company sells automobiles or loaves of bread because risk is measured relative to the portfolio. Second, the price (reward per unit of risk) of risk must be identical across securities, otherwise an investor could, for example, buy a share of automobile systematic risk and sell a share of bakery systematic risk, or vice versa, and make a profit.

Assuming the market portfolio contains all available stocks, the reward/risk ratio for the market portfolio must equal the reward/risk ratio for an individual stock. This relationship is described as:

$$\frac{E(r_j) - r_f}{\beta_j} = \frac{E(r_m) - r_f}{\beta_m}. \tag{7-11}$$

Then, remembering the market beta equals 1 ($\beta_m = 1$), the following formula is arrived at by solving Equation (7-11) for the expected return on stock j.

$$E(r_j) = r_f + (E(r_m) - r_f)\beta_j. \tag{7-12}$$

Equation (7-12) is the CAPM. A graph of the CAPM results in a straight line referred to as the **security market line** (SML). Figure 7-9 depicts the SML and the powerful features of the CAPM. The important concepts that come from the CAPM are

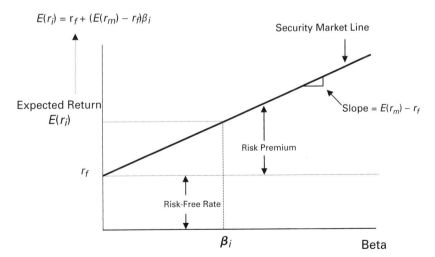

FIGURE 7-9 The security market line.

1. the expected return of a risky security equals the risk-free rate plus a risk premium,

2. the risk premium equals the market risk premium $[E(r_m) - r_f]$ times the security's market (systematic) risk measure, and

3. the security's market risk measure is β, which measures the security's correlation with the market.

The CAPM provides the expected return on a risky security. This is the return an investor would expect from the security. It therefore is an appropriate risk-adjusted discount rate for calculating the (r) in the stock valuation formulas.

7.5 STOCK VALUATION EXAMPLES

Now that you have the necessary tools to value stock, we will show you how to calculate the price of two publicly traded stocks. (IBM and Cisco). IBM is a well-established company with a long history of paying a regular dividend. Cisco is a relatively new technology company that has never paid a dividend. The data for the two companies were collected from the Yahoo! Finance website and is reported in Figure 7-10. The additional data needed for the CAPM were collected from the websites of Standard and Poor's and the Federal Reserve's Board of Governors.[12]

The process will begin by estimating the stock price for IBM. Since IBM pays a regular dividend, the first step is to determine which model for dividends to use: no growth, constant growth, or nonconstant growth. A look at IBM's dividend history shows a steady but small increase in dividends over the last six years; therefore, IBM fits the assumptions for the constant growth in dividends model. Next the risk-adjusted discount rate for IBM needs to be calculated and then the pricing model will be pursued.

The CAPM will be used to calculate the risk-adjusted discount rate. To calculate the CAPM, the following facts are needed: (1) the risk-free rate, (2) the expected return on the market portfolio, and (3) β. The risk-free rate is the current return on a riskless asset. The current rate of return (yield) on a four-week Treasury bill is used to proxy for the risk-free rate. This security is used as our proxy for the riskless asset because it is default free and has the lowest amount of interest rate risk of any available instrument. The current rate of return on four-month Treasury bills is 0.87%. For the expected return on the market portfolio the common practice is to use historical returns from a major stock index. A popular index is the S&P 500 and this index is the one chosen to proxy for the market portfolio. Over the past 10 years, the average annual return on the S&P 500 is 11.36%.[13] Finally, IBM's β needs to be determined. Figure 7-10 shows that β equals 1.45. Therefore, our estimate of the risk-adjusted discount rate for IBM using the CAPM is

$$E(r) = 0.87\% + (11.36\% - 0.87\%) \times 1.45 = 16.1\%.$$

---

[12] The Web addresses used are http://finance.yahoo.com/, http://www.bog.frb.fed.us/releases/, and http://www.spglobal.com/statstotalret.html.

[13] The return used to proxy for the market return should reflect what investors expect for market performance in the future, and the recent past is typically used as the proxy. However, for this example the recent past has been a very unusual period in the stock markets, so we chose to use a fairly long horizon for S&P 500 performance to reflect historical averages.

Data description	IBM	Cisco
Current price	$87.48	$21.65
Earnings growth, last five years.	1.9%	7.3%
Earnings growth, current year	14.1%	20.0%
Earnings growth (estimated), next five years	10.0%	15.0%
EPS	$4.48	$0.61
Beta (β)	1.45	2.20
Current annual dividend	$0.70	No current or past dividends
Dividend yield	0.83%	na
Annual dividend history		
2003	$0.63	na
2002	$0.59	na
2001	$0.55	na
2000	$0.51	na
1999	$0.47	na
1998	$0.43	na
1997	$0.39	na

FIGURE 7-10 Data used for estimating the stock price of IBM and Cisco (May 2004).

Next, to be able to use the constant growth in dividends formula, the growth rate in IBM's dividends needs to be estimated. Using the dividend history from 1997 for IBM, the average annual growth rate is 8.32%.[14] Applying the constant growth formula, the price estimate for IBM is

$$P_0 = \frac{D_1}{(r-g)} = \frac{\$0.70(1+0.0832)}{(0.161-0.0832)} = \$9.75.$$

Our price estimate is considerably less than the current market price of $87.48. Several reasons could account for the discrepancy in the estimated price. Given that the dividend yield for IBM is 0.83% the error could well be the assumption that dividends alone capture the future cash flow stream of an investor in IBM. To address this possibility, IBM's price will be estimated using the EPS growth formula (Equation 7-8).

The data in Figure 7-10 suggest that IBM's earnings will grow 14.1% this year and 10.0% for each of the following five years. With the growth rate over the next five years being less than the discount rate, the constant growth formula can be applied. Using this formula, the price estimate for IBM is

$$P_0 = \frac{EPS_0}{r} + \frac{(EPS_1 - EPS_0)}{(r-g)} = \frac{\$4.48}{0.161} + \frac{(\$4.48(1+0.141) - \$4.48)}{(0.161-0.10)} = \$38.19.$$

[14] The average annual growth rate in dividends can be calculated using the formula for the future value of a single cash flow, which is $FV_t = PV(1+g)^t$. Then, using IBM's dividend history, the growth rate formula is $\$0.63 = \$.39(1+g)^6$. Solving for g provides a growth rate of 8.32%.

This price estimate is considerably higher than the price estimate using the constant growth in dividends, but it is still not close to the current market price of $87.48. This suggests that the price estimates are missing important components of IBM's future growth opportunities and emphasizes the difficulties of pricing stocks even when valuing a well-known company. The solution to the problem is better estimates of IBM's future growth, and better estimates cannot be found in summary numbers like EPS. Instead, a detailed analysis of IBM's future growth opportunities is needed.

Now, take a look at Cisco. Cisco currently does not pay a dividend nor has Cisco ever paid a dividend. This means that one of the EPS formulas must be used to determine Cisco's stock price. In choosing which formula to use, the first step must be to calculate the risk-adjusted discount rate for Cisco. Using the CAPM data from the example with IBM and Cisco's β of 2.20, Cisco's risk-adjusted discount rate is

$$E(r) = r_f + (E(r_m) - r_f) \times \beta = 0.87\% + (11.36\% - 0.87\%) \times 2.20 = 23.95\%.$$

Since Cisco's earnings growth for the next five years (15%) is less than the risk-adjusted discount rate, the constant growth formula will be used. Using the constant growth formula, the estimated price for Cisco is

$$P = \frac{EPS_0}{r} + \frac{(EPS_1 - EPS_0)}{(r - g)} = \frac{\$0.61}{0.2395} + \frac{(\$0.61(1 + 0.20) - \$0.61)}{(0.2395 - 0.15)} = \$3.91.$$

Given the current price is $21.65, the estimate is not very close and again raises the question of what went wrong? Remembering that the second term of the pricing equation values future growth opportunities, the undervaluation suggests that in the dynamic world of tech stocks, EPS growth does not adequately capture the future opportunities available to a company like Cisco. As with IBM, a detailed analysis of Cisco's future opportunities is required to correctly calculate Cisco's stock price.[15]

SUMMARY OF VALUATION AND RISK MANAGEMENT SKILLS

1. Understand the institutional features of stock markets.

The primary equity market is the market for the original sale of the stock. In the primary market the proceeds of the sale go to the issuing firm. The secondary equity markets are resale markets. In a primary market offer, the investment banker serves as either the marketer of the offer or the underwriter of the offer. As an underwriter, the investment banker purchases the entire offer from the issuing firm and then resells the offer to the public. The NYSE is an exchange with a physical location. Trades on

---

[15] Given the need to work with earnings forecasts when valuing stocks, we recommend the reader examine Hong and Kubik (2003). Their abstract is as follows:

> We examine security analysts' career concerns by relating their earnings forecasts to job separations. Relatively accurate forecasters are more likely to experience favorable career outcomes like moving up to a high-status brokerage house. Controlling for accuracy, analysts who are optimistic relative to the consensus are more likely to experience favorable job separations. For analysts who cover stocks underwritten by their houses, job separations depend less on accuracy and more on optimism during the recent stock market mania. Brokerage houses apparently reward optimistic analysts who promote stocks.

the NYSE occur through an auction. The NASDAQ is a dealer network with trades occurring at the best bid and ask price on the network. A dealer network does not have a physical location.

2. Understand the various methods available for valuing stock and be able to use each method to determine the value of a stock.

The price of a stock is the present value of all the future cash flows the investor expects to receive from the stock. The difficulty of pricing stock is in identifying all the future cash flows and the appropriate discount rate. Historically, stocks were valued based on its expected future dividend stream. Today, however, many stocks do not pay dividends. But, for the stocks that do pay dividends, in many cases the dividend is a very small portion of the total annual return. Under the current market conditions, pricing a stock based on its future EPS may be more appropriate.

3. Understand the CAPM (capital asset pricing model) and be able to use it to calculate the appropriate risk-adjusted discount rate for a stock.

The total risk for a stock is measured by the standard deviation of the stock's returns. Total risk decomposes into market risk and company-specific risk. Company-specific risk can be eliminated through diversification. Accordingly, investors in the stock market are only compensated for bearing market risk. Market risk is measured with β. The CAPM uses β to calculate the risk-adjusted expected return for a stock. This expected return is the appropriate risk-adjusted discount rate for calculating the present value of a stock's future cash flows when calculating the price of a stock.

QUESTIONS

1. Describe the function of a primary market. Describe the difference between an IPO and a seasoned equity offer.

2. Describe the process of underwriting a public stock offering. Who bears the selling risk in an underwritten offer?

3. Figure 7-2 shows that in 1999 the closing price after the first day of trading of an IPO is often substantially higher than the offer price. Why should this concern the firm that issued the stock? What is the problem in the market if the price almost always goes up on the first day? Explain.

4. Estimate the price of a preferred stock with a semiannual dividend of $1.20 and a risk-adjusted annual discount rate of 10%.

5. Estimate the price of a common stock with the following characteristics:

   a. Pays a regular annual dividend,
   b. Just paid a dividend of $1.21,
   c. Dividends have been growing at a constant annual rate of 4% which is expected to continue,
   d. The appropriate risk-adjusted discount rate is 9.25%.

6. Using the data from Question 5, estimate the price of the stock if the $1.21 dividend is paid semiannually.

7. What is the appropriate discount rate for a company's common stock if the stock's β equals 1.24? Assume that the risk-free rate is 3.5% and the expected return on the market is 12%.

8. It is projected that a firm's next four annual dividends will be $0.50, $1.00, $1.50, and $1.75. After the fourth dividend, dividends are expected to grow at a constant annual rate of 7%. Assuming that the required rate of return for the stock is 16%, what is your estimate of the stock's price?

9. If a company does not pay a dividend, how would you estimate a share price for its common stock?

10. Estimate the stock price of a company with the following information:

a. The company does not pay a dividend and will not in the future,
b. Current EPS is $1.75 and EPS is expected to grow at a constant annual rate of 10%,
c. The appropriate discount rate for this stock is 14.25%.

11. When estimating the price of a share of common stock, a risk-adjusted discount rate is used. Explain why it is important to make sure that the discount rate is risk adjusted.

12. Diversification is the process of reducing risk through forming a portfolio. Describe the risk that can be eliminated through diversification and the risk that cannot.

13. Define correlation and explain why it is the driving force behind diversification.

14. Explain why the market only provides compensation for bearing market risk.

15. What does β measure and why is β an appropriate measure of the market risk of a stock?

16. If company A provides 4 units of expected return and has 1 unit of market risk while company B provides 10 units of expected return and has 2 units of market risk, which company's stock would you prefer to own? What condition is necessary for you to be indifferent between the two stocks?

17. You are interested in investing in a dot.com stock and have found one that looks promising. You estimate its share price using Equation (7-7). Your estimate for the share price is $50. You look up the market price and find that the market price is $125. Assuming that you applied Equation (7-7) correctly, what can you conclude about the market price?

REFERENCES

AKDOGAN, H., 1996, A suggested approach to country selection in international portfolio diversification, *Journal of Portfolio Management, Fall*, 33–39.
  Akdogan provides a nice framework for discussing international diversification. He discusses market integration versus market segmentation and then suggests that international diversification depends on the degree of segmentation.

BOWER, R., and D. BOWER, 1969, Risk and the valuation of common stock, *Journal of Political Economy*, 77, 349–362.
  This paper provides an early discussion of the pricing of common stock as it presently appears in most textbooks. The authors state that the differences between stock prices depend on differences in (1) earnings growth rates, (2) dividend payout rates, and (3) the risk-adjusted discount rate.

CHEN, S., and A. KEOWN, 1981, Risk decomposition and portfolio diversification when Beta is nonstationary: A note, *Journal of Finance*, 36, 941–947.
  The authors revisit the empirical result that βs are nonstationary in Ordinary Least Squares regressions and show that the nonstationarity of β results in an overestimation of a security's unsystematic risk in OLS regressions. They also show that true unsystematic risk and nonstationarity of β risk are both diversified away in a portfolio of 30 randomly selected stocks.

DEGENNARO, R., and S. KIM, 1986, The CAPM and beta in an imperfect market: Comment, *Journal of Portfolio Management, Summer*, 78–79.
  The authors use the General CAPM with market imperfections to explain the role of financial intermediaries, in this case pension funds and mutual funds. The intermediaries allow small investors access to more assets and thus make their portfolios more mean/variance efficient.

HONG, H., and J. KUBIK, 2003, Analyzing the analysts: Career concerns and biased earning forecasts, *Journal of Finance*, 58, 313–352.
  The authors examine the accuracy of analysts' earnings forecast and how the analysts' forecasts relate to career advancement. They find that accuracy is rewarded with career

advancement. However, after controlling for accuracy they find that optimism was rewarded and this is especially true if the stocks covered by the analyst are underwritten by the analyst's brokerage house.

JAGANNATHAN, R., and E. McGRATTAN, 1995, The CAPM debate, *Federal Reserve Bank of Minneapolis-Quarterly Review, Fall*, 2–17.

The authors provide a nice summary on the ongoing debate about whether the CAPM β describes expected returns or whether firm size and the market-to-book value ratio do a better job. They conclude that, on average, the CAPM provides information about risky expected returns.

LINTER, J., 1965, The valuation of risk assets and the selection of risky investments in stock portfolios and capital budgets, *Review of Economics and Statistics, 47*, 13–37.

This is Linter's version of the CAPM which was developed independently of Sharpe's CAPM and published shortly thereafter.

MARKOWITZ, H., 1952, Portfolio selection, *Journal of Finance, 7*, 77–91.

This is the paper that develops the efficient frontier where investors trade off expected returns and variance.

POON, S., J. TAYLOR, and C. WARD, 1992, Portfolio diversification: A pictorial analysis of the UK stock market, *Journal of Business Finance & Accounting, 19*, 87–101.

The authors provide three-dimensional plots of portfolio mean/variance combinations for various numbers of securities in the portfolio. This presents a very nice visual of the effects of diversification.

POZEN, Robert C., 1999, *The Mutual Fund Business*, The MIT Press, Cambridge MA.

This is an excellent book on all the details of mutual funds.

SHARPE, W., 1964, Capital asset prices: A theory of market equilibrium under conditions of risk, *Journal of Finance, 19*, 425–442.

This paper is the original published article on the CAPM.

SHARPE, W., 1972, Risk, market sensitivity and diversification, *Financial Analysts Journal, January/February*, 74–79.

Sharpe provides a clear, common sense discussion of market risk, nonmarket risk, and diversification.

TREYNOR, J., 1993, In defense of the CAPM, *Financial Analysts Journal, May/June*, 11–13.

Treynor describes how the arbitrage pricing theory (APT) violates neither the assumptions nor conclusions of the CAPM.

KEY TERMS

Beta (β) Beta is a measure of how the returns of a security vary relative to the returns of the market. Beta measures the relevant risk of a security for a well-diversified investor.

CAPM CAPM stands for the capital asset pricing model, which provides a risk-adjusted expected return based on a stock's β.

Common Stock Common stock owners have the residual claim on the firm's earnings and assets. Common stock has voting rights and the common stockholders' responsibility is to oversee the operations of the firm.

Constant Rate Assumption The constant rate assumption for valuing common stock means that we are assuming that dividends will grow (increase) at a constant rate forever.

Correlation Correlation measures how returns of two securities change relative to each other. Correlation is a component of the diversification process.

Dealer Network A dealer network is a group of dealers that work together to trade securities. The best known dealer network for trading securities is NASDAQ.

Diversification Diversification is the process of adding securities to a portfolio to reduce the portfolio's standard deviation.

Dividend A dividend is a cash distribution paid by the company to its stockholders. Dividends are not automatic. Instead, dividends occur when declared by the board of directors. The amount of the dividend is also determined by the board.

EPS EPS is earnings per share. EPS is calculated by dividing net income by the number of shares of common stock outstanding.

Exchange An exchange is a common location for trading. This term usually means a physical location for trading securities, such as the New York Stock Exchange and the Chicago Mercantile Exchange.

Initial Public Offer An initial public offer (IPO) occurs the first time a company offers its stock for sale to the public.

Marketer An investment banker is referred to as the marketer of an offer when the investment banker makes a "best effort" to sell or market the issue to the public.

Mutual Fund A professionally managed portfolio that allows investors to buy shares in the fund.

No Growth in Dividends Assumption The "no growth" assumption for valuing common stock means that the assumption is made that dividends will not grow (increase). This assumption results in a dividend stream that is a perpetuity.

Nonconstant Rate Assumption   The nonconstant rate assumption is that dividends are growing at a very high rate that cannot be sustained in the long run.

Over-the-Counter   Over-the-counter (OTC) trading is trading with a single dealer. Trading over-the-counter may not provide the best price because the price that the individual receives is based upon the dealer's need or desire for the security.

Preferred Stock   Preferred stock is stock that provides its owners with a prior (preferred) claim to the firm's earnings and assets relative to common stock owners. Preferred stock owners generally do not receive voting rights on firm operations.

Primary Market   A primary market is a market for the original sale of a security.

Seasoned Offer   A seasoned offer occurs when a company with stock already publicly traded offers new shares for sale to the public.

Secondary Market   A secondary market is the resale market for securities. This is where investors trade securities.

Secondary Offer   A secondary offer is the first offer of shares to the public of a company that was owned by a government.

Security Market Line   The security market line (SML) is a plot of the CAPM.

Systematic Risk   Systematic risk is the portion of risk in a portfolio that cannot be eliminated through diversification. Systematic risk is also called nondiversifiable risk or market risk.

Total Risk   Total risk is the risk associated with a change in the value of a security or portfolio. Total risk is measured by standard deviation.

Underwriter   An underwriter is an investment banker that buys a securities offer from the issuing firm and then resells the securities to the public.

Unsystematic Risk   Unsystematic risk is the risk that can be eliminated through diversifying a portfolio. Unsystematic risk is also called diversifiable risk or company-specific risk.

CHAPTER 8

FOREIGN EXCHANGE MARKETS

8.1 INTRODUCTION

The foreign exchange market is a highly efficient global market for the exchange of currency. The assets of interest are the different currencies available around the world. However, because currency (cash) is a nonearning asset, the value of currency will *not* be discussed in terms of the present value of its future cash flows. Instead, we will discuss the factors that determine the rate at which traders are willing to exchange one currency for another (the exchange rate) and why that exchange would take place.

At first glance, this approach may seem strange to the reader given the strong interest in international investment and the increased emphasis on an international component to business school education. However, from a financial prospective, the decision to invest is made in the same manner regardless of what country the investor resides in. That is, the value of an asset is the present value of its future cash flows regardless of whether the cash flows are in a foreign currency or U.S. dollars; and the discount rate is based on the riskiness of the cash flows. Therefore, those issues do not need to be revisited here. Instead, the assumption will be made that the companies doing international investing have done their homework and have determined that the investment has a positive NPV. Therefore, the chapter will be on exchanging foreign cash flows for domestic cash flows. In other words, this chapter is about the foreign currency exchange markets and how the exchange rate between two currencies is determined.

Even though the discussion of this chapter will not include the investment decision, the reader should not assume that exchange rates are not a very important topic. In fact, a country's exchange rate is an important topic because a country's exchange rate represents the global investors' average expectations on how the country is run, the soundness of its monetary and fiscal policies, its political stability, and its future prospects. To provide an example of the importance of exchange rates, Figure 8-1 summarizes the reasons behind and the effect of a major foreign exchange rate decline in Zimbabwe.

The point of the Zimbabwe example is that many factors affect a country's exchange rate. This chapter discusses how these factors affect exchange rates. This chapter begins with a discussion of why cash flows cross national boundaries. This is followed with a discussion of spot and forward exchange rates. The spot and forward exchange rates are analogous to the spot and forward interest rates discussed in Chapter 3. Market participants determine exchange rates based on the supply and demand for a country's currency, and the discussion of the factors that influence the supply and the demand for a currency is the next topic covered in this chapter. Finally, the chapter discusses parity conditions in the currency exchange markets. The parity conditions define when an exchange rate correctly fits existing market conditions and, perhaps more importantly, when exchange rates do not

Background to the Food Riots

1997 was a year in which expectations of dynamic growth were replaced by a disappointing performance and increasing pessimism about future prospects. Earlier in the year, excessive rains reduced agricultural output, even though the rains replenished the reservoirs that had run dry due to successive years of drought. Both in dependent analysts and the Government were projecting an economic growth rate of up to 5% for 1997.

The growth projections for 1997 were soon revised downwards, with the Reserve Bank of Zimbabwe (RBZ) estimating it at 4.5%, and other analysts were estimating that the growth rate could be below 3%. The modest recovery in 1996 was too fragile to withstand the increases in taxes, interest rates and inflation that took effect in the middle of 1997. Increases in Government- administered prices to meet spending requirements triggered inflation, that soon ran at over 20%.

The major factors that destroyed confidence in the year were the Government's decision to award excombatants compensation totaling Z$4.5 billion, followed by the expropriation of more than 1,500 large-scale commercial farms [roughly one-third of the country's largest and most productive farms]. The loss in confidence resulted in the country's currency plunging by as much as 75% against most major currencies. The spread between buy and sell rates in the money market reached 73%. The RBZ subsequently increased its rediscount [bank] rate from 28.5% to 31.5% to reduce downward speculative pressures on the Zimbabwe dollar. Unfortunately, the high interest rates made it impossible for companies to occurs the needed money for expansion purposes and drained away a large proportion of the working capital of private sector employers. Increased interest payments severely limited employers' abilities to keep pace with inflation.

The Government, already under siege from war veterans demanding gratuities and pensions, was suddenly engulfed by a crisis of expectations from all fronts: in addition to the veterans, the war collaborators and former political detainees also wanted reparations. The huge civil service was waiting patiently for its annual year-end bonuses, and Western donors were demanding that the Government take visible measures to cut back on its spending if it wanted foreign aid for its reforms, already delayed by lack of funding.

The Government's immediate concern was to find an estimated Z$3 to Z$5 billion before Christmas 1997, to make lump sum gratuity payments to ex-combatants, who had only stopped their violent nation-wide protests earlier in the year after securing government pledges for the payments.

The demands by the veterans could not have come at a worse time; the Government was battling to cut the fiscal deficit while at the same time boosting expenditure on social services such as health and education. The Government was under pressure from foreign aid donors to maintain its target of achieving a budget deficit of 8.9 percent of the Gross Domestic Product.

This lead to a nation-wide civil protest against the tax increases. Analysts observed that the failure by the Government to arrest the economic decline and to address the unemployment crisis had combined to create an explosive situation. Left unchecked, the riots could erupt into social chaos that could seriously challenge the Government's political grip on the country and also force the Government to introduce draconian measures to curb civil liberties.

During 1997, waves of strikes swept the nation as workers fought to ensure wages high enough to keep them above the poverty line. Most workers were demanding wage increases of up to 40 percent. Zimbabwe's poorly paid farm laborers also launched a wave of strikes that brought the country's commercial farming sector to its knees. The countryside was hit by two weeks of work stoppages. Thousands of workers blocked highways for days, in the biggest disruption to large-scale farming since independence in 1980.

In December 1997, the Government announced that it would introduce sweeping cost-cutting measures in the public service during 1998. The measures included a reduction in salary increases and the abolition and/or revision of perks and allowances for senior state officials. The Government was forced to withdraw the tax increases and the five percent war veterans' levy.

FIGURE 8-1 A consolidated report on the Food Riots of 19–23 January, 1998.

Source: Report compiled by the AMANI Trust on behalf of the Zimbabwe Human Rights NGO Forum[1].

---

[1] This report was drawn from a consolidated report on the Food Riots 19–23 January 1998 prepared by the AMANI Trust on behalf of the Zimbabwe Human Rights NGO Forum. It is available online at www.hrforumzim.com/genreps/foodriots98/food9801bl.htm.

fit existing market conditions and an opportunity for arbitrage profits exists. This section of the chapter provides specific examples of arbitrage opportunities in the currency exchange markets.

DEVELOPING VALUATION AND RISK MANAGEMENT SKILLS

1. Understand why cash flows cross country boundaries and how supply and demand for a currency affects the currency's exchange rate.
2. Calculate forward exchange rates from spot exchange rates.
3. Examine the parity conditions to determine when arbitrage opportunities exist and how to take advantage of the opportunities.

8.2 REASONS FOR AND RISK OF INTERNATIONAL CASH FLOWS

There are three primary reasons for international cash flows. The reasons for these cash flows are stated in the description of the cash flows. The three types of international cash flows are (1) investment cash flows, (2) political cash flows, and (3) speculative cash flows. In this section, each of the three international cash flows will be discussed.

8.2.1 Investment Cash Flows

International **investment cash flows** are what the name implies. These investment cash flows are cash flows into a foreign country for the purpose of acquiring a real or financial asset. That is, these cash flows exist because of the desire to make an investment in a foreign asset.

The decision to invest in any asset is determined by the present value of the future cash flows generated by the asset. Once the asset is purchased, the investor faces the usual risks associated with owning a real or financial asset. However, an additional risk is associated with a foreign investment. The risk is known as **foreign exchange risk**, which occurs when revenues are earned in one currency and expenses are paid in another currency.

An investor acquires an asset for the cash flows that the asset will generate for the investor. This reason for investing (acquiring) is the same whether the asset is a foreign or domestic asset. However, the general assumption is that the investor ultimately desires domestic cash flows. Therefore, with a foreign investment, the investor must convert the foreign cash flows into domestic currency. This action exposes the investor to changes in the exchange rate. This exposure is the foreign exchange risk.

Managing foreign exchange risk has both a short-term and a long-term component. In the short term, investors are concerned about having to convert specific cash flows to their domestic currency at an unfavorable exchange rate. Short-term foreign exchange risk can be managed through hedging with forward contracts. This will be briefly discussed later in this chapter and thoroughly discussed in the chapter on forward and future contracts (Chapter 9). In the long term, investors are concerned about earning the appropriate risk-adjusted return on their investment. The parity (equilibrium) conditions for the foreign exchange market function so that investors will earn, on average, a fair risk-adjusted return on a foreign investment. The parity conditions will be discussed in detail later in this chapter.

8.2.2   Political Cash Flows

The second type of international cash flows is **political cash flows**. These cash flows are often referred to as capital flight. Unlike investment cash flows, which flow into a country, political cash flows generally flow out of a country. The reason for the outflow is political instability in a country.

Unstable governments are often unwilling or unable to protect property rights associated with real assets, which, in turn, can lead to the confiscation or destruction of assets. Since corporate securities (stock and bonds) are claims on the real assets of businesses, political instability interferes with investment in the country. Therefore, investor cash flows leave the unstable country for investment in a country where the investor has more confidence in the political system.

Political cash flows are not solely associated with a government's inability to protect business assets. They are also associated with the government's ability to service its own debt. U.S. investors often forget that the debts of national governments have risk because the U.S. government has always paid its debts. However, other national governments are not always as reliable. Non-U.S. national government debt has default risk. Therefore, non-U.S. investors looking for default-free investments transfer cash to the United States for investment in Treasury securities. This transfer to the United States for investment in U.S. government securities is a political cash flow.

To allow the investor to see the default risk of non-U.S. government debt, the non-U.S. government bonds are rated for default risk in the same manner as discussed for corporate bonds in Chapter 3. In Figure 8-2 some examples of country bond ratings from Moody's Investor Services (http://www.moodys.com) and Fitch Ratings (http://www.fitchratings.com) are provided. The examples show that these government bond ratings are fairly similar between these two rating agencies and that ratings are fairly stable across time. Only Argentina's bond rating had a major rating change between the two sets of ratings and that change was major downgrade. The downgrade in Argentina's bond rating followed an October 2001 announcement that the country would default on $38 billion of debt held by foreign investors.

Country	Bond rating	
	Moody's **January 2001**	**Fitch** **May 2004**
Argentina	B	DDD
Canada	Aa	AA
Ecuador	Caa	CCC
Egypt	Baa	BB
Germany	Aaa	AAA
Russia	B	BB
Poland	A	BB

FIGURE 8-2   Bond ratings for selected countries.

The discussion of political cash flows concerns why investors flee countries that have unstable governments. This fact may raise questions for the reader concerning the recent investments by U.S. corporations in Eastern Europe and Russia. These investments are examples where the investors (the U.S. corporations) believe the potential benefit of the investments outweigh the political risks.[2]

8.2.3 Speculative Cash Flows

The third and final type of international cash flows is **speculative cash flows**. Speculation is the bearing of risk in an investment for an expected profit, which usually means taking an investment position assuming the price will change in a manner to create a profit for the speculator. In international finance, a speculator often takes a position in a currency in anticipation of a change in that currency's exchange rate that will allow the speculator to make a profit.

EXAMPLE   *Speculative Profits from Exchanging Currencies*

Assume that the current exchange rate between the Swiss franc (SFr) and the U.S. dollar is 1.50 Swiss francs to $1 but a speculator believes that the exchange rate will change to SFr1.45 Swiss francs to $1. Assuming that the speculator has $1,000 to invest, the speculator will buy SFr1,500 in anticipation of the exchange rate change. If the exchange rate does change to SFr1.45 to $1, then the speculator will buy dollars using the SFr1,500. The speculator will receive (1/1.45 × 1,500) $1,034.48. This is a profit of $34.48 made by the transaction between currencies. However, the exchange rate could have just as easily changed in the other direction, which would have resulted in a loss to the speculator.

The preceding example shows why speculation is often referred to as betting on the direction of the market and why speculation is considered very risky. However, one situation exists for speculation in foreign exchange rates that may be less risky than a normal bet (speculation) on the movement of a market. Under current market standards, the foreign exchange market is a large, highly efficient market where the exchange rates are determined by the supply and demand for the different currencies. Thus, the exchange rates should fairly price each currency under the current market conditions. However, in today's financial environment, countries often talk about their currency being over- or undervalued. Since each currency's exchange rate is set by market supply and demand for that currency, the currency is unlikely to be over- or undervalued. Instead, the statement that a country's currency is over- or undervalued is a statement that the exchange rate is politically undesirable for the country's government.

When a government determines that its currency's exchange rate is undesirable, the government may decide to intervene in the foreign exchange market in an attempt to move its exchange rate to one that is more acceptable to the government. Governments have limited resources; therefore, any intervention in the foreign exchange market must be temporary. Since any such intervention is temporary, the intervention creates an opportunity for a foreign

---

[2] There are two additional reasons for the investments in international assets. First, foreign assets, especially in emerging economies, may provide higher rates of return than in the domestic mature economy. Second, foreign assets tend not to be highly correlated with domestic assets, thus leading to diversification benefits.

exchange speculator to make profits. The speculator anticipates that once the government is finished with its temporary intervention, the exchange rate will turn back toward the exchange rate that existed before the government intervention. Assuming this, the speculator will trade currencies during the government intervention period, and after the government finishes its market intervention will make a subsequent trade to create a profit.

8.3 EXCHANGE RATES

A currency **exchange rate** is the rate at which one currency converts into another. As mentioned earlier, the current market for currency exchange is a large, highly efficient market where the exchange rates are set by the supply and demand for each currency. However, the exchange rates have not always been determined by market forces. For example, from 1944 through 1971 the currency exchange market was governed by the Bretton Woods Agreement. This agreement set the U.S. dollar at $35 to 1 ounce of gold. All other currencies were set at a fixed exchange rate relative to the U.S. dollar. Also, every country agreed to intervene within the currency exchange market to maintain their currency within $\pm 1\%$ of its stated rate relative to the U.S. dollar. The Bretton Woods Agreement worked reasonably well until the United States had a major financial crisis in 1971. After the U.S. financial crisis of 1971 the Bretton Woods Agreement was abandoned.

After the Bretton Woods Agreement was abandoned, the currency exchange market evolved through several phases to its current state, which is freely floating, exchange rate blocs. Floating exchange rate blocs are blocs where sets of currencies are grouped together. There are not specific market rules for forming currency blocs. Currency blocs appear to be geographically defined. However, the blocs are created from economic relationships between a lead currency and some smaller currencies. Within a bloc there is a lead currency to which the other currencies tie their exchange rates. The relationship between the lead currency and the other currencies is fairly constant. Then, between lead currencies (and thus the blocs), the exchanges rates float freely based on market supply and demand for the lead currencies. This system allows the market to operate efficiently by letting supply and demand set the exchange rates for the lead currencies, at the same time providing an orderly system for the exchange of currencies of small countries.

There are two terms often used to discuss changes in exchange rates within the framework of the free-floating bloc system. These two terms are devaluation and depreciation. It is important to understand the difference between devaluation and depreciation because while both mean a currency went down in value, the terms provide very different reasons for the decline. In 1999, for example, the Brazilian real was devalued. The Brazilian real was set at a fixed rate to the U.S. dollar and devaluation means that the fixed rate the government used to value their currency was changed. Devaluation can occur for one of two reasons. One, the government resets their currency to a lower value relative to the fixed standard, or two, the government changes from a fixed to a floating exchange rate system and the value of the local currency falls. Depreciation, on the other hand, refers only to floating exchange rates and means that the value of the local currency has decreased relative to another currency. Given the floating exchange rate blocs seen today, the lead currency of a bloc may depreciate while the other currencies within the bloc can be devalued.

IN THE NEWS

DOLLARIZATION IN ECUADOR: DESPERATION MOVE?[3]

Ecuador's economic crisis is spilling over to a social and political crisis. The government is looking to dollarization of their currency in the year 2000 as a means of stabilizing their economy and creating confidence for both domestic and foreign investors. But this is a high-risk tool, as the country gives up its sovereignty over its monetary policy. Under Ecuador's dollarization plan, the dollar would almost completely replace the current local currency, the sucre.

Ecuador has faced erratic oil prices, capital flight, bank failures, international loan defaults, and devastating floods. Of Ecuador's 12 million people, some 5.1 million are considered impoverished by World Bank standards. Ecuador has had a half-dozen presidents in recent years. And in 1999, the sucre plunged from 7,000 to 25,000 to the U.S. dollar, resulting in skyrocketing prices. With prices constantly in flux, it has become difficult to do business for companies in Ecuador.

Emerging market economies, like Ecuador's, typically lose access to international capital markets during economic crises, and instead, are forced to rely on short-term debt financing. Those debts, often denominated in foreign currencies, are often called on short notice. Dollarization is considered a stabilizing mechanism to overcome a lack of access to capital markets, to repay dollar-denominated debt, and to lessen the swings of prices. For Ecuador, dollarization could help control inflation by removing Ecuador's ability to print money and by pegging its economy to the more stable U.S. dollar. But it will also limit the options of the country's Central Bank to deal with external shocks, such as a sudden fall in prices of oil, Ecuador's main export.

OPIC's inconvertibility insurance coverage can help reduce some of the risks associated with convertibility exposures, because it enables investors to protect their ability to convert profits, debt service, and other remittances from local currency into U.S. dollars and transfer those dollars out of the project's host country. OPIC is currently providing $94.5 million in support for projects in Ecuador, and those projects are expected to generate more than 1,200 jobs and nearly $5 million in government revenue. In addition, OPIC is working with U.S. businesses on 11 other projects worth $222 million in possible investment for the country. In spite of the difficult times it now faces, Ecuador has substantial oil resources and rich agricultural areas. As it works to get its fiscal house in order, OPIC stands ready to assist.

Dollarization in Ecuador

Pros . . .

- Reduces inflation by eliminating the ability to print excess money.
- Attracts investment and reduces capital flight by eliminating likelihood of currency devaluations.
- Reduces the cost of trading with the U.S. and other dollar-denominated trading, by eliminating the transaction costs associated with exchanging currency.

. . . Cons

- May cause havoc with the poor who still need smaller denominated currency.
- No guarantee to bring back confidence. In fact, it may set the stage for huge embarrassment if the country has to return to local currency.
- Dollarization is untested in Ecuador-type conditions.
- Lose control over monetary policy and thus the ability to deal with external shocks.
- Without other necessary reforms, could worsen economic crisis.

"Full dollarization, if credible, eliminates devaluation risk, and, consequently, will likely result in interest rates which are both lower and less sensitive to crisis in other countries. In other words, the incidence of contagion will diminish."

Guillermo Calvo, director of the Center for International Economics at the University of Maryland and former adviser to the International Monetary Fund, quoted in recent testimony before Congress; *The New York Times*, January 18, 2000.

(continued)

IN THE NEWS *(continued)*

DOLLARIZATION IN ECUADOR: DESPERATION MOVE?[3]

"Neither a currency board nor dollarization will serve up 'credibility in a bottle' without the necessary underlying institutions and political will."
Jeffrey Frankel, New Century Chair, The Brookings Institution, and Harpal Chair, Kennedy School of Government, Harvard University; *IMF Survey*, July 19, 1999.

"Any country that abolishes its own currency needs to have an ecomony that is strong and flexible enough to accommodate external shocks, since it cannot ride them out by printing money. Ecuador is not such a country."
"Ecuador Economy: Dollarization and Its Perils," The Economist Intelligence Unit Ltd., January 18, 2000.

8.3.1 Spot and Forward Exchange Rates

An exchange rate is the rate at which one currency converts into another. The timing of the exchange is negotiable between the trading parties and can occur either today or at some time in the future. An exchange, decided on and completed today, is referred to as a spot exchange and the rate of today's exchange is referred to as the **spot exchange rate**. An exchange at some point in the future is a forward exchange, with the rate of the exchange referred to as the **forward exchange rate.** For a forward exchange, the two trading parties enter into a contract that is called a forward contract. The forward contract will specify: (1) currencies to be exchanged, (2) the exchange rate, (3) the amount of one of the currencies in the exchange, and (4) the date of the exchange.

A forward exchange rate contract allows an investor to set the currency exchange rate for an international trade at some point in the future. For example, in July a U.S. corn farmer contracts to sell corn to a U.K. corn importer in October after the fall corn harvest. The contract specifies the amount of British pounds to be paid per bushel of corn. However, the farmer needs U.S. dollars to pay bills so the farmer will need to convert the British pounds paid for the corn into U.S. dollars. The farmer can wait until October and convert the pounds to dollars at the October (spot) exchange rate or the farmer can enter into a forward contract for exchange of pounds to dollars in October. The forward contract allows the farmer to set the amount of dollars per bushel of corn in July that the farmer will receive in October. This forward contract reduces the risk of the trade for the farmer and is the purpose of forward exchange rate contracts. Much more detail about forward contracts will be provided in the next chapter.

An important relationship exists between a spot exchange rate for two currencies and the forward exchange rates for the same currencies. In an efficient market, the forward rate must be an **unbiased predictor** of the future spot rate. That is, at the time the forward exchange rate is set, the forward rate is the market's best guess of the spot rate at the time in the future when the forward transaction will occur.

The farmer example is revisited to explain why forward rates must be unbiased predictors. First, if the farmer always gets a better exchange rate by waiting to do a spot transaction in October, the farmer will never enter into a forward contract and the contracts will cease

---

[3] Source: *OPICNews* is an electronic newsletter published by the Overseas Private Investment Corporation, 1100 New York Avenue, NW Washington, D.C. 20527, 202-336-8400, an Agency of the United States Government.

Currency	Symbol	Value/U.S. $1	
		6/20/01	5/14/04
Australian dollar	AUD	1.9357	1.4568
British pound	GBP	0.7083	0.5698
Canadian dollar	CAD	1.5283	1.3946
Euro	EUR	1.1715	0.8447
Japanese yen	JPY	124.1450	114.4950
Swiss franc	CHF	1.7818	1.3002

FIGURE 8-3 Spot exchange rates.

to exist. Second, if the farmer always get a better rate by using the forward contract, the farmer will always enter into a forward contract and so will everyone. The additional trading pressure will move the forward exchange rate. The rate will continue to move until it equals the expected future spot rate. Therefore, the forward rate must be an unbiased estimate of the future spot rate.

Spot rates and forward rates are reported daily in the *Wall Street Journal*. They are also available online from a variety of websites. For example, spot rates for most currencies are available at http://www.bloomberg.com (Bloomberg L.P.). Both spot and forward rates are available at http://www.bmo.com (Bank of Montreal). These websites need to be explored to develop an understanding of currency exchange rates. An example of the spot rates from Bloomberg is provided by Figure 8-3 and an example of forward rates from the Bank of Montreal is provided by Figure 8-4.

Attention should be paid to the facts in Figure 8-3 that from 2001 to 2004 the U.S. dollar converts to less foreign currency of every country. This shows an example of currency devaluation.

Figure 8-4 shows that the one-year (12 month) forward exchange rate is higher than the spot rate. Using 2001, the spot rate is 0.7083 British pounds (£) per U.S. dollar and the one-year forward rate is £0.7280 per U.S. dollar. What does this imply? It implies that the market is expecting that $1 will buy more British pounds in one year than it does today. In other words, the U.S. dollar is expected to *appreciate* relative to the British pound. Conversely, the value of the British pound is expected to *depreciate* relative to the U.S. dollar

Why is this? The answer is the difference in interest rates between the two countries. Specifics concerning the working of this situation will be discussed later in this chapter when

Term	Value/U.S. $1	
	6/20/01	5/14/04
One month	0.7173	0.5703
Two month	0.7181	0.5719
Three month	0.7192	0.5733
Six month	0.7222	0.5777
Twelve month	0.7280	0.5849

FIGURE 8-4 Forward rates for British pounds per U.S. dollars.

interest rate parity is discussed. At present, an example of how a banker can determine the forward rate will be presented. This example will show the role that two countries' interest rates play in setting the forward rate. Before presenting the example, one important item of institutional detail must be pointed out since this item will affect the nature of the calculations. The primary participants in the foreign exchange (often shortened to *forex*) market are not just forex traders and banks but also hedge funds and the central banks of most countries. As a result, active quotations are available on forex 24 hours per day, seven days a week, somewhere in the world. Therefore, the market convention is to use continuous compounding and discounting techniques when determining exchange rates. This convention will be followed in this example. Continuous compounding and discounting will also be used later in this chapter in the discussion of interest rate parity.[4]

EXAMPLE   *Determining the Forward Rate*

Assume your company has an accounts receivable in British pounds for £100,000 due in one year. You ask the foreign exchange dealer at your bank to quote a price for pounds against the dollar for delivery in one year (a one-year forward exchange rate). If there were no forward markets that the dealer (bank) could look to, how would the foreign exchange dealer come up with a quote?

At the time that you ask for the quote, the foreign exchange dealer would know three spot rates: (1) the spot exchange rate (the 2001 British pound rate from Figure 8-3 which is £0.7083/$1 will be used), (2) the spot one-year interest rate for borrowing British pounds which is 7.09% (continuously compounded), and (3) spot one-year risk-free U.S. rate which is 4.35% (continuously compounded). With these three pieces of information, the foreign exchange dealer can determine the appropriate forward exchange rate in the following manner.

Step 1. The foreign exchange dealer borrows the PV of the pounds account receivable immediately. The amount of the receivable is discounted by the British discount rate.

$$\text{Amt} = £100,000 \times e^{-0.0709} = £93,156.$$

Step 2. The foreign exchange dealer immediately converts the pounds into U.S. dollars at the prevailing spot rate.

$$\text{Amt} = £93,156/0.7083 = \$131,520.$$

Step 3. This money is then invested for one year at the U.S. interest rate. At the end of the year, the bank would have

$$\text{Amt} = \$131,520 \times e^{0.0435} = \$135,367.$$

Step 4. Finally, the foreign exchange dealer calculates the exchange of the dollars received at the end of the year back into British pounds to repay the loan from Step 1 (in the amount of £100,000). The exchange rate necessary to repay the loan using all the proceeds from the investment will be the appropriate forward exchange rate. The effective forward exchange rate is

$$\text{Forward rate} = £100,000/137,367 = 0.7280.$$

By executing a spot deal, borrowing pounds, and investing in dollars, the foreign exchange trader has hedged the complete exposure arising from the forward transaction. This simple

---

[4] For background on continous compounding and discounting please refer to Appendix 8-A at the end of this chapter.

transaction demonstrates that forward exchange rates are really nothing more than a function of the interest rates in the two countries and the current spot rate.

The general formula for calculating any forward exchange rate is

$$\text{Forward exchange rate} = \text{spot exchange rate} \times e^{(\text{foreign interest rate} \times t)} \times e^{(-\text{domestic interest rate} \times t)}$$
$$(8\text{-}1)$$

This formula comes from the interest rate parity condition, which will be presented and discussed later in the chapter. From the previous example the formula is as follows:

$$\text{Forward exchange rate} = 0.7083 \times e^{0.0709} \times e^{-0.0435} = 0.7280.$$

Notice how the forward exchange rates for the country with the higher domestic interest rate indicate that there is an expected *depreciation* in relation to the country with the lower domestic interest rate. That is, the currency for the country with the higher domestic interest rate is said to be *trading at a forward discount*. Trading at a discount means that in the future traders will receive less of that currency. Similarly, the currency for the country with the lower domestic interest rate is said to be *trading at a forward premium*. Trading at a forward premium means that traders expect to receive more of that currency in the future.

In the previous example the British pound is trading at a forward discount. But, how big is the discount? To calculate the size of the forward discount or premium, the following equation will be used.

$$\text{Premium/Discount} = \frac{P_{\text{forward}} - P_{\text{spot}}}{P_{\text{spot}}} \times \frac{12}{\text{no.monthsforward}} \times 100.$$
$$(8\text{-}2)$$

Using exchange rates from the previous example, the premium/discount is

$$\text{Premium/Discount} = \frac{0.7280 - 0.7083}{0.7083} \times \frac{12}{12} \times 100 = 2.78\%.$$

Notice that when the British pound is trading at a 2.78% forward discount, the U.S. dollar will be trading at a 2.78% forward premium.

8.3.2 How Currencies Are Exchanged

Currencies trade in the foreign exchange market. This market does not have a physical location. Instead, it is a global network of currency dealers and central banks that buy and sell currencies. The dealers in this market are generally banks, and these banks operate in the foreign exchange market at two levels: (1) retail and (2) interbank. The retail function for a bank in the foreign exchange market is the exchange of currencies for their customers. Most all banks provide this service to their customers. However, to provide this service a bank needs to hold an inventory of foreign currencies or have the ability to trade currencies quickly. Most banks prefer not to hold this inventory because inventories of currencies are nonearning assets. The ability to trade currencies quickly is the role of the interbank market. The interbank market for currency exchange is a network of preexisting bank relationships established for the quick exchange of currencies. These relationships allow banks to meet their retail currency exchange requests without holding a large inventory of foreign currencies. The *Wall Street Journal* provides rate quotes for $1 million currency exchanges in the interbank market.

8.4 FACTORS THAT INFLUENCE THE SUPPLY AND DEMAND FOR FOREIGN EXCHANGE

As previously discussed, markets determine exchange rates and the rates are based on the supply and demand for a country's currency. In this section, the factors that influence supply and demand are discussed. These factors can be divided into three categories: (1) trade flows, (2) a financial factor, and (3) government intervention.

8.4.1 Trade Flows

The classic economic theory of **comparative advantage** states that a country produces what it can best produce and then trades this product with other countries to obtain other goods or services that it desires. To acquire goods or services from another country, the purchaser must obtain currency of the foreign country. Therefore, factors that influence the supply and demand of a country's goods and services also affect the exchange rate for that country's currency. In this section, the factors that influence the supply and demand for a country's goods and services are discussed.

The first factor to be discussed is the relative cost of production of goods and services. If a country is the low cost producer of a good, then a fair profit can be made for its goods at the lowest sales price in the market. This pricing creates demand for the goods and thus a demand for the country's currency. A country's cost advantage can be in either labor or materials. A current example of a materials advantage is the oil production of OPEC. OPEC nations have a large supply of easily accessed underground oil reserves. Consequently, OPEC produces oil for trade with other nations.

The second factor that influences demand for goods and services is consumer tastes. Prior to the OPEC oil embargo in the early 1970s, U.S. car owners preferred large vehicles. These vehicles provided relatively low miles to a gallon of gas, but conservation was not a concern because gas was very inexpensive. The OPEC oil embargo caused a short-term shortage of gas, but the major effect of this embargo was a large, permanent increase in the cost of a gallon of gas. This large increase in the cost of gas created a shift in U.S. consumer tastes. U.S. consumers wanted more fuel efficient vehicles. The U.S. consumers first looked to their domestic automakers for these fuel efficient vehicles. The U.S. automakers had little to offer; therefore, the U.S. consumers looked to foreign automakers to fill the void. They found that Japanese automakers could fill their needs. The Japanese automakers increased their exports to the United States to meet the new consumer demand for fuel efficient vehicles. However, the Japanese government imposed export quotas on their automakers and these quotas limited the amount of exports to the United States. Since the Japanese exports were not sufficient to meet the new demand, the price of Japanese vehicles increased. This discussion of consumer tastes highlights several important factors that influence supply and demand for goods and services. These factors are

- Consumer tastes determine the demand for a good.
- Domestic producers have an opportunity to meet the demand.

- If domestic producers cannot meet the consumer demand, foreign producers have an opportunity to meet the demand.
- However, a foreigner producers' ability to meet the demand may be limited by trade quotas or tariffs.

The third and final factor for trade flows is the rate of growth in national income. Countries that are rapidly growing (developing) will demand more of all types of goods and services including imports. This increased demand for imports will alter the country's trade flows. Developed countries also demand imports, but this demand will be relatively stable, everything else equal.

8.4.2 A Financial Factor

The real rate of return available in a country's money markets is the primary financial factor that influences exchange rates. The country whose money market provides the highest real rate of return will attract capital flows as investors invest in that country's money market.

Investors prefer higher returns, but recall from Chapter 4 that money market investors are not willing to take on risk. Thus, the return being discussed here is part of the risk-free nominal interest rate. Nominal risk-free interest rates were discussed in Chapter 3 and have two parts: (1) the real rate of interest and (2) the expected rate of inflation. The real rate of interest was defined as the rate earned from investing for delaying consumption. In other words, the country whose money market pays the highest rate of return for delaying consumption will attract capital flows from investors who are attempting to take advantage of the higher real rate. Thus, the higher real rate will influence exchange rates because investors will need the country's currency to purchase that country's money market instruments.

8.4.3 Government Intervention

The final factor that influences the supply and demand for a currency is national governments. As previously discussed under speculative cash flows, governments intervene in the currency exchange market when their exchange rate is undesirable. When a government chooses to intervene to influence exchange rates, it can intervene either in the currency market or the market for goods and services. Governments use their country's central bank to buy or sell currency or to borrow or lend money.

If a government chooses to intervene in its own currency market, it will directly influence the supply or demand for its currency. For example, a government could increase the demand for its own currency by borrowing from a foreign government and then using the borrowed foreign currency to purchase its own currency in the currency exchange market. However, if a government chooses to intervene in the market for goods and services, instead of directly changing the money (currency) supply, the country will indirectly influence the supply or demand for its currency. For example, a government may choose to purchase foreign goods. To do this the government will have to convert its own currency into the foreign currency needed for the purchase. By trading the government's currency for the foreign currency, the government increases the amount of its currency in the currency exchange market. Either intervention will change the country's exchange rate.

INDUSTRY APPLICATION

FOREX (FOREIGN EXCHANGE) AND ECONOMIC ACTIVITY

In this chapter, we outline the various factors that can affect foreign exchange rates. One of the most important factors is the relationship between one country's economic activity and another's. The most common benchmark against which most currencies are measured is the U.S. dollar. As an associate on a forex sales and trading desk, you must be prepared to explain to clients how different economic pressures can affect the exchange rate. Consider the following Australian dollar–U.S. dollar exchange rate chart.

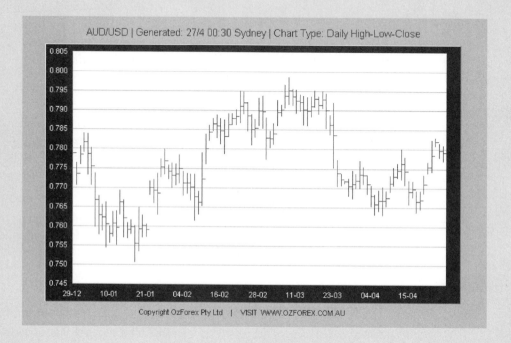

As you can see, since December 29, 2004 (29-12) (the *x*-axis uses the European dating format of dd-mm and the data are from the end of 2004 and the beginning of 2005), the Australian dollar has gained and lost ground against the U.S. dollar. How predictable are these changes and what are the major economic factors involved? Now, consider the following excerpts from OzForex Foreign Exchange Services, an Australian forex dealer. The first is from their Weekly Market Watch for Tuesday, April 26, 2005.[5]

Last Week Recap

Once again the Aussie dollar opened the week below 77 US cents having been unable to consolidate on gains made on the back of mixed US data and suffering from sharp falls in the share market. The Aussie found support around 0.7635 and managed to gain a little against the greenback despite a continuing softening in the share market and commodity prices. Meanwhile the US Dollar retreated from its recent 2-month highs against the Euro as traders focused on signs that the pace of US economic

(*continued*)

[5] This information was drawn from the OzForex website at www.ozforex.com.au.

INDUSTRY APPLICATION (*continued*)

FOREX (FOREIGN EXCHANGE) AND ECONOMIC ACTIVITY

growth may be decelerating. Midweek, the Aussie continued to weather the storm, pushing off lows around 0.7645 to surge higher, eventually pushing above the 0.7700 level to a high of 0.7768, underpinned by higher commodity prices and further losses on Wall St. Towards the end of the week the Aussie dollar consolidated, with no major economic news to provide direction for the local currency. The Aussie dollar closed the week stronger as steady demand pushed the currency closer to the 0.7800 mark.

Notice how the references to the U.S. economy emphasize how important a trading partner the United States is. Also notice how, in the last sentence, the author refers to consolidation in the level of the Australian dollar to which no economic news can be attributed. This might be caused by the political and speculative forces mentioned earlier in this chapter. In contrast, consider the following excerpt which emphasizes how an analyst must be able to provide a coherent explanation of the various influences on a particular forex rate. Note that while anticipated events can be identified, there is little forecasting that is actually done beyond indicating a strengthening or weakening in the rate.

The Week Ahead

USD: A heavy economic calendar provides plenty for the dollar, which is seesawing on signs of slowing economic activity or inflationary pressures, generally ignoring long-term fundamentals. With the dollar focusing on the signals for interest rates from US economic data releases, there will be plenty to provide direction this week. There are also several speeches by Fed officials scheduled, which could provide direction to markets. On the data calendar the following is scheduled for release this week: Mon—Mar existing home sales. Tues—Apr Richmond Fed survey, Apr consumer confidence, Mar new home sales. Wed—Mar durable goods orders. Thurs—Q1 GDP advance, Mar help wanted index, Fedspeak Santomero and Hoenig. Fri—Mar personal income/spending, Mar core PCE deflator, Q1 employment cost, Apr University of Michigan consumer sentiment, Apr Chicago PMI.

AUD: The heavy US economic calendar should provide direction for the Aussie. Locally, traders will be watching for this week's March quarter CPI data, a key measure of inflation. On the data calendar the following is scheduled for release this week: Mon—ANZAC Day holiday. Tues—Q1 PPI, Q1 NAB business survey. Wed—Q1 CPI. Fri—Mar credit.

This excerpt emphasizes just how complicated the "real-world" forecasting of exchange rates can be. Which indicator or indicators should bear the most weight?

8.5 EXCHANGE MARKET PARITY CONDITIONS

A market is in equilibrium when its assets are correctly priced. In most financial markets, to determine if an asset is correctly priced is extremely difficult because many factors are included in the determination of the present value of a security's future cash flows. In the currency exchange market, however, equilibrium is much easier to determine because a currency, in and of itself, does not generate future cash flows. This fact allows currency traders to focus on the current day's market conditions and lead to the development of a set of **parity conditions** that describe when the currency exchange market is in equilibrium and, maybe more importantly, describe when profitable opportunities exist from market disequilibrium. The parity conditions are (1) consistent exchange rates, (2) purchasing power parity, and (3) interest rate parity. Also covered in the process of discussing these parity conditions are (1) the law of one price, (2) the Fisher Effect in international markets, and (3) covered interest arbitrage.

8.5.1 Consistent Exchange Rates

The first parity (or equilibrium) condition in the currency exchange market is **consistent currency exchange rates**. Simply, the exchange rate between two currencies must be the same (consistent) across the various dealers in the exchange network. If the exchange rates between two currencies are not consistent across dealers, profits are available by trading the two currencies between the various dealers.

EXAMPLE   *Consistent Exchange Rates*

Assume that the U.S. dollar/British pound exchange rate is $1.60/£1.0 at a New York dealer. Also, assume that at the same time a London dealer has the exchange rate at $1.50/£1.0. These exchange rates are not consistent. An investor has a profitable opportunity by trading currencies with the two dealers. Profits can be generated through the following two transactions (using £100 as an example),

1. An investor uses the New York dealer to convert £100 to $160.
2. Then with the London dealer the investor converts the dollars back to pounds and receives £106.67.

In the preceding example the investor made £6.67 simply by flipping between currencies. This profitable opportunity would be quickly obvious to all currency traders in the exchange market and the traders would attempt to execute trades similar to the trades in the example. The resulting trading pressure would drive the exchange rates across the different dealers to one exchange rate between the two currencies. Accordingly, one of the parity conditions of the currency exchange market is consistent exchange rates across the currency dealers.

8.5.2 Purchasing Power Parity

The **law of one price** is an equilibrium condition that is vital to international trade. The law of one price states that after adjusting for exchange rates, a commodity has the same price in every country. The formula for the law of one price is

$$P_{\text{foreign}} = P_{\text{domestic}} \times X, \tag{8-3}$$

where

P = the price of the commodity, and

X = the foreign to domestic spot exchange rate.

This relationship must hold because market supply and demand for the one good produced in different countries will adjust prices until buyers can get the same price for the good from those different countries.

To examine the law of one price, a good that is the same around the world needs to be chosen. A popular choice for this analysis is the Big Mac because it is two all-beef patties,

Location	Big Mac price relative to U.S. price (%)	
	1991	**2001**
Australia	86	60
Britain	132	112
Canada	90	85
Denmark	185	115
France	142	98
Germany	114	91
Hong Kong	51	54
Italy	129	77
Japan	125	94
Singapore	70	72
Sweden	191	94

FIGURE 8-5 Big Mac prices around the world.

Source: 1991 data from Pakko and Pollard (1996) and 2001 from *Economist* (4/21/01).

special sauce, lettuce, cheese, pickles, onions, on a sesame-seed bun around the world.[6] Pakko and Pollard (1996) study the law of one price using the Big Mac. They show the prices of the Big Mac around the world relative to the U.S. price in their Table 1, which is reproduced in Figure 8-5 under the column heading 1991. The information in the 2001 column comes from an article in the the *Economist* (4/21/01).

The data in Figure 8-5 show a wide variation in Big Mac prices across countries, but how can that be? Pakko and Pollard offer four factors that can contribute to deviations from the law of one price. The four factors are (1) barriers to trade (e.g., tariffs and transaction costs), (2) nontraded goods (e.g., real estate, utility, and labor costs), (3) imperfect competition that allows price discrimination across markets, and (4) trade imbalances that affect exchange rates. Even though in reality real-world markets contain many factors that make one price difficult to achieve, the law of one price is a useful concept that describes how trading goods should move prices.

Different countries have different rates of inflation; therefore, the price of goods from different countries change at different rates. This means that for the law of one price to work across time, exchange rates must adjust as inflation changes prices. This leads to another powerful concept called relative **purchasing power parity** (PPP). Relative purchasing power parity describes how the exchange rate must change to maintain the same value for the same good across countries.

Relative purchasing power parity shows the relationship between the price changes (inflation) and the change in the exchange rate. The formula[7] for relative PPP can be written as

$$(1 + \Delta P_{\text{foreign}}) = (1 + \Delta P_{\text{domestic}}) \times (1 + \Delta X), \qquad (8\text{-}4)$$

[6] In certain areas around the world, the patties are unlikely to be all beef. However, in those areas the Big Mac still has two patties, special sauce, lettuce, cheese, pickles, onions, on a sesame-seed bun.

[7] Note that the formula for purchasing power parity can be written in continuous form. However, in keeping with the discussion in Chapter 3 and recognizing that the same amount of precision is not required here, we continue to use discrete valuation techniques.

where

ΔP = rate of change in price (rate of inflation), and

ΔX = rate of change in the foreign to domestic spot exchange rate.

Since the usual focus is on how the spot exchange rate must evolve to maintain one price, Equation (8-4) is rearranged to isolate the rate of change in the exchange rate as follows:

$$\frac{(1 + \Delta P_{\text{foreign}})}{(1 + \Delta P_{\text{domestic}})} = (1 + \Delta X) = \frac{X_{\text{new}}}{X_{\text{old}}} \qquad (8\text{-}5)$$

Now, to apply Equation (8-5), the following example will be used.

EXAMPLE   *Using Purchasing Power Parity to Estimate Future Exchange Rates*

Assume that the Canadian annual inflation rate is 5%, the U.S. annual inflation is 3%, and the current spot exchange rate is C$1.31/$1. Under these market conditions what spot exchange rate will be necessary to maintain one price for goods between the two countries one year from now?

The result is

$$\frac{(1 + 0.05)}{(1 + 0.03)} = \frac{X_{\text{new}}}{1.31} \quad \text{then} \quad X_{\text{new}} = 1.34.$$

This result means that the exchange rate must adjust to C$1.34/$1 to maintain one price for goods between the two countries after a year with these different inflation rates.

One example of the importance of understanding how different inflation rates change exchange rates through time is the profitability of a project taking place in a foreign country. This is important because investors require their profits in their own domestic currency. Examining this issue provides another application of the Fisher Effect equation. Recall from Chapter 3 that the Fisher Effect equation is

$$(1 + r) = (1 + R)(1 + E(i)). \qquad (8\text{-}6)$$

Using Equation (8-6) the domestic return on a foreign project can be calculated as:

$$(1 + \text{return}_{\text{domestic}}) = (1 + \text{return}_{\text{foreign}}) \times (1 + \%\Delta(\text{exchange rate})). \qquad (8\text{-}7)$$

Figure 8-6 provides a table of fictitious returns and changes in exchange rates, but was developed to demonstrate the impact of the changes in exchange rates on the domestic return of foreign investments.

Notice that in the case of Nepal, the 3.7% foreign return was magnified to 7.02% by the change in the exchange rate when the funds were translated into U.S. dollars. Similarly, the apparently spectacular 8.9% return in Greenland was reduced to a loss of −0.4% on translation. Changes in exchange rates can enhance or eliminate returns. Therefore, investors should be careful to include an estimate of future exchange rates in any forecast involving returns from foreign investments.

Country of investment	Return in foreign currency (return $_{\text{foreign}}$)	% Change in the exchange rate relative to U.S. dollar (% Δ(exchange rate)	Return in U.S. dollars = (return $_{\text{domestic}}$)
France	+5.3%	−5.2%	−0.2%
Tibet	+4.9%	−2.7%	2.07%
Nepal	+3.7%	+3.2%	7.02%
Greenland	+8.9%	−8.5%	−0.4%
Taiwan	−2.3%	+4.3%	+1.9%
Morocco	−6.8%	+6.6%	−0.6%
Jamaica	+2.7%	−2.0%	+0.6%

FIGURE 8-6 The impact of exchange rates on investment returns.

8.5.3 Interest Rate Parity

The final parity condition to be discussed is **interest rate parity**. The idea behind interest rate parity is that in equilibrium an investor should expect to earn the same risk-adjusted real rate of return in every country. If the market is not in equilibrium, then a profitable opportunity exists. There are several important points in this brief statement about interest rate parity, which are discussed below.

First, revisiting the real rate of interest and the Fisher equation using the approximation formula, the approximation of the Fisher equation states that the nominal risk-free rate equals the real rate of interest plus the expected rate of inflation. The real rate is defined as the rate paid to an investor for delaying consumption. Earlier in this chapter, the fact that different real rates would influence the supply and demand for currency exchange because investors would move money to the country with the highest real rate was discussed. However, different real rates is not an equilibrium condition. As investors move to invest in securities in the country with the highest real rate, they will drive up the price of the securities in that country which drives down the rate of return. Also, as the investors leave their home country, they will reduce demand for their own domestic securities. This move will drive down the price of the domestic securities and increase the rates of return. This process continues until one real rate of interest exists across all countries. Thus, one real rate of interest for all countries is considered the equilibrium condition.

If one real rate of interest is the equilibrium condition around the world, what can be said about nominal risk-free rates of interest across countries? Using the approximation of the Fisher equation, the difference in the nominal risk-free rate of interest between two countries is the difference in the two countries' inflation rates. The approximate Fisher equation as presented in Chapter 3 is

$$r = R + E(i). \tag{8-8}$$

Using this equation the difference in nominal risk-free rates between, for example, Canada and the United States is

$$r_{\text{Canada}} - r_{\text{US}} = [R_{\text{Canada}} + E(i_{\text{Canada}})] - [R_{\text{US}} + E(i_{\text{US}})]$$

then since $R_{\text{Canada}} = R_{\text{US}}$,

$$r_{\text{Canada}} - r_{\text{US}} = E(i_{\text{Canada}}) - E(i_{\text{US}}).$$

Having linked the differences in nominal risk-free rates to differences in inflation rates, interest rate parity can be discussed. Because purchasing power parity links changes in exchange rates to differences in inflation rates, the differences in nominal risk-free interest rates can be linked to the changes in exchange rates. This relationship is the interest rate parity condition and is defined as follows:

$$\frac{X_{forward}}{X_{spot}} = \frac{e^{r_{foreign} \times t}}{e^{r_{domestic} \times t}}, \tag{8-9}$$

where

X = a foreign to domestic exchange rate,

r = a nominal risk-free interest rate, and

t = the appropriate time interval.

When the relationship in Equation (8-9) is true, the markets are in equilibrium and investors will earn the same rate of return in every country. When interest rate parity is violated, investors have an opportunity to earn risk-free profits. The opportunity to earn risk-free profits is referred to as an arbitrage opportunity and occurs from violations of the interest rate parity condition. This profitable opportunity is called **covered interest arbitrage**.

There are two types of covered interest arbitrage and the difference comes from the direction of the violation of the interest rate parity condition.

$$\text{If } \frac{X_{forward}}{X_{spot}} < \frac{e^{r_{foreign} \times t}}{e^{r_{domestic} \times t}}, \quad \text{the investor does an arbitrage outflow.}$$

$$\text{If } \frac{X_{forward}}{X_{spot}} > \frac{e^{r_{foreign} \times t}}{e^{r_{domestic} \times t}}, \quad \text{the investor does an arbitrage inflow.}$$

The terms outflow and inflow refer to the direction of the investment made to take advantage of the arbitrage opportunity relative to the investor's home country. An arbitrage outflow means domestic funds are invested in a foreign security. An arbitrage inflow means that foreign funds are invested in a domestic security. The process for creating both an arbitrage inflow and an arbitrage outflow is best developed through an example as follows.

EXAMPLE *Covered Interest Arbitrage*

For this example, the following data on Swiss and U.S. interest rates and the spot exchange rate of SFr/$ will be used. The rates are

1. The annualized continuous interest rate on a U.S. government three-month instrument is 5.04%.

2. The annualized continuous interest rate on a Swiss government three-month instrument is 4.49%.

3. A spot exchange rate of SFr 7.1/$1.

With this data the interest rate parity condition (assuming a three-month investment) is

$$\frac{X_{forward}}{7.1} = \frac{e^{0.0449 \times 0.25}}{e^{0.0504 \times 0.25}}$$

so $X_{\text{forward}} = 7.09$ is the forward exchange rate necessary for interest rate parity to hold in this example. However, if the forward exchange rate (for a three-month forward) is anything other than SFr 7.09/\$1, then arbitrage profits exist.

Covered Interest Arbitrage Outflow

Assume that instead of SFr 7.09/\$1, that the three month forward rate is SFr 7.0/\$1. Then the relationship is $\dfrac{7.0}{7.1} < \dfrac{e^{0.0449 \times 0.25}}{e^{0.0504 \times 0.25}}$. When the ratio of the exchange rates is less than the ratio of the interest rates, covered interest arbitrage outflow is available. In an outflow, the process requires borrowing in the domestic market and investing in the foreign market. Assuming that the investor borrows \$100,000, the process for arbitrage outflow is as follows:

Today

1. *Borrow* \$100,000 at 5.04% for three months.
2. *Convert* at SFr 7.1/\$1 to SFr 710,000 and *invest* at 4.49% for three months.
3. *Enter into* a three-month forward contract to exchange SFr 718,014.65 (710,000 × $e^{(0.0449 \times 0.25)}$) at SFr 7/\$1.

Three Months Later

1. *Receive* SFr 718,014.65 (710,000 × $e^{(0.0449 \times 0.25)}$).
2. *Convert* SFr 718,014.65 at SFr 7/\$1 to \$102,573.52.
3. *Owe* \$101,267.97 (\$100,000 × $e^{(0.0504 \times 0.25)}$).
4. *Profit* of \$1,305.55 = \$102,573.52 − \$101,267.97.

The profits from this arbitrage outflow is \$1,305.55 and these profits are risk free.

Covered Interest Arbitrage Inflow

Now, an arbitrage inflow will be examined. Assuming a forward rate of SFr 7.2/\$1, the relationship is $\dfrac{7.2}{7.1} > \dfrac{e^{0.0449 \times 0.25}}{e^{0.0504 \times 0.25}}$. When the ratio of the exchange rates is greater than the ratio of the interest rate ratio, covered interest arbitrage inflow profits are available. In an inflow, the process requires borrowing in the foreign market and investing in the domestic market. Using the assumption that the investor borrows SFr 710,000, the process for an arbitrage inflow is as follows:

Today

1. *Borrow* SFr 710,000 at 4.49% for three months.
2. *Convert* at SFr 7.1/\$1 to \$100,000 and invest at 5.04% for three months.
3. *Enter into* a three-month forward contract to exchange \$99,724.26 (SFr 718,014.65/7.2) at SFr 7.2/\$1.

Three Months Later

1. *Owe* SFr 718,014.65 (710,000 × $e^{(0.0449 \times 0.25)}$).
2. *Receive* 101,267.97 (\$100,000 × $e^{(0.0504 \times 0.25)}$).
3. *Convert* \$99,724.26 at SFr 7.2/\$1 to pay SFr 718,014.65.
4. *Profit* of \$1,543.71 = \$101,267.97 − \$99,724.26.

The profit from this arbitrage inflow is $1,543.71, and this profit is also completely risk free. Note, there is no need to limit the borrowing to SFr 710,000. Also, note that for every 0 added to the amount borrowed, the decimal point is shifted one place to the right in the profit. That is, if SFr 7,100,000 is borrowed, the profit from the arbitrage inflow would be $15,437.10.

To conclude the discussion of covered interest arbitrage, a point that cannot be over-emphasized is that the profits are completely risk free. In other words, the moment the arbitrage is started, profits are known because all values are determined at the start of the process. The key to the arbitrage is the forward exchange rate. The reason the forward exchange rate is the key is that investors borrow, convert, and invest today, so the amounts they receive and owe are set today. Only the future exchange rate is open to uncertainty. However, since the forward contract locks in the future exchange rate and the forward contract is entered into at the same time as the borrowing and investing, everything is determined at the beginning of the process. Thus, a risk-free profit is created.

8.5.4 A Final Point about Interest Rates and Foreign Currencies

In previous chapters, changes in interest rates were shown to change the value of financial assets. For example, a fixed coupon bond will decrease in value when domestic market interest rates increase and will increase in value when domestic market interest rates fall. However, in this chapter, the value of a foreign currency (the exchange rate) will change when *the difference between* the foreign and the domestic interest rates changes. That is, the exchange rate for a foreign currency is based on the relative position between two interest rates: (1) the interest rate of the foreign currency's country and (2) the domestic interest rate of the investor.

SUMMARY OF VALUATION AND RISK MANAGEMENT SKILLS

1. Understand why cash flows cross country boundaries and how supply and demand for a currency affects the currency's exchange rate.

Investors exchange currencies for three reasons: (1) investment, (2) political instability, and (3) speculation. Trade flows are determined by: (1) comparative advantage, (2) consumer tastes, and (3) growth in national income. The supply and demand for a currency is determined by three factors: (1) trade flows, (2) the real rate of interest, and (3) government intervention.

2. Calculate forward exchange rates from spot exchange rates.

Exchange rates are the rate at which one currency is exchanged for another. Exchange rates are available for transactions today (a spot rate) and in the future (a forward rate). The difference between spot exchange rates and forward exchange rates is determined by the difference in the two countries' interest rates. The forward exchange rate is the best unbiased estimator of the future exchange rate.

3. Examine the parity conditions to determine when arbitrage opportunities exist and how to take advantage of the opportunities.

Three parity conditions describe equilibrium in the foreign exchange market. The parity conditions are (1) consistent exchange rates, (2) purchasing power parity, and (3) interest rate parity. A violation of any of these parity conditions provides an arbitrage opportunity through exchanging currencies.

QUESTIONS

1. An international investment cash flow is a cash flow across a country border for the purpose of acquiring an asset in the foreign country. What additional risk does an investor face with a foreign investment that is not a factor with a domestic investment?

2. Why are political cash flows often referred to as "capital flight" and what is the reason for capital flight?

3. Explain why speculative cash flows in the foreign exchange market may not be as risky as speculation in other markets.

4. What is the difference between a spot exchange rate and a forward exchange rate?

5. What three factors influence the supply and demand for foreign exchange? Briefly discuss each factor.

6. What is the difference between a currency depreciation and a currency devaluation?

7. Suppose the £/$ spot exchange rate is 0.7083 and the six-month forward rate is 0.7222. Assume that the continuous U.S. interest rate is 4.35%. What does the continuous U.K. interest rate have to be?

8. Suppose the £/$ spot exchange rate is 0.7083 and the six-month forward rate is 0.7222. Assume that the continuous U.K. interest rate is 7.09%. What does the continuous U.S. interest rate have to be?

9. Suppose the £/$ spot exchange rate is 0.7083 and the forward exchange rate is 0.7230. Assume that the U.K. interest rate is 7.09% and that the U.S. interest rate is 4.35%. In terms of months, what forward rate does this represent?

10. Suppose that the one-year forward exchange rate on the British pound was 0.6886. What is the size of the forward discount/premium assuming the spot exchange rate is 0.7083? Is your answer a premium or a discount?

11. One of the foreign exchange parity conditions is consistent exchange rates. Explain what is meant by consistent exchange rates.

12. Define the law of one price.

13. What does relative purchasing power parity describe?

14. Under the following conditions, what is the exchange rate needed at the end of the year for the law of one price to hold?

foreign inflation rate is 32%,

domestic inflation rate is 20%, and

exchange rate is 10 units of foreign currency to 1 unit of domestic currency.

15. The equilibrium condition of interest rate parity means what for investors?

16. Under the following conditions, what type of covered interest arbitrage is available and what are the profits on a three-month loan of $100,000?

U.S. T-bill continuous rate of 7.7% (rate is annual),

Denmark T-bill equivalent continuous rate of 9.53%,

Spot rate of [Danish Kroner] 4 to $1, and

Three-month forward rate of [Danish Kroner] 4.01 to $1.

REFERENCES

BALKAN, E., 1992, Political instability, country risk and probability of default, *Applied Economics*, *24*, 999–1008.
The author examines international loan rescheduling and finds a positive relation between the probability of loan rescheduling and political instability and a finds a negative relation between the probability of loan rescheduling and the level of democracy.

FRENKEL, J., and R. LEVICH, 1975, Covered interest arbitrage: Unexploited profits? *Journal of Political Economy*, *83*, 325–338.
The authors note the existence of apparent arbitrage profits from violation of interest rate parity. They find that adjustments for transaction costs account for most of the apparent arbitrage profits.

HAKKIO, C., 1992, Is purchasing power parity a useful guide to the dollar? *Federal Reserve Bank of Kansas City-Economic Review*, *77*, 37–52.
The author provides a nice discussion of the law of one price, absolute purchasing power parity (PPP), and relative PPP. The author notes that PPP is a useful long-run guide, but not a useful short-run guide.

KANE, A., L. ROSENTHAL, and G. LJUNG, 1983, Tests of the Fisher hypothesis with international data: Theory and evidence, *Journal of Finance*, *38*, 539–551.
The authors examine Eurocurrency rates and find that nominal rates adjust for expected inflation.

PAKKO, M., and P. POLLARD, 1996, For here or to go? Purchasing power parity and the Big Mac, *Federal Reserve Bank of St. Louis-Review*, *78*, 3–21.
The authors use the Big Mac to examine short-run PPP and find persistent deviations from PPP. They examine the Big Mac as a basket of tradable and nontradable goods and discuss why PPP fails.

RHEE, S., and R. CHANG, 1992, Intra-day arbitrage opportunities in foreign exchange and eurocurrency markets, *Journal of Finance*, *47*, 363–379.
The authors find the covered interest arbitrage opportunities are rare using intraday data.

RUMMEL, R., and D. HEENAN, 1978, How multinationals analyze political risk, *Harvard Business Review*, *56*, 67–76.
The authors discuss issues in and methods for analyzing political risk.

TOOTELL, G., 1992, Purchasing power parity within the United States, *Federal Reserve Bank-New England Economic Review*, 15–24.
The author examines PPP within the United States to avoid all the problems associated with trade across country borders and finds that PPP fails within the United States. The author concludes that PPP fails because of the inclusion of nontraded goods in the consumer price index.

KEY TERMS

Comparative Advantage Comparative advantage means that you have something that you are best at and you should conduct this activity because it is the best use of your time. Then you trade your productive output with someone else who is also doing what they do best.

Consistent Currency Consistent currency exchange rates means the exchange rate between two currencies is the same across the financial markets around the world.

Covered Interest Arbitrage Covered interest arbitrage is the risk-free profit opportunity available when interest rate parity is violated.

Exchange Rate The exchange rate is the rate at which one currency converts into another.

Foreign Exchange Risk Foreign exchange risk is the risk associated with changing between currencies. The risk exists because the exchange rate between currencies changes across time.

Forward Exchange Rate A forward exchange rate is the exchange rate on a forward transaction. A forward transaction is an exchange that will occur at some point in the future.

Interest Rate Parity Interest rate parity means that investors should earn equivalent risk-adjusted return in each foreign market.

Investment Cash Flows An investment cash flow in international finance is a cash flow into a country for the purpose of buying a real or financial asset.

Law of One Price The law of one price says that after adjusting for exchange rates a good should cost the same amount across markets.

Parity Conditions Parity refers to equilibrium in the currency exchange markets.

Political Cash Flows Political cash flows are cash flows due to political instability in a country. Political cash flows are cash flows leaving a country and are often referred to as "capital flight."

Purchasing Power Parity Purchasing power parity (PPP) provides the relationship between exchange rates and inflation so that exchange rates adjust with inflation effects on prices to enable the law of one price to hold.

Speculative Cash Flows Speculative cash flows are currency exchanges done to bet on future exchange rates. These are often done when a central bank intervenes in the currency markets to alter the exchange rates for their currency.

Spot Exchange Rate A spot exchange rate is the exchange rate for a currency exchange that occurs today.

Unbiased Predictor An unbiased predictor is a predictor that is not consistently too high or too low. Instead, it is on average correct. This does not mean that it is always correct. It only means that it is not consistently wrong in the same direction.

FUNDAMENTAL MATHEMATICAL CONCEPTS FOR TIME VALUE OF MONEY

8-A.1 GENERAL RULE FOR COMPOUND INTEREST

- The future value (**FV**) of an amount is equal to:

$$FV = S \times (1 + r/n)^{t \times n}.$$

where

S equals the initial value,

r is the nominal rate of interest,

t is the number of years into the future one is compounding,

and n is the number of times within the year that the interest is compounded.

- The formula has nothing to do with the value of S; it has everything to do with the **factor or multiplier $(1 + r/n)^{t \times n}$**.
- Hence, 12% (nominal) compounded quarterly yields a factor of $(1 + 0.12/4)^{1 \times 4} = 1.125509$.

TABLE 8A-1 An Example of Compounding: Let $r = 0.08$ and $t = 1$

Compound n times	Multiplier	Formula
1	1.0800000	$(1 + 0.08)^1$
10	1.0829423	$(1 + 0.08/10)^{10}$
50	1.0832178	$(1 + 0.08/50)^{50}$
100	1.0832524	$(1 + 0.08/100)^{100}$
500	1.0832801	$(1 + 0.08/500)^{500}$
1,000	1.0832836	$(1 + 0.08/1,000)^{1,000}$
5,000	1.0832864	$(1 + 0.08/5,000)^{5,000}$
50,000	1.0832870	$(1 + 0.08/50,000)^{50,000}$
Continuous	1.0832871	$e^{0.08}$

Note that:

- The more frequently we compound, the larger the multiplier and the more money we get.
- As the number of times the compound increases, the amount by which the multiplier changes gets smaller and smaller.
- As we increase the frequency of compounding, the multipliers agree in successively more digits. That is, the product approaches a limit!
- The limit of $(1+r/n)^{t \times n}$, as n grows infinitely large, is written as $e^{r \times t}$.
- This is called the **exponential of r**.
- When $r = 1$, we have e^1 or e and it is approximately equal to 2.71828182845905.
- As n grows infinitely large we think of this as continuous compounding.

8-A.2 THE BASICS OF LOGARITHMS AND EXPONENTS

- You are given the equation

$$2^4 = 16.$$

- The log of the equation answers the question: *"To what power or exponent must the base (2) be raised for the ending value to equal 16?"*
- The log of the equation can be written as:

$$\log_2 16 = 4.$$

8-A.3 THE NATURAL LOGARITHM

- The natural logarithm function is the inverse function of the exponential. If you apply the log function to the exponential function of a number, you get back the number you started with.

$$\ln e^x = x, \text{ and}$$
$$e^{\ln x} = x.$$

8-A.3.1 Solving an Exponential Equation: A Simple Example

$$e^x = 72$$
$$\ln e^x = \ln 72$$
$$x = \ln 72 = 4.2767.$$

- To what power must e be raised to get 72? e must be raised to 4.2767 power to obtain the value of 72.
- The relationship can be written as

$$\log_e 72 = 4.2767 \, (\log_e = \ln).$$

8-A.3.2 Solving a Logarithmic Equation: A Simple Example

$$\ln x = 3$$
$$e \ln x = e3$$
$$x = e3 = 20.0855.$$

- What do you get when you raise e to the third power? You get a value of 20.0855.
- The completed logarithmic equation can be written as:

$$\ln 20.0855 = 3.$$

8-A.4 RULES FOR THE EXPONENTIAL

$$e^0 = 1$$
$$e^x e^y = e^{x+y}$$
$$(e^x)^y = e^{xy}$$

8-A.5 RULES FOR NATURAL LOGARITHMS

$$\ln 1 = 0$$
$$\ln e = 1$$
$$\ln e^x = x$$
$$\ln xy = \ln x + \ln y$$
$$\ln x/y = \ln x - \ln y$$
$$\ln x^y = y \ln x.$$

CHAPTER 9

FORWARD AND FUTURES CONTRACTS

9.1 INTRODUCTION

The next two chapters are going to introduce some of the most exciting instruments in modern finance: derivatives. A derivative is an instrument whose value is based on the value of an underlying asset. The most common categories of derivatives are **forward contracts**, **futures contracts**, *swap contracts*, and *options*. This chapter covers forward and futures contracts. Options and swaps are discussed in Chapters 10 and 13.

The purpose of this chapter is to explain the economic function of forward and futures contracts and to show you how to determine prices for these contracts. Later in this chapter, we provide specific examples of how to price interest rate forward and futures contracts. Financial institutions, such as commercial banks, use these contracts to hedge interest-rate risk exposure from owning fixed-income securities (money market securities, bonds, and mortgages) discussed in earlier chapters. The use of forward and futures is applied to real-world situations in the second half of this book.

This chapter begins with some background and institutional detail on forward and futures contracts. Then the chapter moves into forward contracts with a focus on the interest rate forward contract known as an FRA (forward rate agreement). Next, futures contracts are discussed with a focus on interest rate futures contracts. Detailed examples of using futures contracts to hedge are discussed. This chapter concludes with details on T-note and T-bond futures contracts.

DEVELOPING VALUATION AND RISK MANAGEMENT SKILLS

1. Understand the purpose of forward and futures contracts.
2. Understand the forward rate agreement (FRA) and how to calculate the settlement payments on an FRA.
3. Understand interest rate futures contract and how to calculate the price of an interest rate futures contract.
4. Be able to use an interest rate futures contracts to hedge an exposure to movements in market interest rates.
5. Understand T-note and T-bond futures contracts and their uses as hedging instruments.

9.2 GETTING STARTED IN FORWARDS AND FUTURES

9.2.1 Examples of Uses of Forwards and Futures

Suppose you agree to buy a car manufactured in Greenland from the local automobile dealer at today's price for delivery in three months time. Congratulations, you have just acquired a forward contract! But why bother with the contract when you can just wait three months and buy the car when it arrives? The answer is that the price could change in three months. What you are doing with your contract is locking in today's price for a transaction in the future. Suppose now that the government announces that all future automobile imports from Greenland will be subject to a quota. The government quota will increase the value of the car since they will now be in much shorter supply. However, the quota does not change the terms of the contract you negotiated with the dealer. You still pay the agreed on price. In other words, your contract with the auto dealer locked in a transaction price for a transaction in the future, thus eliminating the **price risk** inherent in waiting until the future to make a transaction.

In Chapter 8, an example illustrated how a foreign exchange dealer could offer a guaranteed quote to exchange pounds for dollars in one year's time based on a customer's accounts receivable recorded in British pounds. That is, the dealer quoted an exchange rate for a forward foreign exchange contract using the existing interest rates in each country. In that example, the pound was currently trading at £0.7083/$1 and was expected to go to £0.7280/$1—a depreciation of almost 3%! Therefore, at the current time £100,000 would exchange to $141,183, but in one year's time £100,000 would translate into $137,367 if the company commits to this exchange rate.* Has the company lost money?

Unfortunately, many people would think so, but this is *not* the correct interpretation. Remember, at the time a company enters into a transaction, the actual future spot exchange rate is unknown even though the forward rate is the best unbiased estimator of the future rate—the future rate could be higher or lower. Remember, also, that the company does *not* have the money yet. One of the responsibilities of the management team of a company that has extensive foreign currency transactions is to *preserve financial value*. In this situation, preserving financial value is done by eliminating foreign exchange risk by entering into the forward contract.

The point of the two examples is that forward and futures contracts exist to reduce or eliminate uncertainty about future transactions. Here is another real-world situation to further demonstrate this point.

Suppose it is December and a wheat farmer in Canada's Quebec province is trying to decide how much wheat he should plant in the following spring. Right now, the winter harvest is about to come in and autumn weather has been terrible. It was unusually dry at planting time and much of the seed did not sprout. The drought was followed by extensive rains that drowned the young plants that did sprout. This dry/wet period was followed by several hail storms that destroyed much of the crop that had managed to survive the unusual growing season. As a result, the current price of wheat per bushel is very high—good in

---

*Amounts differ slightly from those in Chapter 8 due to rounding.

one way for the farmer since he will get a high price for what wheat he can harvest, but bad in another way since only about 30% of his crop survived.

Nonetheless, none of these issues really affect the price of wheat that will be ready for market next summer. The issues that are important for pricing next year's crop are the economic and weather conditions all over the world, but most especially in the rest of Canada and in the other countries that also produce wheat such as the United States, Russia, and China. If the world price for next summer's wheat is low, the farmer may not be able to afford to pay the mortgage on his farm. If the world price of wheat is high, the farmer will make a profit. Not knowing what next year's price of wheat will be and with no way to estimate it, a risk-averse individual may decide not to plant and give up farming. However, if a futures price for wheat is available, the farmer can decide whether or not to plant a new crop on the basis of a known price at which he can sell the crop.

The **futures price**, which is the expected market value of the asset, does not have to be close to the actual cash price in one year's time nor even close to today's cash price. At the time of planting, the farmer, being risk averse, can make a rational decision on the basis of his ability to enter into a contract that pays a specific price in the future. Once again, the example illustrates how futures contracts eliminate uncertainty about the price of a transaction at some point in the future.

This chapter discusses how forward prices for goods and commodities are determined. Also to be examined is how futures contracts work. A futures contract is nothing more than a forward contract that is renewed every day but traded in a public marketplace instead of in the private over-the-counter market. The key to understanding how these contracts work is to remember that the goal of these contracts is to eliminate uncertainty *in the future* so that cash flows can be predicted with greater accuracy. Just as with the forward currency rates, the objective is to preserve financial value by reducing or eliminating price risk.

9.2.2 Institutional Details

Forward and futures contracts provide a means to set the price for a transaction in the future. The main difference between forward contracts and futures contracts is where they trade. A forward contract is an over-the-counter agreement. That is, a forward contract is a private agreement between two parties. As long as the two parties agree, the contract can be for any amount and at any delivery date. Of course, there is the risk that one party to the forward will not perform their obligations under the contract. This risk is known as *counterparty credit risk*.

To avoid counterparty credit risk, futures markets developed. The counterparty to every futures trade is a **clearing house**; for example, the New York Mercantile Exchange or the Chicago Board of Trade. Having the clearing house as the counterparty on every futures contract provides the trader with a guarantee of counterparty performance on every contract. The clearing house can provide this guarantee because it is backed by the financial strength of all of the brokerage firms that use the clearing house to process their trades.

In exchange for this guarantee of performance, futures transactions are for standardized commodities (e.g., number 2 yellow soybeans), in standard amounts (e.g., 1 million bushels) for delivery at a specified point in time; for example, the third week of March, June, September, and December.

Unlike the private forward contracts, futures contracts are traded through an auction-like process with all bids and offers on each contract made public. As a result, a market price is reached for each contract and is based primarily on the laws of supply and demand. However, futures markets are rarely used to actually buy or sell the physical commodity or financial instrument being traded. Futures are used for price estimation, risk management, and, for some people, investment and profit.

The futures markets succeed because they attract two kinds of traders: *hedgers* and *speculators*. Hedgers are market participants who want to transfer price risk and can be either producers or consumers. A producer hedger wants to transfer the risk that prices will decline by the time a sale is made. A consumer hedger wants to transfer the risk that prices will increase before a purchase is made. A speculator takes a position in the futures market in the hope of generating profit.

Traders in the futures market can take two types of positions: (1) a long position or (2) a short position. A long position in a futures contract is an agreement to buy the underlying asset. Hedgers take a long position because they need to buy the underlying asset in the future and thus want to eliminate price risk. Speculators take a long position (agreement to buy) hoping the market price goes up to provide a profit. A short position in a futures contract is an agreement to sell the underlying asset. Hedgers take a short position when they want to sell the underlying asset in the future. Speculators take a short position hoping the market price will drop.

A particular type of speculator who trades in the pits on the exchange floor is known as a local. Typically, this individual provides market liquidity by constantly buying and selling throughout the trading session. These are the individuals that you see on television screaming out prices accompanied with wild hand gestures. These gestures are not chaotic or random. What you are actually seeing is something called price discovery. That is, these locals are determining futures prices. Most U.S. futures and options contracts are still traded in pits on the floors of futures exchanges via a system known as *open outcry*, although a growing number of futures contracts are being traded electronically.[1] Open outcry trading is face-to-face trading with each trader serving as his own auctioneer. The traders stand in a *pit* (an octagon shaped area with several steps along all the sides) and make bids and offers to one another (via shouting or flashed hand signals) to buy and sell designated contracts.

In most cases, only one type of contract is traded in each pit. For example, one pit may be a NASDAQ 100 pit and another a S&P 500 pit. Many other pits exist. In addition to pits being contract specific, each futures exchange trades only specific contracts. A contract trades on a specific exchange because the contract is proprietary to the exchange, or in other cases primarily because that exchange introduced the contract.

---

[1] *After-hours* electronic trading at the Chicago Mercantile Exchange (CME) began in 1992, when currency futures became the first contracts that could be traded electronically after the exchange floor pits were closed. At the time, this was a groundbreaking innovation, introduced to meet the needs of an increasingly global economy. The emerging worldwide marketplace had created demand for access to 24-hour currency price protection. After-hours trading was made possible by the development of the GLOBEX electronic order entry and trade matching system. Now, GLOBEX serves as an after-hours trading vehicle for many different CME contracts. The GLOBEX system has also hosted another innovation in the futures industry: futures contracts developed specifically for online trading. Generally, these contracts are called E-mini contracts ("E" because they're traded electronically and "mini" because the contracts are smaller than their pit-traded counterparts). Most notable among these products are the highly successful E-mini S&P 500 contract and the E-mini NASDAQ-100 contract.

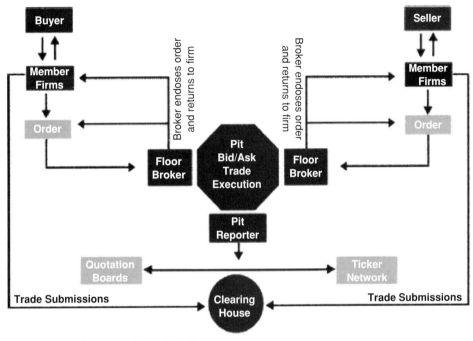

FIGURE 9-1   Structure of a trading floor.

Source: www.cme.com.

Whether trades are executed in the pits or matched electronically, the trading process in both cases consists of an *auction* in which all bids and offers on each of the contracts are made known to the public and everyone can see that the market's best price prevails. This is the price discovery process since the sellers get to see the prices the buyers are willing to pay and the buyers get to see the prices the sellers are willing to accept. Figure 9-1 shows how orders are matched and recorded in a futures trading pit.

9.3   FORWARD CONTRACTS

Many books focus on futures contracts because they are exchange-traded. Forward contracts are over-the-counter contracts between two trading parties. This fact makes forward contracts different from futures contracts, not less important. Section 9.2 will discuss some important characteristics of forward contracts and the discussion will take place in context of interest rate forward contracts.

9.3.1   Institutional Details for Forward Contracts

A forward contract is an agreement to buy (long position) or sell (short position) a specified asset at a certain time in the future for a certain price (the delivery price). The contract is an *over-the-counter (OTC)* agreement between two individuals or companies and the delivery price is usually chosen so that the *initial net present value* of the contract is zero. That is, the current spot price is compounded forward at the appropriate discount rate and adjusted for certain costs and benefits. No money changes hands when the contract is first negotiated, and the payment is settled at maturity. Because forward contracts are negotiated individually, the forward price may vary between different buyers and sellers for contracts of the same maturity and amounts.

One of the most popular forward contracts is one that fixes the interest rate on a loan for some time in the future. These contracts are referred to as **forward rate agreements (FRA)**. These contracts are almost exclusively offered by banks. To facilitate the discussion of how these FRAs are created and valued, the term structure of interest rates will be reviewed before the discussion of FRAs begins.

9.3.2 Understanding Implied Forward Interest Rates

Expected future interest rates are the spot rates investors expect at some point in the future. These expected future interest rates are fundamental to the pricing of all interest-based and foreign exchange-rate-based derivative securities. In the context of forward contracts, the expected future interest rate is referred to as the **implied forward interest rate**. The implied forward interest rate is the market's estimate of the interest rate that will prevail in the future for specific time dimensions or horizons. That is, it is the future rate implied in the term structure of interest rates (see Chapter 3). When the term structure of interest rates was developed in Chapter 3, Treasury securities' rates were used to isolate the effect of time from the other factors such as default risk. When estimating implied forward interest rates, investors often use the term structure of **repo rates** instead of the *term structure of Treasury rates*. The reason for using repo rates is that only the government can borrow and lend at the Treasury rates. The least risky rate that investors can borrow and lend at is the repo rate on T-bills.

When *forward rate agreements* (FRAs) are examined, the implied forward rate is based on the expectations theory of interest rates, which assumes that investors are indifferent to maturity risk and that they will buy and sell debt instruments of different maturities until the expected yields on all instruments are equal over the planning period. That is, the rate of interest on a two-year bond is equal to the compounded rate of interest on a one-year bond rolled over into a second one-year investment at the beginning of the second year, assuming the instruments are of equal risk.

Now, for a quick review of the term structure of interest rates under the expectations theory, assume that an investor has a two-year investment horizon. The investor can either (1) buy a two-year bond with a known investment rate, or (2) buy a one-year bond with a known one-year investment rate and roll that bond over into another one-year bond at the end of one year at a currently unknown rate. Whether an investor chooses a two-year bond or a one-year bond is a function of the investor's expectations, today, of the investment rate at the beginning of the second year.

Using the algebraic notation from the discussion of the expectation theory for the term structure of interest rates in Chapter 3, let the yield on the two-year bond be $_0r_2$ and the yield on the one-year bond be $_0r_1$. Notice how the first subscript tells you the period in which the rate begins and the second subscript tells you when the rate ends. Therefore, $_0r_2$

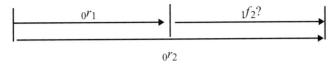

FIGURE 9-2 Relationship between spot and forward interest rates.

refers to the annualized bond yield for two years starting at time 0. Given these two pieces of information ($_0r_2$ and $_0r_1$), the expected yield on a one-year bond starting in one year, $_1f_2$, can be determined. If the investor invests €100 in a two-year bond, at the end of year two, the investor will have

$$€100 \times (1 + _0r_2)^2_0.$$

If the investor invests €100 in a one-year bond and rolls it over into another one-year bond for an additional year, the investor will have

$$€100 \times (1 + _0r_1) \times (1 + _1f_2).$$

The investor will be indifferent between the two investment strategies if the expected value at the end of year two was the same under each investment alternative. That is

$$€100 \times (1 + _0r_2)^2 = €100 \times (1 + _0r_1) \times (1 + _1f_2).$$

For the total dollar amount to be the same under each alternative, then

$$_1f_2 = [(1 + _0r_2)^2/(1 + _0r_1)] - 1.$$

That means that $_1f_2$ is the reinvestment rate which equalizes the two investment alternatives. Take a look at Figure 9-2.

If the investor expects $_1r_2 > _1f_2$, then with a two-year investment horizon, the investor would choose to buy a one-year bond and roll it over for the second year because[2]

$$(1 + _0r_2)^2 < (1 + _0r_1) \times (1 + E[_1r_2]).$$

If the investor expects $_1r_2 < _1f_2$, then the investor would choose to buy a two-year bond because

$$(1 + _0r_2)^2 > (1 + _0r_1) \times (1 + E[_1r_2]).$$

According to the expectations theory of interest rates, the *yield on a multiple period investment instrument must equal the expected yield on sequential one-period debt instruments.* Therefore, a simple formula for deriving a forward rate from the term structure of zero-coupon bonds is

$$(1 + _{n-1}f_n) = (1 + _0r_n)^n/(1 + _0r_{n-1})^{n-1}, \tag{9-1}$$

[2] The term $_1r_2$ means the actual one-period rate the second year. At the beginning of year one (time zero) the investor has an expectation of the value of $_1r_2$ which is referred to as the expected value. The notation for the expected value of $_1r_2$ is $E[_1r_2]$.

where

$$_0r_n = \text{the yield on a zero-coupon bond that matures } n \text{ periods from today,}$$

$$_0r_{n-1} = \text{the yield on a zero-coupon bond that matures } n - 1 \text{ periods from today,}$$

$$_{n-1}f_n = \text{the break-even interest rate that equates the return on an } n\text{-period}$$
zero-coupon bond to that of an $(n - 1)$-period zero-coupon bond rolled over into a one-year bond in year n.

This general equation has a simple interpretation. The numerator on the right-hand side is the total growth factor of an investment in an n-year zero-coupon bond held until maturity and the denominator is the growth factor of an investment in an $(n - 1)$-year zero-coupon bond. Because the investment in the numerator lasts for one more year than the investment in the denominator, the difference in these growth factors must be the rate of return available in year n when the $(n - 1)$-year zero-coupon bond can be rolled over into a one-year investment. In other words, the rate of rate available in year n is the *implied forward interest rate*.

9.4 CHARACTERISTICS OF FRAs

An FRA is an over-the-counter product generally offered by banks to allow borrowers and lenders to reduce the uncertainty of future interest rates. That is, an FRA is *not* a loan contract; it is an interest rate guarantee without a loan commitment. Hence, it is a derivative contract designed to manage potential changes in future loan interest rates for lenders and borrowers.

The buyer of an FRA is referred to as the **notional borrower** and is protected against a rise in interest rates, but must pay if rates fall. The seller of an FRA is referred to as the **notional lender** and fixes the rate for lending. The FRA seller is therefore protected against a fall in interest rates, but must pay if rates rise. The buyer and seller in an FRA are referred to as a notional borrower and a notional lender because no lending occurs in an FRA. The loan amount is identified in an FRA so the interest rate on the loan can be managed, but since no lending occurs, the loan is called a notional loan.

The **notional loan** is for a specified amount in a specified currency that will be drawn on a particular date in the future and will last for a specified term. An FRA is expressed as a combination of digits representing months, with everything measured from time zero (0 on a timeline). For example, a forward rate agreement that covers a three-month period (**coverage period**) but does not start for three months (**deferral period**) is a 3 × 6. Similarly, an agreement for one-year starting in nine-months time would be a 9 × 21. That is, an FRA is described as:

$$\text{deferral period} \times (\text{deferral period} + \text{coverage period}).$$

Because FRAs are over-the-counter instruments, the deferral period and coverage period are negotiated with the bank.

When an FRA is arranged, no lending or borrowing actually takes place. Instead, a notional loan will be made at a fixed rate of interest, which is generally the implied forward rate when the FRA is arranged. What the FRA does is to provide protection against a movement in interest rates. *This protection is in the form of a cash payment—the settlement sum—which compensates each party for any difference between the interest rate agreed to and the rate prevailing when the FRA matures.* If interest rates are higher than the agreed rate, the FRA seller (notional lender) makes a cash payment to the FRA buyer (notional borrower). If interest rates are lower, the FRA buyer (notional borrower) makes a cash payment to the FRA seller (notional lender).

EXAMPLE *Understanding How an FRA Works*

Suppose a company's current borrowing rate is a variable rate defined as three-month LIBOR + 85 basis points. Currently LIBOR equals 5.25%, but LIBOR changes daily. The company likes its current borrowing rate of 6.10% (LIBOR + 85 basis points) and wants to lock-in this rate on a $75,000,000 three-month loan with the loan beginning three months from today.

The company enters into an agreement to *buy* a 3 × 6 FRA on a notional principal of $75,000,000 at a rate of 5.25%. This agreement locks-in the variable rate component (LIBOR) of the company's borrowing rate.[3] However, suppose that in three months, LIBOR is 5.15%. How does the FRA function so the company pays the desired rate of 6.10% (current LIBOR + 85 basis points)?

In 90 days, the interest that the company actually pays on a newly negotiated loan would be equal to the new LIBOR plus the credit spread or 6.00% (5.15% + 0.85%). However, the company expected to pay 6.10% (5.25% + 0.85%) based on the negotiated FRA. A characteristic of forward rate agreements is that they cover only the LIBOR index and the credit spread is ignored. Therefore, the amount of interest actually paid on the loan, which is based on the prevailing LIBOR index, would be[4]

$$\$75,000,000(0.0515/4) = \$965,625.$$

The amount of interest expected to be paid in 180 days based on the negotiated FRA is

$$\$75,000,000(0.0525/4) = \$984,375,$$

which gives us a future value difference of $-\$18,750$.

It is not customary to wait until the end of the contractual coverage period, that is, the end of the 6 part of the 3×6 to pay the interest. Rather, what banks do is to discount the difference in funds at the end of the FRA to the beginning of the contractual coverage period—the end of the deferral period, the end of the 3 part of the 3×6 (see Figure 9-3) at the market rate prevailing at the beginning of the coverage period to arrive at the *settlement sum*.[5]

$$\text{Settlement sum} = \$18,750/(1 + 0.0515/4) = \$18,512,$$
$$\text{Settlement sum} = \$18,512.$$

Since the prevailing LIBOR index is lower than the FRA rate, the corporation (borrower) must compensate the bank for the present value difference in interest amounts. If the company had entered into an agreement to sell an FRA, the bank would have paid instead of being paid the above amount.

---

[3] Technically speaking, the rate on an FRA is a negotiated rate, although in many cases the bank merely states the rate at which it is willing to offer the FRA.

[4] The interest on the loan is paid concurrent with the end of the FRA period which is 180 days from the time the FRA was negotiated (the 6 part of the 3 × 6).

[5] Because the interest rates are known with certainty at the beginning of the deferral period, calculating the amount that is owed is easy. More importantly, however, banks want to get the FRA off their books as quickly as possible to free up the equity capital for other customers' activities.

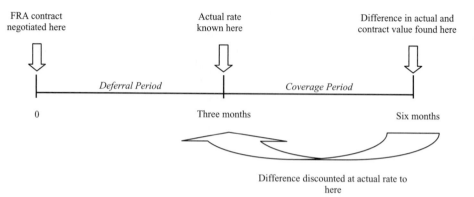

FIGURE 9-3 Example of a 3 × 6 FRA.

In the preceding example, a settlement sum was calculated which is the amount of money that changes hands in an FRA. The standard formula for calculating the settlement sum (S_{FRA}) is

$$S_{FRA} = [(r_R - r_C) \times A \times (\text{days/basis})]/[1 + (r_R \times (\text{days/basis}))], \qquad (9\text{-}2)$$

where

$r_R = $ the **reference rate,**

$r_C = $ the contract interest rate,

$A = $ the notional contract amount,

Days $= $ the number of days in the contract period,

Basis $= $ the day count convention (360 for $, 365 for £).

Using Equation (9-2), the settlement sum for the example above is calculated as follows:

$$[(0.0515 - 0.0525) \times (\$75\text{ MM}) \times (90/360)]/(1 + 0.0515 \times 90/360)$$
$$= -\$1,875/1.012875$$
$$= -\$18,512.$$

Thus, the negotiated rate in the FRA ends up being the effective rate of interest, exclusive of the credit spread, for the period the FRA covers. Here are the calculations to check the effective rate for the company of the $75,000,000 loan.

$ 18,750	(settlement sum paid of $18,512 compounded at 5.15% for three months)
+ $965,625	(interest payment at LIBOR rate of 5.15% in FRA)
$984,375	(total payments on $75,000,000)
5.25%	($984,375/$75,000,000 × 4 = 0.0525)
+ 0.85%	(credit spread)
6.10%	(effective rate on loan)

9.5 INTRODUCTION TO FUTURES

As shown before with the FRA example, the purpose of a forward contract is to eliminate price risk for a transaction in the future. However, because a forward contract is between two individuals or companies, the parties in the contract are exposed to **counterparty risk**. Futures contracts were developed to eliminate counterparty risk by having the clearing house be the counterparty on every futures contract. Another issue in an FRA is finding a bank that is willing to be part of the FRA. Futures contracts are exchange-traded, so all interested parties are in one location, making finding a trading partner much easier. With counterparty risk eliminated, the main function of modern futures markets is to eliminate price risk.

A futures contract is an obligation to buy or sell a specific quantity and quality of a commodity at a certain price on a specified future date, with all the contract features defined in a standardized contract provided by the clearing house. The specific future date identifies the month and year in which the futures contract ceases to exist (expires) and defines when the contract's obligation must be fulfilled. The month in which the futures contract expires is called the **delivery month**.

Figure 9-4 lists several commodities for which futures contracts exist along with the ticker symbol for the futures contract. The figure also provides the expiration month symbol for futures contracts.

Futures contracts are either held to maturity in order to effect delivery, or they are closed out by offsetting transactions. For the vast majority of futures contracts (about 97%), the contract is closed out before maturity. The reason most futures contracts are closed out with an offsetting transaction before maturity (sold if one has bought; bought if one has

Products	
Live cattle	LC
Class IV milk	DK
Feeder cattle	FC
Butter	DB
E-mini feeder cattle	FM
Lumber	LB
Lean hogs	LH
Oriented strand boards (OSB)	BD
Frozen pork bellies	PB
e-Hogs	HM
Milk	DA

Contract Month Symbols			
January	F	July	N
February	G	August	Q
March	H	September	U
April	J	October	V
May	K	November	X
June	M	December	Z

FIGURE 9-4 Ticker symbols for selected futures contracts.

sold) is that most futures contracts are used to hedge price risk. Although holding a futures contract until maturity seldom happens, when it does happen the contract is settled either by the exchange of the physical commodity or cash, as in the case of a financial index futures contract.

For example, if you were a cattle rancher, your objective would be to raise and sell cattle at a price that would give you the most profit. Therefore, your risk would be declining cattle prices. You could transfer (eliminate for you) this risk by selling (taking a short position) cattle futures contracts. If cattle prices fall, you could buy back the futures contracts at a price lower than you previously sold them. This gain on the futures transaction generally will offset your cash loss from selling the cattle in the herd. Hence, the risk of lower prices is eliminated (or transferred to someone else). The buyer can be a speculator who anticipates that cattle prices will increase (accepting the transfer of these risks in hopes of generating a profit) or a commercial user (such as a beef processor) who needs cattle and would be adversely affected by higher cattle prices.

One of the advantages of futures contracts over forward contracts is that there is far more liquidity in futures contracts. Because forward contracts are private two-party agreements, speculators cannot participate in this market and arbitrage any price differences. However, speculators can, and often do, enter the futures market in the hopes of making large profits.

One of the most intriguing cases of futures market speculation involves Hillary Rodham-Clinton, now the junior senator for New York State, once the First Lady of the United States of America. According to the *Wall Street Journal,* Ms. Rodham-Clinton, a lawyer who knew virtually nothing about the cattle futures market, speculated in the cattle futures market between October 11, 1978, and July 31, 1979. Over the 202 days in this period, she was able to make a profit of $99,541 on an initial investment of $1,000. Anderson, Jackson, and Steagall (1994) estimate the probability of obtaining such a sizable return, giving the investor the benefit of the doubt whenever doubt existed. Ignoring transactions costs and commissions, their most conservative estimate of this probability was approximately 1 in 31 trillion. Assuming that the return was made in the most efficient way possible, the probability falls to approximately 1.5×10^{16}.[6]

Now that futures contracts have been introduced, the remainder of this chapter will focus on examples of pricing and hedging using specific futures contracts. Remember, this chapter uses examples instead of a general formula for pricing because every futures contract has its own pricing formula. Therefore, no general formula exists. The first example will cover short-term interest rate futures contracts and compare this futures contract to forward rate agreements. Then, stock index futures contracts will be discussed because these contracts are very similar to other types of futures contracts. Finally, the long-term Treasury bond futures contract will be examined. This contract is perhaps the most interesting of all futures contracts although it also has some of the more complicated pricing techniques.

---

[6] It was subsequently reported that the firm with which Ms. Rodham-Clinton had placed the trades had manipulated the timing of the trades so that any profits would always accrue to Ms. Rodham-Clinton.

9.6 INTEREST RATE FUTURES CONTRACTS

Originally, futures were almost exclusively done with agricultural commodities to solve problems like those faced by the Canadian farmer earlier in this chapter. However, futures contracts do not have to be on commodities. A futures contract is a contract to buy or sell *something* at a specified future date. That *something* could be a physical asset, such as wheat, metal, or oil, but in today's world it could also be interest rates or other financial instruments.

The main difference between forward and futures contract is that in a futures contract you have to buy or sell in *standard* amounts on *standard* assets on *standard* delivery dates. In exchange for agreeing to all of these standard terms, the buyer or seller gets several important considerations. Futures are **exchange-traded** so there is minimal *counterparty* risk. The *clearing house* becomes the counterparty for both the buyer and the seller. Also, because the futures market is an open outcry market, all actual and potential participants know what the current market prices are and there is no possibility of differential pricing as is the case in an OTC market.

9.6.1 How Short-Term Interest Rate Futures Work

The first thing that has to be done when working with an interest rate futures contract is recognize the objective of an interest rate futures contract. The objective is usually to lock in an interest rate so that the correct amount of money will be available when it is needed. Therefore, the amount of money needed at an investment's maturity must be identified. But, the amount available at maturity is a function of *the interest rate which is available at the beginning of the investment period.*

Figure 9-5 shows how this works. Suppose you need a certain amount of money in July. However, the current month is January. You will receive a large amount of money in April, say, from a very reliable customer's accounts receivable. Your problem is that you are not sure now what rate you can invest those funds at in April to get the amount you need in July.

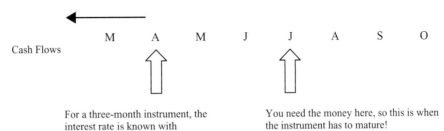

FIGURE 9-5 Identification of the timing of an interest rate futures contract.

Back in Chapter 4, the importance of the money market was discussed. One of the instruments discussed was a three-month Treasury bill, a discount instrument. The importance of this type of debt instrument is that the investor knows with certainty what the yield on the Treasury bill will be at the beginning of the three-months if it is held to maturity.

This same idea shows up here. If you buy a three-month Treasury bill in April, then you will know with certainty the amount of money that you will receive in July from the T-bills. So, in this case, you want an April futures contract (a futures contract that expires in April) to buy new three-month Treasury bills in the amount that will provide the necessary funds in July.

Here, you need to be able to lock the interest rate you earn on T-bills from April to July; therefore, you want a futures contract that expires in April, the point at which you want to purchase the three-month T-bills that will mature in July. You can get T-bill futures contracts that expire in other months. However, they would be of no value to you in this situation because they would not lock in the interest rate for the dates used in this example because the contract would not be for a transaction date in April.

At this point, a helpful reminder is that futures contracts can be viewed as a two-part deal. The first part is the actual futures contract itself, which can increase or decrease in value, and the second part is the underlying asset, which also increases or decreases in value. The combination of these two positions is what locks in the price (rate) for the hedger.

The long position in a future is an obligation to buy; the short position (writing) in a future is an obligation to sell. When dealing with short-term interest rate futures and forwards, it is important to be clear on what the contract is buying or selling. In the case of an FRA, the individual is buying or selling the *interest rate.* In the case of an interest rate future, the individual is buying or selling the *underlying financial instrument which is inversely related to the interest rate—just like a bond!*

Interest rate futures are quoted as 100 minus the rate of interest. This pricing convention affects the decision of whether to be long or short. A borrower is concerned about interest rates rising; therefore, borrowers take a short position in futures contracts to lock in their interest rate. *Because the pricing of futures is inverse, so is the trading.* Obviously, if a borrower takes a short position in the futures contract to lock in the interest rate, then a lender will take a long position in the futures contract to lock in the interest rate. With FRAs, the borrowers take long positions in the interest rate agreements to lock in their interest rate. When hedging with FRAs, investors take short positions in the interest rate agreements but, when hedging with futures, investors take long positions to lock in their rates.

When a trader takes a futures position, the position is described as either being long (a position to buy) or short (a position to sell). A position in a futures contract is referred to as taking a long or short position because the trader is not required to pay a transaction price on the contract. Instead, the trader is required to post the initial margin, which is a small percentage of the contract value. The initial margin is a deposit paid to the exchange at the inception of the transaction. The margin serves as a performance bond. It ensures that the buyer or seller has sufficient wealth to withstand changes in the value of futures contracts.

Trading unit	$1,000,000
Delivery/expiry	Mar, Jun, Sep, Dec
Quotation	100 − rate of interest
Min. price movement	$0.01
Tick value	$25

FIGURE 9-6 Orlando mercantile exchange contract specification of three-month interest rate futures.

Futures positions are **marked-to-market** every day. The exchange automatically calculates the daily gain or loss on the futures. This amount is called the daily **variation margin** and is received from or paid to the clearing house the next day. If the amount in the trader's margin account is insufficient, the broker will contact the customer asking for additional funds to be deposited. This action is referred to as a **margin call**. The amount to be deposited is the amount necessary to return the trader's margin account to the initial margin amount. The clearing house has the right to liquidate the futures positions of anyone who has insufficient margin on hand. The potential of having insufficient margin is referred to as **margin risk**.

Figure 9-6 shows a fictitious three-month interest rate futures contract. Each contract has a notional value of $1 million and contracts mature every year in March, June, September, and December. Contracts are not available for fractions of $1 million nor are they available in any other than the four specified months. The two conditions limit the cost market participants have to pay for the standardized contracts. The minimum price change in any contract is 1 cent. This minimum price movement is known as a **tick** and is essential in figuring out the additions and subtractions from the trader's margin account since each tick results in a $25 change in the margin account.

EXAMPLE *Making Interest Rate Futures Work*

Suppose that the month is March and a company plans to invest $100,000,000 in a project starting in September. That is, the company will spend $100,000,000 in September so it needs to have its money available at that time. To finance this project, the company plans on using the money from the sale of an obsolete division. This sale will occur in June. Therefore, the company gets its money for the September project in June. The first thing the CFO of the company has to do is to compare the dates of the exposure to interest rate changes to the futures dates. See Figure 9-7.

Figure 9-7 shows that the company is exposed to interest rate changes from June to September. Therefore, the contract the CFO needs is the June contract. The fictitious futures contract in Figure 9-6 will be used in the remainder of this example.

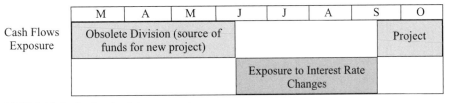

	M	A	M	J	J	A	S	O
Cash Flows Exposure	Obsolete Division (source of funds for new project)						Project	
				Exposure to Interest Rate Changes				

FIGURE 9-7 Project hedging example.

Day	Closing price	Tick change	Margin change
Mon initial position	$ 93.51	0	0
Mon close	$ 93.54	+3	$ 7,500
Tue close	$ 93.53	−1	−$ 2,500

FIGURE 9-8 Evolution of closing prices and margin.

Next, the CFO needs to determine the number of standard contracts needed to cover the amount of money exposed to interest rate changes. Remember, the amount of the exposure may cover more than one futures contract. To determine the number of contracts all the CFO has to do is divide the amount of the exposure by the trading unit of the futures contract. In this case, the CFO is lucky. The result is an even 100 contracts. Later you will be shown what happens if things are a little less exact (see Section 7, Understanding Stock Index Futures).

Now, the CFO has to decide whether to buy or sell the future. Essentially, this question boils down to, *"Am I afraid I will have to pay more interest than I want to?"* If this is the question, then the CFO is a borrower during the exposure period and wants to take the short position in futures to avoid paying more. However, if the CFO is asking, *"Am I afraid I will earn less interest than I need to?"* then the CFO is an investor and wants to take the long position in futures to lock in the rate of interest to be earned. Since the company needs a certain amount of money for its project in July, the company is concerned about interest rates falling, which would cause them not to earn enough. To meet the company's needs, the CFO will take a long position in the futures contract.

Suppose the CFO takes the long position in 100 June futures contracts quoted at $93.51. This means that at the time the CFO enters into the contract, the three-month interest rate must have been 6.49%. Now, its time to see how the hedge works. First, the margin account changes will be examined on a daily basis. Then, the hedge will be examined to determine how well it worked overall to eliminate risk and lock in the interest rate.

The first two days activity in the company's margin account is provided in Figure 9-8.

As you can see, the initial position in the contract corresponds to a rate of 6.49% (100 − $93.51). At the time of the initial position in the contract the tick change and margin change were set at a starting point of 0. At the close of the first day, the three-month interest rate had fallen to 6.46%, from 6.49%, which means the contract value was changed by three ticks. When the interest rate falls, the price of this contract increases. Therefore, the contracts were worth $7,500 more than when originally purchased (100 contracts × three ticks × $25 per tick). Unfortunately, by the end of Tuesday, the three-month interest rate had rebounded a little and the margin account was automatically reduced by the clearing house by $2,500.

When the CFO bought the futures contract at $93.51, the CFO was locking in an interest rate of 6.49%. To determine whether the CFO was successful with the hedge, the gains and losses on the futures contract (these will show up in the margin account) plus the rate of return on investment have to be examined and then compared to the desired rate of 6.49%. That is, the fixed rate of interest at the time of the futures purchase = 6.49%, which is the rate that the futures locks in. This rate of return has to be compared to:

Futures profit	_____	MM
+ Return from investment	_____	MM
= Total return	_____	MM
Rate of return	_____	%

If this rate of return is the same as the lock-in rate then the hedge worked.

Assume that in June the futures contract settles at $94.45. This means that the three-month interest rate at the expiry of the futures contract was 5.55%. Therefore, the profit or loss on the futures contract must equal:

Change in the number of ticks × tick value × the number of contracts.

The CFO bought the 100 contracts at $93.51; therefore, there were 94 tick changes ($94.45 − $93.51) worth $25 each for each of the 100 contracts, which equals $235,000. Since the price of the contracts was higher in June than they were in March, the CFO made a profit of $235,000 on the futures contracts.

The CFO can now invest the $100 million for three months at 5.55%, which means that the company will earn $100,000,000 × 5.55% × 3/12 = $1,387,500. This makes the company's total return equal to $235,000 + $1,387,500 = $1,622,500. The total rate of return is therefore $1,622,500/$100,000,000 × 12/3 = 6.49%. The hedge worked correctly and eliminated the risk from changes in market interest rates. The solution is easier to see in the following form.

Fixed rate of interest at time of futures purchase = 6.49%. This was established when the CFO took the long position in the futures contract. The fixed rate has to be compared to:

Futures profit/loss	$0.235 MM	(94 × 25 × 100 MM)
+ Return from investment	$1.3875 MM	($100 MM × 5.55% × 3/12)
= Total return	$1.6225 MM	($0.235 MM + $1.3875 MM)
Rate of return	6.49%	($1.6225 MM/$100 × 12/3).

Note: while the futures contract is quoted at 100-rate, the actual price of this contract would be: $1,000,000 [1 − 0.0649(\frac{90}{360})] = $983,775.

9.6.2 Summary of FRAs and Short-Term Interest Rate Futures

This chapter began with reference to foreign exchange forwards. Then, forward rate agreements were discussed. The difficulty with FRAs is that there is an exposure to counterparty risk and, since they are traded OTC, every bank has the opportunity to price the instruments differently. To get around this problem, futures markets in financial instruments developed. Even though the futures markets created an environment that avoided counterparty risk and minimized costs, the standardization of contracts detracts from the customization that FRAs can provide investors.

Understanding how interest rate forwards and futures work allows traders to hedge changes in interest rates. In addition, since all forward and futures contracts function in a similar manner, understanding interest forward and futures contracts helps us understand other types of forward and futures contracts. Our attention will now turn to some of these other futures contracts.

9.7 UNDERSTANDING STOCK INDEX FUTURES

In this section, an example of hedging using a stock index futures contract will be discussed along with an *In the News* item and an *Industry Application*. The purpose for discussing stock index futures in this type of contract is similar to many other types of futures contracts, including commodity-based futures contracts and equity-based futures contracts.

EXAMPLE *Hedging with S&P Contracts*

Suppose an investor owns a portfolio of stocks worth approximately $62,300 that is highly correlated with the S&P 500 composite index. Assume that the date is late April and the investor believes that the large capitalization securities in the stock market are likely to decline dramatically in the next month or so. That is, the investor is extremely bearish in the short term and is expecting a 10 to 15% decline in many of the portfolio's stocks.

Clearly, the investor wants to protect the current value of the portfolio against the antici-pated decline. One choice available to the investor is to liquidate the portfolio and hold cash dur-ing the anticipated decline. However, this approach is costly and the investor likes the long-run potential of the portfolio. Therefore, the investor would prefer not to liquidate the portfolio if an-other alternative exists to protect the current value of the portfolio. One available alternative is to hedge the current portfolio value using an S&P 500 futures contract. This hedge is discussed next.

To protect the value of the portfolio, the investor decides to hedge the portfolio using an S&P 500 futures contract. To hedge, investors take a short position in the futures contracts when they expect declines in corresponding cash prices. Why? If prices decline as the investor ex-pects, when the futures contract is closed by buying the contract back (to offset the position), the investor pays a lower price, and thus makes a profit. Specifically, the investor in this exam-ple decides to enter a *short hedge* by taking a short position in one June E-mini S&P 500 futures contract.

Why does the investor sell only one E-mini S&P 500? The value of an E-mini S&P 500 futures contract is calculated by multiplying $50 by the futures index number (notice that this contract pricing method is very different from the contract pricing method for interest rate futures). Suppose that at the time the investor sold the contract, the E-mini S&P futures contract was trading at $1,210, which means it was worth $1,210 × $50 = $60,500. Thus, the investor needs roughly one contract to hedge a $62,300 portfolio. Notice, this does not exactly match the value of the portfolio. This variation means the investor is *not* completely hedged, so the investor is attempting to reduce price risk.

Suppose that the investor was correct and four weeks later the S&P 500 has in fact declined significantly. The investor's strategy to protect against losses with a short hedge on an S&P futures contract would have succeeded at least partially. Now, assume that the value of the investor's portfolio falls by about 10% to $56,200 and the June E-mini S&P 500 futures contract falls to $1,091.

At the end of April, the portfolio was worth $62,300. Four weeks later at the end of May, it was worth $56,200 and the resultant loss is $6,100. Now, look at the decline in the value of the futures contract. When the investor entered into the contract, it was worth $1,210 × $50 = $60,500. When the investor buys it back to close the position, it is worth $1,091 × $50 = $54,550. The investor has gained $5,950 on the futures hedging transactions. When the gain on the futures contract is set against the loss on the portfolio, the investor's net position is a loss of only $150.

In the E-mini S&P 500 hedge example, the hedge provided significant price protection against the portfolio's decline in value. How? The decline in the portfolio was offset by cash gains from closing out (in this case, by buying back) the position in the E-mini S&P futures contract. The profit from the futures contract enabled the investor to show a very small loss despite the significant decline in the market of 10%. Notice that the investor's loss was not completely offset. This happened for two reasons. First, the investor could not match the dollar value of the portfolio exactly because of the standard size requirement of the futures contract. Second, the investor's portfolio was highly correlated with the S&P Index but did not track it exactly. This mismatch in performance is known as *tracking error* or *market risk*.

What if the investor was wrong and the market had increased in value? If this scenario had happened, the investor would have had to consider removing the hedge by closing out the position in the short futures contract. This action would enable the investor to participate in any further upside in the market. Offsetting the futures contract as soon as the advancing market trend was evident would be advisable; otherwise, the portfolio's gains would have been offset by losses in the E-mini futures contract.

IN THE NEWS[7]

One of the most recent developments in the futures market has been the introduction of E-Mini S&P 500 futures contracts at the Chicago Mercantile Exchange (CME). The S&P 500 Index has been the benchmark by which professional money managers measure their portfolio performance. The index is based on the stock prices of 500 large-capitalization companies and represents a broad cross section of the U.S. equity market, including common stocks traded on the New York Stock Exchange (NYSE), the American Stock Exchange (AMEX), and the NASDAQ. The Standard & Poor's Corporation designed and maintains the S&P 500 to be an accurate proxy for a diversified equity portfolio. The S&P 500 Index represents about 70% of the total domestic U.S. equity market capitalization. Standard and Poor's identifies several important industry sectors within the U.S. equity market, approximates their relative importance in terms of market capitalization, and allocates a representative sample of stocks with each sector to the index.

The index is capitalization weighted (shares outstanding times the stock price); each company's influence on the performance of the index is directly proportional to its market value. The daily index values reported in the press are exclusive of dividend income.

Mini S&P 500 futures are legally binding agreements to buy or sell the cash value of the S&P 500 Index at a specific future date. The contracts are valued at $50 times the futures price. For example, if the Mini S&P 500 futures price is at $920.00, the value of the contract is $46,000 ($50 × $920.00).

The minimum price movement of the futures contract is called a tick. The tick value is 0.25 index points, or $12.50 per contract. This means that if the futures contract moves the minimum price increment (one tick), say, from $920.00 to $920.25, a long (buying) position would be credited $12.50; a short (selling) position would be debited $12.50. All futures positions (and all short option positions) require posting of margin. Positions are marked-to-market daily. Additional deposits into the margin account may be required beyond the initial amount if your position moves against you.

Mini S&P 500 contracts are cash settled, just like the standard S&P 500; there is no delivery of the individual stocks. Even better, Mini S&P 500 daily settlements and quarterly expirations will use the exact same price as the S&P 500. The same daily settlement prices allow Mini contracts to benefit from the liquidity of the S&P 500 futures.

Like the S&P 500, which is settled using a special opening quotation (SOQ), all Mini S&P 500 positions are settled in cash to the same special opening quotation on the third Friday of the quarterly contract month. What is the special opening quotation, or SOQ, as it is often called? The final settlement price is an SOQ of the S&P 500 Index based on the opening prices of the component stocks in the index, or on the last sale price of a stock that does not open for trading on the regularly scheduled day of final settlement.

---

[7] This information was drawn from the website for the Chicago Mercantile Exchange at www.opwiz.com/IndexTradingKit/e-minis/e-mini5.html.

INDUSTRY APPLICATION

UNDERSTANDING FAIR VALUE

Very often one of the tasks that falls to an intern in a brokerage house is explaining to clients terms that they hear on financial programs such as CNBC's *Squawk Box*. One such term is "fair value" and often you can hear Mark Haines saying that based on the fair value the market is set to open "up" or "down." But, what exactly does this mean?

First, you have to understand that the discussion centers on the difference between the value of the S&P 500 when it closed on the previous trading day and the value of the futures contract as it trades before the NYSE opens for trading. Before the market opens, everyone knows exactly where the S&P 500 closed (this is referred to as the cash market) and, since it is closed it is not changing. But, the futures are trading in Chicago in an after-hours session. In fact, they trade all night and up to 9:15 A.M. EST. So, during those pre-stock market hours, the spread between the futures contract and the cash market is changing.

Remember that the futures trading on the Chicago Mercantile Exchange is independent of the S&P itself. The contracts expire quarterly in March, June, September, and December. When fair value is discussed, we are referring to the next-expiring futures contract. This is known as the "front month," although no one ever seems to actually use the term because that is simply assumed. So, in late March, after the March contract has expired, and in April, May, and early June, the "front month" is the June contract. A day before the June expires, September becomes the front month, and so on.

The futures contracts, because they are a "bet" on where the S&P will be at a point in the future, almost always trade at a price higher than where the S&P 500 index is at the same time, because most people assume stocks will rise. On rare occasions, the futures will trade below the actual S&P 500, which is referred to as a discount. The difference between the futures and the cash market is called the spread or the premium (since the futures are usually at a premium to cash).

Assume that on February 14, 2005, the S&P 500 closed at $1,206.14 and that in preopening trading the S&P 500 futures contract was trading at $1,210.24. In

this case, the premium was $4.10. But, as stock market trading begins, the futures and the cash can go in different directions. If the spread widens to, say, 5.00, the institutions will find stocks more attractive to own than the futures contract. So, they will buy stocks and sell the futures. If the spread narrows to, say 3.50, in this example, the institutions will sell stocks and buy futures, because their models tell them they will make more profit that way. So, by monitoring the spread, one can get a good idea of whether to expect sudden selling or buying by the institutions through the program trading systems.

One has to be careful, however. Remember that because stock markets are expected to rise, futures contracts tend to have a higher value than the cash market. Just because the futures value is greater than the cash value does not automatically mean a buying opportunity. You have to understand the "fair value" concept.

Let's take another look at our example:

S&P 500 closed at $1,206.14

Futures closed their session at $1,208.34

So, the spread is $2.20

Fair value is $4.10

Here, the futures closed at only a 2.2 point premium to cash (this is possible because the futures continue to trade for a few minutes after stocks have closed). But, in the "after-hours" futures session, the futures are up another 1.90, to 1,210.24. So, at +4.10 we are at exactly fair value. Up 4.10 sounds good, until you realize that what counts is where the futures contract value is relative to the fair value.

Where did that fair value come from? Remember the futures value is equal to the spot price compounded forward to expiry at the T-bill yield minus the S&P dividend yield.

$$F = S\, e^{(r-d)T}.$$

It is possible for a declining futures price to still be a positive. If the futures and cash closed far enough apart, say by 6 points, then a 1-point decline in the futures

(continued)

UNDERSTANDING FAIR VALUE

would still leave a spread of 5 points, which, in our example, would be enough to trigger buy programs at the open.

When dealing with clients, it is always important to cover all of the important issues. For example, while the predictive value of the spread is very certain, it is also very short-lived. In the morning, the effect is gone within the first few minutes of trading. The spread can suggest which direction the market will go at the open, but once trading starts, the market can change direction quickly.

The greatest importance of fair value for the average investor probably lies in the area of "market on open" orders. People who instruct their brokers to buy or sell when the market opens should be aware of how the open is likely to go. A second important point is realizing the effect of program trading based on the relation to fair value will have. Knowing that program trading is more likely at the open, investors should be less concerned if the market drops sharply in the first few minutes while program trading runs its course.

9.8 TREASURY BOND AND TREASURY NOTE FUTURES

Another difference between interest-rate-based futures contracts and the futures contracts on equities or commodities is that the latter generally do not experience differential price changes resulting from the term structure of interest rates. T-bill futures contracts are used to mitigate interest-rate risk in the short term. T-bond and T-note futures are used to mitigate interest-rate risk on a longer-term basis. Futures contracts that deal with longer-term interest-rate instruments will now be examined.[8]

The purpose of T-bond and T-note futures is to hedge price risk stemming from the long end of the yield curve. The good news is that T-bond and T-note futures are the correct hedging instrument; the bad news is *how long is the long end of the curve*? Any long-term bond is eligible for delivery to satisfy a T-bond futures contract if the bond has at least 15 years remaining to maturity on the first day of the delivery month. Obviously, a big difference exists between a 5% coupon 25-year bond and a 9% coupon 16-year bond. So, which bond can be delivered for settlement of the contract? The answer is both of them. However, it is reasonable to assume that the seller in the futures contract will deliver the most economical instrument. In other words, the seller will provide the bond that is **cheapest-to-deliver**. As a result, the T-Bond futures contract tends to trade at the price associated with the bond that is cheapest-to-deliver.

To help solve the problem, the futures clearing house produces a set of tables containing conversion factors. These conversion factors are designed to adjust time to maturity and differing coupon rates to a standard 6% coupon. Remember, however, that price relationships among cash market instruments change daily. Therefore, it is important to reconfirm the cheapest-to-deliver instrument at the close of each trading day.

---

[8] Interest-rate futures contracts are referred to as financial futures contracts in the terminology of the market.

9.8.1 Hedging with T-Bond Futures

Hedging with a T-bond futures contract works the same way as hedging with any other type of futures contract. Suppose a bank has a large portfolio of long-term U.S. Treasury bonds and that the bank's financial officers are concerned that interest rates will rise in the next month and cause a major decline in the value of their portfolio. Having an unhedged position like this would greatly upset the bank's risk manager, so they would probably decide to hedge by taking the short position in U.S. Treasury bond futures contracts. (Note that the hedging position is exactly the same as if they had been dealing with Treasury bill futures.)

Suppose that four weeks later, interest rates have gone up and the value of the bank's bond portfolio has declined. Now the bank's risk managers will offset their position by buying U.S. T-bond futures, which have also declined in value. The profits from closing out the futures position will offset somewhat the decline in the cash market value of the Treasury bonds.

Now, an important fact that must be mentioned is that the market does not always move as expected. However, a hedger accepts that possibility even though the opportunity to gain in the market may be forfeited. Refer to the example in Section 7 of this chapter concerning the investor who was hedging the stock portfolio with the E-mini S&P 500 futures contract. To an experienced hedger, establishing the protection of the investment is more important than worrying about the possibility of a missed profit opportunity.

9.8.2 Basis

The **basis** is the difference between the cash price for a specific commodity at a specific location and the price of a specific futures contract for the same commodity. Whenever basis is spoken about, the assumption is that the difference between the cash price and the price of the futures that is closest to delivery is being discussed unless a very clear statement has been made that the discussion concerns a different contract. Accordingly, the formula for calculating the basis is

$$\text{basis} = \text{cash price} - \text{futures price.} \tag{9-3}$$

Calculating the basis for an agricultural commodity is easy. For example; a farmer in Ohio is selling wheat. The local cash price on April 19 is $2.60 per bushel because a bumper crop is predicted and the May wheat futures contract is $2.65 per bushel. The basis at the Ohio location is −5 relative to the May futures contract. Of course, equally possible is that the crop in Nebraska may be very small because of poor weather conditions. Hence, the local cash crop there on the same day (April 19) is $2.85 per bushel because of the anticipated reduced supply. The basis at the Nebraska location is +20 cents over the May futures contract.

In the case of T-bond or T-note futures, the calculation of basis is a little more complicated because an adjustment must be made to the common 6% coupon base. This requires calculating a conversion factor. To calculate the conversion factor (*cf*) for a Treasury bond or a Treasury note, the price of the *adjusted* instrument priced at a 6% semiannual yield must be divided by the face amount on the T-bond or T-note. *Adjusted* means to round bond maturity and the coupon payment stream down to the nearest three-month period after the first delivery date of the future. For example, suppose that it is April 18, 2002, and a 9% semiannual Treasury bond with 16 years and 7 month's life remaining has a current yield to maturity of 7%. What is the basis of (the cost to deliver) this bond in a September contract? Here are the steps in the calculation.

1. In September the bond will have 16 years and two months life remaining, so round the maturity down to 16 years and assume the coupons are paid every six months after the first delivery date.

2. The price of a 16-year, 9% bond in 6% environment = $130.58.

3. Assuming a face value of $100, the conversion factor $cf = 1.3058$.

4. At a yield of 7% semiannually the bond price is approximately $119.07.

If the current futures contract price is 88.65, then the cost to deliver (the basis) this bond is

$$\$119.07 - 1.3058 \times \$88.65 = \$3.3108.$$

Figure 9-9 shows some of the reasons why the basis can change. Figure 9-10 provides the conversion table from the Chicago Board of Trade for Treasury bonds as of April 18, 2002.

As you can probably tell from Figure 9-9, the basis cannot be predicted precisely, but it is generally less volatile than either the futures price or the cash price. By knowing the basis, the hedger replaces the risk of price fluctuation with the lesser risk of a change in the relationship between the cash and futures price of the commodity, which we define as **basis risk**. Nonetheless, a change in the basis during the time of the hedge can seriously affect the results of the hedging transaction.

Agricultural commodities	Financial instruments
1. Carryover stocks from the previous year	1. Interest rates (cost of credit)
2. Expectations of the current year's production	2. Federal Reserve Board monetary policies
3. Supply and demand of comparable substitutes	3. Fiscal policies (reduced government spending)
4. Foreign production	4. Time to expiration of the futures contract
5. Storage costs	5. Cost of funding margin requirements
6. Availability of sufficient storage facilities	6. Coupon of the cash market instrument being hedged against the 6% futures contract coupon standard
7. Transportation costs	7. Supply of deliverable cash market instruments
8. Transportation problems	8. Domestic and foreign demand for cash market instruments
9. Insurance costs	9. Inflationary expectations
10. Federal policies	10. General level of business activity
11. Seasonal price fluctuations	11. Seasonal factors (e.g., quarterly tax payments)
	12. Liquidity of nearby vs. distant month contracts

FIGURE 9-9 Factors affecting the basis.

	Coupon	Issue Date	Maturity Date	Cusip Number	Issuance (Billions)	Mar. 2002	Jun. 2002	Sep. 2002	Dec. 2002	Mar. 2003	Jun. 2003

CBOT® U.S. TREASURY BOND FUTURES CONTRACT (See Footnotes, Page 1) — Page 3

This table contains conversion factors for all U.S. Treasury bonds eligible for delivery as of March 27, 2002. (The next tentatively scheduled update is April 18, 2002.)

6% Conversion Factors

No.	Coupon	Issue Date	Maturity Date	Cusip Number	Issuance (Billions)	Mar. 2002	Jun. 2002	Sep. 2002	Dec. 2002	Mar. 2003	Jun. 2003
1.)	5 1/4	11/16/98	11/15/28	912810FF0	$10.0	0.9011	0.9014	0.9019	0.9022	0.9027	0.9030
2.)	5 1/4	02/16/99	02/15/29	912810FG8	$10.0	0.9006	0.9011	0.9014	0.9019	0.9022	0.9027
3.)	5 3/8	02/15/01	02/15/31	912810FP8	$15.0	0.9148	0.9152	0.9153	0.9157	0.9159	0.9163
4.)	5 1/2	08/17/98	08/15/28	912810FE3	$10.0	0.9342	0.9346	0.9347	0.9351	0.9353	0.9357
5.)	6	02/15/96	02/15/26	912810EW4	$11.9	0.9999	1.0000	0.9999	1.0000	0.9999	1.0000
6.)	6 1/8	11/17/97	11/15/27	912810FB9	$19.5	1.0162	1.0160	1.0161	1.0159	1.0159	1.0158
7.)	6 1/8	08/16/99	08/15/29	912810FJ2	$10.0	1.0166	1.0166	1.0164	1.0165	1.0163	1.0164
8.)	6 1/4	08/16/93	08/15/23	912810EQ7	$21.8	1.0297	1.0296	1.0293	1.0293	1.0290	1.0289
9.)	6 1/4	02/15/00	05/15/30	912810FM5	$15.0	1.0337	1.0335	1.0335	1.0332	1.0332	1.0330
10.)	6 3/8	08/15/97	08/15/27	912810FA1	$8.6	1.0483	1.0482	1.0479	1.0478	1.0475	1.0474
11.)	6 1/2	11/15/96	11/15/26	912810EY0	$9.4	1.0638	1.0633	1.0632	1.0627	1.0626	1.0621
12.)	6 5/8	02/18/97	02/15/27	912810EZ7	$9.6	1.0799	1.0797	1.0792	1.0790	1.0785	1.0782
13.)	6 3/4	08/15/96	08/15/26	912810EX2	$8.1	1.0951	1.0948	1.0942	1.0938	1.0933	1.0929
14.)	6 7/8	08/15/95	08/15/25	912810EV6	$10.2	1.1088	1.1084	1.1077	1.1073	1.1066	1.1061
15.)	7 1/8	02/16/93	02/15/23	912810EP9	$15.3	1.1324	1.1317	1.1307	1.1300	1.1290	1.1283
16.)	7 1/4	08/17/92	08/15/22	912810EM6	$9.9	1.1453	1.1445	1.1434	1.1426	1.1414	1.1406
17.)	7 1/2	08/15/94	11/15/24	912810ES3	$9.2	1.1839	1.1828	1.1819	1.1808	1.1799	1.1787
18.)	7 5/8	11/15/92	11/15/22	912810EN4	$7.0	1.1902	1.1889	1.1878	1.1864	1.1853	1.1839
19.)	7 5/8	02/15/95	02/15/25	912810ET1	$9.3	1.2001	1.1992	1.1980	1.1971	1.1958	1.1949
20.)	7 7/8	02/15/91	02/15/21	912810EH7	$10.1	1.2092	1.2078	1.2061	1.2047	1.2029	1.2014
21.)	8	11/15/91	11/15/21	912810EL8	$30.2	1.2281	1.2264	1.2249	1.2232	1.2217	1.2199
22.)	8 1/8	08/15/89	08/15/19	912810ED6	$18.7	1.2263	1.2245	1.2224	1.2206	1.2185	1.2166
23.)	8 1/8	05/15/91	05/15/21	912810EJ3	$10.0	1.2390	1.2371	1.2355	1.2336	1.2320	1.2300
24.)	8 1/8	08/15/91	08/15/21	912810EK0	$9.8	1.2405	1.2390	1.2371	1.2355	1.2336	1.2320
25.)	8 1/2	02/15/90	02/15/20	912810EE4	$9.5	1.2706	1.2686	1.2662	1.2641	1.2617	1.2596
26.)	8 3/4	05/15/87	05/15/17	912810DY1	$15.6	1.2695	—	—	—	—	—
27.)	8 3/4	05/15/90	05/15/20	912810EF1	$7.6	1.3002	1.2977	1.2954	1.2929	1.2906	1.2879
28.)	8 3/4	08/15/90	08/15/20	912810EG9	$16.9	1.3024	1.3002	1.2977	1.2954	1.2929	1.2906
29.)	8 7/8	08/15/87	08/15/17	912810DZ8	$11.2	1.2845	1.2818	—	—	—	—
30.)	8 7/8	02/15/89	02/15/19	912810EC8	$13.3	1.3010	1.2985	1.2957	1.2931	1.2902	1.2875
31.)	9	11/22/88	11/15/18	912810EB0	$7.2	1.3115	1.3085	1.3058	1.3028	1.3000	1.2969
32.)	9 1/8	05/15/88	05/15/18	912810EA2	$6.8	1.3186	1.3154	1.3125	1.3092	1.3063	—
				Number of Eligible Issues:	32	32	31	30	30	30	29
				Dollar Amount Eligible for Delivery:	$386.7	$386.7	$371.1	$359.9	$359.9	$359.9	$353.1

FIGURE 9-10 Chicago Board of Trade conversion table for treasury bonds.

The basis for debt instruments is almost completely dependent on interest rates; therefore, the historical basis behavior of debt instruments does not carry the same significance as it would for agricultural commodities. However, certain patterns do exist in the financial markets. For example, quarterly tax payments sometimes have a tendency to affect short-term (usually overnight) interest rates on the 15 of April, June, September, and December. These abrupt changes can affect both the cash and futures markets for a couple of days both before and after the 15 of the months when tax payments are made.

Similarly, because portfolio managers are often measured against the S&P 500 Index for performance appraisal purposes, they have been known to adjust their portfolio's market positions by selling losing positions and/or buying winning positions before the end of the quarter and the required performance report calculations. These actions can affect the 7 to 10 day period around the end of each quarter (March, June, September, and December).

Notice below that distant interest rate futures contracts (those that expire later in the year) are generally priced lower than the nearby contract in a normal market. On April 18, 2002, for example, U.S. Treasury bond futures closed at:

Expiry Month	*Close Quote*	*Close Price*[9]
June 02	100-09	100.281
Sep 02	99-05	99.156
Dec 02	98-07	98.219
Mar 03	97-11	97.344

One reason that distant month contracts are lower than nearby contracts is because of the *positive cost of carry*. The **cost of carry** is the cost of financing the investment and includes any interest payments received minus any short-term borrowing costs and transactions costs. The cost of carry can be either positive or negative. Suppose that a company CFO can borrow at 7.5% to buy a 9% $100,000 Treasury bond currently trading at par:

Annual coupon payment:	$100,000 × 9%	=	$9,000,
Annual finance cost:	$100,000 × 7.5%	=	$7,500,
Annual cost of carry:	$9,000 − $7,500	=	$1,500,
Monthly cost of carry:	$1,500/12	=	$125.

With a *positive cost of carry*, the cash instrument is priced at a premium to the futures contract. Because the gains increase as the holding period increases, the nearby futures contract trades at a premium to the distant futures contracts as noted in the April 18 prices. However, if the cost of carry is negative, as indicated below, the CFO would lose $125 per month until the delivery. Assume a scenario where the CFO must pay 10.5% to finance the purchase of the Treasury bond:

Annual coupon payment:	$100,000 × 9%	=	$9,000,
Annual finance cost:	$100,000 × 10.5%	=	$10,500,
Annual cost of carry:	$9,000 − $10,500	=	−$1,500,
Monthly cost of carry:	−$1,500/12	=	−$125.

[9] Both the cash and futures markets in Treasury notes and bonds are quoted in 32nds, hence to determine what the price has to be, 100-09 has to read as 100 and 9/32 and can be converted to $100.281.

To compensate for the *negative cost of carry*, the CFO would trade the cash instrument at a discount to the futures contract. Because the carrying costs rise as the holding period increases, the futures price of the nearby contract must trade at a discount to the distant contract months.

9.8.3 Hedging with Treasury Bond Futures

Hedging in the futures market involves two actions by the hedger. Depending on the hedger's position, the first step is to take either a long or short position in futures contracts. The second step will be to close this position by engaging in an offsetting position: sell a long position or buy a short position. In both cases, the contract for opening and closing the position must be for the same commodity, the same number of contracts, and the same delivery month.

Short hedges are used as a temporary substitute for a subsequent cash market sale of the underlying commodity because the purpose is to lock in a selling price. When dealing with financial instruments and especially interest-rate-related instruments like Treasury bonds, the short hedge not only locks in a selling price but also it locks in a yield because yield and price are inversely related.

Long hedges are used when the investor is planning to buy a cash commodity at some time in the future. Again, the purpose is to lock in a buying price and, again, for interest-rate instruments, this process not only locks in a purchase price but also a yield.

EXAMPLE *A Hedge with T-Bond Futures*

Suppose that in June, a bank, acting as a primary dealer, had just purchased $100 million of U.S. Treasury bonds (7% maturing in 2017) in the recent auction for 99-00. The bank's risk managers are concerned because interest rates could increase before the bank can complete the selling of the bonds in the retail market. Without completion of the bond sale the value of the bond portfolio would decrease. To address their concern about a possible increase in interest rates, the risk managers decide to acquire a short hedge by selling 1,000 September T-bonds at 98-00.

Once again, the risk managers at the bank were right and interest rates increased, causing the value of the T-bond portfolio to fall to 94-16. To close the bank's futures position, the bank will have to buy the same September futures contract which is now trading at 94-01. Now, review the positions.

Cash Position	*Futures Position*
June	
Buy $100,000,000 T-bonds @ 99-00 or $99,000,000	Short 1,000 September T-bond contracts @ 98-00 or $98,000,000
Now	
Market falls to 94-16 or $94,500,000	Offset short of 1,000 September T-bond contracts @ 94-01 or $94,031,250
Result	
−$4,500,000	+$3,968,750

Because the futures position ended in a profit, the cash market loss was almost completely offset. The bank lost only $531,250 using the hedge instead of losing almost $4.5 million which it would have lost without the hedge. Remember, however, that the bank would have had to pay commissions and transactions costs both when it established the futures position and when it closed it out, but these costs are generally very low.

EXAMPLE *continued*   *A Weighted Hedge*

The bank's hedge in the previous example could have been improved by "adjusting" the number of futures contracts used to hedge the underlying cash position (bond portfolio). What is needed is to compensate for the greater decline in the dollar value of the cash bond versus the decline in the futures price. This is accomplished by adjusting the number of futures contracts in the hedge and is referred to as *a weighted hedge.*

The number of futures contracts needed in a weighted hedge is determined by multiplying the conversion factor of the T-bond by the par value of the cash bonds, divided by the par value of the futures contract. Suppose that in this case the conversion factor for the 7% 2017 T-bonds was 1.130 (see Section 8.2 for how to calculate the conversion factor). Recall that the bank is hedging a bond portfolio worth $100,000,000. In addition, assume that one T-bond futures contract is for $100,000 in Treasury bonds.10

$$\text{Number of futures contracts in the weighted hedge} = 1.130 \times (\$100,000,000/\$100,000)$$
$$= 1,130 \times 1,000$$
$$= 1,130.$$

Assume that the bank's risk managers round their hedge position down to 1,100 contracts. Using the same situation as in the earlier case, notice what happens to the hedge results.

Cash Position	*Futures Position*
June	
Buy $100,000,000 T-bonds @ 99-00 or $99,000,000	Short 1,100 September T-bond contracts @ 98-00 or $107,800,000
Now	
Market falls to 94-16 or $94,500,000	Offset short of 1,100 September T-bond contracts @ 94-01 or $103,434,375
Result	
−$4,500,000	+$4,365,625

The advantage to using the weighted hedge is clear. The risk managers were able to reduce the potential loss on the hedge from $531,250 to $134,375.

Hedges are also used quite frequently by institutional investors to reduce their exposure to the risk of fluctuating interest rates. A classic example is one of a mutual fund manager who wants to take advantage of the high yield offered on U.S. Treasury notes in May, but the company's cash flows are

---

10 The CBOT specifies its T-bond futures contract as one U.S. Treasury bond having a face value at maturity of $100,000 or multiple thereof.

weak because of unexpectedly high payouts and low new summer sales. By September, cash flows are expected to return to normal. Currently, long-term September Treasury note futures are trading at 94-12 while the cash notes are priced at 99-16. The manager wants to buy the 5.5% T-notes that mature in May 2005 and calculates that a weighted hedge requires 103 September T-note futures and takes a long position in them at 94-12.

Over the next few months, the interest rates decline, raising the cash market value of the T-notes to 101-04, and the price of the T-note futures rises to 96-00. Look at the effect of this hedging activity.

	Cash Position	*Futures Position*
May		
	T-notes are @ 99-16	Long 103 September T-note
	$9,950,000 (for $10 million face)	contracts @ 94-12 or $9,720,625
Aug		
	T-notes @ 101-04	Offset long of 103 September T-note
	or $10,112,500	contracts @ 96-00 or $9,888,000
Result		
	−$162,500	+$167,375

If the manager had not established the long hedge, the fund would have paid an additional $162,500 to buy the T-notes in the cash market in August. Using the T-note futures to hedge the purchase price, the manager not only avoided the additional cost but generated a profit of $4,875, which further reduced the purchase price.

Although this example shows that the manager made an additional profit on the futures position, additional profits do not always happen. Suppose the T-note futures and cash prices had fallen to 91-00 and 96-04. Now examine the position.

	Cash Position	*Futures Position*
May		
	T-notes are @ 99-16	Long 103 September T-note
	$9,950,000 (for $10 million face)	contracts @ 94-12 or $9,720,625
Aug		
	T-notes @ 96-04	Offset long of 103 September T-note
	or $9,612,500	contracts @ 91-00 or $9,373,000
Result		
	+$337,500	−$347,624

In this situation, the manager lost money on the futures position. However, even though the manager lost money on the futures contract, the loss on the futures contract would be offset by a lower purchase price on the T-notes in the cash market. One of the main reasons hedging works is because the cash and futures markets tend to follow similar price trends. Therefore, if the cash price of a commodity falls, the futures price tends to follow a similar trend. Even though the manager may have lost $347,625 on this futures position, the price of the T-notes is $337,500 less than anticipated. The manager has to remind himself that in May the purchase price of 99-16 looked very attractive for the notes and it should look even more attractive now.

The cost that hedgers pay for protection is the inability to take advantage of a price move after the hedge has been established. An experienced hedger considers this a good trade-off.

DEVELOPING VALUATION AND RISK MANAGEMENT SKILLS

1. Understand the purpose of forward and futures contracts.

The major characteristics of forward and futures contracts are compared and contrasted in Figure 9-11. Forward contracts and futures contracts are used to reduce price risk by establishing, at the outset of the contract, the delivery price for the commodity in the future.

2. Understand the FRA contract and how to calculate the settlement payment on an FRA.

Forward rate agreements offer protection against a movement in interest rates. The protection is in the form of a cash settlement which compensates each party for any difference between the rate agreed to and the actual rate when the FRA matures. FRA settlement sums are paid on a discounted basis at the end of the deferral period. Borrowers buy FRAs but sell interest-rate futures contracts to lock in interest rates. Investors sell FRAs but buy interest-rate futures contracts to lock in interest rates.

3. Understand interest-rate futures contracts and how to calculate the price of an interest-rate futures contract.

The instruments underlying an interest-rate futures contract is an interest-bearing security or time deposits. The price of the interest-rate futures contract equals $(100 - \text{rate})$, where rate is the interest rate or yield on the underlying interest-bearing security.

4. Be able to use an interest rate futures contracts to hedge an exposure to movements in market interest rates.

Changes in the variation margin account of a futures contract help offset gains or losses in the cash market commodity. Gains or losses in futures contracts may not exactly offset gains or losses in the cash market instrument because of market risk or basis risk.

5. Understand T-note and T-bond futures contracts and their uses as hedging instruments.

	FRAs	Futures
Type	OTC	Exchange
Administration	Low	High
Margins	None	Clearing house
Amounts	Any amount	Standard
Maturity	Any maturity	Standard
Liquidity	High	High
Flexibility	High	Low
Restrictions	Fewer	Restricted
Bid/offer spreads	Wider	Narrower
Credit Risk	Some	Low

FIGURE 9-11 Characteristics of major forward and futures contracts.

For T-bill futures contracts, the deliverable instrument is a three-month T-bill; but for T-bond and T-note futures contracts, the deliverable instrument is the cheapest-to-deliver bond or note.

QUESTIONS

1. Explain how management can preserve financial value if it is selling its products to a country where the interest rate is higher than the domestic rate.

2. One understands why a farmer needs to know what the future price of the crop will be, but who would agree to take the other side of the transaction and why?

3. Why is the repo rate used instead of the Treasury bill rate? What types of institutions can access the repo rate?

4. Suppose the four-year zero-coupon Treasury rate is 7% and the five-year zero-coupon Treasury rate is 7.5%. What is the one-year Treasury rate commencing at the end of year four?

5. What is the difference between the deferral period and the coverage period in an FRA?

6. What is the difference between the reference rate and contract rate when settling an FRA?

7. What role does the tick size play in calculating the variation margin adjustment?

8. Both forward contracts and futures contracts allow investors to eliminate price risk. What risk in forward contracts leads to the creation of futures contracts? What does the investor give up in a futures contract for the elimination of the additional risk from the forward contract?

9. In a T-bill futures contract, is the trader setting the interest rate or the purchase price for the T-bill? Explain.

10. The CFO of a company plans to invest in a new project six months from today. This is because the money for the project becomes available three months from today and the CFO plans to invest the money in three-month T-bills so the CFO will know that the funds will be available for the start of the project. If the CFO wants to lock-in today's market yield on three-month T-bills, what position will the CFO need to take in a T-bill futures contract?

11. What is a margin call? What is margin risk?

12. An investor owns a stock portfolio and is concerned that in the near future economic events may occur that would dramatically reduce the value of the portfolio. The investor's portfolio is positively correlated with the S&P 500 Index. If the investor decides to hedge the portfolio with an S&P 500 futures contract, what position will the investor need to take in the futures contract? With the futures position, will the investor still be exposed to price risk in the stock portfolio? Explain.

13. In connection with T-note and T-bond futures contracts, what is meant by the phrase *cheapest-to-deliver*?

14. Define *basis* in a futures contract. Is the basis more or less volatile than the futures or cash market price? Explain.

15. How do you calculate the conversion factor in a T-note or T-bond futures contract?

16. If a position in a futures contract is designed to eliminate price risk, what is the point of a weighted hedge? What role does the conversion factor play in a weighted hedge?

REFERENCES

ANDERSON, S. C., J. D. JACKSON, and J. W. STEAGALL 1994, A note on odds in the cattle futures market, *Journal of Economics and Finance, 18(3)*, 357–365.
The authors examine the evidence on Hillary Rodham-Clinton's cattle futures trading. Using the rules of the market and the reported initial investment and reported profit, the authors determine that it is virtually impossible to generate the profits reported by Ms. Rodham-Clinton in the cattle futures market.

KEY TERMS

Basis The difference between the cash price for a specific commodity at a specific location and the price of a specific futures contract for the same commodity.

Basis Risk The risk of a change in value in the cash price minus the futures price.

Cheapest-to-Deliver The T-bond or T-note that is the most economical to deliver when adjusted for a 6% coupon.

Clearing House Term for the public institution that is a counterparty to all futures contracts.

Contract Rate The negotiated FRA rate.

Cost of Carry The cost of a particular financial position, usually the borrowing rate minus the investment rate. Some forward contracts include storage and other significant costs as part of the cost to carry.

Counter-Party Risk The risk that the counter-party to an over-the-counter transaction will not honor its obligations.

Coverage Period That part of a forward rate agreement for which interest rate protection is offered.

Deferral Period That part of a forward rate agreement which defines when the interest rate protection will begin.

Delivery Month The month in which actual delivery of the commodity can be made.

Exchange-Traded A public market.

Forward Contract An over-the-counter instrument to buy or sell a particular asset at a defined point, in the future, at a defined price.

Forward Rate Agreement (FRA) An over-the-counter legal contract defining the rate at which a party can borrow or lend over some defined period commencing at a defined point in the future.

Futures Contract An exchange-traded instrument to buy or sell a particular asset at a defined point in the future at a defined price.

Futures Price The expected market value of the asset at a defined point in the future.

Implied Forward Interest Rate The expected repo rate on an appropriate term of Treasury bills used to price forward and futures contracts.

Long Hedge Holding the cash market commodity short and buying the related futures contract.

Margin Call Call from broker to trader requesting that the trader deposit additional funds in the trader's margin account to cover accumulated losses in the futures position and return the margin account to its initial margin position.

Margin Risk The risk that the initial margin will be insufficient to withstand the losses accruing to the futures position.

Marked-to-Market A trader's position is reset each day to the current market price, with the daily gains or losses posted to the trader's margin account.

Notional Borrower The buyer of an FRA.

Notional Lender The seller of an FRA.

Notional Loan The implied principal of an FRA on which the interest calculations are based.

Price Risk The risk that the market price of a commodity will change between today and some specified time in the future.

Reference Rate The existing interest rate for the defined period when the FRA is settled.

Repo Rate The rate of return on a collateralized loan where the collateral is a basket of financial instruments.

Short Hedge Holding the cash market commodity long and selling the related futures contract.

Tick The minimum price movement in a futures contract.

Variation Margin Every buyer or seller posts an initial margin (performance bond) from which daily changes in the valuation of the futures position is posted.

CHAPTER 10

OPTIONS MARKETS

10.1 INTRODUCTION

The purpose of this chapter is to develop an understanding of how options work and an understanding of how to price options. Options provide an opportunity to limit downside risk while retaining the potential for upside gain. Accordingly, options are very powerful tools for the managers of any financial institution as the manager tries to protect shareholders' wealth while not limiting shareholders' gains. Thus, options are a risk management tool that will be used extensively in the second half of this book as we discuss risk management in the various financial markets. To use an option a financial manager must buy or sell the option, so the ability to correctly price an option is vital to the process. This chapter focuses on understanding the features of options and how to price them.

This chapter begins with the institutional details and the basics for options. Option basics are introduced through digital options. Digital options allow for the introduction of vector notation. Next, standard options are introduced and their payoff diagrams are discussed. The payoff diagrams along with the vector notation provide for an introduction to synthetic securities. The remainder of this chapter focuses on two methods for pricing options: (1) binomial option pricing and (2) the Black-Scholes option pricing model.

DEVELOPING VALUATION AND RISK MANAGEMENT SKILLS

1. Understand how digital options function and the vector notation that follows from the digital option.
2. Understand how standard options function and the payoff diagrams for standard options.
3. Understand how to create synthetic securities using the vector notation and the payoff diagrams.
4. Calculate the price of a standard option using binomial option pricing.
5. Calculate the price of a standard option using the Black-Scholes option pricing model.

10.2 INTRODUCTION TO OPTIONS IN A FAMILIAR SETTING

Because options have the aura of being an exotic or mystical vehicle, a very simple premise that should be familiar to all of you—the structure of a firm—will start the discussion. A firm requires a huge investment to be successful, so much money that the dollar amount is often beyond the financial capabilities of any one individual. In fact, even if one individual could finance the entire firm, he or she would be unwilling to do so because the risk of losing one's entire wealth in the case of failure would be too great. Hence, the problem that is being addressed is *how can risk be handled and at the same time be able to raise enough money?* Historically, the answer has been to create shares in the venture and to offer the purchase of these shares to the public. This structure has four major benefits:

1. **Divisibility of the claim.** By offering individual portions of equity at affordable prices that investors can purchase in any amount, the corporation has managed to divide the risk into manageable portions where the purchaser decides how much risk he or she is willing to take on.

2. **Upside financial benefits.** If the company does well, then the value of the common stock will also increase. Hence, the investors have the opportunity to earn a return on the risk they have taken.

3. **Downside risk protection.** Because of the concept of limited liability, investors cannot lose more than their total investment in the company. This concept relates directly to item 1, where the investor can choose the level of their investment and be confident in the knowledge that the worst-case scenario is the loss of the total value of the investment.

4. **Evaluation in an organized market.** Because the shares trade in a public market, the performance of the corporation can be measured in the increases and decreases of the stock price.

This process is an extremely efficient means to transfer risk from a single entity to many individuals. Very often, however, even this market is not sufficient to raise the total amount of money required and, as a consequence, a corporation often acquires debt financing. As an example, assume a construction company is formed to build a dam in Guyana. The company will raise the financing necessary, hire the contractors, buy the materials, build the dam, and, on completion, sell it to the government of Guyana at a fixed predetermined price. The problem here is that the cost of construction is uncertain while the final sales price is known. How profitable will this major project be?

An investment in the company's common stock has the same characteristics as an option. That is, the investor has purchased the opportunity at the initial stock price (the option premium) to earn additional returns. If, at the time when the sale of the dam finally takes place, the value of the firm exceeds the value of the debt (the strike or exercise price of an option), the excess belongs to the shareholders. To the extent that this value exceeds the option premium (the initial stock price), the investors have made a positive return. However, if the value of the firm is equal to or less than the value of the debt, firm ownership passes to the debt holder and the investors lose the initial investment and the opportunity to gain additional returns has expired worthless. Thus, an option (here the common stock) has upside potential and limited downside risk.

The value of an option is based on the value of something else. In our construction company example, the value of the option (the value of the common stock) is based on the profit from the sale of the dam minus the value of the debt. Thus, the value of an option is derived from the value of something else, which is why an option is referred to as a **derivative security**.

10.3 UNDERSTANDING THE BASICS OF PUTS AND CALLS

What is the basic premise of any option? To make things as straightforward as possible, a simple type of option contract called a **digital option** will be used to introduce options. A digital option has a payoff at maturity which is either a fixed amount or zero. As with any other investment vehicle, only two things can be done with an option: buy or sell. A **call option** is the right to buy something and a **put option** is the right to sell something. Suppose that we are dealing with a digital call option where, if a stock rises to the **strike or exercise price** of $10, the option is worth $1. If the stock price never rises to $10, then the option is worth nothing. Take a look at Figure 10-1, Panel A. The vertical axis measures the value V of the digital option, while the horizontal axis measures the price P of the underlying stock. Notice how the value of the digital option varies with the value of the stock. For the time being, ignore any transactions costs or commissions.

An alternate way of depicting this type of option would be to use vector notation such as

$$\text{Call}(C) = \begin{vmatrix} +1 \\ 0 \end{vmatrix}$$

where the $+1$ indicates the payoff if the stock price goes up to $10, and zero is the payoff if the stock price does not.

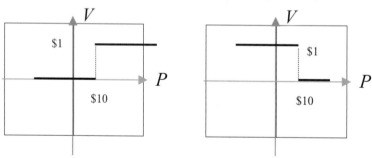

(Panel A) Digital Call Option   (Panel B) Digital Put Option

(Panel C) Combination of Digital Call and Put Options

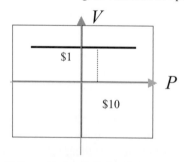

FIGURE 10-1 Payoff diagrams for digital options.

In Figure 10-1, Panel B, a digital put option is depicted. Here, if the value of the stock falls below $10, the digital option will pay $1. If the underlying stock does not fall below $10 then the option will expire worthless. That is, the payoff will be zero. To depict a digital put option in vector notation, we would use

$$\text{Put}\,(P) = \begin{vmatrix} 0 \\ +1 \end{vmatrix}$$

Suppose now that we were to buy both a digital put option and a digital call option on the same stock with the same $10 strike price. In this case, the new (combined) option would payoff regardless of the underlying value of the stock price. See Figure 10-1, Panel C. In terms of the vector notation, the combination of the digital call and the digital put is the sum of the vector for the digital call and the vector for the digital put:

$$\begin{vmatrix} +1 \\ 0 \end{vmatrix} + \begin{vmatrix} 0 \\ +1 \end{vmatrix} = \begin{vmatrix} +1 \\ +1 \end{vmatrix}$$

A 1,1 vector represents a risk-free position[1] in the absence of transactions costs or commissions.

10.4 UNDERSTANDING THE BASICS OF VECTOR ANALYSIS

The purpose of **vector analysis** is to demonstrate the net position an individual can hold as a result of combining various securities and derivatives. The vector is a two-row column where each row can take on one of three possible values: $+1, 0, -1$. The first entry in the vector represents the effect of a price rise in the security. The second entry represents the effect of a price drop in the security. Hence, a $+1$ indicates that the investors will gain from the price change, a -1 indicates that the investors will lose, and a 0 indicates that there will be no change in the investor's position.

Figure 10-2 lists various investment positions. Along with the investment positions are the positions' corresponding vector notation.

Look at some of these positions a little more closely. When an investor owns a stock (long a security) there are two basic possibilities: its value can go up or its value can go down. If the stock price goes up, $+1$ appears in the first row of the vector. If the stock price goes down, -1 appears in the second row. Now look at what happens if the investor had sold short the stock (short a security). The investor's hope is that the stock price will decline and can be purchased later at a lower price. But what happens if the value of the stock rises? In this case, the value of the investor's position has declined; therefore, -1 appears in the

---

[1] This is not the only possible verctor representation of an apparent risk-free position. Any position is risk free if the payoff is the same regardless of whether the strike price is met or not. However, if an investment guaranteed a positive payoff regardless of what would happen, it would be a money machine and would not be offered for sale. Similarly, if an investment guaranteed a negative payoff regardless of what would happen, nobody would want to buy it.

Long a security	$\begin{vmatrix} +1 \\ -1 \end{vmatrix}$
Short a security	$\begin{vmatrix} -1 \\ +1 \end{vmatrix}$
Buy a call	$\begin{vmatrix} +1 \\ 0 \end{vmatrix}$
Sell a call	$\begin{vmatrix} -1 \\ 0 \end{vmatrix}$
Buy a put	$\begin{vmatrix} 0 \\ +1 \end{vmatrix}$
Sell a put	$\begin{vmatrix} 0 \\ -1 \end{vmatrix}$

FIGURE 10-2 Vector description of an investor's position.

first row of the vector. Similarly, if the value of the stock declines, the value of the investor's position has increased and +1 appears in the second row of the vector.

Looking again at the digital call option, a similar payoff structure can be seen. If the value of the stock increases above the strike price, the option has value and +1 appears in the first row of the vector. If the strike price is never achieved, the option will expire worthless and the payoff is 0, the value which appears in the second row of the vector. But what would have happened if the option had been sold instead of bought? If an option is sold, the seller is said to be short the option. If the stock price rises, the buyer of the option will *certainly* exercise the option. But, more importantly, the seller of the option is obliged to honor the buyer's demand and hence will lose value—this result is shown by the −1 in the first row of the vector. If the stock price falls, the buyer of the option will let the option expire worthless since the stock is cheaper in the marketplace than it is under the terms of the option contract. The seller of the option will *not* be obliged to honor any demand to exercise the option and the seller's position will be unchanged. Hence, the 0 appears in the second row of the vector.

The vector notation for a digital put option works in the same manner as for the digital call option but in the opposite direction (take a look a Figure 10-1). The buyer of a digital put has the right to sell the stock at the strike price. If the stock price increases, the buyer of the put will not exercise the option and the value is unchanged; therefore, the first row of the vector is 0. However, if the price of the stock drops below the strike price, the buyer of the option will exercise the option and gain value; therefore, +1 goes in the second row of the vector. The seller of the put has to respond to the choice of the buyer. This means that when the buyer does nothing, there is no change in value for the seller and the first row of the vector is 0. However, the buyer of the put gains when the stock price declines, which means the seller loses and −1 appears in the second row of the vector.[2]

---

[2] In options, and in fact in all derivatives, the buyer and seller of the contract have offsetting positions. This is referred to as a zero-sum game. A zero-sum game means that for every winner in the game there is a loser, and the amount gained by each winner has an exact match in the amount lost by a loser.

EXAMPLE *Using Vector Notation to Create Synthetic Positions*

One of the advantages of vector analysis is that this very simple tool can be used to understand how to solve problems in managing risky positions. Figure 10-3 shows how to combine various instruments to achieve positions that may not be available in the marketplace. These types of positions are called **synthetic positions** because they replicate the same payoff as another vehicle without the investor having to hold the actual position in the other vehicle. This concept is very important and will be fully discussed later in this chapter.

Combination 1: Used if the desired call option is not available in the market.

Long Security	+	Buy a Put	=	Buy a Call

$$\left| \begin{matrix} +1 \\ -1 \end{matrix} \right| \quad + \quad \left| \begin{matrix} 0 \\ -1 \end{matrix} \right| \quad = \quad \left| \begin{matrix} +1 \\ 0 \end{matrix} \right|$$

Combination 2: Used if the desired call option is not available in the market.

Short Security	+	Write a Put	=	Write a Call

$$\left| \begin{matrix} -1 \\ +1 \end{matrix} \right| \quad + \quad \left| \begin{matrix} 0 \\ -1 \end{matrix} \right| \quad = \quad \left| \begin{matrix} -1 \\ 0 \end{matrix} \right|$$

Combination 3: Used if the desired put option is not available in the market.

Short Security	+	Buy a Call	=	Buy a Put

$$\left| \begin{matrix} -1 \\ +1 \end{matrix} \right| \quad + \quad \left| \begin{matrix} +1 \\ 0 \end{matrix} \right| \quad = \quad \left| \begin{matrix} 0 \\ +1 \end{matrix} \right|$$

Combination 4: Used if the desired put option is not available in the market.

Long Security	+	Write a Call	=	Write a Put

$$\left| \begin{matrix} +1 \\ -1 \end{matrix} \right| \quad + \quad \left| \begin{matrix} -1 \\ 0 \end{matrix} \right| \quad = \quad \left| \begin{matrix} 0 \\ -1 \end{matrix} \right|$$

Combination 5: Used to create a risk-free alternative.

Long Security	+	Write a Call	+	Buy a Put	=	Risk-Free Position

$$\left| \begin{matrix} +1 \\ -1 \end{matrix} \right| \quad + \quad \left| \begin{matrix} -1 \\ 0 \end{matrix} \right| \quad + \quad \left| \begin{matrix} 0 \\ +1 \end{matrix} \right| \quad = \quad \left| \begin{matrix} 0 \\ 0 \end{matrix} \right|$$

Combination 6: Used to create a risk-free position.

Short Security	+	Write a Put	+	Buy a Call	=	Risk-Free Position

$$\left| \begin{matrix} -1 \\ +1 \end{matrix} \right| \quad + \quad \left| \begin{matrix} 0 \\ -1 \end{matrix} \right| \quad + \quad \left| \begin{matrix} +1 \\ 0 \end{matrix} \right| \quad = \quad \left| \begin{matrix} 0 \\ 0 \end{matrix} \right|$$

FIGURE 10-3 Using vector analysis to identify combined positions.

Although it is interesting to see how various instruments can be combined to create other positions, it is important to remember that the positions represented by the vectors represent either cash inflows or cash outflows.[3] In the case of Combination 5, the cost [cash outlay ($)] of this risk-free position is equal to the price of the security (S) times the number of securities purchased (H) plus the put premium (P) minus the call premium (C). $\$ = H \times S + P - C$.

10.5 INTRODUCTION TO STANDARD CALL AND PUT OPTIONS

Now, in reality, although digital options do exist and are frequently used by corporations, by far the more popular type of option is one that has a payoff which is equal to the difference between the value of the stock and the strike price. This type of option is the standard type of option. For example, suppose a call option has a strike price of $100. If the stock price at the maturity of the contract is $105, the value of the option is $5. If instead, the stock price at maturity is $110, the option value is $10. Take a look at Figure 10-4. Here, the payoff diagrams to puts and calls that are structured in this fashion are shown. These diagrams are the payoff diagrams of standard options.

Several things should be noted about the diagrams in Figure 10-4. Look at Panel A and notice how the horizontal portion of the diagram is *below* the horizontal stock price axis. This represents the fact that the investor had to *pay a premium* in order to acquire the position. Note how in Panel B, when the investor sells the call, the horizontal portion is *above* the stock price axis and represents the fact that the seller *received a premium* for assuming this position. The actual payoff to the option above the strike price is represented by the angled portion of the diagram. In the case of a purchased call, the angled portion begins below the stock price axis since *the investor will not break-even until the stock price = strike price + premium paid.* Similarly, *the seller of the call option will not start to lose money until stock price = strike price − premium received.*

The relationship between the price paid for an option and the timing of the payoff results in some well-known terminology. The difference between the current stock price and the exercise (strike) price is known as the option's **intrinsic value.** When the intrinsic value is negative, the option is said to be **out-of-the-money.** When the intrinsic value is exactly equal to zero, the option is **at-the-money.** And, when the intrinsic value is positive, the option is **in-the-money.** Note that these terms do not describe the investment value for the investors. Instead, these terms refer to the current value of the option relative to its strike price.

Despite the fact that the payoff diagram of a standard option is somewhat different from a digital option, the usefulness of the vector analysis is not changed. The only difference in the interpretation of the vector notation is that instead of a unit payoff, as would be the case in a digital option, the +1 or −1 in the rows of the vector represent gains or losses.

---

[3] In fact, this is something of a drawback in the use of vector analysis in that while it is easy to assess the net position, it does not give us any indication as to the timing of the cash flows.

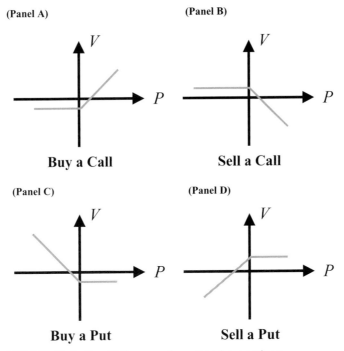

FIGURE 10-4 Payoff diagrams for call and put options.

Note: The diagrams are drawn with the strike price at the vertical axis.

At this point, a summary of the differences between buying and selling put and call options, that is, the differences between buying and selling the opportunities to buy and sell the underlying asset is useful. The following table summarizes the major concerns with the different options positions when they are held *in isolation*.

	Buy	Sell
Calls	• Pay a premium • Expect underlying asset price to rise • Expect to execute • Counterparty (seller) obligated to honor request to exercise	• Receive premium • Expect underlying asset price not to rise above exercise price • Expect not to execute • Counterparty (buyer) not obligated to request exercise
Puts	• Pay premium • Expect underlying asset price to fall • Expect to execute • Counterparty (seller) obligated to honor request to exercise	• Receive premium • Expect underlying asset price not to fall below exercise price • Expect not to execute • Counterparty (buyer) not obligated to request exercise

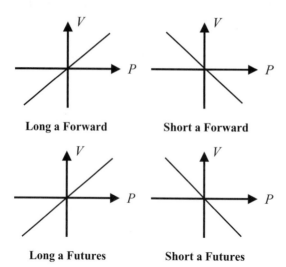

FIGURE 10-5 Payoff diagrams for forward and futures contracts.

In the last chapter, forward and futures contracts were described and the process to correctly price them was discussed. You learned that a forward contract was simply a delayed purchase or sale of an asset. Hence, forward contracts are assets. Chapter 9 also showed how a futures contract was really nothing more than a standardized forward contract with a clearing house that has its value updated every day. Figure 10-5 shows how the payoff diagrams for forwards and futures would be depicted. In terms of vector analysis, a long or short position in a forward or futures contract can be described as:

$$\text{Long position in a forward or futures contract} = \begin{vmatrix} +1 \\ -1 \end{vmatrix}$$

$$\text{Short position in a forward or futures contract} = \begin{vmatrix} -1 \\ +1 \end{vmatrix}$$

Having defined the vector notation for forward and futures contracts, the discussion can progress to how to create a synthetic forward or futures contract by combining standard put and call options. For example, suppose an over-the-counter forward contract to buy gold in three months time is not available. However, standard call and put options on gold are available; therefore, a synthetic forward can be created to meet our needs. Figure 10-6 shows the payoff diagrams and vector notation for the synthetic forward.

10.6 A LAST WORD ON SYNTHETICS—PUT-CALL PARITY

A reasonable assumption can be made that if both a put option and a call option were written on the same underlying asset with the same exercise price and the same maturity, their prices would be related. This assumption is true and the relation between the put price and the call price under these conditions is known as **put-call parity**. Be careful in your

Payoff Diagrams for a Synthetic Forward

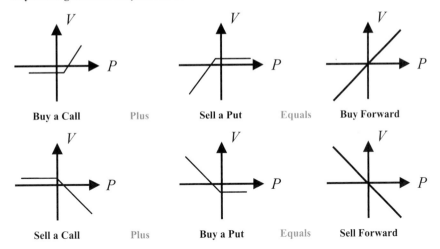

Vector Notation for Synthetic Forwards

Buy a forward   =   Buy a call   +   Sell a put

$$\begin{vmatrix} +1 \\ -1 \end{vmatrix} \quad = \quad \begin{vmatrix} +1 \\ 0 \end{vmatrix} \quad + \quad \begin{vmatrix} 0 \\ -1 \end{vmatrix}$$

FIGURE 10-6 Payoff diagrams and vector notation for synthetic forwards.

reasoning, however, as put-call parity does *not* mean the prices are the same—only that they are *related*. How does this relation work?

Put-call parity is based on the efficient market concept that two investments (single securities or portfolios) with the same cash flows and same risk must have the same price. Put-call parity is usually demonstrated by examining the cash flows from two investment strategies that create different portfolios, with a put option in one portfolio and a call option on that same underlying asset and at the same strike price as the put in the other portfolio. This process for developing put-call parity is discussed next.

Strategy 1 is to buy a share of the underlying asset (S) and buy a put (P) on this stock with an exercise price of X that matures at time T. Strategy 2 involves buying the discounted value of a risk-free bond where the maturity value is equal to X at time T. Strategy 2 also includes buying a call (C) on asset (S) at exercise price X expiring at time T. Now, the payoffs (cash flows) to each strategy (portfolio) at maturity must be examined. These are presented in Figure 10-7.

At maturity (time = T), there are three possible outcomes. Each outcome will be examined in turn, but before the outcomes are examined the payoffs for put and call options need to be defined. For the buyer of a call option, when a call is *in-the-money,* the buyer's payoff is the difference between the stock price (S) and the exercise price (X), but when the call is *not-in-the-money,* the call expires worthless and the buyer's payoff is 0. Mathematically, the payoff to the buyer of a call is defined as:

$$payoff = max[0, S - X].$$

Strategy 1	Strategy 2
Buy stock;	Buy call;
Buy a put	Buy bond that pays X at time T

Investment cash flows:

Strategy 1	Strategy 2
$S + P$	$C + PV(X)$

Value of each investment at maturity (time = T):

		Strategy 1	Strategy 2
Situation 1:	$S > X$	Value = S	Value = S
Situation 2:	$S < X$	Value = X	Value = X
Situation 3:	$S = X$	Value = S	Value = S

Since the outcomes are the same, the investments (price) must be equal, that is, $[S + P = C + PV(X)]$ or $P = C - S + PV(X)$.

This relationship is known as *Put-call parity*.

FIGURE 10-7 Put-call parity.

For the buyer of a put option, when a put is *in-the-money*, the buyer's payoff is the difference between the exercise price (X) and the lower stock price (S); but when the put is *not-in-the-money*, the put expires worthless and the buyer's payoff is 0. Mathematically, the payoff to the buyer of a put is defined as:

$$\text{payoff} = \max[0, X - S].$$

With the payoffs to the options defined, the payoffs from each strategy under the three possible outcomes can be examined. The first possible outcome is $S > X$. Under this condition Strategy 1 is the value of the stock (S) plus the value of the put option ($\max[0, X - S]$.) When $S > X$, the $\max[0, X - S] = 0$, Strategy 1 must be worth S. Under the conditions ($S > X$), Strategy 2 must be worth X (the value of the now matured risk-free bond) plus the value of the call ($\max[0, S - X]$). When $S > X$, the $\max[0, S - X] = S - X$. Thus, Strategy 2 is worth $X + (S - X) = S$.

The second possible outcome is $S < X$. Under this condition Strategy 1 is equal to S plus $\max[0, X - S]$. When $S < X$, the $\max[0, X - S] = X - S$. Then Strategy 1 equals $S + (X - S) = X$, the value of the exercise price. Strategy 2 equals X plus $\max[0, S - X]$. When $S < X$, then the $\max[0, S - X] = 0$. Thus, Strategy 2 equals $X + 0 = X$.

The third possible outcome is $S = X$. Under this outcome Strategy 1 is equal to S plus $\max[0, X - S]$, which equals $S + 0 = S$, the stock price. Strategy 2 is equal to X plus $\max[0, S - X]$, which equals $X + (S - X) = S$, the stock price.

Hence, under every possible outcome, the two strategies yield exactly the same outcome. Remember, under the efficient market hypothesis, if two assets (or portfolios) have the same payoff structures (cash flows), then they have to have the same price! What that means is that Strategy 1 and Strategy 2 have to have the same price. So,

$$\text{Strategy 1 price} = \text{Strategy 2 price}$$
$$S + P = C + PV(X)$$

and then rewritten to solve for P shows

$$P = C - S + PV(X).$$

This relation is known as put-call parity.

This formula has a very practical use other than just describing a pricing relation. Often there is a much greater demand for calls than for puts, so the desired put may not be available. Put-call parity not only demonstrates how to construct a synthetic put instrument, but it also provides the price of the synthetic put.

10.7 PRICING OPTIONS

10.7.1 The Concept of Replication

The previous section showed how to create one type of instrument by combining two or more other instruments. The ability to create an instrument from a combination of other instruments is the basis for a concept called *replication,* which is central to the pricing of options. Before examining the details of the concept of replication, an example from one of the most important annual university sporting events in the United States will be examined. In March of every year, the NCAA holds a basketball tournament in which 64 of the best teams in the country compete. At the end of every round, 50% of the teams win and move on to the next round; 50% of the teams lose and go home.

EXAMPLE *Replication*

Suppose the first round starts in three months and you and your best friend make bets with a bookmaker over whether Duke University (Duke) will beat the University of North Carolina (UNC) in the first round. You bet $52 that Duke will win. If Duke wins, you will win $100. However, if Duke loses, you will receive nothing. Your friend bets $46 that UNC will win. If UNC wins your friend will win $100. However, if UNC loses, your friend will receive nothing. The bookmaker has received $98 from the two bets but will have to pay out $100 at the end of the game.[4]

Where does the bookmaker get the money to pay off the bet? Suppose that the bookmaker can buy a three-month risk-free Treasury bill for $98 that will pay $100 at maturity. Notice that the payoff to the T-bill has exactly the same payoff as the two bets. Since these two "investments" have the same payoff, they should have the same price.

Using the vector notation, the bookmaker's position can be described by assigning a Duke win to row 1 and a UNC win to row 2. The T-bill pays $100 to the bookmaker regardless of the outcome of the game. The two bets will pay out $100. The vector notation shows that the bookmaker has a risk-free position.

$$\text{Buy a T-bill} \quad + \quad \text{Owe on two bets} \quad = \quad \text{Risk-free position}$$

$$\begin{vmatrix} +1 \\ +1 \end{vmatrix} \quad + \quad \begin{vmatrix} -1 \\ -1 \end{vmatrix} \quad = \quad \begin{vmatrix} 0 \\ 0 \end{vmatrix}$$

Now assume that the current prices for the Duke bet is $50 and the UNC bet is $45. A smart investor would be able to take advantage of this miss pricing. What would the investor do? First, the

---

[4] The example assumes no transaction costs. In reality, the bookmaker would charge a fee for handling the bets since he or she would want to make a profit. The fee is not part of the intrinsic value of an investment and thus is outside the framework of the replication, which is why no transaction costs are included in the example.

investor would sell the T-bill short; this will provide $98. Second, the investor would buy both bets for $95. The investor has now made $3. Furthermore, this amount is risk free because in three months, either Duke or UNC will win, thereby paying the investor $100 that will be used to pay off the debt (short position) on the T-bill, which is $100.

Obviously, if an investor could do this once and earn $3 risk free, then repeating this process over and over again would yield even more risk-free money. However, since the T-bill is risk free, the prices of the bets will change until their combined current price is $98. However, the bookmaker will need to price the bets individually. The individual price of a Duke bet to win and a UNC bet to win will be determined by the probability that one team will be able to beat the other. However, notice that a bookmaker does not have to be an expert in probability theory in order to determine the different prices. Suppose the bookmaker knows he can sell any number of bets that Duke will win for $52 but none at $53. Since the current price of a T-bill is $98, the bookmaker knows that the correct price to charge for a UNC bet is $98 − $52 = $46. This is an example of the concept of replication.

10.7.2   Binomial Option Pricing

This section begins the discussion of how to price options. The simplest option to price is a **European option** on non-dividend-paying stocks. A European option is an option that can only be exercised on its maturity date. Having only one day on which the buyer can exercise the option is the criteria that makes a European option the simplest to price. The alternative to a European option is an **American option**. An American option can be exercised on any day through the date of the expiration of the option. The price of American options will be discussed later in this chapter. Also to be discussed later is how to price options on stocks that pay dividends. But first, the basics of option pricing will be introduced using European options on stock that does not pay dividends.

The technique used to begin our discussion of option pricing is called a **binomial tree**. Simply said, a binomial tree is based on the assumption that asset prices will move up or down at known points in time. In a binomial tree, each node in the tree represents the stock at a given price and at a given time. From a node in a binomial tree, the stock can move to one of two other nodes, one period later in time.

For example, consider a tree where the stock can move up by 20% or down by 20%. Assume that the current share price is $125 and that there is a call option on the stock with a strike price of $120. What is the price of the call option? Figure 10-8 provides the binomial tree for the stock and the accompanying tree for the call option given the potential price changes. How the call option tree is developed using replication is discussed now.

If the stock starts at $125, in one period it will either be $150 or $100. Suppose the call option is one period away from expiration. Remember that the call option is a European call with a strike price of $120. Also, assume that the one-period interest rate is 5%. If, at the end of the period, the stock is worth $150, then the value of a call option at that time on this stock will be $30. However, if the value of the stock is $100, then the call option will expire worthless.

Using the replication techniques shown in the previous section, a portfolio of a bond and stock can be created that will replicate exactly the value of the call option regardless of whether the stock goes up or down in price. Notice that the range of call prices is $30. Since one share of stock has a range of prices after one period of $50, only 0.6 ($30/$50)

(Panel A) Binomial Tree of Stock Prices

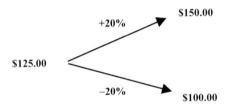

(Panel B) Binomial Tree of Call Prices

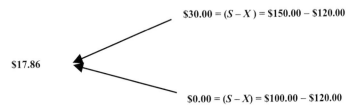

FIGURE 10-8 Binomial trees of stock and option prices.

shares of stock goes into the replicating portfolio. With 0.6 shares of the stock in the portfolio the range of the portfolio will be $30.

However, if the portfolio only contains the stock, after one period the portfolio would have values of $0.6 \times \$150 = \$90$ or $0.6 \times \$100 = \$60$. These values have the same range as the call, but not the same payoff as the call option. However, if a bond that has a repayment value of $60 after one period is borrowed (issued) today, then the portfolio of the stock and the bond has the same payoff as the call. The portfolio now has a value of $0.6 \times \$150 - \$60 = \$30$ when the stock is $150, and a value of $0.6 \times \$100 - \$60 = \$0$ when the stock is $100. This is exactly the same payoff structure as for the call option.

The new combined stock and bond portfolio $((0.6 \times S) + PV(60))$ has the same value as the call at both possible end values for the stock; therefore, it must have the same value as the call today. Mathematically, the value of the call option today when the current (today's) stock price is $125 is

$$c = (0.6 \times S) - PV(\$60)$$
$$= (0.6 \times \$125) - (\$60/1.05)$$
$$= \$17.86.$$

Figure 10-8 provides the binomial tree for the stock in Panel A and the corresponding tree for the option in Panel B.

Now that the process for binomial option pricing is understood, a general formula to calculate the value of a call option using the replication method with a binomial tree needs to be developed. To develop the general formula the following definitions will be used:

let S^u and S^d be the stock prices in the up and down states, respectively,

let c^u and c^d be the call prices in the up and down states, respectively.

The first step is to calculate the number of shares needed to form the stock part of the replication portfolio. This is done by calculating the ratio (H) of the call range $(c^u - c^d)$ to the stock price range $(S^u - S^d)$. Accordingly,

$$H = \frac{(c^u - c^d)}{(S^u - S^d)}.$$

Using the numbers from the preceding example, $H = (\$30 - \$0)/(\$150 - \$100) = 0.60$.

Now, the amount of cash that has to be borrowed must be calculated. This amount will be repaid at the time the call option matures.

$$\text{Let } (1+r) \times B = \text{amount of cash to repay}$$

$$-(1+r) \times B = \Delta S^u - c^u$$
$$= \Delta S^d - c^d$$
$$= (c^u S^d - c^d S^u)/(S^u - S^d).$$

Thus $B = PV[(1+r) \times B]$ is the amount of cash to borrow or lend,

$$-B = [(c^u S^d - c^d S^u)/(S^u - S^d)]/(1+r). \tag{10-1}$$

The value of the call is

$$c = (H \times S) - B. \tag{10-2}$$

Now, solving for H:[5]

$$H = (c^u - c^d)/(S^u - S^d). \tag{10-3}$$

To make the formulation even more general, assume

$$p = [(1+r)S - S^d]/[S^u - S^d], \tag{10-4}$$

where

$$p = \text{probability},$$

and substituting Equations (10-3) and (10-4) into Equation (10-2):

$$c = [pc^u + (1-p)c^d]/(1+r). \tag{10-5}$$

Equation (10-5) is the general formula for the call value at the base of any branch in a binomial tree.

Now, a one-period call option will be extended to a two-period call option. This example continues to use a stock that starts at a price of $125, with the stock price moving up or down 20% each period and the one-period interest rate at 5%. However, the strike price of the call option will be $110. Figure 10-9 contains the binomial trees for the stock price changes and the call option valuation. Notice, with two periods there are now three possible

---

[5] Traders often refer to the H in Equation (10-3) as $-H$ because it represents the short position needed in the stock for self-financing, which will be discussed.

(Panel A) Distribution of Stock Prices

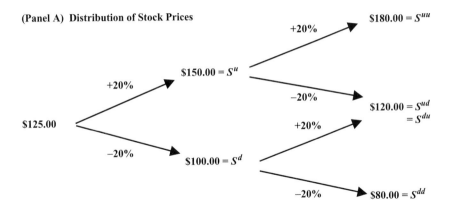

(Panel B) Distribution of Call Option Prices at a Strike Price of $110

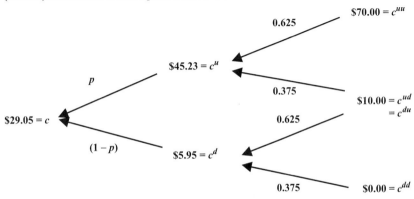

FIGURE 10-9 Distributions of stock and option prices.

final prices because the probability of a stock price increase times the probability of a stock price decrease is the same as the probability of a stock price decrease times a probability of a stock price increase. This type of binomial tree is known as a **recombination tree**. *The tree has the property that, at any time, an up move followed by a down move is exactly the same as a down move followed by an up move.* As a result, three equations have to be used to calculate the call option tree:

$$c^u = [pc^{uu} + (1 - p)c^{du}]/(1 + r),$$

where

$$p^u = [(1 + r)S^u - S^{ud}]/[S^{uu} - S^{ud}].$$

$$c^d = [pc^{ud} + (1 - p)c^{dd}]/(1 + r),$$

where

$$p^d = [(1 + r)S^d - S^{dd}]/[S^{du} - S^{dd}].$$

$$c = [pc^u + (1 - p)c^d]/(1 + r),$$

where

$$p = [(1 + r)S - S^d]/[S^u - S^d].$$

These equations will be used to calculate the value of the two-period call price. *To calculate the price of an option using a binomial tree you must work backwards from the right-hand side of the binomial option valuation tree.* Accordingly, when working from right to left in the option tree the first step must be to calculate the value of the option at the end of period two (the end of the two-period stock tree). The option expires at the end of period two; therefore, the value of the call is calculated using the following equation:

$$\text{payoff} = \max[0, S - X].$$

For the top node in the stock price tree (Panel A, Figure 10-9) the stock price is \$180. At this price the payoff of the call is max[0, \$180 − \$110] = \$70. This option payoff is the value for the top node in Panel B, Figure 10-9. The remainder of the period two option values are calculated in the same manner. Accordingly, the payoff for the middle node is max[0, \$120 − \$110] = \$10 and the payoff for the bottom node is max[0, \$80 − \$110] = \$0.

Next the value of the call at the node where the stock price is \$150 is calculated (see Figure 10-9). From this point the stock price can either decrease to \$120 or increase to \$180.

$$p^u = [(1+r)S^u - S^{ud}]/[S^{uu} - S^{ud}]$$
$$= [1.05 \times \$150 - \$120]/[\$180 - \$120] = 0.625.$$

Thus, the value of the call, if the current stock price is \$150, is

$$c^u = [p^u - c^{uu} + (1 - p^u)c^{du}]/(1 + r)$$
$$= (0.625 \times \$70 + 0.375 \times \$10)/1.05 = \$45.24.$$

This result makes quite a bit of sense since a high price for a call can be expected when the stock price is \$150 and the strike price is \$110.

Now, consider the value of the call where the stock price is \$100 and the stock can increase to \$120 or fall further to \$80.

$$p^d = [(1+r)S^d - S^{dd}]/[S^{du} - S^{dd}]$$
$$= [1.05 \times \$100 - \$80]/[\$120 - \$80] = 0.625.$$

Thus, at the time when the stock price is \$100 the value of the call is

$$c^d = [p^d c^{ud} + (1 - p^d)c^{dd}]/(1 + r)$$
$$= (0.625 \times \$10 + 0.375 \times 0)/1.05 = \$5.95.$$

This result of a low call price also makes good sense, since the likelihood that the final stock price at maturity will be below the strike price is quite high. Notice that the call option can have a positive value even when the strike price is above the current stock price (\$100). A positive call price at this point occurs because of the stock's potential to rise to \$120.

The final step is to calculate the value of the call at time 0, given that the stock price will either increase to \$150 or decrease to \$100.

$$p = [(1+r)S - S^d]/[S^u - S^d]$$
$$= [1.05 \times \$125 - \$100]/[\$150 - \$100] = 0.625.$$
$$c = [pc^u + (1 - p)c^d]/(1 + r)$$
$$= (0.625 \times \$45.23 + 0.375 \times \$5.95)/1.05 = \$29.05.$$

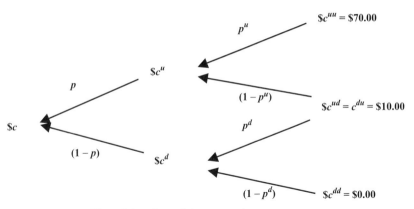

FIGURE 10-10 Binomial option pricing example.

The calculation of the price of the call in this two-period example is shown in Figure 10-9. Figure 10-10 provides supporting details for the option tree in Figure 10-9, and Figure 10-11 provides supporting details for the stock price tree in Figure 10-9. Figure 10-11 reminds the reader of the time that passes between nodes in the tree, which requires discounting of cash flows as the option price is calculated.

Options are priced on the assumption that hedging activity is always taking place. This process is known as taking a **risk-neutral position**. Risk-neutral positions are characterized by an approach that is known as the self-financing trading approach. That is, just as in the case of synthetic positions, an equal but opposite position is taken (the hedge) that will generate the exact same cash flows.

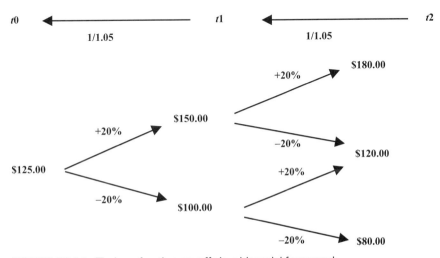

FIGURE 10-11 Timing of option payoffs in a binomial framework.

EXAMPLE   *Self-Financing Approach to Replicating a Call Option*

In order to maintain a risk-neutral position with respect to the call, a dynamic self-financing trading approach has to be used. Recall the two-year $110 strike call example. With the stock at $125 today, the possibility of a 20% up or down move each year, and an annual risk-free rate of 5%, the call is worth $29.05.

Suppose one call is bought at $29.05. This example shows that this call will cover the cost of hedging the put.

Today (time $= 0$ in binomial trees in Figure 10-9):

- Buy the call and pay $29.05.
  Call position $= \$29.05$ (asset).
- Immediately sell H shares of stock.
  $H = (c^u - c^d)/(S^u - S^d) = (\$45.23 - \$5.95)/(\$150 - \$100) = 0.7856$.
  Receive $0.7856 \times \$125 = \$98.20$.
  Stock position $= -\$98.20$ (liability).
- Invest proceeds in money market account.
  MM position $= +\$69.15$ (asset).

In one year (time $= 1$ in binomial trees in Figure 10-9):

- Stock $= \$150$ and call $= \$45.23$.
  Stock position $= -0.7856 \times \$150 = -\$117.84$.
  MM A/C $= \$69.15 \times \$1.05 = \$72.61$.
  Net worth $= \$45.23 - \$117.84 + \$72.61 = \$0.00$.
- Stock $= \$100$ and call $= \$5.95$.
  Stock position $= -0.7856 \times \$100 = -\$78.56$.
  MM A/C $= \$72.61$.
  Net worth $= \$5.95 - \$78.56 + \$72.61 = \$0.00$.

Still at one year (time $= 1$, adjust positions to reflect new prices):

- Stock $= \$150.00$ and call $= \$45.23$.
  Rehedge stock
     New $H = (\$70-\$10)/(\$180 - \$120) = 1.000$.
     Since the number is larger, must sell more stock.
     Sell $(1.000 - 0.7856) = 0.2144$.
     Receive $= 0.2144 \times \$150 = 32.16$.
     Increase MM A/C to $\$72.61 + \$32.16 = \$104.77$.
     Net worth $= \$104.77 - (1) \times \$150 + \$45.23 = \$0.00$.
- Stock $= \$100$ and call $= \$5.95$.
  Rehedge stock
     New $H = (\$10 - \$0)/(\$120 - \$80) = 0.25$.
     Since the number is smaller, must buy back stock.
     Purchase $(0.25 - 0.7856) = -0.5356$ shares.
     Spend $-0.5356 \times \$100 = \$53.56$.
     Decrease MM A/C to $\$72.61 - \$53.56 = \$19.05$.
     Net worth $= \$19.05 - 0.25(\$100) + \$5.95 = \$0.00$.

In two years (time = 2 in the binomial trees in Figure 10-9):

- Stock = $180 and call = $70.
  Stock position = $-1.000 \times \$180 = -\$180.00$.
  MM A/C = $\$104.77 \times 1.05 = \$110.00$.
  Net worth = $\$70 - \$180 + \$110.00 = \$0.00$.

- Stock = $120 (from time = 1 node of stock = $150) and call = $10
  Stock position = $-1.00 \times \$120 = -\$120.00$.
  MM A/C = $\$104.77 \times 1.05 = \$110.00$.
  Net worth = $\$10 - \$120 + \$110 = \$0.00$.

- Stock at $120 (from time = 1 node of stock = $100) and call = $10
  Stock position = $-0.25 \times 120 = \$30.00$.
  MM A/C = $19.05 \times 1.05 = \$20.00$.
  Net worth = $\$10 - \$30 + \$20 = \$0.00$.

- Stock = $80 and call = $0.
  Stock position = $-0.25 \times \$80 = \$20.00$.
  MM A/C = $\$19.05 \times 1.05 = \$20.00$.
  Net worth = $\$0 - \$20 + \$20 = \$0.00$.

As can be seen, since the self-financing worked out perfectly, an option position can always be replicated with a combination of stocks and a bond. This self-financing ensures that options are priced correctly—a market efficiency concept—and that a synthetic option can always be created should the desired option not exist in the marketplace.

10.7.3 Binomial Option Pricing with Dividends

The previous section valued a European call of a stock that does not pay dividends. However, many options are available on stock that does pay dividends. Accordingly, in this section the discussion centers on how to adapt the binomial model to include dividends.

Revisit the example in Figure 10-9 and see how the model can be used when dividends are expected. Assume for the moment all of the same facts except that the underlying stock will pay a $2.00 dividend in period one regardless of whether the stock price goes up or down. Thus, the period-one stock prices are $148 and $98.[6] In period two the prices again go up and down 20% from the period one prices. For simplicity, the period two prices for the middle node will be rounded to $118 ($148 \times 0.8 to $118 and $98 \times 1.2 to $118). Take a look at Figure 10-12.

Once again, starting with the right-hand side of the binomial tree, the payoffs to the call at expiration are calculated first. At a stock price of $177.60 the payoff to the call is max[0, $177.60 - $110] = $67.60. At a stock price of $118 the payoff is max[0, $118 - $110] = $8. Finally, at a stock price of $79.20 the payoff is max[0, $79.20 - $110] = $0. With the payoffs at expiration determined, option values for the period one stock prices can be calculated. At the stock price of $148 the probability for the upper node of the option

[6] The $148 price is [$125 × (1.20)] − $2 and the $98 price is [$125 × (0.80)] − $2.

(Panel A) Distribution of Stock Prices

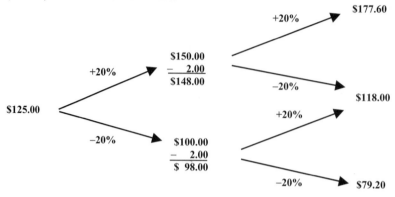

(Panel B) Distribution of Call Option Prices

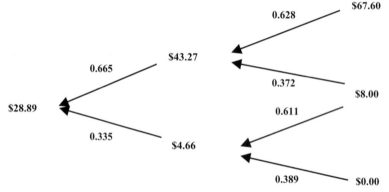

FIGURE 10-12 Binomial call option pricing with dividends.

tree is

$$p^u = [(1+r)S^u - S^{ud}]/[S^{uu} - S^{ud}]$$
$$= [(1.05)\$148 - \$118]/(\$177.60 - \$118)$$
$$= \$37.40/\$59.60$$
$$= 0.628.$$

Thus, the value of the call, if the current stock price is \$148.00 is

$$c^u = [p^u c^{uu} + (1 - p^u)w^{du}]/(1 + r)$$
$$= [0.628(\$67.60) + 0.372(\$8)]/1.05$$
$$= \$45.43/\$1.05$$
$$= \$43.27.$$

Notice that the payment of the \$2.00 dividend has almost an exactly \$2.00 difference in the difference in the call price at this point.

Now, consider the value of the call where the stock price equals $100 − $2 = $98.00 and can rise either to $118.00 or fall further to $79.20.

$$p^d = [(1+r)S^d - S^{dd}]/[S^{du} - S^{dd}]$$
$$= [1.05(\$98) - \$79.20]/(\$118 - \$79.20)$$
$$= (\$102.90 - \$79.20)/\$38.80$$
$$= \$23.70/\$38.80$$
$$= 0.611.$$

Notice here that the payment of dividends causes the probabilities to change, which results in a call value of

$$c^d = [p^d c^{ud} + (1 - p^d)c^{dd}]/(1+r)$$
$$= [0.611(\$8) + (0.389)(\$0)]/(1.05)$$
$$= \$4.66.$$

Here, the payment of the dividend only causes a $1.30 change in the value of the call option at this node. Why is that? Because the dividend cash outflow means that the stock price cannot grow as much as it would without the dividend. Nonetheless, even without the dividend, one possible outcome was that the call option would expire worthless. This is still true. Hence, the effect of the dividend has a smaller effect on the lower part of the binomial tree than it has on the upper part of the binomial tree.

The final step is to calculate the value of the call at time 0, given that the stock price will either increase to $148 or decrease to $98.

$$p = [(1+r)S - S^d]/[S^u - S^d]$$
$$= (1.05 \times \$125 - \$98)/(\$148 - \$98)$$
$$= \$33.25/\$50$$
$$= 0.665.$$

$$c = [pc^u + (1 - p)c^d]/(1+r)$$
$$= [0.665 \times \$43.27 + (0.335) \$4.66]/(1.05)$$
$$= \$28.89.$$

So, the payment of the $2 dividend in year one makes about a $0.16 difference in the price of the call at time 0. What do you suppose would happen to the price of the call if the stock paid another $2 dividend in period 2? The payment of dividends reduces the value of call options. What do you suppose happens to the value of the put options when stocks pay dividends? The put increases in value.

The previous example with dividends showed that the probabilities were different for each node of the option tree. This occurred because the payment of a constant dividend has a differential effect on high-priced versus low-priced stocks. That is, the approach to valuing any node of the option tree is exactly the same—you just adjust the probabilities a little for the different effects of dividends on high-priced stock versus low-priced stock.

10.7.4 Binomial Option Pricing of American Options

So far, one type of option has been priced—a European option. As stated before, this option can only be exercised on its maturity date. Now the other major type of option—an American option—will be discussed. The American options can be exercised at anytime up to, and including, the maturity date. The terms European and American, therefore, have nothing to do with geography.

Because an American option can be exercised at any time, its value can never be less than the maximum of 0 or the stock price minus the exercise price (or the exercise price minus the stock price in the case of a put option).

Suppose that you are trying to value a two-year call option with a strike price of $48. The current share price is $50 and prices can go up or down in each period by 10%. Assume that the risk-free rate is 1%. Will the European and American call options have the same value? Intuitively, the answer is no, because having more choices (in this case because we have different times to exercise the option) is more valuable. The following is a numerical example of the difference between the value of European option and an Amercian option.

Figure 10-13 shows the distribution of the expected stock prices in Panel A and the distribution of expected option prices in Panel B (for a European option). The numbers in both panels were calculated using the same methods used earlier in this chapter.

Take a look at the value of the call option when the stock price is $45. Using the methods introduced so far, which values a European option, the call is worth $0.82. However, since this method values a European call option, the option cannot be exercised at this point in the tree because the expiration point of the option has not been reached. If the option was an American call option, it could be exercised right there in period 1 and the investor would not have to wait until the option matured in period 2.

The question is, "What is the value of the American option in period 1 if the stock price is $45?" If the option must be exercised right away, it must be worth $0 (max[0,($45 − $48)]), not $0.82. However, buyers of American options are not required to exercise an option at any point in time; therefore, at this point in time the holder of an American call would delay exercising the option because the $0.82 represents the discounted value of waiting until the European option matures—a course of action which also exists for American option holders. Hence, an American option can *never* be worth less than a European option. In other words, each node of a binomial tree for a European option is the lower bound for the value of a similar American option at that point in time.

In certain cases, however, an American option can be worth more than a European option. For example, consider a put option on a $40 stock with a strike price of $52. Suppose the stock price would go up or down by 20% in the next period; $p^u = 0.6282$, $p^d = 0.3718$. Therefore the value of this put when valued as a European option is $9.46 because it cannot be exercised until the end of the period when the stock value will be either $48 or $32. However, if the put is valued as an American option it must be worth max[0, X−5] = $52 − $40 = $12. Therefore, the option holder would exercise right away if possible. Clearly, the opportunity to exercise early has value; therefore, an American option is always worth at least as much as a similar European option and sometimes can be worth considerably more.

(Panel A) Distribution of Stock Prices

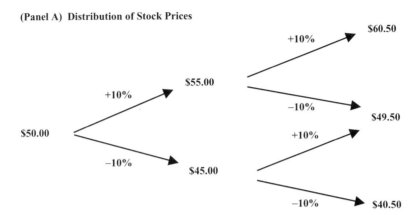

(Panel B) Distribution of Call Option Prices (European option)

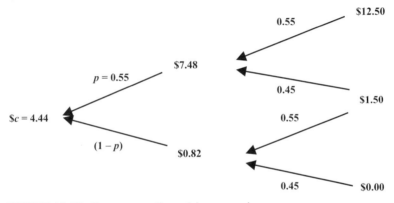

FIGURE 10-13 European option pricing example.

Finally, in the absence of specific information about the stock price going down in the next period a call option on a non-dividend-paying stock will never be exercised early. Instead, the buyer would sell the option because until the option is exercised it has the opportunity to go up in value.

10.7.5 Black-Scholes Option Pricing

Calculating the value of an option using the binomial tree approach can be quite long and involved, especially if the option extends beyond two periods. Thankfully, a mathematical solution has been found that shortens the process. The mathematical solution is the **Black-Scholes option pricing formula**. This formula can be used to value both put and call options. The Black-Scholes formula, as originally developed, priced only European call options on stocks that do not pay dividends. However, the formula has been adapted to include the pricing of put options and the pricing of options on stocks that pay dividends. The original formula and its adaptations will be discussed in this section.

The Black-Scholes formula for a European call on a non-dividend-paying stock is

$$c = (S \times N(d_1)) - (K \times e^{-rT} \times N(d_2)), \tag{10-6}$$

where

$$d_1 = \frac{\ln(S_0/K) + (r + \sigma^2/2)T}{\sigma\sqrt{T}}. \tag{10-7}$$

$$d_2 = \frac{\ln(S_0/K) + (r - \sigma^2/2)T}{\sigma\sqrt{T}} = d_1 - \sigma\sqrt{T}. \tag{10-8}$$

Now, don't panic as you look at this! This formula is much easier to use and understand than first perceived. The d_1 and d_2 terms are used to capture the volatility of the stock insofar as it can move up or down. When combined in the $N(d)$ formula, the probability that the option will expire "in-the-money" is being calculated (loosely speaking). That is, the estimation is being made about whether or not the option will have value. e^{-rT} is the formula for continuous discounting instead of the $1/(1 + r)^T$ or $(1 + r)^{-T}$ formula which you are probably more familiar with and use for discrete discounting. K is the exercise price and S is the current stock price.

Before moving on to a numerical example using the Black-Scholes model to calculate the price of a call option, the formula for the price of the call [Equation (10-6)] will be examined for an option *expiring in-the-money*. Expiring in-the-money means the option definitely has value. Then $N(d_1) = N(d_2) = 1$ and the formula will reduce to $c = S - Ke^{-rT}$. Also, if the option is about to expire, $T = 0$ since there is no time left to maturity. This means that $e^{-rT} = 1$ so the formula reduces to $c = S - K$. That is, a call option expiring in-the-money must have a value equal to the difference between the stock price and the exercise price—just as previously seen in the binomial model. When an option is valued based solely on the difference between the exercise price and the current value of the underlying asset, the option's *intrinsic value* is being calculated.

EXAMPLE   *Pricing a European Call Option Using the Black-Scholes Model*

Consider a European call option with three months (T) to expiry. The stock price (S) is $60, the strike price ($K$) is $65, the risk-free rate ($r$) is 8% (continuous), and the volatility (σ) is 30% per annum. An important point to note about the Black-Scholes model is that all inputs to the model are in annual terms, so an option with three months to expiry means $T = 0.25$ years.

To calculate an option price using the Black-Scholes model, the first step is to calculate d_1 and d_2. For this example, the calculations for d_1 and d_2 are

$$d_1 = \frac{\ln(60/65) + (0.08 + 0.30^2/2)0.25}{0.30\sqrt{0.25}} = -0.3250.$$

$$d_2 = d_1 - 0.30\sqrt{0.25} = -0.4750.$$

The next step is to determine the values of $N(d_1)$ and $N(d_2)$. However, a brief explanation of the role of $N(d_1)$ and $N(d_2)$ needs to be made before the numbers are found. $N(d_1)$ and $N(d_2)$ are cumulative normal probabilities and are used to determine the value of the option given the likelihood the option will end up having value (be *in-the-money*). The d_1 and d_2 calculations evaluate this likelihood by combining the stock's growth rate (r) with the anticipated volatility in the stock (σ) given the current relative position of the stock [ln (s/x)] and the amount of time (T) left to expiry.

The actual probabilities are taken from a cumulative normal table (provided at the end of this chapter). After calculating d_1 and d_2, go to the cumulate normal table and look up the value in the table the corresponds with the calculated values for d_1 and d_2. Here's how. For this example, $d_1 = -0.3253$. Go to the table for $N(x)$ when $x \leq 0$. Under the first column, go down to -0.3, then go across the row to the column entitled .02. You should see 0.3745. Obviously, this value is only approximate. Now, interpolate to find the answer as follows

$$N(-0.3253) = N(-0.32) - 0.53[N(0.32) - N(0.33)]$$
$$= 0.3745 - 0.53[0.3745 - 0.3707]$$
$$= 0.3745 - 0.53[0.0038]$$
$$= 0.3745 - 0.0020$$
$$= 0.3725.$$

That's how simply it is done! Therefore, for this example $N(d_1)$ and $N(d_2)$ are

$$N(d_1) = N(-0.3250) = 0.3725.$$
$$N(d_2) = N(-0.4750) = 0.3173.$$

Finally, $N(d_1)$ and $N(d_2)$ are used along with the other inputs in the call price formula to find the value of the call. Finishing the example, the price of the call is

$$c = 60N(d_1) - 65e^{-0.08 \times 0.25}N(d_2) = 60(0.3725) - 65(0.9802)(0.3173) = \$2.13.$$

To this point, the focus has been on using the Black-Scholes model to value call options. However, the Black-Scholes model can be adapted to value put options. Using put-call parity and the symmetry rules for the cumulative normal distribution, the formula for a European put on a non-dividend-paying stock is

$$P = (K \cdot e^{-rT} \cdot N(-d_2)) - (S \cdot N(-d_1)), \qquad (10\text{-}9)$$

where

$$d_1 = \frac{1n(S_0/K) + (r + \sigma^2/2)T}{\sigma\sqrt{T}}. \qquad (10\text{-}10)$$

$$d_2 = \frac{1n(S_0/K) + (r - \sigma^2/2)T}{\sigma\sqrt{T}} = d_1 - \sigma\sqrt{T}. \qquad (10\text{-}11)$$

Now, how the value of call and put options can change as the different variables used in the Black-Scholes option pricing model change needs to be examined. The previous example will be used and each variable will be changed one at a time. The **bold** variable is the one changed in the set of variables.

Example Inputs

1. $S = \$60, X = \$65, \sigma = 30\%, r = 8\%$ and $T = 0.25$ (used previously).
2. $S = \$65, X = \$65, \sigma = 30\%, r = 8\%$ and $T = 0.25$.
3. $S = \$60, X = \$70, \sigma = 30\%, r = 8\%$ and $T = 0.25$.
4. $S = \$60, X = \$65, \sigma = 40\%, r = 8\%$ and $T = 0.25$.

Examples Results

Call Price	Put Price	Discussion/Result
1. $2.13	$5.85	Initial values for all variables.
2. $4.53	$3.24	Increase in stock price, increase call price, and decrease put price.
3. $0.98	$9.59	Increase in strike price, decreases the call price, and increase the put price.
4. $3.29	$7.00	Increase in stock volatility, increases the price of both the call and the put.

Each of these examples should be calculated to ensure that the mechanical operations necessary to get to an answer are well-understood.

Why were time to maturity and the discount rate not varied in the example? Each will be discussed, one at a time. If the life of the option in the preceding example had been extended from three months to six months and the numbers crunched, the new prices for the call option and the put option were $4.04 and $6.49, respectively. Both prices increased and the conclusion would be that extending the time to expiry on an option increases its value since the underlying asset has more time to either increase or decrease in value. This is true for *American* options only.

European options differ. Because European options can only be exercised on the expiry date, extending the time to maturity may not mean much. Although the fact that the underlying asset has more time to gain or lose value is true, the question remains as to whether or not the underlying asset has gained or lost value on the day the option matures.

A similar argument can be made for changes in the discount rate. Generally speaking, for short-dated options, an increase in the risk-free rate will result in an increase in the value of call options and a decrease in the value of put options. However, as previously discussed, the value of a share is the discounted value of future cash flows. Hence, an increase in the general level of interest rates will *decrease* the value of shares. The question then becomes, "Did the change in interest rates have a greater impact on the underlying asset value or on the discounted value of the exercise price?"

Figure 10-14 provides a table to show how increases in different variables will affect the valuation of both European and American puts and calls, everything else held constant.

Effects on the value of an option				
Variable increased	European call	American call	European put	American put
Stock price	+	+	−	−
Strike price	−	−	+	+
Time to expiration	?	+	?	+
Volatility	+	+	+	+
Discount factor	?	?	?	?
Dividend	−	−	+	+

FIGURE 10-14 Determinants of option prices.

INDUSTRY APPLICATION

OPTION VAR

Because options are levered instruments, option traders are very interested in how small changes in price affect the overall value of a portfolio. Assistants on trading desks are routinely asked to prepare a *daily value-at-risk report* [a detailed discussion of value-at-risk (VAR) appears in Chapter 15]. Options can be used not only to hedge but also to speculate on abnormal price movement. Statistics are often used to determine what the risk of the portfolio is under *normal market conditions.*

Value-at-risk measures the maximum loss that a portfolio might incur over a specific period of time at a specific probability level. On trading desks, this is usually done over a one-day time frame at the 95% level. This is usually done by dividing the volatility measure by the square root of the number of trading days in a year. Black-Scholes models can be used to calculate the implied volatility (implied volatility is the variance necessary for the Black-Scholes model to arrive at the current market price of the option). Consider the following table:

April Calls

Stock	Stock price	Strike	Original call price	Annual volatility	95% adj	Original position	Position change
ASKJ	24.65	22.50	2.85	56.00	6.91	2,850	−1,620
CAH	56.42	55.00	3.20	38.50	4.75	3,200	−1,320
DE	67.34	65.00	3.60	28.00	3.46	3,600	−1,160
INTC	23.68	22.50	1.50	27.50	3.40	1,500	−1,100
PG	52.95	50.00	3.30	20.00	2.47	3,300	−1,050

Ask Jeeves (ASKJ) has an annual volatility of 56% and so the daily volatility is

$$\frac{0.56}{\sqrt{252}} = 0.0353.$$

Multiplying the daily volatility by 1.96 (to obtain the correct measure for the 95% probability level) yields 6.91%. That is, there is a 95% chance that the most the stock price could fall in one day is $24.65 × (−0.0691) = $1.70. If the stock were to fall by this amount the Black-Scholes option value for this stock would fall from $2.85 to $1.23. If the portfolio had 1,000 call contracts, then the value of this part of the option portfolio would fall from $2,850 to $1,230—a loss of $1,620.

This calculation seems rather routine, especially as the table is based on the assumption that each position comprises 1,000 contracts. However, it is the respon-

sibility of the preparer of the document to recognize that the amount of the loss in the individual positions is a function both of the decline in the stock price, the volatility of the stock, and the passage of time.[7] There is, however, a second and perhaps more important responsibility here. The VAR calculation is based on the assumption that the value of options in the portfolio is independent of each other. For example, if ASKJ and INTC were positively correlated, then the portfolio price movements would be greater than expected since the instruments are not truly diversified. It is the responsibility of the preparer to know the statistical relations between the various instruments in the portfolio.

Similarly, more complex option positions can also cause computational problems. For example, the portfolio may comprise option straddles in, say, Proctor & Gamble (PG). But, to add the VAR of call option to the VAR of the put option would not be appropriate.

---

[8] Recall that call options decline in value as the maturity date approaches due to a decrease in the time value premium.

10.7.6 Black-Scholes Formula for Stocks That Pay Dividends

The version of the Black-Scholes option pricing model that has been presented so far does not take dividends into account. Although dividends are normally viewed as good things in equity analysis, dividends do *not* have a positive effect on call options. Remember that the share price generally falls by the amount of the dividend when the stock begins to trade ex-dividend. Since a principal component of a call's value is the value of the underlying stock, the value of the call will also fall.

Extensions have been made to the Black-Scholes model that can account, explicitly, for dividends; however, these models are usually quite complex and difficult to implement. Instead, an ad hoc model can be employed that is based on the assumption that dividends are predictable in both their size and their timing.

Basically, the assumption is made that the dividend yield is constant over the life of the option. This assumption makes the dividend yield analogous to an interest rate. Since the dividend is paid out to the shareholder, it is not retained by the company to be used to fund future growth. Therefore, the current share price (S) is adjusted downward by the present value of the dividends that are expected to be paid during the life of the option. Accordingly, the Black-Scholes option pricing model for call options becomes

$$c = (S \times e^{-yT} \times N(d_1)) - (X \times e^{-rT} \times N(d_2)), \qquad (10\text{-}12)$$

where y is the estimated dividend yield.

There is a second change that needs to be made. Because the payment of the dividends reduces the growth potential of the stock, a small adjustment must be made in the calculation of d_1:

$$d_1 = \frac{1n(S/K) + (r - y + \sigma^2/2)T}{\sigma\sqrt{T}}. \qquad (10\text{-}13)$$

However, d_2 remains the same as

$$d_2 = d_1 - \sigma\sqrt{T}. \qquad (10\text{-}14)$$

Returning to the example where $S = \$60$, $X = \$65$, $\sigma = 30\%$, $r = 8\%$, and $T = 0.25$, add a dividend yield of $y = 3\%$. Using these values, the call and put option values change from \$2.13 and \$5.85 to \$1.97 and \$6.13, respectively. To ensure your complete understanding of the Black-Scholes model with dividends, you should verify these numbers. Notice that paying a dividend reduces the value of the call option but increases the value of the put option.

SUMMARY OF VALUATION AND RISK MANAGEMENT SKILLS

1. Understand how digital options function and the vector notation that follows from the digital option.

A digital option pays \$1 on one side of the strike price and \$0 at and on the other side of the strike price. This allows for the introduction of vector notation where +1 is a gain, 0 is no change in value, and −1 is a loss.

2. Understand how standard options function and the payoff diagrams for standard options.

Standard options allow the buyer unlimited gains while limiting losses to the cost of the option. However, as the buyer gains the seller loses. The buyer gains (seller loses) when the option goes into the money, but the buyer does not make a profit until the gains cover the cost of the option. Out-of-the-money options are allowed to expire with the seller keeping the price of the option and the buyer losing the cost of the option.

3. Understand how to create synthetic securities using the vector notation and the payoff diagrams.

Synthetic securities are payoffs created from combinations of other securities. The vector notation and the payoff diagrams providing a straightforward technique for determining the payoffs from combinations of securities (synthetic securities).

4. Calculate the price of a standard option using binomial option pricing.

Binomial option pricing is a straightforward (but tedious) way to evaluate simple put and call options. The technique can handle most basic issues in option pricing. However, this technique requires many calculations.

5. Calculate the price of a standard option using the Black-Scholes option pricing model.

The Black-Scholes option pricing formula is a mathematical solution to option pricing. The Black-Scholes model was originally developed to price dividend-protected European call options. However, the formula has been adapted to include the pricing of put options and the pricing of options on stocks that pay dividends.

QUESTIONS

1. At the beginning of this chapter, several possible representations were indicated in the absence of transactions costs or commissions of a risk-free position using vector analysis. Explain why the only true risk-free position is depicted by

$$\begin{vmatrix} 0 \\ 0 \end{vmatrix}$$

2. Using forward contracts and options, what combination of these instruments will have the same payoff profile as a long call option? A short call option? Indicate the vector analysis combinations.

3. Using forward contracts and options, what combination of these instruments will have the same payoff profile as a long put option? A short put option? Indicate the vector analysis combinations.

4. Using a two-period binomial tree, find the call and put prices for the stock.

Current stock price = $20
Strike price = $18
Price movement = 10%
Risk-free rate = 3%

5. Using a two-period binomial tree, find the call and put prices for the stock.

Current stock price = $50
Strike price = $57
Price movement = 14%
Risk-free rate = 3%

6. Suppose you had a stock currently valued at $100. One period later, you estimate that the stock price will either increase by 15% (to $115) or decrease by 10% (to $90). If the one-period rate of interest is 5%, at what price would the binomial option pricing model value a call option with an exercise price of $107.50?

7. Use a two-period binomial tree to price the following European put option. Assume that in each period, the underlying stock can exercise or decrease by 20%. Let the current stock price be $125 and the one-period rate of interest be 5%. The exercise price is $130.

8. Reconsider Question 7 and assume risk neutrality. What trades would you need to make (using a dynamic self-financing approach) to hedge this position?

9. Reconsider the situation in Question 7. If this were an American option, would any of the put option values have to change?

10. Using the Black-Scholes formula, calculate the call price based on the following information:

Stock price = $100
Strike price = $95
Interest rate = 10%
Time to expiration = three months
Standard deviation = 50%

11. Using the Black-Scholes formula, calculate the call price based on the following information:

Stock price = $100
Strike price = $100
Interest rate = 7%
Time to expiration = six months
Standard deviation = 30%

REFERENCES

BLACK, F., and M. SCHOLES, 1973, The pricing of options and corporation liabilities, *Journal of Political Economy*, *81*, 637–659.

This is the paper where the Black-Scholes option pricing model is first derived. The authors derive the formula based on the concept of replicating cash flows.

BOYLE, P., and D. EMMANUEL, 1980, Discretely adjusted option hedges, *Journal of Financial Economics*, *8*, 259–263.

COX, J., S. ROSS, and M. RUBENSTEIN, 1979, Option pricing: A simplified approach, *Journal of Financial Economics*, *7*, 229–263.

This is the paper that develops binomial option pricing.

HULL, J., 2003, *Options, Futures and Other Derivations*, 5th Ed., Prentice-Hall, Upper Saddle River, NJ.

This is an excellent reference text on derivatives. The book is very thorough and technically complete.

MANN, S., 1996, Calls are like air conditioners; puts are like heaters, *Journal of Financial Education*, *22*, 61–64.

MERTON, R. C., 1973, Theory of rational option pricing, *Bell Journal of Economics and Management Science*, *4*, 141–183.

This paper is Merton's extension of the Black-Scholes model to price other options including options on stocks that pay dividends.

WATSON, R. D., 1995, Managing the settlement risk of derivatives, *Financial Practice and Education*, *5*, 30–36.

This paper discusses settlement risk. Specifically, it focuses on settlement risk in over-the-counter derivative contracts where money or claims often are not transferred simultaneously. The paper discusses how settlement risk can create problems for the entire financial market system.

KEY TERMS

American Option Options that can be exercised at anytime up to, and including, the maturity date.

At-the-money An option's value when the intrinsic value is exactly equal to zero.

Binomial Tree A time series of prices and option values based on the assumption that asset prices will move up or down at known points in time.

Black-Scholes Option Pricing Formula A mathematical formula that can be used to value both put and call options.

Call Option The right to buy something.

European Option An option that can only be exercised on its maturity date.

Exercise Price Transaction price when an option is exercised. Also referred to as the strike price.

In-the-money An option's value when the intrinsic value is positive.

Intrinsic Value The difference between the current stock price and the exercise price.

Out-of-the-money An option's value when the intrinsic value is negative.

Put-call Parity The relation between the put price and the call price when a put option and a call option are written on the same underlying asset with the same exercise price and the same maturity. This does not mean the prices are the same—only that they are *related*.

Put Option The right to sell something.

Recombination Tree A binomial tree having the property that, at any time, an up move followed by a down move is exactly the same as a down move followed by an up move.

Risk-neutral Position Options are priced on the assumption that hedging activity is always taking place; an equal but opposite position is taken (the hedge) that generates exactly the same cash flows; dynamic self-financing trading approach.

Strike Price See, exercise price

Synthetic Positions Replicate the same payoff as another security, but the investor does not hold the actual position.

Vector Analysis Used to demonstrate the net position an individual can hold as a result of combining various securities and derivatives.

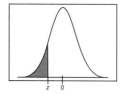

STANDARD NORMAL CUMULATIVE PROBABILITY TABLE

z	.00	.01	.02	.03	.04	.05	.06	.07	.08	.09
−3.0	.0013	.0013	.0013	.0012	.0012	.0011	.0011	.0011	.0010	.0010
−2.9	.0019	.0018	.0018	.0017	.0016	.0016	.0015	.0015	.0014	.0014
−2.8	.0026	.0025	.0024	.0023	.0023	.0022	.0021	.0021	.0020	.0019
−2.7	.0035	.0034	.0033	.0032	.0031	.0030	.0029	.0028	.0027	.0026
−2.6	.0047	.0045	.0044	.0043	.0041	.0040	.0039	.0038	.0037	.0036
−2.5	.0062	.0060	.0059	.0057	.0055	.0054	.0052	.0051	.0049	.0048
−2.4	.0082	.0080	.0078	.0075	.0073	.0071	.0069	.0068	.0066	.0064
−2.3	.0107	.0104	.0102	.0099	.0096	.0094	.0091	.0089	.0087	.0084
−2.2	.0139	.0136	.0132	.0129	.0125	.0122	.0119	.0116	.0113	.0110
−2.1	.0179	.0174	.0170	.0166	.0162	.0158	.0154	.0150	.0146	.0143
−2.0	.0228	.0222	.0217	.0212	.0207	.0202	.0197	.0192	.0188	.0183
−1.9	.0287	.0281	.0274	.0268	.0262	.0256	.0250	.0244	.0239	.0233
−1.8	.0359	.0351	.0344	.0336	.0329	.0322	.0314	.0307	.0301	.0294
−1.7	.0446	.0436	.0427	.0418	.0409	.0401	.0392	.0384	.0375	.0367
−1.6	.0548	.0537	.0526	.0516	.0505	.0495	.0485	.0475	.0465	.0455
−1.5	.0668	.0655	.0643	.0630	.0618	.0606	.0594	.0582	.0571	.0559
−1.4	.0808	.0793	.0778	.0764	.0749	.0735	.0721	.0708	.0694	.0681
−1.3	.0968	.0951	.0934	.0918	.0901	.0885	.0869	.0853	.0838	.0823
−1.2	.1151	.1131	.1112	.1093	.1075	.1056	.1038	.1020	.1003	.0985
−1.1	.1357	.1335	.1314	.1292	.1271	.1251	.1230	.1210	.1190	.1170
−1.0	.1587	.1562	.1539	.1515	.1492	.1469	.1446	.1423	.1401	.1379
−0.9	.1841	.1814	.1788	.1762	.1736	.1711	.1685	.1660	.1635	.1611
−0.8	.2119	.2090	.2061	.2033	.2005	.1977	.1949	.1922	.1894	.1867
−0.7	.2420	.2389	.2358	.2327	.2296	.2266	.2236	.2206	.2177	.2148
−0.6	.2743	.2709	.2676	.2643	.2611	.2578	.2546	.2514	.2483	.2451
−0.5	.3085	.3050	.3015	.2981	.2946	.2912	.2877	.2843	.2810	.2776
−0.4	.3446	.3409	.3372	.3336	.3300	.3264	.3228	.3192	.3156	.3121
−0.3	.3821	.3783	.3745	.3707	.3669	.3632	.3594	.3557	.3520	.3483
−0.2	.4207	.4168	.4129	.4090	.4052	.4013	.3974	.3936	.3897	.3859
−0.1	.4602	.4562	.4522	.4483	.4443	.4404	.4364	.4325	.4286	.4247
0.0	.5000	.4960	.4920	.4880	.4840	.4801	.4761	.4721	.4681	.4641

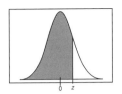

CUMULATIVE PROBABILITIES FOR POSITIVE Z-VALUES ARE IN THE FOLLOWOING TABLE

z	.00	.01	.02	.03	.04	.05	.06	.07	.08	.09
0.0	.5000	.5040	.5080	.5120	.5160	.5199	.5239	.5279	.5319	.5359
0.1	.5398	.5438	.5478	.5517	.5557	.5596	.5636	.5675	.5714	.5753
0.2	.5793	.5832	.5871	.5910	.5948	.5987	.6026	.6064	.6103	.6141
0.3	.6179	.6217	.6255	.6293	.6331	.6368	.6406	.6443	.6480	.6517
0.4	.6554	.6591	.6628	.6664	.6700	.6736	.6772	.6808	.6844	.6879
0.5	.6915	.6950	.6985	.7019	.7054	.7088	.7123	.7157	.7190	.7224
0.6	.7257	.7291	.7324	.7357	.7389	.7422	.7454	.7486	.7517	.7549
0.7	.7580	.7611	.7642	.7673	.7704	.7734	.7764	.7794	.7823	.7852
0.8	.7881	.7910	.7939	.7967	.7995	.8023	.8051	.8078	.8106	.8133
0.9	.8159	.8186	.8212	.8238	.8264	.8289	.8315	.8340	.8365	.8389
1.0	.8413	.8438	.8461	.8485	.8508	.8531	.8554	.8577	.8599	.8621
1.1	.8643	.8665	.8686	.8708	.8729	.8749	.8770	.8790	.8810	.8830
1.2	.8849	.8869	.8888	.8907	.8925	.8944	.8962	.8980	.8997	.9015
1.3	.9032	.9049	.9066	.9082	.9099	.9115	.9131	.9147	.9162	.9177
1.4	.9192	.9207	.9222	.9236	.9251	.9265	.9279	.9292	.9306	.9319
1.5	.9332	.9345	.9357	.9370	.9382	.9394	.9406	.9418	.9429	.9441
1.6	.9452	.9463	.9474	.9484	.9495	.9505	.9515	.9525	.9535	.9545
1.7	.9554	.9564	.9573	.9582	.9591	.9599	.9608	.9616	.9625	.9633
1.8	.9641	.9649	.9656	.9664	.9671	.9678	.9686	.9693	.9699	.9706
1.9	.9713	.9719	.9726	.9732	.9738	.9744	.9750	.9756	.9761	.9767
2.0	.9772	.9778	.9783	.9788	.9793	.9798	.9803	.9808	.9812	.9817
2.1	.9821	.9826	.9830	.9834	.9838	.9842	.9846	.9850	.9854	.9857
2.2	.9861	.9864	.9868	.9871	.9875	.9878	.9881	.9884	.9887	.9890
2.3	.9893	.9896	.9898	.9901	.9904	.9906	.9909	.9911	.9913	.9916
2.4	.9918	.9920	.9922	.9925	.9927	.9929	.9931	.9932	.9934	.9936
2.5	.9938	.9940	.9941	.9943	.9945	.9946	.9948	.9949	.9951	.9952
2.6	.9953	.9955	.9956	.9957	.9959	.9960	.9961	.9962	.9963	.9964
2.7	.9965	.9966	.9967	.9968	.9969	.9970	.9971	.9972	.9973	.9974
2.8	.9974	.9975	.9976	.9977	.9977	.9978	.9979	.9979	.9980	.9981
2.9	.9981	.9982	.9982	.9983	.9984	.9984	.9985	.9985	.9986	.9986
3.0	.9987	.9987	.9987	.9988	.9988	.9989	.9989	.9989	.9990	.9990

VECTOR NOTATION FOR MANAGING CORPORATE ACCOUNTS RECEIVABLE AND ACCOUNTS PAYABLE

One of the things many people tend to forget is that corporate accounts can also be viewed as types of investment vehicles. For example, when a company extends credit to a customer, the accounts receivable the company records is really a long position in an asset whose value will change in relation to any changes in interest rates (remember the time value of money). Similarly, an accounts payable can be viewed as a short position in an asset whose value will change in relation to any changes in interest rates. These points become important especially where large amounts of funds are concerned. (In Chapter 16, we show how exchange rates can be hedged to lock-in the value of international accounts payable and receivable.)

Suppose a company has the opportunity to sell a customer a significant portion of its inventory but only if the customer can pay in 180 days after the goods are received. Assume further that the customer does not want the goods delivered for three months. In this case, the selling company is exposed to interest-rate risk on the accounts receivable for the outstanding period. Hence, the company might want to hedge its interest-rate risk by selling a 3×9 forward rate agreement (FRA). This situation is depicted in Figure 10-A-1. In vector notation, the hedge the company is attempting to establish is

$$\text{Long an accounts receivable} \quad + \quad \text{Short a forward} \quad = \quad \text{Risk-neutral position}$$

$$\begin{vmatrix} +1 \\ +1 \end{vmatrix} \quad + \quad \begin{vmatrix} -1 \\ -1 \end{vmatrix} \quad = \quad \begin{vmatrix} 0 \\ 0 \end{vmatrix}$$

Notice that the neutral (risk-free) position only means that the value of the accounts receivables will not increase or decrease in value due to changes in interest rates. It does not mean that the accounts receivables are noncollectible.

Suppose a company has a large accounts payable that also requires the payment of a floating interest rate payment based on the amount outstanding. Here, the company's concern is that interest rates will increase, thereby also increasing the amount the company will have to repay. In this type of situation, the company that owes the debt often buys an interest-rate call option or *cap* (more on caps in Chapter 18), the purpose of which is to limit

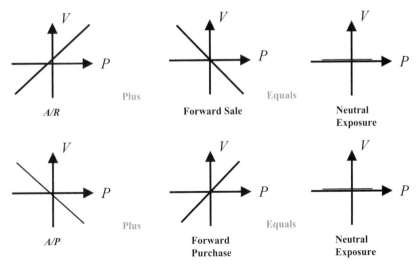

FIGURE 10-A-1   Payoff diagrams for risk management example: forward contractors.

any increase in the interest payment. This combination of a short asset and a call option can result in upside (interest rate) protection. In vector notation, this would be

$$\text{Accounts payable} \quad + \quad \text{long call option} \quad = \quad \text{Upside interest rate protection}$$

$$\begin{vmatrix} -1 \\ +1 \end{vmatrix} \quad + \quad \begin{vmatrix} +1 \\ 0 \end{vmatrix} \quad = \quad \begin{vmatrix} 0 \\ 1 \end{vmatrix}$$

Notice how upside protection in this case is the same as holding a synthetic put in a long position. Figure 10-A-2, shows the payoff diagram is the same as that for a put option.

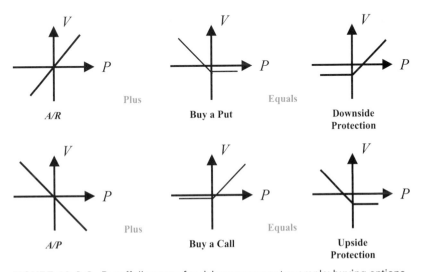

FIGURE 10-A-2   Payoff diagrams for risk management example: buying options.

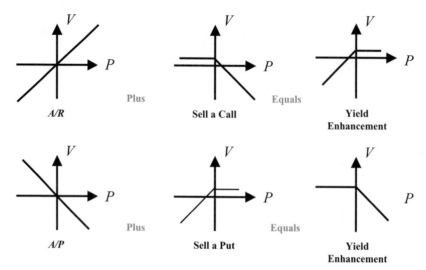

FIGURE 10-A-3 Payoff diagrams for risk management example: selling options.

Very often when a company has interest-rate-sensitive positions, it uses the opportunity to increase returns. Suppose a company has an interest-rate-sensitive accounts receivable. What would happen if the company sold an interest-rate cap (see Figure 10-A-3)? If interest rates go up, then the amount of additional interest the company receives from the accounts receivable will go to paying the obligation they have entered into by selling

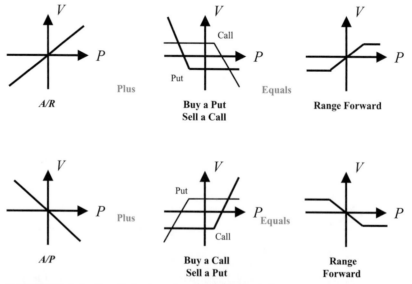

FIGURE 10-A-4 Payoff diagrams for risk management example: combining call and put options.

the cap. However, if interest rates decrease, then the reduced amount received from the accounts receivable will be offset by the premium received from selling the interest-rate cap.

The decision to establish positions that provide protection against changes in interest rates naturally assumes that the company has some sense of the direction of interest rates. In cases like these, companies very often use range forwards (see Figure 10-A-4). The purpose of this type of hedge is to recognize that because of the uncertainty of interest rates, the company is willing to accept some change in interest rates; but if rates change dramatically, then the company has neutralized the adverse effects at the expense of giving up some of the benefits of the interest rate changes.

CHAPTER 11

INTRODUCTION TO RISK MANAGEMENT

11.1 INTRODUCTION

What is risk and why should financial institutions be concerned about it? How should institutions measure risk and manage it? The purpose of this chapter is to define risk, to discuss the different types of risk and general approaches to measuring risk in financial markets, and to describe the importance of implementing a formal risk management policy and evaluating it periodically. This chapter is an important point of departure for the second half of this book, and the concepts described herein are part of the everyday lexicon of financial institutions such as commercial banks, investment banks, mutual funds, and others. In the remainder of this book, you will build on your understanding of how various financial instruments are priced by learning how the risk inherent in each instrument can be measured and managed.

Both in textbooks and in industry practice you will find a myriad of risk measurements and techniques for managing risk. Start with a textbook—say ours. In Chapter 7 we presented from the academic perspective that diversification reduces, but does not eliminate, the risk of a portfolio. The risk that cannot be eliminated through diversification is called **systematic** or **market risk** and that which can be diversified away is called **unsystematic** or **company-specific risk**. Another perspective—from the point of view of many practitioners—suggests **volatility** is the embodiment of risk.

For many years academics and practitioners alike have attacked the extremely difficult task of measuring and expressing risk. One of the latest methods devised to help investors understand the amount of risk is **value-at-risk** (VaR). *VaR is a currency-based measure of the maximum expected loss over a given investment period under normal market conditions at a predetermined level of confidence.* In short, VaR measures the volatility of the value of a company's assets. For example, JP Morgan's 1994 annual report stated that, *"The Daily Earnings at Risk for our combined trading activities averaged approximately $15 million . . . at the 95 percent level."* Based on this measure, shareholders would have been able to determine for themselves whether or not they were comfortable with the level of risk in their investment.

All of the various risk measures have flaws and shortcomings and no technique of measuring or managing risk should be accepted blindly. Relying on a mathematical model of risk without understanding its assumptions and internal workings is surely one of the best ways to *lose* money in the markets. The remainder of this book helps you navigate this morass of risk management techniques by explaining which techniques work well and when the techniques should be treated with caution. As you read the rest of this book, you will gain a framework for understanding how the risk management process should be approached.

This chapter begins by defining the concept of risk and then describes the reasons for managing risk. The next part of this chapter explains the many types of risk faced by financial institutions, paying particular attention to the concept of *operational risk*. The remainder of this chapter discusses how to identify and manage operational risks. This chapter concludes by explaining the role of risk management policy and how to evaluate the performance of the risk policy.

DEVELOPING VALUATION AND RISK MANAGEMENT SKILLS

1. Understand the components of business (unsystematic) risk.
2. Understand the components of market (systematic) risk.
3. Define operational risk and its four components.
4. Know the characteristics of a firm associated with greater operational risk.
5. Understand why a firm should have a risk management policy and how to measure the effectiveness of that policy.

11.2 A GENERAL DEFINITION OF RISK AND THE REASONS FOR MANAGING RISK

Risk management is best defined as the management of risk over a specified time period in situations where volatility exists and managers have the opportunity to change the expected cash flows. *If managers cannot change the expected cash flows, there would be no opportunity to manage risk.* The following **Risk** *is a measure of the potential changes in value that will be experienced in a managed portfolio as a result of differences in the economic environment between now and some specific point in the future.*

The management of risk is important for seven primary reasons. The first four reasons are microeconomic in nature in that they affect the performance of the individual corporation. The last three reasons are macroeconomic in nature since they affect the overall financial system.

The discussion of the seven reasons why risk management, particularly in a financial institution, is important begins with the discussion of the four microeconomic reasons. First, the management of risk *reduces the volatility of earnings*. Since earnings will become more stable with the management of risk, investors are less likely to demand as high a premium for risk. As a result, the value of the firm to the shareholders increases. Second, the management of risk *can reduce the volatility of cash flow from operations*. Since operating income plus depreciation (EBITDA) service debt payments, banks are more willing to lend larger sums to firms with more predictable and/or stable operating income. Thus, the company has greater debt capacity; therefore, it can borrow more funds to invest in both tangible and intangible assets. Third, because the managers of the firm now *have more control over earnings volatility and thus performance,* a firm can more easily achieve its goals and remain competitive. Fourth, the management of risk *reduces the effective corporate tax rate.* If a company is subject to the alternative minimum tax, over time and with proper management of its earnings volatility, the company may lower its effective corporate tax rate.

On the macroeconomic side, there are three reasons why risk management is important. First, from a financial institution's point of view, managers will be able to spend more time on the improvement of financial operations instead of spending time on capital adequacy, thereby *reducing the amount of regulation.* Second, lower volatility *reduces the likelihood that a financial institution will fail.* With lower volatility, depositors are more secure that their funds will be available over longer periods of time; hence, an increase in consumer confidence. Finally, from a global point of view, if *financial systems are safer and less prone to disruption,* world economies, in general, will benefit.

11.3 THE RISK LANDSCAPE

Now that risk has been defined and the importance of managing risk has been discussed, the discussion moves to the risk landscape. The reason for discussing the risk landscape that businesses face is to provide a better understanding of where operational risk fits into the overall risk of a business.

Typically, risks are broken down into systematic and unsystematic categories. However, to get a better understanding of the risk landscape faced by a business and to understand where operational risk fits into this risk landscape, breaking systematic and unsystematic risk into their component parts is most useful. Looking at nonsystematic (company-specific or business) risks is a good place to begin. Figure 11-1 provides a diagram of business risk and its five component parts: (1) operational risk, (2) legal risk, (3) credit risk, (4) liquidity risk, and (5) model risk.

All firms are subject to **business risk**, which is specific to the industry and market within which the company operates. If a firm produces automobiles, its business risks would be those specific to the automobile industry and the market for automobiles. Chief among business risks are the **operational risks**. These are the risks that arise from the failure of internal systems or from errors by the people who actually run the business. These risks can be very minor events such as a failure to update computer programs to the latest revision, or they can be cataclysmic events that result in complete financial failure of the business. After we finish this brief discussion of the risk landscape, operational risk is the focus of the remainder of this chapter.

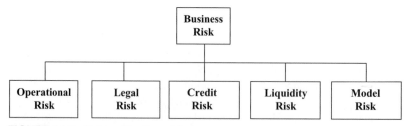

FIGURE 11-1 Types of busines risk.

The next component of business risk to be discussed, **legal risk**, is somewhat related to operational risk. This risk occurs when contracts are *not* enforced. For example, Conseco, a U.S.-based consumer finance company, had been the underlying company in a credit-default swap. Conseco had been in a state of continuous decline in its share price throughout 1999 and 2000 to the point where corporate restructuring became necessary. Under the terms of the credit-default swap, this was a credit event which required payments to the buyers of credit protection on Conseco. The sellers of the protection, however, refused to recognize restructuring as a credit event, even though restructuring had been highlighted in the documentation as one of eight scenarios that would qualify. The sellers of the protection argued that restructuring should not qualify as a trigger (credit) event since restructuring is quite common and banks have little incentive to oppose restructuring. This is a legal risk because it is a problem that the opposing lawyers have to solve. Legal risks will not be discussed to any great depth in this text.

Companies also find that **credit risk**, even though it is often associated with legal risk, can occur independently of legal risk. Here, the problem is that the counterparty to the transactions recognizes their legal obligation but does not have the financial resources to make the promised payment. Approaches to credit risk management will be discussed in Chapter 19. Another business-risk-related exposure is **liquidity risk**. This is the risk arising from the cost of unwinding a position. That is, if a position needs to be divested quickly, a sale at an unfavorably low price may have to be made because buyers may be hard to find. Liquidity risk management problems are discussed in Chapter 12.

A colleague argues that an emerging and serious form of business risk is **model risk**. Since financial models are becoming increasingly complex, designing and implementing the models tend to be extremely technical. Unfortunately, the complexity of a model often obscures the assumptions used to generate a model's outcomes. As a result, the economic validity of the model is increasingly difficult for nontechnical but market-savvy professionals to verify. Model risk is an important component of business risk because business decisions are made based on the outputs from these financial models.

In addition to business risk, all firms are also exposed to market (systematic) risks. Figure 11-2 divides market risk into three components: (1) interest-rate risk, (2) foreign exchange risk, and (3) commodity price risk. In fact, in a 1995 survey by the U.S. Treasury Management Association the researchers discovered that over 90% of the firms in their

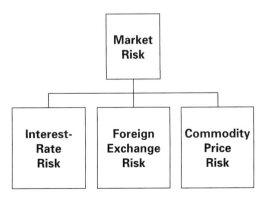

FIGURE 11-2 Types of market risk.

sample faced **interest-rate risk**, 75% faced **foreign exchange risk**, and over 30% faced **commodity price risk**.[1] Interest-rate risk management will be discussed in Chapters 13 and 18. Foreign exchange risk management will be discussed in Chapter 16. The basics of commodity price risk management were discussed in Chapter 9 and Chapter 10. The risk that has not yet been mentioned, the risk of incorrect derivatives usage, will be discussed in Chapter 17.

11.4 OPERATIONAL RISKS

To this point in the chapter risk has been defined and the risk landscape for a business has been discussed. At this point the focus of this chapter narrows to the discussion of operational risk. First will be a general discussion of the operational risk. This discussion will include an example of the role of operational risk in the failure of Barings Bank. The following section will discuss causes of operational risk and provide an example of operational risk found in *Fixed Income Trading* by Joseph Jett at Kidder, Peabody & Co. This chapter concludes with several sections on operational risk in the risk management function of a business.

The British Bankers Association recently published a report examining the nature and extent of *operational risk* problems. The definition they drafted was, *"Operational risk is the risk of direct or indirect loss resulting from inadequate or failed internal processes, people, and systems or from external events."*[2] Notice how this definition of risk incorporates the interaction of individuals with the company and the company's activities with the outside world. In another definition of operational risk, Professor Simons breaks operational risk into four component parts.[3] The four components are:

- **Operations risk** results from a breakdown in a core operating, manufacturing, or processing capability. In an organization charged with investment responsibilities, this risk is associated with the manager, marketing, and sales behavior, as well as technology-related transactions.

- **Asset impairment risk** occurs when an asset loses a significant portion of its current value because of a reduction in the probability of receiving expected future cash flows. This risk centers on the organization's ability to safeguard its assets. Places where transactions are processed or where data can be manipulated are important to maintaining the integrity of the financial system and the value of the assets.

- **Competitive risks** result from changes in the competitive environment that could impair the business' ability to create value and differentiate its products and services. In financial terms, this often means the company has failed to deliver superior performance as a result of a market downturn or from managerial failures.

---

[1] Field, P., 1995, The art, not science, of risk management, *Risk Special Supplement, June*, 2–4.

[2] See, British Bankers Association, RMA Associates, ISDA, and PricewaterhouseCoopers, *Operational Risk: The Next Frontier*, 1999, RMA Associates, Philadelphia, PA.

[3] Simons, RL., 1999, *A Note on Identifying Strategic Risk*, Harvard Business School Publishing, Cambridge, MA.

- **Franchise risk** is a consequence of excessive risk in one of the three other operational risk components listed here. It occurs when the value of the entire business erodes due to a loss in confidence by critical constituents such as shareholders, investors, or customers.

The following story recounts one of the most spectacular cases of operational risk factors resulting in a complete franchise failure.

EXAMPLE *Barings Bank* [4]

When Barings PLC officially failed on February 24, 1995, it was the oldest merchant bank in Great Britain. Founded in 1762, the bank had a long and distinguished history including helping the United States of America finance the Louisiana Purchase in 1803 and helping Britain finance the Napoleonic Wars. Although it was once the largest merchant bank, in 1995, with total shareholder equity of £440 million, Barings was far from the largest or most important banking organization in Great Britain. Nonetheless, it continued to rank among the nation's most prestigious institutions, with clients including the Queen of England and other members of the royal family.

In 1992, Barings sent Nicholas Leeson, a clerk from its London office, to manage the back-office accounting and settlement operations at its Singapore futures subsidiary. Barings Futures Singapore (BFS) was established to enable Barings to trade on the Singapore International Monetary Exchange (SIMEX). The subsidiary's profits were expected to come primarily from brokerage commissions charged to customers and other Barings subsidiaries.

Soon after arriving in Singapore, Leeson passed the required SIMEX examinations and began trading on the exchange later that year. Some time during late 1992 or early 1993, Leeson was also named general manager and head trader of BFS. Normally, the functions of trading and settlements are kept separate, because the head of settlements is expected to provide independent verification of trading records. However, Leeson was never relieved of his original authority over the subsidiary's back-office operations when his responsibilities were expanded to include trading.

Leeson soon began to engage in proprietary trading for the firm's own account. Barings' management believed that this trading involved arbitrage in Nikkei-225 stock index futures and 10-year Japanese Government Bond futures. Since both contracts trade on SIMEX and the Osaka Securities Exchange (OSE), price discrepancies could develop between the same contract on different exchanges, allowing an arbitrageur the opportunity to earn risk-free profits by buying the lower-priced contract on one exchange while selling the higher-priced contract on the other. Unknown to the bank's management, however, Leeson soon embarked on the much riskier trading strategy of placing bets on the direction of price movements on the Tokyo Stock Exchange.

Leeson's reported trading profits were spectacular. His earnings soon accounted for a significant share of Barings' total profits and the bank's senior management regarded him as a star performer. After Barings failed, however, investigators found that Leeson's reported profits had been fictitious from the start. Because his duties included supervision of both trading and settlements for BFS, Leeson had been able to manufacture fictitious reports concerning his trading activities. He had set up a special trading account in 1992, and instructed the clerks to omit information on that account on their reports to the London head office. By manipulating information on his trading activity, Leeson concealed his trading losses, and reported large profits instead.

By the end of 1992, Leeson had accumulated a hidden loss of £2 million. He lost another £21 million in 1993 and £185 million in 1994. By the end of that year, the total cumulative losses were

---

[4] The information in this section is drawn from Kuprianov, A. (1995), *Derivative debacles: Cases of large losses in derivatives markets, Federal Reserve Bank of Richmond, Economic Quarterly, 81,* 1–39.

£208 million. That amount was larger than the £205 million profit reported by the Barings Bank Group as a whole.

The Bank of England's Board of Banking Supervision conducted an inquiry into the collapse of Barings. According to the board's report, total losses directly attributable to Leeson's actions came to £927 million (approximately US$1.4 billion), including liquidation costs. Most of the cost of the Barings debacle was borne by its shareholders and by ING, the firm that bought Barings. Although ING was able to buy the failed merchant bank for a token amount of £1, it had to pay £660 million to recapitalize the firm. SIMEX subsequently reported that the funds Barings had on deposit with the exchange were sufficient to meet the costs incurred in liquidating its positions.[5] It is not known whether the OSE suffered any losses as a result of the Barings collapse.

In the Barings example, the breakdown in the core operating and processing capability (operating risk) brought on by Leeson manipulating records of his trading activity lead to asset impairment because the bank's assets were unable to generate adequate cash flows to meet the margin calls. Consequently, the bank failed and the total franchise was lost.

11.5 CAUSES OF OPERATIONAL RISK

As spectacular as the Barings disaster was, it is a rare type of event. However, lesser problems arising out of operational risk are quite common. How can this happen? Very often these risks arise because the company is initially successful and is growing quickly. Professor Simons identifies nine potential areas that can result in operational risk. He calls these the **levers of control**. These levers detail the places to look for operational risk within a company and later will be used to measure the operational risk of a company. His table presenting the nine levers is reproduced in Figure 11-3.

The first row evaluates a company's *growth*. Errors of omission or commission can occur when senior managers pressure employees to provide a very high level of performance, when the rate of expansion is so high that existing employees do not have enough time to perform their jobs well, or when the company is forced to use untrained or inexperienced employees in important positions.

The second row shows problems related to *corporate culture*. The problems here usually stem from incomplete managerial information. These problems can occur when managers provide high rewards, for example, large year-end bonuses for outstanding performance. As previously stated, higher returns are usually associated with greater risks. Therefore, management may be rewarding employees for taking greater and greater risks. A similar source of difficulty arises when management concentrates too much on the ultimate objective. What this means is that managers only want to hear about events that are in line with achieving their (the managers') goals. As a result, some managers may give employees the notion that bad news is unacceptable, and since many employees choose not to upset their managers, they do not report bad news in sufficient time for managers to take appropriate corrective action. A final cause of insufficient managerial information arises when incentives create an excessively competitive work environment that encourages one employee to compete against another. As a result, employees become reluctant to share

[5] G. Szala, D. Nussbaum, and J. Reerink, Barings abyss, *Futures, 24(May)*, 68–74.

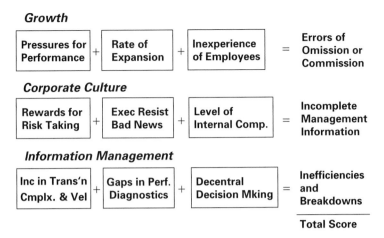

FIGURE 11-3 Assessing internal risk pressures.
Source: R. L. Simons, 1999. *A Note on Identifying Strategic Risk.*

information with their co-workers when certain information is needed to operate the company successfully. These reluctant employees are afraid they will be giving another employee an advantage in gaining recognition that can lead to financial rewards.

The third row discusses problems in *information management*. As a company grows, the nature and extent of the transactions in which it is involved often becomes much more frequent and much more complex. If employees are forced to do more and more complicated functions and have less time to complete them, disasters can occur. A similar type of problem occurs when a company uses a system to evaluate its employees and the system is not adequate for the task. For example, suppose an employee is assigned a task that is not to be evaluated. Do you think the work on that task will be reliable? A final cause of inefficiency and process breakdown occurs when an operation becomes so large that it has to decentralize the decision-making process. If this decentralization is not managed appropriately, transactions *fall through the cracks* because one division believes another division is responsible for performing the task.

The following is another example of a failure in operational risk management. Luckily, this situation did not result in a complete franchise failure.

EXAMPLE   *Joseph Jett* [6]

In January 1994, Kidder, Peabody & Co. (Kidder) named Orlando Joseph Jett as the recipient of the Chairman's Award: the outstanding employee of the year. Nineteen ninety-three had been a good year for Kidder and Jett's best year. As a reward for the profits he had produced as head of its government bond desk, Jett received the second largest bonus in the firm: $9 million. One member of the audience described Jett's acceptance address as a *winning-is-everything* speech.

After high school, Joseph Jett had won a scholarship to MIT where he earned a bachelor's degree in 1980 and a master's degree in 1982, both in chemical engineering. His first job was at

---

[6]This section was drawn from Freedman R, and J. R. Burke, 1998, *Kidder, Peabody & Co.* New York University, Stern School of Business, New York.

General Electric's plastics division in Selkirk, New York. Jett left GE in 1985 to enter the Harvard Business School. His summer internship, working for the group that managed short-term cash at the Ford Motor Company, was his first position in finance. After receiving his MBA, Jett began his trading career at Morgan Stanley as a trainee and worked up to become a junior trader. He was laid off in less than two years.

It took him six months to find his second job, at CS First Boston. In early 1991 Jett was dismissed by CS First Boston. He contends he was dismissed because the firm discovered he was pursuing a position at Kidder. Former colleagues say he was let go because of lackluster performance and for having presented a résumé that exaggerated his experience. After another six months of unemployment, Kidder hired Jett as a government bond trader in the Fixed Income Division. Government bond trading is one of the most straightforward kinds of securities trading, stressing knowledge of yield curves and mathematics. This was a good position for someone with limited trading experience and seemed to be a lucky break for Jett, who had no prior experience trading government securities.

At the end of 1991, Jett received a mere $5,000 bonus along with a warning that if he did not improve his profitability he would be dismissed. In 1992, Jett appeared to have made a complete turnaround. Suddenly, he was very profitable and at the end of the year he received a $2 million bonus. As his profits grew, he was allowed to make larger and larger trades and to risk more and more of the firm's capital. Before his arrival, $20 million in annual earnings had been the best record for the Government Desk. Yet in 1993, Jett's profits ranged from $5 million to $10 million per month. Apparently, Jett's supervisors believed that he had invented a new trading technique that had transformed the Government Bond Desk into a powerful money-making asset for the firm. In March 1993, Jett was promoted to head the Government Desk. Jett, who had joined Kidder only 26 months earlier, now had direct responsibility for 32 people and had a large amount of authority. Jett's apparent performance and money-making ability continued; and, at the end of 1993, he was promoted to Managing Director.

For 1993, Jett generated more than $299 million in profits and accounted for more than one-quarter of the Fixed Income Division's operating profits. This performance led to the Chairman's Award and the $9 million bonus.

Since GE had acquired Kidder in 1986 for $600 million to increase their presence in the financial markets, Kidder reported directly to GE Capital, the financial services arm of GE. Compared to other investment houses, Kidder had access to a tremendous capital base. Firms that operated under the traditional partnership, such as Goldman, Sachs, relied heavily on their partners' capital. This is no match for GE Capital's resources.

Under traditional partnerships, partners are selected from the traders and investment bankers that work for the firm or that have been recruited from other firms. Partners determine the firm's overall investment strategy and consequently the level of risk to which their strategy will expose the firm. Generally, partnerships take a more conservative investment approach because they are investing their own money.

At Kidder, the traders were employees. Their future financial well-being was not as closely tied to the firm's. Since Kidder's traders were not trading with their own money, they were more open to riskier trading strategies that could mean bigger short-term profits for the firm; hence, bigger annual bonuses. At this time Kidder's management was also under intense pressure from GE to produce substantial profits and to demonstrate rapid growth. As a result, senior management at Kidder chose to adopt a relatively risky investment strategy by leveraging Kidder significantly more than many of its competitors.

Under the direction of Jack Welch, Chairman and CEO, GE developed a highly successful diversification strategy. To be included in the GE portfolio, businesses had to be number one or number two in their global market, and demonstrate a high growth rate. If a business's performance did not meet expectations, Welch would *fix, close, or sell* the unit. Under Welch's direction, for the period 1981 to 1991, GE earnings grew at an annual rate of more than 10%, which was $1\frac{1}{2}$ times the GNP's growth rate for the same period. To accomplish this feat, Welch adopted his strategy of diversification and then slashed overhead and decentralized the organization—reducing layers of management and pushing decisions down the hierarchy. GE eliminated *the entire second and third echelons of management*. Welch emphasized a philosophy of leadership, not management. He pushed his employees to become more autonomous in the hopes that they would take responsibility for their actions and decisions.

Welch appointed Michael A. Carpenter to the position of CEO of Kidder. Carpenter had no prior experience on Wall Street. In fact, he was not licensed to run a brokerage firm by the SEC from January 1989 through March 1993. Consistent with GE's growth requirements, Carpenter knew he had to make Kidder a leader in at least one market. He identified mortgage-backed securities (MBSs) as the market segment where Kidder would make its mark. Through the focus on MBSs and on improved profitability, Kidder suddenly became trading oriented. However, there were two weak links in Carpenter's strategy; one was that Kidder lacked the infrastructure (systems and controls) needed to support a heavy-trading environment and the other was that Kidder did not have traders with sufficient skill and experience. As a result, Kidder often promoted less experienced traders (relative to their competitors) into positions of responsibility.

Edward Cerullo, the Head of the Fixed Income Division of Kidder, relied on reports to keep himself up-to-date with the activities of his traders. These reports included inventory reports, profit and loss statements, control reports, and risk management reports. Traders summed up the culture under Cerullo as *produce or perish*. They were expected to produce profits or be fired. Former fixed-income traders were so leery of reporting losses to Cerullo that they would often underreport profits in order to build up a reserve for use in months when they had a loss.

Early in 1994, the computer system began having difficulty in keeping up with the volume of trades that Jett was making. Specialists were called in to fix the computer system. What the Information Systems (IS) specialists found was that Jett had entered $1.7 trillion in trades into the Kidder system (this was almost one-half of the total dollar value of Treasury securities currently estimated to be held in private hands) and that none of the trades were ever consummated. This meant that while no securities had ever changed hands, the profits associated with these trades had been reported as income.

The computer specialists, realizing the seriousness of the situation, called in the accountants and senior executives, including Cerullo, to investigate. Cerullo's risk manager, David Bernstein, began an in-depth audit and found a *distortion* totaling $300 million on Jett's trading book.

By early April, the findings of Kidder's investigation showed that the problem would significantly impact Kidder's profitability for 1993 and 1992. As the accountants continued to dig, the magnitude of the problem grew. Kidder claims that Jett had created some $350 million in false profits and had hidden approximately $85 million in real losses.

Kidder's internal auditors had reviewed Jett's trading desk twice in 1993; but, according to the Lynch Report, the auditors were inexperienced, and Jett had misrepresented his desk's activities to the auditors. Also, employees had raised questions about Jett's trading practices as far back as 1992. A trader who had worked with Jett had raised questions about his sudden profitability with supervisors, believing Jett was mismarking or misrecording his trading positions. The practice of mismarking is illegal and carries heavy penalties by the SEC for the firm and the trader. The trader was fired immediately after raising these questions, for what Kidder described as an unrelated reason. Cerullo never investigated the accusations.

In May 1993, a Kidder accountant realized that there was a defect in the system's setup and suggested that the accounting system be changed to correct this flaw. The suggested change would have exposed Jett's alleged irregular trading activities. Jett is purported to have opposed this change and it was never implemented.

Jett traded government strips, which involves separating the bond's principal and interest components into two separately traded issues. If the demand for bonds is higher than for the strips, as many as 60 interest payments (zero-coupon bonds) could be reconstituted into a traditional coupon-bearing bond (recon). Since Kidder's computer system was not capable of *making dozens of zero-coupon bonds disappear in a reconstitution and then making a conventional bond materialize*, the exchange was recorded as the sale of the zero-coupon-bonds and the purchase of the coupon bond. Kidder's computer system, however, inappropriately allowed recons to be settled up to five days in advance. Jett would enter into forward contracts which joined the principal and interest components together at a later date. This enabled Jett to record profits on the day he entered the recons. The profits should vanish later at the time the trade was settled. However, instead of settling when these forward contracts came due and recognizing a zero profit, Jett would roll them over and leave the profit on the books. To keep the system going, Jett had to continually increase the value of his portfolio, meaning the system operated much like a pyramid scheme.

This is a classic example where efforts to transform a firm into a market leader by using performance-based incentives in a highly competitive environment with an ineffective information system leads to an outcome directly opposite to the desired result.

Using Professor Simons' *levers of control* to analyze the operations at Kidder, Peabody & Co. during the Joseph Jett scandal, refer to the categories in Figure 11-3 and assign a score from 1 (low risk) to 5 (high risk) for each of the nine levers of control components. Then, add the scores. Many students get a total score of 40 or above. What does this mean? Professor Simons uses the following summary to interpret the scoring.

1. **9 to 20: *The Safety Zone.*** Companies that carry this low level are usually safe from unexpected errors or events that could threaten the business. But is the risk exposure *too low*? After all, there is a trade-off between risk and return.

2. **21 to 34: *The Caution Zone.*** Most companies fall here. However, watch for high scores in 2 or 3 dimensions. These scores indicate issues that senior management should address in the near term.

3. **35 to 45: *The Danger Zone.*** Alarm bells should be ringing and immediate action must be taken. A full operational risk audit should be implemented at the insistence of senior management and the Board of Directors.

11.6 MANAGING OPERATIONAL RISK

Now that operational risk has been defined and the causes of operational risk have been discussed, how to manage operational risk needs to be discussed. The management of operational risk was addressed in the 1999 survey by the British Bankers Association (BBA). The BBA found that the evolution of operational risk management with a company involves five stages, which are presented in Figure 11-4. The five stages that the BBA discusses should be viewed as the steps in the evolution of operational risk management that a company must recognize as it becomes more and more sophisticated with and concerned about its risk management process.

The first stage reflects the fact that companies have always known that operational risks exist. Historically, these risks have been managed by relying on internal controls with periodic reviews by the internal auditor. Generally, the responsibility for risk control has remained with the individual managers in the business and specialist functions.

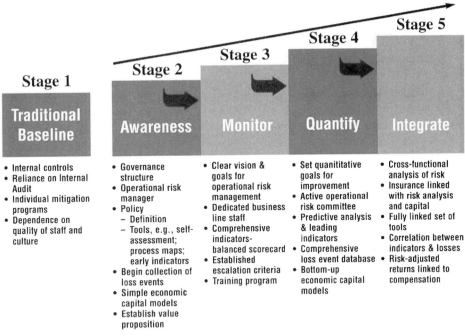

FIGURE 11-4   Five stages of operational risk management.

The second stage recognizes the fact that operational risk can have a significant impact on the profitability of the company. Usually, a particular individual is appointed to be responsible for operational risk and that person is responsible for developing a common understanding and assessment of operational risk. Risk policies are developed, early indicators of risk levels are identified, and operational losses are collected. The purpose at this stage is to provide a framework for risk identification, definition of controls, and prioritization of issues and risk mitigation programs.

Stage three focuses on the current levels of operational risk and the effectiveness of management functions. Risk indicators are established to monitor performance. These indicators are consolidated with other relevant performance measures to provide senior management with an overall assessment of the firm's performance. Because stage three provides a better understanding of the current operational situation, stage four concentrates on quantifying the relative risks and attempting to predict what will happen in the future. Usually, firms in this stage assign specific committees or task forces to develop empirical models and evaluate their validity.

The final stage of risk management recognizes the pervasive nature of operational risk. At this point, the objective is to integrate and implement processes and solutions while, at the same time, recognizing the different levels of management needs. At this stage, operational risk management becomes a fundamental part of the strategic planning process.

Why are there so many concerns with the *how* of the approach to risk management? A business must make a profit (in present value terms) to remain successful and the management of risk requires expenditure of a firm's financial resources. Competent risk management is not inexpensive. The overriding goal of risk management is either the creation or preservation of shareholder value.

To implement a risk management procedure, a risk management philosophy needs to be established that incorporates a knowledge of the effect of risk on the performance of the company, the amount of risk (potential losses) the company can tolerate, and the impact of volatility on financial performance.

11.7 OPERATIONAL RISK IN THE RISK MANAGEMENT FUNCTION

Having defined and discussed the operational risk component of business risk, the remainder of this chapter narrows its focus and discusses operational risk in the risk management function of a business. This discussion of operational risk in the risk management function is divided into three parts: (1) why a business should have a risk management policy, (2) how to create a risk management policy, and (3) how to measure the effectiveness of the risk management operation. Each of the three parts of operational risk in the risk management function will be discussed separately.

11.7.1 Why a Business Should Create a Risk Policy

A **risk policy** establishes guidelines for the management of on- and off-balance sheet financial portfolios and describes the role of the different parties involved in the investment functions and the control of activities related to managing risk. Most policy guidelines are designed to meet or exceed any regulatory standards and to ensure that managers take a prudent course of action in the management of corporate operations and overall financial risk.

The purpose of a policy statement is twofold. First, the policy statement is designed to protect the shareholders of the firm from the management of the firm: that is, to limit the scope of managerial decisions. The second purpose is to protect the managers from themselves. By outlining the specific actions that a manager may or may not take, the policies force managers to work together within a unified framework toward a common goal. With managerial policies in place, departments will have a more difficult time working at cross-purposes with each other. The policy statement should outline the appropriate approval procedures that decision making must follow so that everyone knows who is responsible for what decision. Figure 11-5 is an excellent example of defining authority and responsibility limits in a risk policy.

In the event of a dispute, the policy statement is designed to ensure that a well-informed independent outsider, such as an auditor or a lawyer, can look at the investment decision and understand exactly why it was made. The policy statement should be developed by the senior managers of the firm under the supervision of the Board of Directors.

A brief look at the risks of currency and interest rate volatility is necessary here. In the international markets the effects of these risks on financial performance are too important to be left to technical experts in the treasury department. Treasury groups are not generally strategically (long-term) oriented; they are the tacticians (short-term) of risk management.

The Board of Directors has ultimate authority and responsibility for the management of investment portfolios and financial risk. All new proposals and amendments on limits, products and other parts of the investment policy are also subject to approval by the ING Direct Market & Credit Risk Management Committee (DMC).

In order to ensure accountability, authority to act is delegated to individuals (defined in Delegation of Authority Section below) in the Company, and to ensure maximum control, responsibility for monitoring limits is delegated to Risk Management and the Asset-Liability Committee (ALCO).

In order to ensure an efficient and effective process, authority for the management of investment portfolios and authority for the management of financial risk is delegated to the same individuals.

Delegation of Authority

The authority to manage ING Bank, fsb's investment portfolios and its financial risk, within the limits specified, is delegated from the Board to the President who shall delegate all these authorities of a portion thereof to the Treasurer.

The Treasurer may further delegate all or a portion of these authorities with the approval of the President.

All delegations of the President's and Treasurer's authorities shall be confirmed in writing.

FIGURE 11-5 ING Bank, fsb. Authority and responsibility.

Source: ING Bank, fsb.

For strategic risk management to succeed, the chief operating officer must assume the lead because an integrated risk management system requires coordinated actions across various corporate departments such as treasury, marketing, sales, purchasing, and production to succeed.

For example, assume that the marketing department of a company wants to increase sales by changing the accounts receivable collection period from 90 days to 120 days. Assume, also, that the company funds its operations with variable rate debt. A reasonable assumption would be that the treasury department of the company would hedge any potential changes in the floating interest rate with an interest-rate futures contract. But, what if the longest maturity futures contract were 90 days? There would be no way to hedge completely since the treasurer would have to roll over the futures contract at the end of three months and the treasurer has no way of knowing what the interest rate would be at that time. Does this mean that the collection period should not be increased? Not necessarily. The Chief Operating Officer would have to analyze the costs and benefits of this decision. Does the increased profit arising from increased sales offset the costs and uncertainty associated with the imperfect hedging program? This brief example demonstrates the strategic nature of risk management.

Management must establish the risk management priorities. A good beginning is to determine management's hedging objectives. Is management interested in *total protection*?

Since risk stems from unexpected economic changes, complete protection against any price movement implies hedging against both adverse and favorable outcomes to guarantee the certainty of the costs and benefits of a future financial event. Alternatively, management may want protection against adverse outcomes, yet may want to benefit from any favorable outcomes. If management chooses this hedging objective, they must be able to identify the trade-off between enjoying the upside benefits and the costs of downside protection. Many firms choose this alternative by choosing to avoid potential losses at the expense of giving up potentially large upside earnings.

Choosing the risk management alternative of avoiding potential losses at the expense of potentially large earnings requires enormous management effort. To be successful, management must implement a foreign exposure reporting system, develop exposure reports (balance sheet items, contracts, commitments), create flow of funds reports (future flow of currencies by date and currency denomination), identify currency restrictions by country, and identify any differential tax treatments of income and capital. To reiterate, the first step in risk management is the requirement that management defines the operational, pricing, and financial policies of the firm; attaches accountability and specifies responsibility guidelines that provide for conflict resolution; and specifies responsibilities and criteria for evaluation.

11.7.2 The Process for Creating a Risk Policy

The first step in establishing a company's risk policy is to define risk specific to that organization. The second step is to determine a level of risk aversion based on management's and the other stakeholders' risk appetite. In other words, how much risk exposure will the firm be willing to take? Once management has determined the business's appetite for risk, management must identify and define an investment philosophy. In Figure 11-6, the investment policy of ING Bank fsb is presented. Notice the clear distinction made between

---

Taking risk may result in an enhancement of a financial intermediary's spread and can be an attractive way to boost income. ING Bank, fsb must manage the trade-off between the incremental income received and the potential for losses. These risks are difficult to manage, because no one transaction causes them. They arise from the net of all transactions. The only practical approach is to manage financial risk on a portfolio basis. Credit and settlement risks are inherent in the transactions used to manage the financial position. They do not affect clients' products, but are relevant to the investment activity.

The management of ING Bank, fsb's investment portfolios is not separate from the management of overall financial risk. The risk characteristics of these portfolios are designed to be consistent with the parameters set by the Board of Directors, ING Direct Market & Credit Risk Management Committee (DMC) and consistent with the Bank's prudent risk management philosophy. Placing the management of financial risk and investment portfolios in Treasury under the review of the Risk Management Department is an effective way to ensure a disciplined and integrated process.

FIGURE 11-6 ING Bank, fsb. Investment philosophy.

Source: ING Bank, fsb.

the operational aspect of the bank and the investment aspect. Notice also the clarity of the investment philosophy statement. The risk characteristics of the investment portfolio and the person responsible for managing the portfolio are made very clear.

As stated before, one of the basic purposes of an investment philosophy statement is to define how much risk a firm is willing to accept. The preparation of this document is one of the first steps to ensure that management has accurately identified the nature and extent of the risks faced by their firm. Management must decide whether they want the certainty of cash flows or the flexibility to earn additional profits. Uncertainty over this issue often leads to confusion between hedging and speculation.

The third step is to identify the objectives of the risk management policy. At this point, senior management must decide which exposures are important enough to manage and how much of the corporate resources should be spent in the risk management process of these exposures. This discussion requires that they define and measure the exposures on several dimensions such as present vs. future transactions, the effect of historical vs. accounting reporting, and the economic impact of future cash flows. Some standard policy objectives include the following:

- preserving the value of the firm in the long term regardless of the variation in underlying economic variables,
- ensuring orderly recognition of income without undue variation due to changes in underlying economic variables,
- ensuring the total risk position of the firm is managed in a prudent fashion through the imposition of reasonable and stringently enforceable limits,
- ensuring that within the limits imposed, the firm receives a reasonable return for the risk it does take, and
- pursuing a nonconcentration strategy (including, but not limited to, issuer, industry, and maturity), the selection of solvent counterparties, issuers, and an adequate control of market risk.

The next step is to identify the areas where risk management will be required and the identification of the responsible parties for this risk management. Now, the limitations that the risk managers have to work within must be specifically identified.

To perform effectively in today's environment, a treasurer must understand how risk management instruments perform in both bull and bear markets, must understand the fundamentals of economics, and must be able to quantify as accurately as possible the dollar value of potential gains and losses. Although a treasurer is generally concerned with the tactical (short-term) risk management, the treasurer should also be a permanent member of the strategic (long-term) risk management group so that hedging decisions can be properly inserted into the context of the overall operation. While the position of treasurer is crucial to the success of the corporation, a treasurer must be bound by the risk management policies regardless of economic conditions. In particular, the treasurer may not have the authority to utilize the full range of risk management products. For example, the use of long-term naked (unhedged) options may not be authorized. Alternatively, when instruments are approved, the policy statement will define any limitations on the instrument's use quite specifically. For example, a statement in a risk management policy might be made such as, "No derivative instrument

In general, a policy statement should indicate the following:

- The investment philosophy
- The objectives of the policy
- The authority and responsibility for the management of investment portfolios and financial risk
- The limitations on managers including:
  - Investment limits and definitions
  - Risk measurement
  - Limits on short-term investments
  - Limits on long-term investments
  - How limits are established and revised
  - Eligible investments
  - Trading limits
  - The movement of funds
  - Counterparty limits
- Risk-specific limits
- Reporting
- Auditing
- Policy review and revision

FIGURE 11-7   Major components of a risk management policy statement.

will be used where the potential for loss is greater than 1% of the value of the underlying asset." Figure 11-7 presents the major components of a risk management policy statement.

11.7.3 Evaluating Risk Policy Performance

A major benefit of having a risk management philosophy and a policy statement is that it is much easier to manage and measure the performance of a treasurer. One measure that can be used is to determine the treasurer's degree of **hedging efficiency**. Hedging efficiency is not the same as hedging profitability although the two are often confused. Hedging efficiency relates to how well the hedge achieved the company's risk management goal for hedging. Hedging profitability relates to the profits generated from hedging.

In general, there are five alternative measures of hedging efficiency. The decision of which measure to choose depends on the firm's hedging objectives.

> **Objective 1: Achieve a financial target as close as possible to the target.** This objective is the most common objective of an investment-based hedging position. The desired result may be a target investment rate or profit amount from some transaction. Here, the hedge efficiency measure is
>
> $$\text{Hedge efficiency} = \frac{\text{actual financial result}}{\text{target financial result}}.$$
>
> For example, suppose a company actually invested funds at 8.375% when the target rate was 9.0%; the hedge efficiency would be 93.06%.
>
> **Objective 2: Achieve a financial target subject to a minimum acceptable result.** This investment-based hedging position requires that the hedge yield a minimum

acceptable level. Here, the hedge efficiency measure is

$$\text{Hedge efficiency} = \frac{\text{actual financial result} - \text{minimum target result}}{\text{target financial result} - \text{minimum target result}}.$$

For example, suppose a company wanted to earn $7 million and the break-even level of earnings was $5 million. If the company actually earned $7.3 million, the hedge efficiency would be 115%.

Objective 3: Achieve a financial target that undershoots the target. This objective is the most common objective of a cost-based hedging position. Although it is similar to the first objective, the desired result may be a target borrowing rate or expense amount from some transaction. Here, the hedge efficiency measure is

$$\text{Hedge efficiency} = \frac{\text{target financial result}}{\text{actual financial result}}.$$

For example, suppose a company had targeted estimated costs at £13.2 million but actual costs turned out to be £14.9 million; the hedge efficiency would be 88.6%.

Objective 4: Achieve a financial target subject to a maximum acceptable result. This cost-based hedging position requires that the hedge yield a maximum acceptable level. Here, the hedge efficiency measure is

$$\text{Hedge efficiency} = \frac{\text{actual financial result} - \text{maximum target result}}{\text{target financial result} - \text{maximum target result}}.$$

For example, suppose a company wanted to borrow at 5.5% with a maximum possible rate of 6.5%. After hedging, the company manages to borrow at 5.8%; the hedge efficiency would be 70%.

Objective 5: Maintain the status quo. Maintaining the status quo is different from the four previous cases. The first four objectives have a directional preference. When maintaining the status quo, any deviation from the current situation would be unacceptable. A classic example of this type of objective occurs in portfolios of financial instruments owned by financial institutions. In these situations, the policy is to insulate the portfolio completely from possible changes in market rates. Any movement in the portfolio would indicate an improperly hedged portfolio. Here, the hedge efficiency measure is

$$\text{Hedge efficiency} = \min \text{ of } \left[1 - \frac{\text{change in hedged portfolio value}}{\text{change in unhedged portfolio value}}, \right.$$
$$\left. 1 + \frac{\text{change in hedged portfolio value}}{\text{change in unhedged portfolio value}} \right].$$

The use of these types of performance evaluations highlights two other extremely important issues in risk management. First, risk managers must look beyond the mere application of hedging tools and view risk management as a strategic tool for improving the firm's competitive advantage. That is, the hedging instrument must not be viewed separately from the underlying exposure and the objectives of the firm. Second, the point must be made that hedging creates an element in operational risk. Therefore, regardless of the hedging objectives made, the implementation of the risk management strategy must have the following characteristics:

1. **Acceptability**. The strategies must make sense to professionals who will implement the strategy.
2. **Consistency**. The strategies must make sense in the context of management's stated values and objectives and the strategies must have a logical flow from period to period.
3. **Quality**. The strategies can be seen to improve management decision that is, management's beliefs align with market realities.

Without these characteristics, the risk management process will not have the stature necessary within the organization to become an important element in the strategic planning process.

SUMMARY OF VALUATION AND RISK MANAGEMENT SKILLS

1. Understand the components of business (unsystematic) risk.

Business risks are diversifiable and specific to the industry and the market in which a firm operates. There are five components of business risk: operational risk, legal risk, credit risk, liquidity risk, and model risk. Operational risk results from the failure of internal systems or from errors by people that actually run the business. Legal risk results from failure to monitor and enforce contracts with the firm. Credit risk results when the counterparty to a financial transaction does not have the financial resources to make a promised payment. Liquidity risk results from the cost of having to unwind a position in a security or commodity quickly. Model risk results when nontechnical market professionals naively use complex financial models to make important business decisions.

2. Understand the components of market (systematic) risk.

Market risks are those that are not necessarily diversifiable. Three sources of market risk are interest-rate risk, foreign exchange risk, and commodity price risk.

3. Define operational risk and its four components.

Operational risk is the risk of direct or indirect loss resulting from inadequate or failed internal processes, people, and systems or from external events. The four components of operational risk are operations risk, asset impairment risk, competitive risk, and franchise risk.

4. Know the firm characteristics associated with greater operational risk.

Operational risk is greater in fast growing firms, in firms with cultures that do not foster frank communication between levels of management, and in firms with many complex transactions.

5. Understand why a firm should have a risk management policy and how to measure the effectiveness of that policy.

A risk management policy is designed to meet or exceed any regulatory standards and to ensure that managers take a prudent course of action in the management of corporate operations and overall financial risk. A risk policy statement protects shareholders of the firm by limiting the scope of managerial decisions and by forcing managers to take actions that are not at cross-purposes with those of other members of the management team.

QUESTIONS

1. Why are limitations in risk management measures a good thing?

2. Return to the calculation you performed on the Joseph Jett scandal. Explain why you assigned the scores you did to each of the *levers of control*.

3. Perform a *levers of control* evaluation for the Barings Bank case.

4. What is the purpose of a risk management policy?

5. Explain the difference between *hedging efficiency* and *hedging profitability*.

6. What is the maximum hedge efficiency with a status quo hedge objective? What is the minimum level of hedge efficiency?

7. Suppose a financial institution hedges a portfolio of FRAs with interest rate futures. The yield curve shifts and the value of the hedge portfolio increases by $1,678 while the FRAs alone lost $21,000. What is the hedge efficiency for a status quo hedge objective?

8. What are the three major objectives of a successful risk management strategy?

9. What is operational risk?

10. Define risk.

REFERENCES

DERMAN, E., 1996, Model, *Goldman Sachs Quantitative Research Notes*. Derman provides an excellent overview of the nature and extent of model risk in modern risk management.

British Bankers Association, RMA Associates, ISDA, and PriceWaterhouse Coopers, 1999, *Operational Risk: The Next Frontier*, RMA Associates, Philadelphia, PA. This document provides one of the first analyses of the nature and extent of

operational risk and outlines methods for addressing such risks.

SIMONS, R. L., 1999, *A Note on Identifying Strategic Risk*, Harvard Business School Publishing, Cambridge, MA. This note provides an evaluation tool for determining the nature of operational risk and a means for prioritizing operational risk audits.

KEY TERMS

Asset Impairment Risk Risk that occurs when an asset loses a significant portion of its current value because of a reduction in the probability of receiving expected future cash flows.

Business Risk The risk inherent in a particular line of business. Business risk has five component parts: (1) operational risk, (2) legal risk, (3) credit risk, (4) liquidity risk, and (5) model risk.

Commodity Price Risk Risk associated with changes in commodity prices of production inputs.

Company-Specific Risk See unsystematic risk.

Competitive Risks Risk that results from changes in the competitive environment that could impair the business's ability to create value and differentiate its products and services.

Credit Risk Risk that the counterparty to the transactions recognizes their legal obligation but, does not have the financial resources to make the promised payment.

Foreign Exchange Risk Risk associated with changes in currency exchange rates.

Franchise Risk Risk that occurs when the value of the entire business erodes due to a loss in confidence by critical constituents such as shareholders, investors, or customers.

Hedging Efficiency Relates to how well the hedge achieved the company's risk management goal for hedging.

Interest-Rate Risk Risk associated with changes in market interest rates.

Legal Risk Risk occuring from contracts not being enforced.

Levers of Control Nine potential areas that can result in operational risk.

Liquidity Risk Risks arising from the cost of unwinding a position.

Market Risk See systematic risk.

Model Risk Risk that a highly technical financial model will not have economic validity.

Operational Risk Risks arising from the failure of internal systems or the errors by the people who actually run the business.

Operations Risk Risk that results from a breakdown in a core operating, manufacturing, or processing capability.

Risk A measure of the potential changes in value that will be experienced in a managed portfolio as a result of differences in the economic environment between now and some specific point in the future.

Risk Management The process of managing the risk inherent in owning an asset or security.

Risk Policy Establishes guidelines for the management of on- and off-balance sheet financial portfolios and describes the role of the different parties involved in the investment functions and the control of activities related to managing risk.

Systematic Risk Risk that cannot be eliminated through diversification. This is risk that all businesses and investors are exposed to.

Unsystematic Risk Risk that can be eliminated through diversification. This type of risk is specific to one business or security.

Value-at-Risk Value-at-risk (VaR) is a currency-based measure of the maximum expected loss over a given investment period under normal market conditions at a predetermined level of confidence.

Volatility Change in value of an asset.

CHAPTER 12

MONEY MARKET RISK MANAGEMENT

12.1 INTRODUCTION

This is the first chapter that discusses managing risk in a specific market. The focus of the risk management chapters is how to protect invested funds. The purpose of this chapter is to develop an understanding of how to manage the risk that is associated with investment in money market instruments. The focus in the money markets is on liquidity risk and default risk, stemming directly from the money market's role as the market for trading liquidity. Banks store liquidity in the money markets as a means to meet customer withdrawals while earning a small return on the stored funds. Accordingly, it is vital to banks that they address liquidity risk and default risk in the money markets so that banks have immediate access to the stored funds when customers make withdrawals.

This chapter begins with a brief review of the economic role of the money markets. Then, the discussion moves to the management of liquidity risk and default risk in the different classes of money market instruments that were covered in Chapter 4. The management of these risks in the money markets mainly occurs before any investment takes place. Later chapters will show that risk management in the other financial markets typically occurs after the investment is made. This chapter concludes with a discussion of money market mutual funds.

DEVELOPING VALUATION AND RISK MANAGEMENT SKILLS

1. Understand the economic role of the money markets and how this role drives risk management in the money markets.
2. Understand liquidity risk and how money market securities are structured to manage liquidity risk.
3. Understand default risk and how default risk is managed in the money markets.
4. Understand the basic benefits of mutual funds and how these benefits do and do not apply in money market mutual funds.

12.2 TRADING LIQUIDITY INSTEAD OF TRADING FOR EXPECTED RETURNS

Charles Schwab describes the goal of their **money market mutual fund** as, *"highest current income consistent with stability of capital and liquidity."* They further state that, *"to* *pursue its goal, the fund invests in high-quality short-term money market investments.*"[1] What Schwab is telling investors is that Schwab picks securities for their money market mutual fund with a focus on low default risk and high marketability and then, within those constraints, they try to generate as high a return as possible. Put another way, earnings are not the primary goal of this fund. Instead, earnings are secondary to the preservation of capital and the ability to access that capital when needed.

As discussed in Chapter 4, the economic role of the money markets is the trading of liquidity. This statement means that investors with a temporary excess in cash make these funds available for borrowers with temporary cash shortages. A temporary excess means that the cash will be needed soon to meet foreseeable obligations and thus the protection of principal (cash or, as described by Schwab, capital) is paramount. This investment approach is very different from the approach assumed when an investment is made in stocks or bonds. In stocks and bonds, investors with long-term excess cash make the cash available to issuers of securities with long-term funding needs. The long-term nature of the excess means that the excess is not immediately obligated (this is often called free cash flow) and therefore the investor can put the principal at risk with the intention of earning risky (but higher) expected returns. Another way of looking at this approach is that the investor can make up any short-term losses over the length of the long-term investment.

Investors' willingness to take risk with long-term cash excesses vs. their desire for protection of principal when they have temporary (short-term) excesses, leads to very different approaches to risk management. With long-term cash excesses, investors place their cash at risk and then manage the risks of ownership over the life of the investment. With temporary excesses, investors analyze the borrowers and the market mechanisms before the investment to ensure that the risk exposure of their cash is at a minimum.

12.3 THE RISKS THAT ARE IMPORTANT TO MONEY MARKET INVESTORS AND HOW THOSE RISKS ARE ADDRESSED

Money market investors store temporary cash excesses in money market securities. Because the excesses are temporary, money market investors focus on the protection of their cash in these investments. That is, they focus on getting their money back when they need it. When investors are focused on protection of their cash they are concerned about two types of risk: (1) **liquidity risk** and (2) **default risk**. The remainder of this section discusses these two types of risk and how they are managed.

12.3.1 Liquidity Risk

Liquidity is the process of converting an asset to cash. An asset is considered highly liquid if it can be quickly converted to cash without a major price concession. Money market investors are concerned about liquidity because they are storing temporary cash surpluses that are needed to meet expected near-term obligations. Thus, money market investors

---

[1] Schwab Money Funds Sweep Investments Prospectus, April 30, 2001.

require a high degree of liquidity. A high degree of liquidity is built into the money markets by requiring that money market securities are highly marketable short-term debt securities.

12.3.1.1 *Short-Term Debt*

Money market investors are investing temporary cash surpluses. Being defined as temporary means that the surpluses are short lived. The expected length of the surplus is determined by either a clearly defined near-term obligation or by the normal cash cycle of the investor. In either case, the investor requires that the invested cash be returned at the end of the expected length of the surplus period. The investor attempts to ensure that the cash is returned when needed by putting the return date in a contract. Since the surplus is short term, this contract will be a short-term contract that returns the cash to the investor on a specific date with some interest to compensate for the rental of the investor's cash. This statement is a general description of a short-term debt contract.

A short-term debt contract requires the return of cash on a specific date, with the date chosen by the investor to correspond to the time when the investor expects to need the cash. Since the timing of when the investor needs the cash might change, money market investors also demand that money market securities be highly marketable.

12.3.1.2 *Highly Marketable Short-Term Debt*

Requiring money market securities to be short-term debt instruments meets money market investors' expected liquidity needs. The ability to meet expected liquidity needs is not sufficient to meet all of the money market investors' liquidity concerns. Investors also recognize that the timing of cash flows can and do change. Therefore, money market investors demand flexibility to meet these changing cash flow needs. That is, they demand the ability to get their cash back early if the need should arise. To achieve the early return of cash, the money market contract is sold in the secondary market. The secondary market must be a highly liquid secondary market so that investors can quickly sell their money market securities without price concessions.

The secondary market for money market securities is a dealer market where the dealer stands ready to buy and sell securities. The dealer's role in making the secondary market is extremely important because the secondary money market lacks the one feature most commonly associated with highly marketable securities: high volume. Since the secondary market for most money market securities lacks substantial volume, dealers provide liquidity by standing ready to trade. The exception to low volume in the money market is the secondary market for *on-the-run* Treasury bills.

The on-the-run Treasury bill has substantial secondary market volume. This Treasury bill is the most recently issued bill. However, the length of each bill's run is short. In today's market, the run of a Treasury bill lasts for one week. When a new bill is issued, the previously issued bill goes *off-the-run* and its secondary market volume declines substantially. Figure 12-1 shows a timeline of the run of a 13-week bill. A new bill is on-the-run for one week starting on the Thursday when it is issued. At the end of one week, the next new bill is issued and it starts its one-week run. When the next bill is issued, the previous bill goes off-the-run and is off-the-run for the remainder of its life. In the case of a 13-week bill, the bill is on-the-run for one week and off-the-run for the next 12 weeks.

When regular secondary market volume is low, the dealer's role as a market maker is vital to the marketability of a security and, in the case of the money markets, is crucial to the orderly functioning of the money markets. For example, most commercial paper is

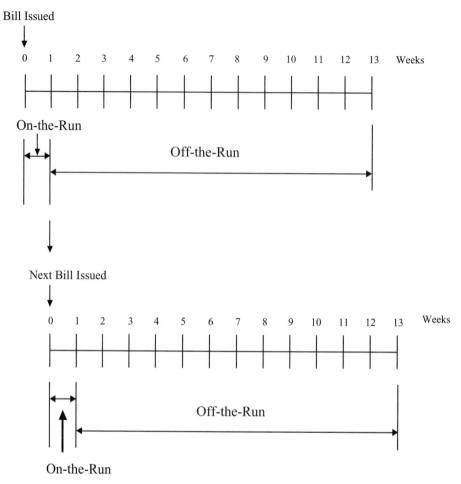

FIGURE 12-1 Timeline showing the run of a 13-week bill.

held by investors until it matures. However, should investors need to sell their commercial paper before maturity, the industry practice is that commercial paper dealers stand ready to buy back any commercial paper they sell to investors. This practice provides the necessary marketability for commercial paper. The dealers offer a similar service by continually quoting bid and ask prices for off-the-run Treasury bills, negotiable CDs, bankers' acceptances, and short-term agency debt. This service ensures that money market investors can quickly sell their securities at prices that reflect current market yields.

Repurchase agreements (repos) and fed funds do not have a secondary market because of the nature of the transactions. A repo is a contract to sell and later repurchase a defined collection of securities. Because the investor in a repo acquires a claim to specific securities (the securities are held by a third party trustee) while the borrower has their money, it would be extremely difficult for investors to transfer their position in the repo agreement to another investor. For this reason, the industry practice is that the borrower will return the investor's cash early if the investor needs the cash before the repo's maturity. Repo market conventions also provide a small price concession for the borrower when the investor requests an early return of the cash. Due to the lack of marketability and the market conventions for early exits, over 50% of the total repo market is in overnight repos. As stated previously, fed funds also lack a secondary market. In a fed funds transaction, the investor (a bank) provides cash to a borrower using a draw against a prearranged line of credit with the investor. As with the repo, the investor's position in fed funds is very difficult to sell because it is a draw against a specific line of credit and, thus, virtually impossible to transfer. To handle the issue of marketability, the industry practice is to issue almost all fed funds transactions with a maturity of one day.

12.3.2 Default Risk

Default occurs when a borrower fails to meet any one of the terms of the debt contract. Long-term debt default usually occurs from a violation of a contract **covenant** or a failure to make payments as scheduled. Covenants are included in long-term debt contracts to identify declining financial conditions in the borrower before the declining conditions deteriorate to the point of threatening a borrower's ability to pay the debt obligations. The short-term nature of money market securities precludes the need for debt covenants; therefore, default in the money markets is associated with failure to make the scheduled payment. As stated in Chapter 4, money market securities require a single payment at maturity; therefore, an analysis of default risk in the money markets is an analysis of the borrower's ability to make that single payment as scheduled at maturity.

12.3.2.1 *Government and Agency Default Risk*   Treasury bills are often described as the ideal money market security, in part, because they are considered default free. Treasury bills are considered default free because the U.S. government has never failed to pay its obligations in full. However, technical defaults have occurred on Treasury bills. On occasion, the Treasury has been late with its payment, a technical default. Being late with a payment is a default because the borrower did not meet the exact terms of the contract. Even though the U.S. government has been late with a few payments, in every case it has paid in full. This is a technical default because the payment was late but the full amount required under the contract was paid.[2]

The debt of federally owned agencies is generally considered to be default free because their debt is backed by the full faith and credit of the U.S. government.[3] However, the debt of a federally sponsored agency is not default free because this debt is not explicitly

---

[2] Technical defaults usually occur because of debt ceiling restrictions during times of increasing government debt. The U.S. government has a maximum amount it can borrow (the debt ceiling), which is established by Congress. During times when the government is increasing its use of debt, it will sometimes reach the debt ceiling, which means it cannot borrow any more money. This creates a problem because during times of increasing debt usage, and since the government pays off maturing debt by issuing new debt, it cannot issue any new debt. When this occurs, Congress has always increased the debt ceiling to allow the issuance of new debt. However, the increase in the debt ceiling has not always occurred in time to prevent late payment on the maturing debt. With late payments, technical defaults occur. See, Zivney, T. L., and R. D. Marcus, 1989, The day The United States defaulted on treasury bills, *Financial Review, 24(3)*, 475–490.

[3] An exception would be debt issued by the Tennessee Valley Authority (TVA). The General Accounting Office stated in April 2001, *(t)he TVA Act states that the federal government does not guarantee TVA's bonds. In addition, TVA includes similar 'no guarantee' language in its ... bond offering circulars. However, because TVA is a wholly owned government corporation, there is the perception in the investment community ... that the federal government would support principal and interest payments on TVA debt if TVA solvency were to be seriously impaired.*

guaranteed by the U.S. government. The debt of a federal-sponsored agency is debt of a privately owned and publicly chartered organization that was created by Congress to support a specific purpose. These agencies are not specifically controlled by the U.S. government. However, investors have long viewed sponsored agency debt to have an implicit guarantee, and that view was strengthened in the mid-1980s when the U.S. government took action to bolster the troubled Farm Credit System. In reality, sponsored agency debt has default risk, but the probability of a default loss in these securities is very near zero.

12.3.2.2 Commercial Paper, Negotiable CDs, and Bankers' Acceptances Default Risk

Other than Treasury bills, federally owned agency debt, and federally sponsored agency debt, the remainder of the money market securities (commercial paper, negotiable CD, bankers' acceptance, repos, and fed funds) has default risk. Because these securities have default risk, money market investors make their temporary cash surpluses available to only the highest quality borrowers.

To assess the quality of commercial paper, negotiable CDs, and bankers' acceptances, a rating agency provides credit risk analyses of companies wanting to issue commercial paper and of banks wanting to issue tradable short-term debt (negotiable CDs and bankers' acceptances) (see, http://www.moodys.com/moodys/cust/ratingdefinitions/rdef.asp).[4] Money market investors provide short-term funds only to those companies and banks that receive high credit ratings, which means that these businesses have low credit (default) risk. Recent evidence has demonstrated the importance of default risk to money market investors. This recent evidence shows that 97% of all commercial paper issued is issued by companies in the two categories with the lowest default risk. This evidence emphasizes that money market investors assess default risk before making an investment and then, after assessment, only provide funds to high credit quality firms.

12.3.2.3 Fed Funds Default Risk

The fed funds market also operates through a credit analysis of the borrower. However, instead of a third party analysis by a rating agency, the investor (lender) does the analysis. Remember, the fed funds market is a market where depository institutions trade reserve balances on deposit at the Federal Reserve. The trade is called a fed funds transaction and the transaction is actually a loan of reserve deposits (funds).

A fed funds trade is a loan which usually has a maturity of one day. Most depository institutions trade every day in the fed funds market, and to facilitate the trading of these funds daily, lines of credit are established for borrowing institutions. To establish a line of credit, a borrower requests a line of credit from a lender. The lender responds with a thorough credit analysis of the borrower. Through this credit analysis, the lender determines the amount of credit that it is willing to make available to the borrower under the line of credit (this amount maybe be zero). Once the line of credit is established, the borrowing institution can request credit, in fed funds, up to the maximum amount available under its fed funds line of credit. Since most fed funds trades have a maturity of one day, the credit line limit is basically a daily trade size limit.

---

[4] In Appendix 12-A, we provide a brief description of how the Moody's rating agency discriminates between the credit risks of issuers of commercial paper.

Requiring fed funds trades to be drawn under lines of credit facilitates the trading process because the lender has prescreened the borrowers and has established the maximum amount that it is willing to lend a borrower. Therefore, when a request to borrow fed funds comes into a bank, the fed funds trading desk of the lending bank needs only to determine: (1) if the borrower making the request is approved and (2) if approved, whether the borrower has credit available in the amount of the request. This process allows fed funds lenders to know their borrowers and to therefore trade only with the borrowers they have prescreened and deemed to have sufficient credit quality.

This process may sound like a cumbersome process for a loan between two banks. However, the big banks often trade fed funds through brokers and often must borrow multiple times each day. The brokers do not have knowledge of the specific lending agreements (lines of credit) between various banks. Therefore, the line of credit for fed funds allows a lending bank to respond quickly to a brokered request for a fed funds loan. This process easily accommodates multiple loan requests during a day.

EXAMPLE *Banks' Aversion to Default Risk in the Fed Funds Market*

To illustrate further the extent that banks will go to minimize default risk in their fed funds loans, a brief story follows. This story, told by a retired banker, tells about the fed funds trading of First National Bank, a small Midwestern bank. Most small banks have excess reserves daily; and, therefore must lend fed funds daily to properly manage their reserve accounts. Because of their size, small banks do not have the manpower to trade fed funds actively. Instead, these smaller banks lend their daily excess reserves to their correspondent bank and receive from the correspondent the average fed funds rate in that day's market. These correspondent banks are large banks with which a small bank has a close working relationship. They provide services for the small bank which, because of the small bank's size, are not economical for the small bank to do for themselves. First National Bank has a correspondent relationship with a large bank in a nearby major city. The correspondent bank is very strong financially; therefore, one might expect that First National Bank would send all its daily excess reserve to this specific correspondent bank. This was not so. First National considered the concentration of all of their excess funds at one correspondent too risky. In other words, they considered sending all their excess reserves to one bank to be the equivalent of *putting all their eggs in one basket*. What did they do? Since the nearby major city had three large banks and all three individual banks were considered financially sound, First National Bank divided their daily excess reserve amount by three and loaned one-third of the daily excess reserve to each of the three banks. By spreading their reserves across three banks they used diversification to reduce their exposure to any potential default risk.

12.3.2.4 Repo Default Risk

A repo is an agreement to sell securities that is combined with a simultaneous agreement to buy them back (repurchase) at a future date. This combination agreement suggests that the original investor is holding someone else's securities while the seller has the investor's cash. In reality, the investor (lender) does not have the collateral (the securities). Instead, the collateral is held by a third party trustee. When the cash is repaid plus interest, the collateral is returned to the borrower. Thus, a repo is a secured loan. It is the only money market security in which the lender is secured with collateral.[5]

---

[5] However, even in the case of default the lender would not automatically be able to seize the collateral. Due process through the legal system would have to be observed.

The market convention in repos is to ensure that the investor has minimal exposure to default risk. The repo market has rules that define the process for providing the securities which are the collateral in a repo. First, the market value of the collateral must exceed the amount of the loan. This rule protects the lender against interest rate increases that would decrease the collateral value below the amount of the loan. Second, should the value of the collateral fall below the amount of the loan, the lender can request additional collateral. Thus, the total collateral will again more than cover the amount of the loan. As an alternative, the lender may request a cash payment that will reduce the loan amount below the value of the collateral. Third, the collateral is held by a third party trustee. The short-term nature of money market repos makes sending the collateral to the lender impractical. Also, placing the collateral with a trustee prevents borrowers from using the same collateral for more than one loan.

The process for a repo is designed to make the lender very secure in terms of the default risk of the loan. Since default is always a risk with any loan, as further protection against default the regular traders additionally recommend that repos only be done with borrowers that are known to be good credit risks.

12.4 INTEREST-RATE RISK

All debt securities are exposed to **interest-rate risk**. Since money market securities are short-term debt securities, they too are exposed to interest-rate risk.

Interest-rate risk is the risk that market interest rates will increase and cause a decrease in the market value of debt securities. If an investor must sell the security when the market rates have increased, the investor will earn less than expected. This can occur in all debt securities. This risk, however, is not a primary concern to money market investors because almost all money market investments are held to maturity. If a money market security is held to maturity, the return expected at the time of the purchase will be earned regardless of the changes in market interest that may have occurred during the holding period. Therefore, as stated previously, for most money market investments interest-rate risk is not a factor. In situations where money market investors must sell before maturity and, hence, are exposed to interest-rate risk, the yield on the money market security will typically still exceed the yield on bank deposits, which is the next best alternative for the money market investor.

However, if a money market investor is concerned about the possibility of an early sell and, hence, about interest-rate risk, this risk can be hedged with short-term interest-rate futures contracts. Futures contracts and hedging with futures contracts are discussed in several other places in this book. This chapter will only briefly mention the products available for hedging interest-rate risk in a money market security. In the United States, the majority of the short-term interest-rate futures contracts are traded on the Chicago Mercantile Exchange (Merc). The Merc has dollar-based money market futures contracts on fed funds, 90-day T-bills, and Eurodollar deposits. The Merc also has futures contracts on one-month **LIBOR** and Euro-yen deposits. These futures contracts allow money market investors to hedge directly interest-rate risk on fed funds and 13-week T-bills and to cross-hedge interest-rate risk on federal agency debt, commercial paper, bankers' acceptances, negotiable certificates of deposits, and repos.

INDUSTRY APPLICATION

FINANCING TREASURY POSITIONS: USING REPURCHASE AGREEMENTS AND EURODOLLAR FUTURES [6]

Back in Chapter 4, the **Industry Application** provided an example of how to finance a Treasury position using a repurchase agreement. This industry application uses basically the same example but with the addition of (1) price volatility and (2) a five-year strip of Eurodollar futures sold against the five-year Treasury note as a hedge. Once again, an example designed by Peter Barker of the Chicago Mercantile Exchange will be used to show how to buy a Treasury note and finance the position for one day and sell a strip of Eurodollar futures. Eurodollar futures work in the same way as T-bill futures.

In this example, the trade is executed in the morning of April 2 at the note price of 99-19+. However, during the day, the market rallies and by the afternoon the note is valued at 100-00. The trader who purchased the bond now has a security that is worth $1,000,543.03, which is the clean price of 100 plus accrued interest. The trader can now use the cash value of this position by entering into a repurchase agreement.

April 2 Buy a Treasury Note and Finance the Position for One Day

Instrument:	five-year T-note 6⅞ of 3/31/02
Trade date:	April 2, 1997
Settlement date:	April 3, 1997
Note price:	99-19+ (morning trade price)
Accrued interest (three days):	$543.03 (3/183 × 0.033125 × $1,000,000)
	[Note : $0.033125 = \dfrac{6\frac{7}{8}}{2}$.]
Full price:	$996,636.78
Settlement price:	100-00 (afternoon closing price)

What happens when the trader enters into the repo agreement? The trader borrows $1,000,543.03 for one day and agrees to repay this original amount plus one day's interest of $152.86 the next day for a total of $1,000,695.89. However, on the settlement day, the trader is obligated to send the original seller only $996,636.78 because that is the price at which the T-note was purchased. The trader's Treasury account at the close of business on April 2 will show a positive balance of:

Repo proceeds:	$1,000,543.03
T-note payment:	$ 996,636.78
Balance:	$ 3,906.25

Note, however, that the actual cash flow for both of these legs of the transaction takes place on Thursday, April 3.

What has happened here? The market rally has a positive effect on the trader's T-note position, but remember that the trader also sold a strip of Eurodollar futures. Because the interest rate has gone down (recall how T-bill futures are valued at 100-rate?; Eurodollar futures are valued in the same manner), there has been a negative effect on the Eurodollar position. Assume that the loss on the short Eurodollar position is $3,500. Just as with Treasury futures, the settlement variation payment must be made on April 3, the morning following the trade. So, what do the next day's cash flows look like?

April 3 (Thursday)

On April 3, the trader receives the five-year T-note and $996,636.78 is wired to the seller. The balance of $3,906.25 in the trader's Treasury account is used to cover the $3,500 settlement variation on the short Eurodollar position. So, the trader's net position on the morning of April 3 shows a profit of $406.25. Just as in the Chapter 4 *Industry Application*, let's assume that the trader now sells the T-note at the unchanged price of 100-00. Further, let's say that the trader also buys back the Eurodollar strip position and that these prices have

(continued)

INDUSTRY APPLICATION (*continued*)

FINANCING TREASURY POSITIONS: USING REPURCHASE AGREEMENTS AND EURODOLLAR FUTURES [6]

also not changed from the previous day's close. Here are the relevant facts:

Trade date:	April 3, 1997
Settlement date:	April 4, 1997
Note price:	100-00
Accrued interest	$724.04 (4/183 × 0.033125 ×
(three days):	$1,000,000)
Full price:	$1,000,724.04

What happens on April 4?

April 4 (Friday) Settlement Day

On settlement day, the trader receives $1,000,724.04 from the previous day's sale of the five-year T-note. The trader then repays the $1,000,695.89 to the overnight repo loan, and receives back the T-note. The Treasury is then sent out to the new buyer, so there is no outstanding Treasury position.

The net cash flow on the previous day, April 3, was $406.25 ($3,906.25 − $3,500.00), to which we need to add one day's interest (at 5.5%), and so on April 4 the balance is $406.31. We then add the difference between the amount received from the bond sale ($1,000,724.04) and the amount repaid on the overnight repo ($1,000,695.89) for an additional $28.15, resulting in a closing balance on April 4 of $434.46.

Balance in cash account:	$ 406.31
Cash received from bond sale:	$ 1,000,724.04
Cash paid to overnight repo:	−$1,000,695.89
Net profit position	$ 434.46

Notice how the interest-rate risk was hedged by using the strip of Eurodollar futures but the appreciation in the T-note was used to generate the cash necessary to pay the settlement variation in the short futures position. The timing of the T-note purchase, repo, and sale of the T-note leads to the profitable trading cash flow.

12.5 MONEY MARKET MUTUAL FUNDS

A mutual fund is a portfolio of securities. A **money market mutual fund** is a portfolio of money market securities. In general, mutual funds provide two primary benefits to investors: (1) low minimum investment increments and (2) low cost of diversification. However, the usual benefits of diversification are not as applicable to money market investments because any amount of default loss is generally unacceptable to money market investors.

Most money market securities trade in large denominations. These denominations are so large that only the wealthiest individual investors can directly purchase money market securities (the primary exception to this rule is Treasury bills).[7] Money market mutual funds allow the small investor to invest in money market securities by purchasing shares in a fund which in turn pools several small investments to acquire money market securities. In addition to providing access to the money market, a money market mutual fund provides a low cost

---

[6] This example is adapted from Peter Barker's *Financing Treasury Positions: Using Repurchase and Reverse Repurchase Agreements* which appears in *CME Interest Rate Products Advanced Topics*, available at www.cme.com.

[7] The Federal Reserve allows individuals to purchase Treasury bills in $1,000 increments.

JP Morgan Prime Money Market Fund	
Floating-rate notes	43.8%
Commercial paper	37.1%
Certificates of deposit	12.0%
Time deposits	4.2%
Repurchase agreements	1.9%
Corporate bonds	1.0%
Strong Heritage Money Fund	
Commercial paper	89.0%
Government agency issues	5.9%
Variable-rate put bonds	5.1%

FIGURE 12-2 Portfolio allocations.

way for small investors to invest in several different types of money market securities. This process creates a low cost method of diversification in the money markets. However, the normal idea of diversification, where good times in some securities offset bad times in other securities, is not as applicable to money markets. In the money markets, good times mean payments are received on time and bad times mean payments are missed. Because of the short-term nature of money market securities, a missed payment usually signifies a substantial decline in the financial condition of the borrower; hence, nonpayment. The nonpayment in one security cannot and will not be offset by higher payments in another security in a money market portfolio because the payoffs from money market securities are predefined. Even though the normal benefits of diversification do not apply here, the fact that the fund holds numerous securities provides some diversification benefits and limits the possibility of catastrophic loss in the fund.

The money market mutual fund industry views any default in a money market mutual fund as unacceptable because the alternative for their investors are bank deposits, and a move to bank deposits removes funds from the mutual fund industry. While bank deposits typically pay lower returns than money market mutual funds, bank deposits are insured up to $100,000 for each depositor by the Federal Deposit Insurance Corporation (FDIC). Not only is the depositor default free up to $100,000 in one bank, the depositor can make deposits in other banks and have no default risk up to $100,000 in each bank. The money market mutual fund industry knows that money market investors are unwilling to accept default risk; therefore, the industry is concerned that if investors perceive money market mutual funds as having default risk, investors will shift their money to bank deposits.

In an attempt to assure investors that their money is safe, the funds provide information about their portfolio allocations. Two money market funds from well-known fund families are presented here. The two funds are the JP Morgan Prime Money Market Fund and the Strong Heritage Money Fund. Their portfolio allocations are reported in Figure 12-2.

Figure 12-2 clearly shows that the two funds invest almost exclusively in traditional money market securities but that they have very different asset allocations. What is not clear from these allocations is the level of default risk. Does one fund have more default risk than the other? To help investors sort out money market mutual fund default risk, Moody's has begun rating money market mutual funds for default risk. Moody's rates the JP Morgan

Prime Money Market Fund at Aaa and it rates the Strong Heritage Money Fund at Aa. These ratings follow the Moody's bond ratings described in Chapter 3. Recall that an Aaa rating is Moody's top rating and suggests an extremely strong financial condition. An Aa rating is Moody's second highest rating and suggests a very strong financial condition. The ratings on these two money market mutual funds suggests that both have low default risk on the bond rating scale, but the Strong fund has noticeably more default risk on a relative basis than the JP Morgan fund.

Remembering that money market investors generally try to avoid default risk, the Moody's ratings for the two funds suggest that money market investors should take extra caution when considering this Strong money market fund. This caution leads to an interesting situation with Strong money market funds and Mercury Finance Company's commercial paper.

EXAMPLE *Strong Money Market Funds and the Problem with Mercury Finance Co. Commercial Paper*

Background on Strong Funds and Mercury Finance Co.

Strong Capital Management was a mutual fund family based in Milwaukee, Wisconsin. The company was founded in 1974 and had grown to the point where it was the 35th largest mutual fund family (out of 677 current families) in the country, based on assets under management of $47 billion. Strong had grown to such prominence because the company had been a consistent industry leader in generating returns. Strong was a broad-based family of mutual funds and its success had been across the board, instead of concentrated in just one area or sector. Its group of money market mutual funds had matched the company success by being a consistent industry leader in generating returns. In fact, Strong's Heritage Money Market Fund was the top yielding money market mutual fund in 1996.

Strong's semiannual reports from the fall of 1996 showed that the Heritage fund along with two other Strong money market funds (Strong Money Market Fund and Strong Institutional Money Market Fund) held about 5% of their assets in Mercury Finance Co. commercial paper. Mercury Finance Co. was a used-car lender that specialized in *below-prime* lending (below-prime refers to credit quality not at the prime lending rate). Below-prime lending is a nice way to say that they specialized in lending to high default risk used-car purchasers. Historically, this segment of the consumer lending market had been ignored, but in recent years a few specialized lenders had stepped into the void. Mercury Finance was one of those lenders, and in their 12 years in business (prior to 1997) had grown into an industry leader. In the years prior to 1997, Mercury Finance had reported strong balance sheets and earnings growth, which led to several stock market analysts recommending Mercury Finance as a stock to buy.

Investment Rules for Money Market Funds

The Code of Federal Regulations contains Securities and Exchange Commission regulations defining the portfolio composition allowable for money market mutual funds (Title 17, Chapter II, part 270.2a-7). The purpose of these regulations is to limit the risk the money market funds can take in forming their portfolios and thus protect investors from unwanted risk.

The regulations limit risk (or in the code's wording "define quality") in a number of ways. The description of quality begins with a general statement that a money market fund shall limit its investments to U.S. dollar-denominated securities that the fund's board deems to present minimal credit risk. The determination of minimal credit risk must be based on factors pertaining to credit quality as well as credit ratings by NRSROs (Nationally Recognized Statistical Rating Organization). Then the regulations take specific steps to limit risk.

First, for taxable funds (the three Strong funds mentioned were all taxable funds) the regulations limit the amount of investment by a money market fund in the securities of one issuer to 5% of the fund's total assets. This is to ensure adequate diversification. Then, a taxable money market fund is limited to having only 5% of its total assets in risky securities and is limited to having 1% of its total assets in the securities of a single issuer of risky securities. The regulations label risky securities as "second-tier securities".

The regulations define a "first-tier security" and then state that any security that is not a first-tier security is a second-tier security. A first-tier security is a security that receives a rating in the highest rating category for short-term debt obligations by at least two NRSROs. Therefore, any short-term debt without two ratings in the highest category is labeled as a second-tier security.

The NRSROs that we are most familiar with are Moody's and Standard and Poor's, although other rating organizations exist. At the end of 1996, Mercury Finance Co. had received a highest rating from two NRSROs, which allowed Mercury Finance Co.'s commercial paper to be considered a first-tier security. The rating agencies that rated Mercury Finance Co.'s commercial paper in their highest rating category were Thomson BankWatch and Duff & Phelps Credit Rating Co.

The Problem for Strong Money Market Funds

The Strong Heritage Money Market Fund was the industry's top earning money market fund in 1996 and this point was being made in early 1997 in an aggressive ad campaign from Strong. The problem with a top earning money market fund is the fact that it is clearly understood and well-documented that higher returns must be accompanied by higher risk in money markets. Logic would then suggest that Strong's money market funds must be consistently among the most risky in the industry, which brings us to Mercury Finance Co.'s commercial paper and Strong's investment in that paper.

In the fall of 1996, Strong reported that three of its money market funds held 5% of their assets in Mercury Finance Co.'s commercial paper. This was acceptable according to the federal regulations because Mercury was considered a first-tier security. Then, in early February 1997, a disaster occurred for Strong. Mercury Finance announced that it would default on $188 million of commercial paper and Strong still had substantial holdings of Mercury Finance commercial paper in three money market funds.

The default of Mercury Finance Co. on its commercial paper and the Strong funds reaction were reported as follows in the *Wall Street Journal* (WSJ). On 2/3/97, WSJ reported that Mercury Finance had failed to repay $17 million of commercial paper that came due on 1/31/97 and had another $100 million of commercial paper maturing within the week. The article also reported that the default came amidst allegations of substantial accounting irregularities. On 1/29/97, Mercury Finance had announced that its 1996 profits were overstated by more than 100%. In a follow-up article on 2/4/97, WSJ reported that accounting irregularities had lead to earnings overstatements for the last four years. The article also stated that the banks that had provided $500 million in backup lines of credit for Mercury Finance's commercial paper had withdrawn the lines of credit due to the accounting irregularities.

After reporting the problems of Mercury Finance Co., the WSJ provided a second article on 2/4/97 discussing the exposure of Strong's money market funds to the default on Mercury Finance Co.'s commercial paper. The article by Julie Creswell and Robert McGough entitled "Money-Market Funds Nearly 'Break the Buck'" appeared on page C1 as one of that day's lead articles in the investment section of the journal. The first nine paragraphs of the article are reproduced below.

Strong Capital Management moved to prevent three of its money-market funds from rattling investors by "breaking the buck" due to the Mercury Finance Co. scandal.

Strong, a Milwaukee mutual-fund-management firm, took the extreme measure of buying back from its funds some Mercury Finance borrowing known as commercial paper. Last week, Mercury, the scandal-tainted used-car lender, failed to meet a payment on the paper.

If Strong hadn't acted, the share price of the money funds would have fallen below the $1 net asset value that money funds strive to sustain, says Peter Crane, managing editor of IBC's Money Fund Report. A money fund's net asset value falling below $1 is known as breaking the buck. It is an almost-unheard-of occurrence, and mutual-fund companies worry that allowing such a thing to happen would frighten investors and cause many to pull their money out of money funds and go back to insured bank deposits.

Strong confirmed that it bought Mercury Finance's commercial paper from the funds, including the $2 billion Strong Heritage Money Market Fund. "We had adequate resources to do right by the shareholders and no one was hurt," a spokeswoman said.

Some money-market funds managed by other fund groups may have some small exposure to Mercury Finance. But the securities are probably not widely held because the two big credit-rating agencies, Moody's Investors Service Inc. and Standard & Poor's Rating Group, had given its debt low credit ratings. Vanguard Group, Dreyfus Corp. and Fidelity Investments, three large managers of money funds, said their funds have avoided Mercury Finance paper.

Analysts and traders said they suspected Strong had the biggest exposure to Mercury among sizable fund firms.

Strong Heritage Money Market was heavily advertised to individual investors, and it has been the top-yielding fund for the past year among taxable money-market funds. Some critics, such as IBC's Mr. Crane, say that Strong was gunning for yield.

The Mercury Finance paper "was an aggressive security bought by someone chasing yield," Mr. Crane said. Money funds that can claim top yields attract billions of dollars in assets, Mr. Crane said, while "being No. 2 means nothing."

Strong denied its funds are too aggressive and said their yields were due to low expenses. It also said it was a victim of misleading financial reports. "Mercury was a leader in their industry," a spokeswoman said.

One very clear point is made in this article. Regardless of why Strong got into the position of holding Mercury Finance commercial paper, Strong took quick and decisive action to make certain that its money market investors did not have any default losses.[8] This is a real-world example that demonstrates that money market investors are unwilling to accept default risk.

12.5.1 Moral of the Story with Strong Fund Example

Two important axioms in finance are reenforced by the Strong Fund example. They are *there is no such thing as a free lunch* and *let the buyer beware.*

 There is no such thing as a free lunch means that everything valuable comes at a cost. In this example, the valuable item is the higher returns and the investors must ask themselves what is the cost? In other words, how does the fund generate the higher return? Strong has suggested their firm provides a higher return by having lower expenses. This approach suggests that Strong intends to generate its profit with higher volume. At first

---

[8] We note that if the $2 billion Strong Heritage Money Market Fund had continued to hold 5% of its assets in Mercury Finance Co. commercial paper, then the fund would have $100 million of Mercury Finance commercial paper.

glance, there appears to be no downside for the investor. However, if as Mr. Crane suggests, being number two means nothing, then Strong must continue to be number one to generate sufficient volume for its low cost strategy. There is a limit to cost cutting, and other firms also claim to be low cost providers. Thus, to maintain its lead Strong had to consistently out-earn the other low cost providers. This means that, on average, it acquired securities that earn more than the securities acquired by the other low cost providers. In the money market, this tactic means taking more default risk. Therefore, even if Strong is a low cost provider, its strategy appears to dictate that it must take more risk than other money market funds. This additional risk is the cost to the investor for the higher returns and eliminates what appears to be a *free lunch*.

The axiom *let the buyer beware* means that the buyers have the responsibility to understand what they are buying. In the case of Strong's money market funds, the fund was in compliance with the regulations that are designed to limit risk taking in money market funds. The investor has to understand that Strong's goal of being the earnings leader dictates that it takes more risk than the other money market funds. To help money market fund investors understand the default risk that money funds are taking, Moody's Investor Services now provides credit risk rating for money market funds. Currently, Moody's rates 157 money market funds, and all but six of the rated money market funds receive a credit rating of Aaa (Moody's highest rating). One of the six funds receiving a credit rating below Aaa was the Strong Heritage Money Fund. It had a credit rating of Aa. Recall that a rating of Aaa means an extremely strong financial condition and a rating of Aa means a very strong financial condition. Therefore, Moody's was not saying that Strong was taking a huge amount of risk, only that it was taking more risk than almost all of its competitors in money market mutual funds. This difference should have been very important to Strong in a market where just about any amount of default risk is unacceptable to investors, but it is up to the investor to understand the implications of the rating. Accordingly, the *buyer must beware*.

12.5.2 Epilogue on Strong Fund[9]

On September 3, 2003, the attorney general of the state of New York announced an investigation into alleged timed trading by Strong Fund founder Richard S. Strong. On October 29, 2003, the attorney general issued an announcement that claimed that Strong had generated some $600,000 in profits for family and friends by personally timing trades. Although not technically illegal, timed trading increases fund costs and compromises fund value for long-term investors. However, timed trading does violate Richard Strong's fiduciary responsibility as a fund manager. The announcement of the investigation triggered $235 million of withdrawals from Strong mutual funds during September and October of 2003. On November 2, 2003, the independent directors of the Strong Mutual Fund announced the resignation of Richard S. Strong as chairman of the funds' board. Wells Fargo & Company became one of the top 20 US mutual funds with the acquisition of $29 billion in assets from strong Financial Corporation in January 2005.

---

[9] The source for the epilogue is an article in the *The Business Journal Serving Greater Milwaukee* dated 11/11/2003 and press releases available on the Strong Funds website.

IN THE NEWS

Breaking the buck in money market mutual funds is in the news once again with the downturn in the economy. An April 9, 2001, *BusinessWeek* article titled "Money Market Funds Enter the Danger Zone," by Lewis Braham, discusses concerns with money market mutual funds and the possibility that some will *break the buck*.

As the article mentions, the idea behind money market mutual funds is simple. An investor puts in a $1; an investor gets back a $1. Along the way the investor earns some interest. This industry has operated this way since its inception in 1969 (with one exception where the value of a share in one money market mutual fund fell to $0.94). The aura of safety surrounding money market mutual funds has allowed the industry to grow to the point where, today, the industry manages over $2 trillion in investor funds.

However, recent decreases in the size of the Treasury auctions and increases in competition (currently there are 1,500 money market mutual funds) have lead some funds into assets that were traditionally not held by money market funds, such as asset-backed credits and unrated commercial paper. On the plus side, these nontraditional securities usually yield more than the traditional securities held by money market mutual funds. On the negative side, these nontraditional securities have higher risk, which means that in economic downturns these securities will tend to have more defaults. The article advises investors who are seeking safe investments to avoid money market mutual funds claiming high yields and, instead, invest in funds that buy securities that are clearly low in default risk.

SUMMARY OF VALUATION AND RISK MANAGEMENT SKILLS

1. Understand the economic role of the money markets and how this role drives risk management in the money markets.

The economic role of the money markets is to trade liquidity. The temporary nature of the investment requires that risk management take place before the investment instead of during the time of ownership. The temporary nature of the investment also places the focus of risk management on liquidity risk and default risk.

2. Understand liquidity risk and how money market securities are structured to manage liquidity risk.

The first risk that money market investors are concerned with is liquidity. Liquidity risk is concern over the ability to convert an asset to cash quickly without a price concession. Liquidity is handled by using only short-term debt and then by providing market mechanisms that ensure that investors can sell their money market securities if needed. Dealers standing ready to trade provide liquidity in the secondary markets for money market securities. Fed funds and repos do not have secondary markets, so the vast majority of these securities have one-day maturities.

3. Understand default risk and how default risk is managed in the money markets.

Default risk is the risk that a borrower will violate some part of the debt contract. The short-term nature of money market securities means the primary default risk is failure to make the single scheduled payment at the end of the contract. The single payment includes both interest and principal, so a failure to make the single payment is a major concern for money market investors (lenders). Accordingly, money market investors only lend to the highest quality borrowers.

4. Understand the basic benefits of mutual funds and how these benefits do and do not apply in money market mutual funds.

Mutual funds have two primary benefits: (1) low minimum investment increments and (2) low cost of diversification. Low minimum investment allows small investors to participant in the money markets where individual securities typically trade in $1 million increments. Diversification, as it is commonly described for a portfolio, does not apply in the money markets because a bad period in one money market security cannot be offset by a good period in another money market security.

QUESTIONS

1. What is the economic role of the money markets?

2. Money market investors have temporary cash surpluses to invest, whereas capital market investors have long-term cash surpluses (free cash flow) to invest. How does the difference between temporary and long-term surpluses affect the risk tolerance of money market investors?

3. What two risks are of primary concern to money market investors?

4. How is liquidity risk handled in the structure of the money markets?

5. Since money market investors choose the maturities of their investments to match the expected length of time of their temporary surplus in cash, why is secondary market marketability important to money market investors?

6. Since there is not a secondary market in fed funds, how is liquidity risk addressed?

7. Since money market investors are willing to accept very little default risk, what kind of borrowers do they demand?

8. What is the difference between the default risk of federally owned agency debt and federally sponsored agency debt?

9. How do investors determine the default risk of a borrower in the commercial paper market?

10. How is default risk handled in the fed funds market?

11. Why is interest-rate risk not a major concern in the money markets?

12. What are the benefits of money market mutual funds for small investors?

13. What is the limitation/difficulty with diversification on money market portfolios?

14. How can investors determine the default risk of a money market mutual fund?

15. What is the problem for a money market investor with a high yield money market mutual fund?

REFERENCES

ALLEN, L., and A. SAUNDERS, The large-small bank dichotomy in the federal funds market, *Journal of Banking and Finance, 10,* 219–230.
The authors find that small banks often pay higher rates for federal funds than large banks. The authors suggests that the rate difference for small banks results from more asymmetric information between the lender and small bank borrowers than between the lender and large bank borrowers.

BAXTER, N., 1968, Marketability, default risk, and yields on money market instruments, *Journal of Financial and Quantitative Analysis, 3,* 75–85.
The author examines survey results showing that money markets investors demand compensation for both default risk and marketability. The author concludes that investors demand a slightly larger premium for marketability than for default risk.

ELLIS, D., and M. FLANNERY, 1992, Does the debt market assess large bank's risk? Time series evidence from money center CDs, *Journal of Monetary Economics*, *30*, 481–502.

The authors examine the effect of the idea that some banks are *too big to fail*. They find evidence of significant default-risk premiums in money center bank CD rates, which suggest that investors believe there is default risk in large bank debt.

General Accounting Office, April 2001, Report to Congressional Requesters, Tennessee Valley Authority: Bond Ratings Based on Ties to the Federal Government and Other Nonfinancial Factors, United States General Accounting Office, Washington, D.C.

The report discusses the role of the federal government in supporting principal and interest payments in the event of a serious impairment of wholly owned government corporations' solvency.

HABERMAN, G., and C. PICHE, 1985, Controlling credit risk associated with repos: Know your counterparty, *Federal Reserve Bank of Atlanta Economic Review*, *70*, 28–34.

The authors discuss that credit risk exists in repos backed by government securities and that the way to limit credit risk is to know your counterparties.

KAMATH, R., S. KHAKSARI, H. MEIER, and J. WINKLEPECK, 1985,

Management of excess cash: Practices and developments, *Financial Management Journal*, *14*, 70–75.

The authors analyze the results from three surveys about cash management practices. The authors have two important conclusions. First, the most important investment criteria for investing in the money market is the preservation of capital. Second, most firms use cash budgeting techniques to forecast cash needs and these firms seldom liquidate their money market investments before maturity, suggesting that cash budgeting is an effective forecasting technique.

OGDEN, J., 1987, The end of the month as a preferred habitat: A test of operational efficiency in the money market, *Journal of Financial and Quantitative Analysis 22*, 329–344.

The author suggests that corporate cash flows create month-end preferred habitats for money market investments.

STIGUM, M., 1990, *The Money Market*, 3 Ed., Dow Jones Irwin, New York.

Stigum is the authoritative reference on the money markets. This book provides institutional detail about all the money markets and includes discussions about the risks in each market and how these risks are handled.

KEY TERMS

Covenant   Covenants are a part of a debt contract that specifies the obligations for the borrower to meet during the life of the loan. Covenants typically cover borrower financial conditions, dividend restrictions, and restrictions on asset sales.

Default Risk   Default risk is the risk associated with a borrower not fulfilling all the obligations of the loan contract.

Interest-rate Risk   Interest-rate risk is the risk of loss of value on an interest-bearing security from change in market interest rates.

LIBOR   LIBOR stands for the London Interbank Offer Rate. This is the rate at which the large London banks loan deposits to other banks. This is similar to a fed funds loan in the United States.

Liquidity Risk   Liquidity risk is the risk associated with having to convert an asset to cash.

Money Market Mutual Funds   Mutual fund portfolio comprising money market securities.

MOODY'S RATING CATEGORIES AND DEFINITION FOR SHORT-TERM DEBT AVAILABLE AT http://www.moodys.com/moodys/cust/

Moody's short-term ratings are opinions of the ability of issuers to honor senior financial obligations and contracts. Such obligations generally have an original maturity not exceeding one year, unless explicitly noted. Moody's employs the following designations, all judged to be investment grade, to indicate the relative repayment ability of rated issuers:

Prime-1   Issuers rated Prime-1 (or supporting institutions) have a superior ability for repayment of senior short-term debt obligations. Prime-1 repayment ability will often be evidenced by many of the following characteristics:

- Leading market positions in well-established industries.

- High rates of return on funds employed.

- Conservative capitalization structure with moderate reliance on debt and ample asset protection.

- Broad margins in earnings coverage of fixed financial charges and high internal cash generation.

- Well-established access to a range of financial markets and assured sources of alternate liquidity.

Prime-2   Issuers (or supporting institutions) rated Prime-2 have a strong ability to repay senior short-term debt obligations. This will normally be evidenced by many of the characteristics cited previously, but to a lesser degree. Earnings trends and coverage ratios, while sound, may be more subject to variation than is the case for Prime-1 securities. Capitalization characteristics, while still appropriate, may be more affected by external conditions. Ample alternate liquidity is maintained.

Prime-3   Issuers (or supporting institutions) rated Prime-3 have an acceptable ability for repayment of senior short-term obligations. The effect of industry characteristics and market compositions may be more pronounced.

Variability in earnings and profitability may result in changes in the level of debt-protection measurements and may require relatively high financial leverage. Adequate alternate liquidity is maintained.

Not Prime Issuers rated Not Prime do not fall within any of the prime rating categories. In addition, in certain countries the prime rating may be modified by the issuer's or guarantor's senior unsecured long-term debt rating.

CHAPTER 13

BOND RISK MANAGEMENT

13.1 INTRODUCTION

Bond investors are exposed to two primary risks: interest-rate risk and default risk. The purpose of this chapter is the measurement and management of interest-rate risk in bond portfolios. We do not directly address managing default risk in a bond portfolio. However, we discuss managing default risk in a mortgage portfolio in Chapter 14 and in a loan portfolio in Chapter 19, and both of these discussions of default risk management are directly applicable to bond portfolios.

All interest-bearing (fixed-income) securities are exposed to interest-rate risk because interest rates are a primary component in the pricing of these securities. Therefore, most fixed-income investors are concerned about the measurement and management of interest-rate risk, and we discuss the measurement and management of interest-rate risk in this chapter in the context of a bond portfolio. The measurement and management of interest-rate risk is of key concern for financial institution managers because the vast majority of financial institutions hold portfolios of fixed-income securities.

This chapter begins with a discussion of bond portfolio yield to maturity and duration. In this discussion the concept of modified duration is introduced and used to immunize a bond portfolio against interest-rate risk. The remainder of this chapter is on swaps. Swaps are a derivative security, but we delayed the introduction of swaps until this chapter because swaps were created to manage interest-rate risk. The focus of the swaps discussion is on the setup and the pricing of plain vanilla swaps. The swaps discussion ends with an overview of other types of swaps.

DEVELOPING VALUATION AND RISK MANAGEMENT SKILLS

1. Calculate modified duration and understand its use in immunizing a bond portfolio against interest-rate risk.
2. Understand the benefits of and the setup for a plain vanilla swap.
3. Calculate the effective interest rate for both parties in a plain vanilla swap.
4. Value both sides of a plain vanilla swap.

13.2 BOND PORTFOLIO YIELD TO MATURITY AND DURATION

As discussed earlier, the yield to maturity for a bond is the internal rate of return that equates the bond price to the discounted value of the instrument's cash flows. The idea is basically the same for bond portfolios, although the calculation is a little more complicated.

This section of the chapter works through a detailed example of a bond portfolio's yield to maturity and duration and discusses why this process is so important.

EXAMPLE   *Bond Portfolio Yield to Maturity and Duration*

Consider a bond portfolio comprising four bonds. For the following example, the bond portfolio consists of the following bonds:

1. U.S. Treasury zero-coupon bond maturing in eight years and currently yielding 7%.

2. BB-rated corporate bond with a 9% coupon paid semiannually currently yielding 11%. This bond matures in 10 years.

3. AA-rated corporate bond with a 9% coupon paid semiannually currently yielding 8%. This bond matures in 7.5 years.

4. AAA-rated corporate bond with a 7.5% coupon paid semiannually maturing in 10.5 years and trading at par.

Portfolio Cash Flows

In the following table, the cash flows associated with this portfolio have been detailed. These cash flows will be used to calculate the yield to maturity of the portfolio. Compare the portfolio's cash flows to those of the individual bonds. Notice how once the bonds are put into a portfolio, the portfolio's cash flows may no longer be in the form of a constant annuity plus a large final payment.

Bond Portfolio Cash Flows

Time	Treasury	BB	AA	AAA	Portfolio
Pr @t = 0	−$576.71	−$880.50	−$1,055.59	−$1,000.00	−$3,512.80
0.5	0	45	45	37.5	127.50
1.0	0	45	45	37.5	127.50
1.5	0	45	45	37.5	127.50
2.0	0	45	45	37.5	127.50
2.5	0	45	45	37.5	127.50
3.0	0	45	45	37.5	127.50
3.5	0	45	45	37.5	127.50
4.0	0	45	45	37.5	127.50
4.5	0	45	45	37.5	127.50
5.0	0	45	45	37.5	127.50
5.5	0	45	45	37.5	127.50
6.0	0	45	45	37.5	127.50
6.5	0	45	45	37.5	127.50
7.0	0	45	45	37.5	127.50
7.5	0	45	1,045	37.5	1,127.50
8.0	1,000	45		37.5	1,082.50
8.5		45		37.5	82.50
9.0		45		37.5	82.50
9.5		45		37.5	82.50
10.0		1,045		37.5	1,082.50
10.5				1,037.5	1,037.50
			Yield to Maturity (IRR) =		0.0423

Portfolio Yield to Maturity

The periodic yield to maturity (IRR) of the bond portfolio cash flows is 4.23%. The annualized yield to maturity for the bond portfolio is $4.23 \times 2 = 8.46\%$, while the individual yields to maturity for the bonds are 7, 11, 8, and 7.5%, respectively. Thus, the yield to maturity for the bond portfolio is not equal to the average of the yields to maturity of the component bonds. Weighting the individual yields to calculate a weighted average also does not provide the correct yield for the portfolio (weighted average = 9.91%). This example introduces a very important point when working with a group (portfolio) of fixed-income securities. The point is *it is the portfolio's cash flows that are important, not the individual bonds' cash flows or yields.*

Portfolio Duration

Having to work with the portfolio cash flows makes the management of a bond portfolio more complicated than it appears at first. However, there is one measure that is a very important tool for managing a fixed-income portfolio that remains a weighted average, and that measure is duration. The following is a spreadsheet for calculating Macaulay duration[1] for the BB-rated bond in the example. Then the duration of the portfolio is calculated and used to estimate the portfolio's exposure to a change in interest rates.

Duration of BB-Rated Bond

Time Pr @ t = 0	BB-rated bond −880.5	PV of cash flow @11%/2	Divide by price	Multiply by t
1	45	42.65	−0.04844	−0.04844
2	45	40.43	−0.04592	−0.09183
3	45	38.32	−0.04352	−0.13057
4	45	36.32	−0.4125	−0.16502
5	45	34.43	−0.0391	−0.19552
6	45	32.64	−0.03707	−0.22239
7	45	30.93	−0.03513	−0.24593
8	45	29.32	−0.0333	−0.26641
9	45	27.79	−0.03157	−0.28409
10	45	26.34	−0.02992	−0.2992
11	45	24.97	−0.02836	−0.31196
12	45	23.67	−0.02688	−0.32258
13	45	22.44	−0.02548	−0.33124
14	45	21.27	−0.02415	−0.33812
15	45	20.16	−0.02289	−0.34339
16	45	19.11	−0.0217	−0.34719
17	45	18.11	−0.02057	−0.34966
18	45	17.17	−0.0195	−0.35092
19	45	16.27	−0.01848	−0.35111
20	1,045	358.15	−0.40676	−8.13519

Sum = duration in periods −13.1308

The duration of the BB-rated bond is 13.1308 (remember that the duration number is really negative although we give it a positive interpretation). To convert to years, the duration of a semiannual coupon

[1]Macaulay duration is discussed in depth in Chapter 5.

bond is divided by two: $13.1308 \div 2 = 6.57$ years.[2] For reference, the duration of the other three bonds is 16 for the Treasury bond duration, 11.34 for the AA-rate bond duration, and 14.9 for the AAA-rated bond duration. Now that a spreadsheet has been developed to calculate duration, that spreadsheet can be applied to the cash flows from the bond portfolio to calculate the duration of the bond portfolio.

Bond Portfolio Duration

Time Pr @t = 0	Portfolio cash flows −$3,512.80	PV of cash flows @ 8.46%/2	Divide by price	Multiply by t
1	$127.50	122.3256	−0.0348	−0.0348
2	$127.50	117.3612	−0.0334	−0.0668
3	$127.50	112.5983	−0.0321	−0.0962
4	$127.50	108.0287	−0.0308	−0.1230
5	$127.50	103.6446	−0.0295	−0.1475
6	$127.50	99.4383	−0.0283	−0.1698
7	$127.50	95.4028	−0.0272	−0.1901
8	$127.50	91.5310	−0.0261	−0.2085
9	$127.50	87.8164	−0.0250	−0.2250
10	$127.50	84.2525	−0.0240	−0.2398
11	$127.50	80.8333	−0.0230	−0.2531
12	$127.50	77.5528	−0.0221	−0.2649
13	$127.50	74.4054	−0.0212	−0.2754
14	$127.50	71.3858	−0.0203	−0.2845
15	$1,127.50	605.6552	−0.1724	−2.5862
16	$1,082.50	557.8843	−0.1588	−2.5410
17	$82.50	40.7922	−0.0116	−0.1974
18	$82.50	39.1367	−0.0111	−0.2005
19	$82.50	37.5484	−0.0107	−0.2031
20	$1,082.50	472.6864	−0.1346	−2.6912
21	$1,037.50	434.6509	−0.1237	−2.5984
	duration in periods			−13.5974

The duration of the portfolio is found to be $13.5974 \div 2 = 6.80$ years. If the portfolio duration had been calculated as a weighted average, the calculation would be as follows:

$$\frac{\$576.71}{\$3,512.8} \times 16 + \frac{\$880.50}{\$3,512.8} \times 13.13 + \frac{\$1,055.59}{\$3,512.8} \times 11.34 + \frac{\$1,000}{\$3,512.8} \times 14.9$$

$$= 0.164 \times 16 + 0.251 \times 13.13 + 0.30 \times 11.34 + 0.285 \times 14.9$$

$$= 2.624 + 3.296 + 3.402 + 4.247$$

$$= 13.569.$$

Dividing by 2 to adjust to years, the answer becomes 6.78 years. The difference between the two calculations is due to rounding. This example demonstrates that the duration of a fixed-income portfolio can be calculated either directly from the cash flows of the portfolio or indirectly from a weighted average of the individual bond durations.

[2]Remember, that the duration of a coupon bond is less than its time to maturity. This knowledge is a useful reality check when calculating the duration of a bond. In this example the BB-rated bond has 10 years until maturity; therefore, the annual duration must be less than 10.

Why is **duration** important? **Macaulay duration**, in general, and **modified duration** in particular, give us a measure for the interest rate sensitivity of the portfolio. However, more important for managing risk is the ability to reprice an asset (or portfolio) quickly and accurately, without having to recalculate all of the tedious mathematics. Duration provides a method for quickly estimating the amount of a bond portfolio that is *at risk* for a given change in market interest rates.

In the process of using duration to estimate the amount of the bond portfolio that is at risk, it is important to remember the fact that the yield to maturity for the bond portfolio is not a weighted average. The reason this is important is because if a weighted average yield is used instead of the correct yield, the value of the portfolio will be mispriced. If the value of the portfolio is mispriced, the portfolio's duration will be incorrect and the measure of the risk that has to be managed will be incorrect.

Modified duration will be used to calculate *the amount of a bond portfolio that is at risk for a given change in market interest rates* (change in value). Modified duration is

$$\text{Modified duration} = \text{Macaulay duration}/(1 + r/n), \tag{13-1}$$

where

$r = $ the annual yield to maturity and,

$n = $ the number of compound periods in the year.

The modified duration for the bond portfolio is $13.5974/(1.0423) = 13.0456$ periods or 6.5 years. A useful working definition of modified duration is as follows: *the approximate percentage change in price for a 100 basis point change in yield*. Hence, if the effect of a 20 basis point change in the yield would have on the portfolio is needed to be determined, modified duration would be used in the formula presented in Chapter 5. The formula is

$$\Delta\text{Bond portfolio price} \approx -\text{bond portfolio price} \times \text{modified duration} \times \Delta\text{yield} \tag{13-2}$$

In the bond portfolio example above, $\Delta Bond\ portfolio\ price = -\$3{,}512.80 \times 6.5 \times 0.0020 = -\$45.67$. That is, the value of the bond portfolio is estimated to fall to $\$3{,}467.13$ ($\$3{,}512.80 - \$45.67$) in response to a 20 basis point increase in interest rates.

13.3 PORTFOLIO DURATION STRATEGIES

Another look needs to be taken at the bonds in the previous portfolio example. In particular, the BB-rated bond and the AA-rated bond will be examined, and the question asked is *what happens to the value of these bonds if the yield curve increases or decreases?* In this examination, the percentage change in value instead of the dollar change in value will be determined. Getting the percentage change instead of dollar change requires only minor modification to Equation (13-2). Specifically, both sides of Equation (13-2) are divided by B. Thus, the percentage change in the value of a bond is

$$\frac{\Delta B}{B} \approx -\text{modified duration} \times \Delta r. \tag{13-3}$$

Now, what happens to the value of the bonds on a percentage basis if yields rise by 100 basis points? For simplicity, a parallel shift in the yield curve is assumed. This means that all rates across the yield curve go up or down by the same amount. Now, the price change using Equation (13-3) can be estimated. Knowing that the duration of the first bond is 6.6 years (13.13 ÷ 2) and that the duration of the second bond is 5.7 years (11.34 ÷ 2), for the BB-rated bond the percentage price change is

$$\text{Modified duration} = 6.6/(1 + (0.11/2)) = 6.26 \text{ and}$$

$$\frac{\Delta B}{B} \approx -6.26 \times 0.01 = -0.0626 \text{ or} -6.26\%$$

and the AA-rated bond percentage price change is

$$\text{Modified duration} = 5.7/(1 + (0.08/2)) = 5.48 \text{ and}$$

$$\frac{\Delta B}{B} \approx -5.48 \times 0.01 = -0.0548 \text{ or} -5.48\%.$$

Notice that the percentage price change is larger for the bond with the longer duration. Since rates are increasing, this would be a decrease in the bond price. *Hence, one strategy that a bond portfolio manager could use to protect the value of a bond portfolio is to move into shorter duration bonds when interest rates are anticipated to increase.*

Suppose you are the manager for the bond portfolio of a pension fund and the policies of the fund allow you to use active strategies in managing the portfolio. It appears that the economic cycle is beginning to improve; inflation is expected to decline; and, in an effort to encourage economic expansion, central bank policy is moving away from monetary restraint. As the portfolio manager responsible for managing the risk that changing interest rates represent, what should your strategy be?

Your first responsibility would be to analyze the economic environment and attempt to determine the future direction of interest rates. In this case, interest rates appear to be likely to decline. As the yields decline, the change in prices will be greater for the longer duration bonds. *Hence, a wise portfolio manager will want to move into longer duration instruments to capture some of the anticipated price gain.* How can this be done? One way would be to sell the shorter duration instruments and purchase the longer duration assets. However, this strategy is likely to be very expensive due to the existence of bid-ask spreads and any commissions that would have to be paid. A lower cost alternative would be to enter into a *swap*. The discussion of swaps begins in Section 13.4.

The key to understanding *active bond strategies* is to understand the concept that the return from fixed income investment comes from only three sources: coupon income, capital gain (or loss), and reinvestment income. Therefore, in addition to changes in bond prices due to a change in the level of interest rates, the following factors will also affect a bond portfolio's rate of return: changes in the shape of the yield curve, changes in yield spreads among bond sectors, changes in option-adjusted spreads (we will talk about these later), and changes in the risk premium for a particular bond. All of these factors can affect the portfolio manager's decision to be in longer or shorter duration instruments.

The primary use of duration is to assist in hedging against **interest-rate risk**. Generally, if a company, pension fund, insurance company, or bank is holding assets to meet anticipated liabilities then, provided the duration of liabilities and assets is the same, the company should be able to meet those liabilities under almost any interest rate condition. That is, if the duration of the assets and the liabilities is the same, the portfolio is said to have been **immunized** against interest-rate risk. Although an increase in interest rates will cause the present value of the assets to decline, this drop in the value of the assets will be matched by a decline in the present value of the liabilities. Because the duration of the assets and liabilities is the same, the absolute change in the present values will also be the same. The following example shows how this works.

EXAMPLE *Hedging Interest-Rate Risk Using Duration*

Suppose an insurance company that offered pension plans needs $7,346,640 in five years' time. Suppose also that the current yield to maturity is 8%, and a six-year 8% (annual) coupon bond with PV = $5,000,000 and a duration of five years is being considered. Assume rates stay at 8%. What happens over the next five years?

Payment	Time left	Value of CF	Amount ($)
1	4	$400,000 \times 1.08^4$	544,196
2	3	$400,000 \times 1.08^3$	503,885
3	2	$400,000 \times 1.08^2$	466,560
4	1	$400,000 \times 1.08^1$	432,000
5	0	$400,000 \times 1.08^0$	400,000
Sale of bond	0	5,400,000/1.08	5,000,000
Total			$7,346,640

Assume a new scenario. Instead of staying at 8%, the yield curve experiences a parallel shift of 50 basis points downward to 7.5%. What happens now?

Payment	Time left	Value of CF	Amount ($)
1	4	$400,000 \times 1.075^4$	534,188
2	3	$400,000 \times 1.075^3$	496,919
3	2	$400,000 \times 1.075^2$	462,250
4	1	$400,000 \times 1.075^1$	430,000
5	0	$400,000 \times 1.075^0$	400,000
Sale of bond	0	5,400,000/1.075	5,023,256
Total			$7,346,612

The difference between the actual amount available and the amount needed is $28—not bad! Now, make a new assumption that instead of staying at 8%, the yield curve experiences a parallel shift of 50 basis points upward to 8.5%. What happens now?

Payment	Time left	Value of CF	Amount ($)
1	4	$400,000 \times 1.085^4$	554,343
2	3	$400,000 \times 1.085^3$	510,916
3	2	$400,000 \times 1.085^2$	470,890
4	1	$400,000 \times 1.085^1$	434,000
5	0	$400,000 \times 1.085^0$	400,000
Sale of bond	0	$5,400,000/1.085$	4,976,959
Total			**$7,347,108**

The difference between the actual amount available and the amount needed is $467—still pretty good! Notice that the combination of the reinvested coupon income and the sale of the bond at the end of year five, whether it be at a premium or a discount, resulted in having almost exactly the correct amount of funds available when they are needed. *These results occurred because the manager matched the duration of the assets used to fund the cash requirement to the duration of that liability.* Also note that the matching was not exact. It was not exact because duration is only a good approximation of risk when interest rate changes are small.

In the previous example, a pension fund with a target obligation at the end of the defined time horizon invested in a bond with a duration that matched the time horizon. This investment decision virtually eliminated interest-rate risk. Notice, however, that this example was motivated with the statement that when duration of the assets and the liabilities is the same, the portfolio is said to have been *immunized*. The point here is that managers work with portfolios of bonds; and, since the process and mathematics for using duration to manage interest-rate risk is the same for a single bond and a portfolio of bonds, a single bond was used in the example to simplify the calculation.

Now, the four-bond portfolio from the example at the beginning of this chapter needs to be revisited to show how duration works for a portfolio of bonds. In the beginning of this section, the modified duration and percentage change in the value of the BB-rated bond and the AA-rated bond were calculated. Recall, that the percentage change in the BB-rated bond for a 100 basis point increase in interest rates was 6.26% and the percentage change in the AA-rated bond was 5.48%. The same calculations need to be done for the other two bonds. The calculations for the Treasury bond are

$$\text{Modified duration} = 8/(1 + (0.07/2)) = 7.73 \text{ and}$$

$$\frac{\Delta B}{B} \approx -7.73 \times 0.01 = -0.0773 \text{ or } -7.73\%.$$

The calculations for the AAA-rated bond are

$$\text{Modified duration} = 7.45/(1 + (0.075/2)) = 7.18 \text{ and}$$

$$\frac{\Delta B}{B} \approx -7.18 \times 0.01 = -0.0718 \text{ or } -7.18\%.$$

Using the portfolio value weights for each bond and the calculated percentage changes, the percentage change in the value of the portfolio from a 100 basis point increase in interest rates is

$$\frac{\$576.71}{\$3,512.8} \times -0.0773 + \frac{\$880.50}{\$3,512.8} \times -0.0626 + \frac{\$1,055.59}{\$3,512.8} \times -0.0548 + \frac{\$1,000}{\$3,512.8}$$
$$\times -0.0718 = -0.0653 \text{ or } -6.53\%.$$

Now, the percentage change in the value of the portfolio using the portfolio duration needs to be estimated. The calculations for the portfolio are

$$\text{Modified duration} = 6.80/(1 + (0.0846/2)) = 6.52 \text{ and}$$

$$\frac{\Delta B}{B} \approx -6.52 \times 0.01 = -0.0652 \text{ or } -6.52\%.$$

The estimate, using the portfolio duration, is virtually identical to the estimate using the individual durations. But the calculation using the portfolio duration is much simpler. The simplicity of the calculation using the portfolio duration is the reason that bond portfolio managers work with portfolio durations when managing the interest-rate risk of their portfolios.

INDUSTRY APPLICATION

THE PROBLEM OF ACCRUED INTEREST IN CALCULATING DURATION

It is unfortunate that in order to teach the basics, many textbooks must simplify "real-world" issues. In the case of bonds this usually means valuing a bond on a coupon date or, at best, recognizing the value of a bond between coupon dates and asking the student to calculate the amount of accrued interest (see Chapter 5, Section 5.3.3). Unfortunately, the effect of accrued interest affects other metrics as well as bond valuation. In particular, it can affect the calculation of duration—the dominant risk measure in fixed-income portfolios. It is often

the task of an associate to recognize when accrued interest can create "anomalies."

One classic error is the assumption that *duration declines smoothly to zero* as maturity approaches. This is *not* true because of accrued interest. For example, use a spreadsheet to create 10 years of days in a column and calculate the duration for a 6% coupon, 10-year bond priced at 6% for every one of those days. Then plot the duration time series for, say, the fifth year. The result should be something like the following graph.

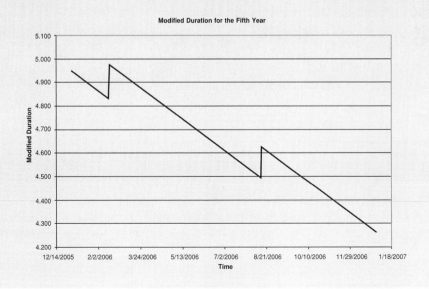

(*continued*)

INDUSTRY APPLICATION (*continued*)

THE PROBLEM OF ACCRUED INTEREST IN CALCULATING DURATION

The reason for the sawtooth pattern is that duration is a weighted average of the accrued interest (duration $= 0$) and the remaining future cash flows (coupons and face value with duration > 0); hence as the amount of accrued interest increases, its weight in the weighted average increases and duration declines. Then when the interest is paid, the weight on accrued interest goes to zero and the duration jumps back up because 100% of the weight goes on the duration of the future cash flows. This phenomenon can cause problems in other areas as well. Consider two bonds now: the first bond has 30 years to maturity and is three months longer in maturity than the second although it has a coupon rate that is 25 bps lower than the second bond.

	Bond 1	Bond 2
Issue date	2/15/2003	11/15/2002
Maturity date	2/15/2033	11/15/2032
Yield	5.30%	5.30%
Coupon rate	5.30%	5.55%
Face value	100	100
Frequency	2	2
Basis (A/A)	1	1

Perform the same duration calculations you did before to create the duration sawtooth pattern, but this time plot *both* bonds on the same graph. You will get something that looks like the following.

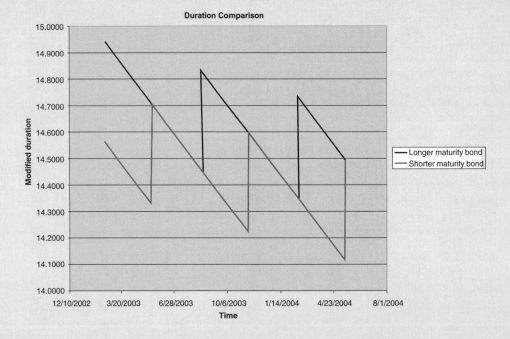

Yes! It is no longer true that *"Bonds with longer maturities and lower coupons have longer durations than bonds with shorter maturities and higher coupons."* And the reason again is due to accrued interest. Notice that if you did not know better, you might think that there was an error in your calculations or programming.[3]

---

[3] This example was drawn from *Duration Crossovers: An Anomaly Explained,* 2006, a working paper by Z. Li, R. Grieves, and M. D. Griffiths.

13.4 SWAPS

Duration is a common technique for managing interest-rate risk for managers with interest-rate-sensitive assets or liabilities. Duration is particularly useful for portfolio managers, managers of financial institutions, and managers of insurance companies and pension funds because these managers work with portfolios. However, some situations exist where a manager is exposed to interest-rate risk, and altering the duration of the obligation is neither practical nor possible. In these situations, a swap may be a viable solution for managing interest-rate risk.

A **swap** is a derivative security. Swaps were not presented in the chapters that discussed the other derivative securities because swaps were originally created to manage interest-rate risk and are easiest to understand if discussed within this framework. Accordingly, the discussion of swaps begins now so that they could be included in the discussion of interest-rate risk. The remainder of this chapter presents swaps, discusses how to use them to manage interest-rate risk, and discusses how to value a swap.

Swaps originated in the 1970s at a time when foreign exchange controls in most countries limited the ability of firms to obtain cross-border financing or for investors to lend overseas. Enterprising companies and investors developed swaps to bypass these restrictions. Swaps involve parallel and back-to-back loans. Basically, this meant that a company in Germany would borrow money in Germany to pay an Argentine company's (then) deutschmark debt. At the same time, the Argentine company would borrow money in Argentina to pay the German company's peso debt. In 1980, the World Bank and IBM engaged in the first official swap, which involved Swiss francs and U.S. dollars. Since that time, the market for interest rate swaps has exploded to more than $25 trillion.

13.4.1 Swaps Techniques for Bond Managers

A swap is an agreement to exchange cash flows at specified future times according to certain specified rules. Although any type of asset that generates a return may be swapped, the most common swaps are single-currency interest rate swaps. These are swaps where one party exchanges a fixed-rate coupon stream for a floating-rate coupon stream. This type of swap is known as a **plain vanilla swap**. The other type of interest rate swap involves the exchange of one floating-rate coupon stream for another. This type of swap is called a **basis swap**. When more than one currency is involved, a swap can be fixed-for-fixed, floating-for-floating, and fixed-for-floating across the different currencies. A point to be made here: A swap is a negotiated contract, and a party who desires a swap must find a second party that is willing to take part in the swap under terms agreeable to both parties.

When a bond manager's expectations differ from the market consensus, the manager may attempt to position the portfolio to capitalize on the manager's expectations concerning price changes resulting from the expected change in interest rates. One method the manager could use is known as a **substitution swap**. Here, the manager exchanges one bond for another bond, identical in every respect except that a temporary price advantage exists because of an imbalance in supply and demand. For example, a manager has some 10-year Aaa utility bonds with a 9% coupon that are currently selling at par. Now, assume there is another 10-year Aaa utility bond with a 9% coupon currently yielding 9.15%. The manager might want to exchange a given dollar amount of the bonds currently held for an equal dollar amount of the second bonds and gain the additional 15 basis points in yield. Why does the manager want the bond with the shorter duration?[4] Because, when the supply and demand come back into balance, the longer duration bond trading at par will be unaffected while the shorter duration bond will increase in price (risk can be on the upside as well!), which lengthens its duration. What the manager has done is to match the duration of the instrument to the period in which the risk exists.

A second type of difference of opinion between the manager and the market might result in a **cross-market spread swap**. Here the manager moves out of one market and into another to exploit an advantageous yield relationship. A cross-market spread swap can occur between any two fixed income markets. However, this type of swap typically occurs between two closely related markets where the typical spread is well-understood. Suppose the manager has a 20-year A utility bond with a 6.5% coupon trading at par and that there is a 100 bps spread between the currently held 20-year bonds and 10-year A utility bonds. If the manager believes that the spread is too low, some of the 20-year bonds can be swapped for the 10-year bonds. Because spreads are expected to increase, the yield on the 10-year bonds can be expected to fall and the resulting price increase will provide an abnormal gain in the holding period return. Again, the more attractive bonds are the ones with the shorter duration. The reason for preferring the shorter duration bonds is the same as discussed for the substitution swap.

Another tool at the manager's disposal is a **rate anticipation swap**, which changes a portfolio's duration by swapping for new bonds that will achieve the target duration. If the manager believes that yields in general are going to rise and that the current portfolio is at risk, since long-term bonds move downward more for an increase in yields than do short-term bonds, the manager might choose to swap the longer-term instruments for the shorter-term instruments.

Swaps can also be advantageous when the manager does not want to make any prediction about future yields. **Yield pickup swaps** are designed to capture long-term price movements. Suppose that 20-year AA *industrial* bonds are currently yielding 8.5%. The manager might choose to swap some 20-year AA *utility* bonds currently yielding 8.25% for some of the 20-year AA *industrial* bonds. The object of this swap is to gain an additional 25 basis points in yield.

13.4.2 Understanding a Plain Vanilla Swap

The discussion of swaps will focuse on plain vanilla swaps because they are the easiest to understand. Once a plain vanilla swap is understood, all the other types become relatively easy to understand.

Why do managers use swaps?

- One reason is to maximize returns by speculating on the direction of interest rates. This may be the motivation of a bond portfolio manager.

- A second important reason is to minimize risk by hedging against fluctuations in the interest rate. This is often the motivation for a corporate client or a bank that is risk

---

[4] Recall, from Chapter 5, that the bond with the higher yield will have the shorter duration.

averse and prefers certainty in the budgeting process. These individuals prefer the certainty of paying or receiving a fixed income stream.

- A third reason is to earn profits by facilitating swap agreements between other parties. This is the role of a bank or other similar financial institution that earns a profit margin based on the difference between the amount it pays to one party and the amount it receives from another.

One important point about swaps is that different parties can and do have different motivations to engage in a swap transaction. Hence a swap can be potentially beneficial to both parties. The following example steps through the process for a plain vanilla swap.

EXAMPLE *Plain Vanilla Swap*

The classic example of a plain vanilla swap for an interest rate hedge is based on the concept of comparative advantage. The basic idea is that sometimes both parties to a swap can lower their costs of financing. Suppose that an AAA-rated company can borrow for five years at a fixed rate of 7.0% or borrow at a floating rate of LIBOR + 25 basis points. Also, a BBB-rated company can borrow for five years at a fixed rate of 10% or borrow at a floating rate at LIBOR + 125 basis points. Assume the AAA-rated company borrows at a fixed rate and the BBB-rated company borrows at a floating rate. The two companies agree to swap interest payments. Because the AAA-rated company is not altruistic, the BBB-rated company must pay the AAA-rated company a premium. Figure 13-1 diagrams this plain vanilla swap.

Now, look at the various cash flows to determine if the swap did benefit both parties. The BBB-rated company will

- *pay* a fixed rate on the swap of   (8%)
- *pay* a floating rate to its funding source of   (LIBOR +125)
- *receive* a floating rate from the swap of   LIBOR +25

Hence, the overall rate to the BBB-rated company will be   (9%). Now, look at the AAA-rated company. The company will

- *pay* a fixed rate to its funding source of   (7%)
- *pay* a floating rate on the swap of   (LIBOR +25)
- *receive* a fixed rate from the swap of   8%

Hence, the overall rate to the AAA-rated company will be   (LIBOR −75).

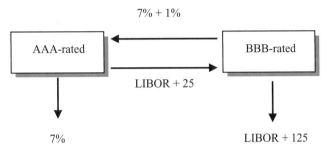

FIGURE 13-1 A plain vanilla swap.

The AAA-rated company will pay LIBOR *minus* 75 basis points when the best rate it could get before the swap on a variable-rate loan was LIBOR *plus* 25 basis points. The BBB-rated company will pay 9% when before it would have had to pay 10% on a fixed-rate loan. Notice that the higher (credit quality) rated company has a comparative advantage in the fixed-rate market and the lower rated company has a comparative advantage in the floating-rate market.

In this example, the total savings from the two firms is 200 basis points. Where did this come from? Before the agreement to swap is made, the difference between the two fixed rates is $(10\% - 7\%) = 300$ basis points. And the difference between the two floating rates is (LIBOR + 125 − (LIBOR + 25)) = 100 basis points. Thus, the difference between the net fixed and net floating rates is $(3\% - 1\%) = 200$ basis points, which is the benefit the two firms have available to share by entering into the swap.

How has the swap in the previous example helped to manage interest-rate risk? Suppose interest rates increase. The managers of the AAA-rated company are disappointed because the cash outflow will increase, but their net rate is still 100 basis points lower than the new variable rate. Now, suppose that interest rates decline. The AAA-rated company managers are pleased because the cash outflow will decrease and their net rate is still 100 basis points lower than the new variable rate. Now look at the BBB-rated company's position. If interest rates increase, the managers of the BBB-rated company are indifferent because the increased cash outflow will be matched by the cash inflow from the AAA-rated company and the management has a fixed rate that is at least 100 basis points less than the new current fixed rate. Now, suppose that interest rates decline. Again, any change in the LIBOR will be matched by a change in the inflow from the AAA-rated company. The BBB-rated company's managers will be disappointed only if their risk-adjusted fixed rates decline below 9%.

In today's market, swap savings are estimated to be in the range of 10 to 25 basis points. In the early days of the swap market, savings as much as 50 basis points could have been obtained. Therefore, the example was exaggerated a little to demonstrate the point. Another small discrepancy in the example is that the variable-rate side was not quoted flat, as it is usually quoted in a plain vanilla swap. That is, in the swap on the variable leg, only LIBOR (and not LIBOR plus a spread) would be exchanged. Nonetheless, what is being demonstrated is how to exploit national or international capital markets that have been segmented due to market or regulatory barriers or due to different perceptions of credit qualities.

Banks play a crucial role in capturing swap savings. Working as an intermediary, a bank is in a good position to find counterparties for the two parts of a swap.[5] A second reason for the bank to be involved is the interest rate sensitivity of the bank's own balance sheet. Since a bank often has variable-rate deposits (liabilities) and fixed-rate loans (assets) and does not really want to take on any interest-rate risk themselves, the bank, itself, is often the counterparty for its clients. In exchange for a small portion of the swap savings, the bank willingly provides the swap service both to help its clients and to help manage its own risk position.

The plain vanilla swap example brought up an important issue that relates to the credit risk of the counterparties. Because no principal is at risk and the net difference

---

[5] Transaction costs for the bank's services are reflected in the bid-ask spread, which appears on the fixed rate side of the swap. The primary determinant of the bid-ask spread is the demand for liquidity. The bid-ask spread is determined by competition in the market and reflects the cost of market-making activities. The bid-ask spread on an interest rate swap generally ranges from 4 to 15 basis points.

between the fixed and floating coupon payments is all that is really exchanged, the relative creditworthiness of counterparties has only a small influence on swap prices. For example, the difference between a company rated AAA and a company rated BBB can be as small as 5 basis points or less in a swap (our example is *really* exaggerated).

Now that the potential interest rate benefits to a plain vanilla swap have been seen, the steps in negotiating a swap agreement will be discussed. Another example, that follows, will further demonstrate the process of a plain vanilla swap with a specific focus on the steps in negotiating a swap.

EXAMPLE   *Steps in Negotiating a Swap*

Suppose you were the Chief Financial Officer for a landfill and had a loan agreement with your bank for the purchase of a fleet of dump trucks and earthmovers. Your bank agrees to charge you a fixed rate on the loan with the rate defined as the 10-year Treasury bond rate plus a credit premium of 200 basis points, and the rate will be fixed at the time the loan is funded to purchase the trucks and earthmovers. At the time of the purchase, the 10-year Treasury bond rate plus 200 basis points was 8% per year payable annually, so you are locked into an 8% fixed-rate loan.

After studying recent announcements from the central bank and reviewing your analysis of the economy and its effect on your company's cash flows, your opinion is that interest rates should fall. As a result, you believe that the interest rate you are paying on the loan will soon be higher than the going market rate.[6] What can you do? You could go to another bank, or you could refinance the loan with the current bank. Both of these choices would be costly. The other choice is to enter into a swap with a new bank.

If you decide on the swap, you will agree to pay a variable rate of interest that will be based on the principal amount of the loan your bank had provided in exchange for the new bank paying you a fixed rate of interest based on the same amount. Your idea is to have the cash flow stream from the new bank pay the interest expense stream to your bank, while you pay the new bank a lower variable rate. Basically, what you want to do is substitute a variable-rate loan (to the new bank) for the fixed-rate loan (to your lending bank). Figure 13-2 illustrates this swap. This swap is not without risk, but this risk will be discussed later.

Now, take a closer look at the steps in a plain vanilla swap. The four basic steps are as follows:

Step 1. First, the business situation has to be analyzed and the current cash flows must be determined. Next determine what cash flows are wanted. In this example, the current cash flows are fixed but you wanted variable cash flows.

Step 2. The details of the swap must be determined. This process comprises several issues. First, you have to identify when the swap will start and when it will end. Remember, a swap contract is a legal document; therefore, you have to be quite specific in identifying who is responsible for what actions. This step includes identifying the counterparty with whom you are dealing.

Step 3. Next, the **notional principal** must be specified. Participants to an interest rate swap do not actually exchange the principal amounts, but the principal amount has to be specified so that interest payments can be calculated. In addition, the rate on the fixed-rate side of the swap is determined.

Step 4. Now, the details associated with each leg of the swap have to be identified. For the landfill, the paying leg is the variable-rate side. Assume the landfill will pay six-month LIBOR on a semiannual basis and will receive the fixed rate on an annual basis. In summary, from the point of view of the landfill, the swap details would look like this:

---

[6] In other words, you want to minimize your perception of the risk by shortening the duration.

Swap Agreement for Landfill with New Bank

Start Date: 01/01/x1   **End Date:** 01/01/x4

Counterparty: New Bank

	Pay side	Receive side
Type	Floating	Fixed
Payment frequency	Semiannual	Annual
Price/basis	LIBOR	8.00%
Day count	Actual/360	30/360

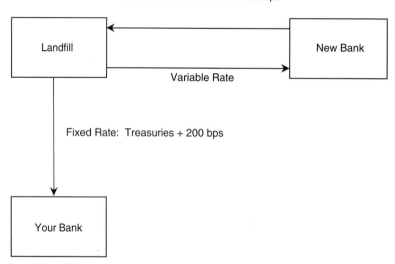

FIGURE 13-2 Illustration of a fixed-variable swap.

Now, assume that three years are remaining on the loan and your reason, as CFO, for wanting to do the swap is something like this. As the CFO, you know that your customers tend to engage in more short-term contracts with you for garbage removal during periods when interest rates tend to decline. Your customers are currently asking for these short-term contracts. Thus, you believe you have some basis for *speculating* that interest rates will decline and you want to profit on the potential difference between the fixed and variable rates as loan rates decline. But what if you are wrong? *If interest rates rise, you will actually be paying a higher rate of interest than you would have paid with the fixed-rate loan.* That is, engaging in *this* swap exposes the landfill to interest-rate risk. Knowing the swap exposes the landfill to interest-rate risk, you believe the risk is worth taking because of the potential profits from a possible decline you expect in interest rates.

In Step 3, the rate on the fixed-rate side of the swap is set. Customarily, banks quote only the fixed side against the floating side. For example, the new bank may have the following quotes for swaps against six-month LIBOR.

New Bank Swap Quotations against Six-Month LIBOR

Two-year	7.92/94
Three-year	8.00/04
Four-year	8.22/27
Day count 30/360	

Here's how to read the quotes: If you want to receive a fixed rate from the bank for two years, you will receive 7.92%. But if you want to pay the bank a fixed rate for two years, you will agree to pay 7.94%. The easiest way to remember which rate you must pick is to choose the one that is most *disadvantageous* to you. (Remember, the bank has to make money!) Therefore, if you want to receive fixed, you will pick the lower rate, but if you want to pay fixed, you will pick the higher rate. The landfill example was a three-year swap contract where you want to receive fixed; therefore, you will receive 8%, which is the rate on a three-year swap.

Finally, you need to calculate the cash flows that will be exchanged. The cash flows for the fixed side are not a problem since they are known in advance. For the floating side, however, the relevant rate is not known until the start of the reset period. Therefore, for every period, other than the one commencing immediately, you will only be able to calculate expected cash flows that are based on the current spot forward rate curve.

13.4.3 Valuing Swaps

Once the swap is in place, the value of the swap needs to be determined since the floating-rate portion will change as market conditions change. Changes in interest rates will change the risk exposure of both of the swap parties. For example, as you learned in the discussion on federal funds, institutions borrow and lend to each other based on a preestablished limit. This limit represents the creditworthiness of the counterparties. Now, assume two banks with a credit relationship enter into a series of plain vanilla swaps. Both banks in the swap would want to track the value of the swaps in case interest rate changes cause the value of swaps to change dramatically. A dramatic change in the value of the swaps could alter the credit quality of the other bank in the swap.

Another reason to value swaps is purely for financial accounting purposes. Every quarter, publicly listed companies are required to report all assets and liabilities on their balance sheets or in the notes to their financial statements. The strength of the companies' balance sheets, in turn, determines their creditworthiness and the valuation investors place on the companies' shares.

Swap values are found by using expected future interest rates. As discussed in Chapter 3, the yield curve represents investors' future interest expectations. However, the yield curve discussed in Chapter 3 was for Treasury securities and reflected the borrowing rate for the U.S. government. Since market participants cannot borrow at the U.S. government rate, an adjustment to the Treasury yield curve must be made to do an accurate swap valuation.

To develop a yield curve for valuing a swap, swap traders start with the Treasury yield curve and then examine other market data to make adjustments to the Treasury yield curve rates. The traders tend to use cash market prices for the rates of less than three months. The next part of the curve is adjusted using interest-rate futures prices or common FRA instruments. Other swaps help determine the intermediate part of the curve while bond prices are used to adjust the long end of the curve. Fitting the curve and adjusting for the various sources of information is not an easy task and requires the talents of men and women trained at the doctoral level in mathematics, statistics, and econometrics.

Both simple and complex methods may be used to build a yield curve for valuing a swap. Since different methods exist for building the yield curve to value a swap, valuations are subject to interpretation. As a result, experts in determining the correct yield curve for market participants should always be consulted when valuing a swap. In the next section, the four basic steps in valuing a swap will be presented.

13.4.3.1   *The Four Steps for Valuing a Swap*   The value of a swap is the net value of the two cash flow streams. That is, just subtract the present value of the paying stream from the present value of the receiving stream to determine the value of a swap. As a result, any gain for one side of a swap is, by definition, a loss for the other side of a swap.

The process for valuing a swap contains four steps. The steps are as follows:

Step 1.   The first step is to calculate the expected cash flows at the end of each period. This calculation multiplies the notional principal, times the rate, times the number of days, and is especially easy to calculate for the fixed side. For the floating side, the calculation multiplies the notional principal, times the *implied forward rates derived from the yield curve for each period,* times the number of days. Although this task seems easy, and it is, one crucial element must be remembered: the **day count conventions**. The day count conventions specifies the number of days in a time period. This convention is very important when dealing with currency or basis swaps. As has been said, *You can swap the returns on virtually anything, but the transaction must be priced correctly*[7].

Step 2.   The second step is to determine the spot discount factors since both cash flow streams must be discounted. The good news is that the same forward rates of interest from Step 1 can be used. The only adjustment to make is the same adjustment that was made in earlier chapters: *multiply the single period discount factors together to obtain the spot discount factors.*

Step 3.   The third step is to discount the cash flow streams to time zero.

Step 4.   The fourth and final step is to subtract the present value of the paying stream from the present value of the receiving stream. This calculation determines the net present value of the swap. Notice that the value of the swap is the NPV of the expected cash flows because the future floating-rate payments had to be estimated from the yield curve. As a result, the value of the swap will change whenever variable rates change. In 2001, interest rates declined dramatically. This dramatic decline made receive fixed, pay floating swaps more valuable and receive floating, pay fixed swaps less valuable.

---

[7] One of our colleagues tells the story of a bond trader who lost $7 million in 10 minutes because he thought he had detected an arbitrage opportunity. Unfortunately, the bonds were priced on a 365-day year, not a 360-day year, as the trader believed.

EXAMPLE *Valuing a Plain Vanilla Swap*

Back to the landfill example. Suppose that your landfill has three years remaining on a fixed for floating swap on a notional principal of $40 million. You receive the fixed payment *annually* but pay the floating rate on a *semiannual* basis. A swap with these terms is known as receiving a three-year annual sixes swap. The convention is to quote the fixed side first with the payment in words (annual) and the floating side second with the payment in numbers (sixes).

Assume that a payment has just been made and the swap needs to be valued. Start with the fixed side of the swap. The following table provides the annual cash flows of the fixed side calculated as: notional principal × rate × days/360.

Landfill, Notional Principal = $40,000,000, Start Date: 6/11/01, End Date: 6/11/04

Payment dates	Days	Fixed rate (%)	Cash flow ($)
6/11/02	360	8.00	3,200,000
6/11/03	360	8.00	3,200,000
6/11/04	360	8.00	3,200,000

The calculation of the cash flows for the floating side will not be as simple as for the fixed side. For the floating side, the *implied forward rates* have to be used. These rates will be derived from the yield curve. Using the implied forward rates, the calculation of the cash flows is the same as for the fixed side; but notice in the next table that there are six cash flows (a three-year annual sixes swap). A common mistake is to believe that the frequency of cash flows from one side of the swap must match the frequency of the cash flows from the other side of the swap. This is not true. A swap can be made with any frequency and on any basis. In the following table, the calculation of the semiannual cash flows is notional principal × implied forward rate × days/360.

Landfill, Notional Principal = $40,000,000, Start Date: 6/11/01, End Date: 6/11/04

Payment dates	Days	Implied forward rate (%)	Cash flow ($)
12/11/01	184	7.10	1,451,556
06/11/02	181	7.26	1,460,067
12/11/02	184	7.72	1,578,311
06/11/03	181	8.13	1,635,033
12/11/03	184	8.60	1,758,222
06/11/04	181	8.94	1,797,933

Now that the expected cash flows have been determined they need to be discounted back to the present. The first thing to do is to calculate the *discount factor from the implied forward rates*. This calculation is easy, but an important fact must be remembered: the relevant rates are the floating rates, not the fixed rates, since the floating rates best represent the market's consensus on what the future rates are going to be. The following equation is used to calculate the discount factor from the implied forward rates.

$$\frac{1}{1 + (\text{rate} \times \text{days}/360)}.$$

This formula is similar to the present value factor for one period. That is, it discounts cash flows back one period. However, when cash flows cover multiple periods, the single period discount factors must be combined so that the cash flows can be discounted back to today. The discount factors are combined by multiplying them together. The results are labeled as the **spot discount factor**. Look at the next table. The discount factor of 0.9650 will discount the cash flow on 12/11/01 to the present (6/11/01). The discount factor of 0.9648 will discount the second cash flow from 6/11/02 to 12/11/01, but for present value the second cash flow needs to be discounted back to 6/11/01. The spot discount factors discount the cash flows back to the present (6/11/01 in this case) and are calculated by multiplying discount factors together. For the second cash flow the spot discount factor is $0.9310 = (0.9650 \times 0.9648)$. The present value of the floating side of the swap is calculated first because the spot discount factors calculated for the floating side will also be used to find the present value of the fixed side.

Landfill, Notional principal = $40,000,000, Start Date: 6/11/01, End Date: 6/11/04

Payment dates	Days	Implied forward rate (%)	Discount factor	Spot discount factor
12/11/01	184	7.10	0.9650	0.9650
06/11/02	181	7.26	0.9648	0.9310
12/11/02	184	7.72	0.9620	0.8957
06/11/03	181	8.13	0.9607	0.8605
12/11/03	184	8.60	0.9579	0.8243
06/11/04	181	8.94	0.9570	0.7888

The next step is to calculate the present value of the cash flows.

Landfill, Notional principal = $40,000,000, Start Date: 6/11/01, End Date: 6/11/04

Payment dates	Days	Implied forward rate (%)	Discount factor	Spot discount factor	Cash flow ($)	PV ($)
12/11/01	184	7.10	0.9650	0.9650	1,451,556	1,400,752
06/11/02	181	7.26	0.9648	0.9310	1,460,067	1,359,322
12/11/02	184	7.72	0.9620	0.8957	1,578,311	1,413,693
06/11/03	181	8.13	0.9607	0.8605	1,635,033	1,406,946
12/11/03	184	8.60	0.9579	0.8243	1,758,222	1,449,302
06/11/04	181	8.94	0.9570	0.7888	1,797,933	1,418,210
					Total PV	**$8,448,225**

The fixed side is easily calculated now because the spot discount factors used when valuing the floating-rate side are used here. Remember that the fixed-rate side only makes annual payments in this example; therefore, the annual spot discount factors are used.

Landfill, Notional principal = $40,000,000, Start Date: 6/11/01, End Date: 6/11/04

Payment dates	Days	Fixed rate (%)	Spot discount factor	Cash flow ($)	PV ($)
06/11/02	360	8.00	0.9310	3,200,000	2,979,200
06/11/03	360	8.00	0.8605	3,200,000	2,753,600
06/11/04	360	8.00	0.7888	3,200,000	2,524,160
				Total PV	$8,256,960

Now for the final step: determining the value of the swap. The landfill wants to receive a fixed rate and pay a floating rate: therefore, the value of the swap is

$$\$8,256,960 - \$8,448,225 = -\$191,265.$$

This swap value shows that the landfill is expected to pay more under the variable-rate scheme than under the fixed-rate contract. Why? Because the market expects interest rates to rise in the future over the life of this three-year swap. Even though the variable rates start out lower, higher rates occur later. The compounding effect in the spot discount factors reduce the value of the floating-rate cash flows more than the fixed-rate cash flows, which more than offsets the benefit of lower rates in the early periods of the swap. As the Chief Financial Officer, you had better be very confident in your forecast of a decline in both long-term and short-term interest rates before you engage in this swap.

IN THE NEWS

One of the reasons to value swaps is that they have to be included in quarterly financial statements. This **In The News** item will show exactly the nature and extent of the reporting that has to be performed under U.S. Generally Accepted Accounting Standards. As an example, the financial statements for Vishay Intertechnology, Inc., a Fortune 1000 Company with annual sales of $2.5 billion will be used. Vishay Intertechnology is the largest U.S. and European manufacturer of passive electronic components and a major producer of semiconductors and integrated circuits. Its headquarters is in Malvern, Pennsylvania. Vishay employs over 20,000 people in 66 plants in the United States, Mexico, Germany, Austria, the United Kingdom, France, Portugal, the Czech Republic, Hungary, Israel, Taiwan, China, and the Philippines. Note 1 to the Company's Consolidated Financial Statements for the year ended December 31, 2001, is a Summary of their Significant Accounting Policies. Contained in this note is the following statement about Vishay's use of swaps:

The Company uses interest rate swap agreements for purposes other than trading and treats such agreements

as off-balance sheet items. Interest rate swaps are used by the Company to modify variable rate obligations to fixed rate obligations, thereby reducing the exposure to market rate fluctuations. The interest rate swap agreements are designed as hedges, and effectiveness is determined by matching the principal balances and terms with each specific obligation. Such an agreement involves the exchange of amounts based on fixed interest rates for amounts based on variable interest rates over the life of the agreement without the exchange of the notional amount upon which the payments are based. The differential to be paid or received as interest rates change is accounted for on the accrual method of accounting. The related amount payable to or receivable from counterparties is included as an adjustment to interest expense and to accrued interest in other accrued expenses. Gains or losses upon terminations of interest rate swap agreements are deferred as an adjustment to interest expense related to the obligations over the term of the original contract lives of the terminated swap agreements. In the event of early extinguishment of an obligation, any realized or unrealized gain or loss from the swap is recognized in income at the time of extinguishment.

13.5 OTHER TYPES OF SWAPS

Having completed the discussion of plain vanilla swaps, the basics of swaps should be understood. Therefore, other types of swaps can now be discussed. This section introduces and briefly discusses currency swaps, commodity swaps, and basis swaps.

A **currency swap** is used to exchange fixed or floating interest payments that are denominated in two different currencies. Unlike a plain vanilla swap, the principals are usually exchanged both at the beginning and at the end of the swap at an exchange rate that was set at the beginning of the swap. These swaps are usually used to hedge against or speculate on foreign currency interest rate movements. They are also used by corporations to gain access to off-shore funding sources without the need to take out a foreign currency loan.

When dealing with a currency swap, day count conventions must be carefully considered. There are six common day count conventions:

1. Actual/actual (in period);

2. Actual/365;

3. Actual/365 (366 in leap year);

4. Actual/360.

   In the calculation of the actual number of days, only one of the two bracketing dates is included. For example: the actual number of days between May 1 and May 15 is 14 days.

5. 30/360;

6. 30E/360.

This example illustrates how the last two, day count conventions, work. Let D1/M1/Y1 equal the day (D1), the month (M1), and the year (Y1) of the first date. Let D2/M2/Y2 represent the same elements for the second date. The number of days between two dates assumes 30-day months based on the following rules: if D1 is 31, change to 30; if D2 is 31 and D1 is either 30 or 31, change D2 to 30; otherwise leave D2 at 31. Then, the number of days between the two dates is $(Y2 - Y1) \times 360 + (M2 - M1) \times 30 + (D2 - D1)$. In the case of 30E, if D2 is 31, change D2 to 30 no matter what D1 is. Confused? The confusion is understandable, but no comforting logic can be provided for this process. All that can be said is that this process is the market convention.

At this point, the day count conventions for several of the major bond types are provided for your reference.

Market	Coupon payments	Day count
U.S. government	Semiannual	Actual/actual (in period)
U.S. corporate	Semiannual	30/360
U.S. government agency	Annual	30/360
	Semiannual	
	Quarterly	
U.S. municipal	Semiannual	30/360
U.K. government	Semiannual	Actual/365
Eurobond	Annual	30E/360
Canadian government	Semiannual	Actual/actual (in period)
Swiss government	Annual	30E/360
German government	Annual	30E/360

A second popular swap type is the **commodity swap**. In this swap, fixed commodity price payments are exchanged for floating commodity price payments. The floating price is usually based on a market index for that commodity. Commodity swaps are based on a set amount such as the number of ounces of gold, the number of barrels of oil, or the number of cubic meters of natural gas. As with other swaps, these swaps can be used to hedge or speculate on the price movements in the underlying asset. They can also be used to allow producers to fix a sales price for their goods and for consumers to fix a purchase price. For example, an airline would use a commodity swap to fix the price of its fuel purchases.

The final type of swap we will deal with here is a *basis swap*. In this swap, floating interest payments are exchanged for different floating interest payments in the same currency. The floating payments are either made at different frequencies based on the same benchmark rate or at the same frequency with different benchmark rates. In general, these swaps are used to hedge against movements in interest rates. For example, when monthly cash receipts from customers have to cover floating-rate semiannual loan payments, this risk of a possible cash shortfall can be minimized by paying floating monthly and receiving floating semiannual on the same benchmark. Corporations also use basis swaps to change the frequency of a cash flow. For example, change monthly payments for quarterly payments.

Basis swaps are another example where the day count convention must be accurately followed. Also, basis such as LIBOR for PIBOR may be swapped. That is, the London Interbank Offer Rate can be exchanged for the Paris Interbank Offer Rate. In some markets and countries, a LIBOR-like rate is not the prevailing rate. For example, in the U.S. housing market, the floating rate for some adjustable-rate mortgages is based on the 11th District Cost of Funds. The 11th District Cost of Funds is computed from reports filed monthly with the Federal Home Loan Bank in San Francisco. The 11th District Cost of Funds is computed using information from reporting savings institutions in Arizona, California, and Nevada. The index measures interest rates paid by the reporting institutions on savings deposits and borrowings. Each month's 11th District Cost of Funds Index (COFI) is calculated as: total monthly interest costs paid for the month divided by the average balances of those deposits and other borrowings. The resulting rate is adjusted for the number of days in the particular month and then annualized. This index is used primarily for adjustable mortgages with a monthly interest rate adjustment.

Some of the more popular floating-rate indexes in the United States are

1. Prime rate
2. LIBOR (one, three, and six month)
3. LIBID (one, three, and six month)
4. LIMEAN (average of LIBID and LIBOR)
5. Federal funds
6. Commercial paper
7. Certificates of deposit
8. 11th District Cost of Funds
9. 91-day Treasury bills

13.6 ANOTHER VIEW OF SWAPS

Before leaving this discussion of swaps, a brief discussion of swaps from a different point of view is presented. It is possible to think of a swap as a series of the forward rate agreements (FRAs) discussed in Chapter 9.

As you know, in a FRA, an amount $(-L)$ is borrowed at time t_1 and the repayment of the loan (L) plus interest (r) is at time t_2.

For the fixed rate, r_K specified by the FRA, the cash flows are

$$\text{Time } t_1 : -L$$

$$\text{Time } t_2 : L[1 + r_K(T_2 - T_1)]$$

And for a floating rate, r_{FL}, the cash flows are

$$\text{Time } t_1 : -L$$

$$\text{Time } t_2 : L[1 + r_{FL}(T_2 - T_1)]$$

Therefore, for the corporation that receives one cash flow (say floating) and pays the other, the combined cash flow would be

$$\text{Time } t_1 : 0$$
$$\text{Time } t_2 : -L[1 + r_K(T_2 - T_1)]$$
$$\text{Time } t_2 : L[1 + r_{FL}(T_2 - T_1)]$$

Therefore, the value of this FRA, which only has one cash flow, is PV(cash flow). In other words, a swap is equal to the present value of a series of FRAs. In diagrammatic form, a swap would look like Figure 13-3.

In Figure 13-4, a diagram is provided to show how to interpret the profit and loss on a swap when it is viewed as the present value sum of a series of FRAs.

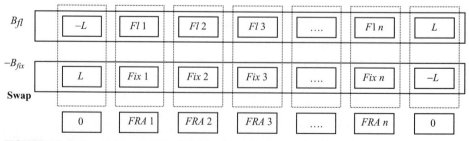

FIGURE 13-3 A swap as a series of FRAs.

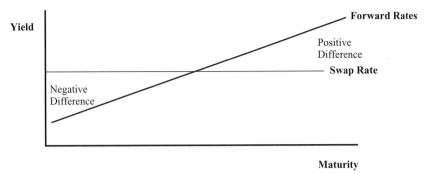

FIGURE 13-4 Profit and loss from a swap.

13.7 SWAP SUMMARY

The key to understanding active bond strategies is the concept that the return from fixed income investments (bonds) comes from only three sources: coupon income, capital gain (or loss), and reinvestment income. However, it is commonly assumed that reinvestment income can be ignored in active bond management strategies.

Therefore, in addition to changes in bond prices due to a change in the level of interest rates, the following factors will also affect a bond portfolio's rate of return: changes in the shape of the yield curve, changes in yield spreads among bond sectors, changes in option-adjusted spreads, and changes in the risk premium for a particular bond. Because bonds have different coupons and different maturities, a standard measure must be established. Duration is that standard measure. Duration is an extremely useful means of determining the effect of a yield change on the value of a bond or a portfolio of bonds. Understanding whether the duration should be increased or decreased is a prime component of any fixed income strategy.

Although portfolio managers can and do buy and sell large amounts of individual bonds, often a less expensive process for them to use in managing their position is swap agreements. Swaps are an excellent way to take advantage of short-term changes in interest rates. Swap agreements are relatively straightforward, but care must be taken when valuing a swap because estimates of the implied forward rates are needed for valuation. Blending the appropriate rates from different sources into a single yield curve to be used for pricing purposes requires a level of expertise that combines academic and practical training and is beyond the scope of this book to address.

The four steps in pricing and valuing a swap are essentially same as pricing a bond. The four steps are

Step 1. Determine the cash flows. The most difficult portion of this step is the calculation of the expected floating rate amounts. These amounts have to be calculated using the implied forward curve.

Step 2. Use the same forward rates estimated in Step 1 to calculate the discount rates. These can then be used to calculate the spot discount rates that are used to discount both the fixed-rate and floating-rate cash flow streams.

Step 3. Calculate the present value of the paying stream and the present value of the receipt stream.

Step 4. Subtract the present value of the paying stream from the present value of the receipt stream. This is the value of the swap. At the time a swap is first negotiated, the present value of the swap is zero.

In this chapter, two major risks associated with swaps are specifically pointed out. The first major risk is market risk, which is the risk of financial loss resulting from movements in interest rates, currency prices, or commodity prices. The second risk is credit risk, which is the risk of a financial loss that arises from the counterparty being unable to meet its obligations. This risk can be somewhat mitigated by running credit checks on counterparties, establishing credit limits, and/or signing standardized ISDA (International Swap Dealers' Association) contracts with counterparties.

Two other sources of risk should be noted at this point. The first is operational risk. This risk results from inadequate internal controls, policies, and/or procedures. Because knowledgeable CFOs recognize the importance of operational risk, any firm that engages in a large number of swaps with different frequencies and bases had better have an excellent accounting and control system established to keep track of and manage everything. Remember, the swap is a formal contract. Any error resulting in a missed or erroneous payment constitutes a default. The second additional risk to mention is legal risk. This risk entails the risk that a contract cannot be enforced in the event of a default. For the most part, the ISDA standard master agreement with recommended terms and conditions covers most possible scenarios, but this is not a guarantee against default. Sometimes, unforeseen events occur even in the best planned circumstances.

For summation, the major features and characteristics of FRAs, futures, and swaps are presented in Figure 13-5.

Feature	Swaps	FRAs	Futures
Traded over the counter (OTC) or exchange-traded	OTC	OTC	Exchange
Period covers	0–30 years	0–3 years	0–3 years
Amount of administration	Medium	Low	High
Credit risk	Medium	Medium	Low
Trade amounts	Variable	Variable	Standard
Can be cancelled or reversed	Cancelled or reversed	Reversed and rarely cancelled	Only reversed

FIGURE 13-5 Comparison of characteristics of swaps, FRAs, and futures.

SUMMARY OF VALUATION AND RISK MANAGEMENT SKILLS

1. Calculate modified duration and understand its use in immunizing a bond portfolio against interest-rate risk.

   Modified duration $=$ Macaulay duration$/(1 + r/n)$, which creates an elasticity measure for bond prices. A useful working definition of modified duration is the approximate percentage change in price for a 100 basis point change in yield. Modified duration can be used to immunize a bond portfolio against interest-rate risk. When the modified duration of a bond portfolio equals the investment horizon for the portfolio, the portfolio is immunized against interest-rate risk. That is, changes in interest rates have a minimal impact of the value of portfolio by the end of the investment horizon.

2. Understand the benefits of and the setup for a plain vanilla swap.

   The idea of a plain vanilla swap follows from the economic concept of comparative advantage, which suggests that traders should do what they do best and then trade for the other things they need. In a plain vanilla swap each party to the swap should get the best interest rate they can from the market and then swap for what they need. There must be an economic benefit for both parities to enter into the swap and the economic benefit is that both parties get a better rate in the swap than they can get directly from the market.

   In a plain vanilla swap the party that received a fixed rate in the market takes the (pay floating/receive fixed) side in the swap so they change to paying a floating rate. The party to the swap that received a floating rate from the market takes the (pay fixed/receive floating) side in the swap and therefore switches to paying a fixed rate. Both parties in the swap switch to a different payment stream at a better rate than they could get in the market.

3. Calculate the effective interest rate for both parties in a plain vanilla swap.

   Both parties in a swap have three cash flows: (1) payment to the market, (2) payment to the other party in the swap, and (3) receipt of payment from the other party in the swap. Thus, each party has two outflowing interest rates and one inflowing interest rate. Then, the effective interest rate for each party in the swap is the net rate on the three flows.

4. Value both sides of a plain vanilla swap.

   Valuing each side of a swap is just an application of classic time value of money principles. That is, for each side of the swap the cash flows are calculated and then discounted back to the point of valuation. The value of a swap is the net present value of the two cash flow streams. The one difficult step in valuing swaps is determining the *implied forward rates derived from the yield curve for each period.* However, this is particularly important because the implied forward rates determine the interest payments on the floating rate side of the swap and determine the discount factors for all the cash flows. Additionally, it is important to apply the correct day count convention when determining the cash flows and the discount factors.

QUESTIONS

1. What is the percent change in the value of a bond portfolio with a modified duration of 4.73 years with an increase in interest rates of 75 basis points?

2. What is the percent change in the value of a bond portfolio with a modified duration of 8.25 years with a decrease in interest rates of 45 basis points?

3. Use the cash flows of a portfolio of the following three bonds to calculate the yield to maturity of the portfolio. Each bond has a face value of $1,000. Use the cash flows and yield to maturity to calculate the duration of the portfolio.

    a. three-year zero-coupon bond with 5% yield,
    b. five-year zero-coupon bond with 7% yield, and
    c. seven-year zero-coupon bond with 6% yield.

Verify your portfolio duration calculation using the weighted average of the individual bond durations.

4. Calculate the yield to maturity and the duration of the following portfolio of bonds.

    a. one-year T-bill yielding 4.65%,
    b. three-year AAA-rated bond paying semiannual coupons at 5% with a yield of 5.25%,
    c. two-year BBB-rate bonds paying semiannual coupons at 5.5% with a yield of 6.75%.

5. Why is portfolio duration a useful tool for a bond portfolio manager?

6. When the duration of a bond matches the investment horizon of the investor, the investor's position is said to be immunized against interest-rate risk. What does immunized mean?

7. The most basic swap is called a plain vanilla swap. How does doing a plain vanilla swap relate to the concept of comparative advantage?

8. Calculate the effective interest rate paid by each party in the following plain vanilla swap.

Company A: AA-rated borrower that can borrow for three years at either 5% fixed or LIBOR plus 50 basis points.

Company B: BBB-rated borrower that can borrow for three years at either 8% fixed or LIBOR plus 150 basis points.

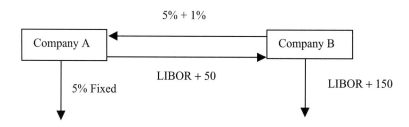

9. What is notional principal and why is the notional principal not part of the cash flows in a plain vanilla swap?

10. What role or roles does the yield curve have in valuing a plain vanilla swap?

11. Use the following annual implied forward rates to calculate the present value of the pay floating side of a three-year plain vanilla swap on notional principal of $25 million.

    Year 1 rate = 7%
    Year 2 rate = 7.5%
    Year 3 rate = 8%

12. Use the following annual implied forward rates to calculate the present value of the pay floating side of a three-year plain vanilla swap on notional principal of $65 million that pays semiannually.

Time period	Day count	Implied forward rate (%)
6 month	181	3.75
1 year	184	3.90
1.5 years	181	4.15
2 years	184	4.22
2.5 years	181	4.50
3 years	184	4.65

KEY TERMS

Basis Swap Floating interest payments that are exchanged for different floating interest payments in the same currency. The floating payments are either made at different frequencies based on the same benchmark rate, or at the same frequency with different benchmark rates.

Commodity Swap Fixed commodity price payments that are exchanged for floating commodity price payments.

Cross-market Spread Swap Where the manager moves out of one market and into another to exploit an advantageous yield relationship.

Currency Swap Exchange of fixed or floating interest payments that are denominated in two different currencies.

Day Count Conventions Methods used to identify the number of days in a month and a year to be used to calculate the amount of interest paid in a contract.

Duration A measure for the interest rate sensitivity of a bond or a bond portfolio.

Immunized Means to protect against something. In this chapter the protection is against changes in interest rates.

Interest-rate Risk The risk that the value of something will change with a change in market interest rate. Interest-rate risk is one of the primary risks to bondholders.

Macaulay Duration Standard duration calculation (see Chapter 5).

Modified Duration = Macaulay duration/$(1 + r/n)$. This provides an approximation for the percentage change in the price of a bond for a 100 basis point change in interest rates.

Notional Principal Amount of principal used in a swap agreement to determine the cash flows of a swap. This amount is referred to as notional principal because it is not one of the cash flows of the swap but instead is only used to calculate interest payment (cash flows) for the swap.

Plain Vanilla Swap Is the most common swap. A plain vanilla swap exchanges a fixed-rate coupon stream for a floating-rate coupon stream.

Rate Anticipation Swap Changes a portfolio's duration by swapping for new bonds that will achieve the target duration.

Spot Discount Factor Discount factor that discounts future cash flows back to the present.

Substitution Swap Exchanges one bond for another bond, identical in every respect except that there is a temporary price advantage resulting from an imbalance in supply and demand.

Swap An agreement to exchange cash flows at specified future times according to certain specified rules.

Yield Pickup Swap Is designed to capture long-term price movements. Suppose 20-year AA *industrial* bonds are currently yielding 8.5%. The manager might choose to swap some 20-year AA *utility* bonds currently yielding 8.25% in order to pick up an additional 25 basis points in yield.

13-A

HOW BANKS HEDGE A PLAIN VANILLA SWAP WITHOUT A COUNTERPARTY

In Chapter 13, swaps were defined and valued. One of the questions that often arises, especially for banks, is *what happens if a counterparty does not exist*? Does this mean that the bank is forced to take an exposure to interest-rate risk while it is trying to find a customer who is willing to take the other side of the swap that the bank has just committed to? The answer is *no*. A financial institution can hedge its position in the capital markets until the appropriate counterparty shows up. This appendix demonstrates how this hedge can be formed.

Before the illustration, one important point must be remembered: when a firm wants to receive floating-rate payments, it receives LIBOR only and *no* credit spread is required in the swap. The additional funds come from operations. In a similar fashion, the rate charged to a firm on the fixed payment side need *not* be the amount that the firm is obligated to pay the fixed-rate lender. Again, the additional funds come from operations.

Assume that the landfill from Chapter 13 wants to engage in a five-year, pay fixed, receive floating swap with your bank. Unfortunately, your bank does not have a counterparty for this transaction. What happens next? Take a look at Figure 13A-1.

Now, suppose that your bank agrees to be the counterparty to the landfill for a five-year fixed to floating interest rate swap. In reality, your bank will only remain a counterparty until it can find another client who will take the bank's place. Your bank will charge the landfill the Treasury bond rate plus a spread. How should the size of that spread be calculated? What hedging actions does your bank have to take?

Your bank will have a potential interest rate exposure since it has agreed to accept a fixed rate while it pays a variable rate. To hedge this position, your bank will go to its Bond Desk and arrange to borrow a sufficient number of five-year Treasury bonds to cover the hedge. These bonds will be sold in the bond market and cash will be received. Because the bonds have been borrowed, the bank is not entitled to receive the coupons; the owner of the bond is. Hence, the five-year Treasury bond rate paid by the landfill to the bank will go to compensate the lender (of the bonds) for the foregone coupon payments.

The cash received by your bank from the short sale of the bonds will now be invested in the money market to buy Treasury bills. Which Treasury bills should be purchased? This decision depends on the nature of the swap contract between the landfill and your bank. Assume that the contract dictates that cash flows will be exchanged semiannually. As a result, your bank will buy six-month Treasury bills. When the T-bill matures, your bank will receive the implied rate of return between the discounted value of the T-bill purchased

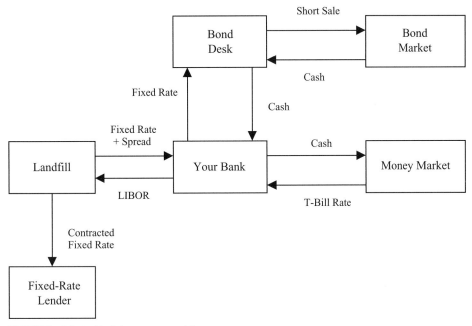

FIGURE 13A-1 Hedging a swap without a counterparty.

and the maturity value of the bill. Nonetheless, at the six-month reset point, your bank will have to pay the landfill the six-month LIBOR rate—*not* the six-month Treasury rate. Note that the six-month T-bill rate will be lower than the six-month LIBOR rate. Therefore, your bank will have a *loss* on this part of the transaction.

What do these transactions mean in terms of cash flows? The left-hand side of the equation will be the landfill's cash flows and the right-hand side will be the bank's cash flows. The equation is

Five-year Treasury rate + spread = five-year Treasury rate − six-month T-bill rate
+ six-month LIBOR.

The use of a little algebra determines that:

Spread = six-month LIBOR − six-month T-bill rate.

The calculation has been simplified here. Since your bank will not engage in any transaction that is not profitable and a small amount will have to be paid to the lender of the bonds, a (small) administrative charge will be added to the right-hand side of this calculation.

Assume the five-year T-bond rate is 7%, the six-month T-bill rate is 4%, LIBOR is 4.5%, and a 5 basis point administrative charge is routinely added by your bank. What rate does the landfill pay?

Spread = six-month LIBOR − six-month T-bill rate + administrative charge

Spread = 4.5% − 4% + 0.05%

Spread = 0.55%.

Hence, the total amount paid by the landfill will be 7.55% (7% fixed + 0.55% spread), and the total amount received will be 4.5%.

PRICING INTEREST RATE SWAPS AT DIFFERENT TIMES DURING THE LIFE OF A SWAP

13B-1 PRICING AN INTEREST RATE SWAP AT INITIATION

Like all financial instruments, a swap transaction has a net present value of zero at initiation. To demonstrate the basic premise of pricing, a one-year fixed for floating interest rate swap with a quarterly reset will be priced. Assume that the floating rate is based on 90-day LIBOR. Let the term structure for LIBOR over the next year be as follows:

$$L_0(90) \ = 0.07,$$
$$L_0(180) = 0.08,$$
$$L_0(270) = 0.10,$$
$$L_0(360) = 0.105.$$

Hence, $L_0(270) = 0.10$ states that the current annualized rate for 270-day LIBOR is 10%. At initiation, the present value of the expected floating rates and the expected value of the fixed rates must be the same. To accomplish this, the present values of the two cash flow streams must be equal:

$$\text{Fixed rate on swap} = \frac{1.0 - PV \text{ factor for fixed term}}{\text{sum of } PV \text{ factors for floating periods}}.$$

In this example, the PV factors for the floating periods would be

$$PV(90) = \frac{1}{1 + 0.07(90/360)} = 0.9828,$$

$$PV(180) = \frac{1}{1 + 0.08(180/360)} = 0.9615,$$

$$PV(270) = \frac{1}{1 + 0.10(270/360)} = 0.9302,$$

$$PV(360) = \frac{1}{1 + 0.105(360/360)} = 0.9050.$$

Therefore, the fixed rate on an interest rate swap with these expected LIBOR rates would be

$$\text{Fixed rate of swap} = \frac{(1 - 0.9050)}{(0.9828 + 0.9615 + 0.9302 + 0.9050)} = 0.02514.$$

For a fixed rate of 10.05% (0.02514×4) per year and given the current term structure, the resulting swap will have an initial value of zero.

13B-2 PRICING AN INTEREST RATE SWAP DURING ITS LIFE

The net present value of a swap need only be zero at initiation. At any other point, because of changing interest rates, a swap can have a positive or negative value depending on whether the floating rates have increased or decreased from the original expectation. For example, suppose that 60 days have passed since the swap in Section 13B-1 was entered into, and the term structure for LIBOR is now:

$$L_0(30) = 0.05,$$
$$L_0(120) = 0.07,$$
$$L_0(210) = 0.09,$$
$$L_0(300) = 0.095.$$

Suppose further the value of the swap is needed for financial reporting purposes. Given the new rates, the value of the fixed rate bond is

$$PV_{\text{fixed}} = \frac{0.02514}{1 + 0.05(30/360)} + \frac{0.02514}{1 + 0.07(120/360)} + \frac{0.02514}{1 + 0.09(210/360)}$$
$$+ \frac{1.02514}{1 + 0.095(300/360)} = 1.0234$$

Remember that the floating rate is paid in arrears; therefore, in 30 days' time, a floating rate payment of $0.07(90/360) = 0.0175$ will be made and the floating rate bond value will reset to 1.0. Hence, the value of-floating-rate bond must be

$$PV_{\text{floating}} = \frac{1.0175}{1 + 0.05(30/360)} = 1.0133.$$

And the value of the swap to each side of the swap must be

$$\text{Swap}_{(\text{receive fixed})} = 1.0234 - 1.0133 = 0.01.$$
$$\text{Swap}_{(\text{receive floating})} = 1.0133 - 1.0234 = -0.01.$$

Given that interest rates have fallen, the pay floating, receive fixed side of the swap has benefited by $0.01 \times$ notional principal and the pay fixed, receive floating side is receiving less than originally anticipated.

13B-3 PRICING A CURRENCY SWAP AT INITIATION

Using the U.S. currency as the domestic currency and the Swiss franc as the foreign currency, assume that at the initiation of the swap the current exchange rate is $0.80/SFr. For this currency swap, two interest rate term structures are involved: the United States and the Swiss. The same term structure of interest rates for the U.S. market as in the previous example will be used (see, Section 13B-1):

$$L_0(90) \ = 0.07,$$
$$L_0(180) = 0.08,$$
$$L_0(270) = 0.10,$$
$$L_0(360) = 0.105.$$

Using these rates, the U.S. dollar fixed rate of 10.05% was calculated previously. Assume that the Swiss term structure is

$$\text{SFr } L_0(90) \ = 0.035,$$
$$\text{SFr } L_0(180) = 0.04,$$
$$\text{SFr } L_0(270) = 0.05,$$
$$\text{SFr } L_0(360) = 0.0525.$$

Hence, SFr $L_0(270) = 0.05$ states that the current annualized rate for a 270-day zero-coupon bond denominated in Swiss francs is 5%. The *PV* factors based on Swiss rates are

$$SFr\_PV(90) = \frac{1}{1 + 0.035(90/360)} = 0.9913,$$

$$SFr\_PV(180) = \frac{1}{1 + 0.04(180/360)} = 0.9804,$$

$$SFr\_PV(270) = \frac{1}{1 + 0.05(270/360)} = 0.9639,$$

$$SFr\_PV(360) = \frac{1}{1 + 0.0525(360/360)} = 0.9501.$$

Therefore, the fixed rate on an interest rate swap with these expected Swiss rates would be

$$\text{Fixed rate of swap} = \frac{(1 - 0.9501)}{(0.9913 + 0.9804 + 0.9639 + 0.9501)} = 0.01284.$$

That is, a fixed rate of 5.14% (0.01284 × 4) per year, given the current Swiss term structure, will have an initial value of zero. Therefore, a currency swap involving U.S. dollars for Swiss francs would have a fixed rate of 10.05% in dollars and a fixed rate of 5.14% in Swiss francs. If the notional principal of the U.S. side were $1, then the notional principal on the Swiss side is SFr1.25 (1/0.8).

Using this information a choice of four possible swap arrangements are available:

Swap type	Pay	Receive
Pay one currency fixed and receive the other fixed	U.S. dollars fixed at 10.05%	Swiss francs fixed at 5.14%
Pay one currency fixed and receive the other floating	U.S. dollars fixed at 10.05%	Swiss francs floating
Pay one currency floating and receive the other fixed	U.S. dollars floating	Swiss francs fixed at 5.14%
Pay one currency floating and receive the other floating	U.S. dollars floating	Swiss francs floating

13B-4 PRICING A CURRENCY SWAP DURING ITS LIFE

Just as with an interest rate swap, a currency swap can be valued at any point in its life. Assume once again that 60 days have passed and now the U.S. term structure is

$$L_0(30) = 0.05,$$
$$L_0(120) = 0.07,$$
$$L_0(210) = 0.09,$$
$$L_0(300) = 0.095.$$

As known from Section 13B-2, the U.S. fixed-rate value was calculated to be 1.0234 and the floating rate value was 1.0133.

Assume that the new Swiss term structure at $t = 60$ is

$$\text{SFr } L_0(30) = 0.02,$$
$$\text{SFr } L_0(120) = 0.03,$$
$$\text{SFr } L_0(210) = 0.04,$$
$$\text{SFr } L_0(300) = 0.05.$$

Using the new Swiss rates and assuming they have a face value of SFr1, the value of the Swiss fixed-rate and floating-rate bonds at $t = 60$ is

$$SFr\_PV_{\text{fixed}} = \frac{0.01284}{1 + 0.02(30/360)} + \frac{0.01284}{1 + 0.03(120/360)} + \frac{0.01284}{1 + 0.04(210/360)}$$
$$+ \frac{1.01284}{1 + 0.05(300/360)} = 1.0104.$$

$$SFr\_PV_{\text{floating}} = \frac{1.00875}{1 + 0.02(30/360)} = 1.0071.$$

Now, to capture the true *PV* of the bonds on the Swiss side of the swap, multiply the *PVs* by 1.25 (the exchange rate) because the notional principal on the Swiss side is SFr1.25. Hence,

$$PV(\text{SFr}1.25, \text{fixed}) = 1.0104 \times 1.25 = 1.263.$$
$$PV(\text{SFr}1.25, \text{floating}) = 1.0071 \times 1.25 = 1.259.$$

Now, assume that over the 60-day period the dollar has weakened, the Swiss franc has strengthened, and the exchange rate is now $0.85/SFr. Using this exchange rate the Swiss present values can be converted to U.S. values as:

PV of Swiss franc fixed payments in U.S. dollars = 1.263 × 0.85 = $1.0736.

PV of Swiss franc floating payments in U.S. dollars = 1.259 × 0.85 = $1.0702.

Thus, the $t = 60$ values for any combination of the four swaps can be found.

Value of swap to pay SFr fixed
and receive U.S. dollars fixed   = −$1.0736 + $1.0234 = −$0.0502.

Value of swap to pay SFr floating
and receive U.S. dollars fixed   = −$1.0702 + $1.0234 = −$0.0468.

Value of swap to pay SFr fixed
and receive U.S. dollars floating = −$1.0736 + $1.0133 = −$0.0603.

Value of swap to pay SFr floating
and receive U.S. dollars fixed   = −$1.0702 + $1.0133 = −$0.0569.

The worst-case scenario is where one side pays Swiss francs fixed and receives U.S. dollars at a floating rate. The combination of the weakening dollar and declining interest rates results in a loss of $0.0603 times the notional principal for a party on this side of the swap. Of course, the counterparty in this swap which receives Swiss francs fixed and pays floating dollars is the beneficiary of these changes in market conditions.

CHAPTER *14*

MORTGAGE RISK MANAGEMENT

14.1 INTRODUCTION

The purpose of this chapter is to develop an understanding of risk management in the mortgage market. As has been discussed before, mortgages are fixed-income securities and therefore share many common features with the other fixed-income securities. Accordingly, mortgages share similar risk features and risk management techniques with the other fixed-income securities, such as the process discussed in Chapter 13 of reducing interest-rate risk by matching the duration to the investment horizon in bonds. The mortgage market is a huge market ($9.3 trillion dollars worth in the United States at the end of 2003), and banks and savings banks (previously savings and loans) originate most new mortgages. Therefore, the issue of risk management in the mortgage market is a significant issue for these financial institutions.

This chapter begins with a discussion of the major risks in the mortgage markets. Next, the securitization of mortgages is discussed, including discussion of the creation of mortgage-backed securities. The remainder of this chapter discusses the mortgage-backed securities (MBS) market, the risks in mortgage-backed securities, and how these risks are managed.

DEVELOPING VALUATION AND RISK MANAGEMENT SKILLS

1. Understand the primary risks of mortgages.
2. Understand the process of securitization in the mortgage markets and how securitization allows specialization in the mortgage markets.
3. Understand mortgage-backed securities (MBS) and how the creation of mortgage-backed securities alters risk management in the mortgage market.
4. Understand interest-rate risk management in the mortgage market.

14.2 MAJOR RISKS OF INVESTING IN WHOLE MORTGAGES

Chapter 6 touched on some of the risks faced by institutions that hold whole mortgages on their balance sheets. Now we discuss more specifics about the most important risks: liquidity risk, interest-rate risk (especially the impact of prepayments), and default risk.

14.2.1 Liquidity Risk

Liquidity risk is probably the most important risk faced by institutions that hold whole mortgages as investments. The problem, to summarize briefly, is that whole mortgages are highly illiquid.

A security's liquidity is a measure of how quickly and at what cost it can be sold or liquidated. Liquidity has two dimensions, the speed of the transaction and the cost associated with the transaction. Some risks can be measured fairly accurately. For example, a security's duration is a good measure of its interest-rate risk. Unfortunately, because liquidity has two dimensions to consider, a precise way of measuring liquidity risk is not available. Further, when it comes to measuring the cost of making a transaction (selling the security), a lot of different elements need to be considered. There are commissions to be paid. There may be a bid-ask spread to include, which is the difference between what it costs to buy the security and what it can be sold for. Depending on the volume one is trying to sell, the seller may have to worry that the supply being brought to the market may overwhelm the available demand and cause the equilibrium price to move. Finally, there's always the chance that a seller will be unable to find a buyer within the time frame needed for the transaction. All of these are liquidity issues.

Single mortgages are illiquid, in part because of the risk that the current owner will engage in a pattern of "cherry-picking" the portfolio. Cherry-picking occurs when the owner keeps the best loans and sells the worst. The current owner of a portfolio of whole mortgages is able to separate the better ones from the worse ones, because the current owner has access to useful information about each borrower that might not show up on a credit report, such as the borrower's payment history. A potential buyer cannot know whether the current owner will engage in cherry-picking or not, but a prudent investor will assume the worst and offer a price that reflects all problems that could exist.

Whole mortgages are also illiquid because the costs of analyzing them are high relative to their size. When an individual borrower refinances a house, the originator insists on a property appraisal, a credit check on the borrower, and a guarantee of clear title (lender's title insurance). The title insurance transfers if the mortgage is later sold to an investor, but the value of the property or the creditworthiness of the borrower might have changed and must be reanalyzed. This must be done for each mortgage.

Finally, there is no established secondary market for whole mortgages. This means that an institution that invests in whole mortgages and later decides to sell them will have to search for a buyer. In addition, it may be difficult to determine what the mortgages are worth because there isn't any public information available about previous transactions.

It may be easiest to see the impact of liquidity risk by looking at the market for a similar security, callable corporate bonds. Both mortgages and callable corporate bonds are fixed-income securities with embedded options and both are subject to default risk. However, an institution that wants to invest in callable corporate bonds can rely on regularly updated, freely available credit ratings from third party rating agencies such as Moody's or Standard and Poor's. The potential mortgage investor must do their own credit analysis. The bond investor will trade in an established market and can see the prices from previous transactions for the same bond and for other bonds with a similar maturity, coupon rate, call provisions, and credit rating. The bond investor can often get price quotes from multiple sellers of the exact same bond. The mortgage investor must analyze each mortgage separately, has no access to previous prices, and must worry about cherry-picking.

In all, whole mortgages are so illiquid that very few of them were ever traded prior to the introduction of widespread securitization. The mortgage market was almost entirely intermediated. The institution that originated the mortgage held it on the balance sheet until it prepaid or matured.

14.2.2 Interest-Rate Risk

Every fixed-income security is subject to some level of interest-rate risk that is closely associated to its maturity and can be measured fairly accurately, for small changes in interest rates, by its duration. Fixed-income security values are inversely related to changes in interest rates, rising when interest rates fall and vice versa. The larger the duration of the security, the bigger the reaction to any particular change in interest rates. Mortgages are fixed-income securities, like bonds and other loans, and therefore subject to the same kind of interest-rate risk as those securities.

If a portfolio of 30-year fixed-rate mortgages was to receive all principal and interest (P&I) payments as scheduled, the duration of the portfolio would be about 10 years. If, instead, the mortgages in the portfolio prepay at a CPR (cumulative prepayment rate, see Chapter 6 for a discussion) of 10%, the duration drops to about five years. At a CPR of 20%, the duration falls to a bit over three years, and at 30% it falls to a bit over two years. And therein lies the problem: the sensitivity of mortgage portfolios to interest rates changes a lot as interest rates change.

At high interest rates, the expected prepayment rate is very low and the duration of the mortgage portfolio is high. Another way of putting this is that mortgages act like very long-term securities when interest rates are high and long-term securities have a lot of interest-rate risk. At very low interest rates, the expected prepayment rate is very high and the duration of the mortgage portfolio is low.

In a sense, one could argue that mortgages are less risky when interest rates are low because they have such short durations in those circumstances. But this misses the point that prepayments cause expected cash flows to change when interest rates change, and the changes always occur in a way that hurts the investor. Figure 6-8 in Chapter 6 showed the impact of prepayments on mortgage values relative to a security for which the cash flows do not change. The prepayment option always makes it worse for the investor. When interest rates drop, the portfolio value goes up less for mortgages than for the security with fixed cash flows. When interest rates rise, the mortgage portfolio value goes down more. It is this pattern of negative convexity that makes interest-rate risk such an important issue for mortgage investors.

14.2.3 Default Risk

The fact that mortgages are fairly safe investments because they are loans secured by real property was discussed in Chapter 6. Further, over the years, standard lending terms have developed that make mortgage lending even less prone to default risk, including the following:

- **Overcollateralization**. The value of the collateral is higher than the loan balance, meaning that the initial loan-to-value (LTV) ratio is less than 100%.

- **Rising property values**. The value of the collateral usually rises over time.
- **Declining loan balances**. Part of each monthly P&I payment is used to pay down the loan balance, so the remaining balance decreases over time.
- **Tax and insurance escrows**. Money is collected each month to make necessary tax and insurance payments.
- **Private mortgage insurance (PMI)**. Typically required if the loan-to-value ratio is higher than 80%.

However, despite all of these advantages, defaults do occur. Further, when borrowers default, the investor holding the mortgage typically suffers a significant loss of value.

To provide a sense of typical default rates for mortgage portfolios, monthly delinquency rates experienced by Fannie Mae (the Federal National Mortgage Association) in 2003 were examined. For non-credit-enhanced, single-family mortgages (mortgages without PMI), loans that were three or more months delinquent or in the foreclosure process represented between 0.29 and 0.32% of the total. For credit-enhanced (low down payments, requiring PMI), single-family mortgages, the delinquency rate rose from 1.34% in January to 1.63% in December. Over the same time period, Fannie's multifamily mortgage delinquency rate rose from 0.03 to 0.13%. Fannie Mae has some limitations on what mortgages it will buy. Therefore, these delinquency rates may understate those that would be experienced in mortgage portfolios that do not conform to Fannie Mae's high standards. Also, delinquency rates will likely rise for all mortgage portfolios if the United States experiences a further economic downturn.

14.2.4 Geographic Concentration Risk

Another risk faced by investors in whole mortgages involves geographic concentration. Because whole mortgages are illiquid (see Section 14.2.1 of this chapter), the commercial bank or savings and loan (S&L or thrift) institution that originates a mortgage once held it until prepayment or maturity. Few of the thousands of banks and thrifts that originate mortgages have national networks of branches. In fact, most operate in only a single city, state, or region (depending on the institution's size).

Traditionally, this meant that many banks and thrifts held mortgage portfolios that were secured by property located in a single geographic region and guaranteed by borrowers who lived and worked in the same region. Although the national news doesn't often emphasize it, in a country as large as the United States with such a diverse economy, it is not at all unusual for some regions to experience economic problems while others experience an economic boom. For example, banks in a region dominated by textile manufacturing might suffer as factories are relocated overseas, workers lose their jobs, housing prices fall, and mortgage delinquencies rise. At the same time, banks in a region with a big population and high job growth might experience record low levels of defaults as rising property values make it possible for everyone to avoid default.

Clearly mortgage investors would be better off holding a portfolio of loans that have been originated in a wide variety of geographic locations just as stock market investors are better off holding a diverse portfolio. But without a secondary market for mortgages, such diversification is not possible.

14.3 MORTGAGE SECURITIZATION

In Chapter 6 the three major parts of mortgage lending—origination, servicing, and investment—were defined, and the fact that the mortgage market has undergone a process of disintermediation over the last 20 years was discussed. Through disintermediation, the three parts have been separated from one another and institutions have developed that specialize in one part or another. Of course, some financial institutions continue to operate in the traditional way, working in all three parts of the mortgage business.

Securitization is the process that has driven disintermediation in mortgage lending and other types of lending. In the **securitization** process, a large number of similar, illiquid loans (such as mortgage loans) are bundled together in an **asset pool**. A new set of securities is issued with promised payments that are based on the cash flows being received by the loans in the asset pool. These new securities are called **asset-backed securities** or ABS. As will be seen later, the cash flows can be divided between the owners of the ABS in a wide variety of ways. The only rule is that every dollar promised to the ABS investors must come from payments promised by borrowers of the loans in the asset pool.

In this section, the securitization process is described in detail, using residential mortgages as an example. This is how a pool of residential mortgages is used to create a **mortgage-backed security** or MBS, but the process described applies to all asset-backed securities. ABS are created from automobile loans, mobile home loans, second mortgages (home equity loans), student loans, credit card loans, small business loans, and other loans, but the volume of MBS is more than five times the volume of all other types of ABS combined. At the end of 2003, government-related mortgage pools totaled about $3.5 trillion and privately issued MBS added another $1.1 trillion. In contrast, nonmortgage ABS totaled $0.9 trillion, $0.6 trillion of which were backed by consumer credit and most of the rest by trade receivables.

The traditional model of mortgage lending is pictured in Figure 14-1. In this approach, the bank or other financial intermediary originates the mortgage according to its own **underwriting standards** using its deposits as a funding source. The mortgage is held on the bank's balance sheet, and the payments received from the borrower are used to pay interest to depositors, to pay the banks operating costs (salaries, buildings, etc.), and to pay dividends to shareholders or owners.

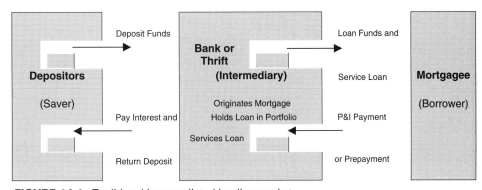

FIGURE 14-1 Traditional intermediated lending market.

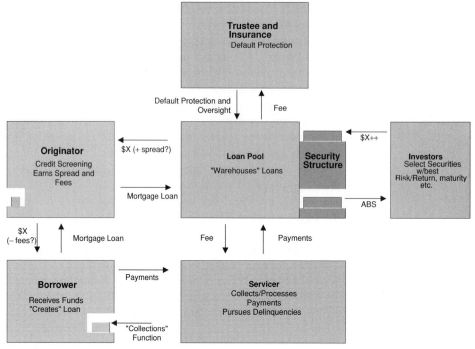

FIGURE 14-2 Securitized lending market.

As shown in Figure 6-2 of Chapter 6, securitization has come to dominate the mortgage market, with about 63% of residential mortgages being held in pools of government agencies or private ABS issuers and only about 30% held on the balance sheets of traditional intermediaries such as commercial banks and thrift institutions (at the end of 2003). Figure 14-2 provides a picture of the securitization process that leads to a disintermediated mortgage market. Each part of this process—origination, creation of the mortgage pool, servicing, trustee services and default protection, and creation of the MBS—is described next.

14.3.1 Mortgage Origination

The mortgage origination business requires that an originator make contact with a potential borrower, assist him or her in completing the loan application, and then make the lending (accept/reject) decision. This business has come to depend on computer models called **automated underwriting systems** that help make the decision to accept or reject the loan application. An originator need only input into the model certain information from the application and the applicant's credit report. The model then creates a score for the applicant. Applicants with high scores are accepted, those with low scores are rejected, and those with scores in between are asked to provide additional information or explanation. For many originators, automated underwriting systems are a **black box**. Numbers go in and a trustworthy answer comes out, but the originator does not necessarily understand how the answer is determined.

In a disintermediated market, the mortgage originator sells the loan on origination. In fact, the originator often enters into a commitment to sell the mortgage before it is originated. It is important to the originator that the mortgage be salable as the originator is not and does not want to be in the mortgage investment business. The originator's goal is to lend the same money over and over—loan the money to create a mortgage, sell the mortgage to get the money back, repeat—and earn fees or even a small profit each time. An originator may enter into an agreement with an MBS issuer such as FNMA, FHLMC, or a private ABS issuer, to sell all originations as they occur. In this case, the originator will follow underwriting guidelines required by the future purchaser of the mortgage and may also rely on an automated underwriting system that has been provided or approved by the purchaser.

When pursued in this manner, the mortgage origination business is fee-based. The goal of the originator is to earn a living from fees charged to the borrower, such as an origination fee, application fee, credit report fee, and so on. The originator may, on some occasions, also be able to sell the mortgage for more than the amount lent, if the coupon rate on the mortgage is higher than the prevailing market rate.

14.3.2 The Mortgage Pool

The institution that intends to issue an MBS must first assemble a pool of mortgages. This pool will usually contain mortgages that are relatively similar to one another. The mortgages might be purchased from a single originator or multiple originators. The mortgage pool may be from a single geographic region or be geographically diverse. Fixed-rate mortgages and ARMs will not be pooled together, nor will 30-year and 15-year mortgages. A pool will usually contain mortgages that were originated over a relatively short period of time and are of similar credit quality. This means that the mortgages will have similar, though not identical, coupon rates and similar LTV ratios.

When investors buy MBS, they want to be certain that the mortgages claimed by the pool actually exist and are owned by the pool. A trustee is hired to verify the existence of the mortgages and to ensure that they are not sold after the MBS is issued. In return for this service, the trustee earns a small fee, typically expressed as a percentage of the remaining principal balance of the pool.

The first MBS were guaranteed against default losses by **GNMA**, an agency of the U.S. government. Since then, MBS have been issued by government-related bodies like **FNMA** and **FHLMC** and by private issuers, but all of these have been insured against default losses, either by the issuer or by a third party insurer. Default protection transfers risk from the investor to the insurer. Insurers demand a fee for this protection, which is usually expressed as a percentage of the pool's remaining principal balance. The extent of default protection varies between insurers. Some guarantee timely payment of principal and interest, so a default by a borrower is treated like a prepayment and the investor does not suffer any kind of loss. Others guarantee only eventual payment of principal, meaning that the investor can lose promised interest payments and suffer time value losses between the date of default and the date of payment by the insurer.

14.3.3 Mortgage Servicing

When a mortgage is sold into a mortgage pool, the responsibility for servicing the mortgage is usually transferred to an independent mortgage servicer. The responsibility of the servicer is to collect the P&I payment from the borrower each month and transfer those funds back to the mortgage pool for distribution to the MBS investors. The servicer also collects tax and insurance escrow payments and makes sure that property taxes and property insurance premiums are paid when due. The servicer interacts with the borrower, answering any questions that might arise and resolving problems. Finally, the servicer is required to pursue delinquent payments and to force foreclosure if the borrower defaults on the mortgage.

The servicer is paid a fee for performing all of these functions, which is stated as a percentage of the remaining principal balance of the mortgage. The customary servicing fee is based on servicing costs from 20 years ago when the process was not very automated and servicers were much less efficient than they are today. The servicing business has become highly automated and servicers have made large investments in computer equipment and programs. This means that, for large servicers, the marginal cost of servicing a loan is much smaller than the fee earned, and the right to service a mortgage is a valuable asset. Servicers will pay for the right to service a loan, based on the value of the fees that are expected to be earned, net of the costs of providing servicing.

Servicing is a business characterized by economies-of-scale. As a servicer grows larger, the fixed costs of computer systems are spread over more and more loans and the average cost of servicing each loan drops. Over the years, a number of servicers have grown very large and the servicing business has become more and more concentrated, with the largest servicers accounting for an ever growing percentage of all servicing.

One potential problem with the servicing business is that the servicer has little incentive to provide high quality services to the borrower. The servicing fee is fixed regardless of how quickly the servicer answers the phone, whether or not mistakes are made in the handling of the borrower's escrow account, and so on.

14.3.4 The Mortgage-Backed Security

Once a mortgage pool has been assembled, the MBS structure must be determined. Some of the choices available are passthroughs, interest-only (IO) and principal-only (PO) strips, and collateralized mortgage obligation (CMOs) of various types. Details about these structures will be provided in Section 14.6 of this chapter.

The goal of the MBS issuer is to create a set of securities that have the highest possible value to investors. Suppose an issuer has spent $100 million putting a pool of mortgages together and is trying to decide whether to issue a passthrough security or a CMO structure. If the expected selling price of the passthrough is $101 million and the expected selling price of the CMO structure is $102 million, the issuer will create and market the CMO structure. If the values are reversed, the issuer will choose the passthrough security.

To design a security, the issuer starts with the expected cash flows of the mortgage pool and determines the rules that will govern how these cash flows will be distributed. The rules must account for possible prepayments and defaults. In essence, the MBS contract is the written instructions (and legal guarantees) describing how the cash flows will be divided up between investors, recognizing that each dollar received by the pool from the mortgage borrowers can be allocated to only one investor.

Once the MBS has been designed and sold, the issuer has no further role. The borrowers make payments (or prepayments) to the servicer, who sends those payments to the pool. The pool pays fees to the servicer, trustee, and insurer and distributes the remaining cash flows to investors according to the rules laid out in the MBS contract. The issuer's profit from creating the MBS came from selling the MBS for more money than was spent to assemble the mortgage pool, designing the MBS contracts, and marketing them to investors.

It is interesting to note that the servicer acts like a shield between the borrower and the investor. The borrower often has no idea whether his or her loan is a part of an MBS and certainly has no idea what investor ultimately receives each part of the monthly P&I payment that is sent in.

14.3.5 Rationale for Securitization

Now that the details of the securitization process for mortgages have been provided, it is useful to remind ourselves why this process has become so popular. In the days before securitization, mortgage borrowers were limited to a few local banks or thrifts. These financial institutions relied on the savings of local depositors.

When securitization is widespread, money (capital) flows much more freely between savers (investors) and mortgage borrowers and other borrowers. In a disintermediated mortgage market, the local supply and demand for savings is immaterial. The mortgage market is essentially national, with a single set of interest rates available to all borrowers, based on the type of loan and the credit quality of the borrower.

Investors who buy MBS do not care about the identity of the borrowers because they don't have to. They are insured against default losses. MBS issuers compete for investors by offering desirable security structures, reliable default protection, and superior returns. They are also anxious to develop new MBS structures that will appeal to additional groups of investors. Borrowers do not care who provides the money that they borrow; all they want is the lowest possible interest rate and low fees. Originators compete for borrowers by offering market rates, low costs, and superior service. Every participant in the disintermediated mortgage market must minimize costs or risk becoming uncompetitive. The result is a more efficient market that benefits both borrowers and investors.

14.4 MBS MARKET

The market for mortgage-backed securities is characterized by its investors, the issuers of securities, and the way that securities are traded after initial issue (the secondary market). Each is described in turn in this section.

14.4.1 MBS Investors

As was noted elsewhere, there were about $9.3 trillion in mortgages in the U.S. market at the end of 2003. These were owned by a variety of investors. Some of them are direct investors who originate mortgages and hold them until maturity or prepayment. Others are indirect investors who buy mortgage-backed securities.

Among direct investors, commercial banks, savings institutions, and credit unions held a significant portion of all mortgages, $3.3 trillion, on their balance sheets. Other direct investors held about $1 trillion. Included in this group were insurance companies and pension funds, which held about $0.3 trillion. Finance companies, mortgage companies, and real estate investment trusts also held about $0.3 trillion. Households and businesses held about $0.2 trillion, as did federal, state, and local governments combined.

The remaining $5.1 trillion were held in federally related mortgage pools ($3.5 trillion), by private issuers of asset-backed securities ($1.2 trillion), and by government-sponsored enterprises ($0.4 trillion). The first group includes mortgage pools guaranteed by the U.S. government (mostly through GNMA). It also includes mortgages held by federally chartered companies and the MBS they have issued (which are held by other investors).

Of the MBS guaranteed by federally related enterprises, U.S. commercial banks hold $0.5 trillion in passthroughs and about $0.2 trillion in CMOs and other structured MBS. They also held about $0.1 trillion in privately issued MBS. In addition, savings and loan institutions (thrifts) held more than $0.1 trillion in mortgage passthroughs.

It is difficult to determine precisely who holds the remaining MBS. In Federal Reserve reports, MBS are grouped together with securities issued by Sallie Mae (which securitizes student loans) and the Federal Home Loan Banks (which make secured loans to mortgage lenders). This group of securities is titled Other Agency and GSE (government-sponsored enterprise) Securities. At the end of 2003, there were $1.3 trillion in GSE-issued securities other than mortgages, which can be added to the $3.5 in federally related mortgage pools, for a total of $4.8 trillion. Figure 14-3 provides total holdings of this category for different types of financial institutions.

14.4.2 MBS Issuers

Ginnie Mae, a federal agency, provides guarantees against default losses for mortgages that are used to back privately issued MBS. The largest issuers of mortgage-backed securities

Type of Institution	2003
U.S. commercial banks	906.4
Savings and loans	198.7
Credit unions	115.5
Life insurance companies	361.8
Other insurance companies	126.3
Private pension funds	246.4
Government pension funds	159.8
Money market funds	326.2
Mutual funds	447.3

FIGURE 14-3 Holdings of other agency and GSE securities (in $billions).

Source: Federal Reserve System, Z-1 Releases.

are **Fannie Mae** and **Freddie Mac**, both of which are federally sponsored, publicly traded institutions. In addition to issuing MBS, both of these institutions buy mortgages to hold in portfolios and issue corporate bonds for funding. Finally, MBS are sometimes issued by private investment banks.

The Government National Mortgage Association (GNMA), more commonly known as Ginnie Mae, is an oddity—a government-owned corporation that is part of the Department of Housing and Urban Development. GNMA provides guarantees of timely payment of principal and interest for certain residential mortgages, mainly loans insured by the Federal Housing Administration (FHA) or guaranteed by the Department of Veterans Affairs (VA). GNMA-guaranteed mortgages are then pooled together and used to back MBS. GNMA charges a fee for providing default protection. The credit quality of GNMA-backed MBS is as high as that of U.S. Treasury securities. Both are backed by the "full faith and credit of the United States," the best guarantee currently available in world capital markets. At the end of 2002, GNMA had existing guarantees on $568.4 billion in residential mortgages.

The Federal National Mortgage Association (FNMA), more commonly known as Fannie Mae, was established by the U.S. government in 1938 to create a secondary market for home mortgages. At that time, all Fannie Mae did was buy FHA-insured mortgages. In 1968, Fannie Mae became a publicly traded, private company, responsible to its shareholders. Fannie Mae buys mortgages from independent originators. Some of these mortgages are packaged into pools and used to create MBS that Fannie sells to private investors. Fannie insures the mortgages in these pools against default losses. The remaining mortgages are held on Fannie's balance sheet. Funding for these mortgages comes from corporate bonds that Fannie issues and from retained earnings. At the end of 2003, Fannie was insuring $1.3 trillion in mortgages used to secure MBS and held $0.9 trillion in mortgages on its balance sheet.

The Federal Home Loan Mortgage Corporation (FHLMC), more commonly known as Freddie Mac, was chartered by the U.S. Congress in 1970. Like Fannie Mae, Freddie Mac is a publicly traded corporation that buys mortgages from originators. Freddie insures some of these mortgages against default losses and uses them to secure MBS. Others are kept on Freddie's balance sheet. Funding for mortgages held in portfolio comes from issuing bonds and from shareholder equity. At the end of 2003, Freddie was insuring $0.7 trillion in mortgages used to secure MBS and held $0.7 trillion in mortgages on its balance sheet.

Clearly, Ginnie, Fannie, and Freddie play a key role in the U.S. mortgage market. Together, they hold or insure about $4.1 trillion in mortgages, or almost 44% of the entire market. There are other issuers and insurers of mortgages, but no other single one plays a noteworthy role in the market. They are niche players, dealing in mortgages that do not conform to Ginnie, Fannie, or Freddie underwriting standards, or creating unusual MBS structures.

Mortgages that do not conform to agency (Ginnie, Fannie, or Freddie) standards are called **nonconforming**. Some are nonconforming because they are too large. These are known as **jumbo** loans. Others are nonconforming because the borrowers are of too low a credit quality. These are known as **subprime** loans. MBS backed by nonconforming mortgages or insured by parties other than Ginnie, Fannie, or Freddie, will offer higher returns than those issued or insured by the agencies.

INDUSTRY APPLICATION

FANNIE MAE (THE FEDERAL NATIONAL MORTGAGE ASSOCIATION) ACCOUNTING AND RISK ISSUES

Back in Chapter 6, we showed you how companies such as Fannie Mae purchased pools of home mortgages by issuing bonds to institutional investors and then issuing highly liquid MBS to the investing public. Companies such as Fannie Mae are overseen by the Office of Federal Housing Enterprise Oversight (OFHEO) to ensure that these institutions do not violate their in-house policy guidelines and thus, do not present an unnecessary risk to the financial markets. Understanding the basics of risk management as described in Chapter 11 is crucial to avoiding problems with regulators. Often, these problems are caught at the entry and "worker bee" levels within an organization.

In 2004, OFHEO identified numerous problems with Fannie Mae's accounting practices, including deficiencies in recording some securities and loan transactions.[1] Like many financial institutions, Fannie Mae must keep a certain amount of capital as reserves against unforeseen problems and illiquidity. In February 2005, OFHEO approved and extended a plan to restore inadequate capital reserves and raise an additional 30% surcharge imposed until the books are in order—Fannie Mae was given until the end of September to raise its capital levels. Fannie Mae itself estimated that correcting the errors identified by OFHEO in September 2004 would show that it had overstated earnings from 2001 through mid-2004 by more than $9 billion after tax.

Alan Greenspan, in testimony before the House Financial Services Committee, called for severe reductions in the mortgage holdings of both Fannie Mae and Freddie Mac (Federal Home Loan Mortgage Corpora-

tion). Dr. Greenspan suggested that these institutions should not hold mortgages totaling more than $100 billion to $200 billion each. At the time, Fannie Mae's portfolio was estimated at approximately $905 billion.

By April 2004, the magnitude of Fannie Mae's accounting problems was still somewhat unclear, although the estimate of the profit restatement had risen to $11 billion. In particular, OFHEO was examining how Fannie Mae accounted for trusts as "qualifying special purpose entities" under FAS 140. By treating these trusts in this fashion, Fannie Mae kept both the assets and liabilities off of the company's balance sheet.

These trusts were used to issue mortgage-back securities (MBS), which Fannie Mae creates by purchasing mortgages in the secondary market and then bundling them into trusts for sale as MBS. If OFHEO decides that Fannie Mae should have accounted for these trusts on its balance sheet, it would substantially boost the amount of capital the company must hold, since reserve capital is determined in part by the amount of assets on its books. The regulator and the Securities and Exchange Commission (SEC) are also looking into accounting problems dealing with FAS 91 on accounting for fees and costs associated with originating or acquiring loans and FAS 133 on accounting for derivatives and hedging activities in addition to several other areas of potential accounting standards violations.

OFHEO has also reported instances where Fannie Mae employees falsified signatures on accounting ledgers and made changes to earnings-related records without following the appropriate procedures.

14.4.3 MBS Secondary Market

The secondary market for MBS is an over-the-counter (OTC) market. Like corporate bonds, many MBS issues are purchased by financial institutions like insurance companies and pension funds as long-term investments. These rarely trade. Other investors, such as mutual funds and various institutional investors, trade more actively.

Common practice when buying or selling MBS is to contact two or three bond brokers and get a quote, picking the lowest (ask) price if buying and the highest (bid) price if selling.

---

[1] For an excellent summary of these issues go to www.nysscpa.org.

However, when comparing ask prices, it is important to recognize that different dealers may be quoting prices for different securities. Even the simplest MBS passthroughs can vary greatly from one another on the coupon rates, remaining maturities, remaining principal balances, LTV ratios, geographic location, and other characteristics of the mortgages in the underlying pool. When comparing complex securities, such as CMOs, even more variation is possible. There are also slight differences in the level of default protection offered by GNMA, FNMA, FHLMC, and private insurers that will affect price comparisons across securities.

It is important to realize that widespread securitization has made it *easier* to trade mortgages (in the form of MBS), but it has not made it easy in the sense that trading a share of common stock is easy or trading a U.S. Treasury bond is easy. Mortgage trading and investing is best suited to fixed-income specialists, not individual investors.

14.5 IMPACT OF SECURITIZATION ON RISK

Widespread securitization of mortgages has reduced many of the risks associated with mortgage investment. But it has also created a few new risks that must be considered. In this section, the reduction in certain risks and the introduction of others that accompanies mortgage securitization will be discussed.

14.5.1 Liquidity Risk

As discussed earlier in this chapter, absent a securitization process, whole mortgages are essentially unsellable. When securitization is widespread, the liquidity of mortgages is vastly enhanced.

First, the presence of MBS issuers in the marketplace creates a demand for whole mortgages. MBS issuers make money by purchasing whole mortgages, bundling them together, and selling securities based on the resultant pool. Therefore, within certain guidelines, MBS issuers stand ready to purchase whole mortgages that conform to their underwriting standards. It is true that **seasoned mortgages**—those that were originated more than a year or two ago—are less liquid than new (unseasoned) mortgages, but the advent of widespread mortgage securitization has lead to a great increase in the liquidity of mortgages.

On top of this, MBS are much more liquid than whole mortgages. If an investor desires securities with mortgage-like characteristics but is concerned about liquidity, investment in MBS is the answer. This increased liquidity is not costless. The fees for trustees and servicing must be deducted from the mortgage pool's cash inflows before payments are made to MBS investors. In addition, MBS issuers will only continue to operate if they are able to earn a profit, in the form of a higher price paid for the MBS than the cost of buying the underlying mortgages and setting up the pool and security structure.

14.5.2 Interest-Rate Risk

The interest-rate risk of the underlying mortgages is not reduced by the securitization process. The weighted-average duration of the MBS that are issued must equal the duration of the underlying pool of mortgages. However, as will be seen when the variety of MBS structures are discussed in the next section of this chapter, it is possible to create a set of securities, each of which has very different levels of interest-rate risk from the underlying pool. The only requirement is that the total risk of the complete set of MBS secured by a particular pool must equal the interest-rate risk of the pool; that is, the sum of the risk of the parts must equal the risk of the whole.

Later, in Section 14.6, using the IO and PO strip structure to create an MBS that has a negative duration will be demonstrated. In other words, this security benefits (rises in value) from increases in interest rates. Using the most common CMO structure, it is possible to create securities that have higher durations and lower durations than the underlying pool of mortgages. In the end, the securitization process cannot get rid of interest-rate risk, but it can allocate it across investors in very creative ways.

14.5.3 Default Risk

Most mortgage securitizations are essentially free from default risk. MBS guaranteed by GNMA or issued by FNMA or FHLMC are insured against losses arising from default. The GNMA guarantee carries with it the full faith and credit of the U.S. government. Further, MBS prices suggest that investors accept FNMA and FHLMC guarantees as very close to the "full faith and credit" guarantee offered by GNMA. Other MBS issuers strive to structure their offerings in ways that do away with default risk, either through use of exceptionally well-regarded private insurers or through overcollateralization. In this context, overcollateralization refers to the practice of having more mortgages in the pool than securities in the MBS structure.

14.5.4 Geographic Risk

Widespread securitization also virtually eliminates problems of geographic concentration. If a traditional financial intermediary, such as a bank, wishes to diversify its mortgage holdings across geographic boundaries, it can sell part of its portfolio to an MBS issuer and use the proceeds to purchase MBS. By intention, the MBS purchased would be based on mortgages originated in geographic regions that the bank does not service. This would diversify away the bank's geographic concentration risk.

Another recent financial market innovation that allows banks to manage geographic concentration in a loan portfolio is credit derivatives. Credit derivatives will be discussed in Chapter 19.

14.5.5 Newly Created Risks

Although widespread securitization has generally decreased the risks associated with mortgage investment, the practice has also introduced some new risks. The first of these is **systemic risk**, which refers to the risk that the market as a whole will experience a breakdown. Because a small group of market participants (Fannie Mae and Freddie Mac) own or are responsible for insuring such a large portion of the residential mortgage market (more than 50% by most accounts), the failure of one of these institutions could have a large, even catastrophic impact on the mortgage market as a whole. Market participants got a glimpse of this when it was revealed that Freddie had engaged in some very questionable accounting practices that significantly misstated its performance (see **In The News**, below). The biggest fear among mortgage market participants is that Fannie or Freddie will fail to manage the risk of its large whole mortgage portfolio and become insolvent.

Another risk that has been introduced by widespread securitization is the **servicer risk** that comes from having a third party service the mortgage. The servicer is the contact for the mortgage borrower. If the servicer does a poor job interacting with the borrower, that poor service may influence the borrower's repayment or prepayment decisions. In addition, the servicer acts as a fiduciary for the insurer of the mortgage pool and the MBS investor by pursuing late payments and, if necessary, foreclosing on the property securing the loan. If a servicer fails, on a systematic basis, to enforce the terms of the mortgage contracts it is servicing, this failure could significantly impact the value of the mortgage pool and the MBS issued from it.

Yet another risk that has been introduced by widespread securitization and investment in MBS is **model risk**. In the traditionally intermediated mortgage market, a bank used its own underwriting guidelines when originating a mortgage, serviced that mortgage, and held it until it was repaid or prepaid. There was little use of complex financial modeling in this market structure. In the disintermediated world of mortgage securitization, automated models are used to make the initial lending decision, and valuation models are used to price MBS. In many cases, an investor purchases a valuation model from a third party vendor and simply trusts that it works. There is always the risk that the model will prove to be inaccurate to a significant degree.

IN THE NEWS

ACCOUNTING PROBLEMS AT FREDDIE MAC: SYSTEMIC RISK IN ACTION

In 2003, another big accounting scandal hit the news; but this time, it wasn't a high-flying Wall Street firm or some "get rich quick" energy company that was at fault. It was Freddie Mac, the company that, together with Fannie Mae, owns or guarantees well over 50% of all U.S. residential mortgages. In many ways, Fannie and Freddie *are* the mortgage market. Suddenly, systemic risk stopped being a dry academic theory or a discussion among regulators, and became a real concern. Investors and *Wall Street Journal* editors began asking, "What would happen if Freddie or Fannie (or both) failed? Could the mortgage market and the housing market survive? Would the U.S. economy survive?"

The odd thing is, Freddie is not, for the most part, accused of hiding losses or pretending to earn a profit it didn't make; it's accused of hiding profits. In 2000

and 2001, Freddie made about $1.3 billion more income than it (or Wall Street) had projected. Freddie's executives did not want to reveal that sharp spike up in profits, because they knew it was not sustainable. Instead, they found ways to hide the profit for a while and move it to future years. What Freddie and every other publicly traded company knows is that investors and Wall Street analysts (those who actually do any analysis, that is) want is a slow and steady increase in profits over the years, not wide fluctuations up and down. Fluctuation equals volatility equals risk, and investors don't want risk. What Freddie's executives should have known is that it is unlawful to manipulate earnings *up or down*. (In addition, it now appears that Freddie did hide some losses in 2002, in addition to hiding big gains in 2000 and 2001.)

(continued)

ACCOUNTING PROBLEMS AT FREDDIE MAC: SYSTEMIC RISK IN ACTION

All told, Freddie undercounted earnings by about $4.5 billion during the 2000 to 2002 period. More importantly, Freddie significantly understated the quarter-by-quarter volatility of its earnings, lying to the investing public about how risky it was. There's been significant reaction. Two consecutive CEOs have lost their jobs because of the scandal. Its stock price has been clobbered by about 20%, despite record profits in the mortgage industry. Further, there is significant talk in Washington about increasing the regulatory oversight of Fannie and Freddie. Specific procedures for liquidating assets should either firm enter bankruptcy have also been drafted.

It is unclear, though, how far these legislative and regulatory efforts will go. Part of the magic that has driven Freddie's and Fannie's growth is the perception that their investors need not worry about bankruptcy. This has allowed them to borrow in the "agency" market, at rates only slightly higher than those on U.S. Treasury securities. These low rates are passed on to mortgage borrowers, which include most U.S. consumers. The existence of Freddie and Fannie in the U.S. mortgage market is estimated to cut about 0.5% off of residential mortgage rates. Multiply that by the $7 trillion in residential mortgages and that's a lot of extra money for U.S. consumers to spend and a lot of big new houses being built and furnished. Neither the U.S. congress nor U.S. regulators are anxious to do anything that might put the breaks on economic growth. What's more, both Fannie and Freddie are experts at lobbying and know just how to use hot-button consumer and housing issues to avoid new regulations and controls.

Ultimately, Fannie and Freddie are likely to remain the powerhouses of the U.S. mortgage market for the foreseeable future. And as long as two firms control more than half of that huge, important market, systemic risk will be a concern.

14.6 MBS STRUCTURES

The structure of a set of mortgage-backed securities is a set of rules that define which investors receive the cash flows that come to the pool in the form of borrower payments. Interest cash flows and principal cash flows are treated differently. When a mortgage borrower makes a payment to the servicer, the payment is credited first to the interest that has accrued on the loan. Any remaining amount is credited against the unpaid principal balance. All servicing, trustee, and insurance fees are paid out of interest.

In this section of the chapter the three common MBS structures will be discussed in detail and an example of each of them will be provided. The three are passthroughs, IO and PO strips, and CMOs. In addition, a brief discussion of some less common types of CMOs, such as the planned amortization class (PAC) and companion pair and the floater and inverse floater pair, will be provided. How the cash flows received by a mortgage pool are divided up according to the MBS structure will be explained. For simplicity, a common example of a fixed-rate mortgage pool will be used. The details of the common example are

1. a mortgage pool with a total remaining principal balance of $100,000,000,
2. a WAC (weighted-average coupon) of 6.50%, and
3. a WAM (weighted-average maturity) of 10 years will be used.

	Balance:	$100,000,000
	WAC:	6.50%
	WAM:	10
	CPR:	20.00%
	Fees:	0.70%

#	P&I payment ($)	Principal cash flow ($)	Interest cash flow ($)	Prepayment cash flow ($)	Fees ($)	Remaining balance ($)	Total cash flow ($)	Total interest cash flow ($)	Total principal cash flow ($)
0						100,000,000			
1	13,910,469	7,410,469	6,500,000	18,517,906	700,000	74,071,625	31,728,375	5,800,000	25,928,375
2	11,128,375	6,313,720	4,814,656	13,551,581	518,501	54,206,324	24,161,455	4,296,154	19,865,301
3	8,902,700	5,379,289	3,523,411	9,765,407	379,444	39,061,628	18,288,663	3,143,967	15,144,696
4	7,122,160	4,583,154	2,539,006	6,895,695	273,431	27,582,779	13,744,423	2,265,574	11,478,849
5	5,697,728	3,904,847	1,792,881	4,735,586	193,079	18,942,345	10,240,235	1,599,801	8,640,434
6	4,558,182	3,326,930	1,231,252	3,123,083	132,596	12,492,332	7,548,669	1,098,656	6,450,013
7	3,646,546	2,834,544	812,002	1,931,558	87,446	7,726,230	5,490,657	724,555	4,766,102
8	2,917,237	2,415,032	502,205	1,062,240	54,084	4,248,959	3,925,393	448,121	3,477,272
9	2,333,789	2,057,607	276,182	438,270	29,743	1,753,081	2,742,317	246,440	2,495,877
10	1,867,032	1,753,081	113,950	0	12,272	0	1,854,760	101,679	1,753,081

FIGURE 14-4 Mortgage pool expected cash flows.

4. The pool is insured against default losses, so any defaults are treated as prepayments. Prepayments, including defaults, are expected to occur at a CPR (cumulative prepayment rate) of 20%.

5. Servicing fees, trustee fees, and default insurance fees are paid out of interest at an annual rate of 70 bps (0.70%) of the remaining principal balance.

In order to make the examples manageable, one *very unrealistic* assumption will be made: all payments are assumed to occur once per year, rather than once per month. The only reason for making this assumption is so that the examples will fit on figures in this textbook. In reality, MBS payments match the underlying mortgage payments and occur on a monthly basis.

Figure 14-4 provides the expected cash flows for this pool of mortgages, given the expected prepayment rate. Notice that a column for fees has been included. The fees include servicing, trustee, and insurance fees. The fees are deducted from the cash inflows when calculating the total cash flow to the pool. In the first year the total expected cash flow of $31,728,375 is equal to

1. the expected P&I payment of $13,910,469
2. *plus* the expected prepayment cash flow of $18,517,906
3. *less* the expected fees of $700,000.

Columns for total interest cash flow and total principal cash flow are included. The total interest cash flow equals the interest part of the scheduled P&I payment less fees. In the first year, the interest cash flow of $5,800,000 is equal to

1. the interest from the P&I payment of $6,500,000
2. *less* the fees of $700,000.

The total principal cash flow equals the principal part of the scheduled P&I payment plus the expected prepayment cash flow. In the first year, the principal cash flow of $25,928,375 is equal to

1. the principal from the P&I payment of $7,410,469
2. *plus* the expected prepayment cash flow of $18,517,906.

The examples only include the calculation of the expected cash flows for each of the MBS examples. The examples will not include an attempt to determine the present value of each. This would require the determination of the appropriate risk-adjusted discount rates for each piece of the MBS, which is difficult to do for many of the more complex MBS structures.

EXAMPLE *Passthroughs*

The mortgage **passthrough security** has a very simple structure. The cash flows from the pool are divided evenly between a fixed number of shareholders. Every dollar received by the pool (net of fees) passes through to the investors on a pro rata basis. The annual expected cash flow for each share is found by dividing the expected cash flow for the pool by the number of shares. For example, suppose that a mortgage passthrough with 800 shares was issued and backed by the example 10-year pool of

##	Pool total cash flow ($)	Passthrough share cash flow ($)
	Number of Shares:	800
0		
1	31,728,375	39,660
2	24,161,455	30,202
3	18,288,663	22,861
4	13,744,423	17,181
5	10,240,235	12,800
6	7,548,669	9,436
7	5,490,657	6,863
8	3,925,393	4,907
9	2,742,317	3,428
10	1,854,760	2,318

FIGURE 14-5 Mortgage passthrough security.

fixed-rate mortgages. The expected cash flow for one share is given in Figure 14-5. Each annual cash flow is equal to the expected cash flow for the pool from Figure 14-4 divided by 800. For example, in the first year, the total expected cash flow for the pool is $31,728,375, so each passthrough share is expected to receive $39,660 (= $31,728,375/800).

Owning a mortgage passthrough security is like owning shares in a mutual fund. It entitles the investor to an equal share of all profits and losses, after fees. Mortgage passthroughs are a good choice for investors who are comfortable accepting mortgage prepayment risk, but uncomfortable with mortgage default risk. They also make sense if the investor wants to own mortgages but is too small or lacks the expertise needed to be able to create a diversified portfolio of whole mortgages. Mortgage passthroughs also share the liquidity benefits provided by all securitizations. An investor who buys a share in a mortgage passthrough knows that there will be an active secondary market available if the investor decides to sell it in the future.

EXAMPLE *IO and PO Strips*

The structure of an **interest-only strip** (IO strip) and **principal-only strip** (PO strip) is only slightly more complicated than the mortgage passthrough. But the characteristics of the resulting securities are very different from the underlying mortgages. This difference provides a reminder that securitization allows the creation of cash flow patterns that are not found elsewhere. This is why different MBS appeal to different investors.

IO strips and PO strips must be created together; you cannot have one without the other. The issuer decides how many identical IO strip securities there will be and how many identical PO strip securities there will be. The number of IO strip shares and the number of PO strip shares can be different. All of the interest cash flow to the pool is divided evenly between the IO strip shares, and all of the principal cash flow is divided between the PO strip shares. It is that simple.

For example, suppose that an MBS with a strip structure was created from the example 10-year pool of fixed-rate mortgages. The issuer decides to create 250 identical IO strip shares and 600 identical PO strip shares. Figure 14-6 shows the annual expected cash flow to each IO strip share and each PO strip share. This is based on the total expected interest cash flow and total expected principal cash flow from Figure 14-4. For example, in the first year, the pool is expected to receive $5,800,000

Number of IO Shares:		250		
Number of PO Shares:		600		

##	Pool interest cash flow ($)	IO strip share cash flow ($)	Pool principal cash flow ($)	PO strip share cash flow ($)
0				
1	5,800,000	23,200	25,928,375	43,214
2	4,296,154	17,185	19,865,301	33,109
3	3,143,967	12,576	15,144,696	25,241
4	2,265,574	9,062	11,478,849	19,131
5	1,599,801	6,399	8,640,434	14,401
6	1,098,656	4,395	6,450,013	10,750
7	724,555	2,898	4,766,102	7,944
8	448,121	1,792	3,477,272	5,795
9	246,440	986	2,495,877	4,160
10	101,679	407	1,753,081	2,922

FIGURE 14-6 IO and PO strip securities.

in interest cash flows, net of fees, so each IO strip share will receive $23,200 (= $5,800,000/250). The pool is also expected to received $25,928,375 in principal cash flows, including prepayments, so each PO strip share will receive $43,214 (= $25,928,375/600).

IO strips will attract a different set of investors than PO strips. This is due, in part, to the fact that IO strips and PO strips react very differently to changes in interest rates. To see this, consider what will happen if interest rates fall. The prepayment rate on the mortgage pool will rise. Higher prepayments mean that principal will be returned to the pool at a quicker pace, which benefits PO investors. PO investors know up front that there is a fixed amount of principal that will be repaid to them. The only question they face is how quickly they will be repaid. Because of time value of money effects, they prefer to receive repayment faster rather than slower. So PO investors like falling interest rates because they imply higher prepayment rates and increasing PO strip values. A PO investor's dream is to buy a PO strip and have every mortgage in the pool prepay in full the very next day.

On the other hand, if a mortgage borrower prepays, he or she immediately stops paying interest, which means that the IO investor's cash flows from that mortgage stop immediately. This means that IO investors dislike falling interest rates because they lead to rising prepayments and prepaid mortgages don't pay interest. An IO investor's dream is to buy an IO strip and have absolutely no prepayments ever occur in the underlying mortgage pool.

The opposite is true for rising interest rates. PO investors hate them because rising rates lead to low prepayment rates and slower return of principal. IO investors love them because low prepayments means that borrowers make interest payments for a longer period of time.

The interesting thing is that by applying a simple rule to mortgage cash flows—give the interest to one group of investors and the principal to another group—we have created securities with very different characteristics. In fact, IO strips are among the most unusual securities available because they tend to *increase in value when interest rates increase*. This would be impossible for a security with fixed cash flows, but the IO's expected cash flows increase substantially when interest rates increase.

EXAMPLE *CMOs*

A **collateralized mortgage obligation**, or **CMO**, is an MBS structure that creates short-term and long-term securities out of a pool of mortgages. The basic idea of the CMO structure is to create a set of securities that receive principal repayments (and prepayments) one after another. Each of these securities is called a **tranche**, which means "a part of something." Each tranche is assigned a letter that indicates the type of tranche and the order in which it will receive principal payments.

A generic CMO offering that is based on a pool of fixed-rate mortgages will contain three types of tranches. The first are the sequential, fixed-rate tranches that will be named A, B, C, etc. Each **sequential tranche**, which will be divided into a number of identical shares, will have a principal balance and fixed coupon rate associated with it. All principal received by the mortgage pool goes to the A-tranche until it is repaid in full. Then the B-tranche receives all principal until it is repaid in full. Then C-tranche (if there is one), and so on, until all sequential tranches have been repaid. Every sequential tranche receives interest each period based on its coupon rate and remaining principal balance at the beginning of the period.

Another tranche commonly found in CMO structures is the **zero-coupon tranche** or Z-tranche. Also called an accretion bond or accrual bond, a Z-tranche has an initial principal balance and an earnings rate. As long as tranches ahead of it in repayment priority are still being repaid, the Z-tranche receives no cash flows, not even interest. Instead, its principal balance grows each period to reflect interest accruing at the earnings rate. The Z-tranche is usually, but not always, the last tranche to be repaid. One issue that arises with a Z-tranche is that its eventual principal balance is unknown. If prepayments occur at a faster rate than expected, the Z-tranche will have little time to grow, so its repayment is certain. If, instead, prepayments slow down, the Z-tranche might grow very large before all of the tranches in front of it are repaid. There is always some risk that there would not be enough principal left in the pool to repay the Z-tranche in full.

The final type of tranche is the **residual tranche** or R-tranche. Sometimes called an equity tranche and other times a junk tranche, the R-tranche gets any cash flow that does not contractually belong to another tranche. As long as other tranches are still being repaid, all principal payments and prepayments go to those tranches, but the total interest due to the tranches may be less than the interest received by the pool (net of fees). If so, that extra interest belongs to the R-tranche. In addition, it is common for CMO issuers to leave some principal unaccounted for after totaling up the principal balances of the sequential tranches and the expected future principal balance of the Z-tranche. At the end of the life of the mortgage pool, if all of the other tranches have been repaid, the R-tranche will receive any remaining principal. In some cases, CMO issuers keep the R-tranche on their books as their equity in the mortgage pool. In other cases, the R-tranche is sold. Obviously, this is the riskiest part of the CMO structure because it has the most junior claim to any cash flow. In addition, many CMO structures require that excess interest payments be placed in escrow until all of the required principal repayments are made, so even if the R-tranche appears to be receiving cash flow, its owners may not be able to access that cash flow for many years.

As an example of a simple CMO structure based on the example 10-year pool of fixed-rate mortgages, Figure 14-7 details a CMO with two fixed-rate, sequential tranches, a zero-coupon tranche, and a residual tranche. The CMO structure is

1. A-tranche with a principal balance of $45 million, the coupon rate is 4.50%, and 400 identical shares;

2. B-tranche with a principal balance of $30 million, the coupon rate is 5.50%, and 300 identical shares; and

3. Z-tranche with an initial principal balance of $12 million, an earnings rate of 7.00%, and 200 identical shares.

			A-tranche	B-tranche	Z-tranche
			$45,000,000	$30,000,000	$15,000,000
Principal Balance			4.50%	5.50%	7.00%
Coupon/Earnings Rate					
Number of Shares			400	300	200

	Pool interest cash flow ($)	Pool principal cash flow ($)	A-tranche Interest cash flow ($)	A-tranche Principal cash flow ($)	A-tranche Principal balance ($)	B-tranche Interest cash flow ($)	B-tranche Principal cash flow ($)	B-tranche Principal balance ($)	Z-tranche Interest accrual ($)	Z-tranche Principal cash flow ($)	Z-tranche Principal balance ($)	R-tranche cash flow ($)
0					45,000,000			30,000,000			1,50,00,000	
1	5,800,000	25,928,375	2,025,000	25,928,375	19,071,625	1,650,000	0	30,000,000	10,50,000	0	1,60,50,000	2,125,000
2	4,296,154	19,865,301	858,223	19,071,625	0	1,650,000	793,676	29,206,324	11,23,500	0	1,71,73,500	1,787,000
3	3,143,967	15,144,696	0	0	0	1,606,348	15,144,696	14,061,628	12,02,145	0	1,83,75,645	1,537,000
4	2,265,574	11,478,849	0	0	0	773,390	11,478,849	2,582,779	12,86,295	0	1,96,61,940	1,492,185
5	1,599,801	8,640,434	0	0	0	142,053	2,582,779	0	13,76,336	60,57,655	1,49,80,621	1,457,748
6	1,098,656	6,450,013	0	0	0	0	0	0	10,48,643	64,50,013	95,79,252	1,098,656
7	724,555	4,766,102	0	0	0	0	0	0	6,70,548	47,66,102	54,83,697	724,555
8	448,121	3,477,272	0	0	0	0	0	0	3,83,859	34,77,272	23,90,285	448,121
9	246,440	2,495,877	0	0	0	0	0	0	1,67,320	24,95,877	61,727	246,440
10	101,679	1,753,081	0	0	0	0	0	0	4,321	66,048	0	1,788,712

FIGURE 14-7 CMO structure.

In the first year, the A-tranche and the B-tranche receive interest as promised. A's is 4.50% of $45 million or $2,025,000 and B's is 5.50% of $30 million. The available principal is just under $26 million (as copied from Figure 14-4), all of which is paid to the A-tranche, leaving a remaining balance of just over $19 million. $1,050,000 in interest accrues to the Z-tranche balance, which grows to $16,050,000. Slightly more than $2 million is left, all of which goes to the R-tranche. In the second year, there is more than enough principal cash flow to the pool to pay off the A-tranche's remaining balance, so the rest of the principal goes to the B-tranche. Similarly, in the fifth year, there is enough principal cash flow to repay the B-tranche's remaining cash flow, so repayment of the Z-tranche begins.

The CMO structure allows issuers to offer securities that appeal to a wide variety of investors. Investors with short-term needs and a willingness to accept prepayment risk can earn yield premiums over shorter-term Treasury securities with no default risk by investing in an A-tranche. Investors with long-term investment needs might be attracted to a C-tranche, a D-tranche, or even a Z-tranche.

14.6.1 Exotic CMO Tranches

In the previous subsection, an example with the three most common types of CMO tranche, the sequential, fixed-rate tranche, the zero-coupon tranche, and the residual tranche was discussed. Now, two pairs of CMO tranches that are a bit more exotic, the PAC and companion and the floater and inverse floater, will be discussed.

The **planned amortization class**, or PAC tranche, and related **companion bond** is a structure that reallocates prepayment risk across investors. Each PAC tranche is similar to a fixed-rate sequential tranche in that it has a principal balance, a fixed coupon rate, and a priority to principal repayment. However, unlike a traditional fixed-rate, sequential tranche, the PAC tranche also has a promised prepayment rate. Each PAC tranche has an associated companion bond that typically has the same principal balance but a higher coupon rate, because the companion bears the PAC's prepayment risk as well as its own. When pool prepayments are higher than the PAC's promised prepayment rate, the companion bond gets the extra prepayments. When pool prepayments are lower than the PAC's promised prepayment rate, the PAC tranche gets part of the companion's prepayments. Unless prepayments to the pool are much different than expected, the PAC tranche ends up with a fixed prepayment rate and no prepayment risk and the companion bond has double the prepayment risk of the underlying mortgages.

A **floater** is a sequential tranche with a principal balance, a priority to principal repayment, and an adjustable coupon rate equal to an index rate plus, perhaps, a fixed spread. The index for the floater is a market interest rate like LIBOR. If market interest rates rise, the coupon rate on the floater rises and vice versa. Associated with each floater is an **inverse floater**. The inverse floater usually has the same principal balance as its associated floater and the same priority to principal repayment. The coupon rate on an inverse floater is equal to a fixed rate minus an index rate. If market interest rates rise, the coupon rate on the inverse floater falls and vice versa. Putting the coupon rates of the floater and inverse floater together gives a fixed rate (index plus fixed spread plus fixed rate minus index). In other words, considered together, the pair equals a fixed-rate sequential tranche. Splitting them creates securities that appeal to two sets of investors, those who think interest rates will rise and those who think they will fall.

In addition to these types of exotic tranches that are typically based on fixed-rate mortgage pools, CMOs that are based on pools of ARMs need to be mentioned.

Because the interest cash flows of an ARM pool will change from year to year, ARM CMOs are unlikely to include fixed-rate sequential tranches. Instead, the structure is likely to emphasize floater tranches (without inverse floaters). The structures get even more interesting when the CMO is based on a pool of hybrid mortgages, such as those that have a fixed rate for five years and then convert to a one-year ARM. Essentially, most tranches in the CMO structure must conform to the type of mortgage in the pool. Some departure is possible, as when a zero-coupon structure or a floater is created from a fixed-rate pool, but there are limits to the ability of issuers to alter the underlying structure of the mortgage cash flows. The cash flows for the complete CMO structure must exactly match the cash flows received by the mortgage pool.

14.7 MANAGING MBS INTEREST-RATE RISK

As mentioned a number of times, both in this chapter and in Chapter 6, mortgage and MBS investors are subject to a lot of interest-rate risk. This is true in part because mortgages and MBS are fixed-income securities. The present value of fixed future cash flows changes as market interest rates change. In addition, mortgages and MBS are subject to prepayments, which increase when interest rates fall and decrease when they rise. Some prepayments are expected by investors, but changes in the prepayment rate lead to changes in the expected cash flows of mortgages and MBS. And these changes, for the most part, hurt investors.

Chapter 5 presented the calculation of duration and its use to measure the interest-rate risk of a security. However, Chapter 6 showed that the duration calculation from Chapter 5 does not work for a mortgage portfolio because a mortgage pool's cash flows change as interest rates change. Instead, a valuation model was used to calculate the mortgage portfolio's effective duration. This method can also be used to calculate the effective duration of various MBS, including passthrough shares, IO or PO strips, and CMO tranches.

Keep in mind, though, that the duration of a mortgage portfolio can change quickly as interest rates change. In the example in Section 6.5.2 of Chapter 6, a 30-year fixed-rate mortgage portfolio was shown to act like it had a duration of about 7.2 years when mortgage rates rose from 7 to 8%, but it acted like it had a duration of about 3.7 years when rates fell from 7 to 6%. Duration is a fairly accurate measure of interest-rate risk, so these changes in duration suggest that mortgages have very different risk characteristics in rising rate environments than in falling rate environments. This instability makes interest-rate risk management very difficult for mortgage portfolios and MBS.

14.7.1 Duration Hedging

In the following discussion of interest-rate risk management of mortgage portfolios and MBS, the assumption will be made that the investor has calculated the effective duration of their portfolio as accurately as possible. This will be the risk measure that is managed to eliminate or reduce risk, depending on the investor's needs. There are more sophisticated ways of measuring the interest-rate risk of complex fixed-income securities, but none that produces a single number like duration. Further, the models used in more sophisticated analysis of mortgage securities are beyond the scope of this textbook.

Recall what the duration model tells us about interest-rate risk. It says that

$$\Delta PV = -MD \times PV \times \Delta i, \tag{14-1}$$

where MD is the modified duration of the security (the Macauley duration divided by $1 + i$) and i is the market interest rate. Suppose that the goal is to create the perfect hedge position to counteract this risk. A perfect hedge will always gain in value exactly what the investment portfolio loses and vice versa. Once the perfect hedge is in place, the hedged portfolio (portfolio plus hedge) will neither gain nor lose value. In other words,

$$\Delta PV_{\text{portfolio}} + \Delta PV_{\text{hedge}} = 0. \tag{14-2}$$

If the right-hand side of Equation (14-1) is substituted into Equation (14-2), the result is

$$[(-MD_{\text{portfolio}} \times PV_{\text{portfolio}}) + (-MD_{\text{hedge}} \times PV_{\text{hedge}})] \times \Delta i = 0. \tag{14-3}$$

For a perfect hedge this needs to be true for every change in interest rates. Performing a bit of algebraic manipulation, the hedge value is

$$PV_{\text{hedge}} = \left[\frac{-MD_{\text{portfolio}}}{MD_{\text{hedge}}} \right] \times PV_{\text{portfolio}}. \tag{14-4}$$

Equation (14-4) tells us how much hedge is needed based on the size of the portfolio, the riskiness of the portfolio, and the riskiness of the hedge instrument. The ratio of the modified durations (in square brackets) is called the **hedge ratio**.

Depending on the particular hedging needs, Equation (14-4) might not be appropriate. Equation (14-2) assumed that the goal was to eliminate the interest-rate risk of the hedged portfolio. An alternative goal might be to reduce the risk to an acceptable level, called a **target duration**. In other words, an investor might want to take on less interest-rate risk but not zero interest-rate risk. The modified duration of a portfolio of two assets is the weighted average of the individual assets' modified durations or

$$MD_{\text{portfolio}} = \left[\left(\frac{PV_A}{PV_{\text{portfolio}}} \right) \times MD_A \right] + \left[\left(\frac{PV_B}{PV_{\text{portfolio}}} \right) \times MD_B \right]. \tag{14-5}$$

The modified duration of a portfolio containing a long asset position and a derivatives position is a bit different. The derivatives position contributes risk (modified duration) relative to its underlying value, but does not increase the size of the portfolio. Employing the target duration, Equation (14-5) is modified to

$$TD = \left[MD_{\text{portfolio}} \right] + \left[\left(\frac{PV_{\text{hedge}}}{PV_{\text{portfolio}}} \right) \times MD_{\text{hedge}} \right]$$

$$\Rightarrow PV_{\text{hedge}} = \left[\frac{(TD - MD_{\text{portfolio}})}{MD_{\text{hedge}}} \right] \times PV_{\text{portfolio}}, \tag{14-6}$$

where TD is the target duration.

14.7.2 Hedging MBS with Treasury Forwards

The goal in this section is to show how forward contracts on U.S. Treasury bonds or notes can be used to implement the type of duration hedge described in the previous section. Forward contracts are used in our example, rather than futures contracts, in order to avoid some of the messy institutional details that arise with Treasury bond futures, including cheapest-to-deliver and margin account (daily mark-to-market) issues. Forward contracts are typically based on a specific bond or note and are not subject to margin requirements. In the real world, however, most investors would use futures contracts rather than forward contracts because futures are free from counterparty risk, are priced in an open market, and have much lower transaction costs than forwards. Further, as will be discussed later, because mortgage securities exhibit negative convexity, their interest rate hedges need frequent rebalancing. This is difficult to do with forward contracts, because the contract must be renegotiated with the specific counterparty, but trivial when futures contracts are used. Presumably, a specialist in mortgage investments and risk management will have experience dealing with the more difficult aspects of using futures to hedge.

The duration hedging models in Equations (14-4) and (14-6) require two pieces of information about the forward contract, the modified duration of the contract and the forward price. The modified duration of the forward contract is equal to the modified duration of the underlying Treasury bond or note. This is a measure of how much the value of the forward contract will change as market interest rates change. The forward price is the price that the parties have agreed to pay or receive at the contract's maturity in exchange for the specified Treasury bond or note.

One issue that has not yet been mentioned is whether the investor should be long or short. That is, does the investor need to agree to buy the Treasury bond or note in the future (long position) or sell it (short position)? This will depend on the risk of the investor's portfolio. In most cases, a portfolio of mortgages or MBS will have a positive duration and the investor will need a short position in the forward contract. Some MBS, however, have negative effective durations (e.g., IO strips). In this case, the investor would need a long position in the forward contract. Luckily, the hedging model will tell us whether the hedge position should be long or short.

The following example will show how hedging MBS portfolio with Treasury forward contracts works.

EXAMPLE *Hedging an MBS Portfolio with Treasury Forward Contracts*

Assume an investor

1. holds an MBS portfolio with a current value of $5 million and an effective modified duration of 4.50 years.
2. The investor has negotiated a three-year forward contract on the 10-year U.S. Treasury bond with a safe counterparty.
3. The parties have agreed to base the contract on a bond with a 6% coupon and a forward price of 107.78% of par (quoted in 32nds as 107-25).
4. The modified duration of this forward contract is 7.39 years.
5. Whether the investor will take a long or short position in the contract and what the size of the contract will be has not been determined yet. The size of the contract is the face value of the bonds that will be exchanged at its maturity.

As a first scenario, assume that the assumptions of Equation (14-4) hold. That is, the investor wants a hedge that eliminates all interest-rate risk. Substituting the example inputs into

Equation (14-4) provides a hedge value of

$$PV_{\text{hedge}} = \left[\frac{-4.50}{7.39}\right] \times \$5,000,000$$
$$= -\$3,044,655.$$

The minus sign tells us that the investor should take a *short position in the forward contract*. Next, the present value of the hedge position is divided by the forward price to determine the volume of the forward contract, which is \$2,824,879 ($= \$3,044,655/1.0778$). This will be rounded to the nearest whole bond amount or \$2,825,000.

As a second scenario, assume the investor does not want to eliminate interest-rate risk, but wants to reduce the modified duration of the portfolio to a target of 2.00 years. Substituting the example inputs into Equation (14-6) the value of the hedge is

$$PV_{\text{hedge}} = \left[\frac{2.00 - 4.50}{7.39}\right] \times \$5,000,000$$
$$= -\$1,691,475.$$

As before, the minus sign tells us that the investor should take a short position in the forward contract. The volume of the forward contract should be \$1,569,377 ($= \$1,691,475/1.0778$). This will be rounded to the nearest whole bond amount or \$1,569,000.

It is important to note that the hedge calculated in the preceding example will *not* be the right one if interest rates change by *more than a small amount*. As interest rates rise or fall, the modified duration of the MBS portfolio will change substantially due to its extreme, negative convexity (which comes from the prepayment option). The modified duration of the forward contract will also change a bit, as will the present value of the MBS portfolio and the forward price. All of these changes will contribute to the change in the appropriate hedge. The investor should respond by adding more hedge or removing some of the existing hedge. Because the correct hedge amount will change as interest rates (the risk factor) change, this kind of hedge is called a **dynamic hedge**. In contrast, a **static hedge** would be one that does not need to be adjusted as interest rates change. As mentioned earlier, one of the reasons forward contracts are rarely used to hedge MBS portfolios is that they are difficult to adjust. In contrast, if the investor is using futures contracts, the investor need only go long or short on additional contracts to adjust the hedge as required.

14.7.3 Hedging with Options

Hedging with forward contracts or futures contracts requires that the investor give up potential return in order to reduce or eliminate risk. This sort of hedge is very inexpensive to put into place because, assuming a balance between supply and demand in the underlying asset market and equal borrowing and lending costs, the expected return on an interest-rate futures or forward contract is zero. However, the hedge position exposes the investor to possible gains and possible losses. If the investor's portfolio loses value, the hedge will gain value. However, if the investor's portfolio gains value, the hedge will lose value. This is called a **two-sided hedge** because the gains and losses in the two sides cancel each other out.

An alternative to two-sided hedging is **one-sided hedging** with options. One-sided hedging is like buying an insurance contract. The investor pays the whole cost of protection, the option premium, in advance. If the investor's portfolio loses value in the future, the option hedge position will gain in value to offset the loss. If, however, the investor's portfolio gains in value, the option hedge will not lose value. Options are limited liability instruments. The most that can be lost in a long call or put position is the premium paid.

Options also provide greater hedging flexibility than futures and forwards because a variety of strike prices are available. Just as using options to create a hedge is like buying an insurance policy, choosing a strike price is like choosing a deductible. If the investor does not want to have any losses, the investor will choose a strike price very close to or at-the-money. This way, the option will pay off when even a small loss of portfolio value is experienced. This is like choosing a low deductible; however, just like an insurance policy with a low deductible, an at-the-money option is expensive. Alternately, the investor can choose to take a risk of some loss and purchase an out-of-the-money option for the hedge. The protection is not as good, but the cost is lower.

The most common options used to hedge interest-rate risk are puts and calls on U.S. Treasury futures contracts. The underlying asset for these options is a futures position. The basic rules of hedging interest-rate risk with options are simple, even if the details can get complex. If the investor's portfolio will lose value when interest rates rise (which causes bond prices to fall), the investor will want to purchase puts on Treasury futures as a hedge. The puts will gain in value when Treasury prices fall. If the investor's portfolio will lose value when interest rates fall (which causes bond prices to rise), the investor will want to purchase calls on Treasury futures. What strike prices to choose—at-the-money vs. out-of-the-money and how far out-of-the-money—is a matter of taste. Different investors will make different decisions.

14.7.4 Basis Risk

Hedging using futures, options, and other derivatives is usually subject to *basis risk*. Basis risk occurs when the price of the risky security (in this case an MBS) and the value of the derivatives hedge change in a way that is not expected according to their historical relationship. Most interest rate derivatives are based on U.S. Treasury securities or LIBOR rates. The U.S. Treasury yield most commonly associated with 30-year mortgage rates is the yield on the 10-year Treasury bond. Figure 6-5 in Chapter 6 showed us that the difference between the 30-year fixed-rate mortgage rate and the 10-year constant maturity Treasury yield is not constant. This difference is sometimes called the basis between the two. This means that the relationship between changes in mortgage values and changes in U.S. Treasury securities is not constant.

When hedges are designed for risky securities like MBS, the assumption generally made is that changes in the value of the derivatives position will exactly counteract changes in the value of the risky security. This assumes that changes in the derivatives and changes in the risky security have a fixed, well-understood relationship. This is not true for an MBS hedge based in Treasury yields, although the hope is that unexpected differences between the two will be minor. What needs to be remembered when managing risk through a hedge is that there may be a time when our risky security loses value and the hedge position does not gain enough to make up for the loss (or even loses value itself). This can happen, even if the hedge is well-designed and appropriately implemented, because of basis risk. *The fact to remember is that no hedge is perfect.*

DEVELOPING VALUATION AND RISK MANAGEMENT SKILLS

1. Understand the primary risks of mortgages.

Mortgages face the same basic risks as other fixed-income securities, which include liquidity risk, interest-rate risk, and default risk. Mortgages also face geographic risk.

2. Understand the process of securitization in the mortgage markets and how securitization allows specialization in the mortgage markets.

Securitization in the mortgage market is the process of creating new securities that are backed by a pool (portfolio) of mortgages. Creating a security backed by a mortgage pool allows financial institutions to sell the mortgages they originate, thus creating a liquid secondary market in mortgages. The ability to sell mortgages allows financial institutions to specialize in one or more of the three parts of the mortgage process: (1) origination, (2) servicing, and (3) owning.

3. Understand mortgage-backed securities (MBS) and how the creation of mortgage-backed securities alters risk management in the mortgage market.

A mortgage-backed security (MBS) is simply a security backed by a pool of mortgages. Some of the choices available are passthroughs, IO and PO strips, and CMOs of various types. MBS passthrough securities pass payments on the mortgages in the pool on to the investors in the MBS, while CMOs are debt securities with defined cash flows that use the mortgage pool as collateral. The ability to sell mortgages for use in MBS pools and the ability to buy MBS allows financial institutions to alter (manage) each risk component of their mortgage loan operation.

4. Understand interest-rate risk management in the mortgage market.

Since mortgages are fixed-income securities, duration matching is available as a technique for managing the interest-rate risk of a mortgage portfolio. Additionally, derivative securities exist that allow for hedging the interest-rate risk in a mortgage portfolio, but remember that care must be taken when hedging with a derivative and remember that no hedge is perfect.

QUESTIONS

1. What is liquidity risk and why are residential mortgages illiquid?

2. How will a decrease in market interest rates affect a portfolio of residential mortgages?

3. To what extent are residential mortgages subject to default risk?

4. What is geographic concentration risk and why are investors in residential mortgages subject to this?

5. Describe the main steps in the securitization process.

6. What fees are paid out of a mortgage pool's cash flows before money is distributed to investors?

7. How do issuers of MBS make money?

8. Describe the market for mortgage-backed securities.

9. How are liquidity risk, interest-rate risk, default risk, and geographic concentration risk affected by mortgage securitization?

10. What risks are created by widespread mortgage securitization?

11. What is the main purpose of an MBS structure?

12. How do the three common types of MBS structure differ from one another?

13. An MBS issuer has assembled a pool of residential mortgages with the following characteristics: $50 million principal balance, WAC = 6.00%, WAM = 8 years. Servicing, trustee, and default insurance fees total 80 bps per year. The issuer expects the pool to prepay (including insured defaults) at a CPR of 22%. Using this information, and assuming annual payments, the issuer has created a table of expected cash flows for the pool. Suppose the issuer creates a passthrough structure with 450 shares. What are the expected annual cash flows for a single share?

				Balance:		$50,000,000			
				WAC:		6.00%			
				WAM:		8			
				CPR:		22.00%			
				Fees:		0.80%			
##	P&I Payment ($)	Principal cash flow ($)	Interest cash flow ($)	Prepayment cash flow ($)	Fees ($)	Remaining balance ($)	Total cash flow ($)	Total interest cash flow ($)	Total principal cash flow ($)
0						50,000,000			
1	8,051,797	5,051,797	3,000,000	9,888,605	400,000	35,059,598	17,540,402	2,600,000	14,940,402
2	6,280,402	4,176,826	2,103,576	6,794,210	280,477	24,088,562	12,794,135	1,823,099	10,971,036
3	4,898,713	3,453,400	1,445,314	4,539,736	192,708	16,095,427	9,245,741	1,252,605	7,993,135
4	3,820,996	2,855,271	965,726	2,912,834	128,763	10,327,322	6,605,067	836,962	5,768,105
5	2,980,377	2,360,738	619,639	1,752,648	82,619	6,213,935	4,650,407	537,021	4,113,386
6	2,324,694	1,951,858	372,836	937,657	49,711	3,324,420	3,212,640	323,125	2,889,515
7	1,813,261	1,613,796	199,465	376,337	26,595	1,334,287	2,163,003	172,870	1,990,134
8	1,414,344	1,334,287	80,057	0	10,674	0	1,403,670	69,383	1,334,287

14. Refer back to the pool of mortgages in Question 13. Suppose that, instead of creating a passthrough structure, the issuer decides to create an IO and PO strip structure, with 150 IO shares and 350 PO shares. Create a table showing the expected cash flows for each IO share and PO share.

15. Refer back to the pool of mortgages in Question 13. Suppose that, instead of creating a passthrough structure, the issuer decides to create a CMO structure. The CMO will have (1) an A-tranche with a principal balance of $25 million, a coupon rate of 4.00%, and 200 shares; (2) a B-tranche with a principal balance of $15 million, a coupon rate of 4.50%, and 150 shares; (3) a Z-tranche with an initial principal balance of $6 million, an earnings rate of 5.50%, and 100 shares; and (4) an R-tranche to be held by the issuer. Create a table (or set of tables) showing the expected cash flows for each tranche.

16. Why is interest-rate risk management more difficult for mortgage and MBS portfolios than for other fixed-income portfolios?

17. The hedge ratio for a fixed-income portfolio is based on what information?

18. What is a dynamic hedging?

19. Explain the difference between one-sided and two-sided hedging.

20. Consider a MBS portfolio with a value of $12.5 million and an effective modified duration of 3.75 years. The investor wishes to hedge this portfolio against interest-rate risk using a two-year forward contract on the 10-year Treasury bond that has a modified duration of 7.69 years and a forward price of 104-00. If the investor wants to completely eliminate interest-rate risk, what position should she take in the forward contract?

21. Reconsider the information provided in Question 20. If, instead, the investor wants to reduce the portfolio duration to a target of 1.50 years, what position should she take in the forward contract?

22. Explain why hedging with options is like buying an insurance policy.

23. Why is hedging MBS portfolios with derivatives on U.S. Treasury securities subject to basis risk?

REFERENCES

BARTLETT, W. W., 1991, *Mortgage-Backed Securities: Products, Analysis, Trading*, New York Institute of Finance, New York.
Comprehensive review of mortgage-backed securities, focused on the investor in MBS, rather than the mortgage lender.

BOEMIO, T. R., and G. A. EDWARDS, Jr., 1989, Asset securitization: A supervisory perspective, *Federal Reserve Bulletin, October*, 659–669.
An early review of the upside and downside of securitization. Particularly useful for understanding the underlying risks that accompany securitization of mortgages and other consumer loans.

BREEDEN, D. T., 1991, Risk, return, and hedging of fixed rate mortgages, *Journal of Fixed Income 1 (September)*, 85–107.
The classic article on mortgage risk.

FABOZZI, F. J., ed., 2001, *The Handbook of Mortgage Backed Securities* McGraw-Hill Education, New York.
The classic collection of articles on MBS investment, recently updated. Fabozzi has edited a large number of other books relating to mortgage and MBS investment.

GILKESON, J. H., and S. D. SMITH, 1992, The convexity trap: Pitfalls in financing mortgage portfolios and related securities, *Federal Reserve Bank of Atlanta Economic Review 77(6)*, 14–27.
The article that explained why prepayments cause mortgage portfolios and MBS to exhibit negative convexity.

SMITH, S. D., 1991, Analyzing risk and return for mortgage-backed securities, *Federal Reserve Bank of Atlanta Economic Review 76(1)*, 2–11.
A good review of MBS risk designed to be (relatively) nontechnical.

KEY TERMS

Asset-backed Security (ABS) A security for which the cash flows come from, and are guaranteed by, the cash flows to a pool of loans or other financial obligations.

Asset Pool A portfolio of loans or other financial obligations grouped together to use as the basis for an ABS issue.

Automated Underwriting Systems A computer model that accepts information from a loan application, including the applicant's credit information, and makes a lending decision.

Black Box Generic term referring to a computer model that is used and trusted but has inner workings that are not understood by the user.

Collateralized Mortgage Obligation (CMO) An MBS structure in which each security (called a tranche) is given a priority to principal repayment.

Companion Bond CMO tranche paired with a PAC. The companion accepts additional prepayment risk so that the PAC can have a fixed prepayment rate.

Conforming Mortgage A residential mortgage with characteristics that meet standards set by the major issuers of MBS, specifically FNMA and FHLMC.

Dynamic Hedge A hedge that needs to be changed when the underlying risk factor changes.

Fannie Mae See FNMA.

FHLMC The Federal Home Loan Mortgage Corporation or Freddie Mac. A federally chartered, publicly traded corporation that issues MBS, insures the underlying mortgage pools against default losses, and holds whole mortgages on its balance sheet (funded by issuing bonds in the capital markets).

Floater A CMO tranche that has an adjustable coupon rate that rises and falls with market interest rates. Paired with an inverse floater.

FNMA The Federal National Mortgage Association or Fannie Mae. A federally chartered, publicly traded corporation that issues MBS, insures the underlying mortgage pools against default losses, and holds whole mortgages on its balance sheet (funded by issuing bonds in the capital markets).

Freddie Mac See FHLMC.

Ginnie Mae See GNMA.

GNMA The Government National Mortgage Association or Ginnie Mae. A public corporation that insures certain residential mortgages against default losses.

Hedge Ratio The ratio that describes the size of the necessary hedge relative to the size of the investor's portfolio.

Interest-only (IO) Strip An MBS that receives all of the interest payments (net of fees) received by a mortgage pool. Paired with a PO strip.

Inverse Floater A CMO tranche that has an adjustable coupon rate that rises and falls opposite of market interest rates. Paired with a floater.

Jumbo Mortgage A residential mortgage with a principal balance higher than allowed under FNMA and FHLMC standards. A type of nonconforming mortgage.

Model Risk When an investor relies on a third party model to perform analysis such as valuation or hedge development, there is the risk that the model will not work as advertised.

Mortgage-backed Security (MBS) An ABS based on a pool of mortgages.

Nonconforming Mortgage A mortgage that does not meet standards for purchase set by FNMA and FHLMC.

One-sided Hedge A hedge in which the investor pays an up-front cost and is protected from any future portfolio losses without additional costs.

Passthrough Security An MBS structure in which the cash inflows to the pool are divided evenly between shareholders.

Planned Amortization Class (PAC) A CMO tranche with a fixed prepayment rate. Paired with a companion bond.

Principal-only (PO) Strip An MBS that receives all of the principal payments (including prepayments) received by a mortgage pool. Paired with an IO strip.

Residual Tranche A CMO tranche that receives all cash flows not due to another tranche. Also called an R-tranche, a junk tranche, or an equity tranche.

Seasoned Mortgage A mortgage that is more than a couple of years old.

Securitization The process of issuing an asset-backed security. Leads to disintermediation of lending markets.

Sequential Tranche A CMO tranche with a fixed coupon rate that receives interest payments each period but principal only when all tranches in front of it have been repaid in full.

Servicer Risk The risk that poor customer service on the part of the mortgage servicer will adversely impact the performance of an MBS.

Static Hedge A hedge that does not need to be changed when the underlying risk factor changes.

Subprime Mortgage A mortgage for which the borrower's credit quality is below the standards required by FNMA and FHLMC.

Systemic Risk The risk that a single market participant is so important to a market that its failure will cause the market to fail.

Target Duration An investor's desired level of interest-rate risk, net of the impact of any hedges.

Tranche A security that is part of a CMO structure.

Two-sided Hedge A hedge in which the investor trades off the risk of portfolio losses against the potential for portfolio gains. The hedge position will always negate the change in the underlying portfolio; it will gain value if the portfolio loses value but lose value if the portfolio gains value.

Underwriting Standards Lending standards.

Zero-coupon Tranche A CMO tranche that accrues interest to the principal balance rather than receiving interest cash flows.

CHAPTER 15

STOCK PORTFOLIO FORMATION AND RISK MANAGEMENT

15.1 INTRODUCTION

This chapter discusses the risk from owning a stock portfolio. Specifically, the purpose of this chapter is to develop an understanding of stock portfolio risk along with developing the ability to measure and manage stock portfolio risk. This is a particularly important issue for mutual fund and pension fund managers as they compete for investment dollars because individual investors are concerned about the potential losses on an investment. For example, the *In The News* item in this chapter shows that Long-Term Capital Management (LTCM) (a hedge fund) calculates its daily dollar value exposure to risk so it can manage its risk exposure. Accordingly, this chapter continues the theme in the second half of this book of identifying, measuring, and managing risk.

This chapter begins by revisiting the basic performance measures of a stock portfolio with a focus on correlation. This is followed by measuring portfolio risk in percentage and dollar terms. The dollar measure of risk is referred to as *value-at-risk* (VaR), which has become a popular risk management measure. The chapter spends some time on both the strengths and weaknesses of VaR. The chapter concludes with a discussion on the use of derivative securities to manage stock portfolio risk, including using protective puts as portfolio insurance.

DEVELOPING VALUATION AND RISK MANAGEMENT SKILLS

1. Understand the basic performance measures of stock portfolios and understand the role of correlation in the risk of a stock portfolio.
2. Calculate stock portfolio standard deviation in percentage and dollar terms.
3. Understand the strengths and weaknesses of VaR.
4. Understand how buying a stock portfolio on margin alters a portfolio's risk.
5. Understand how to hedge stock portfolio risk using derivative securities.

15.2 PORTFOLIO BASICS

The following example describes the basic information for a portfolio of three stocks and calculates the portfolio's expected return and β. It is important to become familiar with the details of this portfolio because it will be used throughout the chapter in examples for calculating portfolio standard deviation and portfolio value-at-risk.

EXAMPLE *Three-Stock Portfolio*

A **portfolio** is a collection of assets: stocks, bonds, and anything else that has value to the owner. The relative importance of each part of the portfolio is measured by its weight or value. For this example, assume an investor owns shares in three fictitious companies: Fly-by-Night Airlines (FLYBY), the Loan Sharks Incorporated (UO), and the Koala Greeting Card Company (GDAY). The total investment in the three companies is £15,000. The investor has £5,000 invested in FLYBY, £6,000 in UO, and the balance is held in GDAY. Thus, the individual securities comprise the following percentages or weights in the portfolio:

$$\text{FLYBY } £5,000/£15,000 = 0.33;$$
$$\text{UO } £6,000/£15,000 = 0.40; \text{ and}$$
$$\text{GDAY } £4,000/£15,000 = 0.27.$$

The investor has done extensive research on these three companies and has compiled the following information.

Investment	Expected return (%)	Standard deviation (%)	Beta
FLYBY	11	10	1.05
UO	9	5	0.95
GDAY	12	7	1.11

The investor has also calculated the correlation coefficients between each pair of securities. The correlation coefficients are

Correlation coefficients	FLYBY	UO	GDAY
FLYBY	1.0	0.8	0.5
UO	0.8	1.0	0.2
GDAY	0.5	0.2	1.0

What is a reasonable rate of return to expect on the portfolio?

The most likely return is determined by calculating the weighted average of the component parts of the portfolio

$$E[R] = w_1 \times r_1 + w_2 \times r_2 + w_3 \times r_3 = 0.33(11\%) + 0.40(9\%) + 0.27(12\%) = 10.47\%.$$

A similar calculation can be made to calculate the portfolio's beta

$$E[\beta] = w_1 \times \beta_1 + w_2 \times \beta_2 + w_3 \times \beta_3 = 0.33(1.05) + 0.40(0.95) + 0.27(1.11) = 1.03.$$

Unfortunately, the same calculation cannot be performed to determine the standard deviation of the portfolio. Why? Diversifiable and nondiversifiable risks differ.

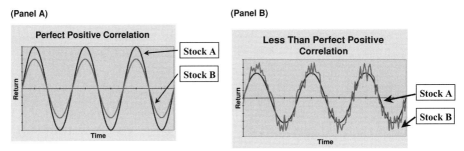

FIGURE 15-1   Correlation and portfolio return.

15.3   CORRELATION REVISITED

As previously discussed, all assets appear to be somewhat correlated to unexpected market-wide risks: for example, changes in interest rates or oil prices. For example, with the possible exception of a handmade Amish quilt taken to market on horseback and traded for handmade furniture, the manufacturing of a product uses oil or oil derivatives in some part of the manufacturing process. Hence, all products are interrelated by the amount they are exposed to market-wide factors. That is, all products tend to be, somewhat, positively correlated.

At this point, a more detailed examination of **correlation** is in order. The degree of correlation is a measure of the extent to which returns on two assets move together. If both move up and down together, they are positively correlated and the correlation coefficient is $\rho_{ij} > 0$. If the relative changes of two assets are exactly together, they are perfectly positively correlated ($\rho_{ij} = 1$). This is shown in Figure 15-1, Panel A. Less than perfect positive correlation is shown in Figure 15-1, Panel B.

If the price of one asset moves up when the other moves down and vice versa, they are negatively correlated. The correlation coefficient is $\rho_{ij} < 0$. Figure 15-2, Panel A shows perfect negative correlation ($\rho_{ij} = -1$). Less than perfect negative correlation is shown in Figure 15-2, Panel B.

If the price of two assets is completely independent, they are uncorrelated. The correlation coefficient is $\rho_{ij} = 0$. This is shown in Figure 15-3.

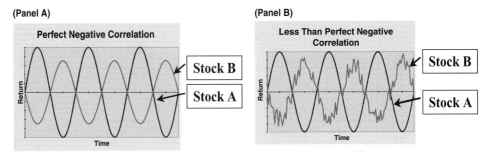

FIGURE 15-2   Portfolio return with two negatively correlated securities.

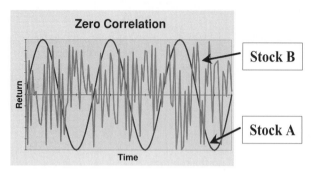

FIGURE 15-3 Portfolio return with two uncorrelated securities.

One professor, known to the authors, compares correlation to dancing the samba. Imagine two people dancing the samba and they are very good together. For every step the man takes to the right, the woman takes a step to the left. For every turn the woman takes to the right, the man takes a turn to the left. These samba dancers are negatively correlated. Now, imagine two people are trying to learn the samba. They bump into each other a lot. This happens because they are moving in the same direction at the same time. These dancers are positively correlated. Now, whenever our colleague steps on the dance floor, his partner tries to ignore him and pretend that they are perfect strangers. No matter how hard he tries, it is usually impossible for him to get a reaction out of his dance partner—they are uncorrelated!

15.4 MEASURING THE RISK OF A PORTFOLIO

The formula used to calculate the **standard deviation** of a portfolio is

$$\sigma_p = \left[\sum w_i{}^2 \sigma_i{}^2 + 2 \left(\sum \sum w_i w_j \rho_{ij} \sigma_i \sigma_j \right) \right]^{0.5}. \qquad (15\text{-}1)$$

What is this? It is nothing more than the square root of the sum of the weighted average of the covariances. What's a **covariance**? A covariance is a nonstandardized measure of the total comovement of two variables. Previously the correlation coefficient was discussed and it is a standardized measure of the relation between two variables. The relationship between covariance and correlation is illustrated by the following formula for covariance:[1]

$$\text{Covariance} = \rho_{i,j} \sigma_i \sigma_j. \qquad (15\text{-}2)$$

EXAMPLE   *Standard Deviation of Three-Stock Portfolio*

Now return to the three-stock portfolio: FLYBY, UO, and GDAY. How is the standard deviation of the portfolio determined? What the investor has to do is determine how all the securities in the portfolio move together as a result of their individual correlations. Equation (15-1) provides this answer. Look at Figure 15-4 and notice that all the cells on the diagonal are shaded. These cells represent the weighted total risk of the individual securities. In the formula, the diagonal is captured by $\sum w_i{}^2 \sigma_i{}^2$ [the first part of Equation (15-1)].

---

[1] Note that in the covariance formula when $i = j$ then $\rho_{i,j} = 1$ and covariance $= \sigma^2$.

Investment	FLYBY	UO	GDAY
FLYBY			
UO			
GDAY			

FIGURE 15-4 Chart for a three-stock portfolio standard deviation.

Figure 15-4 shows two off-diagonal portions exist in the chart and, based on the correlations in the correlation matrix, there should not be any difference between how FLYBY is correlated with GDAY and how GDAY is correlated with FLYBY. Therefore, all that needs to be done is to calculate one off-diagonal portion and then multiply the answer by two. In the Equation (15-1), this part of the operation is captured by $2(\sum \sum w_i w_j \rho_{ij} \sigma_i \sigma_j)$. If this approach is used to calculate the portfolio standard deviation, the chart will appear as in Figure 15-5.

Investment	FLYBY	UO	GDAY
FLYBY	$(0.33)^2(0.1)^2$	$(0.33)(0.4)(0.8)(0.1)(0.05)$	$(0.33)(0.27)(0.5)(0.1)(0.07)$
UO		$(0.4)^2(0.05)^2$	$(0.4)(0.27)(0.2)(0.05)(0.07)$
GDAY			$(0.27)^2(0.07)^2$

FIGURE 15-5 Calculating standard deviation for a three-stock portfolio.

$$
\begin{aligned}
\sigma_p &= \left[\sum w_i^2 \sigma_i^2 + 2 \left(\sum \sum w_i w_j \rho_{ij} \sigma_i \sigma_j \right) \right]^{0.5} \\
&= [(0.33)^2(0.1)^2 + (0.4)^2(0.05)^2 + (0.27)^2(0.07)^2 + 2[((0.33)(0.4)(0.8)(0.1)(0.05) \\
&\quad + (0.33)(0.27)(0.5)(0.1)(0.07) + (0.4)(0.27)(0.2)(0.05)(0.07))]^{0.5} \\
&= [0.001089 + 0.0004 + 0.000357 + 2(0.000528 + 0.000312 + 0.000076)]^{0.5} \\
&= [0.003678]^{0.5} \\
&= 0.0606 \text{ or } 6.06\%.
\end{aligned}
$$

OK! What is the importance of the solution in this example? In statistical terms, it means that if the stock returns are normally distributed, then 68.4% of the time the return to this portfolio should fall within 1 standard deviation (6.06%) of the expected return (10.47%). That is, between 4.41% (10.47% − 6.06%) and 16.53% (10.47% + 6.06%).

If the desire is to reduce risk in a portfolio, the general rule is to include securities that are less than perfectly positively correlated with each other. In Section 15.3, graphs of perfect positive and negative correlation were presented. In the case of perfect positive correlation, some benefit still exists to portfolio formation since the two standard deviations of returns are different. Therefore, combining two such stocks into an equally weighted portfolio will result in an equally weighted expected return and a standard deviation between the standard deviations of the two securities.

Equation (15-1) provides the standard deviation of the portfolio on a percentage basis. However, investors often think of their gains and losses in dollar terms; therefore, having a money-based measure of risk would be useful. The process for determining value-at-risk (VaR) converts the percentage standard deviation into a money-based standard deviation, which is then used to determine a money-based expected loss. Value-at-risk is presented in the next section.

15.5 VALUE-AT-RISK

Investors often define risk as *losing money* or *doing something that feels uncomfortable* rather than in terms of standard deviation. That is, often the absolute dollar values are more meaningful than percentages for individual investors. Therefore, when trying to discuss risk with an investor, a more useful tactic would be to define risk as *losing money*. Further, individuals tend to think of the risk involved usually after the loss has been incurred. Also, their analysis of risk is usually on a single security basis rather than on a portfolio basis and they often measure gains and losses against the original cost instead of incorporating the time value of money.

Because many investors only think in terms of dollars, measuring portfolio risk in terms of dollar losses is helpful. **Value-at-risk** provides a measure of portfolio risk in dollars. Basically, what happens is, the standard deviation of the portfolio is measured using dollar amounts instead of percentage weights.

EXAMPLE *Dollar-Based Portfolio Standard Deviation*

Reexamining our investor's three-stock portfolio and assuming that the investor estimated all of the risk variables using monthly data, the process for calculating value-at-risk begins by replacing the percentage weights with dollar values for estimating a dollar-based standard deviation. For example, for FLYBY the percentage weight is 0.33 and that weight is replaced by the actual amount invested in the stock (£5,000) in the calculation of the portfolio standard deviation. The money-based portfolio standard deviation calculation is as follows:

$$\sigma_p = \left[\sum w_i^2 \sigma_i^2 + 2 \left(\sum \sum w_i w_j \rho_{ij} \sigma_i \sigma_j \right) \right]^{0.5}$$

$$\sigma_p = [(5,000)^2 (0.1)^2 + (6,000)^2 (0.05)^2 + (4,000)^2 (0.07)^2 + 2((5,000)(6,000)(0.8)(0.1)(0.05)$$
$$+ (5,000)(4,000)(0.5)(0.1)(0.07) + (6,000)(4,000)(0.2)(0.05)(0.07))]^{0.5}$$
$$= [250,000 + 90,000 + 78,400 + 2(120,000 + 70,000 + 16,800)]^{0.5}$$
$$= [832,000]^{.05}$$
$$= £912.14.$$

This example shows an estimated money-based standard deviation of £912.14 (variance of 832,000). This is the first step in finding the portfolio value-at-risk, but the process for value-at-risk is not complete, yet! What has to be done now is to put this money-based standard deviation in a context that individuals can understand. This means that the money-based standard deviation needs to be used to measure the *potential for losing money*.

Using the money-based standard deviation to create a measure for the potential for losing money is *value-at-risk*. Value-at-risk provides the expected maximum loss over a target horizon with a given confidence interval. Its greatest advantage is that it summarizes in a single, easily understood number the total exposure of a portfolio position to market

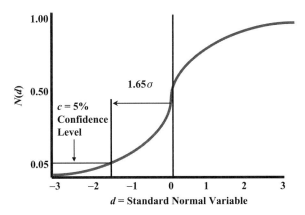

FIGURE 15-6 Cumulative normal distribution.

risk. Shareholders can then assess whether or not they are comfortable with this level of risk.

To calculate value-at-risk from the money-based standard deviation, two additional quantitative measures are needed: (1) the length of the holding period and (2) the confidence interval. Both of these are somewhat arbitrary. The holding periods are usually chosen based on experience. Banks measure daily holding periods. Investment portfolios usually measure the monthly holding period.

The holding period should correspond to the longest period needed for orderly portfolio liquidation. The horizon should be related to the liquidity of the securities and defined in terms of the length of time needed for normal transaction volumes.[2] Confidence levels are a function of risk aversion; and, therefore, higher confidence intervals imply higher value-at-risk figures. A confidence interval is used to quantify the precision or accuracy of a point estimate, such as the mean or median value. That is, the confidence interval around the mean or median equals the point estimate ± (confidence level critical value) × (standard error for the point estimate). Back in your statistics course, you learned how to do confidence intervals. Suffice to say, right now, what you are trying to do is to estimate the lower tail of a normal distribution. So if the standard bell curve shape of the normal distribution curve is taken and summed up for every point along the curve, a curve that looks like the one in Figure 15-6 is the result.

Figure 15-6 shows that at the 5% confidence level, the lower tail of the confidence interval is 1.65 times the standard deviation below from the mean.

EXAMPLE *Calculating Value-at-Risk from Portfolio Dollar-Based Standard Deviation*

In our investor's case, this means 1.65 times £912.14 or £1,505.03. That is, the investor can be 95% confident that the maximum monthly loss will be £1,505.03. In other words, the estimated value-at-risk for this portfolio is £1,505.03.

---

[2] Griffiths, Turnbull, and White (1999) show that it takes 4 to 5 times longer to divest of a portfolio at market prices than it takes to acquire that same portfolio.

The question now is, how comfortable will the investor be with the potential to lose this amount of money? While considering this comfort zone, an investor may want to know which security in the portfolio represents the greatest potential for losses. To answer this question, the incremental value-at-risk can be calculated for each stock in the portfolio.

INDUSTRY APPLICATION

INVESTOR BEHAVIOR AND PORTFOLIO PERFORMANCE

Many portfolios use the annual return on the S&P 500 as the benchmark against which their own performance is measured. This is usually the case for Student Managed Investment Funds classes at most major universities. But what does it mean to earn the benchmark rate of return? As an associate in a money management fund, it is important to remember how various costs and investment horizons affect the risk profiles of the portfolio holders.

Consider the Student Managed Equity Portfolio at a major Midwestern university. The fund started off at the beginning of the calendar with $250,000 under management. These funds are technically part of the university's endowment. The good news associated with this is that the portfolio returns are exempt from taxation. The only new funds the portfolio can be assured of getting would come from dividends and any capital gains. The fund is not allowed to use bonds, futures, forwards, or derivatives of any kind. Because the portfolio is only active when the university is in session—say, nine months of the year—the investment decisions must take into account the three months of inactivity.

Every June, the university assesses a 5% charge against the portfolio since all endowment funds must pay back 5% per year to the school. The university, in this case, uses the money to fund scholarships for the top three students in the portfolio management class. All of the students in the class know of the 5% charge and compete actively for the scholarship.

In poorly performing years, that is, years where the portfolio earns less than 5%, the portfolio suffers a loss of principal. Even in good years, say where the port-

folio earns 8%, the value of the portfolio only grows by 3%. The issue is slightly more complicated for two reasons. First, the university withdraws cash from the portfolio funds but the gains are often in the form of unrealized capital gains. Thus, potentially profitable positions sometimes have to be sold to satisfy the annual budget charge. Second, since the portfolio is not active in the summer months, the student investors often try to earn the annual benchmark rate of return over the nine months they are managing the funds.

Since the students want the fund to succeed, the students often search for short-term high expected return investments. This is not an unusual behavioral response to a *constrained* investment strategy. But notice the true effect. Higher expected return and therefore higher risk stocks are chosen but, in fact, because of the need to withdraw 5% annually, the students actually pick stocks with *marginally* higher returns but *considerably* higher risk. This is exacerbated by the desire to earn the returns over only the school year.

The role of the financial planner or investment advisor is to point out the effect of cash flow obligations on both portfolio performance and investment strategy. Although the portfolio might earn the benchmark return on a predisbursements basis, it is the after disbursements rate of return that should be evaluated. Should the investors choose a growth or value strategy? Would having a large portion of dividend-paying stocks be a good idea? How should questions of market timing and stock picking be answered in the context of such an investment group?

15.6 INCREMENTAL VALUE-AT-RISK

Incremental value-at-risk is an easy extension of portfolio value-at-risk. **Incremental value-at-risk** identifies the dollar contribution of each security to the portfolio's value-at-risk. The best way to present incremental value-at-risk is with an example, so this section continues our three-stock portfolio example.

EXAMPLE   *Process to Calculate Incremental Value-at-Risk*

The whole calculation can be broken down into two steps. The first step is to calculate for each security the sum of its own variance times its dollar position in the portfolio and the covariances times the other dollar positions in the portfolio. Figure 15-7 provides these calculations for our investor's three-stock portfolio.

Stock	Position (£)	Variance	+	Position (£)	Covariance	+	Position (£)	Covariance	= (£)
FLYBY	5,000	0.01	+	6,000	0.004	+	4,000	0.0035	88.00
UO	6,000	0.0025	+	5,000	0.004	+	4,000	0.0007	37.80
GDAY	4,000	0.0049	+	5,000	0.0035	+	6,000	0.0007	41.30

FIGURE 15-7 Calculating incremental VaR: Step 1.

On the first line (FLYBY), the sterling-value of the position is multiplied by the variance of the stock. This value will be added to the product of the sterling-value of UO times the covariance of FLYBY and UO. This sum will, in turn, be added to the product of the sterling-value of GDAY times the covariance of FLYBY and GDAY. The same process is followed for UO (second row of Figure 15-7) and GDAY (third row of Figure 15-7). The result for each row appears in the last column of the figure.

The second step is to divide the results in the last column of Figure 15-7 by the portfolio variance, then multiply the result by the amount of the portfolio value-at-risk and then multiply by the individual sterling-value positions, as shown in Figure 15-8.

Stock	Stock (variance/ covariance)	÷	Portfolio variance	×	Portfolio value-at-risk (£)	×	Stock wealth position (£)	= (£)
FLYBY	88.00	÷	832000	×	1,505.03	×	5,000	795.93
UO	37.80	÷	832000	×	1,505.03	×	6,000	410.27
GDAY	41.30	÷	832000	×	1,505.03	×	4,000	298.94
							Total (rounded)	£1,505.04

FIGURE 15-8 Calculating incremental VaR: Step 2.

Two points need to be noted here. First, notice how UO has the lowest variance/covariance sum (last column of Figure 15-7). This suggests that this security actually represents the least amount of volatility. The reason UO has a larger incremental value-at-risk than GDAY (£410.27 vs. £298.94) is because the UO position (£6,000) is greater than GDAY position (£4,000). Second, notice that FLYBY, the stock with the average sterling-value holding, represents the greatest incremental value-at-risk to the portfolio. Thus, the assumption cannot be made that the position with the greatest monetary value represents the greatest risk to overall portfolio wealth.

15.7   THREE IMPORTANT POINTS

Three points need to be made at this juncture. First, remember that value-at-risk is still an estimate of risk and not a guarantee of the amount of risk. For example, Philippe Jorion[3] analyzed the portfolio risk position of Nicholas Leeson, the rogue trader who bankrupted

[3] Jorion, P., 1997, *Value at Risk*, McGraw-Hill, New York.

Barings Bank. Leeson was reported to have been long $7.7 billion worth of the Japanese stock index futures and short $16 billion worth of Japanese government bond futures. Unfortunately, because of the lack of supervision over Leeson's activities, he actually reported a position with a risk exposure of zero. Jorion computes that the standard deviation of the portfolio was $506 million. Therefore, at the 95% confidence interval, the worst monthly loss under normal market conditions was 1.65 times $506 = $835 million. Leeson's total reported loss was $1.3 billion, a difference of almost 56%! How did this occur? The difference is a result of several factors:

- The position changed over the last two months before his activities were identified.
- Other positions were also in the portfolio, including short positions in options.
- Leeson had very bad luck:

    As a result of the Kobe earthquake, the Japanese government stepped in to control interest rates.

    One week after the Kobe earthquake the Japanese stock market lost 6.4%. However, based on historical estimates of market volatility, the expected value-at-risk at the 95% confidence interval was only 2.5%. This is a very unusual move, even though the normal expectation is to exceed the value-at-risk estimate 5% of the time.

The second point has to do with the way in which a market moves. Most of the models you have seen so far have assumed that stock returns are normally distributed, which is based on the idea that stock prices follow a random walk. What's a random walk? A random walk in stock prices means the next price change of stock is not predictable. In other words, it is random. Stock prices are assumed to follow a random pattern because no one can correctly predict on any given day whether the price is going to go up or down. Both alternatives seem equally likely. But, is this really how the market operates? If half the stocks go up and half go down on any given day, then wouldn't you expect the market index to remain roughly constant? However, when the market goes down, it appears that nearly all the stocks in the market decline in value. This action suggests that, at least in times of major market downturns, securities seem to abandon their historical correlations and tend to become almost perfectly positively correlated.

If this is true, that during major market downturns stocks tend to become almost perfectly positively correlated, perhaps a better way to measure our investor's maximum expected loss at the 95% confidence interval would be to assume that all the correlations between the stocks become 1. If the sterling-value standard deviation of the three-stock portfolio is recalculated on this basis, it is £1,954.07 and, therefore, the value-at-risk must be 1.65 times £1,954.07 = £3,224.22—nearly 2.2 times our original estimate!

The third concern has to do with borrowing money and investing in additional securities. This is known as borrowing on the margin. The market value of the securities represents the collateral value of the assets supporting the loan from the broker. In the United States, the Federal Reserve Board of Governors sets the limit on the value of additional securities that can be financed using margin borrowing. While the rules on margin borrowing are designed to limit borrowing to buy stock, the rules function through specifying the percentage of the purchase the investor must provide. The amount of the purchase that the investor must provide is known as the *initial margin* and is set at different levels (no less than 50%) depending on the volatility of the securities. Figure 15-9 presents a list of high volatility

In response to the recent volatility of certain stocks, the margin maintenance requirements for the stocks listed below are now subject to an 80% maintenance requirement. Maintenance requirements may change without notice. Trades in these stocks should be placed with the new requirements in mind.

The following stocks are now subject to the new 80% maintenance requirement: For securities with an 80% maintenance requirement, the buying power is equal to the nonmarginable securities buying power balance divided by 0.80.

AGIL	Agile Software Corp	MKSI	MKS Instruments Inc.
APNT	Appnet Inc.	MLTX	Multex.com Inc.
ARBA	Ariba Inc.	MMXI	Media Metrix Inc.
ATGN	Altigen Comm.	MPPP	MP3.com Inc.
ATHY	Appliedtheory Corp.	MRBA	Marimba Inc.
AXNT	Axent Tech Inc.	NASC	Ntwrk Access Solns.
BBI	Blockbuster Inc.	NETE	Netegrity
BNBN	Barnesandnoble.com	NETP	Net Perceptions Inc.
BRCD	Brocade Comm.	NPLS	Network Plus Corp.
BRNC	Braun Consulting	NTIQ	Netiq Corp.
BWEB	Backweb Tech Ltd.	NTRO	Netro Corp.
CMDX	Chemdex Corp.	NTSL	Netsolve Inc.
CMGI	CMGI Inc.	ONXS	Onyx Software Corp.
CPTH	Critical Path Inc.	PCLN	Priceline.com Inc.
DIR	DLJ Direct	PCSA	Airgate PCS Inc.
DRTN	Data Return Corp.	PCTI	PC-Tel Inc.
DSCM	Drugstore.com Inc.	PDYN	Paradyne Ntwrks Inc.
ETYS	Etoys Inc.	PRSF	Portal Software
FCOM	Focal Comm Corp.	QSFT	Quest Software Inc.
FCST	Flycast Comm Corp.	RAMP	Ramp Networks Inc.
FDRY	Foundry Ntwrks.	RBAK	Redback Ntwrks Inc.
FFIV	F5 Networks Inc.	RDWR	Radware Ltd.
GNET	Go2Net Inc.	RHAT	Red Hat Inc.
GSPN	Globespan Inc.	RTHM	Rhythms Netconn Inc.
HLTH	Healtheon/Webmd	SBAC	SBA Comm. Corp.
HOOV	Hoovers Inc.	SCMM	SCM Microsystems
ICCI	Insight Comm Inc.	SCNT	Scient Corp.
ICGE	Internet Capital Group	SILK	Silknet Software Inc.
INIT	Interliant Inc.	SLGX	Saleslogix Corp.
INSW	Insweb CorpDigital	SMDK	Smartdisk Corp.
ISLD	Island Inc.	TENF	Tenfold Corp.
ISPD	Interspeed Inc.	TMWD	TumbleweedComm
JNPR	Juniper Networks	TSCM	Thestreet.com Inc.
JPTR	Jupiter Comm. Inc.	VERT	Verticalnet Inc.
KANA	Kana Comm.	VIAN	Viant Corp.
LAUN	Launch Media Inc.	VSTR	Voicestream Wireless
LOAX	Log On America Inc.	WCG	Williams Comm.Grp.
LQID	Liquid Audio	WITC	WIT Capital Grp. Inc.
MCSW	Mission Critical Sware	ZDZ	Ziff-Davis Inc.— ZDNet
MIHL	MIH Ltd.		

FIGURE 15-9 Margin requirements and buying power for volatile stocks.

securities with initial margin requirements of 80% on May 18, 2000. The 80% initial margin requirement on the purchase of these stocks means the investor must provide at least 80% of the purchase price from the investor's personal funds, while the investor may borrow up to 20% of the purchase price.

The brokerage house the investor works with determines the *maintenance margin*. This is based on the net equity value of the investor's portfolio when it is marked-to-market at the end of each trading day. One broker the authors know has a 35% maintenance margin and charges about 7.5% per year for the borrowing privilege. When an investor's net equity position falls below the maintenance margin, the investor receives a call from the broker to inform the investor that their margin is not adequate. This call is referred to as a *margin call*. Margin calls are issued at the end of the trading day and the investor has three business days to resolve any inadequacy in collateral due to falling market prices.

What are the implications of this ability to borrow from the broker? The three-stock portfolio example is continued below, with the addition of using margin to purchase part of the portfolio.

EXAMPLE *Portfolio Risk When Using Margin to Purchase Stock*

Assume that the investor borrows £15,000 at 7% from their broker and invests the £15,000 equally in additional shares of each of the three stocks. Borrowing £15,000 for the purchase of additional stock puts the initial margin of the portfolio at 50%. Figure 15-10 shows the new portfolio's value under different market conditions.

Suppose that the market fell by 20% and the broker required a 40% maintenance margin. The investor's net position would only be 37.5% and the market value of the equity in the portfolio would not represent sufficient collateral for the broker to continue lending money at 7% per year. The investor would receive a margin call from their broker. When a margin call occurs, the investor must return the portfolio value to the level of the initial margin, *not* the maintenance margin. In this example the investor would be required to inject £3,000 into the portfolio. That is, injecting £3,000 into the portfolio puts the margin position of the portfolio at £12,000/£24,000 = 0.5, which is the initial margin. If the investor does not provide the additional funds, the broker has the right to sell the investor's holdings until the collateral is sufficient to cover the loan.

Security	Original portfolio (£)	Initial margin position (£)	Market falls 20%	Market rises 20% (£)
FLYBY	5,000	10,000	8,000	12,000
UO	6,000	11,000	8,800	13,200
GDAY	4,000	9,000	7,200	10,800
Margin loan	0	15,000	15,000	15,000
Total equity value	15,000	30,000	24,000	36,000
Net equity value	15,000	15,000	9,000	21,000
% Margin = $\frac{\text{equity in account}}{\text{value of stock}}$	$\frac{15,000}{15,000} = 1$	$\frac{15,000}{30,000} = 0.5$	$\frac{9,000}{24,000} = 0.375$	$\frac{21,000}{36,000} = 0.583$

FIGURE 15-10 Example of how a portfolio's value changes in response to different market conditions.

	Portfolio value (end of year) (£)	Repayment of principal and interest (£)	Net gain (loss) (£)	Investor's rate of return
Market rises by 20%	36,000	16,050	19,950	$\dfrac{(36,000 - 16,050) - 15,000}{15,000} = 33\%$
Market unchanged	30,000	16,050	13,950	$\dfrac{(30,000 - 16,050) - 15,000}{15,000} = -7\%$
Market falls by 20%	24,000	16,050	7,950	$\dfrac{(24,000 - 16,050) - 15,000}{15,000} = -47\%$

FIGURE 15-11   Portfolio value and margin.

The point at which a margin call will be issued can be easily calculated. If the maintenance margin is 40%, how low does the value of the portfolio have to fall before the investor gets a margin call for additional funds? Let P = the value of the portfolio. All the investor has to do is solve for P in the equation, $(P - £15,000)/P = 0.4$. In this case, the total market value of the stock in the portfolio would have to fall to £25,000.

Why do investors buy securities on margin? Well, they feel bullish about the market and want to increase their rate of return. Of course, the use of debt also implies downside risk. Look at our investor's portfolio after a year and see what the returns would have been under different market conditions. The results are presented in Figure 15-11.

Notice, if the market remains unchanged, the investor loses 7%, the cost of the loan from the broker. If the market increases 20%, the investor earns 33%; therefore, the use of margin has increased the investor's gains. However, if the market declines 20%, the investor loses 47%; therefore, the use of margin also increases the investor's losses. The point is clearly made that buying on margin is a risky business, but can the risk be quantified in terms of money-based losses? Suppose the value-at-risk calculation is tried using the higher sterling-value investments. Recalculating the numbers, the sterling-value standard deviation is now £3,351, which means that the maximum expected loss at the 95% confidence level using historical correlation coefficients is £5,529.15. The value-at-risk estimate with margin is 3.67 times higher than without margin buying.

In addition, the problem was mentioned that when the market declines, correlations tend to move toward 1. In our margin example, if the correlations are 1, then the monthly expected value-at-risk is £6,319.75. The *In the News* section below provides a brief overview of the difficulties experienced by the hedge fund Long-Term Capital Management and its use of value-at-risk.

IN THE NEWS[4]

LONG-TERM CAPITAL MANAGEMENT AND VALUE-AT-RISK

In January 1998, Long-Term Capital Management (LTCM) was one of the world's most respected hedge funds. LTCM was perceived as the master of relative-value trading. Relative-value trading involves the buying of one instrument and simultaneously selling another. The theory was that the portfolio would make money on the increase or decrease in the spread between the two positions and would be unaffected by the absolute level

(continued)

IN THE NEWS[4] (*continued*)

LONG-TERM CAPITAL MANAGEMENT AND VALUE-AT-RISK

of the instruments. Like many other hedge funds, LTCM tended to buy lower quality nongovernment bonds and were short higher quality government bonds. The strategy is designed to exploit the differences in yield that resulted from differences in liquidity rather than differences in credit quality. LTCM used a variety of risk management techniques, including value-at-risk, stress testing, and scenario analysis.

LTCM's firm-wide VaR analysis analyzed the thousands of positions it held and generated predictions about the daily profit-and-loss volatility it was likely to face. During the beginning of 1998, LTCM managers geared their portfolios so that the daily VaR was about $45 million.

Other statistics were generated to lend additional confidence to the portfolio's risk position. A 10% loss in the portfolio was judged to be a three–standard deviation event. That is, it would occur on average only once in a thousand or so trading periods. A loss of 50% was estimated to be a one in ten-to-the-thirtieth day event, an event longer than the life of the universe. A more conservative estimate of the likelihood of a 50% loss resulted in a one in ten-to-the-ninth day event.

LTCM was prepared to adjust its portfolio risk when losses were experienced. If it lost 10% in a particular month, it had to be ready to reduce its risk by an equivalent amount. During May and June 1998, LTCM lost 16% of its net asset value and was prepared to reduce the firm's expected risk from $45 million per day to about $34 million per day. In doing so, however, the firm made a crucial mistake. Instead of taking every single position down 15%, it decided that some investments looked better than others and took off the ones that looked the least attractive. The least-attractive positions tended to be the more liquid investments that generated modest returns. The highest-return trades were usually the most volatile and illiquid.

On August 17, Russia restructured its debt, forcing many institutional investors to reduce their positions.

The flight to quality raised prices for Treasury bonds and sunk prices for lower quality bonds. Naturally, credit spreads moved dramatically as demonstrated by the swap spread, which measures the differential in interest rates paid by high-grade banks and Treasury securities. These spreads that had never moved more than 2 or 3 basis points in a two-day period moved 21 basis points on August 21. As a result, LTCM lost $550 million that day. And, as the losses mounted day after day, the leverage ratio also increased. Before the crisis, the leverage ratio was about 25:1 and the firm had about $4.7 billion in capital and $125 billion in debt. Two days before the firm was finally bailed out by 14 banks investing $3.6 billion in exchange for 90% of the firm, LTCM had a net asset value of under $1 billion with a leverage ratio of approximately 100:1.

The partners of LTCM generally admit that six things went wrong.

1. They were not fully aware of market price dynamics. Although economic theory says buyers should buy cheap bonds, it seems in some markets low prices can repel buyers (flight to quality).

2. Diversification across markets is not always successful especially when other institutions are also trying to liquidate large positions.

3. VaR calculations are based on historic data, but the past can be a poor guide for the future. Stress-testing of the effects of low probability events is important.

4. Returns are more negatively correlated with liquidity than historical data indicate.

5. The individual positions were in some cases too large for the markets they traded in.

6. Experience does not help much with events that are impossible to predict.

[4] The source for the *In the News* item on Long-Term Capital Management (LTCM) is a series of Harvard Business School cases on LTCM by Andre Perold.

Country	E[R]	Standard deviation
U.S.A.	0.0039	0.0255
Egypt	0.0053	0.0154
France	0.0079	0.0283
Germany	0.0045	0.0369
Hong Kong	0.0044	0.0480
Israel	0.0067	0.0313
Japan	0.0021	0.0303
Korea	0.0094	0.0641
Mexico	0.0030	0.0494
So. Africa	0.0030	0.0404
Taiwan	0.0003	0.0417
Canada	0.0023	0.0252
U.K.	0.0022	0.0240

FIGURE 15-12 Average return and standard deviation for various countries' stock indexes, January 1998–December 1999.

15.8 GLOBAL PORTFOLIOS

To demonstrate the LTCM problem discussed before more clearly, suppose you were a very conservative investor and decided that the best course of action would be to invest in the major equity indices around the world. Figure 15-12 presents the indices with their average weekly returns and standard deviations for January 1998 through December 1999.

Now assume that you equally weight your wealth in each of these 13 portfolios. Based on the data provided, you would expect a weekly return of 0.42%. Also, the average of the index standard deviations is 3.5%; however, in a portfolio of these indices the standard deviation would be 1.9% because not all of these indices are perfectly positively correlated. In other words, your portfolio standard deviation is less than the average of the individual index standard deviations because of the effects of **diversification**. The correlations between the indices are provided in Figure 15-13.

	S&P	Egpt.	Fr.	Ger.	H.K.	Isr.	Jap.	Kor.	Mex.	So. Af.	Tai.	Cda.	U.K.
S&P	1.00	-0.09	0.79	0.68	0.47	0.38	0.35	0.19	0.57	-0.12	0.23	0.73	0.69
Egypt		1.00	-0.19	-0.09	-0.02	0.15	0.00	0.06	0.08	-0.07	-0.04	0.02	-0.11
France			1.00	0.83	0.45	0.24	0.29	0.26	0.33	0.13	0.16	0.72	0.71
Germany				1.00	0.43	0.38	0.24	0.20	0.41	-0.07	0.25	0.67	0.71
Hong Kong					1.00	0.09	0.29	0.33	0.40	-0.19	0.23	0.41	0.47
Israel						1.00	0.29	0.20	0.36	0.08	0.26	0.35	0.32
Japan							1.00	0.28	0.39	-0.06	0.19	0.37	0.31
Korea								1.00	0.17	-0.12	0.01	0.26	0.32
Mexico									1.00	-0.11	0.24	0.40	0.38
South Africa										1.00	-0.06	-0.10	-0.13
Taiwan											1.00	0.17	0.11
Canada												1.00	0.67
U.K.													1.00

FIGURE 15-13 Stock return correlations among various countries.

	Incremental Risk
U.S.A.	331.21
Egypt	121.38
France	408.44
Germany	692.12
Hong Kong	1,172.71
Israel	499.31
Japan	467.54
Korea	2,091.72
Mexico	1,240.27
South Africa	828.91
Taiwan	885.61
Canada	323.90
U.K.	293.88

FIGURE 15-14 Incremental VaR for various countries' stock indexes, January 1998–December 1999.

If you assume a $1,000,000 investment in an equally weighted portfolio of these 13 indices, then you can calculate an incremental value-at-risk to determine where to be concerned about possible money losses. The results are shown in Figure 15-14. You would likely conclude that the Hong Kong, Korean, and Mexican indices represented the greatest potential money losses.

Now, suppose the calculations are repeated for the 15 weeks ending April 17, 2000. Based on the previous data a weekly return of 0.42% and an average standard deviation of 3.5% per index would be expected. The actual results show a return of −0.2% and an average standard deviation of 3.8%. The individual values are shown in Figure 15-15.

The data for the first 15 weeks of 2000 yield the incremental value-at-risk results shown in Figure 15-16. You should conclude that, over this shorter time frame, Hong Kong, Canada, and Mexico represented the greatest potential risks.

What is this telling you? First, the estimates are only as good as the mathematics and since there is no way to predict the future, the assumption is made that the past predicts the future. This assumption is often erroneous. When a comparison is made between what is

Country	$E[R]$	Standard deviation
U.S.A.	−0.0053	0.0445
Egypt	0.0038	0.0186
France	0.0012	0.0406
Germany	0.0024	0.0323
Hong Kong	−0.0033	0.0489
Israel	0.0019	0.0364
Japan	0.0051	0.0116
Korea	−0.0166	0.0343
Mexico	−0.0081	0.0701
South Africa	−0.0100	0.0380
Taiwan	0.0069	0.0440
Canada	0.0028	0.0481
U.K.	−0.0038	0.0284

FIGURE 15-15 Average return and standard deviation for various countries, stock indexes, January–April, 2000.

Country	Incremental Risk
U.S.A.	682.48
Egypt	118.55
France	567.50
Germany	359.87
Hong Kong	823.29
Israel	456.73
Japan	46.10
Korea	405.30
Mexico	1,691.40
South Africa	498.00
Taiwan	667.96
Canada	798.54
U.K.	278.63

FIGURE 15-16 Incremental VaR for various countries' stock indexes, January–April 2000.

believed would happen using past data and what actually did happen, the comparison often reveals that there is little correlation between the two estimates. Even measures like value-at-risk can be misleading. In this example, historical data said to expect (at 95% certainty) a maximum expected weekly loss of \$31,678 per million. The more precise figure using actual data was \$38,487 per million—a 21.5% error.

15.9 PORTFOLIO RISK MANAGEMENT STRATEGIES

Now that portfolio risk has been quantified in both percentage and monetary terms, it is time to turn your attention to trying to manage risk. Risk management is usually done in one of two ways. First, over a long time horizon risk is managed through portfolio diversification. Since diversification has been discussed at several points earlier in the book, neither the concept nor the math of diversification will be revisited here. Instead, the short time horizon risk management technique of hedging a portfolio with derivative securities will be discussed. Specifically, the techniques of buying a protective index put or constructing a protective collar will be discussed in Subsections 15.9.1 and 15.9.2. These techniques are short-term techniques because the derivative securities expire and each time a derivative is used to hedge it is costly, so these hedges are not something investors want to use over a long time horizon.

15.9.1 Protective Puts

A **protective put** is a short-term risk management technique used to protect the value of a portfolio against concerns about a near-term decline in the overall market. That is, the concern centers on a temporary decline in the market; and, therefore, a temporary decline in our portfolio, but the belief is that in the long term both will increase. If the belief is that the portfolio will experience a permanent decrease in value then the portfolio should be sold.

Suppose an investor would like to protect a recent increase in the value of the portfolio from an anticipated decline in the market next month due to the possibility of the government raising interest rates. The investor's portfolio roughly matches the composition of the NASDAQ National Market Composite Index (NMCI). The portfolio cost $3.04 million to acquire, and it is currently valued at $4 million. The investor wants to lock in the $960,000 gain, but does not want to sell the stocks because the investor would have to pay capital gains taxes, would likely incur high transactions costs, and would lose any additional gains in the portfolio in the event that the forecast is wrong about the potential market decline.

Recall, a put option gives the buyer of the put the right to sell the underlying asset at the strike price. Buying a put option provides a hedge for the owner of the underlying asset against the price of the underlying asset falling. As the owner of a portfolio, buying a put option on your portfolio provides protection against a decline in the value of your portfolio, which is why this hedge is called a *protective put*. A put option rarely exists on the investor's portfolio. However, put options do exist for most of the major stock market indices; therefore, the investor would want to buy the put on the index that most closely matches the composition of the investor's portfolio. In this example, the portfolio closely matches the composition of the NASDAQ National Market Composite Index (NMCI). Put options are available on this index.

Once the investor has determined which put option to buy, the investor has to determine how many index put options to buy to hedge the value of the investor's portfolio. In this case, the investor needs to hedge a $4 million portfolio. Assume that the NMCI is currently at 1,580. Since each option contract is based on a multiplier of 100, the investor would need to buy $4,000,000/(1,580 × 100) = 25.3 contracts. Unfortunately, a partial contract cannot be bought; therefore, the investor would buy 25 contracts to hedge the portfolio.[5]

If the decision is to lock in as much of the portfolio gains as possible, an *at-the-money* option is needed. An at-the-money option is an option with an exercise price at the current index level, which in this example is at 1,580. Assume this put costs $37. The amount the investor has to pay for portfolio protection is $37 (the put price) × 100 (the multiplier) × 25 (the number of contracts) = $92,500.

Now, see what the protective put does for the investor by examining what happens when the put option expires. If the NMCI stays at the same level or rises, the put option expires worthless and the $92,500 premium represents the *price of insurance* paid to protect the value of the portfolio. Of course, the investor would keep any dividends paid or any additional gains in the portfolio value minus the cost of the put option. If the index falls, the investor receives gains from the options, but be aware that the investor starts out $92,500 in the hole because of the cost of the options. After the gains on the options cover the cost of the options, the remainder of the gains on the put options offsets the losses in the underlying portfolio. Figure 15-17 presents a payoff diagram for an unhedged stock portfolio and the same stock portfolio insured (hedged) with a protective put.

---

[5] We round down the number of contracts because rounding up creates speculation by the portion of the last contract not needed in the hedge.

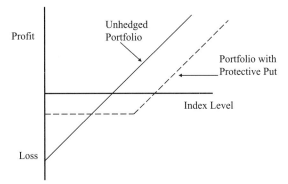

FIGURE 15-17 Protective put payoff diagram.

15.9.2 Protective Collar with Minimum Premium Costs

One of the major problems with using a protective put option as portfolio insurance is the size of the premium that must be paid. One way to reduce the size of the premium is to use a **protective collar**.

A protective collar still provides downside protection because a protective put option is purchased as part of the protective collar. However, the premium paid for the protective put is offset by the sale of index call options. In effect, the protection is being purchased with funds obtained by selling off the rights to some portion of the portfolio's potential upside gains.

This strategy must be executed in the correct order. First, the protective put with the lower exercise price must be purchased. Second, the call options with the higher exercise price will be sold. Remember, the exercise price of the call options and the number of contracts is a function of the put premium and the amount of upside gain that the investor is willing to give up. Figure 15-18 presents the payoff diagram for a protective collar.

Figure 15-18 illustrates that the collar is designed to protect the portfolio at the current index level. Other hedge positions are possible. For example, more calls than required could be sold, but while this sale would yield a net gain on the premiums, it would mean giving

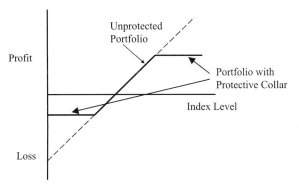

FIGURE 15-18 Protective collar payoff diagram.

up a greater percentage of any upside gain. In practice, the usual procedure is to sell as many call contracts as put contracts are purchased. Another alternative is to allow some downward losses (say 5% of the index level) and create a larger spread between the call and put exercise prices.

If the index rises, the portfolio receives any gains up to the call option exercise price. Above that level, losses from the short call position offsets gains in the underlying portfolio. The puts expire worthless. If the index falls, the portfolio has downside protection. Below the put exercise price, the gain from the long put position offsets losses in the underlying portfolio. If the portfolio remains relatively unchanged (that is, varying between the call and put exercise prices), both the calls and the puts expire worthless. However, the combination is low cost because the cost of the protective put is covered by the premium from selling the call.

SUMMARY OF VALUATION AND RISK MANAGEMENT SKILLS

1. Understand the basic performance measures of stock portfolios and understand the role of correlation in the risk of a stock portfolio.

Stock portfolio return and β are simply the weighted average of the individual stock returns and βs, but portfolio standard deviation is not because of the effect of correlation. Putting stocks that are less than perfectly positively correlated in a portfolio allows for risk reduction through lower portfolio standard deviations.

2. Calculate stock portfolio standard deviation in percentage and dollar terms.

Portfolio standard deviation (the square root of the variance) is typically calculated on a percentage basis because it measures the deviation from the average return on the portfolio. However, investors often think in terms of potential dollar losses. Standard deviation can be calculated on a dollar basis. This dollar-based standard deviation is used in the calculation of value-at-risk (VaR), which is a measure of potential dollar losses.

3. Understand the strengths and weaknesses of VaR.

The strength of VaR is that it uses statistics to quantify potential dollar losses. The weakness comes from too much reliance on the calculated number. It must be remembered that VaR is an estimate based on the assumption that the normal characteristics of the portfolio continue forward through time. In particular, it assumes that the correlations between the stocks in the portfolio continue at past levels. However, often during a significant negative event all stocks move down, suggesting that the stocks become almost perfectly positively correlated. If this happens, VaR will underestimate the dollar losses.

4. Understand how buying a stock portfolio on margin alters a portfolio's risk.

Buying a stock portfolio on margin is the logical equivalent of financing a company with debt and equity. We know that the use of debt financing in a company magnifies both gains and losses. The same magnification of gains and losses occurs when using margin (debt) to finance part of the purchase of a stock portfolio (the cash the investor provides from their own resources is the equity in the purchase). Using margin is one way to increase an investor's risk without changing the stocks in the portfolio.

5. Understand how to hedge stock portfolio risk using derivative securities.

Futures can be used to hedge a stock portfolio, but futures are seldom used because futures eliminate gains along with eliminating losses, and stock portfolio investors do not want to eliminate all gains. Accordingly, protective puts are used as portfolio insurance to limit losses while allowing gains. However, portfolio insurance can be expensive, so the portfolio owner can sell part of the potential gains to pay for the portfolio insurance. This is referred to as a protective collar.

QUESTIONS

Company	Expected return (%)	Standard deviation (%)	Beta	Investment ($)
ABC	21	34	1.75	7,500
XYZ	12	20	1.05	20,000
MNO	9	12	0.85	12,500

Correlation coefficients	ABC	XYZ	MNO
ABC	1.0	0.5	0.2
XYZ		1.0	0.8
MNO			1.0

1. Using the information from the preceding tables, calculate the expected return and beta of this three-stock portfolio.

2. Using the information from the preceding tables, calculate the percentage-based standard deviation of the portfolio.

3. Using the information from the preceding tables, calculate the dollar-based standard deviation of the portfolio and the portfolio's value-at-risk at the 95% confidence level.

4. On a spreadsheet, create a column of 30 cells filled with returns generated by a random number generator. In a second column, multiply each of the items in the first column by 60%, by 20%, and by 113.4%. What are the expected returns and standard deviations of the two sets of returns? What is the correlation coefficient between the two sets of returns?

5. The following is historical data on four companies, NuCo, OlCo, BigCo, and SmlCo.

Company	Annual std. dev. (%)	E[R] (%)
NuCo	8.00	20
OlCo	10.00	20
BigCo	8.00	15
SmlCo	25.00	25

The expected return and standard deviation of return on the market index were 18% and 22%, respectively. The correlation coefficients are OlCo vs. BigCo $= 0.3$, OlCo vs. SmlCo $= -0.2$, BigCo vs. SmlCo $= 0.1$. Assume you have $100,000 to invest and that you believe the market will increase in the coming year. Should 50% in OlCo be invested with 25% invested each in BigCo and SmlCo, or should the entire amount be invested in NuCo? Be clear in justifying your answer, especially, when discussing the issue of risk.

6. Suppose you have $180,000 to invest in two of three currency manufacturing companies. Each is based in the United States; therefore, no currency translation is required. The profit rates and standard deviations are listed in the following table.

	U.S. dollars (%)	U.K. pounds (%)	Brazilian reals (%)
Expected return	15	12	5
Standard deviation	10	9	4
Correlation with U.S. dollars		0.33	0.06

Suppose you want to minimize your risk and invest equal amounts in U.S. dollars and one of the other two currencies. In addition, you want to invest one-third of your wealth in the risk-free asset. Based on the information given, what is the standard deviation of this portfolio?

7. Referring to Question 6, what is the standard deviation if the portfolio is split equally between the U.S. dollars and the Brazilian reals, and 50% is financed using a margin account?

8. Use the following information to calculate the value-at-risk of the four-stock portfolio at the 95% confidence level. Then calculate the incremental value-at-risk of the individual stocks.

Stock	Standard deviation (%)	Investment ($)
A	12	5,000
B	7	10,000
C	15	15,000
D	22	20,000

Correlations	A	B	C	D
A	1	0.5	0.3	0.4
B		1	0.55	0.15
C			1.0	0.75
D				1.0

REFERENCES

GRIFFITHS, M. D., D. A. S. TURNBULL, and R. W. WHITE, 1999, Re-examining the small-cap myth: problems in portfolio formation & liquidation, *Global Finance Journal, 10(2)*, 201–221.

JORION, P., 1997, *Value at Risk*, McGraw-Hill, New York.

KEY TERMS

Correlation A statistical measure of how two assets move relative to each other. Correlation is an important component of the standard deviation of a portfolio because the standard deviation of the portfolio must consider how the assets in the portfolio move relative to each other.

Covariance Another measure of how two assets move relative to each other. However, unlike correlation, covariance is not a standardized measure.

$$\text{covariance} = \rho_{i,j} \times \sigma_i \times \sigma_j.$$

Diversification The process of reducing risk in a portfolio by adding assets to the portfolio that are not perfectly positively correlated with other assets in the portfolio.

Incremental Value-at-Risk Is an extension of value-at-risk that provides the contribution of each stock in the portfolio to the portfolio's value-at-risk.

Portfolio A grouping of assets.

Protective Collar Is a combination of a buying a protective put with selling a call on the same underlying asset. A protective collar is done to reduce the cost of portfolio, insurance.

Protective Put Is a put option purchased on the underlying assets to protect (hedge) the investor's position against a decline in the value of the underlying asset. A protective put is often referred to as portfolio insurance.

Standard Deviation A statistic measure of deviation from the mean. In finance it is a common measure of total risk.

Value-at-Risk Is a measure of maximum expected dollar loss derived from a money-weighted standard deviation and a critical value from the normal distribution.

CHAPTER 16

FOREIGN CURRENCY RISK MANAGEMENT

16.1 INTRODUCTION

The purpose of this chapter is to learn how to manage the risk of foreign currency exposure. When a company (or individual) has a need to exchange one currency for another currency, how does the company (or individual) protect itself against changes in the exchange rate between the two currencies? The examples of exchange risk management in this chapter focus on corporate cash flows, such as the *In The News* item on Lufthansa. However, exchange-rate risk management is also an important issue for banks because the foreign currency exchange market is a dealer market and the dealers in this market are large banks. The reason that foreign currency dealers care about exchange-rate risk is that dealers, by definition, have inventories of different currencies, and as exchange rates change the value of their inventory changes. Accordingly, this chapter continues the focus in the second half of this book on risk management and focuses on the risk associated with exchanging currencies and how that risk is managed.

This chapter begins with an *In The News* item on Lufthansa's exchange-rate risk exposure and discusses the choices that are available to manage exchange-rate risk using the Lufthansa example. One of the risk management choices is to use currency options, so the next section of this chapter discusses how to price currency options with a variant of the Black-Scholes option pricing model. This is followed by a discussion of put-call parity in the currency options market. This chapter concludes with a detailed foreign currency hedging example.

DEVELOPING VALUATION AND RISK MANAGEMENT SKILLS

1. Understand exchange-rate risk exposure and the various choices available to manage this risk exposure.
2. Understand the changes required to the Black-Scholes model for pricing currencies option and calculate the price of a currency option.

16.2 HEDGING CHOICES FOR FOREIGN CURRENCY EXPOSURE

Anytime a company has a **foreign currency exposure**, only six possible choices can be made with respect to the exposure. Those choices are listed next along with the chapter subsection headings under which each will be discussed.

IN THE NEWS

FOREIGN CURRENCY RISK MANAGEMENT AT LUFTHANSA

Perhaps the most dramatic case in recent years of foreign currency hedging and speculation occurred at exactly the same time at the same company, Lufthansa.[1] In January 1985, Lufthansa purchased 20 Boeing 737 jets at a price of $500 million U.S. payable on delivery in one year's time. The U.S. dollar had been appreciating steadily since 1980 and, in January 1985 was trading at approximately 3.2 deutschemarks to the dollar. If the dollar were to continue to rise, the cost of the aircraft to Lufthansa would also rise substantially by the time payment was due.

Heinz Ruhnau, the Chairman of Lufthansa, believed the dollar had risen as far as it was going to go and would probably decline by January 1986. However, Ruhnau realized that the funds at risk actually belonged to the company's shareholders and did not belong to him. As a result, he compromised. He hedged half of the amount

($250 million) by selling a forward contract and locked in a rate of DM3.2/$ in this transaction. Ruhnau left the remaining $250 million uncovered and completely subjected to the volatility in the deutschemark/dollar exchange rate.

Ruhnau was both right and wrong. First, the good news. His expectations of the future deutschemark/dollar exchange rate were exactly right. Over the next year, the exchange rate fell dramatically in Lufthansa's favor to DM2.3/$. Now, the bad news. The total deutschemark cost of the partial forward hedge was DM1.375 billion, a full DM225,000,000 more than if no hedging activity had been done at all! Ruhnau was accused of speculating recklessly with Lufthansa's money, but the speculation was seen as the forward contract and not the dollar exposure that had been left uncovered for the entire year.

1. Remain uncovered (unhedged) (Section 16.2.1, Remain Uncovered)

2. Obtain the foreign currency now and hold it until payment is due (Section 16.2.2, Money Market Hedge)

3. Cover the entire exposure with forward contracts (Section 16.2.3, Full Forward Covers)

4. Cover the entire exposure with futures contracts (Section 16.2.4, Full Futures Coverage)

5. Cover some portion of the exposure, having the balance uncovered (Section 16.2.5, Cover Some Portion—Have a Portion Uncovered)

6. Cover the exposure with foreign currency options (Section 16.2.6, Use Foreign Currency Options)

Although the final cost of each choice cannot be known precisely when the action is initiated, each action's outcome can be anticipated. How to anticipate the outcome will be demonstrated in this chapter. In addition, this chapter will discuss how to price foreign currency options using a version of the Black-Scholes model.

At this point, a mention needs to be made that there is one possible case where a foreign currency exposure does not really pose a problem. Consider Lufthansa's problem from the *In the News* item again. If Lufthansa had sold a sufficient number of airline tickets in U.S. dollars in one year to be able to save up the $500 million U.S., it would not have

---

[1] The authors would like to thank Professor Michael Moffett for bringing this transaction to their attention.

had to worry if the exchange rate went up or down. It would have had the correct amount of cash in the correct currency on hand! However, the likelihood of having enough U.S. sales to cover the dollar cost of the planes is extremely unlikely, even for a company as large as Lufthansa.

Also, before moving on to the discussion of the six choices listed, some important concepts for exchanging currencies that were introduced back in Chapter 8 need to be reviewed. In Chapter 8 the concept of spot and forward exchange rates was introduced. In that chapter exchange rates were discussed as a function not only of the interest rates in the different countries but also of their relationship to the size and timing of three types of international cash flows: (1) investment cash flows, (2) political cash flows, and (3) speculative cash flows. The discussion went on to indicate that in a stable exchange-rate environment, exchange rates were predictable based on the relative levels of the two countries' domestic interest rates. In this situation, the argument was presented that forward exchange rates were **unbiased indicators** of future exchange rates. The example given was one related to the concept of *covered interest arbitrage.* Also, how the relationships between exchange rates and interest rates works was shown, with an example of how a foreign exchange dealer could offer a company a guaranteed quote to exchange pounds for dollars in one year's time. As you recall, in the example, the dealer quoted an exchange rate for a forward foreign exchange contract. Using the existing interest rates in each country, the dealer: (1) calculated the *PV* of the pounds receivable by discounting them at the British discount rate, (2) converted the pounds into U.S. dollars at the spot rate, (3) invested the money for one year at the U.S. rate, and (4) at the end of the year, the dealer exchanged the dollars back into British pounds.

With this brief review, discussion of six choices for handling foreign currency exposure can now begin.

16.2.1 Remain Uncovered

Remaining uncovered represents the position of maximum risk. If Lufthansa had chosen to *remain uncovered,* it would have faced the potential for an unlimited increase in the cost of the planes if the value of the U.S. dollar had continued to appreciate. On the other hand, the company would also have faced the greatest potential benefits if the U.S. dollar depreciated, thereby making the planes much less expensive in deutschemark terms. Remaining uncovered (unhedged) is demonstrated in Figure 16-1 and the figure demonstrates the range of possibilities between DM2.2/$ to DM4.0/$.

Recall from the preceding *In the News* item that in January 1985, the exchange rate was DM3.2/$, which means that the $500 million cost translated into 1.6 billion deutschemarks. If in one year's time the exchange rate had fallen to DM2.2/$, Lufthansa would have paid the equivalent of 1.1 billion deutschemarks. That is, the planes' price tag would have *appeared* to have fallen to $343,750,000. Of course, if the dollar had continued to appreciate to say DM4.0/$, Lufthansa would have paid DM2.0 billion—the equivalent of $625,500,000 at the January 1985 exchange rate. Hopefully, most managers will consider that this range of possible outcomes represents too much risk—especially in terms of cash flows and profit predictability and, therefore, not a viable choice. Most believe that the decision to leave a large exposure uncovered for an extended period of time is currency

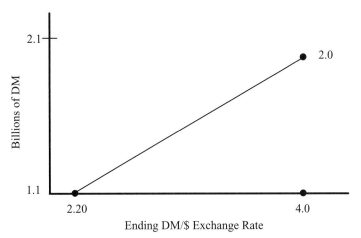

FIGURE 16-1 Lufthansa's exposure if uncovered.

speculation. *Responsible managers usually believe that they should be able to assess and then accept risk in the firm's line of business but not in the payment process.*

16.2.2 Money Market Hedge

A *money market hedge* is basically the same process as covered interest arbitrage, which was discussed in Chapter 8. The idea for Lufthansa would have been to acquire the *present value* of the $500 million in January 1985 and hold the funds in an interest-bearing account until the payment was due one year later. Although this alternative seems to have the potential to eliminate the currency risk completely, it requires the firm to have the capital on hand at the time the order is placed. A money market hedge is often *unavailable* to companies because of covenants attached to bank loans and publicly issued debt. These covenants can restrict the types, amounts, and currencies of the liabilities that a firm can carry on its balance sheet.

16.2.3 Full Forward Covers

A *full forward covers* strategy is for the firm that wishes to be 100% certain of the amount that it will have to pay. Consider the January 1985 Lufthansa decision. At that time, the firm's management believed that buying 20 jets for $500 million U.S. (DM1.6 billion) would be a good price and placed the order. Entering into a forward contract in January 1985 for the conversion of DM1.6 billion to $500 million U.S. in January 1986 would lock in the January 1985 exchange rate of DM3.2/$ (see Figure 16-2).

Notice that just as in the case of the money market hedge, the currency risk appears to be completely eliminated. Of course, the forward contract itself contains certain risks. One or more counterparties must be willing to take the other side of the forward contract in terms of the amount and timing of the cash flows. Also, the counterparty or counterparties should have the financial ability to handle their side of the contract when the time comes.

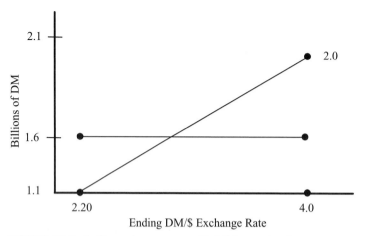

FIGURE 16-2 Lufthansa's exposure with full forward or futures coverage vs. an uncovered position.

16.2.4 Full Futures Coverage

As discussed in Chapter 9, the major differences between forward contracts and futures contracts are

- Futures contracts are traded on specific exchanges, for example, CME, COMEX, CBOT, DTB, SIMEX, HKFE, and LIFFE.
- Futures contracts are regulated and standardized, having pre-set delivery months, contract sizes, margin requirements (about 2% of contract value), transaction costs, and quotation systems.

Originally, futures contracts were available for exchange with U.S. dollars in only seven currencies: the British pound, Canadian dollar, Germany, deutschemark, Swiss franc, French franc, Japanese yen, and Australian dollar. Recently, futures contracts in several other currencies have developed. These include, but are not limited to: euro, South African rand, Mexican peso, Brazilian real, Russian ruble, and New Zealand dollar.

In general, long positions are orders to buy a currency and short positions are orders to sell a currency. If a company is long in a futures currency contract and the futures price goes up, the contract will make money (gain on futures position). Similarly, if the futures price goes down, the firm will lose money (lose on its position). However, if the company is short in a futures currency contract and the futures price declines, the position makes money and vice versa.

Consider the Lufthansa example. At the time, $500 million would have to have been hedged with contracts sized at 125,000 deutschemarks each. This implied a need for 4,000 contracts. If the current exchange rate had been DM3.2/$, this implied a price of $0.3125 per DM. Hence, each contract would have been valued at $0.3125 × 125,000 = $39,062.50. Should Lufthansa want to buy or sell these futures contracts? The easiest way to determine this is by comparing the outcomes in Figure 16-3 to the situation that is being hedged.

Now consider the Lufthansa situation. If the DM/$ exchange rate had increased then the firm would lose money because the jets would become more expensive. Remember

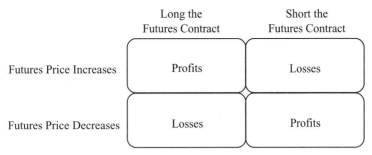

	Long the Futures Contract	Short the Futures Contract
Futures Price Increases	Profits	Losses
Futures Price Decreases	Losses	Profits

FIGURE 16-3 Summary of profits and losses on futures positions.

that the futures contract is quoted not in DM/$ but in $/DM. If the DM/$ increases, then the futures price will *increase*. So Lufthansa (check Figure 16-3) must want to short the contracts. Here is a handy rule: when hedging a foreign currency position, first make certain that the futures price is quoted in foreign units per domestic units. Then buy futures contracts to offset assets and sell futures contracts to offset liabilities. For Lufthansa, the purchase of the planes in the future was a liability.

Remember, whenever an exposure is uncovered, a risky position exists. Hedging the position should be considered. Hedging will lock in a specific exchange rate. Locking in an exchange rate does not necessarily mean you are better off hedging rather than not hedging. It just means you are banking on certainty and not gambling that the exchange rate will move in your favor.

16.2.5 Cover Some Portion—Have a Portion Uncovered

To this point the two extremes for managing foreign exchange exposure have been discussed: either remaining unhedged or becoming completely hedged. Another alternative exists. A manager can choose a middle ground and hedge a portion of the foreign exchange exposure. Lufthansa made this choice. Remember, any hedge that covers less than 100% of the foreign exchange exposure leaves the company open to risk, both favorable and unfavorable, from changes in exchange rates. However, a partial hedge will reduce risk relative to no hedge at all.

Figure 16-1 depicts a completely unhedged position. If only a portion of the exposure is hedged—say 50% as in the Lufthansa case—a position that resembled Figure 16-1, only with one-half the slope, will result. This partial hedge is shown in Figure 16-4.

16.2.6 Use Foreign Currency Options

Foreign currency options provide a useful hedging alternative to forward and futures contracts, which lock in a future exchange rate and thus lock in profits on a transaction. For example, if a sale is made in a foreign currency and the pricing does not include a large profit margin, protection against changes in the exchange rate eroding the value of those cash flows might be desired while, at the same time keeping the opportunity to capture the benefit of a favorable change in exchange rates. This hedge is possible using a foreign currency option.

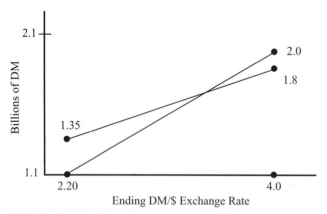

FIGURE 16-4 Lufthansa's exposure with 50% coverage vs. uncovered position.

However, caution must be exercised when dealing with foreign currency options. Foremost in your mind must be the knowledge of the unit of currency that you are working in: foreign or domestic. A short digression is needed here to reevaluate the meaning of *buying or selling* a call or a put.

When dealing with currencies, the discussion of buying or selling puts or calls must be made in terms of domestic or foreign currency. In the Lufthansa example, Ruhnau was working in deutschemarks. Suppose he had bought a one-year dollar-denominated put option at DM3.2/$. That is, he would have bought a *put* on the deutschemarks priced in U.S. dollars. Since the option was dollar-denominated, the strike price would be $1/3.2 = 0.3125$ and the premium would be 0.013467.[2] Hence, in one year's time, Ruhnau would have been able to give up DM0.3125 and receive $1. The dollar value of this put option, if it had expired in-the-money, would have been equal to (the strike exchange rate − the actual exchange rate) $= (1/3.2 - 1/x)$, where x is the DM/$ rate in one year's time.

In the alternative, Ruhnau could have purchased a deutschemark-denominated *call* option to pay DM3.2/$ for 0.1379 deutschemarks. That is, he could have bought a call on dollars priced in deutschemarks. Then, at maturity if the *call* option had expired in-the-money, the option would have been worth (the actual exchange rate − the strike exchange rate) $= (x - 3.2)$ deutschemarks.

Suppose that at maturity the actual exchange rate was DM4/$. Now even though both options were in-the-money, they did differ in a couple of ways. First, the scale of the options was different. The deutschemark-denominated call option was based on DM3.2 to one dollar, while the dollar-denominated put option was based on 0.3125 deutschemarks. Also, the currency of the denomination of strike prices and exercise prices was different.

Now, the scale problem can be solved by holding either more of the smaller option or less of the larger option. For example, the deutschemark-denominated call scale problem can be solved by holding 1/3.2 times of them, or the dollar-denominated puts scale problem

---

[2] The premium calculations are based on theBlack-Scholes model with a dollar interest rate of 5%, a deutschemark interestrate of 4%, an exchange-rate volatility of 10%, and a one-year term toexpiry. We show how to use the Black-Scholes model to price currency options later inthis chapter.

can be solved by holding 3.2 times the number of them. But, what really needs to be known is whether these two transactions have the same result. Let's try this:

1. Buy 1/3.2, one-year deutschemark-denominated call options. When this call is exercised at maturity it will exchange DM1 for $0.3125. The cost of this is $1/3.2 \times \$0.1379 = \$0.04309$.

2. Buy 1 one-year dollar-denominated put option on dollars with a strike of DM3.2. At maturity, the cost of this in dollars is DM3.2/1 × DM0.013467 = $0.04309.

As can be seen, the two transactions have the same cost but will they end up being worth the same at maturity? The deutschemark-denominated call option will be worth $(DM4 - DM3.2) = DM0.8$. Adjusting for the scale difference this is equal to $0.8/3.2 = 0.25$ and translated into dollars at DM4/\$ = $0.0625. The dollar-denominated put option will be worth $(1/3.2 - \frac{1}{4}) = (0.3125 - 0.25) = \$0.0625$. Hence, the two options have the same payoff at maturity as well. Thus, the two positions have both the same cost and the same payoff. Accordingly, either can be used for the hedge.

Take another look at Lufthansa. Ruhnau would want to buy a put option (to sell deutschemarks at 3.2/$) to hedge against further appreciation in the dollar. Remember, Lufthansa is buying Boeing jets; therefore, Lufthansa needs to sell deutschemarks to receive U.S. dollars to pay for the planes. Accordingly, Lufthansa needs to buy put options that sell deutschemarks for U.S. dollars. Figure 16-5 demonstrates the payoff to this option with a strike exchange rate of deutschemark 3.2/$.

If the dollar had continued to appreciate over DM3.2/$, the total cost of the $500 million jet purchase would have been locked in at DM1.6 billion plus the cost of the option premium (Lufthansa would buy put options). This is illustrated by the horizontal portion of the payoff diagram in Figure 16-5. If, however, the dollar had depreciated, Lufthansa would have let the option expire worthless and bought dollars at a lower exchange rate in the spot market. This opportunity is represented by the downward-sloping line to the left

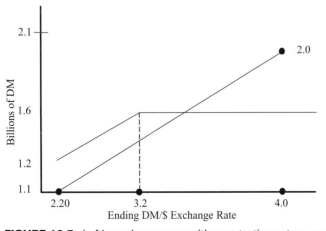

FIGURE 16-5 Lufthansa's exposure with a protective put vs. an uncovered position.

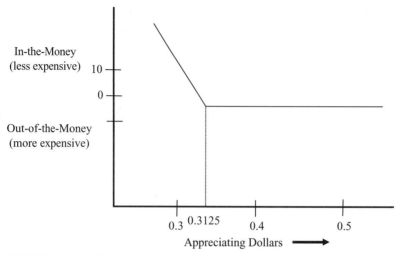

FIGURE 16-6 Lufthansa's exposure with a protective put in dollars vs. profits.

of DM3.2/$. Note also that the option line has the same slope as the uncovered position but does not earn as much (the line is higher) by the amount of the option premium.

But wait! Doesn't the payoff diagram look like that of selling a put option rather than buying a put option? Yes, caution must be exercised at this point relative to Lufthansa's point of reference. Figure 16-5 is drawn with deutschemarks on the horizontal axis and expenses on the vertical axis. Watch what happens in Figure 16-6 when dollars are drawn on the horizontal axis and profits on the vertical axis.

The relationship between Figures 16-5 and 16-6 is a version of put-call parity which will be discussed later in the chapter. However, first foreign currency option pricing needs to be discussed in greater detail.

Therefore, to summarize, care must be taken when using foreign currency options because the option required for the hedge depends on which reference currency is being used. Figure 16-7 is a useful tool to use for determining the correct hedging strategy.

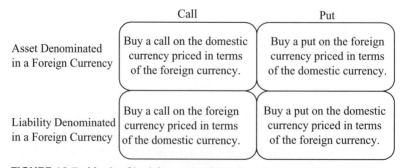

FIGURE 16-7 Matrix of hedging strategies using currency options.

16.3 PRICING CURRENCY OPTIONS

One way for a company to hedge against exchange-rate risk is to use currency options. To use currency options to hedge, the option must be priced so that the cost of the hedge can be determined. The pricing model for a currency option is similar to the standard Black-Scholes option pricing model for a dividend-paying stock index. However, a few minor adjustments that are easy to remember need to be made to the model. Equations for a currency call option and a currency put option are as follows:

$$c = Se^{-r_f T} N(d_1) - Ke^{-r_d T} N(d_2)$$
$$p = Ke^{-r_d T} N(-d_2) - Se^{-r_f T} N(-d_1)$$

(16-1 and 16-2)

where

$$d_1 = \frac{\ln(S/K) + (r_d - r_f + \sigma^2/2)T}{\sigma\sqrt{T}}$$
$$d_2 = d_1 - \sigma_1\sqrt{T}.$$

Following are discussions of the two minor and two major adjustments to the basic Black-Scholes model needed to price a currency option.

Minor Adjustments

1. The first minor adjustment is that S is no longer the stock price but is now the *spot price* for one unit of foreign currency measured in the domestic currency.

2. The second minor adjustment is that K is no longer the exercise price of the stock but is now the *exercise price of one unit of foreign currency* also measured in terms of the domestic currency (for example, if you are working with a U.S. investor who wants to buy a currency call option on Swiss francs). Because the investor is a U.S. investor, the exchange rates entered into the model must be in U.S. dollars. Assume the exchange rate is 1.800 SFr/US$. The spot price for the option pricing model would be input as 0.5556 (US$/SFr) because it takes $0.5556 for one Swiss franc. For a Japanese investor buying a call on SFr with an exchange rate of 82 JY/SFr, the spot would be input as 82 JY/SFr because the exchange rate input must be in yen (the domestic currency of the investor).

Major Adjustments

1. The first major adjustment, as in the dividend version of Black-Scholes, is that S is modified by $e^{r_f T}$, where r_f is the foreign rate of interest. Notice that the exercise price is still discounted by the domestic interest rate.

2. The second major adjustment occurs in the *calculation of d_1 where the foreign interest rate is subtracted from the domestic interest rate*. Why is this? Well, just as in the dividend model where the stock price cannot grow because the firm paid out some of the earnings in the form of dividends to the investors, the exchange rate cannot grow at the domestic rate of interest because some of the funds have to be paid out in foreign interest. Remember the calculation of the forward exchange rate!

In general, currency call options have the following properties:

- *The call price increases when the domestic price of the foreign currency increases* because as the exchange rate increases, the adjusted intrinsic value increases.
- *The call price increases as the domestic interest rate rises* because as domestic interest rates rise the *PV* of the exercise price falls, leading to a larger adjusted intrinsic value.
- *The call price falls when the foreign interest rate rises* because an increase in the foreign interest rates represents an additional return to the seller of the option, thereby reducing the cost of replicating a risk-free portfolio.
- *The call price increases with the time to maturity* for the same reasons as with the standard Black-Scholes model.
- *The call price increases with the volatility of the exchange rate* for the same reasons as with the standard Black-Scholes model.

Another interesting thing about currency options, that is different from the standard Black-Scholes model, has to do with put-call parity. You will remember that put-call parity states that the price of a call option and the price of a put option on the same underlying asset with the same exercise price and the same time to maturity will be related but *will not* be equal. This statement is not true in the world of currency options. The price of a foreign exchange (forex) call option in one currency is equal to the price of the put option in the other currency (with strikes equal). Why? Because in either case the investor has the right but not the obligation to exchange the first currency for the second. The only difference is the number of currency units that are traded. The thing that is really convenient about this parity relationship is that it is really easy to switch from pricing the call to pricing the put. But be careful when drawing the payoff diagrams—remember the payoff diagrams for the Lufthansa example in Figures 16-5 and 16-6.

16.4 PUT-CALL PARITY IN CURRENCY EXCHANGE OPTIONS

For example, if $c_f(S, K)$ and $p_f(S, K)$ are call and put values in the foreign currency, with spot exchange rate S and exercise exchange rate K, and $c_d(S, K)$ and $p_d(S, K)$ are call and put values in the domestic currency with spot exchange rate S and exercise exchange rate K, then the following relationships will hold:

$$c_f(S, K) = S \times K \times p_d(1/S, 1/K) \text{ and,} \qquad (16\text{-}3)$$

$$p_f(S, K) = S \times K \times c_d(1/S, 1/K). \qquad (16\text{-}4)$$

That is, the price of the forex call option in one currency is equal to the price of the put option in the other currency (with exercise exchange rates equal). Perhaps an example will help to demonstrate this point.

EXAMPLE *Put-Call Parity*

Look at six-month options on the Japanese yen and the Swiss franc where the Japanese domestic interest rate is 2% and the Swiss domestic interest rate is 5%. Begin by looking at the problem from the Japanese investor's point of view on a call option. Assume that $S = 82$ JY/SFr and $K = 80$ JY/SFr and that the volatility of the exchange rate is 15% (note that this is independent of how the currency is quoted).

From the Japanese perspective, a call on Swiss francs gives the right but not the obligation to buy Swiss francs and to sell Japanese yen.

$$c_{JY} = 82e^{-0.05 \times 0.5}N(d_{1JY}) - 80e^{-0.02 \times 0.5}N(d_{2JY})$$

$$d_{1,JY} = \frac{\ln(82/80) + (0.02 - 0.05 + 0.15^2/2) \times 0.5}{0.15\sqrt{0.5}} = 0.1444$$

$$d_{2,JY} = d_{1JY} - 0.15\sqrt{0.5} = 0.0383$$

$$N(0.1444) = 0.5574$$

$$N(0.0383) = 0.5153$$

$$c_{JY} = 3.76.$$

Now examine the same problem from the perspective of a Swiss franc investor. A put is the right but not the obligation to sell Japanese yen and to receive Swiss francs. The spot rate and strike from this perspective must be 1/82 and 1/80, respectively. The calculation is straightforward. However, notice that to confirm parity between the call and the put, the relationship in Equation (16-3) is used to switch back to the Japanese investor's point of view. The result is the same value of 3.76 yen per Swiss franc.

$$p_{SFr} = \frac{1}{80}e^{-0.05 \times 0.5}N(-d_{2SFr}) - \frac{1}{82}e^{-0.02 \times 0.5}N(-d_{1SFr})$$

$$d_{1,SFr} = \frac{\ln(0.0122/0.0125) + (0.05 - 0.02 + 0.15^2/2) \times 0.5}{0.15\sqrt{0.5}} = -0.0346$$

$$d_{2,SFr} = d_{1,SFr} - 0.15\sqrt{0.5} = -0.1407$$

$$N(0.0383) = 0.5138$$

$$N(0.1444) = 0.5559$$

$$p_{SFr} = 0.000574$$

$$S \times K \times p_{SFr} = 3.76$$

Note: $82 \times 80 \times 0.000574 = 3.76$.

16.5 A FOREIGN CURRENCY HEDGING EXAMPLE

Now, a currency hedging example needs to be discussed. The purpose of this section is to provide a detailed example that applies the various hedging choices discussed in Section 16.2 of this chapter.

A U.S.-based used-car wholesaler, has just arranged for a fleet sale to a Canadian affiliate. The total US$ value of the cars in the fleet is $2,057,320. At the then current spot rate of 1US$ = Canadian $1.4096, the Can$ value of the contract is Can$2,900,000. The U.S.

wholesaler has agreed to accept payment in Canadian dollars in 90 days time. The day following the signing of the contract, the value of the U.S. dollar closed at 1US$ = Can$1.3590. Since the Canadian dollar has been known to move erratically within a reasonably narrow range relative to the U.S. dollar, this change is not unexpected. In fact, over the past five months, the average exchange rate per month had been 1.4027, 1.3978, 1.4168, 1.4005, and 1.3553. Because of the recent volatility in the exchange rate the Chief Financial Officer at the used-car wholesaler is concerned that the *Canadian dollar might depreciate against the U.S. dollar during the next 90 days*, therefore eroding the already thin profit margin (5%) built into the pricing arrangement. However, over the 55 days since the contract price was set, *the U.S. dollar had depreciated* by Can$0.0502 from Can$1.4096 to Can$1.3594, or 3.6% in absolute terms. If this exchange rate can hold constant for the next 90 days, the wholesaler's profit margin would increase from 5 to 8.6%. However, assuming the exchange rate would remain constant would be a heroic assumption. The CFO knows that a number of hedging alternatives are available if the CFO wants to hedge the position. The alternatives are as follows:

1. **Presell the foreign contract**. The bank that the wholesaler works with has an export finance subsidiary that would purchase the short-term Canadian dollar contract at a discount. The interest rate for this type of transaction is 9.2% plus a transaction fee of 0.5%. Any funds could be reinvested in the United States at 11%.

2. **Arrange a foreign currency loan**. This loan would create a Canadian dollar obligation in 90 days time. The wholesaler could borrow Canadian dollars from the bank and then use the proceeds on completion of the contract to repay the principal and interest. The loan proceeds would be converted into U.S. dollars immediately at the prevailing spot price. Any gains and losses on the receivable due to changes in the exchange rate would be offset by equivalent gains or losses on the loan itself. The bank indicated that the Canadian dollar loan could be made at 12.5% plus a setup fee of 0.125% and could be invested at 11% in the U.S. market.

3. **Use a forward contract**. The use of a forward contract would involve arranging to deliver Can$2,900,000 in 90 days for conversion into U.S. dollars at a predetermined exchange rate. Assume a local bank was quoting the three-month forward rate at 1US$ = Can$1.3995. The wholesaler would want to sell the forward contract. There is no direct transaction cost for this alternative as the bank would earn the bid-ask spread.

4. **Use a foreign currency futures contract**. The current 90-day futures contract was priced at 1Can$ = US$0.735 and came in increments of Can$100,000. The cost per futures contract (round-trip was US$50).

5. **Use a foreign currency option**. Since the wholesaler has a foreign currency contract, it could hedge the position by buying a Canadian dollar put priced in U.S. dollars. Buying the put would protect the company from an unfavorable downward movement in the Canadian dollar exchange rate while allowing the company to benefit from any further appreciation in the Canadian dollar. The current 90-day put exercise price was 1Can$ = US$0.7200 (or 1US$ = Can$1.3888) with a premium of US$0.0225/Can$1.

6. **Use a tunnel forward**. A **tunnel forward** is a special type of contractual agreement between two parties. The contract defines a specific exchange rate band within which

the wholesaler would have to exchange currencies on a specific future date. The upper and lower limits of the contract act as contract settlement rates if the exchange rate exceeds the limits of the range of the contract. The price of a zero cost tunnel (where the premium paid is equal to the premium received) could be created with the exercise rate of the Canadian dollar put set at US$0.7133 and the exercise rate on the Canadian dollar call set at US$0.7533.

Now, look at how each of these alternatives would have worked had they been implemented. The solutions will be in the same order as the hedging alternatives just listed.

1. **Presale of the contract.** The contract is worth Can$2,900,000 and can be sold at an effective interest rate of 9.2%. There is a 0.5% transaction fee and the funds can be invested at 11%.

$$Can\$2,900,000/(1 + 0.092/4) = Can\$2,834,800$$

Less transactions cost

$$Can\$2,900,000 \times 0.005 = \underline{\qquad 14,500}$$

Net   Can$2,820,300

Convert to U.S. dollars = 2,820,300/1.3590 = $2,021,720

Invest and in 90 days = $2,021,720 \times (1 + 0.11/4) = \underline{\$2,077,317}$.

2. **Arrange a foreign currency loan.** The loan would have to be for Can$2,900,000 and would have an interest rate of 12.5%. There is 0.125% transaction fee and the funds can be invested at 11%.

$$Can\$2,900,000/(1 + 0.125/4) = Can\$2,812,121$$

Less transactions cost

$$Can\$2,812,121 \times 0.00125 = \underline{\qquad 3,515}$$

Net   Can$2,808,606

Convert to U.S. dollars = 2,808,606/1.3590 = $2,013,338

Invest and in 90 days = $2,013,338 \times (1 + 0.11/4) = \underline{\$2,068,705}$.

3. **Use a forward currency contract.** The contract is worth Can$2,900,000 and a forward currency contract can be arranged with a three-month forward rate of 1.3995. There is no transaction fee since the bank earns the bid-ask spread.

$$Can\$2,900,000/1.3995 = \$2,072,169.$$

4. **Arrange a foreign currency futures contract.** The current 90-day futures contract is priced at 1Can$=US$0.716 and comes in increments of Can$100,000. The cost per futures contract (round-trip was US$50).

$$Can\$2,900,000 \times 0.716 = \$2,076,400$$

The CFO needs 2,900,000/100,000 = 29 contracts

Less transactions cost

$$29 \times 50 \qquad = \underline{\qquad 1,450}$$

Net $2,074,950.

5. **Use a foreign currency option**. The contract is worth Can$2,900,000 and can be protected by buying a put with an exercise price of US$0.72 with a premium of 0.0225.

> Buy a put on Can$ @ US$0.72
> Premium paid in US$ $= \$2,900,000 \times 0.0225 = \$65,250.$
> Worst case: put expires worthless
> Can$2,900,000 $\times (0.72 - 0.0225) = \$2,022,750.$

> Where would the break-even point with the forward rate be?
> Future spot rate $-$ premium $=$ forward rate
> Future spot rate $- 0.0225 = 1/3,995$
> Future spot rate $= 0.787.$

What are the implications of hedging with a foreign currency option? If the CFO expects the spot exchange rate in 90 days to be greater than 0.7549, the CFO should buy a put. If the CFO believes the expected spot exchange rate will be less than 0.6968, the CFO should sell a forward contract.[3]

6. **Use a tunnel forward**. The contract comprises two positions, essentially a floor and a ceiling representing a best- and worst-case scenario.

> Best case (ceiling) Can $2,900,000 $\times 0.7533 = \$2,184,570$
> Worst case (floor) Can $2,900,000 $\times 0.7133 = \$2,068,570$

16.6 SUMMARY OF HEDGING EXAMPLE

Figure 16-8 summarizes the six hedging alternatives in an easy-to-read chart that shows that the CFO has the opportunity to use a number of different hedging strategies. The question quickly becomes, *Which one is the best?* Perhaps the overriding determinant of the answer to this question rests on three questions.

1. What is management's appetite for risk? The first thing to know is the amount of risk management is willing to accept. This amount of risk frequently rests on the company's policy on the use of performance measures to evaluate and promote its managers.

2. What is the management's rationale for hedging? Management must determine whether external or internal issues dominate the hedging decision. If external issues dominate, management is concerned about what effect hedging will have on

---

[3] The calculation is

> future spot rate $+$ premium $=$ forward rate
> future spot rate $+ 0.0356 \quad = 1/1.3653$
> future spot rate $\qquad\qquad = 0.6968.$

Alternative	Cost	Best case	Worst case
Pre-sell contract	$14,500	$2,077,317	$2,077,317
Foreign currency loan	$3,515	$2,068,705	$2,068,705
Forward contract	Bid-ask spread	$2,072,169	$2,072,169
Futures contract	$1,450	$2,074,950	$2,074,950
Sell a put	Bid-ask spread		$2,022,750
Tunnel forward	No charge	$2,184,570	$2,068,570

FIGURE 16-8   Summary of Forex hedging alternatives.

the firm's share price or how much influence the investor clientele has in influencing management decisions. If internal issues dominate, the concern is usually over the volatility of the cash flows. In the example of the U.S. used-car wholesaler with a thin 5% profit margin, the concern could rest on what the absolute minimum required return on this contract might have to be.

3. What are management's hedging objectives? Four objectives are possible. (1) Management may be concerned about hedging or eliminating translation exposure—this would again relate to the profit issue. Translation exposure may be of concern if the foreign transactions will show up on the firm's balance sheet. (2) Management may feel that it is important to reduce or eliminate volatility in reported results. (3) Minimizing economic exposure is often an issue when firms have to deal with foreign exposures that could affect the companies' competitiveness in delivering its product or services. (4) Finally, management could view the use of derivative instruments in risk management as a means of earning additional returns and thereby contributing to longer-term corporate competitiveness.

Normally, foreign exchange management is not a preoccupation of most senior managers. However, it is one of the many concerns that management of any global enterprise must consider on a daily basis. The treasurer of the firm should be looking at foreign exchange risk management solutions that can solve other problems at the same time or, at least, do not make other problems or situations any worse.

Any solutions that the treasurer decides on should also do the following: they should ensure adequate and timely financing; they should broaden or improve sources of financing or liquidity; they should manage balance sheet risk; they should reduce interest-rate risk and the cost of debt financing; and, if possible, they should reduce any tax liabilities.

Six alternatives for foreign currency hedging and three determinants have been discussed. How the CFO should evaluate this set of alternatives is discussed next.

The first two alternatives, *presale of the contract* and *arranging a foreign currency loan* (a money market hedge), are similar in that both allow for a great deal of certainty in the amount of the cash flow that can anticipated, which helps in the planning process. In addition, arranging a foreign currency loan is relatively easy to understand and can be tailored to the specific situation. Unfortunately, a foreign currency loan has limited flexibility if modifications have to be made after the loan is arranged. Also, arranging the loan can be an onerous affair since substantial loan documentation may be required if the loan is not part of a preexisting loan facility.

The *use of forward contracts* also allows for certainty of cash flows and thus assists in the planning process. Forward contracts are easily understood and as an over-the-counter instrument can be tailored directly to the transaction in question with minimal charges. Using the forward, however, does mean that management must be prepared to forgo any potential gains due to foreign exchange rate movements. Further, the use of the forward means that the firm will have to set up a credit facility with the bank that arranges for the hedge.

A *foreign currency futures contract* should only be used if the firm does not qualify for any forward foreign exchange credit. Although standardized and with minimal charges, the futures contract cannot be tailored directly to a transaction and has high administration costs involved because of the need to monitor any margin requirements. In addition, the treasurer has to consider transactions costs and the potential for basis risk.

The role of *foreign currency option contracts* should be examined from the point in time of the purchase of the contracts forward. These options provide protection against any adverse foreign exchange rate moves, are easy to use, and have a minimal amount of documentation. Unfortunately, the firm will have to pay any up-front fee as a premium. A related concern is the calculation of the appropriate exercise prices since this price determines the amount of self-insurance, that is, the amount of risk the firm is willing to take on.

The *tunnel forward* represents the zero or low cost choice and provides protection against adverse foreign exchange rate moves with minimal documentation. When using a tunnel forward, a treasurer has two major concerns; *How much upside potential gain am I willing to give up in exchange for downside protection?*, and *How much risk am I willing to take on in the form of exchange-rate risk or how wide am I willing to let the tunnel be?*

In general terms, if a company wants certainty of cash flows, forwards and money market hedges are the best tools to consider. The forward would be considered if:

1. The firm has utilized its existing credit lines or does not want to draw on existing credit lines. The forward requires a credit line but a forward credit line is generally significantly larger than a traditional line of credit.

2. The firm has limited or no access to local currency borrowings or is faced with an interest rate surcharge.

3. The firm is in a very liquid position and has limited short-term investment opportunities.

In comparison, the firm would prefer the money market hedge (arranging a foreign currency loan) if:

1. The firm is in need of short-term financing.

2. The firm could use the funds immediately for an investment that yields a higher rate of return than the money market instruments or could use the funds to retire existing debt or meet debt service instruments.

3. No active or well-traded forward market exists for the currency in question.

4. The firm has preferential access to local currency borrowings or is in a strong local currency cash position.

5. Foreign exchange premia and discounts have a less favorable tax impact than do income and interest expenses.

Remember, whenever a firm borrows, it pays a credit spread. The lower the rating of the company, the greater the size of the spread it will have to pay. For a money market hedge to be preferred to a forward market hedge, the firm must recapture that credit spread when it uses the borrowed funds. If the company simply invests in money market instruments, it will fail to recapture the credit spread. This means that the treasurer must compare the differences in lending rates minus deposits rates in each country. Finally, the treasurer must compare the differences between local lending rates and euro lending rates.

DEVELOPING VALUATION AND RISK MANAGEMENT SKILLS

1. Understand exchange-rate risk exposure and the various choices available to manage this risk exposure.

The risk exposure to a company is that exchange rates will change before the company can move foreign cash flows into its desired (domestic) currency. For currency dealers the risk is that a change in the exchange rate changes the value of its inventory. There are a variety of risk management choices for exchange-rate exposure. The company can choose not to manage the risk, but this is likely a bad idea. It can choose to manage part of the risk; however, we saw that managing of part of the risk went badly at Lufthansa. If the decision is to fully manage the exposure to exchange rates, then derivative securities exist to manage this risk exposure. In addition to derivative risk management the company can choose a money market hedge.

2. Understand the changes required to the Black-Scholes model for pricing currencies option and calculate the price of a currency option.

The basic option pricing features of the standard Black-Scholes model remains in the pricing of currency options. However, the model must be adjusted for the fact that cash flows in the different currencies can be invested in that currency and earn that currency's market interest rate. This adjustment is made in both the option pricing formula and in the calculation of d_1. It is also important to remember that the option is pricing currency exchange and not a stock, so the inputs in the pricing formula change from stock prices to exchange rates.

QUESTIONS

1. Futures contracts for currencies are traded on the CME, COMEX, CBOT DTB, SIMEX, HKFE, and LIFFE. Go online and find the locations of these exchanges and the meanings of the initials.

2. What are the rewards and risk of remaining unhedged with foreign exchange exposure on a transaction?

3. What are the rewards and risk of a complete hedge of foreign exchange exposure with forward or futures contracts ?

4. What is the benefit and cost of hedging with a currency option contract over hedging with a currency futures contract?

5. What is the benefit and cost of a hedging with a tunnel forward?

6. What is the primary limiting factor against using a money market hedge?

7. A Euro-based (EUR) investor wants to buy a call on the U.S. dollar (USD). The current exchange rate is 0.95 USD/EUR. The one-year risk-free rate in the Euro area is 5% per annum with continuous compounding and in the United States is 6.5% per annum with continuous compounding. Assume a volatility of 18% on the exchange rate. What is the price of a one-year European-style call option on the U.S. dollar with a strike of 1.00 EUR/USD.

8. Calculate the value of a three-month at-the-money European call option on a currency with a strike price of 1.25. The volatility of the exchange rate is 15%, the domestic risk-free interest rate is 9%, and the foreign risk-free interest rate is 5%. What would be the value of a put with the same characteristics?

9. Calculate the value of a six-month European put option on a currency with a strike price of $0.40 when the current exchange rate is $0.42 and has a volatility of 13%. The domestic risk-free interest rate is 6% per year and the foreign risk-free interest rate is 8% per year. What would be the value of a call option with the same characteristics?

KEY TERMS

Foreign Currency Exposure An obligation to make a payment in a foreign currency.

Tunnel Forward A special type of contractual agreement between two parties. The contract defines a specific exchange rate band. The upper and lower limits of the contract act as contract settlement rates if the exchange rate exceeds the limits of the range of the contract.

Unbiased Indicators An indicator is not consistently too high or too low but, instead, is on average correct (unbiased).

CHAPTER 17

DERIVATIVE RISK MANAGEMENT

17.1 INTRODUCTION

The purpose of this chapter is to discuss the risk associated with taking positions in derivative securities. This continues the risk management theme of the second half of this book, but with a twist. To this point in the book risk management has been about protecting value in an investment and derivative securities are frequently used to protect value. Recall, for example, that forward and futures contracts were created to eliminate price risk in the underlying asset. Accordingly, derivatives are not intended as investments to hold or create value, but instead are intended as positions taken to protect value. Protecting value is important to all investors and is a focus for managers in all the financial institutions as they try to protect shareholder value. The focus of this chapter is the risk associated with derivative positions taken for the purpose of protecting value in the underlying asset.

We motivate the chapter with an *In the News* item that presents a discussion of the Metalgesellschaft debacle. Since the Metalgesellschaft debacle involves the use of futures, the discussion of hedging problems will begin with a discussion of hedging with futures and then proceed to hedging issues in general and hedging issues with specific instruments.

DEVELOPING VALUATION AND RISK MANAGEMENT SKILLS

Stephen Ross, the developer of the arbitrage pricing theory, has said that he is not a financial engineer but a financial pathologist. His point is that by studying financial fiascos, one can learn from the mistakes of others and try to avoid them in the future. The *In the News* item at the end of this section provides his analysis of the famous Metalgesellschaft debacle in the early 1990s. In this case, the oil traders for the company appeared to have perfectly hedged their oil price risk, and on a purely accounting basis, they had. Unfortunately, they had forgotten some basic lessons that all risk managers should remember when dealing with shareholders' funds.

Professor Ross' major points in worrying about risk management can be summarized in the following manner:

1. Understand the nature of the hedge you are trying to establish.
2. Theory is good, but when bad things happen, they happen quickly.
3. Markets are efficient and simple strategies cannot consistently make abnormal profits.
4. Large positions involving large amounts of money are watched closely because concessions must be made to alter these positions.
5. Liquidity is essential in times of crises and cash is the ultimate liquid asset.

6. The more complex the business transaction, the harder it is to hedge and the more vulnerable the business is.

7. Make certain that, to the greatest extent possible, employees' interests are aligned with shareholders' interests.

This chapter covers some of the simpler problems that can arise when dealing with derivatives using Professor Ross's seven points as an outline. Notice, however, that several of the items highlighted by Professor Ross in his article deal with operational risk issues that were discussed in Chapter 11.

IN THE NEWS

METALGESELLSCHAFT (MG) AND OIL[1]

In the early 1990s a group of oil traders employed by MG decided to pursue the following strategy. First, they sold oil and petroleum contracts with delivery commitments extending over periods as long as 10 years and with embedded options for the buyers. Second, for each barrel of oil sold they purchased one barrel of a short duration futures contracts. As these contracts matured, new positions were continually being established to replace them.

When oil prices fell precipitously in 1992, margin payments on the futures contracts exceeded $1 billion and nearly bankrupted MG. MG survived its foray into oil trading, but it was in intensive care for a long time. There are some central lessons that emerge from a careful examination of this case.

To begin with, the oil traders had a theory. Prior to 1990 about 70% of the time the oil futures markets were in backwardation, which is to say that the prices of long-term contracts were lower than those of short-term contracts. As contracts matured, then, their prices were expected to rise, producing cash profits to their holders. Second, from a pure accounting perspective, the delivery commitments were perfectly hedged by the futures contracts. When a one-to-one hedge eventually expires, the holder recovers any margin losses from price changes or pays them back if prices rose. Every dollar made or lost on a futures contract would eventually be offset when the final oil delivery to the customer takes place.

A blind allegiance to a particular theory or strategy is a central feature of all financial debacles. Unfortunately, though, bad things happened that were not anticipated by theory, and this is the second lesson. Enormous and historically unprecedented changes in prices and the busi-ness environment always occur in short time periods. In the oil markets, spot heating oil prices fell by over 50% in a matter of months. The hedge guaranteed that on, say, a 10-year delivery contract, accounting profits would equal accounting losses 10 years out, but that was little comfort when the market demanded approximately $1 billion to cover current margin losses on the futures contracts. These payments had to be financed, and recovering the $1 billion 10 years from now would not begin to cover the interest charges on the financing.

The theory was flawed and the bad event of the price drop only made this flaw painfully apparent. Correctly taking into account interest costs and the relative near and far term volatilities of the oil futures markets showed that the net position with the so-called hedges in place was actually riskier than if MG had simply sold the oil contracts and not bothered to hedge.

The third lesson is a classic one from finance. Financial markets are efficient in the sense that prices reflect up-to-date information. Furthermore, the markets are populated with astute traders whose business is process-ing information and profiting from it. Liquid markets are too efficient for naive and simple strategies to give sure profits. Spreads do narrow and fundamentals do reassert themselves. The drop in oil prices was a consequence of a natural supply response. High prices brought forth more oil supplies and lowered oil demand. But, there is too much competition in the markets for any spread bet, in the case of MG, a simple rolling of futures contracts, to consistently make money. There is always some sig-nificant risk of losing big, and any static, simple system is doomed to failure.

(continued)

IN THE NEWS (*continued*)

METALGESELLSCHAFT (MG) AND OIL[1]

The fourth lesson is that big dollars attract big attention. With their huge short delivery positions, specialists in the oil markets knew that MG would have to roll their expiring positions, and by some accounts, these traders were waiting very eagerly when they did so. It is very costly to move a big position particularly when everyone is watching you, and it is impossible to be nimble. Elephants can waltz but they cannot tap dance.

Lesson five is that in times of distress, liquid debts always beat illiquid assets. Simply put, in a crisis only cash is liquid. The delivery contracts were highly illiquid and difficult, if not impossible, to sell at a reasonable price. Who would finance the MG positions based on the delivery strategy alone? Since the strategy wasn't self-financing, MG had to reach into its general borrowing lines to pay its liquid market debts and avoid bankruptcy.

Lesson six concerns the complexity of the business. While the strategy was relatively simple, its implementation and analysis was not. The complex delivery contracts and the massive size of their futures positions made a simple evaluation of the economics of MG's oil trading difficult. Complexity creates opacity and this makes a business vulnerable; the more opaque and complex a business is, the more difficult it is to finance. Complexity makes controlling risk all the more difficult.

The final lesson, and in some ways the least obvious, but one of the most important, concerns agency costs. The MG traders were employees of MG and their interests were not necessarily aligned with the interest, of the shareholders. This is what is meant by an agency cost; it is the cost to the firm and to its owners of managing this misalignment. It is difficult to align the interests of employees and owners and impossible to do so exactly. The failure to do so in this case puts a greater burden on monitoring and controlling employees, which is a component of agency costs.

17.2 UNDERSTANDING THE HEDGE

The first topic to be discussed is the most important issue in a hedge: understanding the contract and how it is priced. In this section two hedging examples from previous chapters are revisited to show what can happen when the investor does not understand the hedge that is being attempted.

EXAMPLE *The Problem with Not Understanding the Hedge*

Chapter 9 discussed FRAs and T-bill futures. Recall the example in Chapter 9, Section 6.1, where the CFO of a company needed to buy 100 T-Bill futures contracts to hedge a $100 million investment from June through September. Assume all the conditions remain the same but the CFO made a different decision.

Suppose that the CFO remembered that when hedging with FRAs, borrowers buy the rate and that FRAs were basically the same as futures contracts. But the CFO did not remember that because of the different pricing convention, borrowers sold (short) the T-bill futures contracts and investors (lenders) bought (long) the contracts. As a result, instead of going long (buying) in T-bill futures, the CFO went short (sold) at 93.51. What will happen?

---

[1] Abstracted from *Forensic Finance: Enron and Others*, Fourth Angelo Costa Lecture by Stephen A. Ross. See, www.rivistapoliticaeconomica.it/nov_dic02/rossengl.pdf.

At expiry, the yield on the three-month T-bill is 5.55% (as in the example from Chapter 9). Thus, the company will earn 5.55% on its investment in T-bills. However, because the CFO took a short position it also means that $235,000 will be deducted from the company's margin account instead of being added (yields decreased so prices increased). On an annual basis this is ($-$235,000/$100,000,000) $\times$ (12/3) $= -0.94\%$, which means that instead of locking in 6.49% (as in the original example), the CFO locked in an effective interest rate of (5.55% $- 0.94\%$) $= 4.61\%$. The CFO was fortunate that interest rates didn't fall any further!

EXAMPLE   *Taking the Wrong Position in a Futures Hedge of a Stock Portfolio*

Now, look at a different hedging decision the CFO could have to make. Suppose that the CFO had remembered that the pricing convention for T-bill futures was different from the pricing convention for FRAs. However, the CFO now needs to hedge a portfolio of stocks instead of the purchase of T-bills. Assume the stock portfolio is worth approximately $62,300 and is highly correlated with the S&P 500 composite index. This is the portfolio hedging example in Chapter 9, Section 9.7. Like the portfolio hedge, the CFO decides to use an E-mini S&P 500 futures contract, which is trading at 1,210. The CFO is hedging the stock portfolio based on the CFO's knowledge of T-bill futures; the CFO decides to go long (buy) the E-mini S&P 500 futures contract. However, the proper hedge when a stock portfolio is expected to decline in value is to go short (sell) the E-mini S&P 500 futures contract. So, what happens at contract expiry? Using the data from Chapter 9, assume that the value of the portfolio falls by 10% to $56,070 and the June E-mini S&P 500 futures contract falls to 1,091.

Initially the portfolio had been worth $62,300. Four weeks later at the end of May, it was worth $56,070 for a loss of $6,230. Now, look at the decline in the value of the futures contract. When the CFO went long (bought) the contract was worth 1,210 $\times$ $50 $= $60,500. When the CFO sells it to close the position, it is worth 1,091 $\times$ $50 $= $54,550. The CFO has lost another $5,950 on the futures hedging transactions. Combined with the loss on the portfolio, the CFO's net position is a loss of $12,180 or 19.6%!

The lesson in the two examples in this section is ***always know what side of the hedging transaction you want to be on. This will often be determined by the way in which the futures contract is priced. READ AND UNDERSTAND THE CONTRACT!***

17.3 THE PROBLEM WITH THEORY

Notice that the pricing conventions of the contract are not the only issue that can get you into trouble. Remember the Nick Leeson example in Chapter 11 (Barings Bank). Leeson contended that he was perfectly hedged (but remember that he may have been lying) when he held a position that comprised a $7.7 billion long position in Nikkei stock futures and a short position of $16 billion of Japanese government bonds. Unfortunately, the correlation between Japanese stocks and bonds was -0.114 at the time. Hence, this combination of *long and short* positions meant that the total portfolio would move in the same direction regardless of whether bond and stock prices went up or down. This situation is similar to the problem of trying to decide what side of the hedging transaction you want to be on.

Another issue is important when hedging a portfolio against a market downturn. Namely, investors should always remember that portfolio diversification theory only operates under *normal market conditions* and was not meant to operate in cases of crises. When markets crash, correlations between assets tend toward 1.0 and all the benefits of diversification disappear.

Consider the portfolio diversification example you studied in Chapter 15. Recall that an investor owned shares in three companies, Fly-by-Night Airlines (FLYBY), the Loan Sharks Incorporated (UO), and the Koala Greeting Card Company (GDAY). The investor's total investment was £15,000. The investor had £5,000 invested in FLYBY, £6,000 in UO, and £4,000 in GDAY. Thus, the individual securities comprise: FLYBY £5,000/£15,000 = 0.33; UO £6,000/£15,000 = 0.40; and GDAY £4,000/£15,000 = 0.27 of the portfolio. The investor had done extensive research on these three companies and had compiled the following information.

Investment	Expected return (%)	Standard deviation (%)	Beta
FLYBY	11	10	1.05
UO	9	5	0.95
GDAY	12	7	1.11

Suppose now that in cases of financial crises, all of the investor's stocks become perfectly positively correlated with each other and the expected return for each stock falls by one standard deviation. What rate of return might the investor expect on this portfolio? The most likely return is the weighted average of the component parts of the portfolio:

$$\begin{aligned} E[R] &= w_1 \times r_1 + w_2 \times r_2 + w_3 \times r_3 \\ &= 0.33(11\% - 10\%) + 0.40(9\% - 5\%) + 0.27(12\% - 7\%) \\ &= 0.33 + 0.8 + 1.35 = 3.28\% \end{aligned}$$

Notice that this return is very different from the 10.47% the investor had expected under normal market conditions.[2] You should also remember that financial crises rarely involve only one standard deviation. Markets crash dramatically and quickly. In the two largest crashes in American history, the market fell by 20% in 1929 and 22.6% in 1987 *in one day*.

Now, remembering that in times of crises that the correlation between stocks tend toward perfect positive correlation ($\rho = 1$), what is the standard deviation of the portfolio? With a correlation of 1 ($\rho = 1$) between all the stocks in the portfolio the standard deviation of the portfolio becomes the weighted average of the standard deviations of the component securities:

$$\begin{aligned} E[\text{port dev}] &= w_1 \times s_1 + w_2 \times s_2 + w_3 \times s_3 \\ &= 0.33(10\%) + 0.40(5\%) + 0.27(7\%) \\ &= 7.19\% \end{aligned}$$

---

[2] The portfolio expected return calculated in Chapter 15 is

$$E[R] = w_1 \times r_1 + w_2 \times r_2 + w_3 \times r_3 = 0.33(11\%) + 0.40(9\%) + 0.27(12\%) = 10.47\%.$$

This standard deviation is very different from the diversified standard deviation of 6.06%.[3] Why did this happen? The portfolio has lost the benefit of some stocks going up while some stocks were going down under normal market conditions. Notice that the normal expected return of 10.47% minus the crisis portfolio standard deviation of 7.19% yields the crisis expected return of 3.28%.

Markets are generally efficient but efficiency should always be viewed in the context of *normal market conditions*. Assuming that hedges will always work because of negative correlation is foolish. Related to the issue of correlation is the issue of the size of the market response. This is perhaps best demonstrated by the concept of naked strategies in options.

A **naked option** is the writing (selling) of an option without a position in the underlying stock. Writing a naked option is purely a speculative position. You can have both naked puts and naked calls. Of the two, the naked call position is far riskier. The following example will demonstrate.

EXAMPLE   *The Risk in Naked Options*

Suppose you sell five naked put contracts on a stock. Assume that the option price is $5, the exercise price is $70, and the stock price is $72. What have you done?

You have given someone else the opportunity to sell the stock to you for $70 should it fall below that level. You are betting on the market having a positive drift and that the put will expire out-of-the money with the stock price being at or above $70. Notice that you have received $5 × 5 × 100 = $2,500 in premium proceeds.[4]

Suppose now that, on the day of expiry, a huge accounting scandal at the company is discovered, the company is really bankrupt, and the shares of the firm fall suddenly to $50. What is your position? The options will close at $20 ($70 − $50) each and you will lose $20 × 5 × 100 = $10,000 on the options. This loss is partially offset by the premiums you received for a net loss of $7,500 ($10,000 loss on option −$ 2,500 premium).

Now assume that you sell five naked call contracts on the stock. Also, assume the same prices as in the example of the naked put: option price is $5, the exercise price is $70, and the stock price is $72. What have you done?

You have given someone else the opportunity to buy the stock from you for $70 should it rise above that level. You are betting on the market having a downward drift and that the call will expire out-of-the-money with the stock price being at or below $70. Notice that, once again, you have received $5 × 5 × 100 = $2,500 in premium proceeds.

Suppose now that, on the day of expiry, a tender offer for all shares is announced because a competing firm has decided to acquire the company you sold the calls on. Suppose that the shares double in value to $145. What is your position? The options will close at $75 each and you will lose $75 × 5 × 100 = $37,500 on the options. This loss is partially offset by the premiums you received and the result is a net loss of $35,000 ($37,500 loss on option − $2,500 premium).

---

[3] The portfolio standard deviation calculation from Chapter 15 is

$$\sigma_p = \left[\sum w_i^2\sigma_i^2 + 2\left(\sum\sum w_iw_j\rho_{ij}\sigma_i\sigma_j\right)\right]^{0.5}$$
$$= [(0.33)^2(0.1)^2 + (0.4)^2(0.05)^2 + (0.27)^2(0.07)^2 + 2[((0.33)(0.4)(0.8)(0.1)(0.05)$$
$$+ (0.33)(0.27)(0.5)(0.1)(0.07) + (0.4)(0.27)(0.2)(0.05)(0.07))]^{0.5}$$
$$= [0.001089 + 0.0004 + 0.000357 + 2(0.000528 + 0.000312 + 0.000076)]^{0.5}$$
$$= [0.003678]^{0.5}$$
$$= 0.0606 \text{ or } 6.06\%.$$

[4] Note, a standard option contract is for 100 shares of the underlying stock.

One important thing to notice in the naked options example is that with the naked put, you can lose no more than the exercise price of the put times the total number of puts written since the stock price cannot fall below zero. However, notice that there is no such upper boundary for stocks. A share price can theoretically increase without limit; therefore, with a naked call position, you could lose an infinite amount of money. These are the reasons that the central banks require that investors post margin (good faith money), the size of which depends on the nature of the transaction to ensure that losses on such transactions can be covered.

17.4 THE PROBLEM WITH SIMPLE STRATEGIES

The previous section suggests that you should always be careful when making financial decisions because there are times when normal market conditions do not hold. Having said that, in general and on average, normal market conditions do hold. Keeping this in mind, you have to remember that there is a very large number of very talented traders in the market who are constantly on the lookout to make money for themselves and their employers. If you come across a very simple strategy that appears to offer an ongoing profit-making opportunity, you must be suspicious. There is an old adage that says, *if something appears too good to be true, then it probably is!* This infers that you have probably not considered all possible conditions.

One very popular and simple profit-making strategy is the writing of covered calls. This strategy is where you write call options on shares that you currently own. This is less risky than writing naked calls because the worst that can happen is that the investor is required to sell the shares at below their market value. Figure 17-1 presents the payoff diagram for writing a covered call. A covered call is the combination of being long in the stock and short in the call option, which results in the same payoff pattern as being short a put option.

Why do investors do this? Suppose that an investor in the United States owns 300 shares of a stock which he bought last month for $54 and on which he has decided to write three call option contracts on the shares (recall each option contract is for 100 shares). The current stock price is $57, the exercise price is $55, and the price of the option (when the options were written) was $3 and expires in one month. The investor may believe that the stock price will not go any higher over the next 30 days. What has the investor

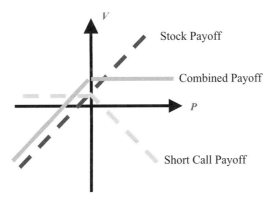

FIGURE 17-1 The payoff diagram for writing a covered call.

done? Assume that the investor is correct about the stock. By the time the option expires the return to the investor will be

$$\frac{\text{(capital gain on stock)} - \text{(loss on option)} + \text{option premium}}{\text{(initial purchase price of share)}}$$

$$= \frac{(\$57 - \$54) \times 300) - ((\$57 - \$55) \times 300) + (\$3 \times 300)}{\$54 \times 300}$$

$$= \frac{\$900 - \$600 + \$900}{\$16,200}$$

$$= 7.41\%$$

for the two-month holding period! Annualized this would be 44.5% (7.41% × 6). Many investors look on this strategy as an easy way to enhance the return of their portfolios. However, very often these same investors make some serious errors in judgment.

Following are four common errors made by investors attempting to increase their returns by writing covered calls:

1. The first major error is that investors picking an option for writing a covered call often pick options that have large premia. From the study of options in Chapter 10, you know that volatility is priced in options. Hence, options with large premia are also options with high levels of volatility, and since options are correlated with the underlying stock, the shares, too, have a high degree of variability. Thus, the option is liable to end up out-of-the-money because the stock declines in value. For example, suppose in our previous example the investor received $3 per option but the share price fell by $6—remember there is no margin effect in this example. What is the investor's position?

$$\frac{\text{(capital gain on stock)} + \text{(option premium)}}{\text{(initial purchase price of share)}}$$

$$= \frac{((\$48 - \$54) \times 300) + (\$3 \times 300)}{(\$54 \times 300)}$$

$$= \frac{-\$1,800 + \$900}{\$16,200}$$

$$= -5.56\%.$$

The point of this example is that options with large premiums have large premiums for a reason, which is often high volatility in the underlying stock. This means that the investor writing a covered call may not make a positive return. However, without the covered call the investor would have lost 11.1%.

2. The second (classic) error is that investors attempt to enhance the returns even further by buying the shares on margin. That is, they may borrow, for example, 50% of the funds from their broker to finance the purchase part of the transaction. In this example, the investor is borrowing a portion of the purchase price of the stock. Ignoring interest on this account, the investor could double the holding period return by using this

strategy. But what if the shares fell by $6 from the original purchase price?

$$\frac{(\text{capital gain on stock}) + (\text{option premium})}{(\text{initial purchase price of share})}$$

$$= \frac{(($48 - $54) \times 300) + ($3 \times 300)}{($54 \times 150)}$$

$$= \frac{-$1,800 + $900}{$8,100}$$

$$= -11.1\%.$$

Notice that the same inputs as number 1 were used, but 50% of the stock was purchased on margin. This did double the return from number 1. *However, the return is negative so the losses were doubled.*

Notice that the investor still owes the broker $54 × 150 = $8,100. In the absence of funds from other sources, the investor will be forced to sell the shares at $48 to repay the broker. Thus, the investor would have to sell approximately $8,100 ÷ $48 = 169 shares to repay the original loan of 150 shares.

3. The third error that investors smitten by the attractiveness of a covered call strategy often make is that they forget the diversification effects of holding securities in a portfolio. For example, they often buy highly volatile stocks that, in turn, have options with high premia. This happened often during the high-tech bubble of the late 1990s when many investors were holding high-tech, Internet stocks in their portfolios. They forgot that these stocks were highly positively correlated so when the bottom fell out of this sector of the market, fortunes were lost because the portfolios were not well-diversified.

   A second diversification issue involves what happens when the investor has to honor the call option. That is, the market value of the shares has increased and the holder of the call option chooses to exercise. Now the investor has to sell the shares and in the process loses the diversification benefits that stock contributed to the overall portfolio. Of course, the investor could always repurchase the stock at the new higher price!

4. The final error an investor makes is to forget that a covered call has the same payoff pattern as writing a naked put. Covered calls are motivated by the investor not expecting prices to rise in the near future. Accordingly, the investor is willing to sell the potential upside on the stock through the call. However, since the payoff diagram of a covered call is similar to a naked put, if the stock price goes down the investor loses. Therefore, a covered call is simply a bet on the future movement of the price of the underlying stock.

17.5 THE PROBLEM WITH LARGE POSITIONS

Many average investors believe that problems involving large positions need only be remembered by large institutional investors like Long-Term Capital Management. This is not true. This problem can actually affect any investor. The question is *How large is large?* In the case of derivative positions, the average investor does not usually have to worry since the clearing house usually takes the other side of trade and guarantees the counterparty performance. But still, difficulties can arise.

For example, recall the discussion in Chapter 1 where Professor Ritter attempted to create profits from a trading strategy only to lose money when another investor, Fisher Black, had better information. Another part of the story around Professor Ritter's trading strategy was that it involved holding 100% of the long positions in the March 1987 Value Line futures contract. Then, when the market started moving to a new price (as Professor Ritter discovered the contract had been mispriced and someone had discovered the error), Professor Ritter could not get out of his position at the current "market" price because the trader that discovered the pricing error was unwilling to take Professor Ritter's contracts until they were correctly priced. This situation created daily margin calls to cover losses until Professor Ritter could hedge his losing position. Professor Ritter states that he discovered the true meaning of an illiquid position.

Liquidity problems also arise during market crises. In the case of market crises, trading can always be suspended pending the dissemination of information so that an adequate number of traders can exist on both sides of an equilibrium value. For example, consider the case of a protective put. An investor has a long position in a stock and a long position in a put. Now suppose that the stock price starts to fall. If the investor has to rebalance their portfolio by selling securities and buying additional puts, this strategy actually creates additional downward pressure on stock prices. (The investor may want to sell positions to lock in previously unrealized gains.) Hence, the simple act of trying to insulate a portfolio from market shocks can actually lead to additional instability in the market.

Stock market **circuit breakers** act to slow trading in times of crises to allow investors to process information in order to make informed trading decisions. As in the stock market, futures markets also use a technique similar to circuit breakers. The technique is to specify a maximum daily price movement. For most contracts, the maximum daily price movements are specified in the contract by the exchange. If the price moves down by an amount equal to the daily price change limit, the contract is said to be trading *limit down.* If the contract moves up by an amount equal to the daily limit price change, the contract is said to be trading *limit up.* A **limit move** is therefore a move in either direction equal to this maximum daily change. When a contract trades limit up or limit down, trading is halted (usually for the day). However, the exchange is the final authority on how long the halt will last.

The purpose of these daily price limits is to prevent large price movements arising from panic or speculation. When trading is allowed once again, the contracts are marked-to-market in the normal fashion. A second way in which large positions are controlled is through *position limits* in the futures markets. A position limit is the maximum number of contracts that an individual can hold. This usually limits the positions of speculators so that they cannot have any undue influence in the market due to the size of their positions.

A second area of concern is the size of the position relative to the average daily traded amount. For example, Griffiths, Turnbull, and White (2000) show that to divest a portfolio of small-capitalization securities takes 4 to 5 times longer than the time to divest a large-capitalization portfolio. This may not be a problem if it only takes a moment or two to sell the shares at the bid price, but for large positions in thinly traded securities, this process can take days or weeks. A similar problem would exist for over-the-counter derivative positions.

17.6 PROBLEMS WITH LIQUIDITY

Derivatives are a **zero-sum game** that is marked-to-market daily. Being a zero-sum game means that for every winner there is an offsetting loser: total gains equal total losses. Marking-to-market daily means that each day the losers pay the winners that day's change in value. The daily payments are made through adjustments in each trader's margin account. When a trader accumulates losses to the point where the trader's margin account reaches the minimum acceptable balance, the trader receives a margin call. The margin call is notification that the trader must put funds in the margin account to return the margin account balance to the initial margin of the trader's position.

Margin calls can create liquidity problems for traders because they must put funds in their margin account the day of the margin call or risk having the exchange close out their positions. Professor Ritter noted that when his position in the March 1987 Value Line futures contract began moving to its new (correct) price, he received a $5,000 margin call several days in a row, which he covered with cash advances on different credit cards. The margin calls continued until he was able to create an offsetting position in another futures contract.

Margin calls can also create a liquidity problem for traders hedging positions in the underlying asset. For example, consider a farmer who wants to lock in today's price for the farmer's field of corn by going short in corn futures contracts. Now, assume the price of corn rises, so the value of the farmer's corn increases and the value of the futures contracts increase. Since the farmer is short in the futures market, the gains in the value of the corn are offset by losses in the futures position and locks in the farmer's sale price of corn. However, the losses in the futures contracts can create a margin call which the farmer will need to cover that day to remain in the hedge. Eventually, the profits from the sale of the corn will cover the losses on the futures contracts; but in the short-term, the farmer must have sufficient liquidity to cover the margin calls. Accordingly, margin calls create liquidity risk even for traders fully hedging the underlying asset.

INDUSTRY APPLICATION

MARGIN CALL

One of the tasks of new associates at brokerage houses is to call investors when the value of their margin (called a performance bond at the Chicago Mercantile Exchange) is insufficient for the position they are currently holding. A second important task is determining the profit or loss on a client's position.

Suppose you have a client who takes a short positioning in five CBOT Treasury bond futures contracts each with a face value of $100,000 at a price of 97 5/32. The initial margin for each contract is $2,700 and the maintenance margin is $2,000. Assume that the client will meet all margin calls and will not withdraw any excess margin. Given the following hypothetical prices, prepare a report for the client to demonstrate when and how much must be deposited in the client's account.

(continued)

INDUSTRY APPLICATION (*continued*)

MARGIN CALL

Day	Beginning balance ($)	Funds deposited ($)	Futures price	Price change	Gain or loss ($)	Ending balance ($)
0	0	13,500.00	97-05			13,500.00
1	13,500.00	0	97-30	25/32	−3,906.25	9,593.75
2	9,593.75	3,906.25	98-21	23/32	−3,593.75	9,906.25
3	9,906.25	3,593.75	98-17	−4/32	625.00	14,125.00
4	14,125.00	0	98-23	6/32	−937.50	13,187.50
5	13,187.50	0	99-04	12/32	−1,875.00	11,312.50
6	11,312.50	0	98-30	−5/32	781.25	12,093.75

On the day the client opens the position, $13,500 must be deposited since each of the five contracts requires an initial margin of $2,700. At the end of the first day, the price has risen from 97-05 to 97-30. That is, the price of the futures contract has increased from $97,156.25 to $97,937.50 and since the client has a short position, this represents a loss of $781.25 per contract. Since this results in a margin position of ($2,700 − $781.25) $1,918.75, which is less than the $2,000 maintenance margin, the client will receive a margin call. The client will be required to reestablish the original margin of $2,700 per contract—this will require a deposit of $3,906.25 to satisfy the margin requirement for all five contracts.

The next day sees another adverse move that again results in a margin call since the loss per contract is ($98,656.25 − $97,937.50) $718.75, reducing the margin balance to $1,981.25. The client will have to deposit another $3,593.75 to reestablish the initial margin on all five contracts. Fortunately for the client, even though the price of the contract moves adversely on days 5 and 6 and falls below the initial margin, in neither case does it fall below the maintenance margin and trigger a margin call.

The client sold the contract at 97-05 and six days later the contract was valued at 98-30, an increase of 1 25/32, which because the client was short represents a loss of 1.78125%. Based on the $500,000 position, this is a loss of $8,906.25. An alternate way to calculate the loss is the original deposit plus the margin call deposits minus the ending balance, that is, $13,500 + $3,906.25 + $3,593.75 − $12,093.75 = $8,906.25.

SUMMARY OF VALUATION AND RISK MANAGEMENT SKILLS

Professor Ross's summary is an important guide to understanding the interaction between market efficiency and derivative risk management and this chapter has provided a discussion or example of each of his seven points. Below, Professor Ross's seven points are again listed with reference provided to the area in the chapter where each point was addressed.

1. Understand the nature of the hedge you are trying to establish.

    Section 17.2 provides two examples of how things can go wrong when the trader does not properly understand the hedge. Specifically, the two examples show that taking the wrong position in the correct derivative security magnifies risk instead of reducing or eliminating risk.

2. Theory is good but when bad things happen, they happen quickly.

Section 17.3 discusses that in market crises the correlation between assets tend toward 1 ($\rho = 1$), which eliminates the benefits of diversification. We point out to the reader that diversification works under normal market conditions, but that dramatic market downturns are not normal.

3. Markets are efficient and simple strategies cannot consistently make abnormal profits.

Section 17.4 discusses the simple trading strategy of a covered call and shows several examples of how this strategy can lead to losses instead of gains. The point is that markets are rational and informed so *something that appears too good to be true, probably is too good to be true!*

4. Large positions involving large amounts of money are watched closely because concessions must be made to alter these positions.

Section 17.5 discusses that Professor Ritter was unable to get out of his large position in the Value Line futures contract at the current market price. The point is that large blocks of any security are difficult to trade quickly, so care must be used whenever a large position is acquired.

5. Liquidity is essential in times of crises and cash is the ultimate liquid asset.

Several situations are discussed in Sections 17.5 and 17.6 where liquidity can be a problem in derivative contracts. For example, futures contracts are marked-to-market daily, which means gains or losses are paid daily. This creates a liquidity problem when a futures position is losing because the losses must be covered daily, but the offsetting gains on the underlying assets are not captured until the transaction in the underlying asset occurs at some point in the future.

6. The more complex the business transaction, the harder it is to hedge and the more vulnerable the business is.

Examples are provided throughout the chapter of what can go wrong with simple strategies using derivatives. It is easy to visualize how the problems increase with increases in complexity.

7. Make sure that, to the greatest extent possible, employees' interests are aligned with shareholders' interests.

The Nick Leeson debacle at Barings Bank (mentioned in Section 17.3 of this chapter and discussed in detail in Chapter 11, Section 11.4) is a classic example of agency problems and agency costs.

QUESTIONS

1. The purpose of hedging with a futures contract is to eliminate price risk. What happens to a trader's return when the trader attempts to hedge with a futures contract but takes the wrong side of the contract (that is, the trader is long when the trader should be short or vice versa)?

2. What tends to happen to the correlations between stocks in a well-diversified portfolio during a major market decline and what effect does the change in correlations have on the standard deviation of the portfolio?

3. Define the term naked option and explain why a naked call is more risky than a naked put.

4. What are the primary benefits and primary risks in writing covered calls?

5. What is the impact on returns of writing a covered call while using margin to purchase some of the underlying stock?

6. What are the problems with large positions in derivative contracts?

7. How can a properly hedged trader have liquidity risk in a futures contract?

8. Consider the following positions and determine what issues an investor must remember before engaging in them as routine strategies:

   a. A short position in a stock combined with a long position in a call.
   b. A long position in a stock combined with a long position in a put.
   c. A short position in a stock combined with a short position in a put.

REFERENCES

GRIFFITHS, M. D., A. TURNBULL, and R. W. WHITE, 2000, Re-examining the Small-firm Myth: Problems in Portfolio Formation & Liquidation, *The Global Finance Journal*, *10(2)*, 201–221.
The authors attempt to capture the profits from the January small firm effect using data on actual transactions from the Toronto Stock Exchange. The authors find that the small stocks do not trade frequently enough to allow traders to profit from the small firm effect. In particular, there is not sufficient volume to sell many the shares of small firms over the first quarter of the year.

KEY TERMS

Circuit Breakers Market mechanism that stops trading following large price declines. The purpose of a circuit breaker is to give traders time to evaluate their positions and make informed decisions.

Limit Move A move in either direction equal to this maximum daily change allowed in the futures contract.

Naked Option The writing (selling) of an option without a position in the underlying stock.

Zero-sum Game For every winner there is an offsetting loser, such that total gains equal total losses.

CHAPTER 18

INTEREST RATE DERIVATIVES

18.1 INTRODUCTION

This chapter covers interest rate derivatives. It continues the risk management theme of the second half of this book, but breaks from the structure used to this point in the book of having a risk management chapter paired with a valuation chapter on the same market. Instead, this chapter (interest rate derivatives) and the following chapter (credit derivatives) discuss fixed-income market risk management techniques not covered elsewhere in the book. These two topics are covered here instead of in previous chapters on specific markets because they are not specific to one market, but instead, apply to all fixed income markets. Specifically, this chapter covers interest rate caps and floors as a technique to limit exposure to changes in market interest rates. Limiting exposure to changes in interest rates is important to all fixed income investors, but it is particularly important to banks that sell interest rate caps and floors to their customers and that use interest rate caps and floors to protect shareholder value from changes in interest rates.[1]

This chapter begins with a discussion of the institutional details and features of interest caps, interest rate floors, and the combination of a cap and a floor, which is called an interest corridor. This discussion includes how to determine the interest rate protection under a cap and floor. Next, how to price a cap is discussed and this is followed by how to price a floor. The chapter concludes with a discussion of how to price caps and floors using an approximation of the Black-Scholes option pricing model.

DEVELOPING VALUATION AND RISK MANAGEMENT SKILLS

1. Understand interest rate caps (caplets), interest floors (floorlets), and interest rate corridors (collars).
2. Calculate the price of a cap using binomial option pricing.
3. Calculate the price of a floor using binomial option pricing.
4. Understand the adjustment to the Black-Scholes model needed to price caps and floors.

---

[1] In this chapter, we focus on OTC (over-the-counter) interest rate options that are obtained directly from a bank. Derivative exchanges, such as the CBOT and the CME, have option contracts that function in a manner similar to the interest rate options discussed in this chapter. However, the exchange-traded options are usually options on financial futures contracts with the financial futures contract for a trade in a short-term debt contract. Accordingly, the exchange-traded options are not interest rate options, but instead are options that change in value with changes in interest rates because the underlying asset is a short-term debt instrument.

18.2 INSTITUTIONAL DETAILS AND FEATURES FOR INTEREST RATE CAPS AND FLOORS

An **interest rate cap** is a portfolio of European call options (referred to as *caplets*) on an interest rate with the payoff coming **in arrears**. Similarly, an **interest rate floor** is a portfolio of European put options (referred to as *floorlets*) on an interest rate with the payoff coming in arrears. Combining a caplet and a floorlet with the same expiration date but different strike rates creates an **interest rate collar**. Combining a series of interest rate collars (or combinations of a cap with a floor) creates an **interest rate corridor**. In practice, many commercial banks offer **zero cost collars** to their clients where, for no charge, the client can lock in a range of potential interest rates.

These instruments evolved from interest rate guarantees on floating rate loans, including adjustable-rate mortgages. Back in the mid-1980s banks began stripping the guarantees out as individual items, much like an FRA is separated from the underlying lending activity. Although still widely used today, caps were very popular in the LBO heydays, as lenders insisted that LBO firms have some cap protection against rising interest rates on their floating-rate loans. Figure 18-1 provides an example of an agreement for caps, floors, and collars.

Interest rate caps and floors are customized, negotiated, option-like contracts between two parties, one of whom is usually a financial institution. Unlike most options that are based on the price of an underlying asset, caps and floors are based on the value of an underlying interest rate. Just as with other option-like instruments, the buyer pays the seller some form of a premium at the inception of the agreement; and if the buyer exercises the option, the seller completes a transaction with the buyer. The transaction in an interest rate option is an interest payment at the strike rate, based on an agreed on amount of notional principal. As a result, *the buyer and not the seller bears all of the counterparty risk in this type of agreement.*

Generally, caps and floors have multiple settlement dates, that create a series of caplets or floorlets, rather than just one maturity date. The cash flows for a cap or floor are based on the difference between a reference rate and the exercise rate times a notional principal.

Payment to cap holder = MAX[0, notional principal × (index rate − cap exercise rate) × (number of days in settlement period/360)].

Payment to floor holder = MAX[0, notional principal × (floor exercise rate − index rate) × (number of days in settlement period/360)].

In the case of a cap, if interest rates are above the exercise price on the settlement day, the seller pays the buyer the difference between the two rates. The actual payment is the difference between the rates times the notional principal divided by the number of settlement periods in a year. In the case of floor, if interest rates are below the floor exercise rate on a settlement day, the buyer will pay the seller the difference in the rates times the notional principal divided by the number of settlement periods in a year.

When a cap is sold and a floor is purchased, the combined strategy is called an interest rate corridor. An interest rate corridor is an interest rate collar that covers multiple time periods (exercise or settlement dates) to create a range of possible interest rates for

FHLBI
MEMBER
LINK

CREDIT

Interest rate caps, floors, and collars

▶<u>Products
and policies</u>
▶<u>Credit
home</u>

Description:	Interest rate caps, floors, and collars are offered in various sizes, sometimes as small as $5 million, subject to availability.
Term:	Various terms may be arranged, usually in the 1 to 10 year range.
Application:	Call the FHLBI by 5:00 p.m. Indianapolis time to request a credit decision and to discuss notional principal amounts. Specific terms will be discussed after credit approval has been made.
Beginning date:	The cap, floor, or collar agreement will begin within 30 calendar days of credit approval; a specific beginning date will be discussed as part of the conditions of the agreement.
Rate:	Specific terms will be negotiated after credit approval.
Commitment fee:	The fee for a cap, floor, or collar will be determined by the FHLBI on the basis of the terms requested.
Collateral:	The member will be required to post collateral in accordance with the requirements set forth in the Collateral Policy.
Capital stock:	For each cap, floor, or collar, a member must hold FHLBI capital stock equal to at least 5% of the amount of collateral required for the agreement. This requirement is in addition to the capital stock required for advances and other credit products, and will be adjusted monthly with changes in the collateral requirement. Members will be notified of any required stock purchases.
Termination:	Terminating a cap, floor, or collar may be arranged with the FHLBI based on market conditions and the requirements of the particular interest rate agreement. Call for details.

FIGURE 18-1   Sample agreement for caps, floors, and collars.

Source: Federal Home Loan Bank of Indianapolis (2003)

the holder of the corridor where the cap exercise rate forms the upper bound and the floor exercise rate forms the lower bound.

All cap and floor contracts must specify the following:

1. **The reference rate**. The market interest rate on which the actual interest payments would be based.

2. **Exercise rate**. The contracted rate on which the interest payments are based.

3. **Term**. The time frame for which the cap and/or floor agreement will be in effect.

4. **Frequency of settlement**. This identifies how often during the term of the agreement the interest rate payments will be calculated. For example, the frequency could be quarterly or semiannually.

5. **Notional principal**. The principal amount on which the interest payments are based.

Following are simple examples of a cap and a floor.

EXAMPLE   *Calculating the Payoff to a Cap*

Assume a company issued a seven-year $50,000,000 note where the coupon is reset every six months to equal PIBOR (Paris Interbank Offer Rate) + 150 basis points. However, the company wants to place a ceiling of 8% as the maximum index rate of interest that they will have to pay. As a result, the company buys the following seven-year cap.

- Notional principal = $50,000,000
- Payments = semiannual
- Reference rate = PIBOR
- Exercise rate = 8%
- Premium (option price) = 200 basis points (premium is calculated by a specific interest rate option model discussed later)

The cost of the cap is equal to the notional principal × premium. Here, this would be $50,000,000 × 2% = $1,000,000. If, at the time of the first settlement, PIBOR is equal to 10%, then the company will receive (from the cap):

$$\frac{(10\% - 8\%)\$50,000,000}{2} = \$500,000.$$

Note that the company would have interest expense from the interest rate index of (10% × $50,000,000)/2 = $2,500,000, but since they receive $500,000 the **effective rate of interest** index paid ($2 million/$50 million) × 2 = 8%. The company has limited the maximum index rate it will pay on the loan at 8%. However, recall that the loan rate is PIBOR + 150 basis points; therefore, by limiting the index rate to a maximum of 8% the company pays an interest rate of 9.5% on the loan at the payment time.

However, if at the time of the second settlement, PIBOR has fallen to 7.5%, the company receives nothing and must pays interest at PIBOR + 150 basis points for an interest rate of 9.0%.

If PIBOR rises above 8%, the company receives payments on the cap, which sets a ceiling on the effective debt cost. If PIBOR falls, however, the company enjoys the benefit of lower interest rates but, in either case, the company has spent the premium paid for the interest rate protection offered by the cap.

EXAMPLE   *Calculating the Payoff to a Floor*

Assume now that an insurance company owns a $20,000,000 five-year floating rate note that pays TIBOR (Tokyo Interbank Offer Rate) plus 50 basis points on a semiannual basis. Further assume that the insurance company purchases a three-year floor to protect their interest payments received from the note against falling interest rates.

- Notional principal = $20,000,000
- Payments = semiannual
- Reference rate = TIBOR

- Exercise rate $= 6\%$
- Premium $= 100$ basis points (premium is calculated from a specific option model discussed later)

The cost of the floor is equal to the notional principal $\times$ premium. The cost of the floor would be $\$20,000,000 \times 1\% = \$200,000$. If at the time of the first settlement, TIBOR is equal to 9%, the company will receive nothing from the floor agreement but will receive interest of

$$\frac{\$20,000,000(0.095)}{2} = \$950,000.$$

If TIBOR falls below the exercise rate of 6%, the insurance company receives the difference between TIBOR and 6% times the notional principal divided by 2. This puts a floor on the insurance company's interest earnings. The minimum interest rate the insurance company will earn over the next three years is

Earnings on note	TIBOR $+ 0.50\%$
Receive on floor	6% $-$ TIBOR
Net interest earnings	6.5%

Note that for the last two years of the note's life the insurance does not have any interest rate protection because the loan covers five years while the interest rate floor covers only three years.

One of the really good characteristics of these instruments is that the binomial option pricing model that you learned in Chapter 10 can be easily adapted to value these types of securities. In the next three sections binomial option pricing will be used to value interest caps, interest floors, and capped floating-rate debt.

18.3 INTEREST RATE CAPS

A cap is a contract that guarantees to the holder that floating rates will not exceed a specified amount, that is, the variable rate is capped. A typical cap contract involves the payment at time t, for example, every quarter, of a variable interest rate on a specified principal. Thus, the payoff on the cap at any point in time is

$$\max((r_{fl} - r_{cap}) \times (n/360), 0),$$

where

$r_{fl} = $ the floating rate, for example, three-month LIBOR,

$r_{cap} = $ the fixed cap rate, and

$n = $ the number of days in the cap payment period.

Payments are made for the lifetime of the cap with the floating rate paid at time t being set at time $t - 1$. Figure 18-2 depicts the payoff to an interest rate cap.

An interest rate cap can be divided into a series of caplets, that is, a series of options where the maturity of the individual options matches the cap payment dates. To value a cap using the binomial method, the following steps need to be followed:

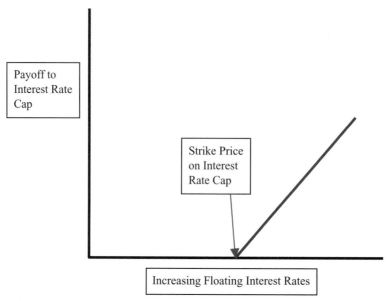

FIGURE 18-2 Payoff profile of interest rate cap.

1. Break the cap into a series of caplets.
2. Value each of the caplets using the binomial model, which requires the following:
   a. Develop the projected interest rate tree of future spot prices around the current forward rate path and calibrate the tree so that it is arbitrage free.[2]
   b. Project the payoff on the caplet at any node on the tree where it can be exercised.
   c. Discount the option payoffs back through the tree to determine its present value.
3. The value of the cap is the sum of the present value of the component caplets.

This technique is best demonstrated by an example. The example will assume the following details and use those details to value an interest rate cap. The details for the cap are

1. a two-year interest rate cap,
2. with annual payments based on the one-year Treasury rate,
3. a strike rate of 4%, and
4. a forward interest rate tree calibrated at 10% volatility (see Figure 18-3).

To value this two-year interest rate cap, the first thing that must be realized is that a two-year cap with annual payments is really a series of two European-style caplets. That is, a one-year caplet and a two-year caplet.

The process of valuing the two-year interest rate cap begins with valuing the one-year caplet. To value the one-year caplet, the payoff is calculated at each of the two nodes' one-year nodes in Figure 18-3 and worked backwards to the root of the tree. This will determine

---

[2] Calibrating the interest rate tree will be done for you, so that the examples are as straightforward as possible.

Today In One Year In Two Years

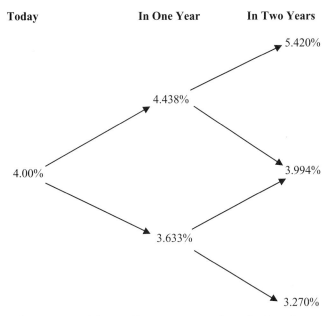

FIGURE 18-3 A forward interest rate tree for valuation of cap.

the present value average of the payoffs. Notice that if the interest rates rise to 4.438%, which is above the exercise rate of 4%, the one-year caplet will pay 4.438% − 4% = 0.438%. However, if interest rates fall to 3.633%, then the caplet will pay nothing. Thus, the payoff to the caplet is

$$c_{1H} = \max(0, 4.438\% - 4\%) = 0.438\%$$
$$c_{1L} = \max(0, 3.633\% - 4\%) = 0.$$

Therefore, the caplet price as a percentage of the notional principal is found by discounting these potential payoffs back to time 0. Recall, from Chapter 10 that the call value at a node of the binomial tree equals:

$$c = \frac{p(C_{1H}) + (1 - p)(C_{1L})}{1 + r}.$$

For all interest rate options, $p = 0.5$ (50%) is assumed; therefore, the value of the caplet is

$$c = \frac{0.5(0.438) + 0.5(0)}{1.04} = 0.2106.$$

If the value of a one-year caplet on a notional principal of $10 million was being examined, the caplet would be worth (0.2106%) × $10,000,000 = $21,060.

But, this was a two-year cap. Therefore, the two-year caplet needs to be valued, which is done by starting at the end of second period and working backwards to time 0 (today, in Figure 18-3). What is being done here is determining the present value (at $t = 0$) of the value of the caplet from $t = 1$ to $t = 2$. This is shown Figure 18-4 with the value of the caplets shown as bold numbers.

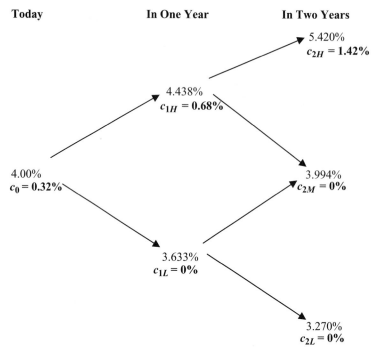

Today	In One Year	In Two Years

5.420%
$c_{2H} = 1.42\%$

4.438%
$c_{1H} = 0.68\%$

4.00%
$c_0 = 0.32\%$

3.994%
$c_{2M} = 0\%$

3.633%
$c_{1L} = 0\%$

3.270%
$c_{2L} = 0\%$

FIGURE 18-4 Binomial tree for valuing a cap.

Calculations for the tree:

$$c_{2H} = \max[0, (5.42\% - 4\%)] = 1.42\%,$$
$$c_{2M} = \max[0, (3.99\% - 4\%)] = 0\%,$$
$$c_{2L} = \max[0, (3.27\% - 4\%)] = 0\%,$$
$$c_{1H} = \frac{0.5(1.42\%) + 0.5(0\%)}{1.04438} = 0.68\%,$$
$$c_{1L} = \frac{0.5(0\%) + 0.5(0\%)}{1.03633} = 0\%,$$
$$c_0 = \frac{0.5(0.68\%) + 0.5(0\%)}{1.04} = 0.32\%.$$

The total value of the cap is equal to the present value of the one-year caplet from $t=0$ to $t=1$ plus the present value of the caplet from $t=1$ to $t=2$. Therefore, the value of the cap must be equal to the value of the one-year caplet (0.21%) plus the value of the one-year caplet one year from now (a two-year caplet) (0.32%), which totals 0.53%. This total, 0.53%, would then be multiplied by the notional principal to determine the cost of the cap. Assuming, for example, a notional principal of $10,000,000 would result in a cost of $53,000 for this interest rate cap.

Note that in determining the value of the two-year caplet, different discount rates were used to calculate c_{1H}, c_{1L}, and c_0. The discount rates are the interest rates for the corresponding nodes of the underlying interest rate tree.

Exactly the same process is used to price an interest rate floor. The process of pricing a floor will be discussed in the next section.

18.4 INTEREST RATE FLOORS

The process for pricing a floor will be demonstrated through an example. The example will use the following details.

1. A two-year interest rate floor,
2. with annual payments based on the one-year Treasury rate, and
3. a strike (exercise) rate of 4%.

As with pricing the cap, the first thing that must be realized is that a two-year floor is really a series of two European-style floorlets. That is, a one-year floorlet and a two-year floorlet.

To value the one-year floorlet from $t=0$ to $t=1$, the payoff at each of the two nodes is calculated and worked backwards to the root of the tree. This process determines the present value average of the payoffs.

Notice that if the interest rates fall to 3.633%, which is below the exercise rate of 4%, the one-year floorlet will pay $3.633\% - 4\% = 0.367\%$. However, if interest rates rise to 4.438%, the floorlet will pay nothing. Thus, the payoffs to the floorlet are

$$f_{1H} = \max[0, (4\% - 4.438\%)] = 0\%$$
$$f_{1L} = \max[0, (4\% - 3.633\%)] = 0.367\%.$$

Then, the floorlet price as a percentage of the notional principal is found by discounting these potential payoffs back to time 0.

$$f = \frac{0.5(0.367) + 0.5(0)}{1.04} = 0.1764.$$

Assuming a notional principal of $10 million, the value of a one-year floorlet would be $0.1764\% \times \$10,000,000 = \$17,640$. But, since this is a two-year floor, the value of the second one-year floorlet which starts at $t=1$ must be calculated. This is shown in Figure 18-5 with the value of the floorlets presented in bold numbers.

Calculations for the tree:

$$f_{2H} = \max[0, (4\% - 5.42\%)] = 0\%,$$
$$f_{2M} = \max[0, (4\% - 3.994\%)] = 0.006\%,$$
$$f_{2L} = \max[0, (4\% - 3.27\%)] = 0.73\%,$$
$$f_{1H} = \frac{0.5(0\%) + 0.5(0.006\%)}{1.04438} = 0.002\%,$$
$$f_{1L} = \frac{0.5(0.006\%) + 0.5(0.73\%)}{1.03633} = 0.355\%,$$
$$f_0 = \frac{0.5(0.002\%) + 0.5(0.355\%)}{1.04} = 0.172\%.$$

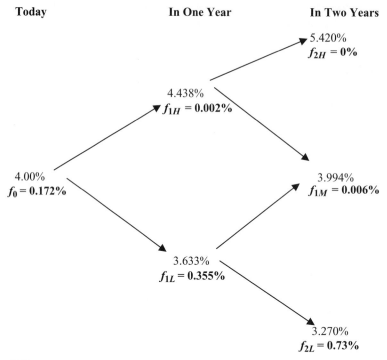

FIGURE 18-5 Binomial tree for valuing a floor.

The total value of the floor is equal to the present value of the one-year floorlet from $t=0$ to $t=1$ plus the present value of the one-year floorlet from $t=1$ to $t=2$. Therefore, the value of the floor must be equal to the value of the one-year floorlet (0.1764%) plus the value of the one-year floorlet one year from now (0.172%) for a total of 0.348%. This total would then be multiplied by the notional principal to determine the value of the floor. Assuming a notional principal of $10 million results in this floor costing $34,800.

Why is the floor important? Assume a company's sales and therefore its profits were negatively correlated with high interest rates. That is, as interest rates went up, profits went down company might examine its budget and decide that profits at an interest rate of 4% are acceptable but lower profits at interest rates above that are not. Unfortunately, they may also believe that $53,000 (the price of the cap in the example) is a substantial amount of money to pay for interest rate protection. But if the company also agreed to pay a minimum of 4%—*that is, they buy the cap but sell the floor*—then they will receive $34,800 for this guarantee and the net cost of the protection against rising interest rates is $53,000 − $34,800 = $18,200. The company might find this amount much more acceptable.

Because banks are always concerned about their customers' credit risk, they are often in a position to recommend what is known as a *zero cost collar*. In this case, a company agrees to buy an interest rate cap and to sell an interest rate floor where the rates are carefully chosen so that the *net cost of the two instruments is zero*.

18.5   CAPPED FLOATING-RATE SECURITIES

A floating-rate security is a bond whose coupon resets higher or lower depending on the change in the level of interest rates. Usually, the coupon paid at the end of the period is set equal to the interest rate at the start of the period. As you can imagine, this type of instrument is riskier than a fixed-rate bond. To reduce the risk of floating-rate securities, some of these bonds are *capped* and are referred to as a **capped floater**. To value a capped floater, the same process used to value a regular bond will be followed with the exception that the coupon rate for each coupon must be determined. The coupon rate is determined at each reset point (node of the interest rate tree) and is set equal to the interest rate at the start of the period or the capped rate, whichever is lower.

For example, consider a three-year floating-rate security with a capped interest rate of 4.5%. How would you determine this bond's value? What you would do is to calculate the value at time 0 by moving backwards through a binomial tree structure, setting the coupon at each node equal to the interest rate at the start of the period or 4.5%, *whichever is lower*. Consider Figure 18-6 where C = coupon rate, f = floating rate, and V = value (price). Notice that at several of the nodes, the coupon can have one or two values depending on the rates leading to that node. The calculations for each of the nodes are

$V_3 = 100$ because a bond redeems at par at maturity and this is a three-year bond,

$$V_{2H} = \frac{1}{2}\left(\frac{100+4.5}{1.05684} + \frac{100+4.5}{1.05684}\right) = 98.88,$$

$$V_{2M} = \frac{1}{2}\left(\frac{100+4.188}{1.04188} + \frac{100+4.188}{1.04188}\right) = 100,$$

$$V_{2L} = \frac{1}{2}\left(\frac{100+3.429}{1.03429} + \frac{100+3.429}{1.03429}\right) = 100,$$

$$V_{1H} = \frac{1}{2}\left(\frac{98.88+4.500}{1.04653} + \frac{100+4.500}{1.04653}\right) = 99.32,$$

$$V_{1L} = \frac{1}{2}\left(\frac{100+3.810}{1.03810} + \frac{100+3.810}{1.03810}\right) = 100,$$

$$V_0 = \frac{1}{2}\left(\frac{99.32+4.000}{1.04} + \frac{100+4.000}{1.04}\right) = 99.67.$$

Note that the cash flows at each node are discounted by the floating rate at each node. This is done because the floating rate is the prevailing market rate at that time. As you can see, the existence of a cap on a floating-rate note tends to reduce the note's value. In fact, the lower the cap rate, the less the floating-rate note will be worth, all other factors constant.

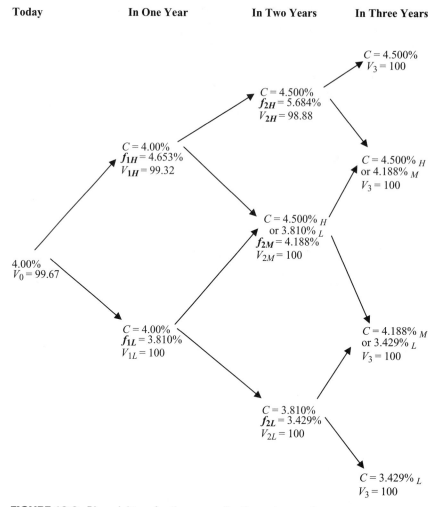

FIGURE 18-6 Binomial tree for three-year floating rate security.

18.6 VALUING CAPS AND FLOORS USING THE BLACK-SCHOLES MODEL

As you have seen, the binomial model is an easy way to determine the value of a derivative instrument whose value can change over time. Also, you probably recognize that the model can get quite cumbersome when it is extended over many periods or divided into many subperiods. Another difficulty is that two values are often obtained at one node. Also, for example, for a one-period option, the binomial model uses two ending possible values for the underlying asset. This is not very realistic because many more than two values are possible. And, as you extend into more periods, you end up evaluating more and more potential end points. While this is bad news, it can be overcome mathematically through the law of large numbers, which you learned in your statistics class. That is, for example, as a one-period model is divided into more and more subperiods, the ending values will tend to converge toward an average. In other words, a mean value will emerge along with a distribution of other possible values. This allows us to use closed-form statistical models, the most famous of which is the Black-Scholes model.

Unfortunately, the Black-Scholes model is not designed to price an interest rate option. However, Fischer Black suggested an approximation of the model and this approximation is used by most practitioners to value options on commodity futures to price caps and floors. While this method is not theoretically correct, it yields surprisingly accurate results. The Black model is

$$c = [r_f e^{-rT} N(d_1) - r_x e^{-rT} N(d_2)]B \times T$$

$$f = [r_x e^{-rT} N(-d_2) - r_f e^{-rT} N(-d_1)]B \times T$$

$$d_1 = \frac{\ln(r_f/r_x) + (\sigma^2/2)T}{\sigma \sqrt{T}}$$

$$d_2 = d_1 - \sigma \sqrt{T},$$

where

$c =$ caplet value

$f =$ floorlet value

$r_f =$ the forward interest rate

$r_x =$ the exercise interest rate

$B =$ the value of the underlying loan

$T =$ the length of the caplet.

The application of this model is best shown by example.

EXAMPLE *Using the Black Model to Price an Interest Rate Cap*

Consider a cap on a 15-month loan where the interest rate resets quarterly and is set to the then three-month LIBOR. The first thing to do is to calculate the present value of the following caplets:[3]

1. Cap on the three-month LIBOR, three months forward.
2. Cap on the three-month LIBOR, six months forward.
3. Cap on the three-month LIBOR, nine months forward.
4. Cap on the three-month LIBOR, twelve months forward.

Assume that the exercise rate on each caplet is 8.5%, and that the principal amount for each caplet is $20,000,000. Assume further that the LIBOR curve is flat at 8.0% with a volatility of 13% for each forward interest rate. (Note that the LIBOR curve will also be used for discounting.) The first objective is to calculate the value of the individual caplets:

---

[3] Note, a cap is not needed for the first three months of the loan because rates reset quarterly; therefore, the rate for the first three months of the loan is set today and held constant for the next three months.

Caplet	r_f (%)	r_x (%)	T	r (%)	σ (%)	B (m)	Value ($)
1	8	8.5	0.25	8	13	$20	2,435
2	8	8.5	0.50	8	13	$20	5,456
3	8	8.5	0.75	8	13	$20	7,969
4	8	8.5	1.00	8	13	$20	10,096
Total value of the cap is the sum of the individual caplets							**$25,956**

Notice from the example the similarities between the interest rate cap and a regular call option. In particular, assuming all other things are equal, the longer the time to maturity the more value the caplet since there is a greater probability that interest rates will increase in the future. Notice also that you need r, which is the spot risk-free rate from $t = 0$ until the beginning of the caplet (or floorlet) since the values must be discounted before they can be added together to determine the final value of the cap or floor.

18.7 SUMMARY

When using the binomial method to value caps and floors, remember to break the instrument into its component caplets and floorlets. For example, if you were valuing a one-year cap that paid off on a quarterly basis, you would have to value the four three-month caplets, one starting at $t = 0$, one starting at $t = 3$, one starting at $t = 6$, and the one starting at $t = 9$.

Caplet Timeline

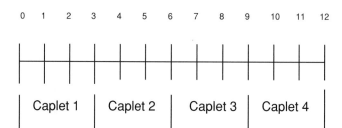

To value a collar, value the component cap and floor and subtract the value of the floor from the value of the cap. Clearly, using the Black model to value these instruments is much simpler than using the binomial model.

Value of Options on Interest Rates

	If Interest Rates	
Value of	Rise	Fall
Long cap	Rises	Falls
Short cap	Falls	Rises
Long floor	Falls	Rises
Short floor	Rises	Falls

SUMMARY OF VALUATION AND RISK MANAGEMENT SKILLS

1. Understand interest rate caps (caplets), interest floors (floorlets), and interest rate corridors (collars).

An interest rate cap is a portfolio of European call options (caplets) that protects the buyer of the cap against interest rate increases. The buyer of a cap receives a payment if interest rates exceed the strike rate on a settlement date. An interest rate floor is a portfolio of European put options (floorlets) that protect the buyer of the floor against interest rate decreases. The buyer of a floor receives a payment if interest rates are lower than the strike rate on a settlement date. An interest rate corridor is a combination of an interest rate cap and an interest rate floor at different strike rates. A zero cost collar can be created by buying a caplet and selling a floorlet. This limits exposure to rising interest rates at no cost by selling a floorlet to cover the cost of the caplet.

2. Calculate the price of a cap using binomial option pricing.

To price a cap using binomial option pricing requires the following steps. First, break the cap into its component caplets. Second, develop an interest rate tree and project the payoffs for each caplet at any node in the interest rate tree where the caplet can be exercised. Third, discount the payoffs back through the tree to determine the present value of the payoffs. Finally, the sum of the present value of the caplet payoffs is the value of the cap.

3. Calculate the price of a floor using binomial option pricing.

The price of an interest rate floor is calculated in exactly the same way as the price of an interest rate cap. However, since a floor protects against falling rates, it pays when interest rates go below the strike rate. Therefore, while the process for pricing a floor is the same process used to price a cap, it is important to remember that the floor pays against falling rates, so the greatest value in the floor will be seen at the bottom of the interest rate tree instead of the top of the tree as with the cap.

4. Understand the adjustment to the Black-Scholes model needed to price caps and floors.

The first major change is that the stock price and the strike price are replaced with the forward rate and the strike rate, respectively. Also, the forward rate (which is a rate for a future period) is discounted back to the valuation point.

QUESTIONS

1. Which options are more expensive and why?

a. A short-dated cap or a long-dated cap.
b. A cap with a lower exercise rate or a higher exercise rate.
c. A floor with a lower exercise rate or a higher exercise rate.

2. Interest rate volatility is an important component of the price of an interest rate option. One important determinant of volatility is the absolute level of interest rates. Why?

3. An important variable in the pricing of an interest rate option is the shape of the yield curve. Why?

4. What are the advantages and disadvantages of buying a collar?

5. Given the binomial interest rate tree below, what is the value of a cap with an exercise rate at 5% on a $10,000,000 loan?

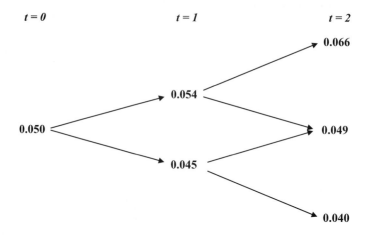

6. Given the binomial interest rate tree below, what is the value of a floor struck at 4.125% on a $10,000,000 loan?

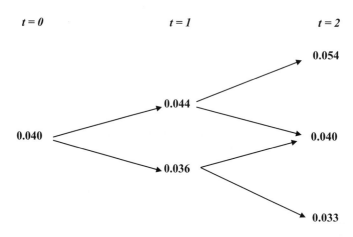

7. The value of a cap is the sum of the values of the caplets included in the cap. Consider a cap on a 15-month loan where the interest rate resets quarterly and is set to the then three-month LIBOR.

a. Calculate the present value of the following caplets:

> Cap on the three-month libor rate, three months forward
> Cap on the three-month libor rate, six months forward
> Cap on the three-month libor rate, nine months forward
> Cap on the three-month libor rate, twelve months forward.

The strike on each caplet is 8.5%, and the principal amount for each caplet is $20,000,000. Assume a flat LIBOR curve of 8.0%, a volatility of 13% for each forward interest rate, and that all rates are quoted quarterly. (Note that the LIBOR curve is to be used for discounting as well.)

b. What is the total value of the cap?

8. Suppose a company wanted to know if its bank had quoted correctly a one-year interest cap on a $20 million loan that resets semiannually. The bank representative said they used the Black model and assumed a 20% volatility, a cap rate of 8%, an implied forward rate of 7% and a spot risk-free rate of 6.5%. The bank representative said the cap would cost $25,000—is that correct?

9. The same bank representative says that a floor on the same loan as in Question 7 struck at 6% would cost $15,000—is that correct?

10. The bank representative also states that an interest rate collar struck with a cap at 8% and a floor at 6% would cost $10,000—is that correct?

KEY TERMS

Capped Floater A variable-rate coupon paying bond with a cap on the interest rate paid for the coupon.

Effective Rate of Interest The actual interest rate paid after taking the effect of interest rate options into account.

In Arrears Means to make the interest payment at the end of the period.

Interest Rate Cap A portfolio of European call options (caplets) on an interest rate with the payoff coming in arrears.

Interest Rate Collar The combination of a caplet and a floorlet with the same expiration date but different strike rates.

Interest Rate Corridor The combination of a series of interest rate collars, or a combination of an interest cap and an interest rate floor.

Interest Rate Floor A portfolio of European put options (floorlets) on an interest rate with the payoff coming in arrears.

Zero Cost Collar A collar where the premium paid for the option that is purchased is the same as the premium received for the option that is sold.

CHAPTER 19

AN INTRODUCTION TO CREDIT DERIVATIVES

19.1 INTRODUCTION

This chapter discusses **credit derivatives**. This is the second risk management chapter that does not link back to a specific market but, instead, applies to all fixed income markets. This book has discussed thoroughly the fact that credit (default) risk is an important structural factor in interest rates and, through interest rates, is an important factor in pricing interest-bearing (fixed-income) securities. However, while the management of default risk in money market securities has been discussed, default risk in the longer term securities has been basically ignored under the assumption that for investment purposes default risk can be diversified away by investors who hold different assets in portfolio. However, in reality many situations occur in the marketplace where diversification does not adequately manage credit risk. A classic example of this problem that is discussed in Section 2 and visited throughout the chapter is the geographic concentration of most bank loan portfolios. Credit derivatives can manage this problem. Specifically, credit derivatives have been created to manage credit risk in the situations where diversification is not adequate. This chapter provides an introduction to credit derivatives, their applications, and their pricing.

This chapter begins with a motivating example of the problem with credit risk from limited diversification. Next, background on the issues in credit risk is discussed and an example is provided where a credit derivative is used by a bank to change its exposure to credit risk. Then, the concept of complete markets is presented and it is shown that credit derivatives are necessary for the completion of fixed income markets. This chapter continues with a discussion of the benefits of credit derivatives and concludes with a discussion on the pricing of credit derivatives. This discussion covers several different methods for pricing credit derivatives because the market has not yet reached a consensus on the best method.

DEVELOPING VALUATION AND RISK MANAGEMENT SKILLS

1. Understand what a credit derivative is and how it helps lenders manage credit risk.
2. Understand how credit derivatives complete the market and why this is important.

3. Understand the strengths and weaknesses of the different pricing methods for credit derivatives.

19.2 A MOTIVATING EXAMPLE

Consider the largest company in a small town, for example, the Hershey Foods Corporation in Hershey, Pennsylvania, the company that makes those marvelous chocolate kisses.[1] This firm employs thousands of workers both directly and indirectly since many of the businesses in the town depend on the Hershey workers to buy their goods and services. Banks making commercial loans to Hershey and the other companies in the town depend on the success of Hershey for the repayment of those loans. Similarly, credit unions and savings and loans making personal and residential loans to the towns people rely on the towns people future employment for repayment of their loans.

Imagine a huge fire destroys the Hershey plant. All of the workers would be unemployed and thus have no money to spend on goods and services. The businesses in town would have to close. Neither Hershey nor the businesses in town would have any sales or cash flow; therefore, repayments to the banks would stop because the towns folk would be unable to repay personal and residential loans. In the absence of any type of insurance, a very grim situation would arise.

To avoid this grim situation, the Hershey Company might carry fire insurance and the employees and small business owners in the town might carry business-interruption insurance. In fact, and theoretically speaking, the only stakeholders who would not be interested in having any insurance would be the shareholders. Insurance is expensive and diversification theory would argue that the shareholders already hold an interest in insurance companies. Therefore, even though the earnings of the Hershey Company would be reduced in years when the insurance was not needed, they would be offset by the increased earnings in the insurance company. Similarly, the losses made whole by the insurance company in the event of a fire would be offset by the loss in the insurance company.

The Hershey example demonstrates that credit risk is important. In particular, credit risk is important to undiversified stakeholders. In this chapter, some of the basic ways in which undiversified stakeholders attempt to minimize their exposure to credit risk will be examined. This is the world of credit derivatives, and the market for credit derivatives has only started to develop in recent years. One of the benefits of this market is that it can serve as an early warning system for impending credit risk problems. The *In the News* item that follows presents a story of one of the most famous credit risk disasters of modern times: Enron.

---

[1] As Milton Hershey's chocolate business continued to thrive in the early 1900s, so did the community he established around it. A bank, department store, school, park, churches, golf courses, zoo, and even a trolley system (to bring in workers from nearby towns) were all built in rapid succession. Although the town was well established by its 10th anniversary in 1913, Mr. Hershey started a second building boom in the 1930s. During the Depression, he kept men at work constructing a grand hotel, a community building, a sports arena, and a new office building for the chocolate factory. See http://www.hersheys.com/about/milton.shtml. The information in this section is drawn from this web site.

IN THE NEWS

SOMEONE KNEW

by Robert Lenzner, 03.04.02, Forbes.com

The Enron belly flop stunned almost everyone, but a select circle of Wall Street pros had an early warning system you can't access.

Tyco, Gap, Ford Motor Credit, and Dow Chemical: Are these the next corporate collapses waiting to happen? Maybe not, but a little-known early-warning system indicates that they are entering dangerous territory.

The warning system is an obscure electronic-trading market where banks and other big players buy and sell credit-protection contracts as insurance against loans going bad. Lately the price of such contracts is surging, for these companies and others.

It's arcane stuff that most investors could ignore but for this: This credit-protection market sounded alarms about Enron months before the scandal-scarred energy giant collapsed. Enron's stock did not begin its most breathtaking plunge until mid-October, when the company's offshore partnerships were uncovered. But two months before that, the trouble signs showed up in credit trading.

On August 15, the day after Enron's CEO, Jeffrey Skilling, abruptly resigned, its stock barely budged, closing just above $40. But on the same day, the price of an Enron credit contract jumped 18%. Contracts bought that day were priced at 185 basis points ($185,000 annually for protection against default on a $10 million loan). By October 25, as the troubles sparked headlines, Enron stock had dropped more than 50%, and the credit contract had soared to $900,000 per $10 million annually.

Even at the much higher price, it was a great deal. Just as Citigroup used the credit-protection approach to insure $1.4 billion in loans to Enron, other banks and security firms shrewdly sidestepped a big hit by purchasing credit-protection contracts on Enron.

"It's like taking out extra fire insurance just as your house starts smoking," says Sunil Hirani, cofounder of Creditex, an intermediary in this relatively new game. "What's the biggest risk in the financial system? Credit risk. Everyone has it. And it's the least-managed risk in the system."

It's too bad that credit-derivatives prices are not published in the paper as stock prices are. You could have seen trouble brewing at Gap well in advance of the downgrades in its credit rating (see the following chart).

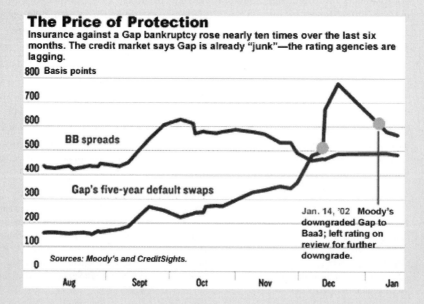

The Price of Protection

Insurance against a Gap bankruptcy rose nearly ten times over the last six months. The credit market says Gap is already "junk"—the rating agencies are lagging.

Sources: Moody's and CreditSights.

Jan. 14, '02 Moody's downgraded Gap to Baa3; left rating on review for further downgrade.

(continued)

SOMEONE KNEW

by Robert Lenzner, 03.04.02, Forbes.com

For now the quotes are known only to a small circle of professionals trading credit insurance in a wholesale-only market. The trades typically cover $10 million tranches of five-year bank debt.

The buyer does not have to be someone wanting to hedge a loan. It could be a speculator betting on financial trouble. Buying credit coverage is roughly equivalent to selling the debtor's bonds short while going long on a comparable U.S. Treasury note.

If the debtor's balance sheet goes from bad to worse, the buyer of the credit derivative will make a profit. If the debtor strengthens, the buyer loses money on the derivative.

Either way, there's money in this for the market makers. It's estimated that middlemen peeled off $1 billion in profits a year on $1.5 trillion in credit-protection trading last year. That is up from $50 billion in 1996.

How much profit or loss is there on a given swing in the pricing of the derivatives? It's a complicated formula akin to the one relating yield swings to bond prices. On a five-year bank loan, a swing of 100 basis points in the credit insurance translates into a gain or loss of not quite 5% of the debt being covered.

Deutsche Bank, JP Morgan, and other international banks started the credit trading market six years ago. You can hedge risks from currencies, energy costs, even the weather—why not credit quality? The Russian default and the Asian crisis of 1998 triggered immense desire by banks to hedge their exposure to calamitous events.

In the wake of Enron, Kmart's bankruptcy filing, and the shocking accounting problems at Global Crossing, Tyco, and others, there is an explosion of interest in the market for insuring against credit defaults.

And nowadays even prime credits are getting harsh judgments in the derivatives market. General Electric Capital gets a triple-A credit rating from the credit-rating agencies; even so, the cost of insuring GE's credit has tripled since early February.

An insurance policy against default by the GE subsidiary over five years will cost you 34 basis points (34-hundredths of a percentage point) of your yield. "The market thinks that [GE Capital's] credit rating should be a low Aa rather than Aaa," says Sanjeev Gupta, head of credit derivatives at Credit Suisse First Boston. Other companies witnessing embarrassing rises in derivatives prices are Household Finance; Deere, the farm-equipment maker; and Countrywide Credit, a home mortgage lender.

Tyco's accounting looks iffy, and investors worry it will not repay its debt. You can see that fear written numerically in the derivatives market. Protection against default on its 6.375% 10-year bonds has soared to 425 basis points. Correspondingly, the bond's price has fallen, from 98 cents on the dollar in late January to a recent 82 cents.

Gap's clothing is not as chic as it used to be. You can see that in the derivatives price. Credit insurance for Gap's bank debt spiked from 82 basis points in late August to 535 recently. The stock is also in trouble but has not seen the same degree of movement. Since August shares have fallen from $21 to $13.

The credit-derivatives market sends warning signals that credit ratings are under pressure to fall from investment grade to noninvestment grade, says Glenn Reynolds, founder of CreditSights, a private credit-research firm.

Reynolds notes that as Nortel Networks, World-Com, and Halliburton get investment-grade credit ratings (BBB and better) from Moody's and Standard and Poor's, they are panned in the derivatives market, where the price of insurance coverage indicates that the debt is of junk status.

At times the market for credit protection can be wrong. The upshot: There is tremendous volatility in the pricing of credit protection. When the retailer J.C. Penney had trouble with suppliers, the premium required to protect loan exposures rose to 750 basis points. But Penney was not headed for default, and the premium went back down to a recent 450.

Someone who bought Penney coverage at the 750-point price is a loser. If he hangs on to the credit insurance until the loan's maturity, he has to cough up 7.5% of the principal amount every year to the seller of the policy. (Should Penney indeed stiff its borrowers, the seller of the policy would owe 100% of the principal less the market value of the loan after default.)

If the buyer at 750 points wants out early, when investors feel better about Penney's prospects, he will have to pay to get someone to take the derivative contract out of his hands.

19.3   WHAT ARE CREDIT DERIVATIVES?

In recent years credit derivatives have burst onto the banking scene and dramatically enhanced the field of risk management. Credit derivatives are off balance sheet contracts whose values are based on the financial strength and creditworthiness of an entity. They are specifically designed to mitigate one of oldest and the most fundamental problems in finance—credit risk. Examples of credit or default events include: bankruptcy, a rating downgrade, failure to pay, a default on a payment obligation, an acceleration of a payment schedule, repudiation of a financial obligation or a moratorium, and/or restructuring of existing debt.

Before going to any greater depth on credit derivatives, back up and take a closer look at credit risk. In general, credit risk stems from two sources: The first is what might be called company and market risk, where the inability to honor a debt stems from a natural disaster such as fire, machinery breakdown, or an unanticipated downturn in the economy. In such cases, the default is outside the normal control of both the borrower and the lender. The second is moral hazard, where the risk is outside of normal control of the lender but within the control of the borrower. Defaults in this case often stem from the borrower diverting funds from their stated original purpose and funneling the money into projects with higher risk/return profiles. This cause of default risk is of little concern for major corporate loans. Therefore, the major risk stems from unanticipated economic changes and these changes are the risks that risk managers attempt to hedge with credit derivatives.[2]

To protect against credit risk, banks first look at the standards for making loans for their portfolio that have shown a low likelihood of default. The risk is then managed on an individual loan basis by requirements for: covenants (by far the most important control mechanism), leverage-based or financial-performance-based grid pricing, blended principal and interest payments, the establishment of sinking or reserve funds, maintenance of business-interruption insurance, cash collateral, third party guarantees, overcollateralization, and the distinction between senior and subordinated debt. On a portfolio basis, credit risk is measured and managed by diversification of the loan portfolio both geographically and on an industry basis, as well as by diversification of the types of loan and other assets. For example, a bank with a 75% loan-to-asset ratio might be more risky than a bank with a 50% loan-to-asset ratio unless the second bank had all of its loans concentrated in the automotive industry while the former was broadly diversified. Diversification is still the major credit portfolio management technique used to minimize **concentration risk**, but it has significant built-in operational constraints and costs.

The concept of concentration risk focuses on the additional risk of credit losses in portfolios where the credit risk is not well-diversified. The presence of concentration risk in credit portfolios is the result of a number of factors.

- **Specialization**. Limited resources and competitive forces often lead institutions into some form of industry, geographic or type of client as classified by credit-rating specialization.

---

[2] Contractual loan covenants are the major device used to prevent risks stemming from moral hazard in middle-market and small commercial enterprises. If moral hazard is a concern for a large corporate borrower, lenders will usually require representation on the Board of Directors.

- **Mismatching between origination capacity and diversification objectives**. The competitive advantage of the institution and competitive pressures from other market participants can limit the ability to competitively enter new markets where the credit assets needed for diversification exist.

- **Incompleteness of credit markets**. A bank located in and/or focusing on a particular area may find a lack of credit assets with the needed term, structure, and industry characteristics necessary for proper diversification. Also, the size of any specific bank credit is often determined by the borrower and not the lender, which leads to a degree of *lumpiness* in the acquisition of credit.

- **Client relationship pressures**. Banks have increased individual loan exposures to clients as a primary resource in establishing and maintaining major relationships. Countering this is the trend by large creditworthy issuers to issuing securities directly to investors instead of resorting to bank financing. Additionally the trend on the part of large corporate borrowers to reduce the size of core banking groups has increased the relative size and scale of bank exposure to individual clients.

These factors are collectively referred to as the credit paradox. These factors have the capacity to increase significantly the concentration risk to unacceptable levels. The use of credit derivatives, in particular credit-default products to mitigate concentration risk, represents a major breakthrough in risk management.

Certainly the age-old techniques designed to reduce concentration risk and to mitigate default risk are successful, but none alleviates this risk quite as efficiently as credit derivatives. Credit derivatives essentially *strip* the credit risk from the associated instrument and allow the lender to concentrate on more fundamental objectives such as the overall profitability of the corporate borrower's relationship to the bank (i.e., treasury, advisory, underwriting, and cash management fees). The following example provides a first look at the use of a credit derivative.

EXAMPLE *Using a Credit Derivative to Reduce Default Risk*

Consider the simple credit-default swap shown in Figure 19-1. Ameriland Bank receives 25 basis points annually for accepting the risk that ABC, Inc. may default on a bond and the bank, therefore, will have to *make good* the shortfall in funds to Euro-Bank. The industry standard in constructing a credit derivative is to base the instrument on a specific bond—for example, the ABC, Inc. bond that matures in 2008. Assume that Euro-Bank has $60 million outstanding to ABC, Inc. through the 2008 ABC, Inc. bond and that Euro-Bank will pay Ameriland Bank 25 basis points annually on a notional amount of $60 million. Thus, Ameriland Bank gets an annual payment from Euro-Bank in the amount

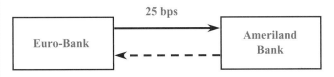

FIGURE 19-1 Simple credit-default swap.

of \$150,000 (0.0025 × \$60,000,000). Ameriland Bank will make a payment to Euro-Bank, if and only if, ABC, Inc. defaults on *this specific bond*.[3]

The structure of the payment by Ameriland Bank in the case of default by ABC, Inc. typically has the following characteristics. ABC defaults and the price of the bond falls from par to 62 cents on the dollar. The amount Ameriland pays will cover the loss in value, which in this example is \$22.8 million ((\$1.00 − \$0.62) × \$60 million). In essence, Euro-Bank is hedged against the effect of default on the market value of its ABC Inc.'s exposure because Ameriland Bank has assumed Euro-Bank's credit risk exposure.

To receive payment for the loss in value of the ABC bond, Euro-Bank, the holder of the option in this case has to deliver to Ameriland Bank the notice of a credit event. Standard convention stipulates that ABC must make a material default—not some minor covenant violation.[4] After a material default occurs, the first thing is to determine the value of the 2005 bond. Generally, a poll of major dealers is taken over the ensuing four weeks. These quotes are averaged to determine the market value. The reason for the delay is to allow the price of ABC, Inc.'s bond to settle and find its true market value.

The brief credit swap example is an example of unbundling loan attributes. The separation or unbundling of loan attributes leads to the more efficient pricing of credit risk and to the reduction of the cost of credit. Although credit instruments are continually being developed in new and different forms, the concepts are similar to standard derivatives. And, like financial derivatives, credit derivatives provide insight into how asset values change due to changing economic conditions and levels of uncertainty. They are instruments that react to views on how market dynamics and conditions will affect credit values and risk.

The major impact of credit derivatives will emerge in the organizational structure of the banking system, where the implementation of a credit derivative strategy will change the way banks have been doing business. Banks will have to reengineer themselves to provide a clear and coherent approach to their new role of suppliers of *value-added financial products* rather than their traditional role of suppliers of credit. This discussion in the remainder of the chapter will provide an overview of the development of credit derivatives and the basic structures used, as well as outlining some of the issues and problems likely to arise in this market.

19.4   CREDIT DERIVATIVES COMPLETE EXISTING MARKETS

Credit derivatives must be understood as another development in a market where there is a progressive refinement of the definition and identification of risk and where derivative instruments are increasingly being used to isolate these risks. As is true with any financial instrument, the management of risk is increasingly becoming one of an asset's attributes.

---

[3] Note that the counterparty exposure of Euro-Bank to Ameriland Bank is similar to that of a currency swap where an exchange of a significant amount takes place at maturity rather than just the netting of cash flows on a periodic basis.

[4] For example, suppose ABC issued commercial paper and for one day its current ratio was less than that required by a covenant in the 2008 bond—this would not constitute a material default.

To demonstrate how an asset can comprise a collection of attributes, consider a simple bond. This instrument can comprise

- liquidity risk (the amount and timing of the cash flows),
- interest-rate risk (sensitivity of price to interest rate changes),
- currency risk (the value of the asset based on the currency in which the cash flows occur),
- contingent risks (the exercise of any embedded options) and,
- default risk relating to the potential failure of the issuer to perform its obligations under the contract.

For example, assume a British company issues

1. a seven-year 7.5% semiannual coupon bond payable in *sterling*,
2. the amount of the issue is £100 million,
3. the issue price is £100,
4. the yield to maturity is 7.5%, which is equivalent to 50 basis points over the equivalent British risk-free rate, and
5. the bond is redeemable at par after three years.[5]

The attributes of this bond can be re-created with derivative instruments by engaging in a number of distinct and separate transactions. From the viewpoint of a U.S. dollar investor, the process would be

- Invest the U.S. dollar equivalent of £100 million in a risk-free seven-year asset yielding floating rate U.S. dollar money market rates.
- Enter into a seven-year cross-currency swap where the investor receives sterling floating rates and pays dollar floating rates (funded by the U.S. dollar investment).
- Enter into a sterling interest rate swap where the investor receives fixed-rate sterling for seven years against payment of sterling floating rates (funded by the cross-currency swap).

These three steps create cash flows identical to the sterling seven-year bond. To add the default risk aspect to the transaction, the following step is needed:

- Invest in a credit-default swap where the default risk of the British company is assumed in return for the receipt of an annual fee.

The effect of this last step is to create a corporate bond where the investor suffers a loss of coupon and/or principal (subject to recovery in bankruptcy) on the default of the issuer (the British company in our example). The spread over the equivalent risk-free rate (derived from the fee received in exchange for the entry into the default swap) is designed to compensate the investor for the credit risk assumed. This fee should be 50 basis points (assuming that there is no liquidity premium).

---

[5] This example is modified from Das, 1998, *Credit Derivatives: Trading & Management of Credit and Default Risk,* John Wiley & Sons, New York.

Risk	Source
Liquidity	Floating-rate investment
Currency risk	Cross-currency swap
Interest-rate risk	Sterling interest rate swap
Call/prepayment risk	Sterling swaption
Default risk	Default swap

FIGURE 19-2 Derivative replication of a risky bond's characteristics.

The call option can also be replicated by having the investor enter into a sale of a sterling-denominated European swaption in which the counterparty has the risk of receiving 7.5% semi annual payment against payment of sterling floating rate for a period of four years exercisable in three years time.*

The pricing of this bond should be equal to the sum of the individual components (ignoring transactions costs, liquidity effects, and counterparty risk). This decomposition shows the separate and distinct risks (summarized in Figure 19-2) that exist in each transaction, the capacity to unbundle the risks, and the potential to trade each risk separately.

The preceding example also highlights the fact that derivatives instruments, in conjunction with a cash investment, can be used to replicate the cash flows of financial assets. Further, this process shows that the deconstruction of financial assets into their constituent cash flow risks facilitates separate trading in the individual risk aspects including credit (default) risk. That is, derivatives facilitate the separate trading of individual attributes of the asset in isolation from the asset itself. This example shows that credit derivatives fill in the last piece of the puzzle for replicating/deconstructing/reengineering/hedging a corporate bond.

19.5 MARKET STATISTICS

The discussion to this point has focused on using credit derivatives to hedge corporate credit risk. However, corporate credit risk is not the only credit risk that risk managers may want to hedge. Recall the discussion that country (sovereign) debt has bond ratings because countries can and do default on their debt (see Figure 8-2). Accordingly, risk managers may also want to hedge the credit risk of sovereign debt. In this section some statistics about market credit risk management activity in corporate and sovereign debt around the world will be discussed.

Figure 19-3 presents the results of a survey conducted by *Derivatives Week*. The survey finds that a considerable amount of trading of credit risk occurs in emerging market debt and provincial/state debt. In North America, the majority of the credit risk trading is on the corporate-risk side. In Europe, most of the credit risk trading is on the sovereign-risk side. The reason for this separation stems from the organization of the market. Many of the international trading desks for emerging markets are based in London rather than New York, while more of the corporate bank loan trading activity occurs in New York and the trading of European corporate loans has traditionally been limited for relationship

---

*A swaption is an option to enter into a swap at a future date. Although they can be designed in many ways, the most common is to pay the fixed rate and receive the floating rate or vice versa. The swaption allows the holder to establish a fixed rate on the underlying swap in advance or to allow the swaption to expire.

	Sovereign risk (%)	Bank risk (%)	Corporate risk (%)
Africa	93.00	2.67	4.33
Asia	55.10	22.14	22.76
Australia/N.Z.	27.36	31.95	40.69
Europe	44.83	29.15	26.02
Latin America	77.94	9.41	12.65
U.S./Canada	10.26	29.48	60.26

FIGURE 19-3 Location of trading activity of credit risk.

Source: Prebon Yamane/Derivatives Week Survey, July 1998.

reasons. Nonetheless, while there is an apparent disparity with Europe dominating trading in the sovereign-risk market and the United States dominating trading in the corporate-risk market, trading in bank risk is relatively similar in both markets, being roughly equal to 29%.

One of the first instances of a credit derivative was an over-the-counter instrument designed in 1991 by Bankers Trust (BT). They introduced a collateralized loan obligation. By doing a repo on a commercial loan portfolio and breaking the package into tranches, BT held the loans and sold the default risk. That same year, JP Morgan is also reported to have made a credit-linked transaction. In general, however, most market participants agree that more general use of credit derivatives really began in 1992. By 1996, the credit derivatives market was estimated to be approximately $1.2 trillion, and according to a BBA (British Bankers Association) survey it was estimated to reach $2 trillion by the end of 2002.[6] To put this in some context, note that the current size of the interest rate swap market is about $25 trillion.

The reason for the phenomenal growth in this market arises from the creation of a larger and more efficient market for credit risk. By way of analogy, suppose there were no organized stock exchanges. How would a quotation for IBM stock be obtained? Obviously, one would have to survey a group of individuals willing and able to sell the stock. This endeavor would take both time and money that may be at a premium and this is precisely today's problem of pricing credit risk. Just as a stock exchange provides an important service in price discovery, so too does the existence of the credit derivatives market. The credit derivatives market is not a public market as is the case of the New York Stock Exchange, but it is a market.

A second reason for the phenomenal growth is the credit paradox of banks. Consider the problem of a generic Canadian bank. In general, the bank is going to have a large number of resource-oriented (e.g., mining and forest products) loans on its balance sheet. What happens if the value of the natural resources declines dramatically? The value of the loan portfolio would decline dramatically, which would reduce the value of the bank. Accordingly, the bank would like to reduce this exposure to resource-oriented loans in favor of exposure to (say) the manufacturing and service sectors. Credit derivatives provide a mechanism to allow banks to make this shift in their credit risk exposures. As will be shown later, the use of these credit-based instruments creates a diversification mechanism for institutions that have a comparative advantage in providing credit to specific market sectors. In effect, the banks substitute counterparty risk for default risk.

---

[6] See www.credit-deriv.com.

The third reason for the growth in these instruments is perhaps the most attractive aspect of credit derivatives, namely, the accompanying flexibility and relative ease of execution that comes with the instrument.

19.6   MAKING CREDIT RISK MARKETABLE

The development of credit derivatives is one of many responses to changes in the field of banking and stems from improvements in technology and information transfer. Capital market advances such as syndicated loans, securitization, secondary loan trading, and collateralized loan obligations have changed the dynamics of corporate banking. These advances have increased competition and the result has been declining loan margins and a trend toward **disintermediation**.

When issued, bonds and loans may have very different price actions due to liquidity and differences in market infrastructure for a company that is performing well. In default, however, the price action for bonds and loans of a given company tend to be very similar. There are exceptions to this, but the important issue is that, in default, both bond and loan credit can be readily sold, assuming that the level of seniority and the collateral backing of each instrument are similar. Loans become indistinguishable from bonds, and bonds become indistinguishable from other defaulted loans. Both become indistinguishable from counterparty credit risk in other derivatives.

The reason why the ability to sell loans in default is so important is that previously illiquid bank loans can now be traded in the much broader and more cash-rich capital markets. The similarity of the price action in the two instruments in default means that banks are indifferent between referencing to a bond or to a loan in a credit-risk swap (but not with a total return swap, which will be discussed later). Referencing to a bond means that the end user can receive (a) their preference of instrument and (b) something that smells, looks, tastes, and feels like a bond.

Recall the simple credit-default swap between Euro-Bank and Ameriland Bank where the latter receives 25 basis points annually for accepting the risk that ABC, Inc. may default on a bond and the bank will have to *make good* the shortfall in funds to Euro-Bank. Why would Euro-Bank want to pay 25 basis points a year to get rid of the ABC, Inc. credit? In other words, how does Euro-Bank benefit in this deal?

First, if ABC, Inc. is a major customer of Euro-Bank, a credit-default swap can be made and ABC, Inc. does not have to be aware of the credit-default swap (for example, in the event that ABC, Inc. notifies Euro-Bank that it wishes to borrow another $150 million). If Euro-Bank has a $200 million credit limit to ABC, Inc., then Euro-Bank could not accommodate its customer because Euro-Bank already has $60 million outstanding to ABC, Inc. (recall the credit swap example in Section 3 and Figure 19-1). However, if Euro-Bank can sell $10 million of its exposure to ABC, Inc. to the credit derivatives market, it can accommodate the loan request and keep the customer happy.[7]

---

[7] The maximum amount that can be loaned to any one customer is determined both by regulation and by in-house guidelines established by the bank. A bank does not want to discuss these limits with a customer because the customer may become concerned about the ability of the bank to handle the customer's needs. This concern can lead to the customer shopping for a new bank.

	Before the credit hedge	After the credit hedge
Asset revenue	$5,800,000	$5,800,000
Liability expense	$4,922,000	$5,264,400
Hedge expense	na	$270,000
Net revenue	$878,000	$265,600
Capital allocation	$8,000,000	$1,600,000
Return on capital	*10.97%*	*16.6%*

FIGURE 19-4   Effect of credit derivatives on bank's rate of return.

Assumes credit pricing is LIBOR +30 bps per annum, bank funding at LIBOR – 15 bps, LIBOR is currently 5.5%. The notional amount is $100 million and the hedger meets regulatory capital criteria.[8]

Second, ABC, Inc. may not be a banking customer of Euro-Bank. Instead, assume Euro-Bank is a derivatives bank that has an interest rate trader who initially acquired the bond without realizing the extent of the credit risk. How can it get rid of the credit risk element? Here is the method. Assume that ABC, Inc. approaches Euro-Bank to do a customized interest rate swap for which there are significant fees. But, Euro-Bank is already up to the limit on ABC credit risk because of the bond it holds. The only way Euro-Bank can do the interest rate swap is by selling the credit risk of the bond. Again, selling the credit risk-only portion into the credit derivative market is the way to do it. Euro-Bank no longer has ABC, Inc. credit risk but Ameriland Bank counterparty risk, and that can be considerably different. Therefore, Euro-Bank can make the much more profitable interest rate swap deal without tying up all of its capital in loans. That is, Euro-Bank can concentrate on more profitable business.

Finally, the issue of regulatory capital exists. When a bank makes a loan to a corporate entity, it has to set aside 8% of the value of the loan for regulatory purposes. No explicit return is earned on this money. If Euro-Bank makes a $100 million loan to ABC, Inc., it has to set aside $8 million in reserves. That is, the 8% required reserve is charged against the full amount of the loan. If, however, Euro-Bank engages in a credit derivative to another bank, the loan is considered by the regulators to be hedged and Euro-Bank must only put up the 8% required reserves against 20% of the face value of the amount.[9] Therefore, instead of putting up $8 million in scarce regulatory capital, Euro-Bank needs only supply $1.6 million (see Figure 19-4). This can, of course, have significant implications for the Euro-Bank's rate of return.

One might ask, *If I am Euro-Bank, why don't I just sell the loan?* Beyond the relationship reasons, the other reason is that if Euro-Bank sells the loan, then it no longer has the right to administer the loan or to vote on covenants on further issues related to the loan. With the credit derivative, Euro-Bank is synthetically selling the risk but is legally keeping

---

[8] This example is drawn from Gontarek and Hegener, 1988, Credit derivatives: the revolution continues, *Credit Risk, A Risk Special Report*, p. 18.

[9] This amount is determined by Basel Accord of July 15, 1988. This accord, designed by the central bankers of the Group of Ten countries, established the 8% capital requirement (the Cooke ratio) as the reserve amount against which losses can be charged.

ownership of the loan. This is a key concept. If ABC gets into trouble, Euro-Bank has retained control and can determine what is best for the client and itself. Many corporate banks want to keep legal ownership of loans simply for this reason. Another reason is because the credit derivative may offer a more liquid market and better pricing in which to sell the credit (for reasons that are stated in the next paragraph).

For Ameriland Bank, the reasons for agreeing to this credit swap are as follows: First, it will be receiving 25 basis points on $100 million ($250,000) annually. In addition, Ameriland might want to establish a corporate loan base in London where it does not have any assets. With credit derivatives, Ameriland does not have to establish a physical London presence or a sterling funding capability. When Euro-Bank calls, Ameriland simply has to agree to accept ABC, Inc. risk and thus forego all the expenses associated with setting up an overseas office. Further, not only will Ameriland get the risk with a good spread, but also it does not have to fund in British pounds. In other words, Ameriland becomes a *virtual* bank. Also, Ameriland may have a very specific investment horizon. For example, it may only want to hold ABC, Inc. risk for two years. However, the only loans outstanding may have a remaining maturity of five or more years. Credit derivatives allow Ameriland to buy a very specific slice. It can buy two-year risk in the credit derivatives market even though there may not be a two-year loan outstanding. These advantages create liquidity and may create better economics for both the buyer and the seller of the credit derivative.

The upper portion of Figure 19-5 shows the basic steps Ameriland Bank would have to take in the absence of credit derivatives in order to take the ABC loan in London. To invest in an ABC bond, Ameriland would have to pay par value to receive the fixed-rate coupon stream (7.25%) plus the principal repayment at the end of the contract. The bank, however, would have to obtain the necessary funds from some funding source to which it would pay LIBOR. The problem of receiving fixed cash flows while owing floating cash flows is easily remedied by swapping fixed for floating in which Ameriland pays 7% and receives LIBOR.

The entire structure can be replicated by Ameriland entering into a credit derivative with Euro-Bank, where Ameriland will make a payment only if ABC declares a credit event. This is shown in the lower portion of Figure 19-5. This situation would be akin to the

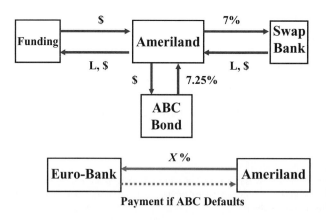

FIGURE 19-5 Ease of the use of credit derivatives.

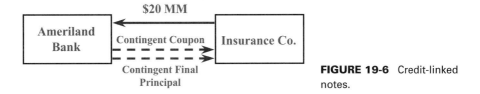

FIGURE 19-6 Credit-linked notes.

case where ABC defaults but the funding source still requires payment. In turn, Ameriland will receive 25 basis points: that is, the difference between 7.25 and 7%. Hence, instead of engaging a series of contracts with different intermediaries, Ameriland Bank can enter into one simple transaction with Euro-Bank that will have exactly the same outcome.[10]

In addition to the default swap shown in the ABC, Inc. example, there are also **credit-linked notes** and **total return swaps**.

Assume an insurance company purchases a $20 million structured note from Ameriland Bank (see Figure 19-6). A structured note is a combination of a bond and a derivative, where the majority of the risky (marginal) return comes from the underlying debt instrument that the derivative references. Assume the note is based on the underlying value of a particular Brazilian bond. At the end of the year, if there is no Brazilian credit event, that is, Brazil does not default or declare an inconvertibility event, then Ameriland Bank will pay the insurance company $22 million. That is, the insurance company will earn a 10% return which is higher than the prevailing rate on straight bonds and will keep its principal. If, however, there is a credit event, Ameriland will repay only $20 million. The insurance company is actually risking only the interest on its $20 million investment. Therefore, the insurance company's principal is protected. The insurance company might lose interest but not the invested principal.

Figure 19-7 examines a total return swap. In a total return swap, two parties agree to exchange the cash flows from specific investments. In the case of banks, the swap might involve the return on two loan portfolios. Recall the credit paradox of banks. A total return swap is a method of hedging the credit paradox. Suppose Chicago Bank believes it is overexposed to Midwest agriculture producers because the producers form 60% of the bank's loan portfolio. Meanwhile California bank has a similar problem with Silicon Valley manufacturers. A swap of the returns on 40% (for example) of the notional amount of their respective loan portfolios can be constructed. With the swap, Chicago bank will receive the income on Silicon Valley manufacturing loans and California Bank will receive income from agricultural producers. Note that if the return to the loans to agriculture producers is −2%, then this amount would be paid by California Bank in addition to the return on the California portfolio. This payment of both positive and negative returns clearly highlights how Chicago Bank has purchased protection on its Midwest portfolio and simultaneously diversified its portfolio to California manufacturers.

---

[10] There actually is a timing issue as the asset swap obligations would continue, while the credit derivative settles at the time of a default. Further, in an asset swap Euro-Bank would still have to unwind the bond position if the remaining maturity of the bond does not match the desired holding period.

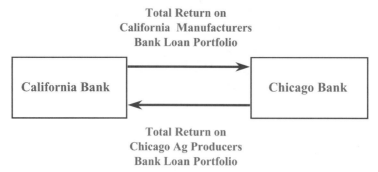

FIGURE 19-7 Total return swaps.

19.7 PRICING ISSUES

This section summarizes some of the current methodologies used to price default-related products. It is important to understand that the field of pricing credit derivatives is evolving with the market; therefore, no explicit or direct methodology for pricing these instruments currently exists. However, several methods for pricing the instruments indirectly through expected values, arbitrage arguments, or through relative comparisons are available. Also important to note is that there is currently no closed-form solution such as, the Black-Scholes option pricing formula, for pricing these types of instruments.

The four basic approaches for pricing credit derivatives are

1. the expected value approach (EVA),
2. the alternative exposure approach (AEA),
3. market quotations (MQ), and
4. comparative market quotations (CMQ).

19.7.1 Expected Value Approach (EVA)

The expected value approach (EVA) is based on the expected value (or the expected loss) of a particular transaction. Consider a one-year default swap where the buyer seeks default protection against an exposure on an investment grade instrument (bond). With this simple instrument, the buyer receives a one-time payment if a credit event occurs, and then the contractual agreement expires. On the other hand, if the credit event does not occur, the swap buyer receives nothing. The expected value of such an instrument is

$$EV = EDP \times ELGD, \tag{19-1}$$

where

EV = expected value (bps)

EDP = expected default probability

$ELGD$ = expected loss given default, in the range from 0 to 1, where 1 corresponds to 100% loss (bps).

The EVA gives the risk-neutral valuation of a given transaction expressed in basis points on a notional amount. The main advantage of this technique is that besides being theoretically and intuitively sound, it is also relatively easy to obtain approximate estimates for EDP and ELGD. The EDP estimate can be derived from either quantitative methods or from using historical default ratios as published by the various rating agencies, such as Moody's and S&P.[11] To estimate the ELGD, inferences based on historical data typically need to be made.

In the case of either a long maturity transaction or a less than investment-grade credit, transition matrices can be used to estimate EDP. These transition matrices are published by Moody's, S&P, or by Creditmetrics. Because credit ratings (and thus credit strength) more commonly deteriorate rather than improve, the associated EDPs should increase with time. The future EDPs would be equal to the probability weighted EDPs for the ratings that the reference asset would carry at future periods of time as shown in Equation (19-2).

$$EDP_n = \sum_{m=1}^{M} P_{m,n} EDP_m, \qquad (19\text{-}2)$$

where

$EDP_n = EDP$ in period n

$P_{m,n}$ = probability that reference credit is rated in state (rating) m in period n

$EDP_m = EDP$ of state m.

$P_{m,n}$ can be calculated in two basic ways. Both Moody's and S&P report multiyear transition matrices based on historical empirical results. These matrices report the probability that a credit of original rating, for example AA, has a given rating after a given time T. A second methodology is to utilize the more popular one-year transition matrices raised to the power of T, where again T is the number of years. The one-year transition matrix, raised to the power of T, should be equal to the T-th year transition matrix. However, interestingly, this is rarely the case.

The main advantage of the EVA pricing is that the model is both easy to calculate and intuitively easy to understand. Further, the model is theoretically sound since it is based on a risk-neutral valuation technique. The model's simplicity and flexibility lends itself to a wide variety of credit derivative structures. For those users with specific future views or advanced default forecasting capabilities, this methodology allows them to directly incorporate their views and techniques into the pricing model.

The major disadvantage of the EVA is that it ignores market perceptions and, in particular, the supply and demand for specific reference names or maturities. The current state of the market is such that the demand for particular names and instruments has developed faster than the pricing methodologies. In addition, liquidity in specific issues may not match the desire for speedy transactions. Many of these transactions are being done within a portfolio context, where not only the individual probability of default but also the marginal probability of default (or correlation of default) are major issues. Therefore, it is

[11] *Moody's Rating Migration and Credit Quality Correlation*, 1920–1996, July 1997, available from http://www.moodys.com/, or *Standard & Poor's Rating Performance 1996: Stability & Transition*, February 1997.

quite common to see market prices that do not reflect any reasonable set of values for EPD and ELGD using EVA.

Arguably, using market-volatility-based quantitative methods to measure the expected default probabilities implicitly incorporates market perceptions. Although this is true as to the expectation of default in general, it ignores the market positions and perceptions of market participants who may utilize different quantitative methods and analysis to calculate defaults. Also, one must consider the different perceptions and viewpoints of the various players in the credit derivatives market. For example, an institutional investor is likely to value a loan very differently than a bank that has a relationship and ancillary business with the underlying company.

An implementation difficulty with EVA is estimating reliable values for EPD and ELGD. Although analytical models exist which are easy to use and intuitively appealing, the difficulty is that there is still significant uncertainty in the estimates as well as variability through time. A variation of the EVA approach is to calculate the credit derivative price necessary to provide a protection provider with a risk-adjusted return on capital (**RAROC**) that meets a predesignated hurdle rate.

The disadvantage of the RAROC hurdle approach is that while it provides an effective floor price below which a bank should not want to trade, it does not take into account market dynamics which may lead to significant pricing mistakes relative to market levels.

19.7.2 Alternative Exposure Approach (AEA)

The alternative exposure approach (AEA) calculates the price of a credit derivative based on what the capital market return would be for taking an equivalent credit exposure. The basic idea is to examine what the costs would be for a funded purchase of the underlying reference asset in the capital market, or alternatively, the secondary loan market.

For example, suppose that a default swap is being proposed with a three-year maturity, and the reference asset is ABC's bond that matures in five years. The yield on the bond is 6.9%. The full funding cost for the bank is assumed to be 6.0%. Therefore, the bank can gain exposure to the underlying credit by going to the markets to fund the purchase of the reference asset. This would lead to a net annual yield of 90 bps (6.9% − 6%). As a result, aside from liquidity and counterparty credit risk, the bank should be indifferent between funding and purchasing the asset or receiving 90 bps annually for buying credit risk through a credit swap.

An interesting fact to note is that this methodology is a slightly refined way of examining the credit risk premium over a risk-free rate that the credit name is trading at in the market. A further refinement is to examine the asset-swap rates for various credits in the capital markets. Observing or calculating the asset-swap rates also takes into account the shape of the yield curve. A further advantage of the asset-swap approach is that prices are readily quoted in the fixed income market and are available on Bloomberg.

When the underlying asset is a bank loan, a similar asset-swap methodology can be used by comparing the cash flows from the bank loan net of funding and then comparing them to the cash flows from a derivative structure. After discounting both cash flow streams, an equivalent credit derivative price can be calculated.

The major benefit of the AEA is that it gives an arbitrageable price level for the derivative because all the pricing variables are based on observed market prices. Further, because the variables are market and traded prices, it eliminates the need for the subjective estimates that are necessary with the expected value approach.

The major drawback to the AEA is for those derivative products where the reference asset is not a public market instrument: for example, derivatives where the underlying assets are nontraded bank loans or receivables. Also, the AEA can lead to mispricing errors due to the basis risk that exists when the reference asset is not the asset that the arbitrage swap is being based on. However, the size of this error should be very small as long as the actual reference asset has the same seniority and a similar maturity to the reference asset being priced.

As with the expected value approach, this method ignores the liquidity and supply and demand issues that may exist for specific derivatives on certain names and for certain maturities. However, this is only an issue if the supply/demand in the credit derivatives market is significantly different from the bank loan or bond trading markets.

19.7.3 Market Quotations (MQ)

Market Quotations are the simplest and most valid prices if a tradable market quote is available. Using this technique, there is no ambiguity whatsoever and there are no subjective variables. The major difficulty is that the market is not yet developed enough for a complete (and deep) set of ready quotes to be available. Therefore, the availability of quotes or quotes in the required size is a major issue. Most activity is still done privately through interbank counterparties without going through the broker market.

Direct private trading can be a major stumbling block for pricing large transactions because it limits the market quotes for that particular instrument. Using a market quote for a transaction size less than the desired position could significantly understate (overstate) the price to buy (sell) protection. For prices of a position of a given size that is larger than the size given in the market quote, a weighted average price to clear the position should be calculated.

The advantage of using market quotations is that it reflects all market perceptions and positions, which gets around the major disadvantage of the EVA approach. The major disadvantage of using market quotations is that prices are often not available. Also, because each deal is unique and each credit is unique, it is unlikely that one will find the exact credit and structure desired in the quoted market. The only time that this is likely to happen is in those few cases where large transactions have been brought to market and a secondary market develops. Strictly using market quotations is also unsatisfactory in that it leaves no room for analysis or stress testing of scenarios.

Finally, a major assumption behind market quotations is, at times, suspect: the assumption that the market is always right. Particularly in the growth phases of a market, such as credit derivatives, pricing may be driven more by exuberance or market imbalances rather than logical and thoughtful value analysis. This is particularly true for quotes provided by brokers who are simply *fishing* and hoping that a market develops.

19.7.4 Comparative Market Quotations

Comparative market quotations (CMQ) is an expansion of the market quotation methods used to price those issues for which a market quotation is not available. The CMQ methodology can be used in two basic situations: either the desired name is quoted but the desired maturity is not, or the desired maturity is quoted but the desired name is not.

If the desired name is quoted, then generally the credit pricing (on an annualized basis) would be relatively insensitive to remaining maturity, and the quoted market price can be used for all maturities. If the maturity that is being priced is significantly longer, this method will understate the true price because the term structure of credit is usually upward sloping.

For derivatives where the underlying name is not quoted, one can often use a quoted name that has a similar credit rating. One should carefully select a reference asset that has similar risk, credit rating, market liquidity, seniority, name recognition, and capital market structure. Where the choice of a reference asset is ambiguous, an average of quoted prices for reference assets of similar remaining maturity and rating should be used.

CMQ pricing has the advantage of utilizing the market's perception of the term structure of credit for both maturity and ratings. What it ignores is any issuer-specific factors that may be important for pricing. However, if liquidity or a market imbalance is not obvious or considered to be a factor, the effects of this drawback should be minimal. A second advantage, which is a by-product of the CMQ approach, is the discipline that it imposes on the analyst and the level of detail about the current structure of the credit markets that it reveals.

The disadvantage of the CMQ methodology is the same as with any comparative pricing technique: the comparability of the proxy securities. With the current state of the credit derivatives market, CMQ could be either a major or minor drawback, depending on the depth of the market for a particular sector. A second consideration is the wide variety of prices observed in the market for similarly rated credits. This drawback can be particularly acute for noninvestment-grade credits. Figure 19-8 ranks the four methods in terms of their strengths/weaknesses on a variety of factors.

	EVA	AEA	MQ	CMQ
Incorporates market opinions and factors	4	2	1	2
Theoretically based	1	1	3	4
Potential basis risk	2	2	1	4
Arbitrageable	4	1	2	3
Ease of calculation	3	2	1	4
Subjectiveness	4	2	1	3
Intuitive	1	1	1	2
Accuracy	?	2	1	?

FIGURE 19-8 Pricing methodologies strengths and weaknesses (1 = better, 4 = worse).

19.8 IMPACT OF THE EMERGING CREDIT DERIVATIVES MARKET

Credit derivatives have dramatically enhanced the field of risk management. They represent the leading edge of new technology in derivative instruments and are potentially a source of great value to the banking system. Like financial derivatives, credit derivatives provide insight into how value changes due to changing economic conditions and levels of uncertainty. They are an instrument that reacts to views on how market dynamics and conditions will affect credit values and risk. Undoubtedly, the market for credit derivatives will continue to expand and grow in significance as market participants become more familiar with the instruments and their applications. However, the major impact of credit derivatives will develop within the organizational structure of the banking system where the implementation of a credit derivative strategy will change the way banks have been doing business for the last century.

Two main points need to be made to enhance the understanding of the implications of the emergence of a credit derivatives market. First, credit derivatives make credit fungible (able to be sold). The importance of this point cannot be stressed too much. The point is, in fact, revolutionary and goes to the heart of the future of banking services. The capital markets are much more efficient suppliers of credit and banks are becoming just an intermediary in the supply of credit. As a result, many commercial banks are, at least to some degree, merging their loan portfolio management, fixed income, and investment banking activities. Credit derivatives might not necessarily be the driving force, but it certainly is the glue that makes credit fungible and facilitates this merging of activities. The implications are as follows: more liquid markets, disintermediation of the *credit judging* role of banks, narrowing of spreads between loans and bonds, more emphasis on structure, more emphasis on the bank's relationship to corporations, and the profitability shift of the relationships from credit supply to fee-based revenues.

Second, loan portfolio management changes from a static activity to a dynamic activity. This statement is oversimplifying, but basically the job of a corporate banker was once to ask, *Can they pay us back in five years when the loan is due?* For all intents and purposes the question was asked once at the inception of the loan and if the answer was *yes*, the money was loaned and the bank waited for it to come back at the maturity of the loan. However, credit derivatives force bankers to think about the market value of credit continuously through time. Now the question is, *Given the level of risk in the bank's portfolio, does holding this individual loan's level of risk increase the bank's risk-adjusted return in today's economic environment?* Combined with the fact that credit derivatives facilitate portfolio diversification and risk management, the arrival of credit derivatives revolutionizes the role and function of a loan portfolio manager.

No ideal pricing method for credit derivatives is available at the current time. Each technique has its own unique advantages and disadvantages. Further, you must remember that the market price is the market price. If it differs significantly from the calculated prices, then the reason behind any discrepancy needs to be uncovered and evaluated. The pricing of credit derivatives is not a completely objective exercise. It involves mostly market analysis which is commingled with both credit and quantitative analysis.

SUMMARY OF VALUATION AND RISK MANAGEMENT SKILLS

1. Understand what a credit derivative is and how it helps lenders manage credit risk.

Credit derivatives are off balance sheet contracts whose values are based on the financial strength and creditworthiness of an entity. They are specifically designed to mitigate one of the oldest and the most fundamental problems in finance—credit risk—by allowing the credit risk of a loan to be separated from the other aspects of the loan and to then be traded. This allows, for example, a bank in Kansas to swap agriculture risk for automotive risk with a bank in Michigan, thus reducing the industry concentration in each bank's portfolio.

2. Understand how credit derivatives complete the market and why this is important.

Risk management is becoming the trading of an asset's risk attributes: liquidity risk, interest-rate risk, currency risk, contingent risk, and default risk. Default risk is a major risk component of all fixed-income securities, so without the ability to trade default risk, a risk manager is limited in the ways default risk can be managed. Traditionally default risk has been managed through diversification. However, managing lending relationships can lead to overconcentration in one or a small set of borrowers. Having credit derivatives allows lenders to trade credit risk and thus focus on the profitability of the banking relationships with their best customers.

3. Understand the strengths and weaknesses of the different pricing methods for credit derivatives.

Credit derivatives are relatively new instruments and currently there are no direct methods for pricing these instruments. However, four indirect methods are available: (1) the expected value approach (EVA), (2) the alternative exposure approach (AEA), (3) market quotations (MQ), and (4) comparative market quotations (CMQ).

The expected value approach (EVA) is based on the expected value (or the expected loss) of a particular transaction. The main advantage of the EVA pricing is that the model is both easy to calculate and intuitively easy to understand. The major disadvantage of the EVA is that it ignores market perceptions and in particular the supply and demand for specific reference names or maturities.

The alternative exposure approach (AEA) calculates the price of a credit derivative based on what the capital market return would be for taking an equivalent credit exposure. The major benefit of the AEA is that it gives an arbitrageable price level for the derivative. The major drawback to the AEA is for those derivative products where the reference asset is not a public market instrument: for example, derivatives where the underlying reference credits are nontraded bank loans or receivables.

Market Quotations are the simplest and most valid prices if a tradable market quote is available. The advantage of using market quotations is that it reflects all market perceptions and positions, which gets around the major disadvantage of the EVA approach. The major difficulty is that the market is not yet developed enough for a complete (and deep) set of ready quotes to be available.

Comparative market quotations (CMQ) is an expansion of the market quotation methods used to price those issues for which a market quotation is not available. The CMQ methodology can be used in two basic situations: either the desired reference name is quoted but the desired maturity is not, or the desired maturity is quoted but the desired name is not. CMQ pricing has the advantage of utilizing the market's perception of the term structure of credit for both maturity and ratings. The disadvantage of the CMQ methodology is the same with any comparative pricing technique: the comparability of the proxy securities.

QUESTIONS

1. What is the purpose of a credit derivative?

2. How does unbundling risk help with diversification?

3. Credit derivatives complete the market for bonds. Why is this important?

4. When a bank enters into a credit-default swap with another bank, what happens to counterparty risk and why would a bank want to make this change?

5. From the standpoint of regulatory capital for a bank, what is the advantage of a credit derivative over holding the original loan in portfolio?

6. Why would two banks from different locations do a total return swap?

7. Four different methods for pricing credit derivatives were discussed. One of those methods is to use market quotes. What is the problem with using market quotes in today's credit derivatives market?

KEY TERMS

Concentration Risk The additional risk of credit losses in portfolios where the credit risk is not well diversified.

Credit Derivative A derivative security created for the management of credit/default risk.

Credit-linked Note A combination of a bond and a derivative where the majority of the risky (marginal) return comes from the underlying debt instrument that the derivative references.

Disintermediation A move away from intermediaries in the financial markets. Specifically, banks are intermediaries in the debt markets and unbundling the attributes of a debt contract makes the intermediary less necessary.

RAROC Risk-adjusted return on capital.

Total Return Swap An agreement to exchange the cash flows from specific investments.

INDEX